WRITING
FOR
TELEVISION

WRITING
FOR
TELEVISION

by Max Wylie

COWLES BOOK COMPANY, INC.
NEW YORK

Grateful acknowledgment is made to the following for permission to reprint: Edwin Granberry for the story, "A Trip to Czardis"; Harvard University Press and Mrs. Kenneth Payson Kempton for excerpt from *Short Stories for Study;* Kirk Gardner for the television script, "A Trip to Czardis"; Donn Mullally for "Creeping Giants" (*Tarzan*); Triangle Publications, Inc., for "I Didn't Want to Play a Nun"; Screen Gems, the Writers Guild, and Bernard Slade for "The Convent of San Tanco" (*The Flying Nun*); Bill Idelson and Sam Bobrick for "Viva Smart" (*Get Smart*); Bill Persky, Sam Denoff, and Carl Reiner (Calvada Productions) for "Coast to Coast Big Mouth" (*The Dick Van Dyke Show*); Time, Inc., for "Success Is a Warm Puppy"; Richard Alan Simmons and Four Star Television for "The Price of Tomatoes"; Paul Monash for "Commitment" (*Judd for the Defense*); Roncom Films-Huggins Productions for "The Committee for the 25th" (*Run for Your Life*); Rod Serling and Finger Lakes Productions for "The Lonely" (*The Twilight Zone*); Roy Winsor, CBS, and American Home Products for *Love of Life;* Steven Shapiro for "Patrol"; Milton Geiger for "In the Fog"; Charles S. Steinberg and *Television Academy Quarterly* for "The McLuhan Myth"; Joan Walker and the *New York Times* for "Of Mikes and Men"; Theodore R. Kupferman and *The Hollywood Reporter* for "How to Protect an Idea."

For Judy Hole

CONTENTS

WRITING
FOR
TELEVISION

1

WRITING FOR THE MARKET

"Why is network programming so poor?" asked J.B., a pair of initials that hide the true identity of one of the sharpest minds in American advertising. His views appear in *Television Age* twice a month. J.B. goes at once to his own answer: "The blame for this must fall directly on the shoulders of the handful of men who pick the programs. Despite their skills, few of these men are equipped with the education, experience, or aptitude that entitle them to exercise good program judgment."

Bob Williams, TV editor of the Associated Press, is equally definite, and much more harsh: "The network program merchants are merely exploiting nightly violence as they chase the sponsor-dollar. Network TV's own contribution to the home screen—the series fare—is a bullet-ridden disgrace."

Harriet Van Horne: "The TV mills are grinding exceedingly coarse grain these days. Too much chaff in the meal, and now and then a few maggots as well."

"TV is killing off its writers," says Leonard Stern, executive producer of *Get Smart.* Where do they go? Broadway. And movies.

Walter Lippmann has scored the trend of killing-is-fun in all our media of mass entertainment: "A continual exposure of a generation to the commercial exploitation of the enjoyment of violence and cruelty is one way to corrode the foundations of a civilized society. . . . Until some more refined way is worked out of controlling this evil thing, the risks to our liberties are, I believe, decidedly less than the risks of unmanageable violence."

And the late Norman Thomas had this to say: "I do not think the First Amendment gives any guarantee to men to seduce the innocent. . . . I think it is nonsense to say that we are so bound by a very extreme interpretation of the freedom of the press that we cannot act."

"If no character in a movie seems to have a past," writes Pauline Kael in *The New Yorker,* "one can be pretty sure it was written and/or directed by people from television. The characters are not likely to have much present, either."

Probably television's best-known network program executive is Michael Dann of CBS. To me there was an ominous overtone in his reply to the question as

3

to whether the *CBS Playhouse* would be discontinued. "It could happen," he said, "if TV plays can't measure up to the best plays on and off Broadway. The mass audience isn't watching anthology drama series on television. And the selective audience—some ten or fifteen million viewers—is insisting on quality drama. We can't get away with the hit-or-miss productions of the fifties. If we fail to capture and hold the audience this time out, television may not see original drama for years to come."

Television, it would appear from the above, is in a critical phase of its short life. And I believe that is true. In the past, it was the writer—no one else—who determined the patterns of television programming. It was his work, the best and the worst of it, that formed those patterns. Today this is true only in a limited way. Today, when all of the complementary skills involved in a good production are in good supply, writers are in short supply. This is getting worse, not better. No one is training tomorrow's television writers. They are finding their way into television by themselves. Or getting lost en route.

This is wrong.

It would be equally wrong, however, to accuse the networks of abdicating a responsibility they do not feel to be theirs. The networks have never recognized this—the actual *teaching* of television writing or the underwriting of a plan for such—as being an activity that might profitably serve their own interests. Yet, if it were properly directed, it would serve these ends richly and at once. Perhaps this is an area that networks, because of their fixed thinking, would not know how to manage, were they to decide to give the thing a try. But it's hard to see how they could get hurt, how they could lose much. Suppose they were to uncover another Rod Serling?

An earnest expression of the problem of writer starvation in television was voiced by one of its most dependable and mature dramatists, Reginald Rose.

"The new *CBS Playhouse,*" he wrote—the *Playhouse* then being in its first year—"does attempt to light one candle, but in the main it is still necessary for us to curse the darkness. The *Playhouse* to date has been an attempt to supply us with serious drama and, hopefully, with new writing talent, but the four or five plays it will present this season are simply not enough. . . .

"ABC's *Stage 67* was a noble but costly flop, proving, I imagine, once again to the decision makers, that the American public is simply not interested in serious drama.

"It becomes increasingly evident that we are not about to spawn a new group of craftsmen such as Robert Alan Arthur, Paddy Chayefsky, *et al*. There is simply no training ground available for them.

"What we are developing today is a kind of computerized writer, an artist who learns his craft writing to formula.

"Without a training ground there will be no new rising young stars, and most of the old ones have turned to other media. J. P. Miller and Sumner Locke Elliot, for instance, are writing novels. The others are writing either for films or theater, or both.

"Television by its very nature has a responsibility to, if you'll pardon the expression, art. Meaningful drama belongs regularly on at least some of those 75 million boxes scattered across the country, if only because there are millions of viewers who want it, who will be entertained by it, and whose insights into the human condition will be deepened by it." (Note: According to latest estimates at the time this book was being written, the number of TV sets in American homes had risen to 78.2 million.)

There are authority and integrity in the foregoing sentences. And a lot of controlled hurt.

Most of the best-known names in television writing, as Reginald Rose pointed out in the same article (*New York Times,* Sunday, September 20, 1966), wrote scripts in their spare time while making their living at something else. For example, Paddy Chayefsky wrote sketches for nightclub comics. N. Richard Nash was a schoolteacher. Rod Serling was on the GI Bill. Tad Mosel was an airlines clerk. Robert Alan Arthur was part owner of a small record company. Horton Foote was an actor. David Shaw was a watercolorist. And J. P. Miller sold airconditioners.

"I myself sold thirteen shows to television before I finally got myself an agent," Rose said.

But for writers, those days were different from today. There was a market for what they wrote. Today there isn't.

I am personally acquainted with most of the writers whose work is included in this book. Often I have asked television writers—the established ones—what kind of advice they had for the young talents who wanted to move into television. Not very encouraging. Said Luther Davis, "I'd tell them to avoid it." Why does he say this? Afraid of the competition you are going to mean to him? Hardly that. His credits are immense; he is very much "in."

A writer of very different slant but large accomplishment—Donn Mullally—said this to me: "The trouble with writing for television is that it can be damn hard work. And there's the slippery bit of scrambling around in your own blood, which is *revision.* Yes, you may correctly assume that all the young men and women are being discouraged, deliberately and overtly, from undertaking this means of making a buck."

Anything encouraging from any writer? Yes, here and there. But you'll have to dig for it. New writers *do* have friends, men who will read them, and five or six are encountered in the pages ahead: Harry Ackerman, Leonard Stern, Sam Bobrick, Jack Elinson, Sheldon Leonard. *Writers* help other writers. Networks do nothing, really. Most producers work with a small (or large) stable of writers they've come to trust. But in the training or steering of talents that have yet to make it, there is neither idealism nor intelligence to help. At the beginning it is better to be tough than gifted.

There is another problem that today's television writer must meet head on: he must live on the West Coast. If he doesn't happen to live there, it is essential for him to move there. But the young writers I know do have a lot of bounce. If they thought they had a chance, they'd go.

Who are "they" and where are they from?

Who, primarily, is doing the discovering now? Colleges and universities.

Every campus in the United States that has a "communications" facility or a structured television installation is attracting new talents and new energies each year, each semester. These energies are brisk and real, and some of the talents

are big ones. During a year of teaching at Temple University I had seven students
—four graduate students and three undergraduates—who will surely become
professional writers. Some of their work is in this book.

Do the networks do anything to help?

ABC is doing something interesting and productive in seeking new *acting*
talents, and through a setup that makes sense. Under the auspices of the American Academy of Dramatic Arts, with Worthington Miner and his actress wife,
Fran Fuller, in charge, twenty-five hundred actors and actresses were heard out of
a list of twenty-five thousand applicants. Each was trying for one of the scholar-
ships established by ABC.

There are sixteen winners and sixteen alternates per year. The plan that is now
operative sends winners to the Yale Drama School for a year. Seven of these
winners receive five thousand dollars apiece. There is a graduated scale for the
others, depending on their (or their parents') ability to pay. Yale makes the final
selections from a recommended list that is put together by Miner and Fran Fuller.

American Broadcasting gives Yale eighty-one thousand dollars for this. But
no "slave" contracts are required by ABC after the winners have had a year at
the drama school. They may seek employment anywhere. At Yale they are
coached and disciplined by Robert Brustein. There are no youngsters in these
classes. Although they have come from all over the United States (via local station
auditions on the ABC network), they have all had, in their own regional careers,
experience comparable to off-Broadway. They've all had a toughening season or
two, maybe more. And they all have potential.

It would be pleasant to report that the same network is doing the same for
writers. Perhaps it is, or at least thinking about it. But it's on a most modest scale.
Editors of high school papers can apply for two available fellowships that will bring
them to Blair Academy for summer work. Blair is in New Jersey, but this is not
just an eastern thing. One of last year's winners was a Texan, the other from
Indiana.

But these fellowships will, and are intended to, steer these young men to TV
journalism, not to television drama. Drama and comedy have recently become
orphaned.

In emphasizing the special contribution of the writer, there is no intent to
slight the importance of other contributions: production quality, publicity, star
value, time-of-show, and the hard effect of competitive factors. A large number
of collateral influences reach into every show. They help it or hurt it. They enhance
or diminish what the writer offers. But it is his offering—whether adult or puerile,
sweet or steamy, whimsical, tough, put-down, turned on, in, out, way-out, up-
tight, funny, or square—that must carry the main load of the production.

The script is the wagon the writer built. All others connected with the journey
either ride on it, drive it, paint it, grease its axles, or push at the spokes. But they
all want the same thing: they want it to move.

This is good. And the units that support most of television's successful efforts
are skillful, approachable, and well disciplined. They get up early and go to work
early.

There is something else. There is a basic honesty, a basic simplicity, about all the successfully produced drama in today's television, whatever its category. This is as true of a happy, tatterdemalion show like *Tarzan* as it is of an excellent thing like "The Price of Tomatoes."

This business of simplicity, of honesty, is no longer quite true of the English-speaking theater. Nor is it true of many of today's novels.

For example, it has within the past few years become more important that a playwright "explain" or exegete his play on the theater page of a newspaper than that he write it for a theater audience. The stage is nostalgically recalled by many Americans—squares, no doubt—as a forum where plays, in days past, did their own explaining. You knew what was going on. You could disapprove, but at least you knew. So did the author. Today, in our passion for the incoherent, we are so contrarily conned by glibness that what is said about a theatrical product is sometimes more significant than what the work says of itself, or what it reveals to beholders, or reveals as to the purpose and integrity of its maker.

For the time being we've mislaid our self-trust.

Television, by contrast, can't be coy, or pawky, or "unresolved." The compound eye of twenty million viewers won't accept such. Perhaps some of the energies in today's theater, and some of the practitioners of the obscure, need a chat with the six-year-old who saw that the emperor had neglected to pull on his pants and was strolling down the boulevard bare as a clam.

A lot of loose naïveté is floating around under the guise of social significance. We'll always have it. Some of it is getting wide attention. In the past four or five years Marshall McLuhan has moved it forward. His mind-catching syndrome about message content in contemporary media, it seems to me, has sharper application to abstract painting and nonbooks than it has to radio or television. I can go along with him about his "hot" and "cold" but only to the limited extent that the contribution of individual imagination makes radio hotter than television. But radio's invitation to the imagination has been known for some time and will serve to explain why serious ghost stories, for example, were big in radio and why they're impossible in television. You want your own ghost, so you create him.

Procter & Gamble long ago learned the risk of photographing Ma Perkins. Radio listeners didn't want to be shown what Ma Perkins looked like. They *knew*. And anything but their own image of this cackling old one-woman matriarchy, hacking around in her sanitary lumberyard, was wrong.

Similarly, many who remember Amos 'n' Andy forget how fast this team died on the screen.

If something isn't understood in television, it's tuned out. If something isn't understood in the theater, it's celebrated.

Television audiences don't have these problems. Marshall McLuhan will never get through to them; they aren't aware of him. He's a university phenomenon and he'll end up there. And not a bad place to end up, either, considering the Joe Namath kind of coin that goes with it.

Even if they had heard of him, TV audiences could shrug off Marshall McLuhan and go right on watching Marshal Dillon accepting warmed-over coffee from Kitty in the Long Branch Saloon.

About thirty million Americans think there is a message there at Dodge.

They're not concerned about the medium, just the message. If there *is* a message, a writer wrote it. Is it important that the message is trivial? No. Or ephemeral? No. It is only important that it is there.

Call it a "story" if you like.

Were the message not there, it is the belief of the network executives that thirty million viewers would not be there either.

In television no one has the handy escape hatch McLuhan has neatly worked into his prose:

"People make a great mistake to read me as if I'm saying something."

Marshal Dillon has to back up all he says. If he doesn't, he's dead. McLuhan doesn't have to back up anything. He can pick up a good fee by advertising his frailties and circumlocuting his adversaries to death by machine gun disgorgements of self-ridicule, self-contradiction, and paradox.

The most intelligent challenge to the thought and the presence of McLuhan that I have read is in this book. It is the work of Charles Steinberg, a CBS Television Network vice-president. Steinberg is the author of *The Mass Communicators* and editor of *Mass Media and Communication.*

Many of the best scripts (of their type) are here, both for comedy and for drama. Some of them are from television series now departed; most of them are from series that will one day be no more. *Titles* of television series are transitory; *types* of series endure. But this is not relevant to the book's purposes since each script is here for a given reason. Each has a claim on the writer's time, whether the script explores the indestructible innocence of Gomer Pyle (nauseating to some) or the abortive hustle of Maxwell Smart.

There is violence in some of these stories. And the violence that will be here encountered *belongs* in these stories. They would not be stories without it. But there is no *gratuitous* violence in any of the material. If you come up against the Mafia and you are caught, you get hurt. The most "violent" story the reader will meet with—"A Trip to Czardis"—is an American classic. It is violent because its violence is withheld, insinuated, never seen. It is the violence of feeling, not of sight or sound. But its swift power will stun. It will leave you hurting the rest of your life.

It is time critics of television's violence review their definitions, time they leave that word alone when they mean brutality. Then it is to be asked: is there not a great deal of brutality in television? Yes, there is. And much too much of it, much that is cynically permitted.

This is the industry's shame.

But any writer who has to rely on it betrays a basic weakness in his talent reservoir. My own hatred of physical violence, more especially of unprovoked brutality, is so extreme that it almost constitutes a violence of its own. The violence in *The Sand Pebbles?* Yes. The brutality in *A Fistful of Dollars?* No.

By the same token, if the aspiring television writer looks down his nose at the *Dick Van Dyke Show* or *Get Smart,* this book is not for him, either. In fact, this book is not for anyone who looks down his nose at anything in television. This does not at all mean that everything is to be approved or applauded or emulated. Or that much isn't to be deprecated. It just means that objective assessment will yield the truth sooner than impassioned dismissal. It means that impartial display of the insides of a great many different types of successful programs will more quickly steer the new writer to where he wants to go, to the thing he would most like to try for in television, to the quality and mood of the show or series to which he feels a natural leaning or a chemical affinity.

Could that include soap operas? Of course. Why not? There has to be something not only valid but unusually viable in a soap opera that has survived for nineteen years. *Love of Life* did it.

Is the writing of a soap opera beneath you? You'd better wait till you try. You think you would never get down to it? Maybe you couldn't get up to it. Actors don't spurn this work. *Love of Life,* which is a part of this book, got Warren Beatty started. And it paid the rent for Carl Betz. They went on to bigger things —Warren Beatty to the springboard of *Bonnie and Clyde,* Carl Betz to *Judd for the Defense.* But neither man considers *Love of Life* a shabby side of his professional background any more than Helen Hayes felt hesitant about taking a role in a *Tarzan* episode. These are professionals, and they are respecters of professionalism.

Most students, in almost any writing course, have a good time criticizing everything they don't like. At Temple University we did this a bit differently. We studied everything that was on the air, good and bad. We followed the full schedules of all three networks, with the films of the shows themselves, week after week, and with exact duplicates of final shooting scripts. But here is what was different: one week the students would act in the capacity of television critic for a metropolitan newspaper; the next week they'd take the role of the network program executive responsible for what was there.

We studied the failures just as diligently as we studied the successes. And we made hard predictions as to what was going to flunk out and why. The same procedure was followed with respect to the shows we believed were going to survive.

The posture of "uninhibited critic" was a lot easier to assume than that of "responsible executive." Impaling television is as popular a sport among educated Americans today as impaling early Christians was to the Romans. Here, for example, is a student comment on *Cimarron Strip:*

> Cameron Mitchell, who plays brother of the star (Stuart Whitman), is a happy-go-lucky, mindless, irresponsible comic relief, chaperone, paraclete, wild spirit and drunk. He possesses all the good, the near-good, and the no-good qualities they couldn't squeeze into John, Victoria, and Blue. He's a sort of human garbage collection of early-American virtue.

On *Cowboy in Africa:* "If you want a story about horse thieves, why go to Africa?"
On *Good Company* (F. Lee Bailey): "Behind Ed Murrow's cloud of cigarette smoke was a professional journalist's intense interest in other humans. Bailey's interest is Bailey."
On *Maya* (which was on against *The Jackie Gleason Show*): "If one has a choice of *two* elephants, the natural selection is Gleason."
Well, that was fun. But it didn't help anything. Suppose, instead of knocking

this stuff down, they had to knock it together? The show called *Custer* was bleeding. Perhaps you saw a few episodes.

"Consider some of its problems," I said. "If you were boss, what could you fix?"

This interested them. They came up with good questions—better questions than answers. But the discipline began to build something into their thinking, something that must be there if a writer is serious about a professional approach to television. He must have *respect* for all its problems. All of them. No other attitude will solve anything. Contempt—the amateur's escape—is fatal.

In the case of *Custer,* for example, what did they find? What did they respect?

It was in a tough time slot. It was fighting *The Virginian,* television's first ninety-minute successful western, solidly established for many seasons. It was also fighting *Lost in Space*. Was that hard? *Lost in Space* was a science fiction show. Yes, but it was pulling pretty much the same audience, agewise, as *Custer*.

Custer brought as the star a new name and new face (to most viewers) in the person of Wayne Maunder. Is that good? Will young people go with him?

"Yes," said some of the students. "He's got this long hippie-length hair. He's got this groovy moustache."

"No," retorted others, and pointed to the risk of supporting players whose acting was noticeably superior to that of the lead. Ralph Meeker and Slim Pickens were just fine. Did they hurt the star they were "supporting"? Especially a first-time-out star? It was a distinct possibility.

Should the show be shifted to another time spot? This always means an elaborate upheaval, jarring many other shows. If you bring in a left-hander, the opposition's bench will get busy.

The students began to take hold of the larger aspects of show survival. At least they began to get the feel of it. They developed a *concern* for the show, a concern for all the shows we studied. That's the point.

When, during intensive study of production problems, they noted vapor trails left in the sky by passing jets, or saw automobile tire marks on the road (during a show cast in the year 1880), or caught "wounded" soldiers limping on the wrong foot, or actors casting shadows in "night" scenes—they no longer howled and hooted. They began wondering how they'd avoid that same mistake if they were in charge of the second unit or of outdoor shooting.

Shifting their interest and their feeling of responsibility to this new angle of sight, they began to mature. They began to think about building, not wrecking.

One thing has amazed me, not only at Temple University but at most of the communications centers I've visited, and that is the vast number of students taking television courses who have never *seen* a television script. I find this generally and appallingly true. It is even true of many of the books on the subject. Few of these available textbooks contain more than a script or two, and I have books on my library shelves that do not contain even a single script.

There seems to me something lazy, or dreamy, or dishonest, about all this, like teaching dentistry without lights or pie baking without flour.

There are eleven scripts in this book, each one included for its special purpose. Most of these are the work of professionals whose names you've seen on the television screen. Some of the scripts represent series now departed. This is not important. The basic, continuing elements—both the obvious and the not so obvious—are all here. And these elements are laid out flat, their secrets opened, their mysteries illumined.

There are two examples of fine student work, as well as some student work that is typically clumsy.

The point is simple: no script is here that doesn't have something important to reveal.

The purpose of television is not to cheapen and distract; it is to refresh, to invigorate, inform, and delight.

The purpose of this book is to help new energies find their way.

2

A TRIP TO CZARDIS

No two stories come into being by the same route. This is Edwin Granberry's account of the genesis of "A Trip to Czardis."

"Here's the way it happened:

"The seed of the story was planted in my subconscious mind by the Judd Gray-Ruth Snyder murder case, and their subsequent electrocution. It was in the late 1920s. I was living in East Orange, New Jersey (Brick Church Station), where Judd Gray also lived. I did not know him. The case was a lurid and sensational one, headlined across the nation, played up especially in the New York papers as a crime of passion.

"He and Ruth Snyder, with Ruth egging him on, had murdered her husband, were caught, tried, convicted, and electrocuted. The morning after the electrocution, while on the train for Hoboken, where I was teaching at Stevens Institute, I read on the front page of the *New York World* a perfectly harrowing report of the electrocution written by Bide Dudley, a well-known columnist of the time and, if I am correct, also the ghoulishy resourceful one who managed to smuggle a camera into the presence of the electric chair (he had it strapped to his ankle and merely had to raise his pant leg slightly to get the unforgettable shot of Ruth rearing back violently as the current hit her).

"Bide Dudley was one of 20 witnesses to this awful scene, and described its horrors with such shattering power I was fairly made sick. One item: when Judd Gray, always a mild and submissive man, seated himself in the chair, he hiked up his trousers, out of long habit, of course, though they were slit clear to the knee to accommodate the electrodes. Dudley's eye missed nothing.

"At the end of the day, while on my way back home to East Orange, I had forgotten Bide Dudley's piece and the emotional shock it had given me. (I rather think that most stories arise from an emotional jolt.) But as we approached Brick Church Station in East Orange, I looked out the train window and saw an altogether abnormally large crowd gaping at the train. For a second I wondered why. Then it hit me—Judd Gray's remains were on the train, being brought home. A grim, silent, morbid crowd had gathered.

"Now here comes the part that interests me most and that I think throws some light on the mysterious business as to how a story gets started. Almost at the moment when realization as to why the crowd had gathered hit me, I happened

12

to see my wife waiting across the street for me, and with her, in a stroller, our year-old son, our first.

"Suddenly it struck me like a thunderbolt: where are Judd Gray's children? Do they know? What age? How will they take it?

"But for the merest chance of my wife having brought my own child to the station to meet me, I doubt that I would have thought about the other man's sons—if he had any.

"I was staggered with pity for the mother and for her children, and with the overwhelming tragedy that faced her in having to tell them.

"When I joined my wife and baby, I must have been pale, for she asked me if something was the matter. I said nothing and she suspected nothing. She hadn't read the Bide Dudley piece in the paper. She didn't know why the crowd had gathered.

"At the time, I hadn't the faintest idea that a story had formed in my sub-conscious mind. It needed, apparently, another spark to set it off. It was coming but it was some ways off. In fact, a couple of months went by. Then one day, accompanied by an artist, I was sent to Florida to do some articles on the Florida Keys. While gathering material, I was showing the artist some of the Florida turpentine country when we came across a row of unpainted shanties lining a sandy road through the pine woods. On the porch of one of the shanties sat a pale, gaunt 'cracker' woman with an equally pale and gaunt baby at her breast. The baby was fretting and wailing hungrily. It may have been my imagination but it looked as if the baby were starving because its mother was too undernourished to have any milk.

"Then occurred one of those things an author can never quite explain: in a flash, the 'starving' baby in the pine woods became one with the emotion touched off back there as the train pulled in at the East Orange station. The story, 'A Trip to Czardis,' was flashed on the screen of my mind as vividly as a motion picture.

"Back home in New Jersey it was written in two days."

The manuscript was uncovered through the happy accident of a severe thunder-storm. The Granberry house was struck by lightning. No damage, but all the lights went out. With a flashlight Granberry went down into the cellar to poke about, looking for fuses. He found the fuses, sitting right beside the typed script of "A Trip to Czardis."

"I squatted down and read the pages again, using the flashlight. It had been a long time. I don't know why I hadn't sent the story out. It seemed all right to me. So I brought it upstairs, screwed in the new fuses, got the light going, and mailed the 'Czardis' story to *The Forum*."

They bought it. That was 1932.

The next year it won the O. Henry Award as the best American short story of the year. It was in this collection that I came across it. I never forgot it. (You won't either.) When, some four years later, I was fossicking about, hunting for material for the "Columbia Workshop" (CBS), the haunting understatements, the brooding implications of this extraordinary piece of work came back clearly to me, and I bought it.

It became the most moving experience I have ever had, in all the radio listening I've ever done.

Now read the story. Then study the thoughtful paragraphs of Kenneth Payson Kempton that follow. You will have a richer and a more practical appreciation of what Granberry created when you see how skillfully Kempton has uncovered and interpreted the technique employed.

A TRIP TO CZARDIS
by Edwin Granberry

It was still dark in the pine woods when the two brothers awoke. But it was plain that day had come, and in a little while there would be no more stars. Day itself would be in the sky and they would be going along the road. Jim waked first, coming quickly out of sleep and sitting up in the bed to take fresh hold of the things in his head, starting them up again out of the corners of his mind where sleep had tucked them. Then he waked Daniel and they sat up together in the bed. Jim put his arm around his young brother, for the night had been dewy and cool with the swamp wind. Daniel shivered a little and whimpered, it being dark in the room and his baby concerns still on him somewhat, making sleep heavy on his mind and slow to give understanding its way.

"Hit's the day, Dan'l. This day that's right here now, we are goen. You'll recollect it all in a minute."

"I recollect. We are goen in the wagon to see Papa—"

"Then hush and don't whine."

"I were dreamen, Jim."

"What dreamen did you have?"

"I can't tell. But it were fearful what I dreamt."

"All the way we are goen this time. We won't stop at any places, but we will go all the way to Czardis to see Papa. I never see such a place as Czardis."

"I recollect the water tower—"

"Not in your own right, Dan'l. Hit's by my tellen it you see it in your mind."

"And lemonade with ice in it I saw—"

"That too I seen and told to you."

"Then I never seen it at all?"

"Hit's me were there, Dan'l. I let you play like, but hit's me who went to Czardis. Yet I never till this day told half how much I see. There's sights I never told."

They stopped talking, listening for their mother's stir in the kitchen. But the night stillness was unlifted. Daniel began to shiver again.

"Hit's dark," he said.

"Hit's your eyes stuck," Jim said. "Would you want me to drip a little water on your eyes?"

"Oh!" cried the young one, pressing his face into his brother's side, "don't douse me, Jim, no more. The cold aches me."

The other soothed him, holding him around the body.

"You won't have e're chill or malarie ache today, Dan'l. Hit's a fair day—"

"I won't be cold?"

"Hit's a bright day. I hear mournen doves starten a'ready. The sun will bake you warm. . . . Uncle Holly might buy us somethen new to eat in Czardis."

"What would it be?"

"Hit ain't decided yet. . . . He hasn't spoke. Hit might be somethen sweet. Maybe a candy ball fixed onto a rubber string."

"A candy ball!" Daniel showed a stir of happiness. "Oh, Jim!" But it was a deceit of the imagination, making his eyes shine wistfully; the grain of his flesh was against it. He settled into a stillness by himself.

"You might could keep a little down."

"No. . . . I would bring it home and keep it. . . ."

Their mother when they went to bed had laid a clean pair of pants and a waist for each on the chair. Jim crept out of bed and put on his clothes, then aided his brother on with his. They could not hear any noise in the kitchen, but hickory firewood burning in the kitchen stove worked a smell through the house, and in the forest guinea fowls were sailing down from the trees and poking their way along the half-dark ground toward the kitchen steps, making it known the door was open and that within someone was stirring about at the getting of food.

Jim led his brother by the hand down the dark way of yellow-pine stairs that went narrowly and without banisters to the rooms below. The younger brother went huddling in his clothes, aguelike, knowing warmth was near, hungering for his place by the stove, to sit in peace on the bricks in the floor by the stove's side and watch the eating, it being his nature to have a sickness against food.

They came in silence to the kitchen, Jim leading and holding his brother by the hand. The floor was lately strewn with fresh bright sand, and that would sparkle when the daybreak got above the forest, though now it lay dull as hoar-frost and cold to the unshod feet of the brothers. The door to the firebox of the stove was open, and in front of it their mother sat in a chair, speaking low as they entered, muttering under her breath. The two boys went near and stood still, thinking she was blessing the food, there being mush dipped up and steaming in two bowls. And they stood cast down until she lifted her eyes to them and spoke.

"Your clothes on already," she said. "You look right neat." She did not rise, but kept her chair, looking cold and stiff, with the cloth of her black dress sagging between her knees. The sons stood in front of her, and she laid her hand on first one head and then the other and spoke a little about the day, charging them to be sober and of few words, as she had raised them.

Jim sat on the bench by the table and began to eat, mixing dark molasses sugar through his bowl of mush. But a nausea began in Daniel's stomach at sight of the sweet, and he lagged by the stove, gazing at the food as it passed into his brother's mouth.

Suddenly a shadow filled the back doorway and Holly, their uncle, stood there looking in. He was lean and big and dark from wind and weather, working in the timber as their father had done. He had no wife and children and would roam far off with the timber gangs in the Everglades. This latter year he did not go far, but stayed near them. Their mother stopped and looked at the man, and he looked at her in silence. Then he looked at Jim and Daniel.

"You're goen to take them after all?"

She waited a minute, seeming to get the words straight in her mind before bringing them out, making them say what was set there.

"He asked to see them. Nobody but God Almighty ought to tell a soul hit can or can't have."

Having delivered her mind, she went out into the yard with the man, and they spoke more words in an undertone, pausing in their speech.

In the silence of the kitchen Daniel began to speak out and name what thing among his possessions he would take to Czardis to give his father. But the older boy belittled this and that and everything that was called up, saying one thing was of too little consequence for a man, and that another was of no account because it was food. But when the older boy had abolished the idea and silence had regained, he worked back to the thought, coming to it round-about and making it new and as his own, letting it be decided that each of them would take their father a pomegranate from the tree in the yard.

They went to the kitchen door. The swamp fog had risen suddenly. They saw their mother standing in the lot while their uncle hitched the horse to the wagon. Leaving the steps, Jim climbed to the first crotch of the pomegranate tree. The reddest fruits were on the top branches. He worked his way up higher. The fog was now curling up out of the swamp, making gray mountains and rivers in the air and strange ghost shapes. Landmarks disappeared in the billows or, half seen, they bewildered the sight and an eye could so little mark the known or strange that a befuddlement took hold of the mind, like the visitations sailors beheld in the fogs of Okeechobee. Jim could not find the ground. He seemed to have climbed into the mountains. The light was unnatural and dark, and the pines were blue and dark over the mountains.

A voice cried out of the fog:

"Are worms gnawen you that you skin up a pomegranate tree at this hour? Don't I feed you enough?"

The boy worked his way down. At the front of the tree he met his mother. She squatted and put her arm around him, her voice tight and quivering, and he felt tears on her face:

"We ain't come to the shame yet of you and Dan'l hunten your food off trees and grass. People seein' you gnawen on the road will say Jim Cameron's sons are starved, foragen like cattle on the field."

"I were getten the pomegranates for Papa," said the boy, resigned to his mother's concern. She stood up when he said this, holding him in front of her skirts. In a while she said:

"I guess we won't take any, Jim. . . . But I'm proud it come to you to take your papa somethen."

And after a silence, the boy said:

"Hit were Dan'l it come to, Mamma."

Then she took his hand, not looking down, and in her throat, as if in her bosom, she repeated:

"Hit were a fine thought and I'm right proud . . . though today we won't take anything. . . ."

"I guess there's better pomegranates in Czardis where we are goen—"

"There's no better pomegranates in Czardis than right here over your head," she said grimly. "If pomegranates were needed, we would take him his own. . . . You are older'n Dan'l, Jim. When we get to the place we are goen, you won't know your papa after so long. He will be pale and he won't be as bright as you recollect. So don't labor him with questions . . . but speak when it behooves you and let him see you are upright."

When the horse was harnessed and all was ready for the departure, the sons were seated on a shallow bed of hay in the back of the wagon and the mother took the driver's seat alone. The uncle had argued for having the top up over the seat, but she refused the shelter, remarking that she had always driven under the sky and would do it still today. He gave in silently and got up on the seat of his own wagon, which took the road first, their wagon following. This was strange, and the sons asked:

"Why don't we all ride in Uncle Holly's wagon?"

But their mother made no reply.

For several miles they traveled in silence through their own part of the woods, meeting no one. The boys whispered a little to themselves, but their mother and their uncle sat without speaking, nor did they turn their heads to look back. At last the narrow road they were following left the woods and came out to the highway, and it was seen that other wagons besides their own were going to Czardis. And as they got farther along, they began to meet many other people going to town, and the boys asked their mother what day it was. It was Wednesday. And then they asked her why so many wagons were going along the road if it wasn't Saturday and a market day. When she told them to be quiet, they settled down to watching the people go by. Some of them were faces that were strange, and some were neighbors who lived in other parts of the woods. Some who passed them stared in silence, and some went by looking straight to the front. But there were none of them who spoke, for their mother turned her eyes neither right nor left, but drove the horse on like a woman in her sleep. All was silent as the wagons passed, except the squeaking of the wheels and the thud of the horses' hoofs on the dry, packed sand.

At the edge of the town the crowds increased, and their wagon got lost in the press of people. All were moving in one direction.

Finally they were going along by a high brick wall on top of which ran a barbed-wire fence. Farther along the way in the middle of the wall was a tall, stone building with many people in front. There were trees along the outside of the wall, and in the branches of one of the trees Daniel saw a man. He was looking over the brick wall down into the courtyard. All the wagons were stopping here and hitching through the grove in front of the building. But their Uncle Holly's wagon and their own drove on, making way slowly as through a crowd at a fair, for under the trees knots of men were gathered, talking in undertones. Daniel pulled at his mother's skirts and whispered:

"What made that man climb up that tree?"

Again she told him to be quiet.

"We're not to talk today," said Jim. "Papa is sick and we're not to make him worse." But his high, thin voice made his mother turn cold. She looked back and saw he had grown pale and still, staring at the iron-barred windows of the building. When he caught her gaze, his chin began to quiver, and she turned back front to dodge the knowledge of his eyes.

For the two wagons had stopped now and the uncle gotten down and left them sitting alone while he went to the door of the building and talked with a man standing there. The crowd fell silent, staring at their mother.

"See, Jim, all the men up the trees!" Daniel whispered once more, leaning close to his brother's side.

"Hush, Dan'l. Be still."

The young boy obeyed this time, falling into a bewildered stare at all the things about him he did not understand, for in all the trees along the brick wall men began to appear perched high in the branches, and on the roof of a building across the way stood other men, all gaping at something in the yard back of the wall.

Their uncle returned and hitched his horse to a ring in one of the trees. Then he hitched their mother's horse, and all of them got out and stood on the ground in a huddle. The walls of the building rose before them. Strange faces at the barred windows laughed aloud and called down curses at the men below.

Now they were moving, with a wall of faces on either side of them, their uncle going first, followed by their mother who held to each of them by a hand. They went up the steps of the building. The door opened, and their uncle stepped inside. He came back in a moment, and all of them went in and followed a man down a corridor and into a bare room with two chairs and a wooden bench. A man in a black robe sat on one of the chairs, and in front of him on the bench, leaning forward, looking down between his arms, sat their father. His face was lean and gray, which made him look very tall. But his hair was black, and his eyes were blue and mild and strange as he stood up and held the two sons against his body while he stooped his head to kiss their mother. The man in black left the room and walked up and down outside the corridor. A second stranger stood in the doorway with his back to the room. The father picked up one of the sons and then the other in his arms and looked at them and leaned their faces on his own. Then he sat down on the bench and held them against him. Their mother sat down by them and they were all together.

A few low words were spoken, and then a silence fell over them all. And in a while the parents spoke a little more and touched one another. But the bare stone floor and the stone walls and the unaccustomed arms of their father hushed the sons with a new and strange fear. And when the time had passed, the father took his watch from his pocket:

"I'm goen to give you my watch, Jim. You are the oldest. I want you to keep it till you are a grown man. . . . And I want you to always do what Mamma tells you. . . . I'm goen to give you the chain, Dan'l. . . ."

The younger brother took the chain, slipped out of his father's arms, and went to his mother with it. He spread it out on her knee and began to talk to her in a whisper. She bent over him, and again all of them in the room grew silent.

A sudden sound of marching was heard in the corridor. The man rose up and took his sons in his arms, holding them abruptly. But their uncle, who had been standing with the man in the doorway, came suddenly and took them and went out and down through the big doorway by which they had entered the building. As the doors opened to let them pass, the crowd gathered around the steps pressed forward to look inside. The older boy cringed in his uncle's arms. His uncle turned and stood with his back to the crowd. Their mother came through the doors. The crowd fell back. Again through a passageway of gazing eyes, they reached the wagons. This time they sat on the seat beside their mother. Leaving their uncle and his wagon behind, they started off on the road that led out of town.

"Is Papa coming home with Uncle Holly?" Jim asked in a still voice.

His mother nodded her head.

Reaching the woods once more and the silence he knew, Daniel whispered to his brother:

"We got a watch and chain instead, Jim."

But Jim neither answered nor turned his eyes.

Here, in part, is what Kenneth Payson Kempton has written about this story:

The telling method here, so restrained and closely tuned to personality, can be called objective. Much of the opening might be coming to us through either or both boys. And at a crucial point in the story—

"But his high, thin voice made his mother turn cold. She looked back and saw he had grown pale and still, staring at the iron-barred windows of the building. When he caught her gaze, his chin began to quiver and she turned back front to dodge the knowledge in his eyes."—suddenly we hear, see, interpret sense impressions, and suffer through and with the mother. Is this arbitrary magic, omniscience? I don't think so. All of them covered by the muted tone and excellently chosen language, these divergencies slip past without for a moment disturbing the illusion of reality. The language is the binding force, the secret behind this telling method just off objectivity. It is so simple and hushed and homogeneous, it would serve as expression for any one of the three persons involved.

It clearly implies both an emotional and an intellective unity in the mother and the two sons, and it precludes even the appearance of self-pity in any one of them, or the faintest tinge of sentimentality in the piece as a whole.

Here technique, as always in a good story, merges and interlocks with content. What of the past of these people in "A Trip to Czardis"? It may strike a reader with surprise that he never learns what crime, if any, the father had committed and whether he was justly or unjustly executed. Yet the story has a strong taproot in the past. If the matter omitted is considered with reference to the persons concerned and the medium of telling used, it is recognized as of little or no importance. It is the imminence of the father's death that overshadows everything. What we do know of the past is of supreme importance. It has been hinted at early, by the mother's warning to her sons, especially Jim, and by Uncle Holly's presence and help; but we discover this taproot in the past rather late, for it has been logically masked by the woman's grief and shame and her nervousness. It is revealed with tragic force in the prison scene near the end.

This family is four persons; it has a head, who will soon be lost. The discovery is no tearjerker; it relates directly to Jim's assumption of authority, his growth, as soon as he knew the truth and from then on. The discovery works, moreover, as a powerful level for prolonged suspense, since we, the reader, aren't yet positive that the worst will happen. And it was to this purpose, this final discovery, that the author constantly refused to dramatize any emotions or tell any more than the barest facts of behavior. Time and again he told less.

Granberry's use of suspense is our main concern. "A Trip to Czardis" is a good example because it shows all kinds.

The personal bond between reader and protagonist that I mentioned is forged at the very beginning, where Jim wakes first, puts an arm around his small brother, and comforts him. Place helps, too, at the point where Jim climbs the pomegranate tree for a gift for his father. By the time his mother has rebuked him, the bond is unbreakable; but it is to grow in strength, as Jim grows, to the end of the story.

Through this early part, the suspense is simple. The reader is as much in the dark as are the two boys, as queasily excited as they at the prospect of going to see their father; but their mother's strange reticence, and her secret conference with Uncle Holly after his question: "You're goen to take them, after all?" increase his tension.

The reader can check back, he can pause on something like "after all" and consider its implication. Already, though still in the dark, he suspects; the boys, excited by the thought of the trip to see their father so long absent, suspect nothing. Complex suspense begins here, on as yet no specific knowledge, merely in the reader's premonition. Detail follows detail—Uncle Holly wanting the top up and the mother saying no, the mother saying nothing when asked why they don't all go in Uncle Holly's wagon, the crowds on the road all headed for town—that withholds information from the boys and the reader but increases his fearful suspicion, while them it only puzzles.

Then, a sympathy-anxiety-fear synergy established in him, the reader's premonition is confirmed by acquisition of knowledge that runs ahead of the boys'. Daniel's knowledge lags throughout; that is, with respect to the younger boy, suspense remains complex, tightening the reader's fear for him. But mercifully—and with a single exception to be noted later, naturally—the ailing and timorous Daniel is not permitted to know what this is all about. Knowledge would be sheer brutality; he couldn't understand. His childlike delight in the gifts provides irony as contrast to and background for what, meanwhile, has happened to his older brother.

Jim's knowledge catches up with the reader's somewhere in the paragraph beginning: "Finally they were going along by a high brick wall on top of which ran a barbed-wire fence." Although the paragraph does not mention Jim, and it is Daniel who sees the man looking over the wall, Daniel who pulls at his mother's skirts and asks: "What made that man climb up that tree?", we can almost see Jim's mind working, adding up the details and reaching the awful truth. Jim knows, now, and what for a while was complex suspense with respect to both boys becomes simple suspense again with respect to him, but a simple suspense that is excruciating, because of the weight of what we have learned that we didn't know before, and because in learning now, Jim has become a part of us. How will he take it? What can he do?

Jim shows that he knows by helping his mother quiet Daniel, by beginning to take his father's place, by beginning to grow; and this sharing of responsibility, though we see its rightness and respect him for it, hurts almost as much as his remaining in ignorance—far more than his simply being crushed by the knowledge—would have hurt.

Does Jim struggle, once he knows? Physically, of course, he cannot; the forces arrayed against him are far beyond his ability to resist. Besides, resistance would be childish, and he is leaving childhood behind him, as shown at the end of the story by his ability to phrase a question that, answered, will tell him what he wants to know without disturbing Daniel; and by his silence, like his mother's silence now, at the very end when Daniel speaks. The struggle, in fact, took place within him, just before he found a way ("papa is sick," etc.) to explain the strangeness of events to his brother, and thus quiet him. It was a tough struggle and he won it. Simply, he takes the truth tight-lipped.

The story shows this, in its characteristic oblique way, by all but ignoring him from the moment when Jim says, "Hush, Dan'l. Be still," and Daniel obeys, until the final sentence. Between those points we have only Jim's *failure* to speak when his father gives him the watch, a powerful implication that he is unable to speak; "The older boy cringed in his uncle's arms," as the crowd presses forward to stare—a concession to childhood weakness that is momentary; and Jim's carefully phrased question, already mentioned, asked to confirm what he knows only too well, but to clear up the mystery of the two wagons and Uncle Holly's presence: "Is Papa coming home with Uncle Holly?" This is very little, considering all that happens in that space; but the story is so packed with implication that in that final sentence Jim's relationship with and emotional response to his brother, his father, and his mother stand out starkly clear: "But Jim neither answered nor turned his eyes."

We come to the single exception in Daniel's behavior, a single word. The child's last line is "We got a watch and chain instead, Jim." At this most important point in the story, where nothing should retard the swift end, "instead" may distract the reader by sending him off into a series of anxious surmises. Could the author possibly have meant that Daniel was willing to substitute the gifts for his father permanently? Or could the author possibly have meant that little Daniel, bewildered and ignorant throughout, has now suddenly come to a partial awareness of the truth? Perhaps the likeliest supposition is that Daniel used the word to mean—since his papa is coming home with Uncle Holly— merely that the gifts will serve as replacement for the trip home. But the irony seems too subtle, and we came too long a way to catch it. Daniel's line would be better if "instead" had been dropped out.

There is strong, simple irony enough as it is. Instead of giving as they had planned, the boys received. In figurative or symbolic terms, each received as much knowledge as—and a gift that—he could understand, enjoy, make use of: Daniel a bright toy to take his mind off his ailments and grown-up matters he would never understand; Jim a watch telling him it is time to grow up, and with it a terrific jolt that started him growing.

The story is notably modest and unpretentious, in manner and matter. Dealing with quite unimportant, uninformed, underprivileged people, it convincingly creates in them a dignity and a sense of unflinching personal integrity seldom found in fiction. It speaks in a low, hesitant, but clear and eloquent voice that, translated, would be understood and found meaningful almost anywhere on earth, at almost any time in history.

The tragedy here does not torture the reader with the presence of implacable and unjust power used to smash the weak; it uplifts and inspires the reader by showing him the weak and lonely holding fast to their ideals in the very face of crushing adversity. He is cleansed in heart by the experience shared with Jim.

"A Trip to Czardis" seems to deserve permanence as part—a small but indispensable part—of the world's literature. (Reprinted from *Short Stories for Study* by Kenneth Payson Kempton, Harvard University Press, Cambridge, copyright © 1953.)

This story, for television, offers any writer a hard test. As adapter, it is his responsibility to tell the same story, deliver it with the same power, sustain the same mood.

The student effort that follows is already in performable shape. No serious mistakes are made, no significant omissions. All implications—both as to character and story progress—are respectably observed and are permitted to "leak" their meanings very much as Granberry did in the unfolding of his simple yet torturing story.

To go through the television versions of this story and "page" it for such hints, arcadings, do's-and-don'ts as this student work reveals will bring to light a few mistakes that are not present in the professionalism of most of the other scripts. Though the author of this script is himself a professional man (a newscaster for

WINS) and a writer, there are some slight amateur blunders. But his story sensitivity is unmistakable.

A TRIP TO CZARDIS
Written by Edwin Granberry
Adapted for Television by Kirk Gardner

CAST

JIM CAMERON	UNCLE HOLLY
DANIEL CAMERON	A MINISTER
MRS. CAMERON	A DEPUTY
MR. CAMERON	SEVERAL PRISON GUARDS

SETS

EXT. CAMERONS' CABIN	EXT. ROAD THROUGH THE WOODS
INT. JIM AND DANIEL'S BEDROOM	EXT. CZARDIS TOWN SQUARE
INT. CAMERON KITCHEN	EXT. PRISON
EXT. CAMERONS' YARD	INT. PRISON VISITING ROOM

ACT I

1 FADE IN ON A BLACK SCREEN. THE TOTAL DARKNESS LASTS ONLY AN INSTANT. SIMULTANEOUSLY, THE TITLES APPEAR, AND BEHIND THEM THE CAMERA APERTURE SLOWLY OPENS. THE VAGUE OUTLINE OF A CLEARING IS GRADUALLY REVEALED. AT ITS CENTER STANDS A SMALL PINEWOOD CABIN. THE POINT OF VIEW IS TREETOP LEVEL, AT THE EDGE OF THE CLEARING. IT IS THE VAGUE TWILIGHT TIME ABOUT AN HOUR BEFORE DAWN. IN THE BACKGROUND, THE ONLY SOUNDS ARE THE FIRST TENTATIVE CALLS OF WAKING BIRDS. THE CAMERA MOVES IN ON A SINGLE WINDOW ON THE SECOND STORY OF THE CABIN.

2 FADE IN TO A CLOSE-UP OF THE WINDOW. THE SCREEN IS FRAMED WITH THE HARSH HORIZONTAL LINES OF THE CABIN, AND IN THE CENTER WE SEE, THROUGH THE VERTICAL SLATS OF THE WINDOW, TWO SMALL FIGURES ASLEEP IN A BED.

3 CUT TO THE INTERIOR OF THE BEDROOM. THE OLDER BOY, JIM, STIRS AND THEN SITS UP SUDDENLY, RUBBING HIS EYES. HE STARES AHEAD FOR A SECOND, OBVIOUSLY THINKING, THEN LEANS OVER AND NUDGES HIS YOUNGER BROTHER, DANIEL.

JIM

Dan'l . . . Dan'l . . .

DANIEL WAKES UP MUCH MORE SLOWLY THAN HIS BROTHER AND SITS UP IN BED.

JIM

(WITH QUIET EXCITEMENT) Hit's the day, Dan'l.

DANIEL YAWNS AND BLINKS HIS EYES, STILL SLEEPY AND CONFUSED. HIS

BODY SHIVERS EVER SO SLIGHTLY WITH THE COLD. HE MAKES A SMALL WHIM-
PERING SOUND AND SNUGGLES CLOSER TO JIM.

4 CUT TO A CLOSE-UP OF JIM AND DANIEL.

> JIM

This day that's right here now, we're goen. You'll recollect it all in a
minute.

> DANIEL

(HIS EYES BRIGHTENING A LITTLE) I recollect. We're goen in the wagon
to see Papa . . .

> JIM

(WITH GENTLE AUTHORITY) Then hush.

DANIEL MOVES EVEN CLOSER TO JIM AND HOLDS ON TO HIM. A LOOK OF VAGUE
FEAR CROSSES HIS FACE.

> DANIEL

I were dreamen, Jim.

> JIM

What dreamen did you have?

> DANIEL

I can't tell. But it were fearful what I dreamt.

JIM GIVES DANIEL A REASSURING HUG, BUT WITH THE ANTICIPATION OF THE
DAY GROWING INSIDE HIM, HE MOVES AWAY FROM DANIEL AND SWINGS HIS
LEGS OVER THE EDGE OF THE BED.

5 CUT TO A MID-ROOM SHOT OF THE BED.

> JIM

All the way we are goen this time. We won't stop at any places, but we
will go all the way to Czardis to see Papa.

JIM PAUSES FOR A MOMENT, THINKING.

> JIM

(CON'T) I never did see such a place as Czardis.

DANIEL CATCHES JIM'S MOUNTING EXCITEMENT AND QUICKLY FORGETS HIS
DREAM.

> DANIEL

I recollect the water tower . . .

> JIM

(JUST A BIT CONDESCENDINGLY) Not in your own right, Dan'l. Hit's by
my tellin it you see it in your mind.

> DANIEL

(HIS SPIRIT COMPLETELY UNDAMPENED BY THIS INFORMATION) And
lemonade with ice in it I saw . . .

JIM

That too I seen and told to you.

DANIEL

(A LITTLE PUZZLED AND SOMEWHAT CRESTFALLEN) Then I never seen
it at all?

JIM

Hit's me were there, Dan'l. I let you play like, but hit's me who went to
Czardis. Yet I never till this day told half how much I seen. There's sights
I never told.

6   THE ROOM BECOMES INCREASINGLY LIT WITH THE ADVANCING DAWN, AND IT
HAS GROWN APPARENT THAT DANIEL IS A THIN, PALE, SICKLY BOY. AS THE TWO
BOYS SIT ON THE BED, WE HEAR IN THE BACKGROUND THE RISING CALLS OF
THE BIRDS. DANIEL BEGINS TO SHIVER AGAIN.

DANIEL

Hit's dark and cold.

JIM

Hit's your eyes stuck. Would you want me to drip a little water on your
eyes?

DANIEL CRINGES EVER SO SLIGHTLY AT THE IDEA.

DANIEL

Oh! Don't douse me, Jim, no more. The cold aches me.

JIM HOLDS HIS BROTHER AGAIN TO SOOTHE HIM.

JIM

You won't have e're chill or malarie ache today, Dan'l. Hit's a fair
day . . .

DANIEL

I won't be cold?

JIM

Hit's a bright day. Hear the birds start'n in a'ready? The sun will bake
you warm.

JIM HESITATES FOR A MOMENT, THINKING. HIS FACE BRIGHTENS.

JIM

(CON'T) Uncle Holly might buy us somethin to eat in Czardis.

DANIEL

What would it be?

JIM GETS OFF THE BED AND STRETCHES.

JIM

Hit ain't decided yet . . . he hasn't spoke. Hit might be somethin sweet.
Maybe a candy ball fixed onto a rubber string.

7   THE CAMERA CLOSES IN ON DANIEL, EXPOSING HIS FRAIL FEATURES. JIM HAS
WALKED AROUND BEHIND THE BED AND STANDS IN THE BACKGROUND.

DANIEL

(WONDERINGLY) A candy ball.

DANIEL'S FACE BRIGHTENS SLIGHTLY, BUT ONLY FOR A MOMENT. HIS BODY SLUMPS A LITTLE, AND HE LOOKS BLANKLY TOWARD THE FOOT OF THE BED.

DANIEL

My stomach would retch it up, Jim. I guess I couldn't eat it.

JIM

You might keep a little down . . .

DANIEL

No . . . I would bring it home and keep it.

8 CUT TO JUST OUTSIDE THE WINDOW AGAIN. WE CAN SEE THE BOYS BEGINNING TO DRESS. THEIR CLOTHES ARE NEATLY LAID OUT ON A CHAIR IN THE CORNER. JIM HELPS DANIEL.

9 AS THE CAMERA MOVES BACK, THE PORTION OF THE CABIN THAT IS THE KITCHEN COMES INTO VIEW. SMOKE RISES FROM A CHIMNEY. SOME OF THE YARD FOWL ARE MOVING AROUND THE KITCHEN STEPS, LOOKING FOR FOOD.

10 DISSOLVE TO A MEDIUM SHOT OF THE KITCHEN, FROM JUST OUTSIDE THE OPEN DOOR. THE CAMERA SLOWLY MOVES INSIDE. STEEP, NARROW STAIRS LEAD DOWN FROM THE BEDROOM, DIAGONALLY ACROSS THE REAR OF THE SET. AT THE LEFT OF THE ROOM IS A WOODEN TABLE AND CHAIRS—ON THE TABLE TWO BOWLS OF STEAMING MUSH. ON THE RIGHT-HAND SIDE OF THE KITCHEN, BRICKS ARE SET INTO THE FLOOR. ON TOP OF THE BRICKS IS AN OLD WOOD-BURNING STOVE, WITH THE DOOR OF THE FIREBOX OPEN. A SINGLE POT STEAMS ON THE STOVE. MRS. CAMERON SITS IN A CHAIR NEAR THE STOVE DOOR. SHE'S WEARING A PLAIN BLACK DRESS, THE CLOTH SAGGING BETWEEN HER KNEES. MRS. CAMERON IS A WOMAN IN HER EARLY THIRTIES, BUT OLD BEFORE HER TIME. HER HEAD BOWED, HER ARMS FOLDED ACROSS HER LAP, SHE MURMURS TO HERSELF. WE CATCH ONLY A PHRASE OR TWO OF WHAT SHE SAYS. . . .

MRS. CAMERON

. . . yet it's hard . . . they'll not understand . . .

THE TWO BOYS COME DOWN THE STEPS, JIM FIRST, LEADING HIS BROTHER BY THE HAND. THEY WALK UPSTAGE TO STAND NEAR THEIR MOTHER. SLOWLY SHE LOOKS UP.

MRS. CAMERON

(GENTLY) Your clothes on already?

SHE REACHES OUT WITH HER HAND, TOUCHING FIRST ONE SON AND THEN THE OTHER.

MRS. CAMERON

You look neat. You'll be good boys today, and do like your father and I raised you.

A SHADOW CROSSES HER FACE, AND SHE RESUMES HER PREVIOUS POSITION. JIM CROSSES THE ROOM TO EAT HIS BREAKFAST, WHILE DANIEL SQUATS DOWN

BESIDE HIS MOTHER ON THE WARM BRICKS BY THE STOVE. AT FIRST, DANIEL
WATCHES HIS BROTHER SIT DOWN, BUT AS JIM TAKES HIS FIRST BITE, HE
SHUDDERS AND BURIES HIS HEAD IN HIS MOTHER'S SKIRTS. JUST AS HE DOES
SO, A SHADOW OF A MAN'S FIGURE FALLS ACROSS THE ROOM FROM THE POSI-
TION OF THE CAMERA. ITS SUDDENNESS IS SLIGHTLY MENACING.

11 CUT TO A NEW CAMERA ANGLE. THE POV IS JUST BEHIND JIM'S BACK. A MAN
STANDS IN THE DOORWAY. HE IS LEAN AND LARGE-FRAMED, HIS FACE DARK
AND WEATHERBEATEN. HE STEPS INTO THE KITCHEN, LOOKS AT MRS. CAMERON,
AND SHE MEETS HIS GAZE. THE CAMERA MOVES BACK AND TO STAGE RIGHT.
JIM RAISES HIS HEAD.

JIM

Uncle Holly. We're all set to go.

12 THE CAMERA CUTS TO A CLOSER SHOT OF UNCLE HOLLY AND MRS. CAMERON.

UNCLE HOLLY

(IGNORING JIM) You're goen to take them after all?

CLOSE-UP OF MRS. CAMERON. SHE PAUSES AN INSTANT.

MRS. CAMERON

(WITH CONVICTION) He asked to see them. Nobody but God Almighty
ought to tell a soul hit can or can't have.

13 CUT TO A MEDIUM SHOT FROM JIM'S POV. MRS. CAMERON GETS UP AND GOES
TO THE DOOR. SHE AND UNCLE HOLLY GO OUT INTO THE YARD.

14 DISSOLVE TO A MEDIUM SHOT OF THE HOUSE, AS THEY COME OUT THE DOOR
TOWARD THE CAMERA. THE CAMERA FOLLOWS THEM AS THEY WALK TO THE
YARD AND STAND NEAR HOLLY'S WAGON. MRS. CAMERON LOOKS INTENTLY
TOWARD THE FAR END OF THE CLEARING. THE CAMERA PANS TO PICK UP
THE SMALL FAMILY BURIAL PLOT NEAR THE ROAD, BUT KEEPS MRS. CAMERON
AND HOLLY IN THE CORNER OF THE FRAME. WE CAN MAKE OUT THREE
MARKERS. AFTER THIS SHORT PAUSE, MRS. CAMERON TURNS TO HOLLY.

MRS. CAMERON

I guess we'll need two wagons. I don't want to stay there.

UNCLE HOLLY

I'll hitch your wagon then.

HOLLY MOVES OFF TO THE SHED BEHIND THE HOUSE, AS MRS. CAMERON'S
GAZE RETURNS TO THE PLOT. THE MORNING FOG IS BEGINNING TO RISE OUT
OF THE SWAMP.

15 DISSOLVE TO THE INTERIOR OF THE KITCHEN. DANIEL, WARMED FROM THE
STOVE, GETS UP AND WALKS TO HIS BROTHER AT THE TABLE.

DANIEL

(HIS EYES BRIGHT WITH AN IDEA) Jim, I'm goen take my shiny penny to
Czardis and give to Papa.

JIM
(EXERCISING THE AUTHORITY OF HIS AGE) A penny won't do for given, Dan'l. What'll Papa buy with a penny?

DANIEL
(AFTER THINKING THIS OVER) How bout that garter snake we found in the yard?

JIM
No, Dan'l. What's Papa goen to do with a garter snake?

DANIEL
(PAUSES, THEN BECOMES EXCITED AGAIN) I know, Jim. Some fruit from the yard.

JIM
Papa don't need food, Dan'l.

THE BOYS FALL INTO A BRIEF SILENCE. DANIEL IS A LITTLE SULLEN.

JIM
Maybe if it were some food Papa liked . . . somethin he might want special. Maybe he'd like a pomegranate from our tree in the yard.

DANIEL
Can I take one, too, Jim?

JIM
Sure . . . I'll get two from the tree and we can take 'em with us.

JIM GETS UP FROM THE TABLE.

16 CUT TO EXT. HOUSE. THE CAMERA PANS TO FOLLOW THEM ACROSS THE YARD TO THE POMEGRANATE TREE. IN THE BACKGROUND, WE SEE HOLLY HITCHING UP THE WAGON. MRS. CAMERON IS STANDING QUIETLY, STILL LOOKING OFF TO THE EDGE OF THE CLEARING. THE BOYS REACH THE TREE AND JIM BEGINS TO CLIMB.

17 CUT TO MEDIUM SHOT OF JIM IN THE TREE AND DANIEL STANDING AT ITS BASE. BEHIND THEM IS A FIELD, AT THE CORNER OF WHICH IS THE FAMILY PLOT. THE MARKERS ARE BARELY VISIBLE THROUGH THE GROWING MIST. JIM PAYS NO ATTENTION TO THIS BACKGROUND.

DANIEL
Find any good'ns, Jim?

JIM FEELS SEVERAL OF THE CLOSEST POMEGRANATES.

JIM
These hain't ripe yet. I'll have to go higher.

JIM CLIMBS UP INTO THE HIGHER BRANCHES OF THE TREE. THE SWAMP FOG WHICH HAS BEEN STEADILY RISING, NOW SHROUDS DANIEL AT THE BOTTOM SO THAT HE IS ONLY A DARK FIGURE. THE CAMERA FOLLOWS JIM TO THE TOP OF THE TREE. JIM FEELS SEVERAL FRUIT, TOUCHING ONE AND THEN ANOTHER. FROM HIS LEVEL, THE GROWING DAYLIGHT, SHINING ON THE GROUND FOG,

MAKES THE EARTH BARELY VISIBLE. AFTER FINGERING A FEW MORE POME-
GRANATES, HE CHOOSES TWO AND PUTS THEM IN A POCKET. AS HE GETS READY
TO DESCEND, HE NOTICES THE FOG THAT IS ENVELOPING HIM. JIM LOOKS
AROUND, OBVIOUSLY TRYING TO GET HIS BEARINGS. A LOOK OF CONFUSION
COMES OVER HIS FACE. MRS. CAMERON'S VOICE COMES THROUGH THE
MIST. . . .

MRS. CAMERON

Jim . . . Dan'l . . . We're ready.

DANIEL, A BARELY DISCERNIBLE FIGURE BELOW, ANSWERS. . . .

DANIEL

Over here, Mama, by the tree.

BELOW, THE SHADOWY FIGURE OF MRS. CAMERON JOINS THAT OF DANIEL.

MRS. CAMERON

Where's your brother, Dan'l?

DANIEL

Up the tree.

MRS. CAMERON

Go watch your Uncle Holly finish hitchin the wagon, Dan'l. Jim and I'll
be right along.

AS JIM HESITATINGLY BEGINS TO DESCEND, THE CAMERA FOLLOWS HIM.

MRS. CAMERON

(CALLING UP TO JIM) Are worms gnawen you that you skin up a pomegranate tree at this hour? Don't I feed you enough?

18 JIM HAS WORKED HIS WAY TO THE BOTTOM OF THE TREE. AT THIS LEVEL WE
CAN SEE THE FIGURES MUCH MORE CLEARLY. THE CAMERA STOPS AT THE
MOTHER'S LEVEL, LOOKING DOWN ON JIM AS HE REACHES THE GROUND. MRS.
CAMERON BENDS DOWN, PUTTING HER ARMS AROUND THE BOY. THERE ARE
TEARS IN HER EYES.

MRS. CAMERON

(TIGHT AND QUAVERINGLY) We ain't come to the shame yet of you and
Dan'l huntin your food off trees and grass. People seein you on the road
will say Jim Cameron's sons are starved, foragen like cattle of the field.

JIM

(WITH RESIGNATION) I were getten the pomegranates for Papa.

MRS. CAMERON STANDS UP, STILL HOLDING HER SON CLOSE TO HER.

MRS. CAMERON

(MORE STEADILY) I guess we won't take any, Jim. But I'm proud it come
to you to take your Papa somethin.

JIM LOOKS DOWN.

JIM

Hit were Dan'l it come to, Mama.

MRS. CAMERON REACHES DOWN, TAKES HIS HAND, AND HOLDS IT TO HER WAIST. SHE LOOKS UP. THE CAMERA, STILL AT MRS. CAMERON'S LEVEL, CLOSES IN, KEEPING JIM IN THE FRAME.

MRS. CAMERON

Hit were a fine thought and I'm right proud . . . though today we won't take anything. . . .

JIM

I guess there's better pomegranates in Czardis where we are goen. . . .

MRS. CAMERON LOOKS DOWN AGAIN AND PLACES HER OTHER HAND ON JIM'S HEAD.

MRS. CAMERON

You're older'n Dan'l, Jim. When we get to the place we are goen, you won't know your Papa after so long. He'll be pale, and he won't be as bright as you recollect. So don't labor him with questions, but speak when it behooves you and let him see you are upright.

A PUZZLED LOOK CROSSES JIM'S FACE, BUT AS HIS MOTHER MOVES OFF TOWARD THE WAGON, HE TAKES THE POMEGRANATES FROM HIS POCKET AND HESITAT-INGLY LAYS THEM ON THE GROUND NEXT TO THE TREE. HE STANDS AND FOL-LOWS HIS MOTHER TOWARD THE WAGONS.

19 DISSOLVE TO A MEDIUM SHOT OF BOTH WAGONS. DANIEL IS SITTING IN ONE WAGON. MRS. CAMERON IS IN THE DRIVER'S SEAT. JIM IS STANDING ON THE GROUND NEXT TO UNCLE HOLLY. THE COVER FOR THE DRIVER'S SEAT IS FOLDED BACK, BARING THE SUPPORTS.

UNCLE HOLLY

You sure you don't want the top up over the seat?

MRS. CAMERON

No, we'll ride with it open under the sky just like we always have. We won't do no different today.

THE UNCLE SHRUGS, THEN BOOSTS JIM UP INTO THE WAGON NEXT TO DANIEL. HE WALKS FORWARD, GETS IN HIS OWN WAGON, AND STARTS OFF DOWN THE ROAD. MRS. CAMERON FOLLOWS WITH HER WAGON.

CLOSE-UP OF JIM AND DANIEL. THE WAGON IS MOVING OUT OF THE CLEARING AND INTO THE WOODS, JUST PASSING THE FAMILY PLOT ALONG THE ROAD.

JIM

Why don't we all ride in Uncle Holly's wagon?

CUT TO A MEDIUM SHOT OF THE WAGON. MRS. CAMERON MAKES NO REPLY. SHE LOOKS STRAIGHT AHEAD AS THE WAGON MOVES INTO THE WOODS. THE CAMERA TURNS TO FOLLOW IT DOWN THE NARROW TRAIL. JIM SEEMS TO HAVE FORGOTTEN HIS QUESTION AS HE AND DANIEL BEGIN TALKING TO EACH OTHER IN THE BACK OF THE WAGON.

SLOW FADE.

END OF ACT I

ACT II

20 FADE IN. LONG SHOT.

WE SEE THE TRAIL THROUGH THE WOODS, AND HEAR THE SOUNDS OF THE HORSES' HOOVES AND THE CREAKING WHEELS. THE TWO WAGONS MOVE UP THE TRAIL. HOLLY AND MRS. CAMERON ARE LOOKING STRAIGHT AHEAD. IN THE BACK OF MRS. CAMERON'S WAGON, THE BOYS ARE TALKING TOGETHER.

21 DISSOLVE TO A LONG SHOT OF THE END OF THE TRAIL WHERE IT MEETS A WIDER, MORE HEAVILY TRAVELED ROAD. WE HEAR THE SOUNDS OF OTHER WAGONS. THE CAMERA PANS TO FOLLOW THE CAMERONS AS THEY TURN ONTO THE ROAD. WE SEE SEVERAL OTHER WAGONS—ALL TRAVELING IN THE SAME DIRECTION.

22 CUT TO A MEDIUM SHOT OF MRS. CAMERON'S WAGON. JIM AND DANIEL NOTICE THE OTHER WAGONS. THEY LOOK FIRST AT ONE AND THEN ANOTHER.

JIM

Look at all the wagons! What day is it?

MRS. CAMERON

It's Wednesday.

JIM

(PAUSES A MOMENT) But if it isn't Saturday, why are there so many wagons goen to town?

MRS. CAMERON

(GENTLY) Hush, and be still.

THE TWO BOYS SETTLE DOWN AND RESUME WATCHING THE OTHER WAGONS. JIM HAS A BEWILDERED LOOK ON HIS FACE.

23 CUT TO A LONG SHOT OF A FORK IN THE ROAD. MORE WAGONS ARE COMING FROM THAT DIRECTION.

24 CUT TO A MEDIUM SHOT OF THE CAMERONS' WAGON. MRS. CAMERON IS STILL LOOKING STRAIGHT AHEAD, BUT HER FACE HAS BECOME ETCHED WITH SOME INTERNAL PAIN. A FANCIER, FASTER WAGON PASSES THEM. AS IT DOES, ITS OCCUPANTS TURN TO STARE—FIRST AT MRS. CAMERON, THEN THE TWO BOYS IN THE BACK. THE ONLY SOUNDS WE HEAR ARE THE THUDS OF HOOFBEATS ON THE DRY, PACKED SAND, THE SQUEAKING OF AN INCREASING NUMBER OF WHEELS, AND THE OCCASIONAL PUNCTUATION OF A SNORTING HORSE.

25 CUT TO A CLOSE-UP OF JIM AND DANIEL. THEY'RE PASSING A SLOWER WAGON CARRYING A LARGE FAMILY. THE ADULTS IN THE DRIVER'S SEAT DO NOT TURN, BUT THE CHILDREN IN THE REAR LOOK WITH CURIOSITY AT THE TWO BOYS. DANIEL SMILES UNDER THEIR GAZE, BUT JIM MEETS THEIR STARES WITH PUZZLEMENT. THEN, SLIGHTLY ANGERED AND AFRAID, HE TURNS AWAY.

26 SLOW DISSOLVE TO A LONG SHOT. THE WAGONS HAVE REACHED THE EDGE OF TOWN. THE RHYTHMIC HOOFBEATS OF THE PREVIOUS SCENES GIVE WAY TO THE SOUNDS OF A LARGE CROWD. THE CAMERONS' WAGONS ARE SWALLOWED UP IN THE RIVER OF PEOPLE, ALL MOVING IN THE SAME DIRECTION.

27 DISSOLVE TO A CLOSE-UP OF JIM. MOUNTING APPREHENSION IS APPARENT IN
HIS EVERY GESTURE. HIS EYES DART BACK AND FORTH ACROSS THE FACES IN
THE CROWD. THE SOUNDS OF THE CROWD BUILD. BEHIND JIM, THE SOLID
SHAPE OF A HIGH BRICK WALL TOPPED BY BARBED WIRE COMES INTO VIEW.
JIM SUDDENLY TURNS HIS HEAD AND STARTS AS HE BECOMES AWARE OF THE
WALL.

CUT TO A MEDIUM SHOT OF THE WALL, JIM'S POV. THE CAMERA ZOOMS IN ON
THE STARK OUTLINE OF THE BARBED WIRE. THE WIRE IS CRISSCROSSED IN
PATTERN.

28 CUT TO A MEDIUM SHOT OF THE SECOND-FLOOR WINDOWS OF THE PRISON—
WINDOWS WITH HEAVY IRON BARS. (STILL JIM'S POV.)

29 CUT TO A MEDIUM SHOT OF THE SQUARE THE WAGON HAS MOVED INTO. THE
CROWD IS PRESSING IN AROUND THE PRISON WALLS. ACROSS FROM THE PRISON
IS A CHURCH. JIM LOOKS UP.

30 CUT TO JIM'S POV. THERE ARE SEVERAL MEN IN THE BELL TOWER OF THE
CHURCH. AS THE CAMERA QUICKLY MOVES ACROSS THE SQUARE, WE CAN SEE
ANOTHER MAN SCRAMBLING UP A TREE. ALL ARE TRYING TO SEE OVER THE
PRISON WALL.

31 CUT TO A CLOSE-UP OF JIM'S FACE. THERE IS SOMETHING APPROACHING PANIC
IN HIS FEATURES AS HIS EYES SCAN THE CROWD.

32 DISSOLVE SLOWLY FROM JIM'S FACE TO A MONTAGE OF THE BARS ON THE
PRISON WINDOWS, THE MEN IN THE BELL TOWER, THE BACK OF HOLLY'S
WAGON, THE CROWD CLOSING IN AROUND IT, AND THE CRISSCROSSED PATTERN
OF THE BARBED WIRE. THE MONTAGE IS FINALLY PUNCTUATED BY DANIEL'S
VOICE. (WITH THE BARBED WIRE STILL ON THE SCREEN.)

DANIEL
What made that man climb up that tree?

33 CUT TO A MEDIUM SHOT OF MRS. CAMERON'S WAGON. MRS. CAMERON SLOWLY
TURNS TO FACE THE BOYS IN THE BACK. AS SHE DOES, HER EYES MEET JIM'S
AND FOR A BRIEF MOMENT THEY LOOK INTENTLY AT EACH OTHER. THE FEAR
HAS LEFT JIM'S FACE, AND A KNOWING SADNESS HAS REPLACED IT. AFTER A
MOMENT, MRS. CAMERON DROPS HER GAZE AND TURNS FORWARD AGAIN. JIM
TURNS TO HIS BROTHER.

JIM
(IN A THIN, HIGH VOICE) We're not to talk today. Papa is sick and we're
not to make him worse.

MRS. CAMERON, LISTENING TO JIM, TURNS AGAIN. THE FEAR THAT HAD BEEN
ON JIM'S FACE IS NOW REFLECTED IN HER OWN AS SHE FULLY REALIZES HIS
AWARENESS. HE MEETS HER GAZE, HIS CHIN QUIVERING A LITTLE. AGAIN, SHE
TURNS AWAY.

34 SLOW DISSOLVE TO A LONG SHOT OF THE SQUARE. IT IS FULL OF PEOPLE. MOST
HAVE GATHERED INTO GROUPS AND ARE TALKING AMONG THEMSELVES IN LOW

TONES. WE CAN SEE THAT A NUMBER OF MEN HAVE CLIMBED INTO THE TREES LINING THE PRISON WALL. IN ONE CORNER OF THE SQUARE, THERE IS A MAN SELLING FRUIT FROM THE BACK OF HIS OPEN WAGON. PEOPLE AND OCCASIONAL WAGONS ARE STILL COMING IN FROM THE SIDE STREETS TOWARD THE SQUARE. THE CAMERA CLOSES IN ON THE CAMERON WAGON AS IT MOVES THROUGH THE CROWD TOWARD THE PRISON GATE.

35 CUT TO A MEDIUM SHOT OF THE CAMERON WAGONS. THEY STOP AS THEY REACH THE GATE. HOLLY WALKS TO THE DOOR OF THE PRISON AND TALKS TO A DEPUTY. THE CROWD IS SUDDENLY QUIET. ALL ARE STARING AT THE CAMERONS. THE ONLY SOUND IS A RHYTHMIC HAMMERING FROM BEYOND THE PRISON WALL.

DANIEL

(QUIETLY, TO JIM) See, Jim, all the men up the trees.

JIM

(GENTLY, WITHOUT EMOTION) Hush, Dan'l, and be still.

DANIEL, PUZZLED, LOOKS AWAY TO THE MEN IN THE TREES ALONG THE PRISON WALL.

36 DISSOLVE TO DANIEL'S POV. WE SEE THE MEN IN THE TREES.

37 AND AS THE CAMERA PANS, THE MEN IN THE BELL TOWER OF THE CHURCH. ALL ARE GAPING AT SOMETHING IN THE YARD ON THE OTHER SIDE OF THE WALL. THE CAMERA PANS DOWN TO PICK UP THE FACES OF THE CROWD. MANY ARE LOOKING IN THE GENERAL DIRECTION OF THE CAMERA, A FEW RIGHT INTO IT.

38 DISSOLVE TO A MEDIUM SHOT OF THE CAMERON WAGONS. THE PRISON IS IN THE BACKGROUND. HOLLY IS MAKING HIS WAY BACK TO THE FAMILY. HE HITCHES HIS HORSES TO THE TREES NEAR THE PRISON GATE. JIM GETS OUT OF THE WAGON AND HELPS DANIEL DOWN. AS HOLLY HITCHES MRS. CAMERON'S HORSES, JIM GIVES HIS MOTHER HIS HAND. SHE STEPS DOWN FROM THE DRIVER'S SEAT.

39 CUT TO A MEDIUM SHOT OF THE CROWD. BEHIND AND ABOVE IT LOOMS THE PRISON. THE CAMERA IS AT DANIEL'S LEVEL. IN THE FOREGROUND, HOLLY LEADS AND MRS. CAMERON FOLLOWS, HOLDING EACH BOY BY THE HAND. AS THEY MOVE THROUGH THE CROWD, THE CAMERA FOLLOWS. THE CROWD OPENS UP AHEAD OF THEM, FORMING A WALL OF FACES AS THEY PASS. AS THEY APPROACH THE PRISON, DARK FACES LOOK DOWN AT THEM FROM THE BARRED WINDOWS ABOVE.

40 AT THE PRISON STEPS, THE CAMERA MOVES AROUND AND UP ON DANIEL. WE SEE THE FRIGHTENED, BEWILDERED LOOK ON HIS FACE. IN THE BACKGROUND ARE MRS. CAMERON AND JIM.

41 THE CAMERA REMAINS STATIONARY, BUT PANS TO FOLLOW THEM AS THEY DISAPPEAR THROUGH THE DOOR HELD OPEN BY A DEPUTY. THE DOOR SHUTS ON THEM.

42 THE SOUND OF THE DOOR SLAMMING DISSOLVES TO THE SOUND OF BOOTS ON THE STONE CORRIDOR INSIDE, AS THE CAMERA DISSOLVES TO THE INT. CORRIDOR. THE FAMILY, LED BY A GUARD, WALKS TOWARD THE CAMERA, UP THE CORRIDOR.

43 THE CAMERA TRACKS BACK AHEAD OF THEM. A DOOR APPEARS TO ONE SIDE, AND THE GROUP STOPS.

44 CUT TO A MEDIUM SHOT OF THE DOORWAY. THERE IS A GUARD BLOCKING IT. JUST TO ONE SIDE ARE HOLLY, MRS. CAMERON, AND THE BOYS. THE GUARD STEPS ASIDE, AND WE CAN SEE THE INTERIOR OF THE ROOM. THERE ARE TWO CHAIRS SET DIAGONALLY ACROSS THE LEFT AND A BENCH DIAGONALLY ACROSS THE RIGHT. APART FROM THESE FURNISHINGS, THE ROOM IS BARE. A MINISTER IS SITTING ON ONE OF THE CHAIRS. ON THE FAR END OF THE BENCH IS THE BOY'S FATHER. HE IS LEANING FORWARD, LOOKING BETWEEN HIS ARMS. HIS FACE IS LEAN AND GRAY. HIS HAIR IS BLACK. HIS EXPRESSION IS ONE OF QUIET RESIGNATION. THE MINISTER STANDS AND LEAVES. HOLLY, MRS. CAMERON, AND THE BOYS ENTER. MR. CAMERON STANDS TO FACE THEM.

45 AS HIS FAMILY APPROACHES, HE PUTS ONE ARM AROUND EACH SON AND BENDS DOWN TO KISS HIS WIFE ON THE FOREHEAD. HOLLY STANDS OFF TO ONE SIDE. AT THIS INSTANT, OUR VIEW IS PARTIALLY OBSTRUCTED AS THE GUARD STEPS BACK INTO THE DOORWAY, HIS BACK TO THE ROOM.

46 DISSOLVE TO A MEDIUM SHOT OF THE INT. ROOM. THE HARSHNESS OF THE STONE FLOOR AND WALLS IS NOW APPARENT. THE FATHER STANDS TO THE LEFT OF THE FRAME, IN FRONT OF THE BENCH. MRS. CAMERON AND THE BOYS ARE TO THE RIGHT. AT THE REAR OF THE SET, WE SEE THE DOORWAY. IN IT, THE SILHOUETTE OF THE GUARD IS VISIBLE.

47 THE CAMERA MOVES SLOWLY IN ON THE FATHER.

MR. CAMERON
(TO HIS WIFE, IN A LOW VOICE) I'm glad you brought them.

MR. CAMERON REACHES DOWN AND PICKS UP THE YOUNGER SON.

MR. CAMERON
Dan'l . . .

DANIEL
Papa . . .

MR. CAMERON PUTS DANIEL DOWN AND RESTS HIS HANDS ON JIM'S SHOULDERS.

MR. CAMERON
Hello, Jim . . .

JIM IS UNABLE TO REPLY. MR. CAMERON SITS DOWN ON THE BENCH. JIM SITS TO ONE SIDE OF HIM, MRS. CAMERON TO THE OTHER. DANIEL CLIMBS INTO HIS LAP. DANIEL LOOKS UP INTO HIS FATHER'S FACE.

DANIEL
(WITH HESITATION DUE TO THE STRANGENESS OF HIS SITUATION) I come
all the way to Czardis, Papa, just like Jim.

MR. CAMERON

You're gettin to be a big boy, Dan'l. It's good you came.

A SILENCE FALLS OVER THE GROUP. AFTER A MOMENT, MR. CAMERON TURNS TO HIS WIFE AND TAKES HER HAND.

MR. CAMERON

(TENDERLY) Are you gettin on alright at home?

MRS. CAMERON

We're gettin on, Jim.

MR. CAMERON

(REMEMBERING) The trees in the yard must be fruited now.

MRS. CAMERON

They are. The boys were goen to bring you some today.

MR. AND MRS. CAMERON EXCHANGE A GAZE, THEN DROP THEIR EYES. AGAIN, A SILENCE FALLS.

48 SLOW DISSOLVE TO A CLOSE-UP OF JIM AND HIS FATHER WITH DANIEL ON HIS LAP. WE HEAR THE SOUND OF FOOTSTEPS AS SEVERAL GUARDS APPROACH THE DOOR. MR. CAMERON LOOKS TOWARD THE DOOR, THEN REACHES IN HIS POCKET AND TAKES OUT A WATCH AND CHAIN.

MR. CAMERON

I'm goen to give you my watch, Jim. You are the oldest. I want you to keep it till you're a grown man. I want you to always do what Mama tells you.

MR. CAMERON NOW TURNS TO DANIEL, PICKS HIM UP, AND STANDS HIM ON THE FLOOR IN FRONT OF HIM. HE KEEPS AN ARM AROUND THE BOY.

MR. CAMERON

I'm goen to give you the chain, Dan'l.

MR. CAMERON UNHITCHES THE CHAIN FROM THE WATCH AND GIVES THE WATCH TO JIM. JIM TAKES IT AND STANDS LOOKING DOWN AT IT IN HIS HAND. THEN HE HANDS THE CHAIN TO DANIEL. DANIEL SLIPS AWAY FROM HIS FATHER, GOES TO HIS MOTHER, AND SPREADS IT OUT ON HER LAP.

DANIEL

Look, Mama, see . . .

MRS. CAMERON BENDS OVER AND HUGS DANIEL, AND THE ROOM IS SILENT.

49 SLOW DISSOLVE TO OUTSIDE THE DOOR, LOOKING IN. AGAIN, OUR VIEW IS OBSTRUCTED BY THE GUARD. THE GUARD MOVES TO ONE SIDE. HOLLY CROSSES THE ROOM AND TAKES EACH OF THE BOYS BY THE HAND. THE BOYS COME THROUGH THE DOOR WITH THEIR UNCLE.

50 MR. AND MRS. CAMERON EMBRACE AS THE MINISTER RETURNS TO THE ROOM.

51 THE CAMERA PANS TO FOLLOW HOLLY, JIM, AND DANIEL DOWN THE HALL AND OUT THROUGH THE FRONT DOOR.

52 CUT TO MEDIUM SHOT OF THE EXT. DOOR OF THE PRISON. A LARGE CROWD SURROUNDS THE STEPS. AS THE DOOR OPENS, THE PEOPLE PRESS FORWARD TO SEE INSIDE. HOLLY COMES THROUGH THE DOOR WITH THE TWO BOYS.

53 CUT TO A CLOSE-UP OF JIM. AS THE CROWD CLOSES IN AROUND HIM, HE CRINGES CLOSE TO HIS UNCLE. THE CROWD BEGINS TO MOVE BACK AS THE CAMERA PANS UP TO SEE MRS. CAMERON COME THROUGH THE DOOR. AS SHE JOINS HER FAMILY . . .

54 DISSOLVE TO A MEDIUM SHOT FROM BEHIND. THE CAMERA FOLLOWS AS THEY MAKE THEIR WAY TO THE WAGONS. AGAIN, THE CROWD OPENS UP AHEAD OF THEM, FORMING A WALL OF FIGURES ON EITHER SIDE.

55 DISSOLVE TO A MEDIUM SHOT OF THE WAGONS AT THE EDGE OF THE CROWD. HOLLY HELPS MRS. CAMERON INTO THE WAGON, THEN BOOSTS DANIEL UP TO SIT BESIDE HER. JIM CLIMBS UP ON THE OTHER SIDE. MRS. CAMERON'S WAGON BEGINS TO MOVE OFF. THE CAMERA LINGERS ON HOLLY STANDING BESIDE HIS EMPTY WAGON.

56 CUT TO A LONG SHOT OF THE SQUARE. WE CAN SEE HOLLY BESIDE HIS WAGON. MRS. CAMERON AND THE BOYS, IN THEIR WAGON, ARE MOVING TOWARD THE EDGE OF THE SCREEN, PAST THE CHURCH. NOW JIM LOOKS AT HIS MOTHER, THEN QUIETLY TAKES THE REINS FROM HER.

SLOW DISSOLVE TO MEDIUM SHOT OF THE WAGON, WHICH HAS REACHED THE EDGE OF THE CAMERONS' CLEARING. IN THE BACKGROUND IS THE SMALL FAMILY BURIAL PLOT. JIM, STILL DRIVING THE WAGON, GLANCES IN THAT DIRECTION, THEN TURNS TO HIS MOTHER.

JIM
(IN A STILL VOICE) Is Papa coming home with Uncle Holly?

MRS. CAMERON NODS HER HEAD. THE CAMERA FOLLOWS AS THE WAGON MOVES TOWARD THE HOUSE. A BRIEF PAUSE.

DANIEL
(MORE RELAXED NOW THAT HE IS HOME AND IN FAMILIAR SURROUND-INGS) We didn't get candy on a string, Jim, but we got a watch and chain instead.

JIM NEITHER ANSWERS NOR LOOKS TOWARD HIS BROTHER. THE CAMERA STOPS AS THE WAGON CONTINUES ITS SLOW PACE TOWARD THE CABIN.

SLOW FADE.

THE END

In his cast lineup, it is important (I feel) to indicate the ages of the two boys. We don't need to know the ages of the others. Either we can accurately guess their ages, or the matter is not material to the story. It is important, though, that we fix an age for Jim and for his younger brother. Classes I have taught have disagreed as to how old Jim is. How do you tell? We have no clues about his schooling. We have to guess at his age by attitudes, by Jim's "in-take" comprehension, his protectiveness of Daniel, his response to his mother, his deference to his uncle (they exchange no words), the depth of his self-control, his brief loss of it, followed by his sudden stiffening and recovery.

Students have guessed at the age of the younger Daniel as being anywhere from five to ten, and for Jim, seven to fifteen. But the man writing the script must have an *exact* fix on this and have it from the beginning. There are two reasons. The writer must prepare more dialogue than Granberry has given us. And the writer must tell a casting director what kinds of youngsters to look for. Just in passing, it's safer to suggest ages for all cast members. In this script, however, the two boys are of chief importance in this regard.

In Shot 1, the house so well seen in this predawn moment sets the right mood, the same mood the story sets. For television, since we know there's a fire in the stove and that Mrs. Cameron is up and doing, perhaps we should see that one of the rooms (the kitchen) is lighted. And our establishing shot might also include chimney smoke.

The scriptwriter uses his cameras well. The getting-up details are nicely handled. Very early we come to know the exact relationship of the two brothers, the continuous dependence of the younger, the fraternal comfort of the older. And there is an almost direct transplant of the original dialogue.

In Shot 5, note the line direction, "his spirit completely undampened by this information." This indicates that the adapter is absorbing, in his own emotions, the extreme sensitivity that is immanent in each line and gesture in the original. The *feeling* of the story has really hit him and the suffusion of it warms and colors (and controls) his words, his camera suggestions, and cast directions. He, the adapter, is giving back to us the story's values and undertones with full integrity. The patience of Jim with Daniel, for his fretting, his chilling, his little fears (huge to him, as are all children's fears), his sickliness—all this is well projected by the lightly prodding insinuations of the camera and the undecorated speech.

Kenneth Kempton, a part of whose penetrating critique you have read, was disturbed by the very last spoken word in the original, the word "instead." It has puzzled no student to whom I've exposed this story. Here, in Shots 5, 6, and 7, the several references to what Uncle Holly might possibly buy for the boys in Czardis seem to me—and to the students—the reason we have the word at the end. The story seems so brief that all its impacts, all its details, big or little, are held close together in the mind. All are contained in active memory as we race to the bitter conclusion. So, to the students, the word "instead" has meant, "We got a watch and chain instead of a candy ball," or "instead of lemonade with ice."

And if the word is to be dropped, assuming it does throw a distracting preoccupation to an engrossed reader, perhaps its element of distraction is even stronger in the script than in the story: a matter of time, six or seven minutes for the reading, twenty-five for the watching. But it is the adapter's privilege to use it or leave it out.

See how much Kirk Gardner, the student whose work we're looking at, has let the viewer see in Shots 8, 9, and 10. Think now how much stress Professor Kempton put on the word *implication* in discussing and dissecting the story. Now we have a fine convergence of both sight and implication. The camera tells us a tremendous lot—all of it through tiny touches, brief focusings on the simplest of household materials, on gestures. We know (for example) that Mrs. Cameron is a good housekeeper. How? "Their clothes neatly laid out on a chair." We know much about their economic circumstances.

I doubt if the line spoken to herself by Mrs. Cameron is needed. Or even useful. Jim's gradual understanding, or rather his sudden absorption of all the irreversible horror of it and what he does with this dreadful knowledge, how he "manages" it—this is the story's climax. No need to palpate it here, even though the mother is more prayerful and in-looking than revelatory.

Her line, "Your clothes on already?" is to be delivered "gently," the adapter instructs. That is right. He should have retained "right" from the original, "You look right neat," to preserve the idiom that is theirs.

Toward the end of the breakfast scene, as Jim takes his first bite, Daniel "shudders and buries his head in his mother's skirts." The significance of this minor bit of action might not be immediately discerned, except we saw it earlier, in Shot 7. Gardner took care not to mislead his viewer.

Should Jim recognize Uncle Holly? No words are exchanged between the uncle and the boys in the original. Again, this is an adapter's prerogative. Here the scriptwriter has elected to have Jim recognize the man. For character purposes—since our impressions of Uncle Holly are almost identical to those we entertain toward Mrs. Cameron—Uncle Holly should have some word, however slight, for the boys. He loves them. He's been foster father to them for a year. The mission is almost as tormenting to him as to the others.

One thing for sure, the blunt question he puts to Mrs. Cameron—"You're goen to take them after all?"—should be directed to her out of earshot of the boys. Grief and anxiety could make him blunt, but they would not make him hard. It hurts the quality of Uncle Holly, the implied quality of him, that he would ignore Jim.

Mrs. Cameron lets her guard down, too, something she would never do before the boys. Any woman who can take the crucifixion she is about to endure (going to Czardis with herself publicly exposed), and do so voluntarily, would hide her anguish (her last line in Shot 12) from her sons. The moment is too adult, far too private, for their hearing. And it threatens to light up the tragedy she is for these few hours trying to spare them.

Simple repairs could fix this: a nod of the head by Uncle Holly that would bring her to the door; an ECU (extreme close-up) on his face as he whispers the question. It would emphasize the anguish of her ringing response were it to take place even farther from the boys' hearing than the question that provokes it. Out in the yard, for example. A nice graduation has been missed here.

The tree-climbing scene is well handled, except for one arguable moment—in the middle of Shot 17 there is this direction: "Jim looks around, obviously trying to get his bearings. A look of confusion comes over his face."

I find this of doubtful value, even though it's in the original. It is even a little misleading. Confusion over what? He's been up the tree for the same fruit a hundred times. Anyhow, there's no place to go but down. (This item would clear itself in rehearsal.)

In Shot 18, some of the size of Jim's character is realized, for he takes the rebuke quietly. And he gives his kid brother credit for the idea of taking something appropriate to their father. However, in the playing of this little scene—most moving, by the way—would it not be even more effective if Mrs. Cameron were standing up when she scolded her sons? It would also be preferable, when she recognizes her error, to have her crouch down and gather them in. She is quickly touched by their thoughtfulness, by the rightness of it. By doing it this way she would suggest that she's letting their right action rebuke her. Furthermore, it would be appropriate, for there is nothing ungenerous in any of these people.

Mrs. Cameron's speech is direct and simple. Not much "school-larnin' " to it and that is right. But it jars me a little to hear her guilty of "We won't do no different today." I think "We won't do different today" is preferable.

In Act II, Shot 20, the boys "talking together" will distract the viewer from the thing the writer most wants us to see: Holly and Mrs. Cameron in their respective wagons looking straight ahead. A traveling, or trucking, shot of Uncle Holly first, with Mrs. Cameron entering the shot a few seconds later, would give us the rigidity that is needed here, the rigidity that is intended.

The implications picked up by the camera in Shots 21 and 22 are excellent. So is the bewilderment of the boys as the wagons reach the confluence of their rutted trail and the high road.

Would it be proper for Daniel—this is just a thought—to wave at some group that he personally knew? At some other five- or six-year-old? And be shushed by his mother? Yes. Why not? Or could he not be lightly pinched by the epicritic Jim? Jim knows something's wrong without knowing what. I think it might be very touching. Gardner has suggested this possibility to the reader of his script, if not actually to himself: "Children . . . look with curiosity at the two boys. Daniel smiles under their gaze . . . Jim meets their stares . . . slightly angered and afraid."

"Afraid" is a new and powerful word here.

When does the horror of their journey burst upon Jim at a conscious level? I think in Shot 27: "Behind Jim, the solid shape of a high brick wall topped by barbed wire comes into view. Jim suddenly turns his head and starts as he becomes aware of the wall."

The jolts and clashing emotions; the inexorable advance through this thicket of slavering ghouls; the unbearable interchange between Jim and his mother when at last he knows all; when she knows he knows; the sight inventions Kirk Gardner has given us (changing "building" to the bell tower of a church); fitting the barbed wire into an effectively delirious montage; the fruit seller; the fearful insinuation of the steady hammering in the prison yard; the gruesome fiesta atmosphere that includes small children; these combine to bring an overwhelming experience to the eye and heart. No one could watch this sequence without being most cruelly wrenched. It strikes us a paralyzing blow.

This is an unusually fine piece of work for any student, a real achievement, spare, well organized, and in slow continuous crescendo. It is almost solidly professional from Shot 27 on to the finish. How well Gardner has used his cameras to tell Edwin Granberry's story. All the Granberry dialogue is well used, and what this student has invented is simple, natural, appropriate, and easy to play. The transfer of the reins, and the symbolism of this, was an extraordinarily happy inspiration.

I've found the following to be excellent drill in preparing any class in dramatic writing for television: (1) Select any short story that has more feeling than it has plot or dialogue. (2) Have a member of the class read the story aloud to the rest of the class. (3) Immediately, while details are fresh, have a written impromptu quiz.

Here are some of the questions, after a class reading of "Czardis," that I put to one of my writing groups at Temple University:

1. What are we given in the way of people?
2. Will these be enough to tell the same story in television?
3. Where does the story take place?
4. Could you relocate the story without damaging it, giving it a locale with which you are familiar?
5. What is the economic situation with the people we are exploring?
6. Why is it necessary to know this?
7. Write a one-sentence description of each of the principals.
8. We've mentioned place. What about time? If you don't feel secure in the handling of this story in the time in which it is now set, can you update it to your own advantage without hurting the original?
9. Mr. Cameron is to be hanged for murder. Is his guilt or innocence important?
10. Should you touch on this matter?
11. Is Uncle Holly the brother of Mr. Cameron? Or of Mrs. Cameron?
12. Should this be made clear?
13. How old are the boys?
14. How many sets do you need to handle this story? Interiors? Exteriors?
15. What sound effects are suitable?
16. What music are you going to ask for?
17. Flashbacks?
18. Do you want (or need) a narrator? (If you don't need him, you don't want him.)
19. What would you tell a director (who had not read the script or story) as to the relationship of the brothers to each other?
20. Of the boys to their mother?
21. Of Uncle Holly to the Cameron family?
22. What was the father's occupation?
23. How much time does the story consume?
24. Describe Mrs. Cameron's kitchen.
25. Is she a good housekeeper? Bad?
26. Why don't they have a car?
27. Is there linoleum on the kitchen floor?
28. Is there anything about this story you don't believe?
29. What do you wish the camera to pick up first?
30. If you had only one word to describe the main characteristic of the Cameron family, what word would you pick?
31. What did Mrs. Cameron give her boys for breakfast?
32. Does the stairway have a banister?
33. What do the boys wear?
34. What does their mother wear?
35. What does Uncle Holly look like?

36. Has he ever been married?
37. Name a character actor to whom you'd give this role.
38. How long has Mr. Cameron been in prison?
39. How does Mrs. Cameron warn the boys to prepare for their father's appearance?
40. Does the word *jail* or *prison* appear in the story?
41. On what day does this story take place?
42. Had Daniel ever been to Czardis?
43. Are you tempted to reconstruct the trial scene?
44. Describe the room where the farewell scene occurs.
45. If you craned a camera to peer over the prison wall, what would you see?
46. Should you do this?
47. When does Jim know for sure his father is to be executed?
48. How much schooling has young Jim had?
49. How much for his mother?
50. What's the population of Czardis?

In this practice it is not important that this particular exercise be observed. However, the out-loud reading is extremely valuable, especially when students know they are to be quizzed immediately after listening. A companion set of questions, different for each story, disciplines their in-take remembrance, sharpens their interest in the story, forces them to retain first impressions (always the best) and to catch detail, nuance, and what we might call the harmonics of any fine story.

No student is going to go off on an autistic excursion, even in mid-May, and after a heavy lunch, if he knows he must absorb every detail and refinement of what he's listening to and if he knows his recall is to be presently challenged.

For students of writing, this drill offers new areas of respect: the secrets of decoration without the use of a flock of adjectives; the secrets of revealing character by what people do or what they refrain from doing, not what they say or what the author says of them; the secrets of restraint, insinuation, the beeline of indirection; the summoning of the senses to make plausible interpretations to the brain; the cunning of the senses to set the brain's function temporarily to one side.

The fiction route is the route of *feeling*, of people in trouble, their response to this trouble and their management of it. Nothing more. Nothing else.

Many students succumbed to the temptation to reconstruct, in whole or in part, the murder trial. There is no need for this at all. And there is one extreme hazard: going into the full background of Mr. Cameron's story and his character; giving him attributes not intended by the author; suggesting guilt, compromise, or complicity—all of which would go far beyond the author's original intention and would, in the long run, be unpardonably presumptive.

To me the most haunting, most illuminating line in the entire story is said by the mother, as she tries to prepare her boys for the confrontation with their father: ". . . and let him see you are upright."

With this simple statement we know the true inner core of that whole family, the true grain of character that runs in them all. If I had to answer question 30, *upright* would be my word.

Another temptation that was better avoided concerned flashbacks to happier times. These attempts on the part of some students were not very successful. Dad took the boys hunting. Or fishing. Or did something nice for mother. Bought her something. Remembered an anniversary. The family frolicked. This is (and was) a little sickening—like looking at snapshots of neighbors.

The main point is that flashbacks aren't needed. Mr. Cameron's affection for his sons is self-revealing in his welcome when they come to say good-bye. There is no parade or show of false feelings, nothing mawkish, no prepared statements. Their responses are controlled, reflexive, genuine.

It is tough for all four of them, and all four behave well in their worst extremity. A fine relationship between the boys and their father can be assumed by the naturalness of their mutual acceptance of each other here. A flashback to "prove" a good relationship would be redundant. It needs no playing out. It is already there.

I would like to close this chapter by looking at some student dialogue that is typically bad.

Student writers who write good prose often have serious dialogue trouble. They "run too long in one place." They don't write dialogue. They write a nice little speech for one character. Then they write another nice little one for another. Then they pass these to and fro with oriental charm and patience. But it isn't talk an actor can deliver, nor talk to which another actor can respond. Worse, audiences won't listen to it. It is both unreal and boring.

We have to wait too long for the slow trajectory, the lazy descent. Our mind wanders. We know no one ever said such a thing.

However, there is one fortunate aspect to the problem of sluggish dialogue. It is easy to correct. It is an easy habit to break. Here's how to do it: Chop up your speeches. Pare them down. Say one short thing at a time.

Here is an example of dialogue that has become so costive it is inert:

JIM

But I worry, Papa.

MR. CAMERON

Bout what?

JIM

Bout whether I'll ever get big. Get to be a man like you.

MR. CAMERON

That ain't no serious worry, Jim. That's just growin up worry. It's when you're all growed up that you get the special worries.

JIM

Like what?

MR. CAMERON

Like whether you're going to have enough to eat for the winter. Or whether you're going to be able to make money to get some of the things that might be nice for your wife and kids. If you have a family, you feel for the way they feel, too. Like I feel for your worries, as if I was growin again myself.

JIM

But, Papa, you don't act like you're worryin all the time.

MR. CAMERON

It ain't the kind of frettin that shows. You carry it round inside you. Most of the time you forget it's there, but every now and again you hear it loud and clear, sayin "Jim Cameron, what you going to do about your family? You ain't doin right by them."

JIM

But you always done right by us. Why, just t'other day Momma told me, "Jim, your father's the finest man in the world." And then she said what you said today, how you didn't like spendin so much time in the mountains, that you wished you didn't have to cut lumber for a livin.

MR. CAMERON

That's the truth, Jim. I just wish there was some way I could be home with your momma and you boys all the time, stead of runnin off every so often to the timberlands. I'd like to have a real nice farm, like that Timson place, where all of us, 'cludin Holly, could run it real proper.

JIM

Do you think we could, Papa?

MR. CAMERON

Sure enough, soon's I get the money, that's exactly what we're goin to do.

JIM

I'll be growed up soon, Papa. Then you won't have to fret about me. And I'll take care of Dan'l and Momma, too, so when you're gone, you won't have to fret about them, either.

MR. CAMERON

You'll be old soon enough, son, so you needn't worry yourself with what I been tellin you. All you got to do now is worry about bein a boy—the rest your papa'll take care of like he's supposed to do.

It is easy to envision this weary exchange on a stage. Both father and son are standing, perhaps moving slowly toward the gate, or the outside pump. The more the director encourages them to move about, the more business he invents (plucking grass, kicking at dollops of earth, father-patting-son-on-the-shoulder), the more static the whole thing becomes. Nothing is being said. It is not dialogue. It is a belabored sequence of pious declamations.

We've all seen dialogue far more stationary than this example. And we have squirmed in our seats through lethargic spasms of this kind in amateur theatrics. For anything intended to reflect the character and quality of the Camerons, the quoted fragment is doubly inappropriate. They just didn't speak this way. The adapter is talking, not the Camerons. Certainly not Edwin Granberry. He's in the wings, wincing.

The quoted section could be redone without trouble, restricting each speaker to eight words or less per side.

PART II / TELEVISION FOR CHILDREN AND TEEN-AGERS

3

TARZAN

Though *Tarzan* is currently not on the air, it will return. Its formula answers a primitive need of mankind—a need running through a segment of American mankind a good bit less than grown-up. Is this a large segment? Yes. It takes in about 340 degrees of the full circle.

There is nothing wrong with this phenomenon. Anyhow, no one is grown-up all the time. And no man, however adult, is grown-up in all departments.

To say that *Tarzan*'s appeal is to the immature is not to belittle the validity of its concept, nor to fault the quality of production this favorite has enjoyed through the years. Some shows have been better than others. So have some of the *Tarzan* series. So have some of the "Tarzans" who played Tarzan.

All have made money. And there will be other *Tarzans,* in one medium or another, in the future.

Old-timers today claim to prefer their memories of Johnny Weissmuller over a more recent Tarzan—Ron Ely. And it is possible Weissmuller brought more primitive virility to his Tarzan than some of the others have. But it should be noted that in the Weissmuller days we didn't have the plethora of heroes who now crowd our media schedules. Today we're choked with heroes. This situation may be related to the appearance—now also in oversupply—of antiheroes.

The *idea* of Tarzan, a permanent part of American folklore by now, appeals to both sexes and to all ages. But most of its appeal is to children and teen-agers. It is escape drama of the purest sort. Psychologically well-grounded, the Tarzan symbol satisfies many yearnings we all feel: omnipotence, purity, infallibility, indestructibility. Plus, of course, the full decalogue of the Scout Law.

Periodically recasting Tarzan through the decades has supplied another valuable attribute not figured on by Edgar Rice Burroughs when he first machined this unusual athlete so many years ago. It has given Tarzan a kind of immortality. In fact, Tarzan's youth, always splendid, is constantly renewed. New actors keep bringing new bodies to the Tarzan jungle.

In each show Tarzan must suffer. But he must also always prevail. Always, too, his commendable restraint keeps him tall and dignified, at least till that instant when evil threatens to take over. Then he can crouch and run. But when he must descend to this, look out.

He loves his "subjects." He cares for them. And they love him. Snakes never bite him. Elephants never trample him. They toss him into high boughs, out of danger. Tarzan is fearless, all-seeing, all-hearing, all-sensing, in true harmony with nature— a marvel of arboreal symbiosis.

He has other attributes of the demigod. Because he is untouchable, women more than ever want to put their hands on him— to tousle his hair, cook his dinner. But he never needs such ministration. He is too exalted, too much a loner. A swing or two in one of his ubiquitous lianas is about all the girls get. Then they're packed off safely to England or the States.

Tarzan is above the needs of other men. He is superior to the blandishments of women. He bathes in waterfalls, alone, with nothing around except giraffes.

Among Tarzan's male television viewers, some of the more adventurous probably respond to the atavistic carry-over that is here—not in the person of Tarzan himself but in the mixed fellowship of his African jungle (most recently Mexican!). Men of outdoor persuasion sense some evolutionary linking up to our ancestral past; they feel themselves very much right there *in* the jungle.

Why shouldn't grown men feel this way? Tarzan is having one grand, leaping smash of a time while we just sit around in our smoky living rooms, slowly expiring in the pollution of our cities.

Looked at another way, Tarzan, as hero, is peculiarly similar to *Gunsmoke*'s hero. How so? Tarzan is really Marshal Dillon with his clothes off. This is not meant to be facetious. It is the truth. If you don't believe it, examine some of these character parallels:

Both men are basically in the same business—they are against evil.

Both inhabit a hostile environment.

Both are in weekly peril.

Both are weaponed, strong, relentless, protective, gentle, and ready.

Both have built-in charisma.

Both are bachelors.

Matt Dillon, to be sure, must go about his work with a somewhat less interesting menagerie. But he's equipped with a comparable language facility. He knows all the Indian dialects as Tarzan knows animal talk. The purpose, nature, and variety of their adversaries (their adversaries have no variety) are identical.

Both Matt Dillon and Tarzan can take a quick look at the ground and tell you which way anybody traveled. And they can also determine how many people were involved and the approximate time of their passage.

Both heroes are always right in their judgment of character. And these judgments are usually made instantly.

Though both are lovers, this quality or capacity is confined to social and philosophical manifestations only, for their strength seems to be rooted in their celibacy. If the U.S. marshal has to go to Kitty's room, does he charge right up and enter? No. He knocks first. If he goes in at all, he leaves the door open.

Similarly, Tarzan never enters the tent of the distressed but bosomy Vassar graduate whose father—a dedicated missionary with more zeal than sense—has just been eaten by a carefree tribe that Tarzan has warned him against to no avail. But with this desiring and now available daughter, does Tarzan make even a first suggestive move or gesture? No. He keeps his distance, just as he did back in 1920. He waits by her tent fly till she hurries into something and comes out to *him*. He never goes in.

There is a deliberate sanctification about Tarzan that, if altered, would pull down everything, including his tree house.

There are some *musts* about *Tarzan* scripts, and most of these musts apply to all adventure melodrama. One of the first is simple: Tarzan must be involved in the story *at once*. There is no circling around, no easygoing setting of atmospheres, no polite chatter. A *threat* of some sort must establish itself in the very first few seconds of the show—establish itself by a flung spear, a flaming arrow, a spent runner, a malign face peering through parted foliage.

The vehicle of its arrival doesn't matter. Anything in jungle character will do. It just has to be done *early*.

We'll go through a fine *Tarzan* script now, the product of a solid professional, and dissect his work shot by shot and scene by scene to lay bare everything that is significant. In this manner we will perceive, by looking at the isolated parts, how they are fitted together to make this jungle come alive, and to make you, the beholder, emotionally participate in the action.

It is not necessary to discuss the quality of this emotion, the quality of the bundle of feelings thus aroused—how deep they go or how long they last. It is only important to discuss the *reality* of our involvement and to reveal the means, often mechanical, by which this reality of involvement is achieved.

TARZAN
"Creeping Giants"
By Donn Mullally

Act I

FADE IN: STANDARD FILMED OPENING.

1 EXT. JUNGLE—FULL SHOT—DAY. CAMERA IS SITUATED ON SOME HIGH POINT OF GROUND . . . PANS OVER THE GREEN RAIN FOREST.

2 ANOTHER ANGLE—A NATIVE STUMBLES INTO SHOT. PHYSICALLY, HE IS NEARLY SPENT . . . HAS BEEN BLOODIED BY A FALL OR ENCOUNTER WITH AN ANIMAL. HOWEVER, HE PUSHES HIMSELF ON . . . ALMOST BLINDLY. HE FALLS, RISES, AND STAGGERS ON.

3 INT. TREE HOUSE—TIGHT ANGLE—DAY. JAI IS SEATED AT A TABLE, FROWNING AT AN OPEN BOOK IN FRONT OF HIM. FROM HIS EXPRESSION, HE'S BORED STIFF. HE TOYS WITH THE PENCIL IN HIS HAND . . . TRIES BALANCING IT ON ONE FINGER . . . GLANCING AROUND GUILTILY. CAMERA PANS TO A WIDER ANGLE AND WE SEE TARZAN, EATING, LOOKING UP AT JAI.

Tarzan
(MILD REPROACH) Jai . . . you're supposed to be studying your history lesson . . . not physics.

JAI HAS DROPPED THE PENCIL AND IT ROLLS OFF THE TABLE TO THE FLOOR.

TARZAN

(CONTINUING) Besides ... Sir Isaac Newton already discovered the law of gravity.

JAI

Aw, Tarzan ... who cares about all those old English kings?

TARZAN

Right now ... you do. Besides, Newton wasn't a king. (INDICATES) And those cubs have your pencil. Better get it away from them before they chew it up.

4 LOW ANGLE—A COUPLE OF LION CUBS ARE ON THE FLOOR AND LIKE ALL KITTENS THEY ARE PLAYFUL. THE PENCIL IS A FINE TOY AND THEY ARE BATTING IT AROUND, CHASING AFTER IT. AND, LIKE ALL BOYS, JAI IS IN FAVOR OF ALL GAMES . . . PARTICULARLY WHEN THEY COME BETWEEN HIM AND STUDY. HE JOINS IN WITH THE CUBS . . . MAKING LARGE VOCAL PROTESTS, OF COURSE.

JAI

Come on ... let me have my pencil. (BEAT) You don't want to get your mouths all full of splinters.

HE HAS HOLD OF ONE OF THE CUBS BY NOW, BUT THE OTHER ONE SWATS THE PENCIL AGAIN, SENDING IT SPINNING ACROSS THE FLOOR. AT THIS POINT, CHEETAH GETS IN THE GAME, POUNCING ON THE PENCIL AND LEAPING AWAY FROM THE LION CUB TO A PERCH IN THE WINDOW.

5 ANOTHER ANGLE—FAVORING THE CHIMP AS IT PLACES THE PENCIL BEHIND ONE EAR AND LOOKS VERY SCHOLARLY, INDEED. TARZAN AND JAI ENTER SHOT . . . JAI LAUGHING, TARZAN AMUSED.

TARZAN

Cheetah looks more like a scholar than you do, Jai.

JAI

Maybe we ought to send her to the mission school.

AS HE SAYS THIS, THE WEARY VOICE OF THE NATIVE IS HEARD O.S.

NATIVE'S VOICE

(O.S.) Tarzan!

TARZAN LOOKS DOWN AND OUT OF THE TREE HOUSE.

6 TARZAN'S POV—FROM TREE HOUSE AS THE NATIVE, LOOKING UP, GASPING FOR BREATH, COLLAPSES.

7 BACK TO TREE HOUSE. TARZAN RUSHES DOWN, FOLLOWED BY JAI, WITH A MEDICAL KIT, AND CHEETAH.

8 EXT. TREE HOUSE—DAY. MED. ANGLE—FAVORING THE NATIVE AS, WIND WHEEZING IN HIS TORTURED CHEST, HE OPENS HIS EYES, CHOKING AS HE TRIES TO SPEAK, AS TARZAN BENDS DOWN TO HIM.

TARZAN

Easy . . . you'll be all right.

HE LOOKS AROUND AS JAI REACHES THEM, HAS THE MEDICAL KIT OPEN ON THE SPOT . . . WHIPS OUT COTTON AND A BOTTLE OF ALCOHOL AND STARTS IMMEDIATELY TO CLEANSE THE MAN'S WOUNDS. THIS CAUSES THE NATIVE TO OPEN HIS EYES WIDE.

JAI

I know it stings. But it must be done.

TARZAN STUDIES THE ELEPHANT HAIR WRISTBAND THE NATIVE IS WEARING.

TARZAN

You are one of Lwutumba's tribe?

THE MAN NODS.

TARZAN

(CONTINUING) The Chief sent you here?

NATIVE

(GASPS IT) The Creeping Giants, Tarzan. (BEAT) They . . . they're . . .

THE MAN GRINDS HIS TEETH TOGETHER, CANNOT SPEAK FOR A MOMENT.

TARZAN

What about the mountains . . . what's happening to them?

NATIVE

(STRAINED) Blow . . . into . . . river . . .

TARZAN

The mountains are being dynamited into the river?

NATIVE

(BRIEF NOD) Lwutumba asks . . . you come.

TARZAN

Why didn't he send this message by the drums?

NATIVE

They would hear it, too. Send men to border to kill you.

TARZAN NODS . . . QUICKLY EXAMINES JAI'S FIRST AID.

TARZAN

Jai, bring the doctor to him.

HE RISES AND JAI SQUINTS UP AT HIM.

TARZAN

(CONTINUING) And then—back to your homework.

HE ROUGHS JAI'S HAIR AS THE BOY LOOKS DISGUSTED WITH THIS PROSPECT, RESUMES ADMINISTERING TO THE NATIVE WHILE CHEETAH HOLDS THE KIT.

TARZAN RUNS OFF INTO THE JUNGLE, AS WE:

BLUR OUT TO:

9 EXT. RIVER GORGE—FULL PAN SHOT—(STOCK)—DAY. POSSIBLY STARTING WITH

THE WHITE WATER OF A CASCADE, THIS PORTION OF THE RIVER CARVES ITS COURSE THROUGH MOUNTAINOUS COUNTRY. THE SLOPES OF THESE GIANTS ARE LARGELY COVERED WITH RAIN FORESTS . . . A SLASH OF BARE ROCK ONLY OCCASIONALLY VISIBLE. SOME OF THESE OUTCROPPINGS OF ROCK RISE ABRUPTLY FROM THE WATER'S EDGE . . . ALMOST SHEER WALLS OF STONE UPWARD TO SEVERAL HUNDRED FEET IN HEIGHT.

10 ANOTHER ANGLE—AT ONE OF THESE ROCK CLIFFS THAT RISES OUT OF THE RIVER. HIGH UP ON THE FACE OF IT, WE SEE THE TINY FIGURE OF A MAN IN A BOSUN'S CHAIR. HE IS BEING LOWERED FROM THE TOP OF THE CLIFF . . . SWINGING FREE AT THE END OF OVER A HUNDRED FEET OF LINE. HE USES HIS FEET TO KICK AND WALK HIMSELF OVER THE FACE OF THE CLIFF. TO THE BOSUN'S CHAIR IS ATTACHED A BIG ELECTRIC DRILL WITH A HEAVY-DUTY POWER LINE LOOPING DOWN FROM THE TOP OF THE CLIFF.

11 TIGHT ANGLE—FAVORING THE MAN IN THE BOSUN'S CHAIR. THIS IS WALTER WILSON, THE RENOWNED AMERICAN ENGINEER. WILSON IS A MAN IN HIS EARLY FORTIES . . . MUSCULAR, LEAN, THE STAMP OF EXCEPTIONAL INTELLIGENCE AND DEDICATION IN HIS FEATURES. THE FACT THAT HE IS A NEGRO IS COMPLETELY INCIDENTAL. WHAT HE IS DOING AS HE WORKS HIS WAY ENERGETICALLY AND BREATHTAKINGLY OVER THE FACE OF THIS CLIFF IS TO DRILL THE ROCK WALL AND PLACE DYNAMITE STICKS IN THE HOLES. HE THEN TAMPS AND WIRES THE CHARGES. HE GLANCES UP THE LENGTH OF ROPE HOLDING HIM TOWARD THE TOP OF THE CLIFF . . . MAKES A GESTURE TO BRING HIM UP.

12 MED. ANGLE—FAVORING THE MAN IN CHARGE OF THE PARTY AT THE TOP OF THE CLIFF AS HE REPEATS WILSON'S GESTURE . . . WHICH IS A SIMPLE POINTING OF HIS FOREFINGER DOWN AND MAKING A SMALL CIRCLE WITH IT. THE LINE STARTS TO PAY OUT OVER A PULLEY SET IN AN A-FRAME AT THE EDGE OF THE CLIFF. COLIN YAEGER IS A BIG MAN, WEARS HIS BUSH JACKET WITH A CERTAIN DASH THAT BESPEAKS AN EARLIER CAREER AS A WHITE HUNTER. HIS EVEN, SUN-BRONZED FEATURES AND A MANNER OF ALMOST OVERWHELMING MASCULINE COMPETENCE MUST'VE BEEN THE LANDMARK EXPERIENCE FOR MANY AN OTHERWISE BORED LADY ON A HUNTING SAFARI.

YAEGER

Hoist 'im up. (STOPPING GESTURE) Hold!

HE SINGS THIS OUT WITHOUT A GLANCE BACK AT THE "TROOPS" WHO ARE EXECUTING THE ORDER. THESE ARE AFRICANS. THEY, TOO, ARE WEARING BUSH JACKETS AND SHORTS. SOME OF THEM EVEN WEAR SHOES. THOSE WHO DO WEAR SIDE ARMS AND CARRY CARBINES. ONE MAN IS SEATED IN A LAND ROVER WHICH IS EQUIPPED WITH A POWER WINCH, WHICH HE OPERATES ON YAEGER'S ORDERS. THERE'S A TRAILER ON WHICH IS MOUNTED AN ELECTRIC GENERATOR. THE POWER LEAD SNAKES FROM IT TO THE CLIFF'S EDGE.

13 TIGHT ANGLE—(INTERCUTS)—WILSON BEING RAISED SLOWLY UP THE FACE OF THE CLIFF, GESTURES FOR A STOP AND BEGINS DRILLING THE ROCK.

14 FULL SHOT—ANGLED ACROSS THE CLIFF FROM A POINT DISTANT ENOUGH TO TAKE IN THE ENTIRE OPERATION. IN THE F.G., THE SCENE IS FRAMED BY FERN

FRONDS OR OTHER JUNGLE GROUND GROWTH. THESE MOVE AND WE SEE AN ARMED AND WAR-PAINTED NATIVE GLOWERING OFF AT THE ACTIVITY ON THE FACE OF THE CLIFF. CAMERA PANS TO INCLUDE A DOZEN OR SO MORE PAINTED BLACK FACES. THE FIRST NATIVE MAKES A GESTURE AND THE WHOLE GROUP MELTS OFF INTO THE JUNGLE . . . MOVING IN THE DIRECTION OF YAEGER'S GROUP.

15 SERIES OF BRIEF CUTS WHICH ESTABLISH AN ENCIRCLING MOVEMENT BY MANY NATIVES . . . ALL OF THEM ARMED AND PAINTED. THE "MILITARY HARDWARE" RANGES FROM SPEARS AND BOWS AND ARROWS TO A FEW ANCIENT MUSKETS TO A COUPLE OF WORLD WAR I RIFLES. THEY MOVE AS SHADOWS THROUGH THE DAPPLED LIGHT OF THE JUNGLE. THE LAST CUT OF THE SERIES IS ONE OF YAEGER'S MEN (IDENTIFIED BY HIS BUSH JACKET AND SHORTS) LYING ON TOP OF A BARE OUTCROPPING OF ROCK, SWEEPING THE JUNGLE AROUND HIM WITH BINOCULARS. HE SEES SOMETHING, REACTS . . . THEN SLIDES BACK OFF THE ROCK AND DASHES OFF.

16 MED. ANGLE—FAVORING YAEGER AS HIS SENTRY DASHES IN TO HIM . . . MAKING A BROAD GESTURE BACK THE WAY HE HAS COME, AND CHATTERING EXCITEDLY IN A NATIVE TONGUE. YAEGER REACTS, SHOUTING TO HIS WINCH OPERATOR IN THE LAND ROVER.

YAEGER
(SHOUTING) Bring him up . . . fast! (BEAT) Stand by to stop on my hand signal.

HE HAS RAISED HIS HAND, POINTING THE FOREFINGER AT THE SKY AND ROTATING IT.

17 TIGHT ANGLE—WILSON IS LOOKING UP AT THE TOP OF THE CLIFF, NODS AND WAVES, HANGS ON AS THE BOSUN'S CHAIR STARTS TO RISE, RAPIDLY NOW, OUT OF SHOT. AS IT GOES, HE USES HIS FEET TO KEEP HIMSELF FROM BEING SCRAPED ON THE PROJECTING ROCKS OF THE CLIFF . . . SOARING IN A SERIES OF GIANT LEAPS EACH TIME HE KICKS OUT.

18 BACK TO YAEGER. HE BARKS TO ONE OF THE AFRICANS WEARING SHOES WHO ALSO HAS A CHEVRON SEWED TO THE SLEEVE OF HIS BUSH JACKET.

YAEGER
Get your riflemen ready for prone firing.

THE CORPORAL CONVERTS THAT ORDER INTO THE NATIVE LANGUAGE AND HIS MEN MOVE OUT INTO THE ROCKS IN A SEMICIRCLE AROUND THE LAND ROVER.

19 TIGHT ANGLE—THE TROOPS FALL PRONE, TAKING COVER BEHIND ROCKS AND STUMPS, ETC. UNDER CAMERA, WE SEE ONE OF THE TROOPERS LEVER A SHELL INTO THE FIRING CHAMBER OF HIS CARBINE.

20 BACK TO YAEGER AS HE MAKES A STOP GESTURE TO HIS WINCH OPERATOR, THE ROPE STOPS WITH WILSON'S HEAD JUST APPEARING AT THE EDGE OF THE CLIFF . . . THEN YAEGER INDICATES A SLOWER LIFTING OF THE BOSUN'S CHAIR, TURNING HIS FINGER IN THE AIR, SLOWLY. THE LINE IS BROUGHT IN SLOWLY AND YAEGER REACHES OUT AND GRASPS WILSON'S HAND, PULLING HIM AND THE CHAIR UP ONTO LEVEL GROUND AWAY FROM THE EDGE OF THE CLIFF, AS:

YAEGER

Stop the winch!

HE ASSISTS WILSON, WHO IS UNBUCKLING THE BELT THAT HOLDS HIM IN THE BOSUN'S CHAIR.

WILSON

What's happened, Yaeger?

YAEGER GLANCES OFF TOWARD THE JUNGLE, NODDING.

YAEGER

We're about to have visitors. (SHOUTS OFF TO CORPORAL) Hold your fire!

WILSON

(REACTS) Visitors?

21 ANOTHER ANGLE—OVER WILSON AND YAEGER AS THEY MOVE TO A POINT BESIDE THE LAND ROVER. IN THE B.G., WE HEAR THE CORPORAL RELAYING THE ORDER TO HIS MEN . . . AS THE JUNGLE BEYOND SUDDENLY BECOMES ALIVE WITH THE ARMED NATIVES ESTABLISHED EARLIER. THEY CLOSE UNTIL STOPPED BY THE UPRAISED HAND OF THEIR LEADER. DURING THE ABOVE, WILSON HAS CAST A TROUBLED LOOK AT YAEGER.

WILSON

They're hostile?

YAEGER

(DRYLY) How do they look to you, Mr. Wilson?

WILSON

I don't understand. Why should they be?

YAEGER HAS REACHED INTO THE LAND ROVER AND TAKEN OUT A REPEATING SHOTGUN. HE SMILES SLIGHTLY AND MOVES OUT TO MEET THE CHIEF. AS HE DOES, A SPEAR FLASHES INTO SHOT AND BURIES ITS BLADE IN THE ROCKY SOIL INCHES AHEAD OF HIM. YAEGER SNAPS THE SHOTGUN TO HIS SHOULDER.

22 TIGHT ANGLE—FAVORING WILSON AS HE RUSHES IN AND GRABS THE BARREL OF YAEGER'S SHOTGUN AND THRUSTS THE MUZZLE TOWARD THE SKY.

YAEGER

Whose blood do you want to see on the ground . . . yours . . . *Mr.* Wilson?

WILSON

We don't know why they're here!

YAEGER

Did we send for them . . . ask them to bring their weapons? (ACIDLY) Look, Mr. Wilson . . . I wouldn't think of telling you how to build a dam. (BEAT) Let me handle this.

23 ANOTHER ANGLE—(INTERCUTS)—FAVORING THE CHIEF AS HE STRIDES FORWARD SEVERAL PACES AND SPEAKS VERY RAPIDLY IN HIS NATIVE TONGUE.

24 BACK TO SCENE

WILSON

What did he say?

YAEGER

(TIGHT-LIPPED) He says we're not to move. (BEAT) I have an answer for that!

HE STARTS TO RAISE THE SHOTGUN AGAIN, SHOUTING:

YAEGER

(CONTINUING) Lwutumba . . . clear your people out of here. I'll give you to the count of three. You understand . . . three! (BEAT) One . . .

25 ANOTHER ANGLE AS TARZAN STRIDES OUT FROM THE JUNGLE TO STAND IN FRONT OF THE CHIEF. YAEGER LOWERS HIS GUN, SLOWLY.

TARZAN

I want to talk to the American engineer in charge of this project.

YAEGER

(BEAT; SMILES) Mr. Wilson . . . (INDICATES) . . . this is Tarzan . . . lord of the jungle. (BEAT) When he speaks the king of beasts runs off and hides—so they say.

WILSON HAS STEPPED FORWARD, NODDING ACKNOWLEDGMENT OF THE INTRO-DUCTION.

WILSON

What can I do for you?

TARZAN

(SHAKES HEAD) Not for me, Mr. Wilson . . . for yourself . . . for this country. (BEAT) All I ask is that you listen.

WILSON

I'm listening.

TARZAN

The dam cannot be built here in this gorge. (SOLEMNLY) If you go ahead with it, thousands of people in the valley below will die.

WILSON

I can't believe that. I've been studying the abutment and foundation loca-tions personally. All the footings for the dam will be in solid rock.

TARZAN

The dam will fail, Mr. Wilson.

YAEGER

Why don't you ask the lord of the jungle where he studied engineering?

TARZAN

Mr. Wilson . . . Chief Lwutumba and his people call these mountains that are to hold the lake behind the dam . . . the "Creeping Giants."

WILSON

(AMUSED) "Creeping Giants." Sounds like something out of *Gulliver's Travels*.

TARZAN GESTURES OFF TOWARD THE MOUNTAINS.

TARZAN

It's not. They're moving, Mr. Wilson. The entire west side of the range is undercut by a great rift . . . an earth fault.

WILSON

I've read all the government survey reports on those mountains, Tarzan. There's not a word about an earth fault!

YAEGER

(TO TARZAN) You expect Mr. Wilson to value a native superstition over a half-million dollars worth of government surveys?

TARZAN

This has nothing to do with native superstition! I've seen the rift.

AS HE'S SPEAKING, YAEGER PASSES A BARELY PERCEPTIBLE NOD TO THE COR-
PORAL IN CHARGE OF THE TROOPS.

26 TIGHT ANGLE—FAVORING THE CORPORAL AS HE SIGHTS HIS RIFLE AND FIRES.

27 ANOTHER ANGLE—FAVORING ONE OF THE TRIBESMEN WHO IS HOLDING AN
ANCIENT MUSKET AS THE WEAPON IS KNOCKED FROM HIS HANDS, THE FORCE
OF THIS CLOSE-RANGE SHOT SPRAWLING HIM TO THE GROUND.

28 MED. ANGLE—FAVORING YAEGER AS HE SEEMS TO REACT WITH SURPRISE AND
ANGER TO THE SHOT COMING FROM HIS SIDE. HE SHOUTS A FEW WORDS OF THE
NATIVE LANGUAGE AT THE CORPORAL, WHO REPLIES IN KIND.

YAEGER

(TO WILSON) Sorry that happened, Mr. Wilson. The man was taking dead aim at you.

WILSON

Why would he do that?

YAEGER

(SHRUGS) You're his enemy.

YAEGER HAS TURNED AND REACHED INTO THE LAND ROVER AS TARZAN GRABS
HIM BY THE SHOULDERS AND WHEELS HIM AROUND.

TARZAN

(COLDLY ANGRY) He wasn't your enemy, but he is now.

YAEGER

That worries me, Tarzan . . .

HE HAS PULLED THE PIN ON A HAND GRENADE WITH HIS TEETH, SHRUGGED
AWAY FROM TARZAN, ADDING:

YAEGER

(CONTINUING) You'd bett⁻r tell your *friend* Lwutumba and his men to get out of here or I'm going to start throwing these firecrackers in about one minute.

TARZAN STARES UNFLINCHINGLY AT YAEGER.

TARZAN

Not until Wilson assures me he'll look at the rift.

WILSON

All right, all right—put that grenade away, Yaeger.

YAEGER RELUCTANTLY REINSERTS THE PIN IN THE GRENADE.

YAEGER TURNS AND SNAPS TO THE DRIVER AS HE TOSSES THE GRENADES BACK IN THEIR BOX:

YAEGER

Let's turn this van around . . . we're getting out of here.

29 ANOTHER ANGLE—FAVORING TARZAN AS HE STEPS UP TO WILSON.

TARZAN

If no one else can show you that rift . . . I'll take you there. Just come to Lwutumba's village.

YAEGER MOVES INTO THE B.G., LOOKS GRIM. THE LAND ROVER HAS BACKED AWAY FROM ITS POSITION NEAR THE EDGE OF THE CLIFF AND COME ABOUT. ALSO IN THE B.G., WE HAVE SEEN YAEGER'S NATIVE TROOPS PILING INTO THE BACK OF THE VEHICLE.

YAEGER

We're ready to go, Mr. Wilson.

WILSON NODS ABSTRACTEDLY . . . MORE IN RESPONSE TO TARZAN THAN TO YAEGER.

WILSON

I'll check into the matter.

HE HAS CLIMBED INTO THE LAND ROVER BESIDE THE DRIVER. BEFORE YAEGER SWINGS IN NEXT TO HIM, HE HAS A PARTING REMARK FOR TARZAN.

YAEGER

(HARD) Ape man . . . don't try climbing on my back again.

HE CLIMBS IN THE ROVER, GESTURES TO THE DRIVER, AND THE VAN ROARS OUT, LURCHING HEAVILY OVER THE UNEVEN GROUND, ITS TIRES SPINNING UP A CLOUD OF DUST THAT SETTLES OVER TARZAN.

DISSOLVE TO:

30 EXT. CASA GRANDE—FULL SHOT—DAY. THIS IS A CONSIDERABLE RESIDENCE TO FIND ALMOST HIDDEN IN THE JUNGLE. IT COULD NEVER REALLY BE HIDDEN . . . NOT THIS MOORISH-SPANISH CASA OCCUPYING ITS HILLTOP, MAGNIFICENTLY

LANDSCAPED TO THE JUNGLE'S EDGE, THE GROUNDS A RIOT OF COLOR FROM THE
TROPICAL FLOWERS. A DRIVEWAY CURVES UP TO THE FRONT ENTRANCE, WHICH,
IN THE MANNER OF THIS KIND OF ARCHITECTURE, IS NOTABLE FOR AN ALMOST
MILITARY-POST SIMPLICITY . . . AND WE SEE THE LAND ROVER, WITH WILSON,
YAEGER, AND THEIR SURVEY PARTY, TOOL UP THIS DRIVEWAY AND STOP AT THE
STEPS WHICH LEAD TO THE MASSIVE WROUGHT IRON GATES WHICH (FOR LACK
OF A BETTER TERM) MIGHT BE CALLED THE FRONT DOORS OF THE CASA.
YAEGER, THEN WILSON ALIGHT FROM THE LAND ROVER.

31 ANOTHER ANGLE. AS WILSON STARTS TO EXIT INTO THE HOUSE, A MAN ON A
RANGY, BEAUTIFULLY MADE HUNTER RIDES UP. MIGUEL JIMENEZ BROWN III
IS A MODESTLY PROPORTIONED MAN IN EARLY FORTIES. HIS DARKER, SPANISH,
BLOOD HAS BEEN DOMINANT . . . IN FACT, HE COULD BE OF PURE CASTILIAN
STOCK. HE REINS IN HIS MOUNT AND A NEGRO SERVANT DASHES OUT OF THE
HOUSE AND TAKES THE REINS, AS:

BROWN
(WARM SMILE) Everything go well today, Mr. Wilson?

WILSON
I'd like to talk to you about that . . . inside.

BROWN
Certainly . . . my study. I'll be right in.

WILSON NODS AND EXITS INTO THE HOUSE. BROWN FROWNS BRIEFLY, TURNS
TO YAEGER.

BROWN
(CONTINUING) What's the matter with him?

YAEGER
He met Tarzan.

YAEGER SMILES CROOKEDLY AS HE SAYS THIS, BUT BROWN NODS SOLEMNLY,
WHEELS, AND EXITS INTO THE HOUSE.

32 INT. ENTRANCE HALL—DAY. MED. ANGLE—AT DOOR WITH ITS BRIGHT SUN-
LIGHT MAKING A SILHOUETTE OF BROWN AS HE ENTERS AND STRIDES QUICKLY
TO A DOOR WHICH OPENS INTO HIS STUDY. AS HE REACHES THE DOOR, HE STOPS
MOMENTARILY.

33 INT. BROWN'S STUDY—DAY. MED. ANGLE—OVER WILSON WHO HAS BEEN PAC-
ING IMPATIENTLY, NOW TURNS AND LOOKS AT BROWN AS HE ENTERS. BROWN
HAS TURNED UP HIS "INSTANT" CHARM, SMILES . . . GESTURING:

BROWN
Mr. Wilson. May I have a boy bring us a drink? What is your pleasure?

WILSON
Thank you. I'm not interested in a drink at the moment.

BROWN
Allow me to insist that a tall, cool drink is precisely what you should find
interesting at the moment.

BROWN

AS HE'S SPOKEN, BROWN HAS PRESSED A BUTTON ON HIS DESK AND A HOUSE SERVANT POPS IN.

(CONTINUING) Two Scotch and soda . . . tall, much ice.

THE SERVANT BOBS . . . ALMOST CRACKING THE STARCHY WHITE UNIFORM HE WEARS . . . EXITS. BROWN SEATS HIMSELF AT HIS DESK AND SMILES ACROSS IT AT WILSON.

BROWN

(CONTINUING) So—you met Tarzan today?

WILSON

(NODS) I did. (BEAT) He told me something I find very disturbing. Yaeger insists it's only native superstition, but—

BROWN

(INTERRUPTS) I must admit to surprise that a man of your background would give any importance to superstition.

WILSON

I'm not certain that's all it is.

BROWN SMILES AGAIN.

WILSON

(CONTINUING) In the case of many primitive beliefs . . . there's a basis in fact.

34 ANOTHER ANGLE—FAVORING BROWN AS THE SERVANT RETURNS WITH THE DRINKS. BROWN GESTURES WITH HIS.

BROWN

Suerte, amigo! (DRINKS) May I tell you about my grandfather . . . the poor immigrant boy who came to Gwamba . . . and made the family fortune by ignoring native witchcraft?

WILSON PEERS DOWN INTO HIS DRINK, NODS.

WILSON

I didn't know superstition was a factor in the discovery of the Gwamba tin fields.

BROWN DIPS INTO HIS DRINK AGAIN.

BROWN

(AMUSED) It's native dogma that only death rewards the man who disturbs the sacred soil of Gwamba.

WILSON SHAKES HIS HEAD.

BROWN

(CONTINUING) Most of the natives still believe that . . . won't even dig a grave for their dead . . . build *burial* platforms up in the trees, instead.

WILSON CONSIDERS THIS THOUGHTFULLY FOR A MOMENT.

                                  WILSON
That's the reason they don't want the dam?

                                  BROWN
Unquestionably. We haven't changed their minds at all . . . we even have
to work the tin mines with imported labor.

BROWN SIPS HIS DRINK, SMILES.

                                  BROWN
(CONTINUING) Of course, I blame this on my grandfather.

                                  WILSON
(REACTS) What did he do?

                                  BROWN
Horse fell with him during a wild boar hunt, broke his neck. He was dead
by the time they brought him in from the bush . . . exactly as the natives
had predicted all along.

BROWN FINISHES HIS DRINK, RISES . . . ADDS:

                                  BROWN
(CONTINUING; SMILES) But, he died in his ninety-fifth year . . . after
making a hundred million dollars. (BEAT) Will you have another drink?

                                  WILSON
No, thanks.

HE HAS ONLY PARTIALLY FINISHED THE ONE HE HAS; PUTS THE GLASS DOWN,
ADDING:

                                  WILSON
(CONTINUING; BRIEF SMILE) I think I get the point. (BEAT) However, an
earth fault . . . a rift . . . is a geological fact. It exists or it doesn't. Tarzan
offered to show this one to me.

35 MED. ANGLE—OVER BROWN'S SHOULDER AS HE LEANS FORWARD TO AN INTER-
COM BOX ON HIS HUGE DESK . . . DEPRESSES A TALK KEY.

                                  BROWN
(TO WILSON) Excuse me . . . (TO BOX) Yaeger . . . would you come into
my study, please.

BROWN FLIPS THE TALK KEY UP AND SMILES ACROSS AT WILSON.

                                  BROWN
(CONTINUING; TO WILSON) I want Yaeger's thoughts on this. He knows
every inch of that country.

BROWN GLANCES OFF TOWARD THE DOOR AS THERE IS A TAP ON IT AND THE
DOOR OPENS TO ADMIT THE WHITE HUNTER.

                                  YAEGER
Yes, bwana?

BROWN

Come in, Colin . . .

YAEGER DOES . . . LOUNGES OVER THE BACK OF A TALL CHAIR ON WHICH HE
RESTS HIS ELBOWS.

BROWN

(CONTINUING) Before you came to work for me . . . I believe you made a
specialty of taking hunting parties back into the mountains the natives
call the "Creeping Giants"?

YAEGER

(NODS) That's correct . . . you might say the "Giants" were my personal
playpen for over five years.

BROWN

(WRY SMILE) Did you ever see them do any creeping?

YAEGER

Only when I knew I'd had too much warm gin.

WILSON

On the way back today, you told me there was no rift in those mountains.

YAEGER NODS.

WILSON

(CONTINUING) You're absolutely positive?

YAEGER

(SOLEMNLY) Absolutely.

WILSON

Then why would Tarzan offer to make a fool of himself . . . why would
he say he could show this fault to me?

BROWN

(TO YAEGER'S SURPRISE) If it will ease your concern—then, of course,
you should go.

WILSON IS RELIEVED, RISES AND STARTS PURPOSEFULLY TOWARD THE DOOR OF
THE STUDY . . . STOPS TO NOD.

WILSON

We'll go out to Lwutumba's village and see what kind of an answer this
Tarzan can give us . . . tomorrow morning.

BROWN

Anything you say.

WILSON EXITS.

YAEGER FOLLOWS HIM TO THE DOOR AND CLOSES IT AFTER HIM, TURNS TO
REGARD HIS BOSS WITH A PUZZLING LOOK.

YAEGER

Well, bwana?

BROWN

(FLATLY) Get Tarzan for me. I mean, *get* him—now.

YAEGER NODS AND EXITS.

DISSOLVE TO:

36 EXT. LWUTUMBA'S VILLAGE—FULL SHOT—DAY. A CLUSTER OF BEEHIVE-SHAPED MUD HUTS, THE VILLAGE IS SITUATED IN A SMALL CLEARING. THE SHADOWS ARE VERY LONG, SUGGESTING LATE AFTERNOON. THE ACTIVITY IN THE VILLAGE IS LARGELY CONFINED TO THAT OF THE WOMEN COOKING OVER THEIR OPEN FIRES IN FRONT OF THEIR HUTS.

THE MEN ARE GATHERED IN FRONT OF LWUTUMBA'S SLIGHTLY LARGER HUT. TARZAN, THE CHIEF, AND SEVERAL OF THE ELDERS ARE SEATED IN A CIRCLE SURROUNDED BY THE OTHER MEN.

37 ANOTHER ANGLE—LWUTUMBA ADDRESSES THE SILENT TRIBESMEN IN THEIR NATIVE TONGUE . . . REACTING TO THE O.S. SOUND OF A HELICOPTER. LWUTUMBA STOPS SPEAKING, LOOKS OFF TOWARD THE SKY. ALL HEADS TURN WITH HIS.

38 THEIR POV—(STOCK)—A BIG CHOPPER SWEEPS ACROSS THE SKY AT TREETOP LEVEL.

39 MED. ANGLE—FAVORING JAI AS HE AND CHEETAH RUN TOWARD CAMERA, STOP, AND STARE UP AT THE CHOPPER, SOUND OF WHICH COMES FROM DIRECTLY OVERHEAD.

40 SERIES OF CUTS—(STOCK)—WHICH SHOW THE ABOVE CHOPPER CIRCLING TO LAND IN A CLEARING, THEN COME DOWN WITH THE USUAL DUST CLOUD BILLOWING UP FROM THE DRY GROUND.

41 FULL SHOT—FAVORING TARZAN AS THE WHOLE GROUP OF NATIVES NOW STANDS AND LOOKS OFF TOWARD THE SOUND OF THE CHOPPER . . . A SOUND THAT NOW CUTS OFF, WHILE THE DUST BEGINS TO FILTER IN FROM THE LAND-ING. THE ENTIRE GROUP STARTS MOVING OFF ACROSS THE VILLAGE COMPOUND TOWARD THE RIM OF TREES THAT SCREEN THE ACTUAL LANDING PLACE. CHEETAH GOES ALONG, EXCITEDLY SCRAMBLING UP INTO THE TREES.

42 ANOTHER ANGLE—JUNGLE PATH—THROUGH THE TREES WHERE TARZAN AND THE NATIVES COME FACE-TO-FACE WITH YAEGER AND SEVERAL OF HIS HEAVILY ARMED SECURITY FORCE. YAEGER IS ALSO CARRYING A LONG GUN . . . WHICH LOOKS SOMETHING LIKE A CARBINE. THE TWO GROUPS STOP WITH SEVERAL YARDS SEPARATING THEM. YAEGER SMILES.

YAEGER

Tarzan . . . I only half expected to find you here.

TARZAN

I told the engineer I would be in this village.

YAEGER

(SHAKES HEAD) That's *why* I thought you'd be any place else. You can't really want to produce that rift you're talking about?

TARZAN'S EYES NARROW.

TARZAN

Is that what you came to tell me?

YAEGER

No . . . I came to invite you to have dinner with Senor Miguel Brown.

TARZAN EXCHANGES A BRIEF GLANCE WITH LWUTUMBA AS YAEGER ADDS, SMILINGLY:

YAEGER

(CONTINUING) One of my dinner jackets should about fit you.

TARZAN

Please thank Senor Brown for me . . . but I have already accepted Chief Lwutumba's invitation.

YAEGER

You can break that. I'm sure the Chief won't mind. (BEAT) Wilson wants to talk to you.

TARZAN

I'll wait for him here . . . tomorrow.

43 TIGHT ANGLE—A FRIGHTENED JAI, WITH CHEETAH, PEERS OUT OF THE UN-DERBRUSH, AT:

44 HIS POV—YAEGER'S GUN HAS MOVED INTO FIRING POSITION, AIMED AT TARZAN. THE CORPORAL AND THE OTHER TROOPS HAVE TAKEN THEIR CUE AND ARE COVERING THE NATIVES WITH THEIR AUTOMATIC WEAPONS.

YAEGER

Have it your way.

HE SQUEEZES THE TRIGGER. TARZAN SPINS AND FALLS TO THE GROUND, DOES NOT MOVE AS THE NATIVES AND THEIR CHIEF STARE IN DISBELIEF.

45 BACK TO JAI. HE REACTS . . . EYES NOW BIG WITH TERROR.

FADE OUT.

END OF ACT I

ACT II

FADE IN:

46 FULL SHOT—(CONTINUOUS ACTION)—DAY. ANGLED FROM JAI'S POSITION IN THE JUNGLE AS THE BOY RACES FORWARD, FOLLOWED BY A SCREAMING AND SCOLDING CHEETAH. WE SEE TARZAN LYING ON THE GROUND.

47 ANOTHER ANGLE—JAI ATTACKS YAEGER WITH HIS SMALL FISTS. YAEGER BRUSHES HIM ASIDE, STEPS OVER TARZAN, AND TAKES HIS KNIFE.

YAEGER

Well, Lwutumba . . . your friend doesn't look so tall now, does he?

JAI

(CRYING NOW) You killed him . . . you killed Tarzan!

YAEGER

Only put him to sleep, Sonny. He'll be all right.

YAEGER BENDS OVER TARZAN AND REMOVES A TRANQUILIZER DART FROM HIS SHOULDER.

LWUTUMBA

You leave Tarzan here . . .

YAEGER

No. He's coming with us.

48 ANOTHER ANGLE—FAVORING LWUTUMBA AS A COUPLE OF YAEGER'S MEN, ON HIS GESTURE, START TO TAKE TARZAN BY THE SHOULDERS.

LWUTUMBA

You leave him!

LWUTUMBA AND HIS PEOPLE START TO SURGE FORWARD . . . ARE STOPPED BY A BURST OF AUTOMATIC WEAPON FIRE THAT CHIPS THE JUNGLE TREES ABOVE THEIR HEADS. LWUTUMBA RESTRAINS JAI.

YAEGER

(FLATLY) There are going to be a lot of widows and orphans in your village, Lwutumba . . . if you and your men make another move like that one.

HE GESTURES WITH HIS HEAD, AND TARZAN'S LIMP BODY IS CARRIED BACK THE WAY HE AND HIS MEN HAD COME.

LWUTUMBA

Where do you take Tarzan?

JAI

Don't let them, Lwutumba!
Don't let them take him away!

YAEGER

I'm not going to hurt the ape man, Sonny, not if Lwutumba does what I tell him. (DELIBERATELY) I will bring the engineer tomorrow. He will ask questions and you'll give the answers I want to hear—or Tarzan will be dead. You can count on it. (BEAT) You understand what I say?

LWUTUMBA NODS SOLEMNLY AND YAEGER SMILES.

YAEGER

(CONTINUING) You Africans get smarter all the time.

HE NODS TO THE CORPORAL AND WHEELS . . . MOVING OFF IN THE DIRECTION TARZAN WAS TAKEN. THE CORPORAL BARKS A COMMAND IN THE NATIVE LANGUAGE AND THE GROUP BEGINS TO FALL BACK . . . COVERING LWUTUMBA AND HIS PEOPLE ALL THE TIME. LWUTUMBA HAS TO HANG ON TO A STRAINING, DISTRAUGHT JAI.

AFTER A LONG BEAT, LWUTUMBA AND HIS PEOPLE BEGIN TO MOVE AFTER

THEM . . . STOP AFTER A FEW STEPS WHEN THERE IS THE O.S. SOUND OF THE CHOPPER'S MOTOR BEING REVVED UP. JAI BREAKS AWAY AND RUNS TOWARD THE SOUND.

49   MED. ANGLE—AT JUNGLE'S EDGE—TREES IN F.G. AS JAI, LWUTUMBA, AND HIS PEOPLE APPEAR AND ARE ENGULFED IN THE BILLOWING DUST CLOUD THAT RISES FROM BEHIND CAMERA. THE NOISE OF THE CHOPPER'S MOTOR IS NOW VERY LOUD. JAI MOVES INTO MARKS THAT APPROXIMATE A TIGHT ANGLE AS HE LOOKS OFF.

50   HIS POV—(STOCK)—THE CHOPPER LIFTS OFF AND SLANTS ACROSS THE JUNGLE CLEARING. AS ITS BEATERS CARRY IT OVER THE TREETOPS AND OUT OF SIGHT, WE:

DISSOLVE TO:

51   EXT. SMALL JUNGLE CLEARING—FULL SHOT—DAY. THE CHOPPER COMES IN FOR A LANDING. AS SOON AS THE ROTORS STOP AND THE DUST BEGINS TO SETTLE, MIGUEL BROWN MOVES OUT TO MEET THE PLANE. HE IS BACKED UP BY A GROUP OF ARMED AND UNIFORMED MEMBERS OF HIS SECURITY FORCE.

52   ANOTHER ANGLE—AT PLANE AS THE DOOR OPENS AND YAEGER STEPS OUT. HE REACHES BACK AND HELPS A STILL GROGGY BUT CONSCIOUS TARZAN TO THE GROUND . . . PRESENTS HIM TO BROWN AS THE SECURITY GUARD IMMEDIATELY COVER TARZAN WITH THEIR AUTOMATIC WEAPONS.

YAEGER

Here's your trophy animal, bwana . . . as ordered.

BROWN

Very good. (INDICATING) If you don't mind, Tarzan . . . this way.

TARZAN LOOKS AROUND AT THE ARMED MEN WHO ALMOST RING HIM, NODS.

BROWN

(CONTINUING) Forgive me . . . I should introduce myself.

TARZAN

(FLATLY) Not necessary. I know who you are.

HE MOVES OFF IN THE DIRECTION BROWN HAD INDICATED . . . BROWN MOVING BESIDE HIM.

53   EXT. PRISON CAMP COMPOUND—MED. ANGLE—DAY—THROUGH THE BARBED WIRE GATE AS TARZAN IS BROUGHT UP TO IT BY BROWN AND HIS MEN. A HEAVILY ARMED GUARD OUTSIDE THE GATE UNLOCKS IT TO ADMIT THEM. WE PAN TO REVEAL THE UNPAINTED, CRUDELY CONSTRUCTED CORNERS OF A COUPLE OF PRISONER DORMITORIES . . . AS THE PARTY MOVES INTO THE COMPOUND, THE GATE LOCKED AFTER THEM.

BROWN

(SMILINGLY) I call this my rest and recreation camp, Tarzan. When laborers at my tin mines become peevish . . . I transfer them up here for a few weeks. (BEAT) They come back to the mines new men.

TARZAN

(GLANCING AROUND) If they come back at all.

BROWN

(SHRUGS) Some *do* refuse to take full advantage of the facilities here.

54 MED. TRAVEL SHOT—WITH THE GROUP AS THEY MOVE OUT INTO THE COM-
POUND . . . THE CAMERA BRUSHING A COUPLE OF MEN STRUNG UP BY THEIR
WRISTS IN THE PROCESS.

BROWN

Others have been known not to believe that for their protection the fence
is electrified . . .

TARZAN

For *their* protection?

BROWN

Of course. I insist these men get their rest . . . free of any outside dis-
turbance.

THIS HAS BROUGHT THE PARTY TO A CEMENT SLAB ABOUT SIX FEET SQUARE
WHICH SHOWS ABOUT EIGHT INCHES ABOVE THE GROUND. IN THE CENTER OF
THIS SLAB IS A ROUND GRATING WITH A LARGE PADLOCK ACTING AS A HASP
BETWEEN TWO IRON STAPLES . . . ONE ON THE OUTER EDGE OF THE GRATING
AND ONE ON ITS RIM.

BROWN MAKES A BRIEF HEAD GESTURE AND ONE OF THE GUARDS MOVES UP
ONTO THE SLAB TO UNLOCK THE PADLOCK . . . OPENING THE GRATING.

BROWN

We call this the well, Tarzan. As you can see . . . we'll have no one dis-
rupting your tranquillity during your stay with us.

TARZAN

And your tranquillity won't be disturbed, either.

BROWN

(NODS) Very perceptive.

TARZAN

I wonder if I am. There's something I don't understand. How can you
keep me alive in there for the years it will take to build the dam? (BEAT)
And if I'm not alive . . . how will you control the natives?

BROWN

There will be no dam. (BEAT) When Wilson detonates his probing
charges, this situation will be resolved. The rift is loaded with dynamite;
those exploratory charges of Wilson's will create a seismic shock and
blow an entire mountain into the river.

TARZAN

And thousands of people will die just so progress won't invade your
vicious little empire.

BROWN
(SMILES) Precisely—and the eminent Mr. Wilson's disaster will discourage any future progress in this part of Gwamba. (SHRUGS) I am very grateful to this land, of course. I may rescue it from this disaster.

BROWN GESTURES TOWARD "THE WELL."

BROWN
(CONTINUING) If you don't mind, Tarzan . . .

TARZAN NODS . . . SEEMS ABOUT TO COMPLY MEEKLY. HE STEPS UP ON THE SLAB, AS THOUGH HE WERE GOING TO CLIMB INTO THIS TORTURE CHAMBER WILLINGLY. BUT SUDDENLY HE SPRINGS BACKWARD, DROPPING BROWN WITH A BLOW TO THE SIDE OF THE JAW. TARZAN WHEELS TO MEET THE SWARM OF GUARDS WHO ARE IMMEDIATELY ON TOP OF HIM.

55 ANOTHER ANGLE. NATURALLY, TARZAN KNOCKS A FEW HEADS TOGETHER BEFORE HE IS FINALLY SKULLED BY A GUN BUTT, GOES LIMP WITH THE SECURITY GUARDS PILING ON. BROWN, MEANWHILE, HAS SHAKEN OFF THE EFFECTS OF TARZAN'S BLOW . . . BELLOWS:

BROWN
All right . . . that's enough! Stand back . . . get off him!

HE GRABS A COUPLE OF THE NATIVE COPS BY THE SCRUFF OF THE NECK AND HURLS THEM BACK. HE STANDS OVER TARZAN'S LIFELESS-LOOKING FORM FOR A MOMENT, THEN GESTURES TO THE GUARDS.

TWO OF THE GUARDS PICK TARZAN UP BY THE SHOULDERS, DRAG HIM ONTO THE SLAB, AND DROP HIM, FEET FIRST, INTO "THE WELL." THE GRATING IS SLAMMED SHUT AND PADLOCKED. THIS ACCOMPLISHED, BROWN TURNS ON HIS HEEL AND WALKS OFF TOWARD THE CAMP GATE . . . FOLLOWED BY THE GUARDS.

56 INT. "THE WELL"—NIGHT. TIGHT ANGLE—TARZAN IS SLUMPED IN A CRAMPED POSITION AT THE BOTTOM OF THIS PIT. HE DOESN'T MOVE, BUT IN THE LIGHT THAT DOES FILTER DOWN FROM THE FLOODLIGHTED COMPOUND, WE SEE HIM OPEN HIS EYES AND STARE UP AT THE GRATING. HE LIFTS ONE HAND WHICH HE HAS CLOSED INTO A FIST . . . OPENS IT SLOWLY.

57 INSERT—TARZAN'S HAND. WE SEE A FULL CLIP OF CARBINE AMMO . . . THE STEEL JACKETS ON THE SHELLS CATCHING THE FEEBLE LIGHT FROM ABOVE.

DISSOLVE TO:

58 INT. CASA GRANDE LIVING ROOM—NIGHT. CLOSE ANGLE—A BRANDY GLASS WHICH REFRACTS THE SILKEN LIGHT OF A CANDLE. THE GLASS IS HELD BY SENOR MIGUEL BROWN AND AS WE PAN TO A WIDER ANGLE, WE FIND WALTER WILSON, SEATED ACROSS A HUGE COFFEE TABLE FROM BROWN . . . AT ONE END OF AN IMMENSE BROCADE-COVERED SOFA.

BROWN
Our home government has made it very clear, Mr. Wilson. Gwamba must be brought into the twentieth century. (BEAT) This dam and hydroelectric

plant you are going to build is considered the cornerstone of that whole effort.

WILSON
That's the reason for my position that we can't gamble. Until we can *prove* otherwise, we have to assume Tarzan knows something we don't or he would never have come forward.

BROWN
Mr. Wilson . . . can you imagine yourself in Tarzan's position? (BEAT) I mean, *any* man whose entire way of life is that primitive. (BEAT) Surely you can understand—to this man, every advance of civilization, every step of progress . . . is a direct and lasting threat. In your own United States . . . what chance would there be for a man in a loincloth?

WILSON BROODS OVER THIS, NODDING.

WILSON
But, if he's right. If he can show us a rift that has somehow been overlooked . . .

BROWN HAS FINISHED HIS DRINK, RISES SMILING.

BROWN
He'll be doing us an immense favor.

WILSON
(NODS HIS AGREEMENT) Think I'd better turn in now, Senor Brown. I want an early start for that native village in the morning.

BROWN NODS.

BROWN
(LIFTING GLASS) Goodnight, Mr. Wilson.

AS WILSON EXITS . . .

DISSOLVE TO:

59 EXT. PRISON CAMP COMPOUND—FULL SHOT—NIGHT. ONLY THE ARMED GUARDS ARE SEEN MOVING ALONG THE FENCE LINE . . . THE ONLY SOUNDS ARE THOSE OF THE NEARBY JUNGLE.

60 INT. "THE WELL"—NIGHT. INSERT—ONE OF THOSE STEEL-JACKET CARBINE SHELLS IS BEING JABBED INTO THE CEMENT BESIDE THE IRON FRAME THAT HOLDS THE GRATING WHICH COVERS TARZAN'S PLACE OF CONFINEMENT. THIS WORK HAS BEEN UNDER WAY FOR SOME PERIOD OF TIME AND, IN THE DIM LIGHT THAT FILTERS IN FROM THE COMPOUND ABOVE, WE CAN SEE SOME OF THE CEMENT HAS BEEN CHIPPED AWAY.

61 TIGHT ANGLE—TARZAN. HE'S CROUCHED AGAINST THE NARROW WALLS OF THIS PIT, PUNCHING AT THE CEMENT WITH THE BUSINESS END OF THE CARBINE SHELL. CHIPS OF CEMENT, DUST CLING TO HIS SWEAT-GLISTENING BODY. HIS EFFORT PRODUCES A FAIR-SIZED CRACK BESIDE THE IRON FRAME AND HE

WEDGES THE SHELL INTO IT, BREAKING OUT A SLIVER OF CEMENT. HE KEEPS
WORKING, AS WE:

DISSOLVE TO:

62 INT. "THE WELL"—DAY. CLOSE SHOT—AT THE HOLE TARZAN HAS CHIPPED
INTO THE CEMENT WHERE IT JOINS THE GRATING FRAME. IT IS A JAGGED
OPENING, BUT LARGE ENOUGH TO EXPOSE PART OF THE OUTER EDGE OF THE
RIM. CAMERA TILTS DOWN AND WE SEE TARZAN CAREFULLY COVERING ALL
TRACES OF CEMENT CHIPS IN A HOLE HE HAS DUG INTO ONE CORNER OF THE
PIT. HE EXAMINES HIS HANDS AND ARMS TO BE SURE THERE IS NO TELLTALE
CEMENT DUST ON THEM. THEN HE RUBS HIS HANDS OVER HIS FACE AND HAIR,
HIS NECK . . . EXAMINING HIS HANDS. THERE IS NOTHING ON THEM THAT WILL
GIVE HIM AWAY. THEN HE CUPS HIS HANDS TO HIS MOUTH . . . SHOUTS:

TARZAN

Guard . . . guard!

63 EXT. PRISON COMPOUND—DAY. MED. ANGLE—AT "THE WELL" WITH ITS
CEMENT SLAB AND IRON GRILLE . . . SHINING IN THE BRIGHT SUNLIGHT, AS
WE HEAR:

TARZAN'S VOICE

(O.S.) Guard!

ONE OF THE ARMED GUARDS STROLLS UNCONCERNEDLY PAST THE CEMENT
SLAB. THEN SQUATS DOWN TO PEER THROUGH THE GRATING.

64 TIGHT ANGLE—AT GRATING—THROUGH THE BARS OF WHICH WE CAN MAKE
OUT TARZAN'S FACE, STARING UP AT THE GUARD WHO HUNKERS IN THE F.G.

TARZAN

Water . . . bring me water!

CAMERA TILTS UP AS THE GUARD RISES AND WALKS OFF TO A CISTERN ON THE
OTHER SIDE OF THE COMPOUND. HE DRAWS A BUCKET OF WATER AND RETURNS
WITH IT . . . MATTER-OF-FACTLY POURS THE WATER THROUGH THE GRATING.

65 INT. "THE WELL"—DAY. TIGHT ANGLE—THE WATER FROM THE BUCKET POURS
DOWN THROUGH THE GRATING, DRENCHING TARZAN. AS HE CATCHES SOME OF
THE WATER IN HIS HANDS, DRINKS IT, WE:

DISSOLVE TO:

66 EXT. JUNGLE—MED. ANGLE—DAY. WHILE CHEETAH WATCHES, JAI BENDS
OVER A JUNGLE POOL . . . CUPPING WATER OUT WITH ONE HAND, DRINKING IT.
THE CHIMP ALERTS TO SOMETHING O.S., SCRAMBLES AWAY FROM THE BANK
OF THE POOL, AND SWINGS UP ONTO THE NEARBY TREES AS WE PAN WITH HER.
NOW WE'RE AWARE OF THE THROBBING SOUND OF A CHOPPER. JAI RUNS TO A
SMALL CLEARING.

JAI

Hurry, Cheetah—they're coming back with Tarzan!

67 ANOTHER ANGLE—JAI REACHES A POINT OF VANTAGE, PEERS OFF AND UP . . .

UP IN THE TREE, CHEETAH BEGINS TO SCREAM EXCITEDLY. THE SOUND OF THE CHOPPER INCREASES.

68 JAI'S POV—(STOCK). THROUGH AN OPENING IN THE TREES, WE SEE THE CHOPPER COMING IN FOR A LANDING.

69 BACK TO JAI. HE RACES OFF THROUGH THE JUNGLE, FOLLOWED BY CHEETAH.

70 TIGHT ANGLE—AT UNDERBRUSH AS IT MOVES SLIGHTLY, PARTS, AND JAI PEERS OUT. HIS FACE FALLS IN DISAPPOINTMENT.

71 EXT. LWUTUMBA'S VILLAGE—DAY—JAI'S POV. FULL SHOT—LWUTUMBA STANDS BEFORE HIS HUT. WILSON, YAEGER, AND SEVERAL OF THE LATTER'S ARMED SECURITY POLICE MOVING TOWARD HIM. THE NATIVES OF THE VILLAGE STARE AT THE PARTY SILENTLY.

72 BACK TO JAI. HE MAKES A SILENCING GESTURE TO CHEETAH AND THEN THEY BOTH "MELT" BACK INTO THE JUNGLE.

73 MED. ANGLE—FAVORING LWUTUMBA AS WILSON AND YAEGER REACH HIM. HE STANDS LIKE A STATUE, STARING AT THE SPACE BETWEEN THEM.

WILSON

Chief Lwutumba . . . I have come here to meet Tarzan.

LWUTUMBA

Tarzan not here.

WILSON

(REACTS) Yesterday he said I could find him at your village. (BEAT) I want him to show me the rift in the mountains.

LWUTUMBA

Tarzan not here.

WILSON

Can you tell me where he is?

LWUTUMBA

No.

WILSON GLANCES AT YAEGER, WHO SHRUGS. AFTER A MOMENT'S THOUGHT, WILSON TRIES AGAIN.

WILSON

Chief . . . do *you* understand what is meant by rift . . . what Tarzan was talking about yesterday?

LWUTUMBA

No.

WILSON

(BEAT) These mountains you call "Creeping Giants" . . . you understand, "Creeping Giants"?

LWUTUMBA NODS.

WILSON

(CONTINUING) Do they move . . . or is there some other reason for that name? Do you understand my question, Chief Lwutumba? I'm trying to find out what makes the mountains move . . . if they do.

LWUTUMBA

The mountains do not move. Only Tarzan calls them by that name.

LWUTUMBA STARES AT THE SPOT BETWEEN THE TWO MEN FOR ANOTHER MOMENT, THEN, WITHOUT A WORD OR SIGN, TURNS AND EXITS INTO HIS HUT. YAEGER SMILES AND SHAKES HIS HEAD.

YAEGER

Had enough?

WILSON NODS GRIMLY.

WILSON

I have a lot to learn about Africa. Let's go.

HE STARTS BACK THE WAY THEY CAME . . . YAEGER AND THE ARMED GUARD TROOPING OUT BEHIND HIM.

74 HIGH ANGLE SHOT—THROUGH THE BRANCHES OF A TREE. CHEETAH'S HEAD FIGURES IN THE F.G. OF THE SHOT AS SHE AND JAI WATCH WILSON AND THE PARTY LEAVE THE NATIVE VILLAGE.

75 FULL SHOT—JAI AND CHEETAH MOVING THROUGH THE JUNGLE. SUDDENLY THERE IS THE O.S. SOUND OF THE CHOPPER'S MOTOR. WE SEE JAI AND CHEETAH SCRAMBLE TO A POSITION HIGH IN THE TREETOPS.

76 TIGHT ANGLE—JAI AND CHEETAH PEERING O.S. AS THE NOISE OF THE CHOPPER ALMOST SHAKES THE TREE.

77 JAI'S POV. THE CHOPPER RISES ABOVE THE TOPS OF THE TREES, CIRCLES . . . THEN TAKES ITS COURSE.

78 BACK TO JAI. HIS HEAD SWIVELS AS HE WATCHES THE CHOPPER . . . THEN GOES ON "POINT" WHEN THE COURSE IS ESTABLISHED.

JAI

Come, Cheetah! If we want to find Tarzan, that must be the way to go.

AS THEY SCRAMBLE DOWN THE TREE:

DISSOLVE TO:

79 INT. "THE WELL"—DAY. TIGHT ANGLE—TARZAN IS TAKING A STRAIN ON A 30-30 CARBINE SHELL, SEPARATES THE STEEL JACKET FROM THE BRASS SHELL CASE. HE VERY CAREFULLY EMPTIES THE CONTENTS OF THE CASE INTO THE LEATHER SCABBARD IN WHICH HE CUSTOMARILY CARRIES HIS HUNTING KNIFE. AS HE TAPS THE LAST OF THE POWDER INTO THE SCABBARD, WE NOTE HE HAS A PILE OF EMPTY CASES, ONLY ONE BULLET STILL INTACT. HE TAKES IT APART. HOWEVER, HE DOES NOT EMPTY THIS CASING INTO THE SCABBARD, BUT FILLS THE OPEN END OF IT WITH A BALL OF MUD HE SCRAPES UP FROM THE FLOOR

OF "THE WELL." THEN, HE INSERTS THIS (OPEN END FIRST) INTO THE SCABBARD AND SECURES IT BY WRAPPING THE SCABBARD WITH THE THONG ATTACHED TO IT.

80   INSERT—VERY CLOSE ANGLE OF THE ABOVE ACTION.

81   BACK TO SCENE. TARZAN NOW STUFFS THE SCABBARD INTO THE HOLE HE HAS PREPARED BESIDE THE IRON FRAME OF THE GRATING . . . SO THAT ONLY THE FIRING CAP ON THE LAST CASING IS EXPOSED. HE PACKS THE SCABBARD INTO THE HOLE WITH MUD. HE EXAMINES THE PROJECT . . . FINDS IT SATISFACTORY, FLOPS DOWN TO THE DAMP FLOOR OF "THE WELL" IN A SQUATTING POSITION, LEANING BACK AGAINST THE DIRT WALL OF THE HOLE, AND CLOSES HIS EYES. A BEAM OF SUNLIGHT THAT FALLS ON HIS EXHAUSTED FEATURES DOES NOT DISTURB HIS REST.

CAMERA TILTS UP TO HOLD ON THE BARS IN THE GRATING . . . THE SUN BLAZING IN THE SKY . . . THE TINY PATCH OF IT WE CAN SEE THROUGH THE BARS.

DISSOLVE TO:

82   INT. "THE WELL"—NIGHT. TIGHT ANGLE—ON THE GRATING THROUGH WHICH THE LIGHT VALUES ARE NOW THOSE OF THE FLOODLIGHTS IN THE PRISON COMPOUND. CAMERA TILTS DOWN AS TARZAN STIRS, AWAKENS. HE RISES STIFFLY . . . EXAMINES HIS HOMEMADE BOMB PLANT.

83   VERY CLOSE ANGLE. THIS EXAMINATION IS DONE MOSTLY BY FEEL AS THERE IS LITTLE LIGHT FILTERING INTO THIS HOLE. TARZAN NOW PICKS UP THE CLIP THAT HAD HELD THE CARBINE SHELLS, TWISTS IT IN HIS HANDS . . . MUSCLES BULGING WITH THE STRAIN . . . UNTIL HE HAS SPRUNG IT APART.

THIS PROVIDES HIM WITH A SHARP EDGE FOR A FIRING PIN. HE PLACES THIS AGAINST THE CAP . . . TAKES A LARGE ROCK IN HIS OTHER HAND AND MAKES A PRACTICE PASS AT HITTING IT AND FALLING TO THE FLOOR OF "THE WELL" IN ONE LIGHTNING MOVEMENT.

84   EXT. PRISON COMPOUND—NIGHT. FULL SHOT—OVER THE CEMENT SLAB WHICH COVERS "THE WELL"—TOWARD THE MAIN GATE OF THE PRISON CAMP. WE SEE THE GUARDS MAKING THEIR ROUTINE PATROLS. SUDDENLY AND VIRTUALLY UNDER CAMERA, THERE IS ONE HELL OF AN EXPLOSION . . . THE SMOKE AND DUST FROM WHICH MOMENTARILY OBSCURE SHOT.

85   SERIES OF VERY FAST CUTS. WE SEE TARZAN CROUCHED IN THE BOTTOM OF "THE WELL," PROTECTING HIS HEAD FROM DEBRIS AND BLOWBACK . . . THE REACTION OF THE GUARDS TO THE EXPLOSION (THEY'RE MOMENTARILY SUR- PRISED AND BEWILDERED—MILL ABOUT UNCERTAINLY) . . . TARZAN IS ON HIS FEET, STRAINING TO DISLODGE THE GRATING RIM WHICH HAS BEEN ONLY PAR- TIALLY FREED FROM THE CEMENT.

86   TIGHT ANGLE—AT GRATING—(FROM THE EXT.)—AS IT IS MOVED, THEN BROKEN FREE. TARZAN'S HEAD APPEARS IN THE OPENING AND HE PULLS HIM- SELF UP TO EYE LEVEL . . . LOOKING OFF.

87 HIS POV—TOWARD THE MAIN GATE WHERE SEVERAL GUARDS HAVE CONGRE-
GATED. ONE OF THEM IS POINTING TOWARD CAMERA (AND "THE WELL").
THERE ARE FLASHES OF FIRE AS THE GUARDS OPEN UP WITH THEIR AUTO-
MATIC WEAPONS, SPRAYING SHOTS AT CAMERA.

88 THEIR POV. THERE IS STILL SOME SMOKE FROM THE EXPLOSION PARTIALLY
OBSCURING THE IMMEDIATE AREA OF THE CEMENT SLAB THAT COVERS "THE
WELL," BUT NOT SO MUCH THAT TARZAN'S APPARENT EFFORT TO ESCAPE IS
EFFECTIVELY HIDDEN. WE SEE HIM COME PARTIALLY OUT OF THE HOLE IN
THE SLAB AS THE GUARDS CONTINUE TO FIRE . . . RUNNING TOWARD THE SPOT.
TARZAN APPEARS TO BE HIT, BUCKLES, AND FALLS BACK DOWN INTO THE HOLE.

89 CLOSE SHOT—MUZZLE OF AUTOMATIC WEAPON IN THE HANDS OF ONE OF THE
GUARDS AS THE FLASHES FILL THE ENTIRE FRAME AND WE:

FADE OUT.

END OF ACT II

ACT III

FADE IN:

90 EXT. PRISON COMPOUND—NIGHT. TIGHT PAN SHOT—AT THE "WINDOWS" OF
THE PRISON DORMITORY WHERE THE LIGHT FROM THE FLOODLIGHTED PRISON
COMPOUND REFLECTS ON A LINE OF SOLEMN BLACK FACES WHICH ARE PEER-
ING THROUGH THESE HOLES IN THE WALL AT THE SCENE IN THE COMPOUND.

91 ANOTHER ANGLE—AT "THE WELL" WHERE THE GUARDS ARE IN THE ACT OF
REMOVING AN APPARENTLY DEAD TARZAN FROM THE HOLE IN THE CEMENT
SLAB. TWO GUARDS ARE IN THE HOLE . . . PASSING HIM UP TO TWO MORE,
WHILE TWO OTHER GUARDS WATCH . . . THE GUNS OF THE FOUR HANDLING
TARZAN ARE LYING ON THE SLAB. THE REMAINING TWO GUARDS HOLD THEIR
WEAPONS CASUALLY. AS TARZAN COMES OUT OF THE HOLE, WE SEE A TRICKLE
OF BLOOD FROM A SCALP WOUND, AT LEAST MOMENTARILY VISIBLE.

92 TIGHT ANGLE—FAVORING TARZAN AS HIS COMPLETELY LIMP AND LIFELESS
FORM IS SUDDENLY EXPLOSIVELY IN ACTION. HE KNOCKS THE HEADS OF THE
TWO GUARDS WHO HAVE LIFTED HIM OUT OF THE HOLE TOGETHER AND HEAVES
THEM AT THE TWO ON THE GROUND. CAMERA PANS TO A WIDER ANGLE AS THE
FOUR GUARDS SPRAWL TO THE DIRT. AND TARZAN IS OFF . . . RUNNING.

ONE OF THE GUARDS MANAGES TO GET TO ONE KNEE AND BRING A GUN TO
BEAR, FIRING OFF A BURST IN TARZAN'S DIRECTION.

93 ANOTHER ANGLE—TARZAN REACHES THE CORNER OF THE PRISON DORMITORY
WITH BULLETS CHIPPING THE SIDE OF THE BUILDING AND KICKING UP THE
DUST BEHIND HIM. CAMERA PANS AS AT LEAST FOUR OF THE GUARDS ARE NOW
IN THE CHASE, FIRING AS THEY RUN.

94 MED. ANGLE—(INTERCUTS)—AT DORMITORY WINDOWS AS ALL SORTS OF
OBJECTS SUDDENLY FILL THE AIR . . . THROWN IN THE DIRECTION OF THE
GUARDS.

95 BACK TO SCENE. THE GUARDS LOSE SEVERAL STRIDES DODGING THIS RAIN OF LOOSE OBJECTS FROM THE DORMITORY.

ON THE GESTURE OF ONE OF THE GUARDS, THE FOUR SPLIT UP . . . STARTING OUT TO SURROUND THE BUILDING. THIS BRINGS ONE OF THEM CLOSE TO THE ELECTRIFIED FENCE . . . JUST AS A HEAVY WOODEN PLANK COMES SAILING OUT OF THE DORMITORY WINDOW. IT HITS HIM ON THE SIDE OF THE HEAD, STAGGERS HIM . . . AND HE FALLS INTO THE FENCE. THERE IS A TREMENDOUS ELECTRICAL ARC WHEN HE HITS IT . . . LIGHTING UP THE SKY.

96 EXT. JUNGLE—NIGHT. MED. ANGLE—FAVORING JAI AS HIS FEATURES ARE LIGHTED BY THE REFLECTED GLOW OF THIS ELECTRICAL ARC. HE'S SCARED, BUT HE AND CHEETAH PUSH ON. NOW THEY HEAR THE SOUND OF AUTOMATIC WEAPON FIRE.

97 EXT. PRISON COMPOUND—NIGHT. TIGHT ANGLE—A GUARD FIRING TOWARD THE ROOF OF THE DORMITORY.

98 TIGHT PAN SHOT—TARZAN IS RUNNING ALONG THE ROOF OF THE DORMITORY, KEEPING LOW SO THAT THE PEAK OF THE ROOF AFFORDS SOME PROTECTION.

99 TIGHT ANGLE—(INTERCUTS)—ANOTHER GUARD HAS COME AROUND THE CORNER OF THE DORMITORY BUILDING AND IS FIRING FROM THE HIP.

100 BACK TO TARZAN. HE REACHES THE END OF THE BUILDING AND LAUNCHES HIMSELF INTO SPACE.

101 ANOTHER ANGLE—FROM THE GROUND OUTSIDE THE FENCE AS TARZAN FLASHES OVER THE FENCE . . . CATCHES A VINE THAT DANGLES FROM A TREE AND SWINGS OFF AND OUT OF SIGHT . . . UNDER A HAIL OF AUTOMATIC FIRE. CAMERA PANS TO DISCOVER A WIDE-EYED, FRIGHTENED JAI WITNESSING ALL THIS. NOW HE REACTS TO THE ACTION INSIDE THE COMPOUND.

102 HIS POV—(INTERCUTS)—THE GUARDS HAVE STOPPED FIRING AND ARE RUNNING TOWARD THE MAIN GATE OF THE PRISON CAMP.

103 BACK TO JAI. HE AND CHEETAH MOVE OFF.

104 ANOTHER ANGLE—AT PRISON GATE AS IT IS SWUNG OPEN AND THE GUARDS RUSH OUT . . . HEADING FOR THE POINT WHERE TARZAN VANISHED. WE PAN TO A WIDER ANGLE AS THEY SPLIT UP AND PLUNGE INTO THE JUNGLE.

105 EXT. JUNGLE—NIGHT. TIGHT PAN SHOT—TARZAN RUNNING, GLANCES BACK AND SEES THE SILHOUETTE OF SOMEONE CHARGING AFTER HIM, BACKLIGHTED BY THE FLOODLIGHTS OF THE PRISON COMPOUND. TARZAN SWINGS UP INTO THE TREES.

106 TIGHT PAN SHOT—THE GUARD CRASHING THROUGH THE JUNGLE. SUDDENLY HE'S LIFTED OFF HIS FEET AND DANGLES BY HIS ANKLES FROM A LOOPED VINE WHICH HAS BEEN SNAPPED INTO THE AIR BY A TREE BRANCH. HE DROPS HIS GUN. A MOMENT LATER, JAI POPS OUT OF THE UNDERBRUSH, GRABS THE GUN, AND THROWS IT AWAY . . . THEN HURRIES OFF AFTER TARZAN.

107 ANOTHER ANGLE—JAI AND CHEETAH "MELTING" INTO THE JUNGLE NIGHT.

DISSOLVE TO:

108 INT. WILSON'S WORKROOM—TIGHT ANGLE—NIGHT. THIS IS ACTUALLY THE LIVING ROOM OF THE SUITE, BUT IT HAS BEEN CONVERTED BY WILSON TO HIS WORK AREA. HE AND A YOUNG ASSISTANT, RICHARD PARRIS . . . A WHITE MAN . . . ARE BUSY AT A LONG LIBRARY TABLE ON WHICH THERE ARE ROLLS AND STACKS OF DOCUMENTS, CHARTS, ETC. THEY REACT TO A KNOCK AT THE DOOR . . . WILSON TURNING TO CALL:

WILSON

Come in.

CAMERA PANS TO INCLUDE THE DOOR AS IT IS OPENED BY BROWN. HE SMILES.

BROWN

Thought I'd better come up and rescue you . . . from yourself. It's possible to overdo this work thing.

WILSON

(RISING) I agree, but my rather stupid adventure this afternoon . . . the hours I wasted trying to meet with Tarzan . . . had to be made up. However, we're back on schedule. (INDICATES ASSISTANT) Richard and I just completed our checklist for tomorrow.

BROWN

Then you plan to detonate?

WILSON

(NODS) Seven A.M. (BEAT) This is how we have set it up . . . if you'd care to see it on paper.

BROWN NODS AND ON WILSON'S GESTURE MOVES TO THE TABLE WHERE WILSON UNROLLS A CONSIDERABLE TOPOGRAPHICAL MAP.

109 ANOTHER ANGLE. PERMITTING US TO SEE THIS MAP AS WILSON INDICATES THE POINTS OF INTEREST.

WILSON

This scale drawing of the face of the proposed abutment shows where I have placed the dynamite charges. (POINTING) Up here on top of the cliff we have our detonation device in place and programmed for the seven A.M. firing. It is fully automatic and is tied into the seismograph by its own radio beam, which cuts out precisely at the moment of firing.

BROWN

Completely remarkable.

WILSON

(NODS) Richard will be my backup. In fact, he's leaving for there immediately. (SMILES) We can't take a chance on anything as humiliating as a flat tire on a Land Rover scrubbing this whole effort.

DURING THE ABOVE, RICHARD HAS BEEN GETTING INTO HIS BUSH JACKET . . . MOVING TOWARD THE DOOR.

WILSON

(CONTINUING) I'll see you out there at six-thirty, Richard. However, if I'm not there . . . proceed with the count.

RICHARD

Will do.

RICHARD EXITS AND WILSON ROLLS UP THE MAP AND CHART, SHAKES HIS HEAD, WEARILY.

WILSON

Been a long day.

BROWN

I could have a boy bring us a nightcap.

WILSON

(SHAKES HEAD) Thank you, but I'll pass. Better turn in.

BROWN NODS AND MOVES TOWARD THE DOOR TO THE BALCONY. WILSON CROSSES WITH HIM.

110 TIGHT ANGLE—AT THE DOOR AS THEY REACH THIS POINT AND FOR THE FIRST TIME, WILSON APPEARS TO BE AWARE OF THE NATIVE DRUMS BEATING OUT THERE IN THE NIGHT. BROWN CONCEALS HIS CONCERN OVER THE SOUND OF THE DRUMS.

WILSON

What's that all about?

BROWN

Nightly ritual. Don't let it disturb your sleep. Goodnight and good luck tomorrow.

BROWN EXITS.

111 EXT. CASA GRANDE—FULL—NIGHT—AS YAEGER RUSHES ACROSS THE GROUNDS TO MEET BROWN AS HE EMERGES. THE DRUMS CONTINUE TO SOUND.

YAEGER

Tarzan has escaped . . . exactly as the drums have it.

BROWN

How did it happen?

YAEGER

I don't know. But I never worry about bagging an animal—when I know I have the right bait.

AS HE SAYS THIS, YAEGER MAKES A SMALL HEAD GESTURE TO INDICATE WILSON'S LIGHTED WINDOW.

BROWN

I'll be waiting in my study. (QUIETLY OMINOUS) I expect to hear from you *very* shortly, Yaeger.

THEY MOVE OFF IN DIFFERENT DIRECTIONS, YAEGER MOVING HURRIEDLY.

DISSOLVE TO:

112 EXT. JUNGLE STREAM—NIGHT. MED. ANGLE—FAVORING TARZAN. THERE IS A PATH OF MOONLIGHT ACROSS THE BLACK WATER. FROM ITS REFLECTED LIGHT,

WE SEE TARZAN BATHING THE WOUND IN HIS SCALP. HE ALERTS TO AN O.S. SOUND, WHEELING, BUT NOT BEFORE A RATHER LARGE ANIMAL SHAPE FLASHES INTO SHOT, KNOCKING HIM OFF HIS FEET.

113 ANOTHER ANGLE—FAVORING CHEETAH AS THE CHIMP JUMPS AWAY FROM TARZAN'S GRASP, CHATTERING HAPPILY. TARZAN LAUGHS.

TARZAN

Jai . . . what're you doing here?

JAI

Thought you might need help.

TARZAN

(SOLEMNLY) You mean . . . you saw a chance to get away from your books?

JAI

(CHEERFULLY) That, too. But the man who was shooting at you back there is now hanging by his ankles high in a tree!

TARZAN STUDIES THE BOY, CAN'T CONTROL A GRIN. BUT HE SHAKES HIS HEAD.

TARZAN

And you didn't learn that trick out of a book.

JAI

(SMILES) But it has something to do with Sir Newton's gravity, doesn't it?

TARZAN

All right, come on.

THE THREE EXIT, AS WE:

DISSOLVE TO:

114 EXT. CASA GRANDE—FULL SHOT—NIGHT. IT IS A VERY QUIET SCENE . . . EXCEPT FOR VARIOUS O.S. JUNGLE NOISES. WE CAN PICK OUT A COUPLE OF SENTRIES MOVING ABOUT THE GROUNDS . . . HEAVILY ARMED, WITH LARGE DOGS ON LEASHES.

115 TIGHT ANGLE—FAVORING TARZAN, WHO IS PEERING OFF AT THIS SCENE. CAMERA PANS TO A WIDER ANGLE AND WE DISCOVER JAI AND CHEETAH IN A TREE BESIDE HIM.

TARZAN

Jai . . . you stay here. And I *mean* right here.

JAI

But, Tarzan—I could act as decoy.

TARZAN

You stay put. Cheetah can handle that.

JAI NODS AND TARZAN NODS TO CHEETAH.

TARZAN

Cheetah . . . you go . . . that way!

HE POINTS AND THE CHIMP TAKES OFF.

116 ANOTHER ANGLE—FAVORING YAEGER. HE'S WEARING A LUGER, IS IN THE PATIO BELOW WILSON'S SUITE. SUDDENLY, THERE IS ONE HELL OF AN UPROAR ON THE OTHER SIDE OF THE HOUSE . . . DOGS BARKING. YAEGER TAKES OFF, RUNNING . . . WITH HIS GUN.

117 FULL SHOT. THIS IS THE OTHER SIDE OF THE HOUSE . . . IDENTIFIABLE BY THE DIFFERENCE IN PLANTING, THE ABSENCE OF THE SWIMMING POOL. IF THERE IS SOMETHING LIKE A FORMAL GARDEN AVAILABLE AT THE LOCATION, THIS WOULD BE IDEAL . . . OR A SWEEP OF LANDSCAPED LAWN WITH TREES AND SHRUBS FALLING AWAY FROM THE HOUSE. IN ANY EVENT, THE AREA IS BEING COMBED BY GUARDS WITH DOGS STRAINING AT THEIR LEASHES. THE DOGS ARE MAKING A FUSS. YAEGER RACES IN WITH HIS GUN, SHOUTS:

YAEGER

(IMPATIENTLY) Let the dogs go!

THE GUARDS RELEASE THE DOGS AND THEY CHARGE OFF INTO THE SHRUBBERY, YELPING AND BARKING. THE MEN AFTER THEM.

118 ANOTHER ANGLE—FAVORING CHEETAH—WITH THE SOUND OF THE DOGS VERY LOUD . . . AS THE CHIMP SWINGS BOLDLY THROUGH THE TREES OF THIS PARK-LIKE SETTING. IN THE B.G., WE SEE SEVERAL OF THE DOGS BRIEFLY AS CHEETAH STOPS AND LOOKS BACK. THEN YAEGER AND A COUPLE OF THE GUARDS APPEAR IN THIS SMALL OPENING THROUGH THE TREES. CHEETAH MOVES OUT.

119 INT. WILSON'S BEDROOM—NIGHT. TIGHT ANGLE—WILSON IS LYING AWAKE . . . LISTENING TO THE RACKET THE DOGS ARE MAKING. HE REACTS . . . STARING OFF TOWARD THE WINDOW. CAMERA PANS TO INCLUDE THE WINDOW . . . THE OPENING OF WHICH IS FILLED BY TARZAN'S SILHOUETTE. TARZAN MOVES QUICKLY TO STAND BESIDE WILSON'S BED. THE LATTER SITS UP.

WILSON

What are you doing here?

TARZAN

I came to get you.

WILSON

(IMPATIENTLY) Isn't it a little late for that? (BEAT) I went to Lwutumba's village this morning . . . to meet you. Where were you?

TARZAN

I was unavoidably detained. (BEAT) Cheetah can hold Yaeger's interest only so long. Get dressed.

TARZAN HAS PICKED UP WILSON'S CLOTHES FROM A CHAIR, TOSSED THEM TO HIM. WILSON STARES AT HIM WITHOUT MOVING.

WILSON

I'm not leaving.

TARZAN

Mr. Wilson—put on your clothes or I'll take you as you are.

YAEGER'S VOICE

(O.S.) I don't think so, ape man. I really don't think so.

120 MED. ANGLE—FAVORING YAEGER AS HE MOVES INTO THE ROOM . . . HIS LUGER LEVELED AT TARZAN, ADDING:

YAEGER

You rose to the bait, didn't you, old boy?

AS TARZAN STARES INTO THE MUZZLE OF THE BIG HANDGUN, WE:

FADE OUT.

END OF ACT III

ACT IV

FADE IN:

121 INT. WILSON'S BEDROOM—NIGHT. MED. ANGLE—YAEGER HAS THE GUN ON TARZAN . . . HIS EYES NEVER LEAVING HIM AS HE SPEAKS INTO THE PHONE.

YAEGER

(TO PHONE) We have a caller, bwana. I have him here in Mr. Wilson's room . . . at gunpoint.

BROWN'S VOICE

(FILTER) Splendid! I'll be right there!

YAEGER HANGS UP, SMILES AT TARZAN.

YAEGER

I hope Senor Brown turns you over to me this time, Tarzan. (BEAT) I consider you a genuine trophy animal.

122 MED. ANGLE. THE CAMERA IS SITUATED ON THE BALCONY, SHOOTING THROUGH THE OPEN FLOOR-TO-CEILING WINDOW.

WILSON (WE NOTE) IS STILL SEATED ON THE EDGE OF HIS BED, WATCHING TARZAN AND YAEGER. THERE'S NO NONSENSE IN THE WAY THE LATTER KEEPS THAT LUGER POINTED AT TARZAN. NO NONSENSE IN TARZAN'S RESPECT FOR THAT WEAPON. THEN, FROM DIRECTLY OVER CAMERA, A SMALL, BROWN SHAPE FLASHES THROUGH THE OPEN WINDOW AND JAI LANDS ONLY A FEW FEET FROM YAEGER . . . WHO REACTS BY TAKING HIS EYES OFF TARZAN FOR A SPLIT SECOND. THAT'S ALL TARZAN NEEDS. HE SCOOPS UP A LARGE ASHTRAY, SCORES A HIT WITH IT ON THE SIDE OF YAEGER'S HEAD. AND HE'S ACROSS THE ROOM BEFORE YAEGER CAN RECOVER SUFFICIENTLY TO BRING HIS GUN INTO PLAY. HE KNOCKS THE GUN FROM YAEGER'S HAND AND PULPS HIM WITH A RIGHT TO THE JAW.

TARZAN

All right, Mr. Wilson . . . let's go. (BEAT) Jai . . . get his clothes. He'll have to dress later.

WILSON

(FLATLY) I'm not setting foot outside this room tonight. I don't know what your game is, but . . .

TARZAN

(INTERJECTS) Sorry . . . it's no game.

AS HE SAYS THIS, HE LIFTS WILSON OFF THE BED, CREAMS HIM, AND TOSSES HIM UNCONSCIOUS OVER HIS SHOULDER.

TARZAN

(CONTINUING) Hurry, Jai!

JAI HAS AN ARMLOAD OF WILSON'S CLOTHING . . . DASHES OUT THE WINDOW AHEAD OF TARZAN AND HIS BURDEN. CAMERA PANS TO HOLD ON YAEGER BRIEFLY. HE'S NOT MOVING. O.S., WE HEAR SOUND OF A KNOCK ON THE DOOR.

123 ANOTHER ANGLE—AT THE DOOR AS THE KNOCK IS REPEATED AND WE HEAR:

BROWN'S VOICE

(O.S.) Yaeger . . . open up!

THE KNOB TURNS WHEN THERE IS NO RESPONSE FROM THE ROOM. BROWN BURSTS IN, LOOKS AROUND, AS:

BROWN

(CONTINUING) Yaeger . . . Wilson?

A GRIM MIGUEL BROWN SPOTS YAEGER WHERE HE'S LYING ON THE FLOOR, ALMOST HIDDEN BY WILSON'S BED. HE MOVES TO STAND OVER HIM, AFTER PICKING UP THE LUGER ON THE WAY.

BROWN

(CONTINUING; SHOUTS) Yaeger!

YAEGER STIRS, STRUGGLES TO SIT UP.

BROWN

(CONTINUING) Get on your feet!

YAEGER MANAGES TO SWAY ERECT . . . BUT HAS TO HANG ONTO THE BED-STEAD FOR A MOMENT.

BROWN

(CONTINUING) So you had Tarzan at gunpoint. What happened? He take this toy away from you?

YAEGER

(DULLY) That . . . that little boy . . .

BROWN

(BITINGLY) So it was a child who disarmed you. (BEAT) If your brains are not too addled to understand this . . . Tarzan not only got away from you, but he took Wilson with him!

THIS PENETRATES YAEGER'S CONSCIOUSNESS. HE STRIDES AWAY FROM THE BED TO THE WINDOW, STARING OUT INTO THE NIGHT. THEN, HE WHEELS AND STARTS FOR THE PHONE.

YAEGER

I'll call out the guard . . . stop them!

BROWN

(ANGRILY) You'd be wasting time. Never find them out there in the dark.
(BEAT) He'll have Wilson at that rift by daybreak. Then Wilson poses
as big a threat as Tarzan. You get there in the helicoptor and kill them—
both of them.

YAEGER STUDIES BROWN FOR A MOMENT, THE EASE WITH WHICH HE HAS MADE
THIS STATEMENT. HE SHAKES HIS HEAD . . . REMARKING WRYLY:

YAEGER

And I thought I was a hard case.

BROWN

(COLDLY) I don't know where you got that idea. (BEAT) You've never
been anything but an overgrown child, playing children's games . . .
pretending you're a man. You shot dumb beasts . . . because that was
supposed to be dangerous. You helped other child-men prove their
manhood that way.

YAEGER FLUSHES WITH ANGER . . . HE SNAPS BACK:

YAEGER

You don't have to prove anything. You can hire men to do your proving
. . . just point your finger at who or what you want killed.

BROWN

That's a fair statement and I wouldn't forget it if I were you. (BEAT)
What you have to understand is that this land has belonged to my family
for three generations. I'm not opening it up to a group of fuzzy-minded
African nationalists. Nor to anybody else!

A STRANGE, SEMIFANATICAL GLEAM HAS COME INTO BROWN'S EYES. HE BITES
OUT HIS WORDS.

BROWN

(CONTINUING) The hydroelectric dam was *their* big dream. After tomorrow the dream will be a nightmare. (SHAKES HEAD) I have brought them
along . . . step by step, to this particular brink. I'm not going to be
stopped from pushing them over it!

YAEGER HAS FALLEN UNDER THE SPELL OF BROWN'S DEMAGOGUERY, NODS.

YAEGER

All right, bwana. It's your show.

AS HE IS SPEAKING, BROWN HAS CROSSED TO THE DOOR, EXITS AS YAEGER
STARES AFTER HIM AND WE:

DISSOLVE TO:

124 EXT. JUNGLE SKY—DAY. FULL SHOT—THE SUN IS BARELY UP . . . THE SKY
PALE BLUE, CAPPING THE BLACK SEA OF TREES BELOW. THE COPTER "SWIMS"
INTO VIEW . . . FLYING LOW.

125 INT. COPTER—DAY. TIGHT ANGLE—(INTERCUTS)—YAEGER, A HEAVY RIFLE

BETWEEN HIS KNEES, IS PEERING DOWN AND OFF AS THE CHOPPER SKIMS ALONG.

126 BACK TO SCENE. THE CHOPPER MAKES A BIG CIRCLE AND STARTS A CRISS-CROSS FLIGHT PATTERN.

127 EXT. JUNGLE—DAY. MED. ANGLE—FAVORING TARZAN. HE, WILSON, JAI, AND CHEETAH ARE STANDING UNDER THE SHELTER OF A BIG TREE . . . LOOKING UP AS THERE IS THE SOUND OF THE CHOPPER PASSING ABOVE THEM.

TARZAN

They're out early . . . looking for us.

WILSON

(DRYLY) Does that surprise you . . . or is kidnapping only bad manners in this part of Africa?

THE SOUND OF THE CHOPPER IS NOW DISTANT AND TARZAN GESTURES THEM ON.

128 ANOTHER ANGLE—AT THE EDGE OF THE RIFT AS TARZAN LEADS THEM UP TO IT, STOPS, AND NODS TO WILSON.

TARZAN

The rift . . . Mr. Wilson. It runs over two hundred miles north and south. At its deepest point, it is . . . very deep.

HE PICKS UP A ROCK AND TOSSES IT INTO THE SLASH IN THE JUNGLE EARTH (ANY DRY WASH PROPERLY PHOTOGRAPHED . . . OR A BARRANCA . . . SHOULD DO THE JOB FOR US). IT TAKES SEVERAL SECONDS FOR THE SOUND OF THE ROCK LANDING IN THE BOTTOM OF THE RIFT TO REACH THEM. WILSON IS TRULY SHAKEN.

WILSON

(DRY-MOUTHED) I don't understand how this can be possible. All the surveys of this whole section of Gwamba which I have studied . . . there's not a word about this!

TARZAN

Let's just say Senor Brown is a very influential man in Gwamba. All of those surveys had to clear through him.

WILSON

But why . . . why would anyone want to spend Gwamba into bankruptcy to build a dam where it has to fail?

TARZAN

No dam will be built, Mr. Wilson.

WILSON

Then what am I doing here? I'm being paid a great deal of money . . .

TARZAN

(INTERJECTS) That's an important part of Brown's plan. He wants the best engineer of African descent that Gwamba's money can buy.

WILSON

(NO LONGER UNDER ANY ILLUSIONS) What's the rest of it?

TARZAN

What would happen if portions of this rift were mined . . . the mines detonated by your seismic charges in the gorge?

WILSON

(THOUGHTFULLY) A large landslide.

TARZAN

Could that divert the river into the rift?

WILSON

(NUMB ASTONISHMENT) Yes.

TARZAN

(DRYLY) Very likely an idea Brown picked up from a survey report he didn't have passed along to you.

WILSON

(NODS) I'm with you, Tarzan . . . at least, I think I'm catching up. That landslide will be blamed on me . . . my work?

TARZAN NODS . . . THEN THEY ALL ALERT TO THE O.S. SOUND OF THE CHOPPER RETURNING. THEY SCATTER FOR COVER.

129 EXT. JUNGLE SKY—DAY. FULL SHOT—THE COPTER CHURNS OVERHEAD IN A GIANT SWEEP . . . THE SOUND DIMINISHING AGAIN.

130 EXT. JUNGLE—DAY. MED. ANGLE—FAVORING JAI AS HE IS THE FIRST ONE TO PEER OUT FROM UNDER SOME HEAVY UNDERBRUSH. THE OTHERS GROUP NEAR HIM.

WILSON

Those charges are set to fire at seven A.M.—whether I'm there or not.

HE GLANCES AT HIS WRIST WATCH, ADDS:

WILSON

(CONTINUING) It's five fifty-two, now. Can we reach the gorge in time?

TARZAN

We'll have to.

HE GLANCES AT JAI, ADDING:

TARZAN

(CONTINUING) I want you to get to Lwutumba's village as quickly as you can. (BEAT) You and Cheetah. Tell Lwutumba to have the drums warn the people who live below the rift to move out to higher ground. Understand?

JAI

Yes.

TARZAN
As fast as you can go!

JAI NODS AND TAKES OFF, SHOUTING BACK:

JAI
(SHOUTING) Come on, Cheetah!

THE CHIMP RACES AFTER HIM. TARZAN NODS TO WILSON AND THEY START JOGGING THROUGH THE JUNGLE IN ANOTHER DIRECTION, AS WE:

DISSOLVE TO:

131   EXT. JUNGLE SKY—DAY. FULL SHOT—THE CHOPPER IS CONTINUING ITS TREETOP-LEVEL SWEEPS.

132   INT. COPTER—DAY. TIGHT ANGLE—A GRIM YAEGER STUDIES THE RAIN FOREST BELOW. SUDDENLY, HIS FACE LIGHTS WITH EXCITEMENT AND CAMERA PANS TO INCLUDE HIS PILOT AS HE GESTURES FOR HIM TO BANK TO THE LEFT. HE KEEPS HIS EYES ON WHAT HE HAS SEEN BELOW AS HE OPENS THE HATCH BESIDE HIM AND PREPARES TO FIRE.

133   EXT. JUNGLE SKY—DAY. FULL SHOT—THE COPTER MAKES A LEFT BANKING TURN AND SWEEPS EVEN LOWER.

134   EXT. JUNGLE—DAY. MED. ANGLE—FAVORING TARZAN AS HE AND WILSON TAKE COVER UNDER A TREE. THE SOUND OF THE CHOPPER BECOMES VERY LOUD AND SUDDENLY THIS IS AUGMENTED BY THE SOUND OF AUTOMATIC WEAPON FIRE AND THERE'S A PATTERN OF DUST SPURTS ACROSS THE GROUND AND SPLINTERING OF A TREE UNCOMFORTABLY NEAR THEM. THE CHOPPER HAS COMPLETED ITS PASS.

TARZAN
We can't stay here. Come on!

THEY MAKE A DASH FOR AN OVERHANGING ROCK FORMATION.

135   ANOTHER ANGLE—UP THROUGH THE TREES AT THE CHOPPER AS IT BANKS AND TURNS AND COMES BACK WITH A RUSH. WE PAN IT IN ANOTHER PASS . . . THIS ONE CHASING THE TWO MEN LITERALLY AND OPENING FIRE.

136   TIGHT ANGLE. THEY DIVE UNDER THE PROTECTION OF THE ROCK JUST IN TIME . . . THE BULLETS FROM YAEGER'S AUTOMATIC WEAPON BUTTONING THE GROUND AT THEIR HEELS. WE PAN UP AS THE CHOPPER BANKS IN ANOTHER TURN . . . COMES BACK AND MAKES ANOTHER FIRING PASS. AS THE BULLETS FROM THIS ONE CHIP A PATTERN ACROSS THE ROCK, WE TILT BACK TO TARZAN AND WILSON HUDDLED TOGETHER.

137   INT. COPTER—DAY. TIGHT ANGLE—FAVORING YAEGER AS HE GESTURES TO HIS PILOT TO LAND.

138   EXT. JUNGLE—DAY. FULL SHOT—THE COPTER HOVERS OVER A SMALL CLEARING NEAR THE ROCK WHERE TARZAN AND WILSON HAVE TAKEN COVER, BEGINS ITS LANDING.

139   TIGHT ANGLE—TARZAN AND WILSON WATCHING THE ABOVE.

TARZAN
(INDICATING CHOPPER) As soon as it starts to make dust . . . follow me.

140 THEIR POV—(INTERCUTS)—THE CHOPPER BEGINS TO KICK UP A BILLOWING CLOUD OF DUST AS IT NEARS THE GROUND.

141 BACK TO SCENE.

TARZAN
(NODS) Now . . . do what I do!

HE BREAKS FROM THE COVER OF THE OVERHANGING ROCK WITH WILSON AT HIS HEELS . . . CAMERA PANNING AS THEY RUN TOWARD THE LANDING CHOPPER. WILSON IS A GOOD STUDENT . . . KEEPS LOW AS HE RUNS . . . EXACTLY AS TARZAN IS DOING. THEY ARE ALMOST OBSCURED IN THE DUST CLOUD.

142 ANOTHER ANGLE—TARZAN AND WILSON RUNNING TOWARD THE CHOPPER WHICH IS JUST TOUCHING DOWN IN THE B.G. THEY ARE ALMOST THROUGH THE "DOUGHNUT" OF DUST. TARZAN GESTURES TO WILSON AND THEY BOTH HIT THE GROUND BEHIND ROCKS THAT BARELY SUFFICE TO PROVIDE VISUAL COVER.

THE ROTORS ON THE CHOPPER STOP TURNING AND THE DUST BEGINS TO SETTLE. THE HATCH IS ALREADY OPEN AND YAEGER PILES OUT WITH HIS AUTOMATIC WEAPON, FOLLOWED BY ONE OF THE SECURITY COPS . . . OR THE PILOT . . . ALSO ARMED. THEY START RUNNING TOWARD CAMERA.

143 TIGHT ANGLE—FAVORING YAEGER AS HE GESTURES OFF.

YAEGER
They were over there . . . that big rock. Come on!

CAMERA PANS AS THEY RUN TOWARD THE OVERHANGING ROCK WHERE THEY HAD PINNED TARZAN AND WILSON DOWN.

144 LOW ANGLE—FAVORING TARZAN AS HE GLANCES BRIEFLY AT WILSON, WHO NODS GRIMLY. TARZAN HOLDS HIM WITH A SMALL HAND GESTURE. YAEGER AND THE MAN WITH HIM RUN BETWEEN THEM. AS THEY PASS, TARZAN SIGNALS WILSON AND THEY JUMP THE TWO.

145 SERIES OF BRIEF CUTS—TIGHT ANGLES—OF THE FIGHT. YAEGER AND HIS MAN ARE TAKEN BY SURPRISE. TARZAN HAS YAEGER . . . KNOCKS HIS GUN OUT OF HIS HANDS AND THEN JUDO CHOPS HIM TO HIS KNEES . . . CREAMS HIM. WILSON IS NOT AS EXPERT . . . BUT HE STRUGGLES WITH HIS MAN AND GETS HIS GUN AWAY FROM HIM . . . SKULLS HIM WITH THE BUTT.

TARZAN STEPS OVER YAEGER, TAKES THE GUN FROM WILSON, AND FIRES A BURST INTO THE CHOPPER'S AFTER ROTOR.

146 ANOTHER ANGLE.

TARZAN
(BEAT) How is our time?

WILSON

(LOOKS AT WATCH) Twenty-two minutes to zero.

TARZAN

(NODS) We can make it.

THEY HURRY OFF, AS WE:

DISSOLVE TO:

147 EXT. RIVER GORGE—DAY. TIGHT SHOT—ON THE DETONATING DEVICE REPLETE WITH DIALS, TIMER, WIRES. CAMERA, AFTER ESTABLISHING THAT THERE ARE SEVEN MINUTES TO ZERO, PULLS BACK TO A FULL SHOT AT THE GORGE, REVEALING WILSON'S ASSISTANT WATCHING THE DIALS OF THE DETONATING DEVICE CLOSELY. CAMERA PANS TO HIGH GROUND WHERE BROWN IS CHECKING OUT HIS GUARD, WHO IS ALERTED FOR ANY POSSIBLE INTERRUPTIONS. BROWN TURNS AND WALKS TOWARD THE DETONATING DEVICE AND WILSON'S ASSISTANT.

148 ANOTHER ANGLE AS BROWN JOINS THE ASSISTANT WHO HOLDS UP A HAND AND A FINGER TO HIM, INDICATING THERE ARE SIX MINUTES TO GO.

149 GUARD SWEEPING THE JUNGLE WITH HIGH-POWERED FIELD GLASSES. HE COMES ON POINT.

150 HIS POV—(MATTE)—(INTERCUTS)—TARZAN AND WILSON ARE RUNNING ALONG THE EDGE OF THE GORGE.

151 BACK TO SCENE. THE MAN HOLLERS TO BROWN, WHO RUSHES TO HIS SIDE. HE LOOKS, REACTS. HE TAKES THE GLASSES FROM HIS EYES AND PICKS UP A HUNTING RIFLE, PUTS IT TO HIS SHOULDER, SIGHTING IT.

152 HIS POV—(MATTE)—WILSON IS IN THE SIGHT . . . THE CROSSHAIRS MOVING WITH HIM. THE SOUND OF THE SHOT IS VERY LOUD.

153 MED. ANGLE—FAVORING WILSON AS HE'S KNOCKED OVER. TARZAN TURNS AND DIVES FOR HIM . . . ROLLS HIM TO COVER.

154 TIGHT ANGLE—WILSON GRIPS HIS SHOULDER WHERE THERE IS A SPREADING PATTERN OF BLOOD.

WILSON

I'm all right! But, the detonator—

TARZAN MOVES OFF, IN THE MIDDLE OF WILSON'S WORDS, CIRCLING AROUND TO COME IN ON THE DETONATING SITE FROM HIGH GROUND. CAMERA SWINGS BACK TO WILSON, WHO STRUGGLES TO HIS FEET AND CONTINUES, IN A DIRECT ROUTE, FOR THE SITE.

155 AT THE GORGE—CLOSE—THE DETONATING DEVICE. THE TIMER SHOWS FOUR MINUTES TO GO.

156 MED. SHOT—BROWN LOOKING OFF WITH A SLIGHT SMILE, AS:

157 HIS POV—WILSON APPROACHES.

158 BACK TO BROWN.

BROWN

Let me have a hand grenade.

ONE OF THE GUARDS UNCLIPS A GRENADE FROM A SHOULDER STRAP AND HANDS IT TO BROWN. THE GUARDS BACK OFF AS BROWN TAKES THE PIN FROM THE GRENADE, HOLDS THE HAMMER DOWN, AS WILSON APPROACHES.

BROWN

(CONTINUING; CALLING) Wilson . . . in four minutes you will be famous . . . as the engineer who kept Gwamba unspoiled by the twentieth century. At least, that will be *my* view.

159 WILSON, OUT OF BREATH, HIS FACE WORKS WITH PAIN AND HELPLESSNESS.

160 BACK TO BROWN, WHO HAS RELEASED THE HAMMER OF THE GRENADE . . . IS ABOUT TO THROW IT, WHEN WILSON'S ASSISTANT TRIES TO STOP HIM, IS RIFLE-BUTTED BY THE GUARD.

161 TIGHT ANGLE—FAVORING TARZAN AS HE RISES QUICKLY ON HIGH GROUND, THROWS A ROCK.

162 BACK TO SCENE. THE ROCK HITS BROWN IN THE SHOULDER, CAUSING HIM TO DROP THE GRENADE AT HIS FEET. HE HAS ONE BRIEF MOMENT OF TOTAL TERROR AS HE FREEZES, STARING AT THE GRENADE . . . THEN THE EXPLOSION OBLITERATES CAMERA.

163 FULL SHOT—THE SMOKE AND DUST FROM THE EXPLOSION CLEAR. WILSON MOVES TO THE DETONATING DEVICE BUT COLLAPSES BEFORE HE CAN REACH IT. CAMERA SWINGS TO TARZAN, WHO ROARS DOWN, FIGHTS THE GUARD, AS:

164 INSERT—TIMER. IT IS NOW SO CLOSE TO SEVEN O'CLOCK THAT THE DIFFERENCE CAN HARDLY MATTER.

165 BACK TO FIGHT. TARZAN SUBDUES THE GUARD, MOVES TO THE DETONATING DEVICE, STARES DESPERATELY AT IT FOR A MOMENT, THEN RIPS THE WIRES CONNECTED TO IT FROM THEIR TERMINALS.

TARZAN HOLDS HIS BREATH . . . LETS IT OUT AS THE GROUND UNDER HIM DOES NOT SPLIT WITH AN EXPLOSION. HE RISES SLOWLY . . . MOVES TO WILSON'S SIDE.

FADE OUT.

END OF ACT IV

TAG

166 EXT. LWUTUMBA'S VILLAGE—DAY. MED. ANGLE—AT THE CHIEF'S HUT. PRESENT ARE: LWUTUMBA, TARZAN, A PATCHED-UP WILSON, JAI . . . AND, OF COURSE, CHEETAH. SEVERAL OF THE TRIBE ARE ALSO THERE, AS:

WILSON

Gwamba will have its hydroelectric plant, Chief . . . if I have to build it with my bare hands. (SMILES) But, it will be built where it should be built—not near the "Creeping Giants."

HE SHAKES LWUTUMBA'S HAND.

WILSON

(CONTINUING) I'll return. You have my promise.

LWUTUMBA

My people will help . . . when it is time to build the dam.

HE STARTS TO SAY SOMETHING TO TARZAN, BUT REALIZES WORDS CANNOT EXPRESS HIS GRATITUDE. THEY SHAKE HANDS.

WILSON MOVES OFF TO A LAND ROVER. WILSON AND HIS ASSISTANT DRIVE OFF. TARZAN SMILES DOWN AT JAI.

TARZAN

Now, young man . . . suppose we get you back to cracking your books?

JAI

Aw, Tarzan . . . can't you ever forget anything?

BUT HE GRINS UP TO TARZAN AND AS THEY WAVE TO LWUTUMBA AND START BACK HOME, HOLDING AS CHEETAH JUMPS INTO TARZAN'S ARMS.

FADE OUT.

THE END

Now that you have read the script, turn back to the beginning. Notice how, after the opening fade-in and the standard footage—the waterfall, the seventy-five-foot swan dive into the foamy linn below, the quick cuts of wild animals (all the "set" stuff, in short)—we get our first hint of trouble. It's the first new material in the show—in Shot 2.

Look at it now. A native is in trouble. We know he's headed our way. If he weren't, the camera wouldn't bother with him. We realize he's hurt. We also know he'll have something to report, that this something will be big news, that the news will involve us.

Our viewer knows all this in just the three seconds the camera inspects this bleeding man. Something serious is in motion, and presumably on its way—with its message—to Tarzan.

Now with a quick cut—no fading, no dissolves—we leap to something quite different, a switch from an exterior shot to an interior. It is a jump from the alarming to the amusing. And for every teen-ager in America, it is an about-turn to something wholly familiar: a kid who doesn't like to do homework. Every young person watching will identify right there with Jai.

This brief domestic moment does something important at the very top of the show. It establishes the *relationship* between these two characters. In stories, in novels, in most motion pictures, there is time to let these things develop more gradually. But in this kind of nonliterary, commercial, popular television, all characters must be quickly recognized for what they are—good or bad (there are no other kinds). Also, we must be made aware of what they mean to each other. These considerations, plus a real promise of coming danger, must be set very early.

In Shot 3 the mildness of Tarzan's reproach (he kids Jai slightly) indicates his prevailing attitude toward this attractive youngster. Tarzan reveals a big-brother-is-watching protectiveness and a real concern. Tarzan is a bit too old for his regard to be fraternal. It's closer to the avuncular. The main thing, however, is this: if you had tuned in this show for the first time and were just sampling it, your understanding of the relationship of these two people would be correct. It's been made completely clear at the start, and that's good television.

In any fast-moving action show—and all adventure shows are fast-moving—it is wise to be clear about your principals from the beginning, who they are and what can be expected of them. Always try to establish this at once.

To recapitulate, it is important at the very outset in an adventure show of this kind to establish the two prime and basic features—danger and character relationships.

In Shots 4 and 5 we have several tricks, instinctively used by professional television writers irrespective of the show they're writing.

Here's one: *contrast* of quick visual interests.

Reread the indicated business with Jai, the lion cubs, and Cheetah. No one—not even an animal hater—can tune out your show at this point. Not only is the eye held, but the human feelings of the viewer are completely captured. One delight tumbles over another—comical, charming, unexpected. And for each shot, the eye is given a new angle of fix.

This little scene is pure fun, innocent, spontaneous. We enjoy everything we're looking at, including Tarzan and Jai who are themselves enjoying it. People love to watch other people enjoying themselves. This was common knowledge long before television.

Suddenly all this fun is interrupted—and without warning. We hear the native. What does he bring? A complete alteration in mood. A radical change of interest. And with these elements comes a shift of feeling. Meanwhile, we change our angle of sight again. Why? Because we're elevated above the ground, in Tarzan's tree house, looking down. This change eliminates the animals and fixes our mind on new material, plot material. The story is about to begin.

Is this slow? No, it's fast. Since we've been on the air, we've had a lot of preliminary clutter, to be sure—the regular filmed opening, logos, wild animals, a few credits and commercial billboards—but we haven't had forty-five seconds of the *Tarzan* show.

This is getting it off fast. Do the same when you are writing adventure fiction. Grab your audience. The lion cubs guaranteed the attention of most of the kids and some of the women; the chimp pulled in some more. The spectacular Tarzan, now about to show his muscles and place himself in danger, will pull in the rest—envious men, marveling women.

Remember, too, that motion invites continuous attention. Changing of camera angles from one POV (point of view) to another is an additional stimulus of great power. The maneuver provides new things to look at, new reactions to pick up.

Tarzan looks down. Now *he* sees the gasping native whom we saw at the very start. The native is in poor shape. But our crew—Tarzan, Jai, and Cheetah—are resourceful. And right here is another good trick: giving the boy a man's responsibility.

Use this in your own work. It explains half the holding power and identifying value Jim Hawkins enjoys in *Treasure Island*. The situation is no different here. Jai has something to do. He carries the first aid kit. And later Jai comforts the native. Who will be most impressed by Jai's "adult" compassion here? That's easy —all the twelve- and fourteen-year-olds who are watching the episode. This puts *them* in the scene. They *become* Jai.

Now let's take a close look at Shot 8.

Would the native know the meaning of the word "dynamite"? No. But the matter isn't really important. (Maybe the Peace Corps has been there.) The significant factor is that you, the writer, *have this license*. You may give him that understanding. It is your duty to make your story clear. Haven't you seen fifty science fiction shows in which the captured Venusians speak perfect English? How did they learn? It was easy—intercepting earth's radio programs. Implausibles are skipped over so fast they aren't picked up.

We need the privilege of free communication. If conditions suggest that the freedom we need isn't there, we take it anyhow.

This same shot is crowded with examples of good carpentry. Menace appears here. It's in the native's last line and it's the word "they." "They" unmistakably means the wrong people, the enemy.

There's a reference to drum signaling—a good element in any jungle show. We have people in trouble, the essence of all drama. Who are they here? A tribe we like—or that Tarzan likes, which amounts to the same thing. Is Tarzan himself in trouble? Yes, deep trouble. His life is threatened. With that disclosure, the scene is really finished. Accordingly, it must be killed in a hurry. And that is exactly what happens. How? The native has delivered his message. And he's been patched up. So we can forget him. We can forget Jai, too. He's on his way for the doctor.

With these summary clearances, the writer has demonstrated something of great basic value to the student writer: the quick dispatch of any character once his dramatic use has been terminated. If one word should be italicized in that sentence, it is the word *quick*. The clean cutoff is what we are seeking. In this little scene everyone is accounted for, even Cheetah. Meanwhile, Tarzan carries the story forward. Now, you ask, how can he, when he's also leaving the same scene? He does it by *running*.

Use devices of this nature to maintain pace, to keep your show *moving*. With this kind of show, it's a vital necessity.

In Shot 9 we encounter a different sort of script matter. Read carefully the great detail this writer has requested from stock. What is stock? Stock is cataloged film that has been taken before and usually for other purposes, other shows. The material may never have been used or, if used, has been retired. Millions of feet of all kinds of film is racked in vaults and is available on a rental basis.

This is a reservoir into which you, as the writer, are allowed to dip. When patched into location shooting, judicious use of stock film footage saves a lot of money. In addition, it often elaborates the overall effect of a production, making it appear bigger and richer than it really is.

Stock is there to be used. Ask for it.

In Shot 9 see what Donn Mullally, the writer of this particular *Tarzan* script, has demanded from stock. He knows he'll be lucky to find all those effects in just the way he has described them. But even the mere asking for the material, and the laying out of particulars, gives his producer a fine understanding of the scene the writer is attempting to create and how he wants it mounted. In my judgment, it is the most artfully conceived "television" scene in the script. I'm referring to its almost automatic acceptance by the eye, rather than to the action that occurs.

Now look at Shot 9 again, and select *one item only* and pretend that it is all that stock is going to be able to deliver to your show. If you have to sacrifice all but one item, you'll lose some fine picture material (or have to do without it). But one of the features requested by the writer is a must.

It is the cliff. Why so? For the next several minutes the cliff becomes his stage. A vertical stage? Yes. And it is very exciting to watch the work that is put together there.

The reason the cliff, functioning as a stage, is so satisfactory and essential from a television point of view is because of the exquisite *isolation* in which the actor is able to perform. This isolation will demand an exclusivity of attention from the viewer.

In my opinion, the two most important words in the production of successful television drama are these: *isolation* and *simplicity*. The reasons are obvious. If you present the viewer with a lot of things to examine all at once, or inundate him with a mass of people to look at, you don't intensify his interest. You scatter it.

Look at the line (we are now in Shot 10) that describes Walter Wilson at work: "He uses his feet to kick and walk himself over the face of the cliff."

This is enormously visual. It is excellent TV because of the isolation. We react to it exactly as we do when we suddenly come across the precarious movements of a steeplejack at work, the topping out of a skyscraper, or the painting of a gold ball atop a flagpole set on the roof of a building.

Now look at something else (in Shot 11) that's very different from anything encountered so far. Read these nine or ten lines, then answer this question: How do we know Walter Wilson is "the renowned American engineer"—among other things? We don't actually know. All we really know is that he's a muscular Negro on a perilous working surface, doing something dangerous and masculine.

There's good visual direction in Shot 12. You've all seen the "hoist" and "lower" gestures used by construction crews in erecting new buildings. The same hand signals are universally used. But in this same shot how do we know Colin Yaeger is our enemy? We can't really be certain, but the producer knows. However, we can make an educated guess because the character description is half flattery, half contempt.

Note the next action: the makeshift militia under Yaeger's command is being spied upon. And they become aware of this. What does that telegraph to the viewer? That a collision is coming. An emergency is building up. Work on the cliff face is suddenly halted. The calm Mr. Wilson is unceremoniously hoisted to the top, using his feet to keep from being scraped on the projecting rocks of the cliff, soaring in a series of giant leaps each time he kicks out.

This is intensely visual, especially for a sitting, nonacrobatic audience. This kind of television isn't for students of August Strindberg. This is *Tarzan*. Don't laugh at it. It has its own rules, and this script is an excellent example of the category.

Look at the *physical props* the writer has brought to his action. See what authority these props bring to the action. Aside from the armed men, the list includes an A-frame, a Land Rover, a trailer, bosun's chair, cable winch, power generator, drills, rope, wires, dynamite.

Character? Very little, and such as there is carries the most obvious stamp. This is all that's needed. We're looking at men in action. We're looking at disciplined strength, trained skills, strong men involved in perilous endeavors.

Tarzan is muscle, nerve, and hazard. The mechanical gear isn't wasted. It's well used. There is no fumbling and the equipment is handled by men used to the feel of these things. Look at Shot 20, for example. Wilson is now reaching the top. The winch slows, Wilson is pulled in, he unbuckles a safety belt. This attention to physical detail, and to the handling of gear, can be very clumsy when requested by amateurs.

If you don't know how to give the signals for the use of the equipment you require, don't use it. Leave it out. Provide a substitute.

On this same point—or at least a related one—pick up and use the idiom and abbreviations employed by television writers. We've had several here: F.G. is foreground. Beat is a pause (but never more than two seconds—a long time in television). Pan is panorama—a slow, lateral sweeping of the camera to left or right, usually at horizon level. Intercut is the shifting back and forth, in rapid succession, between two or more people, scenes, or objects. (The amount and duration of intercutting are at the discretion of the director.) O.S. is offscreen, that is to say, the acting is heard or indicated but not seen.

Earlier I mentioned the necessity of being clear in regard to all character relationships. There are some exceptions. Here, with the emergence of Wilson, now moving about with the others, are we clear about his relationship to Yaeger? Do we really know who Wilson is? In whose pay? Is he Yaeger's man, or vice versa? The answer is that we don't know.

Isn't this, therefore, inconsistent with what has been said on the subject? No. This delay in settling Wilson's exact role in the drama has three purposes: to enrich the villainy of Yaeger; to show the integrity of Wilson (who finds out important things *after* the viewer does); to set up frictions—frictions within the group that is planning to dynamite these mountains. As you will see, this dissension in the ranks builds constantly.

All this adds yeast to the mix the writer is kneading. We aren't left in doubt very long. Wilson wants to know his enemy before any shooting starts. He's controlled and circumspect. As proof of his desire to get the full picture, he aborts Yaeger's first impulsive attempt at mayhem by shoving Yaeger's gun barrel at the instant of firing and making him miss.

Who was his target? Chief Lwutumba. Where did we hear about him? At the very beginning, from the *gasping native*. Tight-lipped Yaeger wants to kill the chief. Why? Obviously because Wilson will find out things Yaeger doesn't want him to know.

Is Yaeger a paper villain? Or is he a villain to be reckoned with? He's the real thing—a man of action, used to command, a white hunter, a good shot, a man among-men, even of the low order he chooses to move with. He's strong. And he'll take large risks. He lies convincingly, seems to enjoy killing, and is devious.

All these men are given outward attributes, enough business and flavored dialogue to tell us what their essential characters are. In action melodrama, this is sufficient.

The purity of speech, thought, and action that is part of Tarzan (and one of the reasons the show is easy to caricature) appears when Tarzan enters in Shot 25. Examine his lines. His words are composed, civilized, and to the point. If some of the dialogue has university overtones, remember these two things: Tarzan is no hippie, he's educated. That's one thing. The other relates to the fact that the *Tarzan* show isn't supposed to entertain *you*. (Very little in television is supposed to entertain *you*.) Your purpose in looking at this dissection is to learn how the thing is done. And the purpose behind that is to remind you that the *Tarzan* type of entertainment will always have a proper place in the front yard of television's hardy perennials.

The main reason—and let's not kid around about this part of it—is that TV writing fees are excellent. The reason I am including in this volume network material that is or has been popular is to show you what is being *presented* by the networks and *consumed* by the public. And the reason for showing only that kind of material is because I assume you want to explore typical commercial fare that pays good money to the people who have learned how to write it—and that you'd like to do the same.

To get on with Mr. Mullally's *Tarzan*, we know that Yaeger is a villain when he is sassy to Tarzan, when he ridicules the prestige that Tarzan enjoys in his jungle. What Yaeger says is an insult to the throne. Does it bother Tarzan? No. He's above noticing it, as is any king. He just wants to get the record straight. He tells Wilson the truth about the rift. He offers to take him to the very place. Yaeger tries a desperate diversionary tactic (that sneaky shot), but Tarzan sees through it. The "Creeping Giants" confusion is cleared up—at least the aspect of mountains-on-the-move.

The full motivation behind the next large segment of action is Yaeger's determination to prevent Wilson from seeing the rift. Before departing, Yaeger insults Tarzan again by deliberately showering him with dust from the Land Rover.

One of the great attributes of all melodrama is the pleasure we take in revenge. We're building to it here as our hatred of Yaeger is nourished by the writer. When President Roosevelt told America the Japanese attack on Pearl Harbor was a "day of infamy" that would live forever in history, we gave this our best approval. Somewhat later, when he said, "They have asked for it. And they are going to get it!" we all leaped up cheering.

Pared down to its bones, this is the difference between the editorial and the visceral, the intellectual and the emotional. All responses in Tarzan are to be visceral, emotional, primeval, immediate, reflexive, nonthinking.

Not having Wilson committed to either side is well employed by the writer. It gives him a hod of cement to splash among a lot of loose bricks, letting them harden as his story strengthens. Wilson is entitled to some honest doubts. The tussle between scientific fact and native superstition (Shot 25), for example, would bother any engineer's mind. Besides, he doesn't know the tribal language. And he doesn't know Tarzan. In fact, he doesn't know what to believe. And this, as you realize, presently thickens. (It has to or we'd only have a half-hour show. Tarzan was an hour show.)

For Wilson *not* to know which man to trust—Yaeger or Tarzan—sharpens the contest between these two, and intensifies our interest in watching.

In passing, let us consider something else. Look at Shot 30. Would this *Tarzan* television crew, working on location, be so unexpectedly lucky as to encounter a Moorish-Spanish *casa* in the African jungle? Of course not. This latest version of *Tarzan* was filmed in Mexico. The writer just made an astute accommodation in geography, architecture, and casting (Miguel Jimenez Brown!). Do the same whenever you're confronted with a similar problem.

Do we know the relationship of Senor Brown and Yaeger? Yes. This one is really billboarded:

> BROWN: What's the matter with him? (meaning Wilson)
> YAEGER: He met Tarzan.

The reaction to this? Here it is: "Yaeger smiles crookedly . . . Brown nods solemnly." This tells us all we need to know.

Incidentally, in pure adventure shows of the *Tarzan* type it is important to remember that the heavy drinker is an evil man. The light drinker or the total abstainer is on our side. This is well set forth in Mullally's script. Note the direction in Shot 34: "Wilson peers down into his drink." Is he enjoying it? No. He's an abstemious fellow. He never did finish his first highball. But Brown burrows right in, a sure sign of turpitude. People sometimes drink a little to be polite, but only rascals really *enjoy* their liquor.

These signals, or character labels, while not quite so dependable in television as they have been in radio, still point up the difference between the good guys and the bad guys. Gin and whiskey—in television—perform somewhat the same purpose that cigarette smoking did for actresses in yesterday's soap operas. A woman who kept a pack of cigarettes in her pocketbook was an evil woman. In large segments of today's Bible Belt, it is still no joke.

While we are on the subject of good and evil, examine the script to determine the appurtenances of Brown's layout that help establish him as the master villain. You will note several. The capable but dangerous Yaeger is in his employ. Brown pretends to a certain amount of cultivation: well-starched servants, dinner jackets, fine riding horses, palatial home. His desk is equipped with an up-to-date intercom. He's an undeniable big shot. And he's filthy rich. But his courtesy—when he tries to show it—is spurious. It has the awkwardness of Mafia members trying to give you a pleasant hour. They don't know how it's done. They've seen it in the movies but have never really tried it themselves. Brown's efforts to be a congenial host are grotesque.

There is a good kicker at the end of Shot 35. Yaeger is going after Tarzan. Is he going to kill him? Perhaps. At least he's going to immobilize or hurt him. This is another important bit of business.

A powerful physical threat against the hero of any adventure melodrama must be mounted in every show.

Brown's line, "I mean, *get* him!" has a clear-cut and unmistakable implication.

The next bit of action, which calls for Yaeger to arrive in Lwutumba's village by helicopter, is an excellent maneuver because it makes use of new gadgets that excite wonder and surprise. It's worth noting, for example, that Bell Aerosystems has just developed a jet-powered belt that you strap on like shoulder harness. You can fly like lightning. You can hover, fly backward like a hummingbird, even leap over mountains. It's twenty times the gadget the rocket belt was. And you can go for miles.

Make use of such new inventions whenever possible in your own adventure scripts. Keep your toys contemporary. Stay modern. It impresses the young. In fact, they expect it and demand it.

Often the use of modern equipment affords effective sight contrasts. It does here, for the helicopter lands within sight of a "cluster of beehive-shaped mud huts."

The frequent juxtaposition of symbols of today's civilization to the opulence, beauty, and challenge of the forest primeval is one of the chief charms of this series, or of any series that pits moderns against primitives. Accordingly, you would be wise to use such tools whenever the opportunity offers.

Act I ends abruptly, as it should (as all of the first three acts should), with Tarzan in such a mess you don't see how he'll ever extricate himself. This, of course, is the *classic* situation in which to have him suspended. We're in that business. Here the poor man has been shot. Fortunately, in all shows of this broad adventure phylum, for good guys there are only two kinds of wounds (and for westerns, too)—flesh wounds and scalp wounds.

This early in the play, there is hell to pay. How does Mullally emphasize the poignance of it all? By having little Jai a witness to it.

An important consideration to keep in mind with respect to the *structural mechanics* of this script and all one-hour scripts is that they contain four acts. The current practice is to spell these out as such in the script itself, even though they are seldom declared so on the screen. There is a hard reason for this, a reason that must be respected. The physical partitioning of long shows into acts of more or less equal length is required to give an even time spread between the commercials the show is permitted to carry. On nighttime schedules, in prime time (7:30 to 10:00), it amounts to about six minutes of commercial time per hour. This pertains to shows seen in regular series.

In many specials, other patterns have been appearing in the scheduling of commercials, including arrangements that permit the viewer to see more of the show without interruption. Another variation is to expand the length of the commercials themselves. This involves bunching the elements, as it were—employing longer segments of each with less jumping back and forth.

Does this put an extra burden on the dramatist? You bet it does. He must think just as realistically of the proper *commercial* demands of his show as he does of its artistic merits. This often means that he can't tell his story the way he might prefer to tell it. If he had a choice, he might wish to tell his story in three acts, or even two. Or he could conceivably opt for a swift sequence of thirty or forty scenes.

These commercial requirements—this need to space the selling elements at equal intervals throughout the production—make it imperative for the writer to *create rising action before each curtain*. He must do this three times. In most hour shows, he must do it for all but the final curtain.

This introduces the problem of artificially created excitement. It is not so serious as some feel. Most of the world's commercial entertainment is structured around artifice, not around genuineness of motivation or authentic emotionalism. Thus the matter of creating these hypos is more a matter of advance planning than painful compromise. You work cold-bloodedly from a blueprint. Get used to the idea. In shows of this kind, you're not trying to build something for posterity.

Writers like Donn Mullally, writers of shows like *Tarzan*, don't expect their work to be remembered. They just want to be reasonably well paid for their efforts. They don't expect their shows to be subjected to serious criticism nor to receive more than a brief notice in newspaper listings. They don't have to explain their work. And under only one condition do they have to defend it—when the show begins to slide.

These writers and their teleplays are feeding the crowded hoppers of television's "B" pictures. Their structural form is determined not by artistic discrimination but by the demands imposed upon them by the commercials they carry.

There is nothing wrong with the system. Without the commercials, the shows wouldn't be on the air. Something else would be there.

Look at the early shots of Act II. We find Tarzan alive, even though we just saw him shot—or thought we did. But it turns out to be a nonlethal shooting. He's been knocked down and put to sleep by a dart. However, now he's in worse trouble than before. Cut off from his friends, drugged, and in the clutches of the scummiest of men, his value as a hostage is so great that it forces the noble Lwutumba to betray him—to go along with the plot to keep the truth away from Wilson. "Do this or I level your village." So he agrees, with little Jai pleading and, as before, plucky but impotent.

The takeoff of the helicopter once more insults the good people, blasting them with dust as the Land Rover did before. This is good symbolism. Good contempt. Bad manners. All this is building up to the fun we'll have when it's our turn to powder Yaeger.

Any personification of rectitude—as is Tarzan's posture before the villainous Brown—must necessarily present the man as pretty much a complete square. But, again, don't laugh at this. Rather, understand it. For Tarzan to trade tough talk with anyone, for Tarzan to descend to the use of the sordid weaponry of "civilized" man, would dethrone him spiritually. It would be like giving Mahatma Gandhi a girl friend. To be coarse in speech, no matter what the provocation, would be equivalent to Tarzan's taking a chaw of tobacco. The fine clarity of his image could never find its way back after such a collapse. It is his apartness, his large forbearance, that is his strength. Standard and effective is the sadistic chatter we get out of Brown before Tarzan's entombment. And standard and effective is Tarzan's failure to respond to it.

Here the camera gives us a good look at the place where he's to be sealed up. It is a torture chamber and it's called such. The camera thoroughly inspects Tarzan's new surroundings, with C.U.s (close-ups) on the escape-proof features of "the well." We think of historical equivalents: the Iron Maiden, Boger's Swing, Calcutta's Black Hole—a cruel way to house a fine man.

Tarzan is suddenly fed up with his multiplying frustrations. He strikes his cruel captor, sends him spinning. We are simply delighted. Then we have this bit of business: "Naturally, Tarzan knocks a few heads together before he is finally skulled by a gun butt."

This is another *must*. So is Tarzan's being flung into the dungeon (or cave, temple, cellar, tomb, cistern, grotto, grain bin, tank, or cavern—a different oubliette every week). It is a transplant of Poor Pauline to the jungle.

It could be pointed out that there is a slight departure from the classic line of Tarzan in Shot 57. Normally Tarzan scorns anything man-made in his coming to grips with evil people. He disarms them, flings their pistols into swamps. But this time he *uses* some of the white man's gear—gunpowder and steel-jacketed shells. The show has tolerance for occasional inconsistencies. There is another one. How did Tarzan ever smuggle these into the well? Dressed in nothing but a loincloth, he'd have trouble hiding a match.

The answer in this instance is that we don't know how Tarzan accomplished it. The author does not enlighten the viewer. I feel some credibility has been unnecessarily lost here. Tarzan has just been through a good scrap with Brown's guards and has whacked and disabled a few. Could he not have ripped one of the guards' tunics or snatched up a cartridge belt and dropped it down the well? In other words, couldn't Tarzan have gained possession of the bullets in some logical fashion, and preferably under circumstances the viewer could observe? Such a contrivance might appear a bit awkward, but to bypass the matter seems more awkward still. If we could see how he grabbed the shells, our belief would be complete.

Part of your license as a writer of melodrama permits minor departures from logic and probability, but you must never be guilty of what we might call the flagrantly improbable.

There are a few slow scenes—the after-dinner brandy, for example. But anything going on around "the well," even if it borders on immobility, is not really slow for the simple reason that it is jammed with lively *feeling*—the most powerful ingredient in all writing. What is the feeling at this precise point in time? The man we're cheering for is plotting his own escape. And we are given suggestive progress shots to clue us in. (See Shots 60 and 62, for example.)

Nothing ever stands still.

At Lwutumba's place, all of Yaeger's careful plotting is going forward without a hitch. Our spirits are pretty low here. They're supposed to be. We wish Jai could be activated in some manner. He appears to be the only remaining hope. But he has some suffering to do, too. He and Cheetah witness the scene in which Lwutumba is forced to lie to Wilson. The scene, itself static, is infused with considerable emotion just through the eavesdropping of Jai. We share his pain. Then we rally, as he does, when he watches the chopper leave and starts to follow.

Shots 79 through 83 are commonly called work shots, e.g., cleaning a gun, changing a tire, something that takes a little time—not interesting in itself but necessary to the story plan. Here Tarzan, with his inexhaustible ingenuity, is completing preparations to fire his impromptu bomb. By this time we've seen enough of the detail to know what he's doing.

From what we've observed, would the thing work? Would it really go off? No. Do we believe it? Yes. Why? Because we saw it.

There is a nice moment (another *must*) when, if this were an old Tom Mix movie, every kid in the theater would cheer. It occurs right after the explosion. The grating *moves*. "Tarzan's head appears in the opening." That's the moment. (Then, of course—*zap!*—he's back down again.)

But is he? No. He's just pretending. He begins knocking heads together as soon as guards lift him out of the well. Other prisoners, still penned up, give him support out of kinship with the underdog. A guard is electrocuted. How right! Equally positive, Tarzan "launches himself into space," a Superman gesture. But we know he'll get his hands on a vine.

There's a short chase. A guard gets derricked into the air. He drops his gun. Jai grabs it and throws it away. (Tarzan never uses the white man's weapons, remember. It's beneath him. And this situation holds true for Jai as well.) Biceps, knife, cunning, body oil—Tarzan needs no more.

Tarzan, Jai, and Cheetah, while hiding in a tree, sketch out a plan. Below, the hunt for them continues. Yaeger, on the prowl, knows what he's doing. Tarzan *does* come to the *casa grande* to grab Wilson. Yaeger immediately acts to capture Tarzan, a play that's been in his mind all along. This makes a fine curtain for Act III. If Yaeger had mustachios, he'd be twirling them now. And, of course, his weapon is a Luger—another sure sign of villainy. (Colts, Webleys, Berettas for our side.) This menacing tableau ends the act. Tarzan is *surely* doomed.

Now review the endings of Acts I, II, and III. You'll learn something about suspense.

> ACT I: He (Yaeger) squeezes the trigger. Tarzan spins and falls to the ground, does not move.
> ACT II: Tarzan appears to be hit, buckles, and falls back down into the hole.
> ACT III: Tarzan stares into the muzzle of the big handgun.

See? You're in the suspense business. You've put your hero in extreme trouble. How will he extricate himself? That's all your viewer cares about. While waiting to find out, is there a better time to sell a little margarine?

Turning to Act IV, the viewer is again worried about Tarzan. Is he doomed? Of course not. (He has to be on next week, doesn't he?) Jai saves him. He jumps into the picture now and distracts Yaeger's aim on Tarzan just long enough for Tarzan to slug him.

And now Tarzan goes to work. If this be violence, let us celebrate it! Every fourteen-year-old in America has been waiting for this instant. Tarzan does much better than merely slugging Yaeger. Look at the script. He "pulps" him—the only thing you can do with folks like Yaeger. The undecided, recalcitrant Wilson he "creams" (not so permanent as pulping), then slings him over his shoulder like a bag of meal and strides away.

Think of this fight from the point of view of the observer. Is it a cluttered free-for-all? No. The reverse. The hits are well isolated, with a continuous fix on Tarzan in action.

Suddenly, and for the first time, things are going badly for the *villains*. But they aren't through, and they play for keeps: "You get there in the helicopter and kill them—both of them." There's an exchange of vicious recriminations, but it's between our enemies, Brown and Yaeger. Brown turns into a Hitler. Tarzan points out the rift to Wilson, so Wilson is converted. He also sees how Brown had intended to use him: "That landslide will be blamed on my work" (Shot 128). It sure would, too. Any kid can see that. Even a grown-up can see it.

The mechanical rigging of the explosion is familiar stuff, but an unbroken continuity of action hides the mechanics as such and gives tremendous pace to the story from here to the finish. "They dive under the protection of the rock just in time, the bullets from Yaeger's automatic weapon buttoning the ground at their heels." That's a fine picture, those last few words. It took a writer to phrase it.

The show builds to its finish with a race against time: running, firing, bad men spotted through binoculars, Tarzan wrecking the chopper, Tarzan disposing of Yaeger (but with Brown still up and dangerous), and the seven o'clock deadline right on top of us.

Now, to make up for the big explosion that we *don't* see—the explosion Tarzan is preventing—we get solid satisfaction when Brown gets shredded by the grenade intended for Wilson. Tarzan rips out the firing circuits, the villains are dead or unconscious, and Africa is saved. Tarzan sends Jai back to his homework, permitting the production to inherit the blessing of the PTA.

What producer could ask for more?

Before leaving *Tarzan*, let me identify two terms commonly used in television writing. The word "matte" appears in Shot 150. You will see this frequently. The same goes for "process" or "process shot."

Technically a matte is a light modulator, or an obstruction to the passage of light on its way to form a photographic image. In the *Tarzan* script, on location, the guard sees Wilson and Tarzan "running along the edge of the gorge." This was probably photographed full aperture and at the proper distance. There are two ways of handling such a shot:

1. The camera crew may have put a matte in front of the lens of the camera and photographed the scene right there on location. The matte, or masking, would cut out everything but the area pinpointed by the circle of the binocular. The crossed hairs could be put across the opening of the matte.

2. The scene observed could also be shot full aperture and later, at the lab, they would make up the binocular matte and shoot it on the optical printer. An optical printer is for certain rephotographing operations such as fades, dissolves, wipes, and so on. The optical printer has many advantages over doing a binocular shot on location. The printer makes the operation as flexible as possible, so as to produce image modifications of almost any kind. Bartosch, the great French director, is reported to have superimposed as many as thirty images on a single strip of film.

A process shot can best be defined as a studio technique whereby the actors, sets, and props in front of the camera are combined with a background consisting of a translucent screen on which a picture (moving or still) is projected from behind. Some scriptwriters and producers refer to it as back projection, background projection, rear-screen projection, or transparency projection. It creates the convincing illusion of motion when you see two characters chatting in a taxi (for example) with scenery whirling by. Actually the taxi is stationary.

Scenes in dining cars, moving trains, planes, ships—where we are watching and listening to the actors before us but are conscious we are in motion with them (because of moving landscape, traffic, other planes, waves, clouds)—are effected through this device. A scene of bank robbers being chased through midtown traffic is process. The moving pictures in the background are merely thrown on a semi-transparent screen that is set up behind the actors. For most shots, this screen is suspended within a frame about seven or eight feet high and four or five feet across. It's tilted to give the exact visual effect needed. The frame looks like an upended bed.

Process shots are made in the studio and are used to save the expense (again, note the item of expense—the costs of television are diabolical) of sending a company to Paris, for example. Films of Paris rented from stock would be likely to have shots of the Eiffel Tower. If sufficient footage can't be found in a stock library, or if the exact right footage can't be found there, a small camera crew can go to Paris and photograph all the backgrounds needed, and then have this film developed back at the Hollywood studios. The actors play the scene in front of the translucent screen, and if the cameraman is skillful, the viewer can't possibly tell that the actors aren't on the actual site. Today, however, most producers prefer going to the actual location.

Whenever you see young lovers driving in an expensive car down the lovely Monterey Peninsula, with the Pacific rolling in easily just beyond them, it's likely to be a process shot. If the car shows no vibration or jiggling at all, and if the driver seems not to have his mind on the wheel and no other cars are coming or going, then you *know* it's a process shot.

Now we'll proceed to a few "inside" notes to the student writer from Donn Mullally, who wrote the *Tarzan* script we've just studied. These are excerpts from articles Mullally has published.

They spare no one, including himself. He thinks that writing commercial television is a great deal less than ideal, but that if you want to make it, you'd better put up with its realistic and less pleasant aspects.

Here is his first comment:

> The trouble with writing TV for a living, boys and girls, is it can be damn hard work. The simple act of facing a blank sheet of paper with a blank mind every day is an exercise in courage and will. Then there's the herculean task of shoveling out words (any words) to fill the page. And finally, there's the slippery bit of scrambling around in your own blood and sweat—which is *revision*.
>
> You may correctly assume at this point that you are being discouraged, deliberately and overtly, from undertaking this means of making a buck. Who needs *you* for competition? And besides, honestly, writing is a drag.

In an interview some few years back with Dave Kaufman, feature writer for *Variety*, some of the above leaks through, but with proper illuminations and well-weathered professionalism.

> One of the more common and frequent gripes from TV writers [writes Kaufman] is that they can't turn out good material because of the many hands

involved in their scripts before they reach the screen. "They" refer, of course, to the producer, the story editor, ad agency, network and director, all of whom often have a hand in a script before it is finally okayed.

Another gripe of the telescripters is that it's difficult to write for a series with set characters because there are dramatic restrictions tailored to fit the leading thesps in the series, so that instead of truly being original, they have to come up with something in which the creative mold has already been cast.

Both of these charges are legitimate, but none of the gripers get much sympathy from Donn Mullally, vet TV writer and former prexy of the TV-Radio branch of the Writers Guild. Mullally, who estimates he has sold over 300 television plays since starting in TV in 1951, contends that "when someone charges TV writing has become more pedestrian and that writers are unable to produce the things they want, what they are really complaining about is the system."

By "system," Mullally means that massive collaboration involving so many people in what started out as one man's script.

A realist, Mullally says this is of the TV "system":

"It's the kind of world we live in, and a satisfactory world if you accept it. If you fight it, you wind up on a psychiatrist's couch. There is no way of fighting it. I accept it. Anybody who doesn't is not a professional."

Mullally also contends there is no true freedom in any media. Publishers change manuscripts. . . .

"This will probably get me creamed by a lot of writers, but the thing that makes a script—at least sometimes—is the presence of all these collaborators peering into the writer's typewriter. Proof of that is the low incidence of men who move out of TV and pictures. Deadlines and pressure actually help some writers. Then too, if I'm writing a *Bonanza,* for example, I know right away if it's wrong by checking the story editor or producer. Good things come from collaborations. They provide instant challenge. They provide an interplay of writing muscle. But of course, without the writer's original contribution, all these other collaborators couldn't get anything off the ground."

I will restrict comment on the above to a single observation: the most effective collaborations I've ever seen have been among not more than three people.

4

THE FLYING NUN

There have been so many stories written about the origins of *The Flying Nun,* about its many misadventures before it became a reality, that it will save time, answer questions, and bring a fresh voice into this book if the reader will now see Dwight Whitney's account of the whole thing. His piece in *TV Guide* is the most accurate that has appeared. And he didn't get the story from reading other releases. He talked to the people involved, and here is what he learned:

I DIDN'T WANT TO PLAY A NUN
by Dwight Whitney

Reprinted from TV Guide®, with permission.
Copyright © 1968 by Triangle Publications, Inc.

One day about two years ago Max Wylie, the author, TV executive and sometime ad man, lunched with a friend, LeBaron R. Barker, a top editor at Doubleday in New York. The two men were woolgathering together, as great idea men will. Barker said he had a feeling that Doubleday had published a lot of books with TV potential. But how to recognize and find them?

Wylie, a cool hand at this sort of game, volunteered to do something about it. Poring over old Doubleday catalogs, he came up with a slim volume called "The Fifteenth Pelican," about a nun who weighed 90 pounds and flew. At first glance the project appeared unpromising. While fantasy had gained a certain measure of success in shows like *Bewitched* and *I Dream of Jeannie, religious* fantasy was something else again. "Miracles" were not to be taken lightly in the Catholic Church.

Still, the little wheels went around in Wylie's mind. He thought of the box-office receipts of "The Sound of Music" and "The Singing Nun," and the thought proved intoxicating. He wrote a "rationale" for a TV series to be called *The Flying Nun,* in which he specifically answered this objection. He pointed out that the Church was becoming less conservative and he believed that it would not be offended by the idea. He said the way was clear for his nun with an aerodynamically designed cornette and the embarrassment its miraculous quality brings to a strait-laced Mother Superior. If "the exact right performer" could be found, the fantasy might even be extended to the point where young Sister Bertrille "talked to pelicans." Possibilities were endless. What he really had here, he wrote, was "a nun with sex appeal."

He personally took the prospectus to Leonard Goldberg, ABC vice president in charge of programming, who, he understood, was hungry for ideas. Goldberg's minions, after stifling a few impolite yawns, turned it down. Later Wylie was to chide Goldberg about this, but he "failed to find the reference amusing." Wylie sent it to the Batboss, William Dozier of *Batman* fame, who was quite frank to say he thought Wylie had taken leave of his senses. Later, when *Nun* became the big new hit of the season, Dozier wrote Wylie a note "plucking the egg off my face and eating large portions of humble pie." Likewise CBS, Warners and MGM could see no humor in it but only large "religious obstructions" which none of them cared to try to circumvent.

Then Wylie thought of his old friend Harry Ackerman, who had had a lot of successes with a more sophisticated fantasy, *Bewitched*. It so happened that the producer was looking for a vehicle for Sally Field, a talented young woman whose previous effort, *Gidget,* had been sunk in a sea of saccharine. He also happened to be talking to then ABC-TV president Thomas W. Moore about the network's plans for *Bewitched*. As Ackerman was leaving, Moore asked if there was anything else cooking. "Yes," replied Ackerman, "but you wouldn't like it." Moore demanded to know what he wouldn't like and Ackerman told him. "I want it," Moore said, and promptly placed it on Goldberg's schedule.

When the word got out about what Ackerman was up to, eyebrows shot up like picket signs at a love-in. Most people assumed that the nun would do her do-gooding by Piper Cub, an idea so cloying that it might even have turned Moore off. Those who understood that the intent was fantastic rather than scientific went around referring to the show as "Sister Terrific." Ackerman told his story developer, Bernard Slade, the Canadian comedy writer who had been a mainstay of *Bewitched,* about his plans in a San Francisco taxicab.

"I said he was crazy," Slade, a Protestant married to a Catholic, recalls. "Then he turned to my wife and asked what she thought. 'I think it's cute,' she said. I shuddered. The modern nun had some appeal, but this was something else. We would have to make her resemble an everyday human being and for that we needed Sally Field."

But Sally Field, nonpracticing Catholic, was not available. An intense, serious young woman then just 19, she had taken the failure of *Gidget* very hard. Moreover, Ackerman had made the mistake of treating her like a child, not telling her what was going on, relaying everything through her agent and her stepfather, Jock Mahoney. Sally came away with the feeling that somehow she was responsible for *Gidget*'s flop and that no one would tell her why. When *Gidget* was canceled, no one bothered to call *her*. She left the studio "feeling defeated," hibernated for a month to lick her wounds, and embarked on a movie career, determined that TV should never darken her door again.

"Besides, I didn't want to play a nun," Sally said recently. "You're not allowed to kiss or show your belly-button."

Now Ackerman proceeded to compound his error by failing to supply Miss Field the "personal contact" which would have solved all problems. Consequently the pilot started shooting in December 1966 with another actress, Bobby Troup's daughter, Ronne. Then, on impulse and after-the-fact, the line producer, Bill Sackheim, called Sally in for a heart-to-heart.

"It was what I had been wanting all the time," she says. "He understood that losing *Gidget* was like having someone call your kids ugly. The business doesn't interest me. Acting does. Just the thought of doing 'The Graduate' for

Mike Nichols [a part she lost to Katharine Ross] got me so excited I could hardly stand it. Sackheim made me see it was presumptuous to think I could step into movies. Idiot, I told myself, you're not Liz Taylor! *The Flying Nun* would give me time to learn and still keep me in the public eye. So—I changed my mind."

Insiders estimate that Sally's emotional needs combined with Ackerman's reticence cost Screen Gems about $2000 a week, the salary offers having escalated from $2000 to $4000 during this period (not to mention the first day's shooting, which had to be scrapped). Quite a status change for a girl who thought she was rich on the $450 a week she got for *Gidget*.

As if by magic the word raced around Madison Avenue: Ackerman had a hit—or, as one old hand observed, "It didn't smell like anything else you'd ever heard of." It seemed that all that was left was to collect the money, provided the Church could be kept happy. For this delicate diplomatic task Screen Gems procured the services of a politician, former Los Angeles councilwoman Rosalind Wyman.

Mrs. Wyman's job was to demonstrate that *"The Flying Nun* was no 'Going My Way' and that instead it brought the Church up-to-date." She showed the pilot in the principal archdioceses. She screened it for Cardinal McIntyre in Los Angeles, for Archbishop Hannan in New Orleans, and procured the tacit approval of the late Cardinal Spellman. "We just wanted to be sure the Catholic community dug it," says the forthright Mrs. Wyman.

Actually, the studio's fears were groundless. Everybody was worried *except* the Catholic Church. Indeed the National Catholic Office for Radio and Television looked upon it as an excellent recruiting poster and could thus afford to be lenient. "The show is positioning nuns as human beings," Charles Reilly, the executive director, said a few weeks ago. "Only the studio, the agencies and the sponsors were worried. I guess they thought Catholics might stop buying toothpaste."

When the show proved to be the hit Wylie had said it would, it was Sackheim's job to make it work on a week-to-week basis. This was not easy, since the studio had decided that Sister Bertrille must fly in every episode, come what may. He found himself ejecting her through flues in caves, or inserting comic but unrelated bits showing pelicans and painters doing double takes. Moreover, he found that many stories which ordinarily might be expected to work, secularly-speaking, didn't work with nuns. "For instance, you can't have her kidnaped because you can't get her out of the habit. Or say you have a baby dropped on the doorstep of San Tanco, the oldest cliché story in the world. No good. They have orphans there already."

Back in Madison, Wis., the author of the book watched with bemusement. She was Tere Rios, the half-Irish, half-Puerto Rican wife of a retired colonel of artillery named Versace (West Point 1933). She got the idea 15 years ago when "I saw a little Sister of Charity in her big white bonnet nearly blown off her feet in Paris." Since she was also a flyer who learned her flying in the Georgia Civil Air Patrol, the story came easily. She wrote "The Fifteenth Pelican," one of three published novels, in 1963, saw it published in 1965 and saw it achieve a small but steady sale over the following years.

She says she wrote it because "I had known nuns all my life and was tired of all this serious stuff about them." Generally speaking, she is pleased with what happened to her modest little tale. "It is like watching old friends get into new trouble." She may be even more pleased when Doubleday gets around to reissuing the novel. If Screen Gems can sell a million dollars' worth of Flying Nun bubble gum, think what Lee Barker can do with the Flying Nun book.

As for Sally, she was having a ball. Instead of a child, she was a personage, a $4000-a-week personage. In fact, the cash registers were ringing so prettily that, last November, Screen Gems production chief Jackie Cooper was moved to "show our appreciation." He put in a call to Herb Tobias, Sally's agent, and inquired what Sally wanted most in the world. "Well," replied Tobias lightly, "she always said she'd be driving around in a Ferrari one of these days." Cooper bought the little girl from Portola Junior High acting class a midnight-blue Ferrari 330 two-plus-two convertible with stereo tape deck. It cost about $16,000. "Is that all right, Sally?" asked Cooper at the presentation. "You're putting me on," Sally said. To top it all off he threw a birthday party (her 21st) at The Factory, the discotheque in West Hollywood. She wore a bright-orange, cut-velvet Rudi Gernreich mini-dress with a ropette neck, had her first legal drink (Kahlua and cream) and frugged the night away with Davy Jones (of the Monkees), her sometime escort.

"I just couldn't believe it," said the Flying Nun. "There was little me where all the big stars are."

Much of Tere Rios's life has been spent in U.S. Army camps or in military installations outside the United States. In passing, consider some of the reasons for the authentic sound and the assured touch she brings to such things as soldier talk, soldier attitude, military descriptions, flight terminology, convents, nuns, Puerto Rican scenery. She was *there*. That is the thing. That's where her authority comes from. Being a writer, she took note of what and who were around her.

In our correspondence, many gleams and glimpses of writer problems and writer trials crept into her paragraphs. I've picked out a few that seem either relevant or refreshing.

"About the 'Pelican,' " she writes, "I always loved the kooky uniforms worn by the Daughters of Charity. There was one big nun in Pornichet (France) who used to march the orphans to the sea, kick off her shoes, tuck her skirt hem into her belt, and wade in. Then she'd pick up the kids and throw them over the tops of the small breakers."

"But the Sister Bertrille inspiration came in Paris. A Daughter was apparently late for something and she came bucketing around a corner, hit a gust of wind, and when she reached to save her cornette, it looked as if she'd taken off."

"I thought that would be great fun. But to make a story, you have to get your character in trouble. And what kind of trouble can a nun get into? [This was all fifteen years ago.]

"At a cocktail party in Petit Beauregard, someone suggested she land in a nudist camp. But Thorne Smith had already done that with the Methodist bishop—'The Bishop's Jaegers.'

"One night at Fort Meade (Maryland) somebody said: 'How about letting the nun land in a security area?'

"That did it. I had studied aerodynamics—I fly some—so that part was okay.

One of my husband's friends was a security-area lieutenant. I asked him what he'd do if he found a nun there. He muttered. He said he'd shoot himself. So I called his CO, the commandant of the Rocket Brigade. He said if they found a nun in a security area, they'd question her, then turn her over to the CIC (Civilian Investigation) and the local police."

"Then I wrote the story and sent it to my agent, who read it and said it wasn't commercial. Then a long series of rejections. One house kept my manuscript 10 months! Another wanted the illustrations, not the book. One day a friend called me and told me about Doubleday's Catholic contest. Doubleday wrote that the book wasn't eligible for the contest but they'd like to publish it anyway, if I'd change two words, 'spik' and 'gook,' I think. Soldier talk, with no malice to it."

"I teach beginner's writing to classes of grown-ups. Most of it is just standing there and letting them see that if an ordinary dope like me with a high school education can get published, so can they. Wisconsin audiences are kind and friendly. . . . My toughest audience was a class at Johns Hopkins (Baltimore, where we used to live). The easiest was the seminarians (Capuchins) at Marathon, Wisconsin. They booed when I said I'd come in from Baltimore. Which shook me. How did I know the Baltimore Colts had beaten the Green Bay Packers the day before?"
(You catch the whole spirit of this writer from these happy fragments.)

What else has Tere Rios written? And how did she get started? She's done two other novels, *Brother Angel* and *An Angel Grows Up,* and she's written about sixty stories. Her stories indicate a personal familiarity with many skills. This is natural, since her enthusiasms include painting, sailing, flying, and horseback riding. She's published in *The Atlantic Monthly, Collier's, Ave Maria,* and a dozen or so magazines in England, Ireland, and Germany.

Currently she is an instructor in creative writing, Rhinelander School of the Arts, University of Wisconsin, where most of her time is given to showing fledgling authors how to get started.

When you find a fine property that you feel has a chance to become a television series, what is the first thing to do?

That is simple: get the right to adapt it, to offer it, and to participate in the earnings, if any. The property, if published, will most likely already be represented by an agent. Call the publisher and ask who the agent is. Then write the agent, and tell him who you are, what you've done, and what you want. (If you don't have an agent yourself, this is a good way to get one.) Ask for a free option of six months. This will give you time to prepare the kind of work we will look at next. And it will give you time (and your agent time) to circulate the presentation, or treatment.

That's the first thing. The next: write your presentation. The presentation should give the full flavor of the original. It should strongly suggest the commercial durability of the main story, that the series can go on and on, for thirty weeks, a year, several years.

You should also inhabit the *same climate of doubt or uncertainty* that your potential producer is living in. Do this to anticipate all his objections. Do this to meet them.

The presentation has to sell itself. It has to be easy to read. It has to be fun to read, or exciting to read. It has to suggest the full dimension that the series, if happily cast and professionally produced, can ultimately realize for itself and for its backers.

It has to be a good money risk, a good popularity risk, that is, and not out of sight financially. It has to be politically nonpartisan. It has to be short.

It will pay you, after your own work is done, to have this work professionally typed, or Xeroxed. Always keep two protection copies in your possession. *Never* leave yourself stranded without at least one.

Now, what does a presentation look like? What should the first *page* look like? Center your title.

THE FLYING NUN

Now this:

TYPE OF SHOW:	Comedy (or Situation Comedy)
LENGTH:	Half-hour
FREQUENCY:	Once a week
SETTING:	San Juan
TIME:	Present
DAY OR NIGHT:	Night

Written by

....

Adapted from

....

On this same page, put agent's name in this corner.

Dress up your presentation. If the original contains a fine, illustrative sampling of the main story, if it has a juicy or colorful paragraph that sets mood and tone and atmosphere, include it. Use it as a frontispiece. Like this:

San Juan is on a high cliff on an island. Across it sweeps the trade wind of the Spanish Main. At 30 miles per hour this wind catches the edges of bedspreads and whips them off. At 50, it blows out everything blowable in the whole house.

The above is the opening paragraph of *The Fifteenth Pelican*. What kind of comedy does it suggest? Light and fast and colorful, clean and fresh. You haven't been "on" long, and you are ahead.

Now the presentation itself. Short paragraphs. Short sentences. Fast reading. Fun reading. And no "writing." Just simple, honest exposition.

Break up your sections with rows of dots. Scatter a little dialogue through your suggested scenes. Limn in character with an adjective or two.

If it is fantasy, force belief in the unbelievable right away. Do this by immediately *assuming* its naturalness.

At the end of your presentation, do a page emphasizing why right now is a good time to go with this kind of show. Mention scenery advantages, if any. Mention cost cuts, if any.

Here, now, is the presentation that sold *The Flying Nun* concept to Harry Ackerman, executive producer and vice-president at Screen Gems. He has built more radio and television programs than any man in the industry's history, has a great knack for casting, is possessed of a fine business head, a tough streak of persistence, and an open willingness to gamble on his own show instincts. His success record is phenomenal. He is the most versatile man in television today.

He knows and loves Puerto Rico, and this, as it turned out, was a happy plus in getting the show off the ground.

Here is the TV presentation I wrote:

> On top of San Juan's highest hill is a convent run by the Daughters of Charity. Though most of the Catholic sisters are used to the trade winds here —even the strong blows—they have learned how to hold on to their dignity, and to their cornettes.
>
> Their cornettes are long, peaked bonnets—pointed triangles really, shaped like the paper airplanes children fold when pretending to study.
>
> These cornettes aren't flattering to the older nuns, giving them the appearance of secretary birds. But they make young nuns look like swans in flight. Young or old, however, San Juan's whimsical air currents treat them all alike. When the wind strikes, all the nuns suddenly look like water birds trying to remain on the ground, and barely managing.
>
> A few of the nuns, privately to each other, had reported they had experienced a sensation actually of being lifted from their feet. Frightening but exhilarating.
>
> It was never discussed openly since it might imply disapproval of the way they had been dressing for 400 years.
>
> But they'd all *felt* it once or twice. That was the thing.
>
> It was the arrival of a new nun—a tiny American nun from New York City who weighed only 90 pounds and who was being sent to the Daughters of Charity to teach kindergarten—who, without at all meaning to or expecting to, brought up the question of the strange sensations that accompanied sudden gusts of these Puerto Rican trade winds.
>
> By New York standards Sister Bertrille, 24, was a good nun. Obliging, adaptable, well-read (even sciences). Vigorous, too, for one so small.
>
> But the sister-in-charge—Sister Placido—was not aware of any of these virtues. At first. She had come to the pier to meet the new young American teacher and feared she'd seen Sister Bertrille at the foot of the gangplank, "hob-nobbing with a gang of sailors."
>
> This was true. "But they were so helpful to me on the voyage, Sister Placido. We played cards every night."

Sister Placido was unable to reply to this.

Sister Sixto, who always came to the pier with Sister Placido because she was big and strong and could lug things—a few called her "Big Six"—realized the new nun from New York had just stunned the Placid One. So she tried to smooth it out:

"In Puerto Rico, we nod and lower our eyes. And that's *all*."

She began reaching for little Sister Bertrille's bags, books, and umbrella. But the sailors had everything. Including an immense basket of fruit that Sister Bert's cousin—Bernie the Bartender—had given her when she left Spanish Harlem in New York.

Sister Placido had not seen such fruit since her own girlhood in the Pyrenees so did not interfere when villagers began to help carry the baggage to the top of the hill.

Near the summit, they passed the grocery store of Don Scarpo, a thin man, very correct. But also unusually discerning, for he was a retired pilot and had been in many places in the world.

It was at this point, and in the physical presence and sight of Don Scarpo, that the thing happened.

Invisible in its approach, a warm gust of Puerto Rico's trade wind lifted the young New York nun into the air. Briefly and harmlessly. And not very high. But positively.

Sister Sixto pretended it had not *really* happened, and that she could "remonstrate" everything back to normal: "Less haste, and more grace, Sister."

"Yes, Sister. Excuse me. I was nearly blown off my feet."

So the three nuns got safely up to the convent with the help of the villagers.

Don Scarpo watched the youngest one, the new nun. His little store supplied vegetables to the sisters and he knew how breezy it was up there on the very top. Being a man of the world and familiar with its air currents, he was not amazed at what he had just seen. To his trained eye, he recognized that what all these Sisters of Charity were compelled to wear did have some significance in the field of aerodynamics, given the right conditions.

He knew, for example, that their white cornette was merely a bonnet to them but to the amiable atmospheres of the island it was a perfect airfoil. With such a pointed front, it would tend to give lift to anything wearing it, especially if it were moving into the wind.

He had seen the little nun run to keep up with the others, which could possibly give her just enough thrust. And her body, visibly small despite the blue folds of her habit, would offer little load and practically no drag.

Being a grocer, he was used to adding things up. And having been a flier in his youth and seen everything, he now added what he knew to what he had seen:

If *lift* and *thrust* is greater than *load* and *drag*, anything will fly.

Even a nun.

To Don Scarpo, a man of the world, it did not seem remarkable. It seemed inevitable. What else could you expect?

But because he delivered groceries to the Daughters of Charity who lived on top of the hill where you couldn't see the wind coming, he realized that life for this newcomer would not be the same in the Caribbean as it had been in New York.

In Puerto Rico most of the Spanish houses have flat roofs, so hurricanes can't catch under eaves and rip them off. And these roofs have low walls around them so that the people won't fall off, because the people *use* their roofs, unlike New York people who have balconies.

The convent where the Daughters of Charity lived was called San Tanco and had a good roof. Not for sitting or sunbathing, of course, for they were nuns. But for hanging out the laundry.

Sister Bert was drinking in the sun with a clothespin in her mouth, the next time it happened.

One minute she was anchoring the corner of a sheet to the clothesline. The next she was in the air, higher than before.

Don Scarpo, from the doorway of his grocery store down the street, watched with interest and smoothed his wavy mustache. He could see she was clinging to a free corner of the sheet and that to let go would either be the end of her or the beginning of experiences hard to explain to people of small learning.

He hoped that sooner or later she'd get the hang of it and learn how to use her cornette, learn how to fold in her arms, or spread them, as the situation required. She was perhaps twenty-five feet in the air this time. Then she plopped out of sight. He winced just a little, for he was not unkind, and went into his store.

Coming down, she hit the clothesline just as Sister Sixto came up the steps with another basket. She slid it quickly under the descending American, who crashed into the mound of soft linen, splitting one side of the basket and skinning herself.

Sister Sixto, in a spirit of compassion and dismay, flung her broad self on top of everything.

"You're new here," she said, as they sorted themselves out of the laundry and tried to adjust their cornettes. "But were you being blown about? Or were you . . . I mean . . . *flying?*"

"Well, I just don't know!" she answered honestly. "I was lifted right up. Like a bird! I couldn't get down! I'm sure—without your basket, I'd have had the most awful crash."

"If you'll accept a little advice, I think you better not come on this roof without me to hold you down."

"Oh, I wouldn't. But I suppose now we'll have to tell Sister Placido."

"I don't know. She had a heart attack last year. And then she saw you waving at all those sailors—the day you got here—and that *same* day—going by Don Scarpo's grocery—"

"She didn't see that, did she?"

"No. But I saw it. And so did he. About Sister Placido, I'm familiar with the situation here and you are not. We shall not tell Sister. Not now. But please, Sister Bert, don't go out when it's windy. If you have to go, please take me!"

This was the beginning of a good friendship, valuable to both.

Sister Bert each day took her kindergarten class on nature walks. And taught them manners and how to hold a fork and say thank you in English, Spanish, and even Latin, in case the Bishop ever visited.

But she found it was harder and harder not to think about flying. Everything reminded her of it, gulls and pelicans especially. And she often dreamed at night of extensions of the two flights she had already taken.

She shared a third-floor balcony outside room with Sister Cook, Sister

Laundress, and Sister Narcisco. Sometimes when they were asleep, she'd study the flight of birds at night. Every night, at the same time, the same flight of pelicans would pass her balcony. The same fourteen, every night. One night it was too much. Though they were awkward as they crouched on the pilings in the daytime, in the air at night they sailed with unbelievably beautiful grace.

That night, just as the fourteenth passed, Sister Bert stepped onto the railing, lifted her head, spread her arms, and took off after the last one.

The next morning at breakfast, everyone was ominously silent. Later, for the spiritual hour, Sister Placido read to all the nuns from the life of Saint Joseph Cupertino. He was a saint who had had some good qualities but who had embarrassed his superiors by floating about in the air. Levitating, they called it.

Then Sister Placido told all the sisters that levitation was being off the ground without visible means of support. And that bilocation was being in two places at once. She told them that no San Tanco nun, missing during the night, should show up calmly with a pelican feather in her hair and offer no explanation. So Sister Bertrille would do the garlic preparations for the week.

At Don Scarpo's, who sold her a rope of garlic, she was interested to hear the grocer tell her about his cousin, a ship's chandler.

"He owns a marina, Sister. Many fascinating things to show the little children you teach. And he also has a tame brown pelican. You'll love to talk to it."

"It" and not "him"? Don Scarpo had said it that way. He meant she should talk to the pelican, not the cousin? If he did, then he also knew she was flying around with pelicans. He must. But he wasn't spreading it around. He was keeping it to himself. He was a man of the world. The good kind. He was a real friend. Like Sister Sixto.

But Sister Bert was having a struggle with her conscience. The soft whirr of the pelicans' flight and their long cries on the wind lifted her heart to God, to praise Him for this great gift: flight.

Then, thinking about the wisdom of the Holy Founder of her Order, she began to wonder why he hadn't made the promises more *specific*—since he must have known that he was dealing with the minds of women, even if they were nuns. Poverty, chastity, obedience—these were pretty broad terms—and flying—something quite natural for half of Creation—how could this be a violation?—yet it kept bothering her.

But what could be the matter with flying? Even a nun flying? The pelicans knew her now, and accepted her. Counted on her. She had an obligation to them, just as she had to the little children in her charge.

Sister Placido never seemed to object when she saw Sister Bertrille teaching six-year-old Spanish girls how to play American basketball—something Sister Bert had learned in the American capital in Washington, at Saint Scholastica. There was a lot more jumping around in basketball than there was in flying. And no dignity. None at all.

So why all the fuss?

Her conscience told her: it was sport, it was selfish, and unnecessary.

But the pelicans kept coming by to pick her up.

Sister Bert vowed to fly no more. But she had no say in the matter. She just got swept off her feet.

And this time she got caught by Sister Placido.

In her office:

"Were you aware of your actions last night?"

Sister Bertrille lowered her eyes: "Yes, Sister."

There was a pause. Then: "When did you discover that you had—this—ability?"

"The day I got here, Sister."

"But I was with you. The whole day."

"Yes, Sister. But not *right* with me. I flew up in the air in front of that grocery store."

Sister Placido realized that the little American nun who waved at sailors and played cards was truthful.

"How do you explain your flying—? Do other New York nuns know how to fly?"

"I don't think so. And it isn't *really* flying. It's just a sort of formula—if you fit the conditions, you *have* to fly. A matter of lift and thrust, Sister."

"The world is changing too fast," Sister Placido decided. "Are you sure—that your special ability has nothing to do with the Russians?"

"Oh, I'm quite sure. I've never *seen* a Russian."

"And not something from God?"

"Oh, good grief, *no*, Sister! Probably all the laws of motion, even the stars, come from God."

Sister Placido felt this a fitting summary.

"You'll have to make all this clear to Sister Sixto. She has an over-developed tendency to organize. She thinks you should be canonized. If what you're doing gets out, we'll have no peace here. Just tell Sister Sixto your formula and get it out of her mind."

Early that evening Sister Placido was relieved to hear Sister Bert telling the simple truth to Sister Sixto:

"What I was getting to is that, if something is light enough, and moves fast enough, and has wings, it will fly. My cornette is almost like wings. What men call an airfoil. That's what happened there on the roof. When you slid your laundry basket to catch me. And that's *all*. Do you understand?"

"Oh, yes, Sister Bert. You can *fly*!"

Tooey Maynard, who ran a charter helicopter service from San Juan to Eleuthera and who was a drinking man, told a mechanic at the hangar, while he hooked his chopper to a cable for the night, that he had seen a nun fly around a convent on top of San Juan's highest hill.

So his friend, knowing Tooey took a drink now and then and sometimes several and had stopped going to Mass, agreed with him.

But Tooey saw through it. He saw he was being indulged instead of being believed. He would stop in at the grocery store and ask Don Scarpo the next time he was near the place. They used to fly together as young men and still had a good understanding.

Even after 100 hours in the air Sister Bert couldn't fly as well as the pelicans, though they had helped her in many ways. They just knew their stuff better and they also knew San Juan better, having been raised right there.

One night the fourteen pelicans that Sister Bert traveled with, with herself as number fifteen at the end of the string, shot down in a swift, steep, dizzy glide, aiming directly at a blaze of light that came up so strong as to blind her.

Sister Bert blinked her eyes and ducked her cornette, which was a mistake. The pelicans zoomed off just in time, knowing it was a floodlighted military enclosure with dogs and wire mesh outside and secret stuff inside.

Sister Bert zeroed right in and hit the fence.

"Halt!" It sounded like a good strong American accent.

"I am halted. I'm just trying to get up."

A strong light was put on her. A man with a gun appeared.

"How the hell did you get in *here*! Excuse me. How in heaven's name did you get in here?"

"I—just lost my way, I guess."

"Over the top of a 30-foot fence you lost your way? This is a security area, ma'am. Nobody loses their way into this joint."

He took her inside a building. Three soldiers were playing cards at a table. They all jumped and spilt their coffee. Then rushed to phones and communicators.

"She says she's an American nun," said the guard who had put the gun on her.

"Did you frisk her?"

"No. I ain't never frisked a nun."

"Sit down, Sister. And don't try anything funny. You got a camera?"

"No, sir. I don't even own a camera. I don't own *anything*. I'm a nun."

"You can't frisk a nun, for Pete's sake," one said.

"She *could* be a Puerto Rican in disguise," said another soldier, giving her a good admiring look. "They come that little."

Sister Bert tried to look grown-up and professional, though her feet didn't reach the floor. She recited a lesson she had learned years ago in the Mission Training School: "Puerto Ricans are Americans, too."

Since she didn't quite believe it herself—never having been down here where Puerto Ricans came from—she sounded a little mechanical. So she caught up her rosary and began to tell beads and pray.

"Hey!" shouted a sergeant. "None of that!"

A lieutenant looked coldly at him. "Why not?"

"Okay, okay, I'm sorry, miss. Go ahead." Turning to the lieutenant, he said: "Everything's a bomb these days. Or a receiving set." He wanted all to know he spoke from rich experience. "Why, I saw a Joe get killed in a soda fountain. With a soda fountain straw. Only it was no such thing. It was a blowgun. Zwatch!" Here he slapped himself dramatically right in the eye.

"Right through the eye!"

"Oh, the poor man," said Sister Bert.

The phones began to get answers. Men questioned her while other men barked back and forth near a small switchboard.

"Age?" "Place of birth?" "Yes, a blue dress! And a big white bonnet." "Convent of San Tanco!" "That checks." "How do we know she's a real nun?" This voice whirled around in a swivel chair and looked accusingly at his colleagues: "Hey, how-do-we-know-she's-a-real-nun-they-want-to-know?"

"You a real nun?" someone asked her, quick but hopeful.

"Oh, yes. I'm the kindergarten teacher."

"Well, *I'm* a Catholic, Sister." And she knew he was because he said "s'tr" for "Sister."

"Sisters who travel have to carry travel orders. Just like army people."

The other soldiers were relieved. This should clear it all up. And save embarrassment.

"Well, you see—" she began, "—I hadn't really planned this trip—"

A sergeant whirled around. He was wearing a loop of phone around his head. "San Juan Police on the way. Counter-Intelligence too."

"Good. Maybe we could get a priest in here. Maybe he could frisk her."

"No, no! Never. Only another nun! Don't you know *anything*!" This was Lieutenant Shannon.

"Would you gentlemen like to hear me speak in Latin? Would that be enough?"

But the lieutenant shook his head.

"No, Sister. If the Russians wanted to send a spy who looked like a nun, they'd make darn sure she knew Latin. And prayers. Things like that. Now wouldn't they?"

Sister Bert had to admit it. "Yes, they'd certainly make sure of that."

"Exactly. So *we* don't have the authority to turn you loose."

To Sister Bert, the phrase "turn you loose" made her sound like something with fangs, but being a military prisoner she said nothing.

"Now, Sister—kindly tell us exactly how you got into this restricted zone." This was the lieutenant.

"Yes," she said. "You have a right to know."

Every man in the room grew tense, the sergeant, the corporal, the men with guns, the man with the flashlight, the lieutenant.

"The truth is—I flew in. Behind some pelicans."

"Oy!" The sergeant screamed this out. "A *nut*!"

"Shut up, Sarge!" More sensibly he asked Sister Bert: "If you flew, where'd you leave your parachute?"

"No. No plane. Just *me*. I hit a downdraft."

"How do you know about downdrafts?"

"I've studied aerodynamics." She tapped her feet against the chair legs. "My feet are going to sleep. How long . . . ?"

"Not long." Gallantry was alive among these men.

Very soon the door opened. From outside came the chief of the San Juan Police, Colonel Liebermann. He spoke both English and Spanish with a strong German-British accent, and filled the room with all three languages at once.

Behind him was a short civilian the soldiers saluted and called "Captain Bork." And behind him, and preceded by three feet of cornette, was Sister Placido.

The civilian captain seated himself at Lieutenant Shannon's desk, shoving everything aside.

"What were you doing in that enclosure?"

Before she could answer, Colonel Liebermann said: "May I remind you, sir, the lady is a civilian. Therefore under my jurisdiction. Not Counter-Intelligence."

The two men glared, fighting for priorities.

The colonel went on: "But it's a good question. What *were* you doing?"

They summoned the radarman, Corporal Page.

"I saw fifteen blips. Very clear. Pelicans by size and flight pattern. Then the last one fell out."

"At what angle? What degree from horizon?"

"That's classified, sir. Let's say, below a certain point. She fell out of formation about sixty feet. Did a fast falling leaf . . ."

"*She!* You could tell it was a she on the *radar?*"

Then they asked Sister Placido some hard questions.

"Do you recognize this nun and acknowledge her?"

"Oh, yes, sir."

"Can she fly?"

"It is thought that she has a certain—ability—"

"Have *you* ever seen her fly?"

"I've never actually seen Sister Bertrille in the air."

"Have you ever *actually* seen Sister Bertrille trying to get into the air? Or trying to get out of the air?"

"I saw her skidding along the balcony once."

Colonel Liebermann stood up. "This is a civilian prisoner. I shall take her before Judge Torres." He looked at Counter-Intelligence. "If you wish to come along—strictly as a guest of the Insular Government—"

Captain Bork got to his feet.

"I wouldn't miss it."

The two sisters, the colonel, and the civilian captain sat in a small semicircle facing Judge Torres.

Sister Bertrille told him the story just as it happened.

The judge didn't move or say anything when she finished.

She felt the silence might be damaging to her or to the Order or to Sister Placido, whom she had embarrassed enough, so she added:

"So, from the point of view of known principles, I was not actually flying, but *gliding.* Unless conditions are just right, I can't get off the ground."

But Judge Torres was a firm man:

"Sister Bertrille—we are here not attempting to decide *whether* you flew. Or how. The legal point is clear enough: You have intruded upon a Security Area. You have made an unauthorized entry. This offense comes under the Espionage Act."

"Espionage!" The sound of the word was abhorrent. "But all they asked me was how I got in. I just *flew* in."

"Sister"—the Judge seemed tired and it was certainly late for everyone—"that is what 'they' wanted to know. But that is not going to satisfy Washington!"

Captain Bork was a direct man. He turned to Sister Placido: "Did she ever tell you she was bombing around nights with a bunch of pelicans?"

Sister Bert interrupted: "It's only I never had this problem in New York. Not so windy there, you know—"

"I'd like to believe you," said the judge.

"What would convince you of her innocence?" asked Sister Placido.

"You're the sister in charge," the judge answered. "Do you believe in this little nun?"

"I attest to Sister Bertrille's absolute honesty in all things," came her reply.

"I'd like to *see* her fly," suggested Bork.

But the judge shuddered. "Not me. You'll have to stand trial, Sister."

"But if I go on trial, I could never be a Sister anymore."

"What do you care?" asked the practical Bork. "If you can fly without a plane, you can make a fortune!"

"My fortune is San Tanco and the little children I teach."

"Oh, you foreigners!" shouted Bork, the German. "Always trying to make a bum out of the United States!"

Don Scarpo, the grocer, came in. He looked at Sister Bert.

"You flew in some place?" She nodded, and he said to the judge, "I knew it."

"Who's this?" asked the judge.

"He's the grocer."

"I was seeing Sister flying—several times. I used to fly. When I was seeing Sor Placido leave tonight with Colonel Liebermann, I suspected, yes, something is amissing so rapidly checking with allabody, I came to finding you here."

Here he beamed cheerfully and went right on: "And I am having to say only this, that this Sister Bertrille is being as innocent as any new being born baby, for I was seeing first flight she was taking and this being purely by accident, by the wind too much strong for this very smallness. So I am here by witnessing to her very goodness of character which is excellent superb for honesty."

They all decided to get into the biggest police car in San Juan and escort the two sisters back to San Tanco.

Sister Bertrille thanked them, then flew up to the balcony where her little cot was neatly made up and waiting for her.

"Light little thing, isn't she?" Judge Torres said pleasantly. "This time of night you could swear she flew right up to the balcony."

"Yes, it certainly looked that way," agreed Sister Placido.

Don Scarpo, the man of the world who was aware of its truths and forgiving of most of them, thought he'd ask his cousin, the ship's chandler, if he could make a rosary out of those little lead weights they use as sinkers on fishing lines.

The previous pages describe the spirit and the attitude the author (Tere Rios) has brought to her pleasant story about the American nun transferred to Puerto Rico.

For projection into a week-to-week television series, other comments seem appropriate. Different readers will have different reactions, to be sure, but perhaps most would agree to the following:

That in view of the Catholic-Protestant dialogues that have opened these two religions to each other's inspection, right now would be an advantageous time to offer the public a spirited and unusual nun;

That half the success of her adventures, however, would depend on the proper casting of Sister Bert;

That the setting of these stories in Puerto Rico and areas nearby would offer three important commercial advantages:

   a) Continuously good climate (for filming purposes)
   b) Great variety of unexploited scenery and locations
   c) Lower cost

That a "flight" in each story would be looked forward to, as are Elizabeth Montgomery's and Agnes Moorhead's lighthearted deviltries in *Bewitched*;

That unusual visual plusses can be supplied *The Flying Nun* by the frequent use of footage filmed from a helicopter;

That a nun with sex appeal is acceptable if presented without comment.

If you wish, and if your subject lends itself to this added support, wind up with a rationale for the whole series. Give your producer some strong arguments that he can bring to his own meeting with "the money."

In this respect, here are some of the plusses I thought worth mentioning in the brief rationale that follows.

Producers or writers familiar with the Caribbean, or with Puerto Rico itself, would no doubt have favorite locales of their own for story settings. The area is rich in scenic change. The sudden contrast between extreme wealth and the most egregious poverty is a brutal fact of these lands. But the quiet activities of the Catholic Church would be percolating through all levels, giving Sister Bert plausible access to any situation—funny, pathetic, unexpected, grotesque, or insoluble.

Her "gift," because it belongs to a devout if somewhat jumpy nun, supplies the convent with this continuing dilemma: how to make quiet, legitimate use of her ability to fly without openly admitting that such a miracle is actually part of San Tanco's resources. How to keep the secret in the family, in other words, yet use it.

Just let it go on as the air dictates? Or study it and exploit it? (Always, of course, for the purest of causes.) Make scientific use of it? Can she learn to *talk* to pelicans, for example, as we are trying to do with porpoises?

But the nuns don't want to turn their happy hilltop into another Lourdes. Or even a lab. Certainly they don't want to get "touristy." Anyone snooping about with a camera is discouraged.

Sooner or later, of course, San Tanco will have to come to grips with *Life* magazine, which sooner or later will hear rumors.

Because of the dramatic "opening of the windows" of the Catholic Church by the late Pope John; the commercial success of Catholic nuns, both real (Sister Sourire) and made up (Debbie Reynolds, a Congregationalist); because the secular treating of an imaginary order will offend none yet put no restraints on story inventiveness, *The Flying Nun*—were a producer fortunate enough to find the *exactly* right performer for the central role—could catch the public's affection very early and hold it for many seasons.

Puerto Rico maintains a well-staffed, versatile publicity apparatus. Its offices could clear the producer's way in securing permits to places and properties; the right to film them: hotels, golf courses, private clubs, casinos, campuses, concert halls, the local townspeople of entire villages, churches, dignitaries, fiestas, festivals, conventions, distilleries, joints, cantinas, airports, the Governor's Mansion, military installations, marinas, factories, farms, and cathedrals.

Puerto Rico is *extremely* self-conscious, not just normally so. It has spent many millions in the past nine years trying to repair the squalid image which it is sure exists in the minds of most mainlanders. (More or less a fact.)

A happy partnership could be built between the producer and the PR facilities of this pretty island.

Finally, the Catholic Church is a living force in almost every land on earth. Foreign markets would likely find quick acceptance of this American-Latin American product, especially if the action moves and the nun is pretty.

Here are some revealing notes on Bernard Slade, the young Canadian writer who wrote the pilot that sold *The Flying Nun* to the network. He was the choice of Harry Ackerman, executive producer of the series, for the very good reasons that follow. Bernie Slade's credits are indeed impressive. As is the case with so many, his skills and his self-training began very early in his life.

When he was eighteen, after a dozen years in England, Slade embarked on an acting career. And he should have. In less than six years he played over three hundred roles in summer stock, touring companies, and television. In 1954 he and his wife, the actress Jill Foster, founded the Garden Center Theatre in Vineland, near Niagara Falls, and produced the first of a twenty-five-week season of plays.

Any writing yet? No. But in 1957 he did write a television play, with the happy result that it was bought by both the Canadian Broadcasting Corporation and NBC. He gave up acting right then and there and has given his talents exclusively to writing ever since.

In 1964 he moved to Hollywood and began writing for the *Bewitched* series. He did fourteen originals for this most delightful half hour, then became story consultant for *My Living Doll*. Screen Gems, one of the most successful "package" creators in television history, sent for him, asked him to take on the job of head writer and story consultant for *Bewitched*. In addition he has done four pilot scripts for Screen Gems.

Earlier credits include three originals for the *U.S. Steel Hour,* plus original contributions to *Matinee Theatre, Bob Hope Chrysler Theatre, Encounter,* and a long list of originals for the Canadian Broadcasting Corporation, as well as the BBC. Two of his plays have been seen in Canada: *Simon Says Get Married* (produced in Toronto) and *A Very Close Family* (in Winnipeg).

The tough disciplines for so much output came in Canada, not here. For six years he was the head writer on a weekly TV variety show, creating jokes, sketches, playlets. *Liberty Magazine* has twice awarded him "Best TV Playwright."

I have never seen a better TV pilot script for a comedy series than the one he prepared for *The Flying Nun*. For a full appreciation of this man's skills— what he had to work from and what he thought he needed to invent, in order to promise longevity to Tere Rios's sweet little novella—the two efforts should be studied together, the teleplay and the novel. *The Flying Nun* is now a paperback (Anchor Books), so it should be easy to pick up.

Now read Bernard Slade's pilot script. He missed none of the fun. He caught the full quality, the essential human fragrance, of the original. And he built a marvelously useful comic boisterousness into the show with his invention of the girl-chasing casino operator, winningly played by Alejandro Rey. Bernie Slade enriched and broadened a fine architectural story plan and put up the building.

A fine property got into the right hands, a miraculous accident in television.

It should also be pointed out that when the show was finally cast, and then filmed, it was tested before an audience in Hollywood. This is a regular routine and an important one. Packagers and show builders for sure know what they have (or don't have) before exposing their newest candidate to a network, for sale and acceptance. There is a singular irony about this: *The Flying Nun,* shown to an audience in Hollywood—as all other shows are exhibited—ran the highest test rating of any show ever offered in the twelve-year history of these tests. Yet as a written presentation it was everywhere rejected.

It is hard to get executives to read anything. It is even harder to find an executive who can read a script and see the show's potential. One of the finest scripts in this book—"The Price of Tomatoes"—was rejected by a top network official. But this is no more amazing and no more regrettable than the odd ricochet through which *Get Smart* had to bounce before getting on CBS. Television programming would improve overnight if the networks fired their programming heads.

CAST

THE CONVENT SAN TANCO

SISTER BERTRILLE	An enthusiastic, impulsive young novice from the United States. She weighs only ninety pounds.
SISTER JACQUELINE	American. Early forties with a warm personality and a nice, dry sense of humor.
MOTHER SUPERIOR	She is in her sixties and has very traditional ideas. One of the "old school."
SISTER SIXTO	Puerto Rican. A jolly, big woman in her early forties.
SISTER ANA	Puerto Rican. A very timid, young nun who acts as the Mother Superior's secretary.
SISTER MARGUERITA	Puerto Rican. A pretty nun in her twenties who teaches art.
SISTER TERESA	Puerto Rican. She teaches home economics.

ALSO SEVEN OR EIGHT PUERTO RICAN AND AMERICAN CHILDREN RANGING IN AGE FROM FIVE TO SEVEN.

OUTSIDE THE CONVENT

CARLOS RAMEROS	Puerto Rican. A very handsome, dashing, charming man. One of the richest gamblers and casino operators on the island.
CONSUELO MARIA LOUISE JULIE	Four extremely beautiful young girls. All work as dancers in the discotheque owned by Carlos.
KORMAN	A young sailor serving on a United States submarine.
COMMANDER	Captain of the submarine. Forties.

EXTRAS REQUIRED IN DISCOTHEQUE, TOWN SQUARE, LAUNCH, PIER, AND CONVENT SCENES.

THE FLYING NUN

PROLOGUE

FADE IN

EXT. SAN JUAN, PUERTO RICO—DAY

1 ANGLE

THIS SHOULD BE AN AERIAL SHOT THAT EMBRACES BOTH LAND AND SEA.

SISTER JACQUELINE'S VOICE

This is San Juan, Puerto Rico.

EXT. CONVENT SAN TANCO—DAY

2 SHOT

THIS IS A VERY OLD, RUN-DOWN CONVENT WITH CRUMBLING WALLS. AN OLD, BEATEN-UP STATION WAGON IS PARKED OUTSIDE THE CONVENT.

SISTER JACQUELINE'S VOICE

And this is the Convent San Tanco, high on a cliff in Old San Juan over-looking the Caribbean.

3 ANOTHER ANGLE

TWO NUNS, FOLLOWED BY A GROUP OF POORLY DRESSED CHILDREN, MOVE ACROSS THE SQUARE. THE ENTIRE GROUP IS BENT ALMOST DOUBLE AGAINST THE VERY STRONG WIND.

SISTER JACQUELINE'S VOICE

Whoever called Chicago the "windy city" just hadn't been to San Juan. Most of the sisters are used to the trade winds that swirl around and through the convent and have learned how to cope with them—

THE NUNS STOP, MAKE A SIGNAL TO THE CHILDREN. THE ENTIRE GROUP DOES AN ABOUT-FACE AND PROCEEDS BACKWARD ACROSS THE SQUARE!

SISTER JACQUELINE'S VOICE

—in one way or another.

INT. CLASSROOM IN CONVENT—DAY

4 SHOT

THE CLASSROOM IS SMALL AND DILAPIDATED. SISTER TERESA IS LECTURING TO A CROWDED CLASSROOM. SHE HAS PINNED A DRESS AROUND A DRESS-MAKER'S DUMMY AND IS STANDING BY IT, TALKING TO THE CLASS.

SISTER JACQUELINE'S VOICE

This is Sister Teresa, who teaches home economics—

A GUST OF WIND BLOWS THROUGH THE ROOM, WHIPPING THE DRESS OFF THE DUMMY AND OUT THE OPEN WINDOW! SISTER TERESA DOESN'T REALIZE DRESS HAS GONE AND INDICATES THE NOW BARE DUMMY WITH POINTER.

SISTER JACQUELINE'S VOICE

—or anatomy—depending upon which way the wind blows.

INT. ANOTHER CLASSROOM IN CONVENT—DAY

5 ANGLE

SISTER MARGUERITA MOVES AMONG STUDENTS WHO ARE SKETCHING ON PAPERS WITH CHARCOAL.

SISTER JACQUELINE'S VOICE

And this is Sister Marguerita, who teaches art. As you can see, our classrooms leave something to be desired—

THE WINDS BLOW THROUGH THE ROOM, LIFTING ALL THE PAPERS AND

SCATTERING THEM IN THE AIR. COMPLETE PANDEMONIUM AS THE STUDENTS
AND SISTER MARGUERITA FRANTICALLY TRY TO RETRIEVE PAPERS.

SISTER JACQUELINE'S VOICE

But at least they're air-conditioned.

INT. MOTHER SUPERIOR'S OFFICE—DAY

6 ANGLE

MOTHER SUPERIOR IS SEATED BEHIND HER DESK TALKING TO SISTER JACQUE-
LINE AND SISTER SIXTO, WHO STAND BEFORE HER DESK. ALL IS CALM AND
SERENE.

SISTER JACQUELINE'S VOICE

This is the Reverend Mother Placido. Now you may be wondering why
the wind doesn't blow in her office. The answer is simple. The Reverend
Mother just wouldn't allow it!

EXT. CONVENT—PLAZA—DAY

7 ANGLE

SISTER SIXTO AND SISTER JACQUELINE FIGHT THE WIND AS THEY MOVE
ACROSS SQUARE TO OLD STATION WAGON.

SISTER JACQUELINE'S VOICE

One day a few months ago, Sister Sixto and I were instructed to meet a
young novice who was arriving that day by steamer from New York to
teach kindergarten.

THEY BOTH GET INTO STATION WAGON. SISTER SIXTO BEHIND THE WHEEL.
THE CAR WON'T START. SISTER JACQUELINE GETS OUT, RAISES HOOD, GIVES
SOMETHING A HEARTY WHACK WITH WRENCH. THE ENGINE SHUDDERS TO LIFE
AND SISTER JACQUELINE SLAMS DOWN HOOD AND RACES INTO CAR. JUST
AS SHE GETS IN, THE ENGINE DIES AGAIN.

8 ANOTHER ANGLE—FRONT SEAT—SISTERS JACQUELINE AND SIXTO

SISTER SIXTO

(SPANISH ACCENT) Did you give the thingamejog a real bolt?

SISTER JACQUELINE

Thingame*jig* a real *belt,* Sister. And I did. Funny, it started yesterday.

SISTER SIXTO

(TRIUMPHANTLY) Well, one out of two ain't bad. Right?

SISTER JACQUELINE

(SMILES) You've been studying that Dictionary of American Slang again.

SISTER SIXTO

(NODS) When I go teach in U.S.A. I really know my way around. I got
it made!

SISTER JACQUELINE

I'm afraid not. Hold on to your cornette, Sister Sixto—we're going to
have to walk!

9 ANOTHER ANGLE
THE TWO SISTERS GET OUT OF STATION WAGON AND START OFF, THE WIND
SWIRLING AROUND THEM.

EXT. DOCK—DAY
10 ANGLE
A STEAMER HAS DOCKED AND THE DOCK IS CROWDED WITH PASSENGERS.

SISTER JACQUELINE'S VOICE
We didn't reach the dock in time for Sister Bertrille's arrival.

11 ANOTHER ANGLE—SISTER BERTRILLE
SHE IS MOVING ALONG THE DOCK, HER YOUNG FACE EAGER AND ALIVE. SHE
CARRIES A BATTERED SUITCASE.

SISTER JACQUELINE'S VOICE
She came bursting off the boat in high spirits—and a high wind.

SISTER BERTRILLE STOPS, LOOKS AT SEA.

SISTER JACQUELINE'S VOICE
Now, the reason I keep mentioning the wind is that it's as important to
our story as it was to the Wright Brothers.

DURING FOLLOWING SISTER BERTRILLE PUTS SUITCASE DOWN (A MISTAKE!)
AND TURNS TO LOOK TOWARD SAN JUAN.

SISTER JACQUELINE'S VOICE
You see, one of the many things we didn't know about Sister Bertrille
was that she only weighed ninety pounds—

AS SISTER BERTRILLE HAS TURNED TOWARD WIND IT BOWLS HER OVER BACK-
WARD. SHE DISAPPEARS OVER DOCK, A STARTLED EXPRESSION ON HER FACE.
WE DON'T SEE HER HIT WATER, ONLY THE SPLASH THAT RISES ABOVE DOCK.

12 ANOTHER ANGLE—SISTER BERTRILLE FLOUNDERING IN WATER

SISTER JACQUELINE'S VOICE
—dripping wet!

SISTER BERTRILLE STRIKES OFF IN THE DIRECTION OF A VERY EXPENSIVE
LAUNCH THAT IS ANCHORED.

13 ANOTHER ANGLE
CAMERA PANS OVER A NUMBER OF VERY BEAUTIFUL GIRLS, ALL IN BIKINIS,
SUNBATHING ON LAUNCH. CAMERA PANS TO COCKPIT AT BACK OF BOAT
WHERE WE SEE CARLOS RAMEROS, A VERY HANDSOME MAN IN HIS LATE
THIRTIES, WHO IS TALKING IN A LOW, PERSUASIVE VOICE TO A BEAUTIFUL
GIRL NAMED CONSUELO. HIS BACK IS TO THE STERN OF BOAT.

CARLOS
Look, St. Thomas is only forty-five minutes away. We'll fly over on
Friday and be back Sunday night. Your father will never know.

CONSUELO
I don't know, Carlos. It just doesn't seem right.

CARLOS

Now, do I seem the sort of man who would take advantage of a girl? (SHE LOOKS DOUBTFUL) Trust me, Consuelo.

CONSUELO

Well, maybe I'll go if you promise not to—

SHE STOPS AND A PECULIAR EXPRESSION COMES TO HER FACE.

CARLOS

What's the matter?

CONSUELO

There's a nun on the back of the boat.

HE TURNS TO LOOK.

14 ANOTHER ANGLE—POV
SISTER BERTRILLE, DRIPPING WET, HAS HALF PULLED HERSELF OVER STERN.

SISTER BERTRILLE

Hi there!

15 ANOTHER ANGLE—BACK TO SCENE

CARLOS

Who—who are you?

SISTER BERTRILLE

I'm Sister Bertrille. I just arrived from the United States.

CARLOS

(STUNNED) You swam all the way?

EXT. DOCK—DAY
16 ANGLE
SISTER SIXTO AND SISTER JACQUELINE HURRYING ALONG DOCK. THEY LOOK AROUND FOR SISTER BERTRILLE. SISTER SIXTO SEES HER, REACTS, NUDGES SISTER JACQUELINE AND INDICATES:

17 ANOTHER ANGLE—POV—LAUNCH
SISTER BERTRILLE IS SEATED ON TOP OF CABIN PLAYING CARDS WITH THREE OF THE BIKINI-CLAD GIRLS. SISTER BERTRILLE TRIUMPHANTLY SLAPS CARDS DOWN.

SISTER BERTRILLE

Gin!!

18 ANOTHER ANGLE—SISTERS SIXTO AND JACQUELINE
THE GOOD SISTERS REACT.

19 ANOTHER ANGLE
SHE LOOKS UP, SEES SISTERS, WAVES.

SISTER BERTRILLE

(CALLING) Oh, hello there! I fell off the dock! (TO GIRLS) Sorry to break up the game, girls, but I have to get to the Convent. (GETTING TO HER FEET) See you on Sunday at Mass.

CONSUELO

It's a deal, Sister.

CARLOS

(WHO HAS BEEN WATCHING FROM COCKPIT) Sunday? But what about St. Thomas?

CONSUELO

Sister Bertrille blitzed us. We agreed if we lost we would attend Mass for three weeks.

CARLOS REACTS. SISTER BERTRILLE CLAMBERS BACK TO COCKPIT.

SISTER BERTRILLE

Thank you for your hospitality, Senor Rameros. I'll say a prayer for you.

CARLOS

Do not bother. I am not a religious man, Sister.

SISTER BERTRILLE

All the more reason I should say a prayer for you.

SHE WAVES GOOD-BYE AND STARTS UP LADDER.

20 ANOTHER ANGLE—DOCK

AS SISTER BERTRILLE APPEARS. SHE IS STILL SOMEWHAT DAMP. THE TWO NUNS LOOK AT HER.

SISTER JACQUELINE

Sister Bertrille, this is Sister Sixto and I'm Sister Jacqueline.

SISTER BERTRILLE

(SURPRISED) Oh, you speak English.

SISTER JACQUELINE

I'm from Boston—it goes with the territory. Sister Sixto is from Puerto Rico.

SISTER BERTRILLE

(IN SPANISH) Very nice to meet you, Sister Sixto.

SISTER SIXTO

(TRIUMPHANTLY) You are a little wet behind the ears!

SISTER BERTRILLE

(PUZZLED) Well—I'm still a novice.

SISTER JACQUELINE

Sister Sixto is studying the Dictionary of American Slang. She means you're a little damp around the edges.

SISTER BERTRILLE

(CHEERFULLY) In the middle, too.

SISTER JACQUELINE

Uh—where are your bags?

SISTER BERTRILLE

Over here.

AS THEY MOVE DOWN THE DOCK TO BAGS.

SISTER BERTRILLE

Senor Rameros was so nice to me. Did you know all those girls work for
him in his discotheque? He puts them in cages.

SISTER JACQUELINE

(DRILY) I don't doubt it. His reputation is not exactly flawless. (THEY
HAVE REACHED SUITCASES. CURIOUSLY) You play cards often, Sister
Bertrille?

SISTER BERTRILLE

I only learned three weeks ago. (PICKING UP SUITCASES) It helped pass
the time while I was in jail.

SISTER JACQUELINE

Prison?

SISTER BERTRILLE

I was arrested at a civil rights protest rally.

THEY START OFF DOWN DOCK, SISTER BERTRILLE LUGGING HER HEAVY SUIT-
CASES.

SISTER JACQUELINE'S VOICE

It was at this point I had the feeling the Convent San Tanco would never
be the same again. *That* turned out to be the biggest understatement of
the year!

EXT. NARROW COBBLED STREET IN OLD SAN JUAN—DAY

21 ANGLE

THE THREE SISTERS MOVE THROUGH THE CROWDED STREET. SISTER BER-
TRILLE IS UNASHAMEDLY RUBBERNECKING. AT TIMES SHE HAS TO BREAK
INTO A LITTLE JOG TROT TO KEEP UP WITH THE OTHER TWO.

SISTER JACQUELINE'S VOICE

Sister Bertrille eagerly drank in all the sights and sounds of Old San Juan.

EXT. TOWN SQUARE IN OLD SAN JUAN—DAY

22 ANGLE

THEY MOVE THROUGH SQUARE, STOP BY VENDOR'S CART (RATHER LIKE POP-
CORN CART BUT ACTUALLY THE TRANSPORTATION FOR A PORK DISH PECULIAR
TO PUERTO RICO AND SOLD ON STREETS). SISTER BERTRILLE WATCHES A
SMALL BOY EATING THIS DISH.

SISTER JACQUELINE'S VOICE

She was curious about everything and possessed the gift of infecting
everyone around her with her enthusiasm.

UNDER ABOVE NARRATION SISTER BERTRILLE ASKS THE LITTLE BOY SOME-
THING. HE IS SURPRISED AND SHYLY HOLDS WHAT HE IS EATING UP. SISTER
BERTRILLE TAKES A BITE, CHEWS, HOLDS UP HER FINGER AND THUMB IN
AN "OKAY" GESTURE. THE LITTLE BOY GRINS.

EXT. CREST OF STEEP HILLSIDE ROAD—DAY

23 ANGLE
SISTER BERTRILLE IS POINTING UP AT BALCONY ON BUILDING. SISTERS SIXTO
AND JACQUELINE ARE ANSWERING HER QUESTIONS.

SISTER JACQUELINE'S VOICE
By the time we neared the Convent, Sister Sixto and I were looking at
San Juan as if for the first time.

CUT TO:

EXT. CONVENT—DAY
24 ANGLE
THE THREE SISTERS MOVE ACROSS SQUARE, STOP, AND LOOK AT CONVENT.

25 ANOTHER ANGLE—CLOSE ON SISTERS
SISTER BERTRILLE'S EYES ARE SHINING.

SISTER BERTRILLE
(OVERCOME) It's beautiful.

SISTER SIXTO
The plumbing. She is on the blank.

SISTER JACQUELINE
Blink, Sister. So is everything else in the Convent, I'm afraid.

SISTER BERTRILLE
But it looks so well preserved.

SISTER JACQUELINE
Someone willed a fund to keep up the actual building. Unfortunately, it
doesn't cover the cost of new classrooms or modern plumbing. (SISTER
BERTRILLE IS STILL DRINKING IN THE CONVENT) I'll show you where
you can change. (SISTERS SIXTO AND JACQUELINE START OFF, STOP, AS
SISTER BERTRILLE DOESN'T MOVE) What is it, Sister Bertrille?

SISTER BERTRILLE
Somehow I have a feeling of—coming home.

THEY SMILE AT HER.

DISSOLVE TO:

INT. SISTER BERTRILLE'S ROOM—DAY
26 ANGLE
THE ROOM IS VERY SMALL, FURNISHED ONLY WITH THE NECESSITIES. SISTER
BERTRILLE IS NOW IN A DRY HABIT. SISTER JACQUELINE ENTERS.

SISTER JACQUELINE
The Reverend Mother has gone to Mayaguez for a few days. She asked
me to look after you. (PICKS UP SISTER BERTRILLE'S WET HABIT) I'll
show you where to hang your wet clothes.

SISTER BERTRILLE FOLLOWS HER TO A DOOR LEADING TO A BALCONY.

CUT TO

EXT. BALCONY—DAY
27 ANGLE

AS THEY ENTER. THIS IS ABOUT TWENTY FEET SQUARE AND OVERLOOKS THE
OCEAN. THERE ARE SHEETS HANGING FROM CIRCULAR CLOTHESLINES.

SISTER JACQUELINE

Thank goodness the wind has died down. It seems to blow in gusts.

AS SISTER JACQUELINE MOVES TO CLOTHESLINE WITH WET HABIT, SISTER
BERTRILLE LOOKS UP AT SKY.

28 ANOTHER ANGLE—HER POV
SEAGULLS DIVING AND WHEELING AGAINST BLUE SKY.

29 ANOTHER ANGLE—BACK TO SCENE

SISTER BERTRILLE

Oh, look at the seagulls! Aren't they beautiful. (STILL LOOKING UP)
When I was a little girl I often wished I were a bird. They seemed so
free and graceful.

THE WIND HAS STARTED TO BLOW AGAIN. SISTER JACQUELINE HAS HER BACK
TO SISTER BERTRILLE AND IS HAVING DIFFICULTY PINNING HABIT ONTO LINE.

SISTER JACQUELINE

And you weren't?

SISTER BERTRILLE

Oh, I was the klutz of the neighborhood. (SISTER JACQUELINE TURNS TO
LOOK AT HER) Fell out of the treehouse nine times in the fourth grade
alone.

SISTER JACQUELINE

(TURNING BACK TO WASHING) No wonder you wished you were a bird.
And you almost got your wish. Some people think our cornettes make
us look like birds.

A STRONG GUST OF WIND BLOWS. SISTER BERTRILLE IS TAKEN STRAIGHT UP
AGAIN! SHE IS TOO SURPRISED TO SAY ANYTHING, BUT THROWS OUT HER ARMS
AT THE ALTITUDE OF TEN FEET AND HOVERS!

SISTER JACQUELINE

I suppose it's true in a way. Have you ever seen the secretary birds in
the—

SISTER BERTRILLE

(FINDING HER VOICE, HOARSELY) Sister!

SISTER JACQUELINE TURNS, IS PUZZLED TO SEE SISTER BERTRILLE HAS
DISAPPEARED.

SISTER BERTRILLE

Sister!!

SISTER JACQUELINE LOOKS UP, SEES HER.

SISTER JACQUELINE

Good grief!

SHE GRABS AT SISTER BERTRILLE'S FEET, BUT MISSES.

SISTER JACQUELINE

Have faith, Sister, don't panic—have faith! I'll get you down somehow!

CUT TO:

EXT. ANOTHER PART OF THE CONVENT—DAY

30 ANGLE

SISTER ANA, A VERY SHY YOUNG NUN, IS READING. HER EYES COME UP FROM THE TEXT AS SHE MEDITATES. HER EYES BECOME SAUCERLIKE.

31 ANOTHER ANGLE—POV

SHOOTING UP FROM GROUND WE SEE THE WALL OF BALCONY AND HOVERING A GOOD SIX FEET ABOVE WALL, HER ARMS SPREAD—SISTER BERTRILLE!

32 ANOTHER ANGLE—SISTER ANA

SHE CROSSES HERSELF AND MURMURS A PRAYER.

EXT. BALCONY—DAY

33 ANGLE

SISTER JACQUELINE HAS SISTER BERTRILLE BY ONE ANKLE AND IS TUGGING FURIOUSLY.

SISTER JACQUELINE

Try to get your other foot down!

SISTER BERTRILLE LOOKS DOWN SO THAT HER CORNETTE IS POINTED DOWN-WARD AND SHE PROMPTLY CRASH-LANDS INTO SISTER JACQUELINE! THEY DISENTANGLE THEMSELVES. SISTER JACQUELINE STANDS, PUTS TWO FIRM HANDS ON THE SHOULDERS OF SISTER BERTRILLE, WHO IS STILL SITTING, A LOOK OF WONDERMENT IN HER EYES.

SISTER JACQUELINE

Are you all right?

SISTER BERTRILLE LOOKS UP AT HER.

SISTER BERTRILLE

(WIDE-EYED) Sister Jacqueline, when I was—up there—I—I had the strangest feeling. I felt that if I had really wanted to—I could have flown!

THEY ARE LOOKING AT ONE ANOTHER IN SURPRISE, AS WE:

FADE TO:

ANIMATION AND CREDITS

THE FLYING NUN

FADE IN

INT. REFECTORY—DAY

34 ANGLE

SISTERS SIXTO, MARGUERITA, TERESA, AND JACQUELINE ARE AT THE BREAK-FAST TABLE.

SISTER TERESA

Where is our new little member of the family this morning?

SISTER JACQUELINE

(PUZZLED) I don't know. She can't afford to miss breakfast.

SISTER SIXTO

Yes. Sister Bertrille is as thin as a rook.

SISTER JACQUELINE

Thin as a *rake*, Sister.

SISTER BERTRILLE BUSTLES IN, CHEERFULLY.

SISTER BERTRILLE

(BREATHLESSLY) Good morning, Sister! Sorry I'm late. (SITTING) I went to the library to try and find out why I became airborne last night.

SISTER MARGUERITA

Airborne?

SISTER BERTRILLE

I had some trouble with the wind.

SISTER TERESA

(PUZZLED) Wind?

SISTER JACQUELINE

Sister Bertrille only weighs ninety pounds and sometimes it lifts her.

SISTER MARGUERITA

(STILL PUZZLED) Lifts here where?

SISTER JACQUELINE

(POINTS) Uh—up.

THE NUNS ALL LOOK UP AND THEN AT SISTER BERTRILLE.

SISTER BERTRILLE

Oh, it's okay. I've figured it all out. It's all to do with the cornette.

SISTER TERESA

Cornette?

SISTER BERTRILLE

Yes. You see, if *lift* plus *thrust* is greater than *load* plus *drag* anything will fly.

SISTER SIXTO

(BAFFLED) Load plus drag?

SISTER BERTRILLE

Yes. (SHE STANDS UP. THE OTHER NUNS WATCH, AS IF HYPNOTIZED) Look, think of me as drag. Only ninety pounds of drag, unfortunately. (DEMONSTRATES WITH HANDS) Therefore—when the peak of my cornette is forced into the wind it *lifts* me. The theory is aerodynamically sound. (SITS, CHEERFULLY) I'll just have to keep my cornette tilted a certain way.

SISTER TERESA

I—I see. Well, you are very small, Sister Bertrille. (EARNESTLY) Perhaps it might help if you had more starch in your diet.

SISTER JACQUELINE

(NOT SO EARNESTLY) Or less in your cornette.

SISTER BERTRILLE

(A LAUGH) I'm afraid everything I eat turns to energy, Sister Teresa.

DURING THE FOLLOWING THE OTHER NUNS LEAVE THE TABLE.

SISTER BERTRILLE

I'm anxious to meet the Reverend Mother. When will she be back?

SISTER JACQUELINE

In a few days.

SISTER BERTRILLE

What is she like?

SISTER JACQUELINE

(CAREFULLY) Well, of course the Reverend Mother is quite old. (SISTER BERTRILLE WAITS) Sister Bertrille, you must understand that when the Reverend Mother entered the order perfection was reached by discipline —discipline, which destroyed all traces of self-will or—or "rebellious-ness." At least that was the idea. (SISTER BERTRILLE IS STILL LISTENING) I suppose what I'm trying to say is that her ideas are rather—traditional.

SISTER BERTRILLE

But times are changing so fast, Sister Jacqueline.

SISTER JACQUELINE

I know, and the Reverend Mother tries to understand, but for her some-times it's—difficult.

SISTER BERTRILLE

Thank you for the advice, Sister Jacqueline, but you don't have to worry. The Reverend Mother and I will get along fine.

SISTER JACQUELINE

You think so?

SISTER BERTRILLE

Of course. We young sisters are just approaching things a different way. Our aims are still the same.

AS THEY SMILE AT EACH OTHER SISTER ANA (THE SISTER WHO SAW HER FLY) SCURRIES IN. SHE IS A TIMID SOUL AND HER WIDE, RATHER FEARFUL EYES REFLECT A WORSHIPING ATTITUDE WHEN IN SISTER BERTRILLE'S PRESENCE.

SISTER JACQUELINE

Ah, this is Sister Ana. She'll take you to your kindergarten class.

SISTER BERTRILLE

Lead on, Sister Ana!

THEY EXIT. SISTER JACQUELINE RISES, STOPS AS SHE THINKS OF SOMETHING. SISTER SIXTO, WHO IS CLEARING TABLE, NOTICES HER.

SISTER SIXTO

Something the matter, Sister Jacqueline? You look as if you have a flea in your bonnet.

SISTER JACQUELINE

Bee, Sister. I just hope Sister Bertrille doesn't tell Sister Ana about her tendency to go up.

SISTER SIXTO

Why not?

SISTER JACQUELINE

Sister Ana has a tendency to overorganize. (SISTER SIXTO DOESN'T UNDERSTAND) She may want to canonize her.

INT. CORRIDOR OF CONVENT—DAY

35 ANGLE

SISTER ANA SCURRIES ALONG BESIDE SISTER BERTRILLE, HER EYES STILL UPON HER. SISTER BERTRILLE NOTICES THIS AT ONE POINT, FLASHES A FRIENDLY GRIN AT HER, AND SISTER ANA DROPS HER EYES. SISTER BERTRILLE IS PUZZLED. AS THEY REACH THE TOP OF SOME STAIRS LEADING DOWN, SISTER ANA FINALLY HAS GATHERED ENOUGH COURAGE.

SISTER ANA

(BLURTS) Sister! (SISTER BERTRILLE STOPS, LOOKS AT HER) When did you discover you had the—ability.

SISTER BERTRILLE

(PUZZLED) Ability?

SISTER ANA

(IN HUSHED VOICE) To—(RAISES HER HAND UP AND DOWN) you know.

SISTER BERTRILLE

(CASUALLY) Oh, just yesterday. But it's nothing to get excited about. It's all a question of aerodynamics, you see.

SHE MOVES ON DOWN STAIRS. SISTER ANA DOESN'T UNDERSTAND, FOLLOWS HER. AS THEY REACH THE BOTTOM OF THE STAIRS.

SISTER ANA

(TENTATIVELY) Sister? (SISTER BERTRILLE STOPS, LOOKS AT HER. TIMIDLY) Many—very holy people don't realize they're holy because they're so humble.

SISTER BERTRILLE

What do you mean?

SISTER ANA

(IN A HUSHED VOICE) Some of the—the saints.

SISTER BERTRILLE

Saints?!

SISTER ANA NODS AND SCURRIES AHEAD TO A DOORWAY. SISTER BERTRILLE, VERY PUZZLED, FOLLOWS HER.

INT. CLASSROOM—DAY

36 ANGLE

THIS IS REALLY A LAUNDRY ROOM. IT IS SMALL, WITH ONLY ONE SMALL WINDOW. TEN FIVE- AND SIX-YEAR-OLDS SIT ON ORDINARY BENCHES. THEY

ARE HOT AND LISTLESS, WITH LONG HAIR. ALL ARE DRESSED BADLY AND SOME ARE WEARING DRAB GRAY CLOTHES MADE OUT OF THICK MATERIAL. SISTER ANA ENTERS, FOLLOWED BY SISTER BERTRILLE, WHO LOOKS AROUND ROOM IN SURPRISE.

SISTER ANA

(IN SPANISH) Children, this is Sister Bertrille, who has come all the way from America to teach you. She is a *very* special person.

SISTER BERTRILLE

Hi, kids! Buenos días, niños! (TO SISTER ANA) This is the classroom?

SISTER ANA

We have no space, Sister Bertrille. Most of the Convent is taken up with hospital wards for the old people.

SISTER BERTRILLE

But, good grief, this looks like something out of Charles Dickens! (SISTER ANA DOESN'T UNDERSTAND) Why are some of the children wearing those awful thick gray clothes?

SISTER ANA

They are the orphans who live here at the Convent. That is the uniform.

SISTER BERTRILLE

But the poor dears look so hot with all that hair and those uniforms. (LOOKS AROUND "CLASSROOM") Is there no equipment?

SISTER ANA

No money.

SISTER BERTRILLE

(FIRMLY) Well, something has to be done about all this! Oh, thank you, Sister.

SISTER ANA MOVES TO DOOR, TURNS.

SISTER ANA

Sister Bertrille? (SISTER BERTRILLE LOOKS AT HER) Maybe if *you* prayed.

SHE EXITS BEFORE SISTER BERTRILLE CAN ANSWER. SHE TURNS TO CLASS.

SISTER BERTRILLE

(CHEERFULLY) Well, now, you're all a sorry-looking mess, you know that?

BOY

(PUSHING HAIR OUT OF EYES—IN SPANISH) It is very hot, Sister.

SISTER BERTRILLE

I know it's hot. (IN SPANISH) But let's not talk about the weather—let's do something about it. (IN ENGLISH) English translation—let's not talk about the weather—let's *do* something about it!

FLIP TO:

INT. STRIPED SHEET FILLS SCREEN—CLASSROOM—DAY

37 ANGLE
THE SHEET IS WHIPPED AWAY.

SISTER BERTRILLE

Next!

WE SEE HER WITH LARGE SCISSORS IN HER HAND. SHE HAS WHIPPED SHEET
FROM BOY WHO NOW HAS SHORT CREW CUT. THE FLOOR AROUND HER
COVERED WITH HAIR.

38 ANOTHER ANGLE
WE NOW SEE SHE HAS CUT EVERYONE'S HAIR. THE BOYS HAVE CREW CUTS, THE
GIRLS EAR-LENGTH PAGE BOYS. SISTER BERTRILLE SURVEYS THEM.

SISTER BERTRILLE

(IN SPANISH) Very good! Now we are going on a hunt!

LITTLE GIRL

(IN SPANISH) A hunt?

SISTER BERTRILLE

A hunt—for remnants!

LITTLE BOY

(PUZZLED, IN ENGLISH) Remnants?

SISTER BERTRILLE

(IN ENGLISH) Right! Remnants. (TRIES TO THINK OF SPANISH WORD)
Uh—el remnants!

FLIP TO:

EXT. NARROW STREET IN OLD SAN JUAN—DAY
39 ANGLE
SISTER BERTRILLE AND THE CHILDREN IN A DOUBLE FILE ARE MARCHING
THROUGH THE STREETS SINGING.

SISTER JACQUELINE'S VOICE

Fortunately, the wind didn't blow too hard for a few days, but Sister
Bertrille managed to create quite a stir—even with her feet on the ground!

FLIP TO:

EXT. ANOTHER STREET IN OLD SAN JUAN—DAY
40 ANGLE
SISTER BERTRILLE AND THE CHILDREN MARCHING AND SINGING, BUT NOW
THEY CARRY ROLLS OF MATERIAL ON THEIR SHOULDERS.

SISTER JACQUELINE'S VOICE

She introduces a new word to the Convent San Tanco—(SPANISH WORD)
—English translation—credit!

FLIP TO:

EXT. SANDY BEACH AND OCEAN—DAY
41 ANGLE
SISTER BERTRILLE AND CHILDREN, STILL SINGING, MOVING ALONG BEACH.

THE CHILDREN ARE ALL IN NEW CLOTHES—BOTH GIRLS AND BOYS IN NEAT SHORTS AND SHIRTS. HOWEVER, EACH COSTUME IS A DIFFERENT COLOR. THE COLORS KNOCK YOUR EYES OUT! WILD POLKA DOTS, STRIPES, ORANGES, PURPLES, GREENS.

SISTER JACQUELINE'S VOICE

As a dressmaker she had a unique feeling for color—all kinds of color! The next problem Sister Bertrille tackled was how to raise money for the remnants and classroom equipment.

FLIP TO:

INT. CLOSE ON SISTER BERTRILLE PAINTING SIGN—DAY

42 ANGLE

SISTER JACQUELINE'S VOICE

Of course she had an idea for this, too.

WE NOW SEE THE SIGN WHICH READS (IN SPANISH AND ENGLISH)—"ALL PROCEEDS TO CONVENT SAN TANCO." SISTER BERTRILLE ADMIRES HER WORK. CAMERA PANS WITH HER AS SHE MOVES TO SISTER MARGUERITA, WHO IS PAINTING A LANDSCAPE. ABOUT TWENTY NEWLY PAINTED PICTURES SUR-ROUND HER.

SISTER JACQUELINE'S VOICE

And managed to infect the other sisters with her enthusiasm. Sister Marguerita painted—

SISTER BERTRILLE NODS ENCOURAGEMENT, MOVES TO TABLE WHERE SISTER TERESA IS BUSILY CUTTING COOKIES. THE TABLE IS COVERED WITH COOKIES.

SISTER JACQUELINE'S VOICE

Sister Teresa baked—

SISTER TAKES BITE OF A BAKED COOKIE, SIGNIFIES APPROVAL, AND MOVES ON.

43 ANOTHER ANGLE—CLOSE ON SISTER SIXTO WHO IS MAKING A STRAW HAT.

SISTER JACQUELINE'S VOICE

Sister Sixto made hats—

44 WIDER ANGLE

BESIDE SISTER SIXTO WE NOW SEE A PILE OF HATS REACHING TO CEILING.

SISTER JACQUELINE'S VOICE

—and more hats!

FLIP TO:

EXT. SQUARE OUTSIDE CONVENT—DAY

45 ANGLE

THE CHILDREN ARE ALL OVER THE OLD STATION WAGON HAPPILY SPLASHING A BRIGHT PURPLE PAINT ALL OVER IT.

SISTER JACQUELINE'S VOICE

The children became involved in the project—

46 ANOTHER ANGLE—CLOSER SHOT

WE SEE THE CHILDREN HAVE AS MUCH PAINT ON THEM AS THE STATION WAGON.

SISTER JACQUELINE'S VOICE

—and were given a chance to express themselves at the same time.

47 ANOTHER ANGLE
SISTER JACQUELINE STOPS AND WATCHES, A SMILE ON HER FACE. SHE LOOKS DOWN, HER SMILE FADES.

48 ANOTHER ANGLE—HER POV
TWO CLERICALLY CLAD FEET AND LEGS PROTRUDE FROM UNDER THE CAR. A BODY GLIDES OUT (ON MECHANIC'S TROLLEY). THE BODY TURNS OUT TO BE SISTER BERTRILLE, SOMEWHAT GREASY, BUT TRIUMPHANT! SHE GRINS HAPPILY AT SISTER JACQUELINE.

49 ANOTHER ANGLE—FULL
SISTER BERTRILLE MOVES TO CAR, GETS IN, TURNS IGNITION, AND THE MOTOR COMES TO LIFE—SMOOTHLY AND EFFICIENTLY. THE CHILDREN ALL CHEER WILDLY AND DANCE UP AND DOWN ON TOP OF THE STATION WAGON IN HAPPY EXCITEMENT.

DISSOLVE TO:

EXT. TAXICAB NOSING THROUGH TOWN SQUARE—DAY
50 ANGLE
WE SEE THE MOTHER SUPERIOR IN BACK SEAT. IN THE B.G. WE HEAR A STRANGE TINNY BANGING COMBINED WITH A WHEEZY ACCORDION.

SISTER JACQUELINE'S VOICE

Unfortunately, Sister Bertrille's plans came to fruition the same day our Reverend Mother returned to San Juan.

WE SEE MOTHER SUPERIOR REACT—CAN'T BELIEVE HER EYES! SHE SIGNALS DRIVER TO STOP, STARES HORRIFIED!

51 ANOTHER ANGLE—HER POV
THIS IS WHAT SHE SEES. IN THE MIDDLE OF THE TOWN SQUARE A BILIOUS-COLORED STATION WAGON WITH CRUDELY PAINTED SIGN, "CONVENT SAN TANCO STEEL BAND," SERVES AS A BACKGROUND FOR THE STRANGEST LOOKING "COMBO" IN THE WEST INDIES. THE CHILDREN, IN THEIR COLORFUL NEW CLOTHES, ARE ENTHUSIASTICALLY BANGING A DEAFENING BEAT OUT ON STEEL DRUMS, ONE LITTLE BOY IS GOING CRAZY ON THE MARACAS, AND THE ENTIRE "ENSEMBLE" IS BEING LED BY SISTER BERTRILLE, WHO IS PROVIDING THE "MELODY" ON A WHEEZY ACCORDION.

THE BEAT IS TERRIFIC BUT THE BAND DOESN'T REALLY SWING—ONLY A TRAINED EAR COULD DISCERN "WHEN THE SAINTS COME MARCHING IN!" THE BAND IS SURROUNDED BY SMALL BOOTHS WHERE SISTERS SIXTO, MARGUERITA, AND TERESA ARE DOING A ROARING TRADE SELLING COOKIES, PAINTINGS, AND HATS. SIGNS IN ENGLISH AND SPANISH PROCLAIMING THAT ALL PROCEEDS ARE FOR THE CONVENT SAN TANCO COMPLETE THE PICTURE.

52 ANOTHER ANGLE—MOTHER SUPERIOR
FIRE IN HER EYES, GRIMLY STARTS TOWARD SQUARE.

53 ANOTHER ANGLE—THE "BAND"
MOTHER SUPERIOR MARCHES UP TO SISTER BERTRILLE.

SISTER BERTRILLE

(EXCITED, HAPPILY YELLING OVER DIN) Hello, you must be Reverend Mother Placido! I'm Sister Bertrille! Reverend Mother, we've raised sixty-two dollars so far! Isn't that wonderful?

MOTHER SUPERIOR

Sister Bertrille—(SISTER BERTRILLE CUPS HER EAR)

54 ANOTHER ANGLE—CLOSE ON MOTHER SUPERIOR

MOTHER SUPERIOR

(YELLING) Sister Bertrille!

                                                        DIRECT CUT:

55 ANGLE

WE ARE STILL CLOSE ON MOTHER SUPERIOR BUT SHE IS NOW SPEAKING IN A QUIETER VOICE, TRYING HARD TO CONTROL HER ANGER.

MOTHER SUPERIOR

In six days you have managed to totally disrupt the Convent San Tanco.

WE NOW SEE WE ARE IN:

INT. MOTHER SUPERIOR'S OFFICE—DAY

56 ANGLE

MOTHER SUPERIOR

First those ridiculous costumes you made.

SISTER BERTRILLE

Well, I know the colors are a little spectacular, Reverend Mother, but I had to make do with remnants.

MOTHER SUPERIOR

It is unbecoming for girls to wear shorts! (FIRMLY) Girls wear dresses, boys wear trousers—gray trousers, not dotted polkas! And then that undignified exhibition in the town square. Do you realize how much attention you attracted?

SISTER BERTRILLE

But that was the whole idea. (EARNESTLY) Reverend Mother, something must be done about this building. The classrooms are overcrowded, there is no equipment, there is no—

MOTHER SUPERIOR

(REALLY ANGRY) Do you think I don't know that! For thirty years I have been fighting a losing battle against inadequate space, not enough books, bad plumbing, and not enough money—thirty years, Sister! And you spend one week here and tell *me* what is needed!

SISTER BERTRILLE

(TRULY PENITENT) Forgive me, Reverend Mother. Sometimes I speak first and think after.

MOTHER SUPERIOR

Sister Bertrille, you are young and you are American, with different—

attitudes. I am trying to take all this into consideration. (RISES) Let me acquaint you with the realities here at San Tanco. First, there is the question of money.

SISTER BERTRILLE
(EAGERLY) I have some ideas about that.

MOTHER SUPERIOR
(SHARPLY) Yes, I have seen some of your ideas! (SISTER BERTRILLE BITES HER LIP, RELENTING) I am sorry, Sister Bertrille. I know your intentions are good. You see, it is not only money. Even with funds we would have no land to build on.

SISTER BERTRILLE
(EAGERLY) I saw a vacant lot in Old San Juan. That would be a perfect location!

MOTHER SUPERIOR
I know the land you speak of. It is owned by a man named Carlos Rameros, who absolutely refuses to sell.

SISTER BERTRILLE
Oh, I know Senor Rameros!

MOTHER SUPERIOR
(WEARILY) Somehow I am not surprised. Now, you are new here so I am willing to overlook your breach of conduct, but in future please remember, Sister Bertrille—dignity!

SISTER BERTRILLE NODS AND EXITS.

CUT TO:

INT. SMALL OUTER OFFICE—DAY

57 ANGLE

AS SISTER BERTRILLE COMES OUT. THIS CONTAINS SISTER ANA'S DESK AND COULD BE PLACED IN CORRIDOR IF NECESSARY. SISTER ANA IS BEHIND DESK, SISTER JACQUELINE IS WAITING.

SISTER BERTRILLE
Sister Jacqueline, what are you doing here?

SISTER JACQUELINE
I thought you might need some cheering up.

SISTER BERTRILLE
(GRATEFULLY) Thank you, but I'm fine, Sister Jacqueline. I only have one problem.

SISTER JACQUELINE
What is that?

SISTER BERTRILLE
How to get that land we need.

THE BUZZER ON SISTER ANA'S DESK SOUNDS. SISTER ANA, WHO HAS HEARD ABOVE DIALOGUE, EXITS INTO OFFICE WITH LETTERS.

SISTER BERTRILLE

I think I'll go and see Senor Rameros.

SISTER JACQUELINE

Did the Reverend Mother say you could?

SISTER BERTRILLE

Well, she didn't say I *couldn't*.

CUT TO:

INT. MOTHER SUPERIOR'S OFFICE—DAY

58 ANGLE

MOTHER SUPERIOR IS SIGNING LETTERS.

SISTER ANA

Isn't it wonderful, Reverend Mother? Sister Bertrille is going to get us our land!

MOTHER SUPERIOR LOOKS UP.

MOTHER SUPERIOR

What are you talking about? How can she possibly get us our land?

SISTER ANA

(IN WORSHIPING VOICE) Oh, Sister Bertrille can do *anything!!*

MOTHER SUPERIOR LOOKS AT HER WORSHIPING FACE, AND WE:

FADE OUT

FADE IN

INT.—CLOSE ON A GO-GO DANCER GYRATING IN CAGE—DISCOTHEQUE—LOUD MUSIC—NIGHT

59 CLOSE

THE DANCER LOOKS DOWN, STOPS DANCING, REACTS.

60 ANOTHER ANGLE—HER POV

TOP SHOT OF CROWDED FLOOR FILLED WITH FRANTIC DANCERS. SISTER BERTRILLE MOVES THROUGH DANCERS MURMURING "EXCUSE ME'S." AS EACH COUPLE SEES THERE IS A NUN IN THEIR MIDST THEY REACT AND STOP DANCING.

61 ANOTHER ANGLE—CARLOS AND MARIA

THEY TALK AS THEY DANCE.

CARLOS

I have a beautiful house in St. Thomas. We'll leave Friday night and spend a marvelous, relaxing weekend—getting to know each other.

MARIA

I haven't said I'll go yet, Carlos.

CARLOS

Trust me, Maria. Will you come?

SISTER BERTRILLE APPEARS BEHIND CARLOS.

MARIA

Well, if you promise not to—(BREAKS OFF, PUZZLED)

CARLOS

What is it, Maria?

MARIA

Carlos, there is a—a nun behind you.

HE TURNS, SEES SISTER BERTRILLE.

SISTER BERTRILLE

Hello there! Sorry to cut in, but could I see you for a few minutes?

CARLOS

(ASTOUNDED) Uh—this way.

SISTER BERTRILLE

See you in Mass on Sunday, Maria.

MARIA

Yes, Sister.

CARLOS REACTS AND LEADS SISTER BERTRILLE THROUGH THE NOW STATIONARY DANCERS. SHE REACHES THE EDGE OF THE FLOOR, TURNS.

SISTER BERTRILLE

Please carry on. You all dance beautifully!

INT. CARLOS'S OFFICE—NIGHT

62 ANGLE

THE OFFICE IS VERY LUXURIOUS AND IS DECORATED WITH VARIOUS TROPHIES ADVERTISING CARLOS'S ATHLETIC ABILITY. HE ENTERS, TURNS ON SISTER BERTRILLE.

CARLOS

(STILL HASN'T RECOVERED FROM HIS SURPRISE) You know, I don't believe it. How can you come here like this?

SISTER BERTRILLE

(TEASING) You mean what's a nice girl like me doing in a place like this?

CARLOS

(A TOUCH OF SARCASM) There is dancing, drinking, and gambling here, Sister. Aren't you afraid of being "contaminated"?

SISTER BERTRILLE

Are all the young people out there contaminated?

CARLOS

But you are a *sister!*

SISTER BERTRILLE

All the more reason I should set an example.

CARLOS

(OFF BALANCE AGAIN) At a discotheque.

SISTER BERTRILLE

To show that the Christian life can flourish in the land of reality.

CARLOS

(SHAKES HEAD) Boy, you're some nun, you know that? (SHE COCKS AN EYEBROW) When I was a child the sisters never—

SISTER BERTRILLE

(GENTLY) Excuse me, Senor, but you must stop thinking of *the* sisters as if we were all turned out on an assembly line. We're all different, with different personalities. (SMILES) We're really like everybody else, Senor Rameros.

HE LOOKS AT HER FOR A MOMENT, MOVES TO POUR HIMSELF A DRINK.

CARLOS

What did you want to see me about, Sister?

SISTER BERTRILLE

Your vacant lot. We are desperately in need of space, Senor Rameros.

CARLOS

I am going to build a house on that land.

SISTER BERTRILLE

When is that?

CARLOS

When I settle down—when I find the right girl.

SISTER BERTRILLE

Well, you certainly seem to be looking hard enough.

CARLOS

In any case, I will not sell that land, Sister.

SISTER BERTRILLE

No, I didn't think you would. I believed you might donate it.

HE LOOKS AT HER FOR A MOMENT, ASTOUNDED.

CARLOS

(FINALLY) You certainly have some strange beliefs, Sister.

SISTER BERTRILLE

I agree with St. Ireneaus.

CARLOS

St. Ireneaus?

SISTER BERTRILLE

That the Glory of God is man fully alive and that whatever promotes life or growth is good. It's all a matter of potential, really.

CARLOS

And what has this to do with me and my land?

SISTER BERTRILLE

I thought you might donate your land because you have a potential for good within you.

HE LOOKS AT HER IN AMAZEMENT.

CARLOS

(SMILES) You should have been a lawyer, Sister, you missed your calling!

SISTER BERTRILLE

I don't think so, Senor.

CARLOS

(GRINS) You know, I like you. I really do. But I am a businessman first—a friend second. I'm sorry.

SISTER BERTRILLE

Thank you for your time, Senor Rameros.

SHE MOVES TO DOOR.

CARLOS

Sister Bertrille. (SHE TURNS) Please do me a favor and don't come to my discotheque again. (WRYLY) You'll give the place a bad name.

DISSOLVE TO:

EXT. BALCONY AT CONVENT—DAY

63 ANGLE

THIS IS THE PATIO-BALCONY THAT IS USED FOR HANGING THE WASHING. SISTER JACQUELINE IS SEATED AND SISTER BERTRILLE IS STANDING BESIDE HER GENTLY BALANCING ON THE BALLS OF HER FEET. THE WIND IS BLOWING AGAIN AND WHIPS HER HABIT AROUND HER LEGS.

SISTER BERTRILLE

I asked, but Senor Rameros absolutely refused. He's a very stubborn man.

SHE LIFTS HER CORNETTE, FLOATS UP ABOUT TWO FEET, PUTS OUT HER ARMS, AND HOVERS. SISTER JACQUELINE IS LOOKING OUT OVER SEA AND DOESN'T NOTICE.

SISTER JACQUELINE

Well, perhaps your timing could have been a little better.

SISTER BERTRILLE

Hey, I think I have the hang of it!

SISTER JACQUELINE TURNS TO LOOK.

SISTER JACQUELINE

Be careful, Sister Bertrille.

SISTER BERTRILLE

Don't worry. You see, now I just lower my cornette and—(SISTER BERTRILLE LANDS) I land! Pretty good, huh?

SISTER JACQUELINE

(SMILES) Worthy of Charles Lindbergh.

SISTER BERTRILLE FLOATS UP ABOUT TEN FEET.

SISTER BERTRILLE

(AS SHE GOES UP) Anyway, I'm not giving up. I'm sure Senor Rameros will donate the land.

SISTER JACQUELINE

(LOOKING UP AT HER) How can you be so sure?

SISTER BERTRILLE

Because he's basically a *good* man. (SHE LANDS AGAIN) I can tell.

SISTER JACQUELINE

(TURNING TO LOOK AT SEA) Well, perhaps you're a very discerning person but you should know some facts about Senor Rameros.

SISTER BERTRILLE LIFTS HER CORNETTE AND TAKES OFF MUCH FASTER THAN SHE INTENDED. SHE DISAPPEARS OUT OF THE PICTURE. SISTER JACQUELINE DOESN'T NOTICE AND GOES ON TALKING.

SISTER JACQUELINE

You see, he's notorious for being the biggest gambler and confidence man on the island.

64   ANOTHER ANGLE—SISTER BERTRILLE (PROCESS)

SHE GULPS, LOOKS DOWN.

65   ANOTHER ANGLE—HER POV

BIRD'S-EYE VIEW OF PATIO.

66   ANOTHER ANGLE—SISTER BERTRILLE (PROCESS)

SHE SMILES BLISSFULLY.

67   ANOTHER ANGLE—BACK TO SCENE

SISTER JACQUELINE IS STILL TALKING, STILL UNAWARE OF SISTER BERTRILLE'S "DEPARTURE."

SISTER JACQUELINE

Oh, he's never actually been convicted of anything, but he's not above cutting a few corners.

MOTHER SUPERIOR COMES ONTO PATIO AND SEES SISTER JACQUELINE APPARENTLY TALKING TO HERSELF.

SISTER JACQUELINE

His private life is not exactly beyond reproach either. Apparently his whole life is dedicated solely to the pursuit of pleasure. Now, I'm only telling you this because—

MOTHER SUPERIOR

Sister Jacqueline, who are you talking to?

SISTER JACQUELINE TURNS.

SISTER JACQUELINE

Why, to Sister Bert—(SHE TRAILS OFF, PEERS AROUND, BEWILDERED) But she was here a moment ago. (SHE LOOKS UP) Good—grief!

MOTHER SUPERIOR

What is it?

SISTER JACQUELINE WORDLESSLY POINTS—UP. MOTHER SUPERIOR LOOKS UP.

68 ANOTHER ANGLE—THEIR POV
A SMALL DOT WAY, WAY UP IN THE SKY!

69 ANOTHER ANGLE—BACK TO SCENE

MOTHER SUPERIOR

What is it? A pelican?

SISTER JACQUELINE

No. Sister Bertrille.

MOTHER SUPERIOR REACTS, LOOKS UP AGAIN AS WE

DISSOLVE TO:

EXT.—SISTER BERTRILLE HOVERING AGAINST BLUE SKY (PROCESS)—DAY
70 SHOT
WE SEE HER EXPERIMENTING WITH A FEW SIMPLE MANEUVERS. SHE DIVES,
DOES A LEFT BANK, A RIGHT BANK, AND FINALLY A LOOP-THE-LOOP. THIS
LAST ONE IS A LITTLE CLUMSY. SISTER BERTRILLE GRINS, LOOKS DOWN.

71 ANOTHER ANGLE—HER POV
BIRD'S-EYE VIEW OF SAN JUAN.

EXT.—SISTER BERTRILLE (PROCESS)—DAY
72 ANGLE
SHE IS NOW ON HER BACK FLYING UPSIDE DOWN.

EXT.—SISTER BERTRILLE HOVERING AND LOOKING DOWN (PROCESS)—DAY
73 ANGLE
SHE IS ALARMED.

74 ANOTHER ANGLE—POV
BIRD'S-EYE VIEW OF OCEAN—NO LAND IN SIGHT.

75 ANOTHER ANGLE—SISTER BERTRILLE
VERY ALARMED, SHE PEERS DOWN AGAIN.

76 ANOTHER ANGLE—HER POV
DOWN BELOW HER WE SEE A SUBMARINE SURFACING IN THE OCEAN.

77 ANOTHER ANGLE—SISTER BERTRILLE
SHE GOES INTO A DIVE.

EXT. CONNING TOWER—SUBMARINE—DAY
78 ANGLE
THE CONNING TOWER IS OPENED AND THE HEAD AND SHOULDERS OF A YOUNG
AMERICAN SAILOR APPEAR. HE TAKES A BREATH OF FRESH AIR, LOOKS AROUND
—GAPES.

79 ANOTHER ANGLE—HIS POV
A VERY TIRED, VERY SMALL NUN IS KNEELING ON THE BOW OF THE SUB-
MARINE, PRAYING.

80 ANOTHER ANGLE—CONNING TOWER
THE SAILOR DISAPPEARS, FAST.

INT. SUBMARINE—DAY

81 ANGLE
THE SAILOR PRACTICALLY FALLS DOWN THE LADDER AND INTO THE CAPTAIN.

SAILOR
Beg—beg your pardon, sir, but there's a nun topside.

CAPTAIN
What?

SAILOR
A nun, sir, kneeling on the bow, sir—praying, sir.

CAPTAIN
Korman, have you lost your mind? We just surfaced.

SAILOR
I'm as surprised as you are, sir.

THE CAPTAIN GIVES HIM A LOOK, STARTS FOR LADDER FOLLOWED BY SAILOR.

CUT TO:

EXT. BOW OF SUBMARINE—DAY

82 SISTER BERTRILLE
STANDS AND THE WIND PROMPTLY TAKES HER UP AND AWAY!

83 ANOTHER ANGLE—CONNING TOWER
THE CAPTAIN AND THE SAILOR APPEAR. CAPTAIN LOOKS.

84 ANOTHER ANGLE—HIS POV—BOW, NO NUN

85 ANOTHER ANGLE—CONNING TOWER

SAILOR
(BEWILDERED) She—she was there, sir, I swear it—a nun—in her uniform.

CAPTAIN
A nun?

SAILOR
(NODS) With a—(PANTOMIMES CORNETTE) you know—hat and everything.

THE CAPTAIN CONSIDERS FOR A MOMENT.

CAPTAIN
(GENTLY—THE PSYCHOLOGIST) Korman, are you a religious man?

SAILOR
Yes, sir—Jewish, sir—so that doesn't explain it.

CAPTAIN
Explain what?

SAILOR
A vision, sir.

CAPTAIN
Why not?

SAILOR

Sir, wouldn't I have seen a rabbi?

THE CAPTAIN JUST LOOKS AT HIM AND WE

DISSOLVE TO:

EXT.—DAY

86 SISTER BERTRILLE FLYING AGAINST SKY
SHE PEERS DOWN, FROWNS, IS OBVIOUSLY LOST. SHE SPOTS SOMETHING.

87 ANOTHER ANGLE—HER POV
DOWN BELOW WE SEE A SMALL, SILVER SEAPLANE FLYING OVER THE OCEAN.

88 ANOTHER ANGLE—SISTER BERTRILLE
AS SHE DIVES TOWARD THE PLANE.

INT. CABIN OF PLANE

89 ANGLE
IT HAS ONLY TWO PASSENGERS—CARLOS RAMEROS AND LOUISE, ANOTHER
BEAUTIFUL GIRL. A PILOT IS AT THE CONTROLS. CARLOS HAS THE WINDOW SEAT.

LOUISE

Do you know this is the first time I've been to St. Thomas? Does it have
beautiful scenery?

CARLOS

Not compared to you, Louise.

LOUISE

(PLEASED) Oh, Carlos!

CARLOS GLANCES OUT OF THE WINDOW AND FREEZES. THROUGH THE WINDOW
WE SEE SISTER BERTRILLE PEERING INTO THE CABIN FROM OUTSIDE. SHE
WAVES IN RECOGNITION AND MOUTHS "ARE YOU ON YOUR WAY TO ST. THOMAS?"
HE IS TOO STUNNED TO ANSWER AND THE WIND DRAWS SISTER BERTRILLE UP
AND OUT OF SIGHT. THE LAST THING HE SEES IS HER FEET DISAPPEARING.

LOUISE

I understand St. Thomas is a free port. What can I buy there? (SEES
HIS WILD LOOK) Carlos.

CARLOS

(IN STRANGLED VOICE) We're not—going—to St. Thomas.

LOUISE

You're kidding!

CARLOS

(TO PILOT) Pedro, turn back to San Juan! Turn back!

LOUISE

What for?

CARLOS

To donate my land to—to the Convent.

LOUISE

Do you have to do it right *now*?! (HE NODS) But *why*?

CARLOS

(ALMOST AS MUCH TO HIMSELF AS HER—IN WONDER) I—just—had a—a religious experience!

DISSOLVE TO:

INT. MOTHER SUPERIOR'S OFFICE—NIGHT

90 ANGLE

SISTER JACQUELINE IS AT THE WINDOW, PEERING OUT AND UP. MOTHER SUPERIOR IS PACING THE FLOOR.

MOTHER SUPERIOR

Sister Jacqueline, why don't you try and get some rest? I will notify you the moment Sister Bertrille—uh—lands.

SISTER JACQUELINE

But maybe she doesn't know *how* to land! (TURNS AWAY FROM WINDOW, VERY WORRIED) Oh, I can't bear to think of her out there all alone flying without instruments. (MOTHER SUPERIOR WEARILY PASSES HER HAND OVER HER EYES) You not feeling well, Reverend Mother?

MOTHER SUPERIOR

No, I am well. It is just that I find it hard to—to assimilate everything that has happened today.

SISTER JACQUELINE

It has been a strange day. Why do you think Senor Rameros suddenly changed his mind and donated the land?

MOTHER SUPERIOR

I do not know. The Lord moves in mysterious ways, Sister Jacqueline.

SISTER JACQUELINE

Somehow I have a funny feeling Sister Bertrille had something to do with it.

THERE IS A TERRIBLE CLANGING CRASH! THE TWO LOOK AT EACH OTHER AND RACE FOR THE WINDOW AND PEER OUT.

91 ANOTHER ANGLE—THEIR POV

LOOKING DOWN INTO THE PLAZA WE SEE SISTER BERTRILLE. SHE IS SPREAD-EAGLED ON A PILE OF GARBAGE CANS, HER CORNETTE DENTED AND ASKEW.

CAMERA ZOOMS IN FOR CLOSE-UP.

SISTER BERTRILLE

(HAPPILY—WITH GREAT RELIEF) I made it!

92 ANOTHER ANGLE

MOTHER SUPERIOR AND SISTER JACQUELINE.

93 ANOTHER ANGLE—SISTER BERTRILLE

SHE SEES THEM AND WAVES HAPPILY AS WE

FADE OUT

TAG

FADE IN:

INT. MOTHER SUPERIOR'S OFFICE—DAY

94 ANGLE

SISTER BERTRILLE IS STANDING BEFORE THE MOTHER SUPERIOR. SOME ANDIRONS ARE ON EITHER SIDE OF HER ON FLOOR. SISTER JACQUELINE IS ALSO PRESENT.

MOTHER SUPERIOR

I have pondered the problem all night, trying to arrive at a solution. Sister Bertrille, do you want to keep on flying?

SISTER BERTRILLE

(EAGERLY) Oh, yes—(STOP) But only if you wish it, Reverend Mother.

MOTHER SUPERIOR

I understand you believe in *responsible* freedom? (SISTER BERTRILLE NODS) I know you do not wish to bring any undignified attention to the Convent San Tanco. Therefore, I leave the matter of flying to your conscience.

SISTER BERTRILLE

Oh, thank you, Reverend Mother.

SISTER BERTRILLE BENDS DOWN TO ANDIRONS, LIFTS THEM WITH EFFORT, STAGGERS TO DOOR.

MOTHER SUPERIOR

Sister Bertrille? (SHE TURNS) You can't go around clinging to heavy objects all the time.

SISTER BERTRILLE

I'll try and work something out.

SISTER JACQUELINE

I have something for you. (SHE PRODUCES A STRING OF FISHING WEIGHTS, HANDS THEM TO HER) Sew them in the hem of your habit.

SISTER BERTRILLE

Fishing weights?

SISTER JACQUELINE

Fifteen pounds worth. (SISTER BERTRILLE IS STILL PUZZLED) Sister Bertrille, everyone knows a one-hundred-and-five-pound nun can't fly!

SISTER BERTRILLE AND SISTER JACQUELINE GRIN AND, AFTER A MOMENT, MOTHER SUPERIOR SMILES TOO. THE TELEPHONE RINGS. MOTHER SUPERIOR PICKS IT UP.

MOTHER SUPERIOR

(INTO PHONE) Yes, Sister Ana—I see. (TO SISTER BERTRILLE) There is a long-distance call for you from a Mr. Sullivan in New York.

SISTER BERTRILLE

(PUZZLED) I don't know any Mr. Sullivan.

SISTER JACQUELINE

Sullivan. He's probably Catholic.

MOTHER SUPERIOR

You'd better take it.

SISTER BERTRILLE PICKS UP PHONE.

SISTER BERTRILLE

(INTO PHONE) Hello—yes, this is Sister Bertrille.—Ed Sullivan?!—Oh, no, Mr. Sullivan, I'm afraid I couldn't possibly appear—yes, I know it helped Sister Dominic's record sales, but it's really out of the question for me. I'm sorry—no, even if I did have permission it wouldn't work. You see, it's all a question of wind—

AS SHE IS TALKING WE

FADE OUT

PREVIEW SCENE

FADE IN:

INT. SECURITY OFFICE—ARMY—NIGHT

95 ANGLE

TWO GUARDS WITH RIFLES STAND EITHER SIDE OF THE DOOR. A VERY FORLORN SISTER BERTRILLE SITS OPPOSITE A SERGEANT, WHO HAS A NOTEBOOK READY TO TAKE DOWN ANYTHING SHE SAYS, AND MAJOR CHARLES OVERLAND. THE MAJOR IS IN HIS FIFTIES, A REGULAR ARMY OFFICER, WHO HAS BEEN IN THREE WARS AND IS NOT ABOUT TO BE SURPRISED BY ANYTHING.

MAJOR

But how do we know you're a real nun?

SISTER BERTRILLE

(GLANCES DOWN AT HABIT) Don't I look like one?

MAJOR

(NOT UNKINDLY) Sister, it would be very easy for an enemy agent to *look* like a nun.

SISTER BERTRILLE

Agent?

MAJOR

We're on an island thirty miles at sea, and this is a highly restricted area. Now, can you prove you're a nun?

SISTER BERTRILLE

(HOPEFULLY) Would it help if I spoke some Latin to you?

MAJOR

An agent would be taught Latin.

SISTER BERTRILLE

I could recite the unchangeable parts of the Mass?

MAJOR

I'm sorry, we need more positive proof than that.

AT THIS POINT LIEUTENANT CARMICHAEL ENTERS. HE IS YOUNG, OFFICIOUS, EFFICIENT, AND ALL SPIT AND POLISH.

LIEUTENANT

It checks out, sir. The Mother Superior at the Convent San Tanco verified there is a Sister Bertrille in the order who answers to the description of the prisoner.

MAJOR

(WRYLY) You sound disappointed, Lieutenant.

LIEUTENANT

(EAGERLY) That doesn't rule out the possibility of espionage, Major. The Commies are infiltrating everywhere. This alleged sister could have been using the Convent as a front for—

MAJOR

(WEARILY) Sit down, Lieutenant. Well, now, since Sister Bertrille is a civilian it means she's also under the jurisdiction of the San Juan police.

LIEUTENANT

(ON HIS FEET AGAIN) I'm aware of that, sir. I phoned Captain Gonzalez and he is on his way.

MAJOR

Always thinking, aren't you, Lieutenant?

LIEUTENANT

I try, sir.

MAJOR

Now, Sister, there is a thirty-foot-high wire fence around this base. How did you get in here? (SHE HESITATES) Sister Bertrille, I think it would be better if you told the truth.

SISTER BERTRILLE

(FINALLY) I—I flew in.

LIEUTENANT

(POUNCING) The area was searched. There was no sign of a parachute!

SISTER BERTRILLE

Oh, I didn't use a parachute. I just—flew.

MAJOR

In what, Sister?

SISTER BERTRILLE

Oh, not in a plane. Just *me*. You see, I'm light—and when the wind's right I just ride the currents.

THERE IS A PAUSE. THEY ALL STARE AT HER.

MAJOR

(SLOWLY) You—*fly*—on your own?

SISTER BERTRILLE

Well, I *glide,* really. But I hit a downdraft—you see, this was my first flight. (ANOTHER PAUSE)

MAJOR

Let me get this straight—you glide—on your own—like—like Peter Pan?

SISTER BERTRILLE

Well, Peter Pan is a *fantasy.* No, my flying is more like the—the pelicans.

MAJOR

(NUMBLY) Pelicans?

SHE LOOKS AROUND AT THEIR BLANK, UNBELIEVING FACES, TRIES A NEW TACK.

SISTER BERTRILLE

Look, does lift plus thrust mean anything to you?

THEY JUST LOOK AT HER.

FADE OUT.

Most writers who have any respect for television at all, and all writers who have a favorite show or two, often wonder how they could offer a single story, a happy inspiration of their own invention. They ask what such a story outline ought to look like, how long it ought to run, what form it should assume.

While we are still on the subject of *The Flying Nun,* I'll include an original for this series, the work being a collaborative effort put together by Frank Woodruff* and myself. We had worked together on many shows during the twelve years we were both at Lennen & Newell, have the same sense of humor, and the same convictions about the kinds of situations the nun should be allowed to get herself into.

Here is our story. It is short, fun to read, informal. Its main pictorial and dramatic values can be perceived at once. It goes into no unnecessary detail. It suggests a few cautions. The quality of its fun is quickly visualizable. So is the use of the principals in the series. We called this one "Avenging Angel."

For many months Carlos has been trying to reach relatives (and a few former girl friends) living in a nearby "Island Republic." No luck. His phone calls never get through. His letters, sliced open but patched again, are returned. The only time he ever tried to anchor his yacht in the island's harbor, the local coast guard shooed him off.

The situation, exasperating to many, is well understood: a whimsical dictator has fenced off the island to suit himself.

For reasons quite different from those of Carlos, the Bishop has been

---

*Director of fifteen feature films for Columbia, RKO, and Universal; thirty films for the U.S. Army Signal Corps; director or stage manager for Theatre Guild, William Harris, A. H. Woods, the Shuberts; for eight seasons the director of the *Lux Radio Theatre.* Woodruff is one of the most experienced veterans in television today, with uncommon show savvy and sensitivity. His background is rich, not only in the theater but in the world of professional music. For many seasons he sang with the Metropolitan Opera chorus; moved, as director, to radio's first "hour" ("Roses & Drums"). He is with the Ted Bates agency in Hollywood.

trying to visit this same island. Many of his parishioners live there but all contact has been cut off. Nothing is known of their welfare. The matter is building into a diocesan crisis.

Carlos hears of the Bishop's frustration one afternoon while making a friendly call on the Reverend Mother.

Being Carlos, he wonders if he can't somehow "use" the situation. For the Bishop and the Convent San Tanco, of course. Nothing for himself.

Candidly Carlos suggests an interesting idea to the Reverend Mother, with the following result:

As the first step toward getting the Bishop back on the island, Carlos invites the Bishop, the children's choir, and the sisters to an outing on his yacht. But it's a bit more than an outing, actually—a two-day overnight cruise. They agree and sail.

Everyone knows just what kind of dictator El Presidente is—flashy, theatrical, unstable, arbitrary. But Carlos knows one thing more: El Presidente, possibly to impress his people or possibly because he believes he's communing with the Almighty, stands on a high promontory near his palace each morning and there conspicuously prays.

He is always flamboyantly uniformed. His subjects think he is receiving divine guidance and "the general orders of the day." He has told them to think so. He has told them he gets these orders from his Commander in the Skies, a posture and a relationship the dictator is pleased to insinuate.

During his early morning show of worship he is always surrounded—at a respectful distance—by a gathering of his people. And, of course, by a backup force of his soldiers.

Carlos has witnessed the ceremony more than once as he has sailed by. He has not only noted it, but has recorded its exact timing. His understanding of the psychology of power leads him to think that a sudden confrontation of the praying dictator by the Bishop would be something El Presidente could not publicly disavow in the presence of the faithful. Especially if the confrontation were backed up a phalanx of innocent nuns and singing children. Carlos reasons that El Presidente will have to go along with it and reopen his island.

Anticipating the "surprise" aspect of a confrontation between these two powers, Carlos has brought aboard his yacht a small transistor microphone and an equally tiny but powerful transmitter. It is his plan to coast up quietly on El Presidente's devotional, then hand the equipment to the Bishop, and let the Bishop's rich appeal and religious challenge boom over the water with full dramatic effect. Loud enough for all to hear. Rev it up.

It's a good plan. But it doesn't come off that way.

After a happy cruise under the stars and a rehearsal of the songs they plan for El Presidente, all get into their bunks.

Toward dawn, the yacht moves into heavy fog. Carlos is alerted by his navigator and comes on deck. He knows the yacht is now close to its target. He also knows he has to be dead on this target; he must have it physically in sight or his whole scheme will abort.

They take a sonar depth measurement. The water below is too deep to anchor. So they must keep in motion, maintain seaway. Yet they are now so close to land as to make this risky. The danger to sleeping children is another problem.

Though it's just dawn, Sister Bertrille is up and on deck.

"Sister"—Carlos is thinking fast now—"I wonder if you could—well, I mean —do you think there's enough wind? If you took off from the rigging, perhaps? You see, we can't navigate through this fog. And we're too close to land . . . I was thinking, if you could get above this—"

Here Carlos equips Sister Bertrille with the tiny mike and transmitter.

"If you could get *above* the fog, you could direct us how to get in."

Sister Bertrille takes off.

The yacht comes to life. Nuns and children appear. Carlos anxiously waits for a report. And presently gets one.

Sister Bert has successfully sailed above the fogbank, spied the shore, and also spied the odd ceremony taking place there. She hovers over the yacht briefly, points to the direction of land, then gracefully settles in the stern.

The Bishop appears. He is astonished at Sister Bert's report, that she has seen the so-called morning devotion of El Presidente.

"It's all a pose and a pretense," Sister Bert tells the Bishop. "A pure piece of showmanship. I'd like to go back and give him a piece of my mind!" she adds.

"I wish you'd give him a piece of mine!" the Bishop interjects. "You tell him, if he doesn't repent—"

Sister Bertrille is off through the fog. We go with her into the sunshine, high above the promontory where the dictator in his phony splendor is going through his ritual.

Sister Bertrille bombs him once, to get a good look at him. Out of a cloud in the sky he sees her coming. He's certain his eyes behold an angel, flying right at him. When he hears the trumpet voice of an angel, he's positive. Sister Bert has turned on her equipment. As her amplified voice reaches him, the ship's whistle blasts warningly through the fog. Now there can be no doubt. He is in the very presence of a Divine Visitation.

Sister Bert has decided to scourge the offender in her own way. She feels she has the Bishop's support in doing so. Well, almost. With the wrath of the Archangel Michael, she hurls her anathemas down upon the dictator:

"Get thee to a monastery!"

"Let these people go!"

"Hypocrite!" "Pharisee!" *Bang! Swoosh!*

She dives back and forth, making a series of close passes, her message clear and terrifying.

El Presidente falls to his knees, trembling and amazed. His hands go up as if shielding himself from lightning. The soldiers flee. Only the faithful remain.

Sister Bert disappears as she came. The fog lifts. She sets herself down on the deck of the yacht.

"I didn't expect you'd be quite so—so direct," the Bishop says. Her imprecations have been audible to all.

"Well, I just lost my temper. When I saw what a faker he is! He wasn't praying at all!"

"Sister Bertrille, you do indeed have a most remarkable voice. I suppose— perhaps the altitude—"

Carlos summons them all to the foredeck. They are approaching the harbor of the island now.

Clearly distinguishable, en route to the tying-up area, are the townspeople.

The yacht moves in slowly. Carlos takes the electronic equipment from Sister Bertrille. Then they go ashore in orderly but triumphant procession, the children singing as they march down the long pier. The island has been joyously, unexpectedly liberated.

   Two notes:
   (a) For purposes of Latin harmony, the character of El Presidente in appearance, age, color, and manner should be totally different from any present-day dictator. Stylishly uniformed, perhaps, but not bearded, nor even very dark.
   (b) Optional but not mentioned in teleplay: reactions on the yacht of the Bishop and the older nuns as they hear (but don't see) Sister Bert dive-bombing and excoriating the dictator.

That's the story, good for a single episode in the *Flying Nun* series. What does it tell the producer?

A producer has to make a quick, solid, important estimate of a story's usability on three counts: *satisfactory nature* (or playability) of the story; *suitability* to the series; *cost*.

Keep cost in mind always.

In a quick reading of your teleplay outline, the producer will be getting answers to other questions important to him:

Does your story have the right *flavor?*

Does it make *good use of the principals* in the series?

Does it have an *ending* consistent with this series?

In the teleplay outline just seen, what are the story elements? How would this narrative break down, for example, if its ingredients were to be entered like a grocery list? How elaborate a production is being called for? What could be dropped if there is a money shortage?

Here is the story's rundown:

 1. A West Indies island is secured against all outsiders
 2. Strongly but illegally
 3. By a demagogue
 4. Who is feared by his people
 5. But who is vulnerable in one area:
 6. He makes a public show of morning worship each morning which Carlos knows is phony.
 7. Carlos also knows the Bishop would like to visit his parishioners on this same island,
 8. The same as he, Carlos, would like to visit some of his former girl friends there.
 9. How to do?
10. Invite the nuns of San Tanco, the kindergarten choir, and the Bishop on a pleasure cruise to the island.
11. Arrive at the moment the dictator is praying.
12. Have the Bishop challenge the dictator across the water

13. By amplified electronic equipment
14. And expose his hypocrisy before his own people.
15. Heavy fog spoils this plan.
16. Carlos privately asks Sister Bertrille to "pilot" them in, by flying above the fog, and fastens equipment to her.
17. She makes this flight, taking note as well of the "praying" dictator.
18. Sister Bertrille returns, giving her report to the Bishop
19. Who is so outraged he wishes Sister Bert would "tell him off"
20. Which she at once construes as license to do so and
21. Disappears in the fog
22. To reappear above the dictator and his people
23. Where she dive-bombs him into collapse,
24. Assisted by the amplifying system she carries and
25. The ship's whistle, sounding its position in the fog.
26. The dictator panics, terrified by this visitation and the trumpets of heaven.
27. His "army" flees.
28. The faithful remain, marveling at the sight.
29. Sister Bert flies back to the yacht
30. Which moves to a pier in the harbor
31. Where all go ashore, triumphant—the children singing, the island liberated, the townspeople rejoicing.

Simple enough? Yes, after a number of years these tidy little enthusiasms learn how to shake themselves down into disciplined order and economic brevity. Or better to say *you* learn how to shake them down.

Suppose your production is short of money. Exceeding the budget is a common occurrence. Can you think how to make a ten-thousand-dollar saving in "The Avenging Angel" without harming the basic idea of the story?

Something's got to give. Tough compromises will have to be made. Certain elements will have to be eliminated. What are these elements? Can you put your story in a different setting? No, you can't. Can you cut out the yacht? Pretty hard to do that. Eliminate all the nuns but Sister Bert? Not feasible, and it would save nothing.

What, then, does it *have* to be? Yes, the children. And their happy singing.

This is another fierce reality in television: production costs. If your show has to come in under the budget (and most do); if you can't "steal" money from one production to use in another; or if you've already done all the stealing of that kind and have no other sources to tap and no other savings you can make, you just have to drown the children.

All that beauty? That wide-eyed enchantment? Those wavering, earnest harmonies? Yes, drown them. Every one. For this story they are decoration only.

But don't grieve. They'll be back in a week or two, when the overhead on another story is lighter.

What kind of press has *The Flying Nun* enjoyed? Quite complimentary. And it deserves it all. It's that happy rarity in an industry crowded with quarrels, self-doubt, and amateurs in high places—a family show that is clean, free of violence, pure of speech, but one that has been a commercial success despite these appalling demerits.

Joan Walker, one of television's fairest but hardest to please critics, has said in a few words what many others have run into swollen columns of praise:

> I take back everything I thought about *The Flying Nun* (Ch. 7, Thurs., 8 p.m.) before its premiere. I had been insulted by the title, by the obvious attempt to cash in on the success of *The Sound of Music* and *Mary Poppins,* and by the casting of Sally Field, who had not endeared herself to me when she was masquerading as that bubbling little surf-bunny named Gidget. It turns out that *The Flying Nun* is enchanting, and Miss Field is enchanting. She is beautiful without being Hollywood-beautiful; she is hoydenish without being tough; she is sunny without being sticky about it. The show is one of those things that television producers keep trying to put together but seldom do —a show for the entire family. One group I know that looked at the first two episodes together consisted of a 5-year-old, an 8-year-old, a very sophisticated 10-year-old, and parents who, although they might not admit it, I happen to know are 36 and 40. A fine time was had by all. P.S.: Puerto Rico has never looked as beautiful as it does in color on this show.   By Joan Walker

PART III / COMEDY

5

GET SMART

When you're in the television business yourself and have to look at a large number of shows every week, those you seek out for your personal delight are few. If I'm at home, I never miss *Get Smart*.

This show bounces around the world in a deadpan zigzag of fast absurdity, specious logic, misfiring master plans, phony calm, and fluttery idealism. Maxwell Smart, its hero, has about him a Ben Turpin resourcefulness of such tattered splendor as to impose on the whole cast a fierce control not to giggle.

Almost everything aborts. One dreadful blunder leads right into a worse one. All final rescues owe more to fortuity than to good thinking, and the stories ricochet happily among burlesque, travesty, lampoon, parody, and caricature. There's neither time nor depth for satire, and who needs it! Decisive battle actions are stalled by etiquette problems in sleazy hotels. The planet earth is imperiled by chewing gum wrappers.

Smart's monumental poise—a kind of mobile atrophy—is secure in any calamity. Actually he has no poise—only a glyptic inability to be shaken. But it serves! Why not? If it's a war, he merely brushes it off his clothes. "Sorry about that" has become the Americanized version of Britain's "he dropped a clangor."

Max walks confidently up to the registration desk or to the fuming general or sputtering fuse or toothy *presidente* or venal tycoon or armed-to-the-teeth annihilator or departing space rocket and addresses each one with such a fracture of the plausible as to turn every head around and down (Don Adams is short) to see if they heard right.

Which of course they did.

We get mock-heroic treatment of the trifling, labored inspection of the non-existent, curt dismissal of the immense. We also get fine running gags and sight gags.

As to the characters in *Get Smart*, every one has a large sign hanging from his neck that instantly flashes his role and meaning to the viewer. In this kind of comedy, for anything going by so fast as Maxwell Smart, you need labels. And you get them.

Now read the script, "Viva Smart," just for fun. Just to get its story and its flavor.

GET SMART
"Viva Smart"
by Bill Idelson
and
Sam Bobrick

CAST	EXTRAS

CAST
MAXWELL SMART
99
CHIEF
DON CARLOS
GENERAL SANCHEZ
ISABELLA

BITS
LOPEZ
DELIVERY MAN
SERGEANT
CART DRIVER
PEON (SOUVENIR MAN)
FIRST SOLDIER
GUARD
VOICE (Spanish Accent)
PEASANT

EXTRAS
PILOT
SOLDIERS
PEOPLE IN LINE
2 ACROBATS

SETS
INTERIOR:
　SMART'S APARTMENT
　CHIEF'S OFFICE

EXTERIOR:
　SAN SALUDOS AIRPORT
　PLAZA
　BUILDING

FADE IN:

1　INT. SMART'S APARTMENT

MAX AND 99. MAX IS SITTING ON THE COUCH READING A MAGAZINE. HE IS DRESSED IN A SMOKING JACKET AND IS SMOKING A CIGAR. 99 IS IRONING HIS SHIRTS. SHE HOLDS ONE UP.

99

I just have to do the pajamas and I'll be all finished.

SMART

I sure appreciate this, 99. Do you know what they want for shirts at the Chinese laundry? Twenty-four cents apiece.

99

Well, I enjoy spending an evening like this. It's so domestic. It's almost as if we were . . . well . . .

SMART

Twenty-four cents apiece. And they don't even put them on hangers.

JUST THEN THE DOORBELL RINGS.

SMART

(CONT'D) Who can that be? It's almost midnight.

MAX GOES TO THE DOOR AND OPENS IT. A MAN IN WHITE MEXICAN PEON CLOTHES, WEARING A SOMBRERO, IS AT THE DOOR WITH A PACKAGE OF FOOD.

SMART

(CONT'D) Yes?

MAN

Maxwell Smart?

SMART

Yes.

MAN

Chile Delight. I have your order.

SMART

Chile Delight? There must be some mistake. I didn't order anything.

MAN

Take it anyway. It's very good. Especially the tortillas.

SMART

Don't be silly. With my stomach? I'd be up all night.

MAN

(LOOKS AROUND) Take it! Take it! Please!

99

Who is it, Max?

SMART

(TURNING TO HER) Why, it's a delivery man from Chile Delight.

99

(WALKING TOWARD DOOR) Oh, Max. How sweet of you to buy me dinner.

SMART

I didn't. This isn't my order, 99. This guy made a mistake . . . (TURNS TOWARD MAN) Listen, Mister, I absolutely refuse to accept this . . .

AS SMART TALKS, THE MAN CRUMPLES UP IN FRONT OF HIM AND FALLS DOWN ON HIS FACE. THERE IS A KNIFE STICKING OUT OF HIS BACK. (NOTE: SHOW HANDLE, BUT NOT POINT OF CONTACT WITH BODY.)

SMART

(CONT'D) Oh, come on, now. Don't take it like that. It's nothing personal.

HE STOPS, REACTS, AS HE SEES THE KNIFE.

99

Max! He's been stabbed!

MAX LEAPS INTO THE HALL, COMES BACK.

SMART

No one out there—

99

Max, who could have done this to him?

SMART

Well, I'm sure it wasn't a satisfied customer. If I were you, 99, I wouldn't touch that food.

MAX BENDS OVER THE BODY.

99

Is he dead?

THE MAN LIFTS HIS HEAD.

MAN

Not yet.

SMART

Who are you? What's this all about?

MAN

(GASPS) The third tortilla from the bottom.

HE SLUMPS OVER DEAD.

SMART

Now he's dead.

99

The poor man. Max, do you think this was the work of KAOS?

SMART

Either that or those home delivery outfits are pretty fierce competitors.

FADE OUT:

END OF TEASER

ACT I

FADE IN:

2 INT. SMART'S APARTMENT—LATER
MAX AND 99 ARE GOING THROUGH THE TORTILLAS.

99

He said the third tortilla from the bottom. (SHE PULLS ONE OUT) Look, Max. This one has a hole in it.

SMART

Well, there's no use asking him to take it back.

99

Max, you know what I think this is? A recording.

SMART

That's exactly what I was going to think it was. (TAKES THE RECORD) I'll play it.

SMART GETS UP AND GOES TO HIS PHONOGRAPH. 99 FOLLOWS HIM.

SMART

(CONT'D) I wonder if it's 45 or 33⅓?

HE PUTS THE TORTILLA ON. WE HEAR A ROTTEN MARIACHI BAND.

> SMART

(CONT'D) That's one of the worst tortillas I ever heard.

> 99

Play the other side.

> SMART

Right. I hope it's the Tijuana Brass.

HE TURNS THE TORTILLA OVER.

> ISABELLA'S VOICE

(ON RECORD) This is the daughter of Don Carlos Hernandez, the president of San Saludos. My father is being held prisoner in a dungeon beneath the palace of General Diablo Sanchez, an agent of KAOS and an enemy of our people.

> 99

Why, that's terrible, Max.

> SMART

Yes, but not as bad as the mariachi band on the other side.

> ISABELLA'S VOICE

Please, Mr. Smart, my father has often talked about how brave and courageous you are. You must come to San Saludos and save him before he is killed. P.S. Please destroy this tortilla after you have played it.

> SMART

How do you like that, 99? Don Carlos Hernandez of San Saludos a prisoner of KAOS.

> 99

And he's depending on you for help. Did you save his life once?

> SMART

No. I just met him at an embassy party.

> 99

Then how does he know how brave and courageous you are?

> SMART

I told him.

99 REACTS.

> SMART

(CONT'D) I better call the Chief and tell him about this.

HE STARTS OFF.

> 99

(HOLDS OUT TORTILLA) Wait, Max. What about this? She wanted it destroyed.

> SMART

Oh, yes. Give it here, 99.

HE BREAKS THE TORTILLA IN HALF, GIVES ONE PIECE TO 99. THEY BOTH START
EATING THE TORTILLA TO CRACKLING NOISES.

DISSOLVE TO:

3 INT. CHIEF'S OFFICE—DAY
CHIEF, MAX, AND 99. THERE IS A SATCHEL ON THE DESK.

CHIEF

Now, Max, 99, we've got everything worked out for you. Once you get
through customs, you'll be met by our San Saludos agent—numero cinco
y ocho y quatro y seis y nuevo y uno y tres.

SMART

Gee, that's a long number, Chief. I'll never be able to remember it.
Couldn't I just call him Lopez?

CHIEF

(SURPRISED) You know his name?

SMART

Naturally. Who else is numero cinco y ocho y quatro y seis y nuevo y
uno y tres?

CHIEF

(REACTS) All right. When you meet him you'll give him the password—
Fernando Lamas loves Dolores Del Rio . . . He'll take you into the
capital.

99

Fernando Lamas loves Dolores Del Rio. Right, Chief!

CHIEF

You will take this satchel with you . . . The lining contains thirty-
thousand pesedas . . . That should be plenty to bribe your way into the
dungeon . . . and get Don Carlos out.

99

Right. But after we get him out of the dungeon—then what, Chief?

CHIEF

This satchel has a false bottom. Look at this.

THE CHIEF PRESSES A BUTTON AND THE BOTTOM FALLS OUT.

CHIEF

(CONT'D) It's a collapsible balloon that when filled with special high-
expansion gas is powerful enough to safely lift three people. The air
currents at San Saludos should carry all three of you right to the coast
where we can pick you up.

SMART

Great gimmick.

99

Fantastic!

CHIEF

I suggest that as soon as you get into San Saludos you plant the satchel in a field just outside of town, so it will be ready for your escape.

WHILE THE CHIEF IS TALKING, MAX HAS PICKED UP ONE OF SEVERAL CIGARS THAT ARE ON THE CHIEF'S DESK AND STARTS TO LIGHT IT.

SMART

Got you, Chief.

THE CHIEF SEES MAX LIGHTING THE CIGAR AND KNOCKS THE MATCH OUT OF HIS HAND.

CHIEF

Max, don't light that cigar!

SMART

(HURT) Well, I'm sorry, Chief. I'll be glad to pay you for it. They couldn't be more than two for fifteen.

CHIEF

No, no, Max. Those are not real cigars. They're explosives. Each has the power of a small bomb. You're going to take these with you in case of emergencies.

SMART

Oh.

99

Getting out seems to be all taken care of, but how do we get in? Won't they be suspicious of us?

CHIEF

I've taken care of that, too, 99. As you may or may not know, for years Control has been publicizing certain fictitious celebrities just for situations like this.

SMART

I don't get you, Chief.

CHIEF

We've created people, Max. People that are known all over the world except that they don't exist. For instance . . .

THE CHIEF PICKS UP A SMALL POSTER SHOWING A MAGICIAN PULLING A RABBIT OUT OF HIS HAT. THE RABBIT COVERS THE MAGICIAN'S FACE. ON THE POSTER WE READ "XANDU THE MAGICIAN. MIRACULOUS MAGIC."

CHIEF

(CONT'D) Xandu the Magician.

SMART

I've heard of him! He's great. He does the famous barrel trick. He puts an elephant in a barrel.

99

And then what?

SMART

What do you mean and then what? That's the trick. Getting an elephant in a barrel.

CHIEF

But you've never seen Xandu, have you, Max?

SMART

Well, now that you mention it, Chief, no.

CHIEF

Because he doesn't exist. We created and publicized him. And if you ever do see him he'll be one of our agents.

99

That's brilliant, Chief.

CHIEF

We also have Zubin Rubin and the Santa Barbara Philharmonic.

THE CHIEF HOLDS UP A POSTER SHOWING THE BACK OF A MAN CONDUCTING A HUGE ORCHESTRA. THE POSTER READS "ZUBIN RUBIN. ONE NIGHT ONLY."

CHIEF

(CONT'D) We use him when we have to get a big group in someplace.

SMART

How do you like that? No Zubin Rubin!

THE CHIEF HOLDS ANOTHER POSTER SHOWING AN ICE SKATER SPINNING. IT IS BLURRED SO THAT YOU CAN'T MAKE OUT HER FACE. THE POSTER READS: "THIS WEEK: THRILLS ON ICE. GLORIA DURSHLAG AND HER DANCING SKATES."

CHIEF

Gloria Durshlag and Her Dancing Skates.

SMART

I'm dazed, Chief. I hope you're not going to tell me there's no Debbie Reynolds.

CHIEF

There are a lot more, but here's the important one for you two.

THE CHIEF HOLDS OUT A POSTER OF TWO SPANISH DANCERS. THE MAN'S BACK IS SLIGHTLY TOWARD US. BOTH OF HIS HANDS ARE HELD HIGH COVERING HIS FACE. THE GIRL'S WHIRLING DRESS AND LONG HAIR COVER HER FACE. "JOSE OLE AND CONCHITA. WORLD FAMOUS FLAMENCO DANCERS. SEE JOSE DO HIS FAMOUS DEATH-DEFYING LEAP OVER FOUR HORSES."

99

(READING) Jose Ole and Conchita. World Famous Flamenco Dancers. See Jose do his famous death-defying leap over four horses.

SMART

Wow, I'd give anything to see them, Chief. I flip over flamenco dancers.

CHIEF

Max, you and 99 are going to be Jose Ole and Conchita.

SMART

What?

CHIEF

That's right, Max. San Saludos is having their annual fiesta and we've already booked you as the featured attraction.

SMART

Think of that, 99. We're going to be stars. Listen, Chief. Just out of curiosity, what are they paying us for this?

CHIEF

A thousand pesedas. Less ten percent for Control. After all, we did book the deal for you, Max.

SMART

Fair is fair.

99

But, Chief. Max can't dance. He can't even do the boogaloo. How could he possibly do a flamenco and leap over four horses?

CHIEF

He won't have to, 99. The fiesta is on Thursday. You're scheduled to arrive Wednesday afternoon. You'll make your escape that very night.

SMART

Oh, but what about all those people? Won't they be disappointed? After all, they came to see me, Chief.

CHIEF

(IGNORES MAX) Your plane leaves in twenty minutes. You'll fly to Buenos Aires where you'll make connections with a local airline that will bring you into San Saludos. Max, this is a difficult assignment and your lives will be in constant jeopardy. But there's one supreme danger you've got to be on guard against every moment.

SMART

What's that, Chief?

CHIEF

The entire time you're there, don't drink the water.

DISSOLVE TO:

4 CLOSE SHOT—LOUD SPEAKER

VOICE (from speaker)

(SPANISH ACCENT) Welcome to San Saludos. All first-class passengers on the Supreme royal deluxe red carpet flight please line up at Customs to inspect your luggage.

CAMERA PULLS BACK TO:

5 EXT. SAN SALUDOS AIRPORT—CUSTOMS

A TABLE IS SET UP NEAR THE OUTSIDE OF A BUILDING. SIGN READS: "EL CUSTOMS." TWO SOLDIERS, A SERGEANT AND A PRIVATE WITH A RIFLE, ARE OUR CUSTOMS AGENTS. THERE ARE FOUR OR FIVE PEASANTS IN THE LINE HAVING THEIR LUGGAGE INSPECTED. A COUPLE, CARRYING A BABY; ONE HAS A CHICKEN, ETC. WE CAN TELL IT IS NOT TOO CLASSY AN AIRLINE OR AIRPORT.

6 ANOTHER ANGLE
MAX AND 99 NOW STEP UP TO THE END OF THE LINE. THEY ARE DISGUISED AS JOSE OLE AND CONCHITA. MAX HAS LONG SIDEBURNS AND A MOUSTACHE. 99 HAS A BLACK WIG TIED IN A BUN, VERY SPANISH LOOKING. SHE HAS A BEAUTY MARK ON HER CHEEK, A TYPICAL SPANISH BEAUTY. THEY HAVE A SUITCASE PLUS THE SECRET-BOTTOM SATCHEL.

99

Max, what an awful flight. Just one engine and it kept missing, the wings kept flapping . . . and I've never been on such a slow plane.

SMART

You're right. (POINTS TO COUPLE WITH CHILD) When that couple got on they weren't eligible for the family plan.

99

Frankly, Max, I was frightened.

SMART

You think you were. Look!

HE POINTS O.S.

7 THEIR POV—THE PILOT
HE IS DRESSED IN OLD-FASHIONED PILOT'S CLOTHING, GOGGLES, LEATHER CAP, SCARF AROUND NECK, ETC. HE HAS A LIQUOR BOTTLE IN HIS HAND. HE WAVES HAPPILY TO MAX, TAKES A SWIG FROM HIS BOTTLE, AND THEN GETS DOWN ON HIS KNEES AND KISSES THE GROUND.

CUT TO:

8 MAX AND 99

SMART

Thank goodness we're going back by balloon.

99

Do you think we'll have any trouble getting the balloon through customs?

SMART

Of course not, 99. This false-bottom satchel is too clever. They've never seen anything like this.

9 ANOTHER ANGLE
THE LINE HAS MOVED. THERE IS ONLY ONE MAN IN FRONT OF SMART. THE MAN HAS A SATCHEL EXACTLY LIKE SMART'S. THE SERGEANT HAS DISCOVERED THE FALSE BOTTOM.

SERGEANT

What? Another false-bottom suitcase?

10 CLOSE SHOT—SMART
   HE LOOKS AT 99.

11 BACK TO SCENE

SERGEANT

You stupid pig! You think you can outsmart us with this foolishness?
What are you smuggling in here? (LOOKS AT IT, AMAZED) Coffee?

PEASANT

But, senor sergeant! This kind is Mountain Grown.

SERGEANT

Take this dog out and shoot him!

THE SOLDIER TAKES THE PEASANT OUT.

PEASANT

No . . . no.

IT'S NOW MAX AND 99'S TURN. THEY HAND THE SERGEANT THEIR PASSPORTS.

SERGEANT

Ahhh. The famous Jose Ole and Conchita. You have come to perform
at the fiesta.

SMART

(NERVOUS) Yes. We've come to perform at the fiesta.

99

Si. We've come to perform at the fiesta.

SMART

Si.

SERGEANT

(ENRAPTURED) Jose Ole and Conchita! For years I have admired you,
for years I knew of your famous leap over the four horses. Tell me, do
you still do the famous leap over the four horses?

SMART PUTS HIS LUGGAGE UP ON THE TABLE.

SMART

Si, but I've improved on it.

SERGEANT

You have? (HE EYES THE SATCHEL)

SMART

Now I leap over four horses and a false-bottom satchel.

SERGEANT

Ha, ha—you know, senor, it is my duty to inspect that satchel.

SMART

Actually, I prefer you didn't.

SERGEANT

Oh. How much would you prefer I didn't?

SMART

I would prefer five hundred pesedas you didn't.

SERGEANT

For just five hundred pesedas I would prefer I did.

99

We might prefer a thousand pesedas you didn't.

SERGEANT

For a thousand pesedas and a beautiful lady I would still prefer I did. (TO MAX) Senor, you are trying to bribe me, yes?

SMART

In one word, si.

SERGEANT

Then you are not very good at it. Do you know a thousand pesedas is only fifty cents in American money?

SMART

(INDIGNANT) Fifty cents! That's not bribing, that's tipping.

99

Look. How much do you want?

SERGEANT

(THINKS A MINUTE) Two thousand pesedas.

SMART

(STILL INDIGNANT) Two thousand pesedas. That's only a dollar.

SERGEANT

You're right. Four thousand pesedas.

SMART

But even that's . . .

99

Pay him, Max. Pay him!

SMART

I've got nothing against bribing, but tipping is still against my principles.

MAX OPENS THE SATCHEL, PULLS OUT SOME BILLS, AND GIVES THEM TO THE SERGEANT.

SERGEANT

Thank you.

SMART

Gracias.

THE SERGEANT SEES THE CIGARS IN MAX'S SUITCASE. HE TAKES ONE OUT.

SERGEANT

Wait a moment—What is this—American cigars? Do you mind?

SMART

Well, ah, ah . . . (HELPLESS) No. Help yourself. But you'll forgive me if I don't light it for you. Come on, 99.

THEY RUSH OFF.

12 SERGEANT

THE SERGEANT LOOKS AFTER MAX AND 99 FOR A MOMENT. HE BITES OFF THE END OF HIS CIGAR AND SPITS IT OUT. HE THEN PICKS UP A PHONE. THE PRIVATE RETURNS.

SERGEANT

(ON PHONE) Get me General Sanchez. (TO PRIVATE) I am calling the General. I have a strong suspicion about our last two visitors.

THE PRIVATE STRIKES A MATCH AND BRINGS IT TOWARD THE SERGEANT'S CIGAR.

SERGEANT

(CONT'D) Hello, General . . . Listen to this, please . . .

THE CIGAR IS LIT. THERE IS AN EXPLOSION.

13 EXT. ANOTHER AREA NEARBY

MAX AND 99 ARE HURRYING. THEY TURN AT THE BLAST AND LOOK UP IN THE AIR IN THE DIRECTION OF THE EXPLOSION.

99

Oh, those poor men.

SMART

Don't waste your sympathy on them, 99. They were killers and they would have killed us, too, if we hadn't given them a dollar.

99

You're right, Max.

SMART

Now the Chief said after we got through customs we would be met by our agent down here, Lopez. Where do you suppose he is?

99

There's a fellow over there, Max. I wonder if that could be him.

14 THEIR POV

THERE IS A PEON SITTING AGAINST THE WALL IN THE CLASSIC TRADITION OF THE PEASANT TAKING A SIESTA. A HUGE SOMBRERO IS OVER HIS FACE. MAX AND 99 WALK TO HIM.

SMART

Lopez—?

LOPEZ

(NOT LOOKING UP) Si, senor.

SMART

Fernando Lamas loves Dolores Del Rio.

LOPEZ

Oh, senor. You want Lopez the spy.

99

You are not Lopez the spy?

LOPEZ

No, I am Lopez the Informer.

SMART

Oh . . . Listen, Lopez the Informer, can you inform me where I can find Lopez the spy?

LOPEZ

I can give you that information but first I must inform you that I must be paid for my information.

SMART

How much must you be paid for your information?

LOPEZ

Would four thousand pesedas be too much?

SMART

No. That sounds reasonable.

LOPEZ

Then the price is eight thousand pesedas.

SMART

That's still only . . .

99

Pay him, Max! Pay him!

SMART TAKES MONEY OUT OF SATCHEL AND GIVES IT TO LOPEZ.

LOPEZ

Gracias, senor . . .

SMART

Now. Where is Lopez the spy?

LOPEZ

He is hanging around the plaza, senor.

99

Hanging around the plaza? What's he doing there?

LOPEZ

Just hanging. They hung him this morning.

99

Oh, Max, think of that . . . Numero cinco y ocho y quatro y seis y nuevo y uno y doce is dead.

SMART

Yeah. Well—I guess his number was up.

DISSOLVE TO:

15 EXT. PLAZA—LONG SHOT

IT IS A VERY SLEEPY PLAZA. THERE ARE JUST A FEW PEONS AROUND, ALL
VERY INACTIVE. A BURRO CART MOVES TOWARD THE CENTER. IN THE CART
ARE MAX AND 99. THE BURRO IS BEING LED BY THE DRIVER, AN OLD MAN. IT
STOPS RIGHT IN THE CENTER OF THE PLAZA. THE DRIVER PUSHES DOWN THE
METER.

DRIVER

Here you are, senor, senorita, the heart of town. Just as you wished.

99

How do you like this, Max? This is the capital of San Saludos.

DRIVER

(SADLY) Yes, it has changed a great deal since I started driving here.
It's not the same peaceful little town. All this hustle, bustle, the noise,
the traffic . . .

SMART

Well, you can't stop progress. How much do we owe you for the ride?

DRIVER

One hundred pesedas.

SMART

One hundred pesedas? All the way from the airport here? Boy, that's
cheap.

DRIVER

You're right. Two hundred pesedas.

SMART

But that's only . . .

99

Pay him, Max. Pay him!

MAX HANDS HIM SOME MONEY. THE DRIVER HANDS THE SUITCASE AND SATCHEL
TO MAX. JUST THEN A PEON WITH A PUSHCART COMES INTO SHOT AND STOPS
IN FRONT OF MAX. HE IS HOLDING A PIGEON IN HIS TWO HANDS.

SOUVENIR MAN

Souvenirs of San Saludos! Wallets, bedroom slippers, funny hats, mellow
yellow . . . (TO SMART) You care to buy a souvenir to remind you of
your glorious visit to San Saludos, senor?

SMART

No, thanks. Not right now.

SOUVENIR MAN

Perhaps the senor would like to buy a pigeon?

SMART

Sorry. Not interested.

THE SOUVENIR MAN SHRUGS HIS SHOULDERS AND RELEASES THE BIRD. IT FLIES
OFF.

SOUVENIR MAN

Every year the tourists get harder to please.

HE GOES OFF.

16 ANOTHER ANGLE

GENERAL SANCHEZ IS BEATING HIS WAY THROUGH A CLUSTER OF SEVERAL PEASANTS. ISABELLA IS BEHIND HIM. THE GENERAL IS MENACING. ISABELLA IS BEAUTIFUL.

SANCHEZ

Out of my way, you filthy peasants! Dogs, scum of the earth. Out of the way before I have you shot!

17 MAX, 99, AND DRIVER

99

Who is that?

DRIVER

It's our beloved General Sanchez, friend and defender of the common people.

GENERAL SANCHEZ AND ISABELLA COME INTO THE SHOT.

SANCHEZ

Ahh. Greetings, distinguished visitors to our humble country. You are the magnificant Don Jose and Conchita. (HE KISSES 99'S HAND) I recognized you on sight. I am General Diablo Sanchez, beloved leader, friend and defender of the common people.

WITH HIS WHIP HE SWINGS AT SEVERAL PEASANTS WHO HAVE MADE THE MISTAKE OF COMING TOO CLOSE.

SANCHEZ

(CONT'D) Back, you pig, you dog! You are breathing on my boots.

99

It is a pleasure to be here in your fair country, General Sanchez.

SMART

Yes, it's a real tropical paradise.

SANCHEZ

Thank you. I try to keep it that way. Of course at times it is difficult. We are constantly beset with spies, foreign agents, college students, those who would interfere with our domestic tranquillity.

SUDDENLY WE HEAR A VOLLEY OF SHOTS.

99

What was that?

SANCHEZ

Oh, it is just my soldiers rehearsing for the fiesta.

99

Rehearsing?

SMART

By the way, General Sanchez, what is this fiesta in honor of?

SANCHEZ

One of the most important holidays in my country. National Firing Squad Day.

WE HEAR ANOTHER VOLLEY OF SHOTS.

SANCHEZ

(CONT'D) They are rehearsing on a few peasants.

SMART

I wonder if AFTRA knows about this?

SANCHEZ

May I present Senorita Isabella Hernandez, my future bride.

ISABELLA STEPS FORWARD AND GIVES HER HAND TO SMART. SMART BENDS DOWN TO KISS IT.

ISABELLA

(WHISPERING) I am the one who sent you the tortilla. Did you get it?

SMART

(WHISPERS) Yes. It was delicious.

SMART STEPS BACK.

SMART

(CONT'D) I compliment you on the choice of a bride, General Sanchez.

SANCHEZ

Thank you. And I compliment you on the choice of a dancing partner, Senor Ole.

99

Thank you.

SANCHEZ

I cannot tell you how I have looked forward to seeing your world-famous performance.

SMART

Thank you. I am honored. Tomorrow you shall see the performance of your life.

SANCHEZ

Tomorrow? You do not dance tomorrow, Jose. You dance this afternoon.

99

This afternoon? I thought the fiesta was tomorrow.

SANCHEZ

Senorita, we have two fiestas. One on the afternoon before National Firing Squad Day. And the other on the next afternoon. The performance is always at the first fiesta.

SMART

But why?

SANCHEZ

Well, by the time of the second fiesta we seldom have enough people left for an audience.

SMART

Just a minute. Our contracts say that we dance tomorrow. We just got off the plane. It's impossible for us to dance this afternoon. Right, Conchita?

99

Oh, yes. It's impossible.

SEVERAL SOLDIERS RAISE THEIR GUNS.

SANCHEZ

Impossible?

SMART

(LOOKING AT RAISED GUNS) . . . Make that improbable.

THE SOLDIERS COCK THE GUNS.

SMART

(CONT'D) Dubious?

THE SOLDIERS COME FORWARD.

SANCHEZ

You will dance this afternoon or you will die.

SMART

(CONFIDENT ATTITUDE) General, we shall dance this afternoon.

SANCHEZ

Good. What made you change your mind?

SMART

Well, nobody ever explained it to me like you before.

HE AND 99 LOOK AT EACH OTHER.

FADE OUT:

END OF ACT I

ACT II

FADE IN:

18 EXT. BUILDING

SMART, IN FLAMENCO DANCING OUTFIT, HAS FINISHED CLIMBING DOWN FROM THE FIRST-FLOOR WINDOW BY MEANS OF BED SHEETS. HE IS HELPING 99 DOWN. SHE IS ALSO IN HER DANCING OUTFIT.

19 CLOSE SHOT—SMART AND 99

SMART

Well, we made it, 99.

A RIFLE IS PRESSED INTO THE SMALL OF HIS BACK. CAMERA PULLS BACK
REVEALING A SOLDIER—

SOLDIER

Si. Just in time to dance at the fiesta.

THERE IS ANOTHER SOLDIER THERE, AND THE TWO PROD SMART AND 99
FORWARD.

99

(WHISPERING) Max, what do we do now?

SMART

We dance. Oh, why didn't I stay up late and watch more Ricardo
Montalban movies.

AS THEY START TOWARD SQUARE WE HEAR CROWD NOISES.

CUT TO:

20 EXT. PLAZA—MAIN AREA

IT IS SET UP FOR THE ENTERTAINMENT. THERE ARE A FEW TABLES, A FEW
PEOPLE ON THE GROUND. ON A LOW PLATFORM AN ACT IS IN PROGRESS—TWO
CHEAP NONUNION ACROBATS. GENERAL SANCHEZ AND ISABELLA ARE SITTING
IN A SPECIAL LITTLE BOX. ISABELLA IS SAD. THE GENERAL IS ENJOYING
HIMSELF.

SANCHEZ

Why are you so sad, my little pigeon? In the midst of this wonderful fiesta?

ISABELLA

You know why I am sad, General. My father lies rotting in your dungeon.

SANCHEZ

It won't be for long. Right after the wedding we will let him out.

ISABELLA

Yes, to be shot by the firing squad.

SANCHEZ

(HURT) Isabella, I gave you my word that if you married me no harm
would come to Don Carlos.

ISABELLA

But I do not trust you.

THE GENERAL SHAKES HIS HEAD REPROACHFULLY. THE ACT IS OVER. THE
PEOPLE APPLAUD. THE MC COMES ON THE STAGE.

MC

And now, ladies and gentlemen, the act you've been waiting for, the really
big attraction of the fiesta, the world-famous, everybody knows them,
Jose Ole and Conchita.

THE PEOPLE APPLAUD.

SANCHEZ

Ahhh, now we shall see something. Even you, my sad little canary, should
enjoy this.

SANCHEZ STANDS UP APPLAUDING. ALL THE PEOPLE LOOK OFF IN THE DIREC-
TION THEY EXPECT JOSE OLE AND CONCHITA TO COME IN FROM. THEY DO NOT
COME IN.

SANCHEZ

(CONT'D) Where are they? Where are Jose Ole and Conchita? Bring them
on! Bring them on!

JUST THEN THE TWO SOLDIERS WITH RIFLES BRING ON MAX AND 99.

SANCHEZ

(CONT'D) What is the meaning of this?

FIRST SOLDIER

We found them at the rear of the hotel, General. They were sliding down
bed sheets from their hotel window.

SANCHEZ

Sliding down bed sheets? Why would you do a thing like that, senor?

SMART

Well, uh . . . uh, I heard someone yell fire.

SANCHEZ

But there is no fire. Why would anyone do that?

SMART

Come to think of it, he also yelled ready, aim.

SANCHEZ

Anyway, you are here and we are ready for your performance. You are
prepared for your leap over the four horses?

SMART

I've been meaning to talk to you about that, General. You see, I've got
this ingrown toenail . . .

SANCHEZ

So?

SMART

Well—would you settle for three chickens and an iguana?

SANCHEZ

Enough of this nonsense. I am growing impatient. Begin now. No more
delay. Escort them to the stage.

THE SOLDIERS LEAD MAX AND 99 TO THE STAGE. THE PEOPLE APPLAUD.

SANCHEZ

(CONT'D) (SITTING DOWN, MUSING) I wonder if Lopez the Informer was
right.

ISABELLA

What do you mean?

SANCHEZ

He told me these two were impostors, that they are not dancers at all, but Control Agents.

ISABELLA

(WORRIED) You cannot believe Lopez. You know that.

SANCHEZ

We shall see what we are to believe. When they dance I will know.

21 MAX AND 99

THEY ARE ON THE STAGE. THE MUSIC STARTS.

SMART

99, I have a dreadful feeling that this is going to be Jose Ole's farewell appearance.

99

Max, we can't afford to think negative. Think positive.

SMART

I am. I'm positive we're gonna be shot.

MAX AND 99 GO INTO THEIR DANCE. 99 CARRIES THE BALL. WITH A ROSE IN HER MOUTH SHE STARTS DANCING ABOUT. SHE ISN'T BAD AT ALL. THE AUDIENCE GETS WITH HER.

SMART

(CONT'D) Hey, not bad. Where did you learn that?

99

We had a Spanish maid.

SHE CONTINUES DANCING.

22 SANCHEZ AND ISABELLA

ISABELLA

They are very good. They cannot be impostors.

SANCHEZ

Maybe. We shall see.

THE MUSIC CONTINUES. IT STARTS TO GET TO MAX. HE FINDS HE CAN HARDLY CONTROL HIMSELF AND STARTS CLAPPING AND STAMPING HIS FEET AND YELLING "OLE! OLE!" THE AUDIENCE LOVES IT.

SMART

(TO 99) Hey, 99, they love me—

HE STARTS TO STAMP HIS FEET A LITTLE MORE, SNAPPING HIS FINGERS AND GRADUALLY BUILDING UP STEAM.

99

Take it easy, Max . . . Max!

SMART

Look at them, 99. I'm a hit! I'm a hit! They're eating it up!

NOW MAX REALLY CARRIES THE BALL. HE DANCES AROUND 99, SNAPPING HIS FINGERS.

99

Please, Max . . .

MAX IS IN ANOTHER WORLD, CARRIED AWAY BY IT ALL.

SMART

Don't bother me, 99. I'm in the *mood!*

23 SANCHEZ AND ISABELLA

SANCHEZ

The leap! The leap! Bring in the horses.

24 MAX AND 99

99

(TERRIFIED) Max, they're bringing horses for your leap.

SMART

Marvelous! Bring 'em up . . .

99

But Max, you'll be . . .

SMART

I can do it, 99. I know I can do it. Si! Ole!

THE MUSIC CONTINUES. THE SOLDIERS BRING FOUR HORSES UP TO THE EDGE OF THE STAGE. THE AUDIENCE STARTS TO YELL, "THE LEAP! THE LEAP!"

99

Max! Max!

SMART

Out of my way, 99. Here I go.

MAX TAKES A FLYING LEAP INTO THE SIDE OF THE FIRST HORSE AND FALLS DOWN. THERE IS A DISAPPOINTED NOISE FROM THE CROWD.

99

Ooooh, Max.

SMART

I wonder if they'd let me have two out of three.

25 SANCHEZ AND ISABELLA

SANCHEZ

Seize them! Take them to the dungeon.

DISSOLVE TO:

26 INT. DUNGEON

MAX, 99, AND DON CARLOS. DON CARLOS IS AN OLD WHITE-HAIRED MAN. HE SITS ON A CRUDE BENCH AGAINST THE WALL.

SMART

I feel terrible, Don Carlos. I messed this whole thing up.

DON CARLOS

Don't reproach yourself, my son. You did your best. You were very brave to come here at all.

99

That's right, Max. You can't go through life blaming yourself.

SMART

Who's going through life? We'll be shot in an hour.

THE DOOR TO THE CELL OPENS AND A GUARD THROWS ISABELLA IN. THEY AD-LIB "ISABELLA." SHE RUSHES TO HER FATHER'S ARMS.

DON CARLOS

Isabella, why are you here?

ISABELLA

Oh, father. I could not let you die alone so I confessed to General Sanchez that it was I who sent the tortilla to Mr. Smart.

99

Oh, Max. This is terrible. Isn't there anything we can do?

SMART

I don't know . . . Wait a minute, 99. Of course there's something we can do. My shoe phone. I'll put in a call to the Chief. He'll think of something.

MAX REMOVES HIS SHOE AND TAKES OUT THE PHONE. IT'S IN SEVERAL PIECES. WIRES HANG DOWN.

SMART

(CONT'D) You know something? Flamenco dancing is not the greatest thing for shoe phones.

WE HEAR THE FIRING SQUAD.

99

What was that?

DON CARLOS

The firing squad. Another poor soul has gone to his reward.

A GUARD APPROACHES THE CELL DOOR.

GUARD

(WHISPER) Psst! Psst! Senor!

MAX APPROACHES THE BARS.

SMART

(WHISPERS) Yeah?

GUARD

(WHISPERS) In just a few minutes you are scheduled to die.

SMART

Why are you whispering? Everybody knows it.

GUARD

You do not understand, senor. Perhaps I can help you. It has been some-times arranged that for a certain number of American dollars the firing squad could be persuaded to use blanks.

SMART

You mean the firing squad can be bribed? Why, that's terrible! Corrupt! They should be ashamed of themselves.

99

Max, Max, listen to him. We may be able to save our lives.

SMART

Right, 99. (TO GUARD) What's the deal?

GUARD

Eighty American dollars, senor.

SMART

Eighty dollars! Are you out of your mind? I'd rather die first.

99

Max!

SMART

(TO 99) You have to bargain with 'em, 99. They expect it. Do you want us to look like tourists? (TO GUARD) Forty dollars!

GUARD

Seventy!

SMART

Fifty-five!

GUARD

Sixty-three!

SMART

Fifty-nine!

GUARD

Sixty!

SMART

No. You've had my last offer.

GUARD

Senor, we are only a dollar apart.

SMART

I don't care. It's the principle of the thing.

99

Max!

SMART

Listen, 99. He's trying to take us. You can get the same deal in Panama for thirty-nine ninety-five.

WE HEAR THE FIRING SQUAD GO OFF.

SMART

(CONT'D) All right, sixty dollars. Will you take a credit card? When I travel, I never carry more than fifty dollars in cash.

99

Max, here. I've got ten dollars.

99 LIFTS HER DRESS AND TAKES OUT TEN DOLLARS FROM HER STOCKING AND HANDS IT TO MAX.

SMART

All right.

MAX REACHES INTO THE POCKET OF HIS FLAMENCO PANTS, PULLS OUT HIS EMPTY HAND, REACHES IN AGAIN, PULLS OUT HIS EMPTY HAND.

99

What's the matter?

SMART

(PUTTING HIS HAND BACK IN HIS POCKET AND CLOSING IT) When I hold onto the money, I can't get my hand out of my pocket.

HE MAKES AN EXTRA EFFORT, PULLS HIS HAND OUT OF HIS POCKET, AND HANDS SOME BILLS TO THE GUARD.

GUARD

Gracias.

THE GUARD LEAVES. 99, DON CARLOS, AND ISABELLA CONGRATULATE MAX.

99

Max, you did it!

SMART

Yeah. I hope it's deductible. Now listen, everyone. Here's what we do. When the firing squad shoots, we all fall down and play dead. When I see the coast is clear, I'll give you a signal, and we run to that field just west of the plaza.

DON CARLOS

But, Senor Smart, we will be captured.

99

No. We have an aerial balloon hidden there that will take us to safety.

DON CARLOS

We owe you our lives.

THE GUARD APPROACHES.

GUARD

Pssst! Senor!

MAX GOES OVER TO THE GUARD.

SMART

Back already? That was quick. Did you do it? Did you bribe the guards?

GUARD

Well, yes and no, senor.

SMART

What do you mean, yes and no?

GUARD

I could only bribe half of them.

SMART

Half of them? That's terrible.

GUARD

Well, it's not all bad, senor. You get half your money back. Here. Twenty-seven dollars.

SMART

Twenty-seven? I should get thirty.

GUARD

Well, there's ten percent for me, senor. After all, I booked the deal.

MAX SIGHS.

WIPE TO:

27 EXT. PLAZA

MAX, 99, DON CARLOS, AND ISABELLA ARE LINED UP AGAINST THE WALL. THE FIRING SQUAD IS IN POSITION. GENERAL SANCHEZ IS TALKING TO THEM.

SANCHEZ

Well, my friends, we come to the end of the road, eh? You do not know how it grieves me to have to say good-bye to you all . . . especially to you, Isabella, my little hummingbird. If only you had not chosen to betray me we could have been so happy together.

ISABELLA

I would much rather die than marry you, you pig, you dog, you rotten filthy swine, you lowlife . . .

SMART

Shhh, Isabella, don't make trouble.

SANCHEZ

Would any of you like a blindfold? A last cigarette?

SMART

No, I'm trying to break the habit.

SANCHEZ

Please, senor, it is no time for stupid jokes.

DON CARLOS

Sanchez, I have only one thing to say to you! You can enslave some of the people all of the time and all of the people some of the time, but you cannot enslave all of the people all of the time!

THE GENERAL PUTS BOTH THUMBS TO HIS EARS, WAGGLES HIS FINGERS.

SANCHEZ

Yeah, yeah, yeah!

SMART

General—do you mind if we say good-bye to each other?

SANCHEZ

Why, certainly—go ahead.

SMART

Good-bye, 99.

99

Good-bye, Max. Good-bye, Don Carlos.

DON CARLOS

Good-bye, senorita. Good-bye, Mr. Smart.

SMART

Good-bye, Don Carlos. Good-bye, Isabella.

99

Good-bye, Isabella. Good-bye, Max.

SMART

Good-bye, 99. Good-bye, General.

SANCHEZ

Good-bye, Smart. Good-bye, Don Car . . . (REALIZES HE'S BEEN SUCKED IN) That's enough!

HE GOES BEHIND THE FIRING SQUAD TO GIVE THE ORDERS. THE SQUAD COMES TO ATTENTION.

99

Max, I just want you to know it's been wonderful knowing you.

SMART

We're not dead yet, 99. Don't give up hope. Remember, those are soldiers. They respond to commands automatically.

99

What do you mean, Max?

SMART

Ssshhh . . .

SANCHEZ

Firing squad, attention! . . . Ready! Aim!

SMART

About face!

THE SQUAD TURNS AROUND POINTING THEIR GUNS AT SANCHEZ. SANCHEZ DOES NOT REALIZE THIS.

SANCHEZ

Fire!

THE FIRING SQUAD FIRES. SANCHEZ DROPS. THERE IS CONFUSION.

99

Max, that was brilliant!

MAX TAKES 99'S HAND.

SMART

The old about-face routine and they fell for it. Come on, let's get out of here.

MAX, 99, DON CARLOS, AND ISABELLA RUN OFF AMIDST THE CONFUSION.

DISSOLVE TO:

28 EXT. FIELD

MAX, 99, ISABELLA, AND DON CARLOS COME TO A SPOT IN THE FIELD WHERE THE SUPER SATCHEL IS. MAX STARTS TO REMOVE THE BALLOON.

SMART

I'll just inflate it and we'll be off.

MAX PULLS OUT THE PACKET, A CYLINDER OF GAS, AND PRESSES A BUTTON.

29 CAMERA ON THE FACES OF DON CARLOS, ISABELLA, AND 99 AS THEY WATCH THE BALLOON INFLATE.

WE HEAR THE SOUND OF THE GAS.

DON CARLOS

Ingenious!

ISABELLA

Marvelous!

99

It really works, Max!

30 SMART IN BALLOON

THE BALLOON IS INFLATED AND HELD DOWN BY A ROPE. ALL WE SEE IS THE BASKET AND ROPES GOING UP.

SMART

Come on, get in. We'll get out of here. Hurry, the soldiers are coming.

THEY ALL SCRAMBLE IN.

31 LONG SHOT—SOLDIERS

RUNNING TOWARD THEM.

32 BACK TO BALLOON

99

Wait, Max. We can't all go. There's four of us. The balloon will only take three.

SMART

That's right. Well, you three go.

MAX JUMPS OUT AND STARTS TO CUT THE ROPE TO RELEASE THE BALLOON.

SMART

(CONT'D) I'll stay behind.

99 JUMPS OUT.

99

No, no, Max. If you stay, I stay.

SMART

(STILL CUTTING ROPE) Get back in, 99.

DON CARLOS JUMPS OUT.

DON CARLOS

No, no. You three go. I am an old man. It makes no difference to me.

SMART

Don Carlos, get back in. And you too, 99.

ISABELLA JUMPS OUT. THE BALLOON IS EMPTY.

ISABELLA

No, I will not go without my father. If he stays, I stay.

SMART

Look, please, will the three of you get back in there and . . .

THE ROPE SNAPS. THE BALLOON RISES.

DON CARLOS

The balloon!

ISABELLA

It's escaping!

SMART

Ohhhh!

THEY ALL WATCH HELPLESSLY AS IT GOES UP.
SOUND OF SOLDIERS YELLING. THEY ALL LOOK O.S.

99

Max, I'm afraid it's all over now.

33 MED. SHOT—POV
THE SOLDIERS ARE RUNNING TOWARD THEM.

34 MAX, 99, ISABELLA, AND DON CARLOS
THEY ARE HORRIFIED.

99

What are we going to do, Max?

SMART

There's only one thing we can do. Good-bye, 99. Good-bye, Isabella.
Good-bye, Don Carlos.

THEY ALL START SAYING GOOD-BYE.

FADE OUT.

END OF ACT II

TAG

FADE IN:

35 EXT. FIELD

MAX, 99, ISABELLA, AND DON CARLOS ARE SURROUNDED BY SOLDIERS.

99

Oh, Max.

SHE CLUTCHES HIS ARM.

SMART

(TO SOLDIERS) Well, what are you waiting for? If you're gonna shoot, shoot. Get it over with.

DON CARLOS

Yes, shoot, but there's just one thing I want to say first. You can shoot all of the people some of the time and some of the people all of the time but you cannot shoot all of the people all of the time!

SMART

Maybe not, but they seem to be trying.

FIRST SOLDIER

I think there is some mistake, Don Carlos. We have not come to shoot you. Now that the General is dead, we are free and we want you to come back and take your rightful place as President of San Saludos.

DON CARLOS

What?

ISABELLA

(HUGGING FATHER) Oh, father, father.

SMART

What do you think about that, 99?

FIRST SOLDIER

The fiestas were much better when you were in power. This last one . . . (TURNS THUMBS DOWN AND GIVES IT A RASPBERRY)

THE SOLDIERS AD-LIB AGREEMENT. "SI! SI!" THEY ALL TURN THUMBS DOWN AND GIVE A RASPBERRY.

DON CARLOS TURNS TO SMART.

DON CARLOS

Well! I am president again. How can I ever repay you.

HE KISSES MAX ON BOTH CHEEKS.

SMART

That's not exactly what I had in mind.

DON CARLOS

What can I do for you? Name it.

99

Thank you very much, Don Carlos. But all we want is to get back to our country.

DON CARLOS

Very well, I will arrange for first-class tickets for you on our airline.

SMART

Don Carlos, I have changed my mind. I do have a small request.

FLIP TO:

36 EXT. ROAD

MAX AND 99, WITH THEIR LUGGAGE, ARE NOW IN THE CART. DON CARLOS, ISABELLA, AND THE CROWD ARE WATCHING THEM.

SMART

All right, Pedro, Washington, D.C., and don't spare the burro.

THE CART STARTS OFF AS THE CROWD CHEERS AND WAVES GOOD-BYE.

FADE OUT:

THE END

It reads fast and smooth, does it not? Even with a kind of nutty coherence and plausibility.

Studied more closely and more coldly, this script will be found to be jammed with clues for this kind of comedy writing, jammed with tricks and treasures that will have great practical value to the new television writer. For the most part, as in the dispatch of any professional work, the actual *technique* is neatly hidden in the speed of the story's execution. You don't see the moving parts working until you slow down the mechanism and look for them, look *at* them. But they're here, and some of them are so well displayed, so neatly delivered, as to stand out to the practiced editorial eye almost as if they were in italics.

Let us go over it now.

Professional script values, easy to pass by unnoticed, begin with the very first shot in the first scene. What are these values?

Here's one, and it's immediate: the stamp of *relationship* between the two principals. This appears at once. And there is just the faintest romantic tug to it, to 99's part of it, anyhow. And therefore to ours: "It's so domestic. It's almost as if we were . . . well . . ." She's ironing his things and enjoying it.

We know what she means. But does Smart? He does not. Nor does he ever know. He's television's most unconquerable square. But 99 is loyal anyhow, even though Max kept going through season after season ignoring her vast availability. And with a dish like 99, expertly played by Barbara Feldon, this takes a curious brand of ignoring. For she is a very considerable bundle. In a single side-glance this girl can be roguish, skeptical, sexy, weak, or indomitable. To us she is winning and lovable and exquisitely feminine. To Smart she's office furniture.

What else is present Much. Notice how Max almost always talks to the *circumstance,* rather than to others in the cast. It's almost as if he sees the action, then turns his back on it in order to address the audience at home, saying, "Well, you saw it. Now let me tell you what *I* make of it."

In other words, we very early get a pronounced character *attitude* from Smart, an attitude that maintains itself consistently in every scene. He is a congenital misser of overtones. He believes he thinks in practical terms and he sometimes does, but this seldom relates to any observable practicality in his actions. Though totally unprepared for every exigency in life (despite his shoe phone), he remains unharmed through self-belief. And this grand charade of self-belief continues firmly through every show, masking his massive incompetence from himself.

Max bypasses 99's wistful little reference to domestic living, made while she labors at the ironing board. He just hasn't heard. His mind is on the high price of Chinese laundries. Fixing him early (or fitting it early into the viewer's mind) as a man who is excessively money-conscious has an important plot purpose. The writers deliberately emphasize it and do so at the start. Max misses 99's insinuation about the pajamas and stays with the cost of shirts. We are told twice. Twenty-four cents apiece. "And they don't even put them on hangers."

He's doing the talking. She's doing the ironing. (And the dreaming.)

Do we like him? Sure. He's smug and comfortable and unmanly and self-approving and elaborately stuffy. But we know he's vulnerable. And we know he's about to get knocked around something awful. We know, too, that, though incompetent, he'll be game at the end, that if such were needed he'd instantly die for 99.

We also like him because 99 does. And this affectionate allegiance, although quiet, is one of the most persistent elements in the series. The writers give this another nudge when the Chile Delight arrives and 99 thinks (hopes) he's ordered dinner for her. But no. "This guy made a mistake."

This guy, a peon, now falls on his face. There is a knife sticking out of his back. Which 99, ever compassionate, notices. It is important to note the following: scrupulous attention is paid to the abundantly obvious throughout this series. That is a "must" for this kind of comedy. Do it this way yourself. It is part of the fun.

The stabbing is our first emergency. Does Smart act? Yes. To any effect? Of course not. But another ingredient to his character shows itself here. He is unshakably phlegmatic. He never blinks. Nothing jars his matter-of-factness.

Just before the end of the "Teaser" there is a great though tiny moment. Can you see what a good time the camera (and the director) had in the comic death scene? The "corpse" contradicting his own passing, then gasping the magic clue then dying. Max's line—"Now he's dead"—is a marvelous redundance, telling us something we already know because the camera has just got through showing it to us.

In Shot 2, with the action still in Smart's apartment, it is clear the writers are well into their own frenzy, that they're happily caught in their own mood. It's a subtle revelation but a true one, and it occurs in this direction: "Max and 99 are going through the tortillas."

The writers have bought their own illusion. They're *treating* the tortillas like something you can sort, like cards, or records, or photos in an album.

There is a quality to the writing, a quality that belongs to all good professional work, that must by now have suggested itself to the reader, even though the quality is an invisible one. It is the quality of *assurance*. We buy the story because, consciously or not, we know the writers know where they are taking us.

Why is this important? It is important because the attribute of assurance enhances our enjoyment and does so by intensifying our sense of participation. We are in the hands of experts and we know it. A good crew is at the controls. So we can relax. We know that insinuated promises are going to be kept, that suspicions will be realized. We know that the worst that could happen is now about to.

How does the writer *find* this assurance? For the veteran it has become automatic through long practice. For the new writer, much trouble can be cleared away at the start if he writes from a plan, if he works from a detailed breakdown.

This plan should have two parts: first, a listing of the story's *main elements;* second, a structured scene-by-scene schedule of the story's *progress*. Let this second part read like a railroad timetable. That is really what it is. If you adhere to it, you won't lose your cars in the switchyards of momentary inspiration. These moments are seldom inspired. Usually they just confuse or delay. Almost always, even though they may be individually pretty, they clutter your script. They slow it down. Actors have to stand around waiting for the dragging line to be delivered.

This is poor in any script—fatal in comedy.

In the *Get Smart* script under study here there is no stammering. Its very stumblings are surefooted. The deadpan silliness that accompanies their getting the tortilla spinning around on the turntable has a swift progressiveness and brings us quickly to the point: Isabella's voice. This is the third fixture in the plot, the first two being the dying delivery boy and the "third tortilla from the bottom."

By the time Max and 99 destroy the tortilla (they eat it—great pantomime here), a great deal of forward motion is visible. We're going somewhere, and KAOS, most pandemic of all villains, is the cause of it all.

Shot 3 sets up the mission we're to undertake. It also produces some of the equipment which (naturally) won't work at the right time, some simple instructions we know will be flivvered, and a pile of furnishings valuable for such missions—exploding cigars, bribe money, passwords, a "contact," a satchel with a false bottom. And disguises.

This kind of nonsense has to be fast. And continuous. Any letdown breaks the illusion. Once broken, it can't be patched together in the same scene.

Notice how the writers have contrived to make the satchel conspicuous. It's first displayed on the Chief's desk. Then its magic is demonstrated. We *see* the false bottom, see it pop out. We don't have to see the balloon, but we have to know it's there and functional.

There's something else right in here, too. Somehow we must be persuaded to go along with the creation of all those imaginary people: Xandu, Zubin Rubin, Gloria Durshlag. Do we do this? Of course. How? The Chief makes a convincing sell, producing posters to prove his point. Max himself has heard of Xandu. We, the audience, buy it because we've just seen Max and 99 buy it. In fact, Max is already imagining himself in his new role. And loving it.

After learning of these new roles, there is another mention of money. And good reason for this. The writers are building up to the running gag they have so much fun with, beginning in Shot 11. They are setting this up. And setting up another at the same time. Note the line, "After all, we did book the deal for you, Max." When we hit this same line in Shot 26, much later and under quite different conditions, it explodes a tremendous laugh. *But the preparation for it is going on here.*

Another important element is being moved into the story here—the "leap over the four horses." It becomes firmly planted. We know we're headed for early catastrophe. This is sharpened, not diminished, when the Chief tells Max he probably won't have to go through with it. But we know better. It's too good to lose.

The most perfect comedy line of the whole script is in this exchange. Max, in his imagination, is already performing. He can't bear the idea of disappointing the crowd: "After all, they came to see me, Chief." This bit of vanity is so mountainously fatuous that the Chief does the only thing possible, he ignores it.

Shot 3 has given us all the props our leads will have to carry into the coming action. The scene has been fun. It has also been a long one. And a more or less static one; no exits or entrances, no new people, no movement. The pace and speed of the show need a shot in the arm right here, and quickly get it. How? By *a sequence of fast, short scenes:* arrival in San Saludos; airport and Customs; Max and 99 in disguise; the airlines atmosphere (flight passenger with chicken, pilot with scarf, goggles, whiskey); lineup for Customs; first embarrassment with false-bottom suitcase.

Note how very much, in both mood and movement, has been brought to the viewer's eye and to his feelings in such a short time span. A matter of seconds, not minutes. Fine flavors are added to the fun by the Spanish disguises, of course, and Smart's impassive, confident blundering with the satchel is consistent with his impeccable pattern of mismanagement.

What has been illustrated there is the effectiveness of *speed*. In your own work, use this trick for fast pickup after any needed expository slowdown.

Use juxtaposition, too. We have it here. It can always deliver a jolt when a jolt is needed.

Nearly everything Smart does, or says, is almost immediately contradicted by action. Thus, "They've never seen anything like this" false-bottom satchel is instantly followed by the sergeant's disgust: "What? Another false-bottom suitcase? ... Take this dog out and shoot him!" Besides being good juxtaposition, this is good comedy *timing*. Why?

Because we're next.

Passing through the Customs line, the writers have missed nothing. The leap over the four horses gets another notice. The trick satchel goes on display again. And Smart, in one of his best moments of mental lapse, *points out* that he has a false-bottom satchel.

This leads to the bargaining scene—the first of three in the running gag (a device developed in vaudeville) that ends each time with, "Pay him, Max. Pay him!" This is the best single scene in the script—from the point of view of comedic ingenuity. We've had three distinct reminders about what a tightwad Max is, or at least how cost-conscious he is: the shirts, the cigars, and the matter of their getting paid for their flamenco act. Now we get a complete *reverse* on all this. When the currency exchange between the dollar and the peseda is made clear to Smart, and he realizes the bribe he's being asked to pay is peanuts, is this penny-pinching opportunist relieved? No. He's outraged! "That's not bribing, that's tipping." The bargaining stumbles absurdly forward till 99, ever practical, closes it out.

We get "Pay him, Max!" twice more, as you'll remember from your reading of the script, and each one with its own buildup. This incremental repetition—just as it does in English balladry—enriches the flavor with each new utterance. You will seldom find a more easily spotted, effectively employed illustration of the running gag than this example. Here it is as conspicuous as a clump of birches in a stand of fir. Use the device. It's in the public domain.

Something else to note right here, the business with the cigar. This illustrates another rule of comedy writing: don't plant anything unless you exploit it. No matter how pleasant it may seem to you, the writer, when you first set it down, no matter how decorative, you will learn that your little piquancies and conceits and fillips of cleverness are *not* decorative. They are debris.

If your momentary invention doesn't add a brick to the staircase you're building, *leave it out*. Regarding all such incidentalism, here's a good rule, simply stated:

Use it or lose it.

The new writer, the beginning scriptwriter, can go over almost any script that is a fine example of its particular sort and make new findings even after several readings, just as a good orchestra conductor can find new meanings by rereading a good score. Illustrating this point is the delicate little touch at the start of Shot 13. We've just had the explosion that ended Shot 12. Look, now, at the reaction scene. The direction here instantly infuses this new scene with its special quality: "They turn at the blast and look up in the air." At home, we who are watching Max and 99 see that their eyes follow trajectories. Of what? Of bodies hurtling through space. It is much funnier that we *don't* see, that our heroes do it for us.

Should we feel sorry for anyone here? Certainly not. This is a rough crowd. "They would have killed us, too, if we hadn't given them a dollar."

Keep the script clear and open. Keep the script obvious and fast. About the obvious, always give it deadly weight. Another bit of license should be mentioned here. If you're afraid your audience is going to forget something, use a reminder. For example, it's been some time since we heard about Lopez. This is the agent Smart and 99 are to contact. We're going to bring him on now, so we need to know who he is. And so we do; his name is just lugged in.

The writers have some fun with this little scene. They get an obliging Lopez but they get the wrong one. Visually, something else quite charming occurs here. Did you notice? The scene is played without his ever looking up.

We also get a repeat of the money haggle. This is the second time we've bumped it. And we bounce one more laugh off the 007 nonsense that's been played with earlier—the long string of Spanish numerals. In going out of this scene, 99 pumps in just one more: "Doce." After so many numbers, the tag line writes itself.

Something else that is useful for new writers to absorb and to use is present throughout this script: *economy* of scene setting. An immediate impression of San Saludos' main plaza is swiftly delineated by a couple of drowsing peons, just as the whole character of the airport was earlier limned in by chickens, just as the villainy of General Sanchez is billboarded by his self-complimentary title ("beloved leader") and his whip. As to the quality of fiesta entertainment, the writers have completely informed us, and in the fewest possible words: "Two cheap nonunion acrobats." The word "nonunion" says everything any casting director is going to need.

How much more do we need to know about the general than this: "The general is menacing"? Or of Isabella than "Isabella is beautiful"?

The above has to do with economy. A great burden of detail can be insinuated or made clear, even vivid, by a single phrase, often by the use of the exact word.

Here's the rule: Better brief than labored.

You'll get quicker response from all three of the sources you wish most to influence: your producer, your cast, and your audience.

One more note on economy and we'll drop the subject. This one (see Shot 30) has a most precious importance but an importance that has nothing to do with the script. It has to do with production. Do we really have a balloon? No. No one ever sails away in it, so there is no real need for it. The illusion is sufficient, the ropes, the basket, the compressed air to inflate the bag. But we don't have to see the big bag tugging at its mooring. Or see it escaping, once freed. Because it is not absolutely necessary, it's left out.

Several thousand dollars are saved. And comedy writers who think in terms of budget are far more welcome than those who think in terms of Cecil B. De Mille. To any treasurer, unit manager, producer, or budget-control executive, that single sentence in Shot 30—"All we see is the basket and ropes going up"—is the true mark of the established professional.

The writer who makes a habit of indicating cost cuts and production economies can always find a team to play on.

Scattered through this same script are some lovely ironies that should not be missed. How many can you spot? Shot 20 contains my favorite. It's Isabella's line, "You cannot believe Lopez. You know that." Another (Shot 26) is Smart's line, haggling over the amount of the bribe that will fix the firing squad: "I'd rather die first." Later, lined up against the wall, he's offered a last cigarette and refuses: "I'm trying to break the habit."

Much of the comedy in the *Get Smart* series—and this is true of many comedy shows—lies in the principals never trying to be funny, never thinking they are funny, never seeing anything as funny, and never milking a line. Their own responses are primitive and literal. The use of clichés is conscientious and deliberate. There is a childish quality to all the talk. And all the whispered, secret plotting is, of course, desperately public. Farewell scenes before firing squads become so moving as to envelop everyone, and cab meters find their way into burro carts.

In this one script we have had fine comedy coming from:

The unexpected
The irrelevant
The anachronistic
The juxtaposed
The ambiguous
The incongruous
The contradictory

The surest way there, however, is first things first. Here the first thing is the laydown of your story's main elements. This is followed by the schedule of your story's progress, scene by scene. The story must exist before anything at all can happen. The breakdown of the story, by scenes, should exist as your guide to dialogue. *And no dialogue should be written without this preliminary diagramming.*

Notes on Sam Bobrick and Bill Idelson

All through this book I have deliberately scattered notes and quotes by, or about, writers. Teams and collaborations have always intrigued me, the fortuity by which they seem to occur and the once-in-a-thousand happy result. You have just seen some fine work by a most odd couple.

Here is how Sam Bobrick got into television. He has the daffiest background of any television writer I know. Nothing seems to have served him as an assist toward the happy elevation he enjoys today. (He has done much of the extremely high-paid work for the Smothers Brothers.) But how did he begin?

While a student of accounting (a subject he loathed) in Chicago, he enlisted in the air force and went down to Lackland AFB outside of San Antonio. Here it was discovered that he'd been studying accounting. It was never discovered that he couldn't fly. He was assigned to accounting in Texas (the Korean War was on—this was in 1951). Then he was sent to the accounting school at Lowry Field, outside Denver. Then next to New Jersey (Camp Kilmer), then Clinton County AFB in Ohio, then back to Lowry for more accounting.

Did he fly, back and forth? Only once. It made him violently ill. Thereafter, he was shunted around by train. At Lowry he poked into the air force library to see if he were developing a mere neurosis or a true psychosis. He puzzled air force psychiatrists. He was permitted to work on *The Tribe Scribe*, a service paper that tried for a low-key Earl Wilson kind of gossip. "It had the lowest rating of any of the air force newspapers," Bobrick said, with a kind of candid mournfulness.

He was honorably discharged and entered the University of Illinois. He wanted to get into television. He didn't know why. His professors at Illinois all gave him the same advice: "Don't go to New York till you have some local credits. Get a job near here first. Then try New York."

There was an opening in Peoria, Illinois, not too far away. He went there. It was April. "There's nothing here till the fall."

He sold market baskets for a produce dealer—his uncle. The uncle bought the produce. The farmers took what they wanted of the baskets. In one month there was a thousand-dollar loss. "I was on a reading kick and I kept no records. Anyhow, I didn't like the work."

In 1956 he went to New York. It was summer. "I sweated all the way down Madison Avenue in my gray flannel suit. It was my only suit."

He tried advertising agency mail rooms. Every four months, for two years, he kept getting the same letter from one of the agencies: "There's nothing available for you in the mail room." But he was working in the mail room of ABC, so this continuing turndown didn't hurt.

Sam Bobrick applied for the job of office boy on the Ray Bolger show (called *Washington Square*—a sweet show that failed). Here he met George Shapiro, the agent who was responsible for the team of Persky and Denoff—responsible for teaming them up, a brilliant piece of perception. (One of their Dick Van Dyke scripts is in this book.)

Shapiro saw what Bobrick had and became his agent, a relationship that brought forth the following observation by Bobrick about agents: "A writer is as good as his agent. There are a lot of good writers who have bum agents and they get nowhere. But bum writers with good agents get work."

It was George Shapiro who, after persuading Persky and Denoff they should team up, got them to the attention of Carl Reiner, creator-producer of the *Dick Van Dyke Show*. When Persky and Denoff were taking their bows, two years later, on receiving an Emmy for this best-of-all-comedies, they made a genuinely spontaneous personal mention of what George Shapiro had done for them. This seldom happens in the credit-grabbing guerrilla warfare of television.

Bobrick struggled and suffered (as office boy) on another show—quite a dreadful show. You may remember it—*Make Me Laugh*. Robert Q Lewis was host. At a Robert Q party one night, Bobrick got tight (he seldom drinks), was very funny, and Lewis hired him. But the show folded. So he wrote for anything he could get: *Music Bingo*, where writers prepared the sick dialogue you always hear on these things—"How did you meet your wife?" etc. He wrote on the *Captain Kangaroo Show* one summer.

Then he wrote the lyric for a song that Elvis Presley turned into a quick hit, "The Girl of My Best Friend." Somebody told Bobrick, "You'll make ten grand in a month." So he quit writing television. And he starved. For a long time it was England's number-one song, but the ten grand never showed. He lived on unemployment insurance. "I figured the city was giving me a scholarship." He cranked out things for *Mad Magazine*. Then suddenly he ran into George Shapiro again, who said, "Want to come back to work?"

George Shapiro was big by then, representing Jim Nabors, Wayne Newton, Ron Clarke, Persky and Denoff, the Smothers Brothers. Sam Bobrick began writing on a quiz show called *People Will Talk*. This was 1963. He did much work on *Hey, Landlord!* and *Flintstones*, then met Bill Idelson and with him did some of the Andy Griffith scripts, one of which, "The Shoplifters," won the Writers' Guild Award. The team of Bobrick and Idelson wrote the *Andy Griffith Show* for several seasons.

As a team they did very few of the *Get Smart* shows, perhaps only two.

In any case, one of those they did do—"Viva Smart"—is one of the most amusing and most constantly amusing scripts this series has had, beautifully *carpentered* from its opening shot to the final, unlikely getaway.

It would perhaps earn the scorn of any professor in America if it were to be claimed that radio soap opera had ever delivered a genius. Probably it never did, but it came close. Or so I feel. Paul Rhymer—who created and wrote *Vic and Sade* for many years—had no competitive skill threatening him in the daytime field of comedy, with the exception of Goodman Ace.

Rhymer was constantly and continuously original. And he never had more than three people on the microphones. (Amos and Andy had only themselves, though they "created" more than five hundred others.)

Vic and Sade had a son named Rush. The part was played by Bill Idelson. He won a competitive audition for the role when he was only eleven. And he played Rush for twelve years without a break.

Idelson has been an actor—radio, movies, television—most of the time since he left the *Vic and Sade* show—and still appears now and then. But writing had always been a hobby of his. On the West Coast he "took courses wherever they were given"—notably UCLA. He mentions one book (why I'm plugging another author's book, I don't know) as being of great value to him—Uzzell's *Narrative Technique*.

6

THE DICK VAN DYKE SHOW

This is the happiest script in the book. And from the best-scripted comedy half hour that television has given us. I do not think it will ever be topped. To expect a repeat pattern, to expect the convergence of so many "perfect" talents working together on one show over a long period of time, seems mathematically unlikely. Just remember that you had some marvelous fun with some great people. Take heart that you can still catch this great series. It's syndicated. Look for it.

The most pleasurable experience I ever had in the too-much-of-the-time-dreary business of advertising was the privilege of being agency supervisor—a rapidly obsolescing activity—for this show. I had many others, more than eighty shows, in fact, many of them exciting or satisfying or fun. And one whose title you may recall—*Hennessey*—was really a great comedy for two and a half seasons. But nothing in all television has ever equaled the *sustained* excellence of the *Dick Van Dyke Show*.

Nothing in television has ever equaled the sustained excellence of Dick Van Dyke, for that matter, except perhaps the sustained excellence and the inventiveness of the real creator of this series—Carl Reiner. Both these men are prodigiously gifted.

Read the story now just for the enjoyment of it. In the critique that follows, I have departed from the practice of referring to shots. There is a purpose in my doing so. There are so many professional tricks hidden away in this fast-reading, fast-playing script, tricks that relate far more to *writing* than merely to writing for the camera.

What kind of tricks? This kind: how to keep a motionless scene from going dead on you; how to get a lot said in a few words; how to get a lot said with no words; how to set and sustain comic suspense; how to exploit to the fullest the known abilities of your cast; how to change mood; how to introduce and build a running gag; how to build comedy characterizations that are real. Thirty or forty other tricks.

Little reference is made to numbered shots as such. The marginal numbers here are used merely to identify the exact spot as to where, how, and why these stratagems are being used. Some occur at scene endings, many others in mid-sentence.

Now read the script.

THE DICK VAN DYKE SHOW
"Coast To Coast Big Mouth"
By Bill Persky and Sam Denoff

CAST

ROB PETRIE .... DICK VAN DYKE
LAURA PETRIE .... MARY TYLER MOORE
SALLY ROGERS .... ROSE MARIE
BUDDY SORRELL .... MOREY AMSTERDAM
ALAN BRADY .... CARL REINER
MEL COOLEY .... RICHARD DEACON
MILLIE HELPER .... ANN MORGAN GUILBERT
JOHNNY PATRICK .... DICK CURTIS
CAROL HACKETT ....

SETS

INT. TELEVISION STUDIO
INT. ALAN BRADY'S OFFICE
INT. PETRIE KITCHEN
INT. ROB'S OFFICE

TEASER

FADE IN:

INT. TELEVISION STUDIO—DAY

1 THIS IS THE SECTION OF THE AUDIENCE AND THE STAGE. THE AUDIENCE IS FILLED WITH PEOPLE . . . MOSTLY WOMEN. MILLIE AND LAURA ARE SEATED ON THE SIDE. THE STAGE AREA IS SET UP FOR A TYPICAL DAYTIME GAME PARTICI- PATION SHOW. A LECTERN FOR THE EMCEE . . . PLUS MIKES AND TABLES FOR THE CONTESTANTS. THE SHOW IS NOT YET ON THE AIR. THE JOVIAL, CLEVER, WITTY, HANDSOME EMCEE, JOHNNY PATRICK, IS STAGE CENTER. UPSTAGE WALL OF STAGE IS A MAP OF U.S., PLUS A SIGN: "PAY AS YOU GO."

PATRICK
(READS CARD) Okay. Now for our final contestant. Where is Miss Carol Hackett? Miss Hackett is from Sacramento, California. Miss Hackett?

LADY WAVES HAND.

PATRICK
2 (CONT'D) Come right up here, Miss Hackett . . . and if anything gets in your way . . . hack it! (HE LAUGHS) (TO AUDIENCE) Love ya!

LADIES IN AUDIENCE LAUGH. MILLIE DOES . . . LAURA DOES, POLITELY. MISS HACKETT WALKS UP TO STAGE. AT THIS POINT MISS HACKETT JOINS HIM. AS HE LEADS HER TO THE WINGS HE ADDS:

PATRICK
(CONT'D) (LOOKING AT WATCH) Gals . . . we go on the air in a little while . . . it's exactly ten minutes to one . . . in case anyone has to take a pill.

3 Come on, Miss Hackett . . . meet our producer . . . (WINKS) And watch out for him.

THEY GO OFF . . . AUDIENCE LAUGHS.

MILLIE

4 (WATCHING MISS HACKETT GO) You see . . . another sexy one. I didn't stand a chance.

LAURA

Sure you did. They pick them out of that bowl.

MILLIE

Yeah, but the only thing that comes out of that bowl is sexy out-of-towners.

LAURA

Millie . . . you are so phony!

MILLIE

5 (INDIGNANTLY) What do you mean phony?

LAURA

If they ever picked you to go on, you'd die!

MILLIE

Well, I'd live long enough to win a dishwasher. I know Rob could have 6 used his influence to get me on.

LAURA

Millie . . . it took him half a day just to get us the tickets. (SIGHS)

MILLIE

7 (APOLOGETICALLY) I already thanked you for that.

JOHNNY PATRICK ENTERS WITH MISS HACKETT.

PATRICK

Girls . . . girls . . .

THEY QUIET DOWN.

PATRICK

(CONT'D) There's still a chance for one lucky lady. We had to disqualify Miss Hackett. She doesn't speak English. Right.

HACKETT

(SMILES) Gracias. . . . gracias . . .

SHE WALKS OFF STAGE AND GOES BACK TO HER SEAT.

PATRICK

You don't have to apologize . . . we'll have to pick another contestant.

Let's see . . . (LEAFS THROUGH CARDS)

AUDIENCE BRIGHTENS WITH EXPECTATION. MILLIE STIFFENS . . . AND WRINGS HANDS.

MILLIE

Laura . . . did you ever have a sudden flash of blind intuition hit you?

LAURA

8 What???

MILLIE

He's gonna call me . . .

PATRICK

Uh . . . Mrs. Mildred Helper.

LAURA

(TURNING IN EXCITEMENT) Oooh!

SHE TURNS IN TIME TO SEE MILLIE FREEZE IN HER CHAIR.

MILLIE

Oooh!

PATRICK

9 (LOOKING AROUND) Mildred Helper.

LAURA

(RAISES HER HAND TO TELL HIM WHERE MILLIE IS) Uh . . . Mr. Patrick.

PATRICK

There she is.

LAURA

10 No. (POINTS TO MILLIE) Here she is . . . I'm her friend . . .

PATRICK

What's wrong with her?

LAURA

Oh . . . nothing . . . she, uh . . .

PATRICK

Nothing? She always look like that?

LAURA

Well, no . . . (TO MILLIE) Mil . . . come on . . .

MILLIE

I'll die . . . Laura . . . I'll die . . .

PATRICK

We'll have to pick someone else.

LAURA

Millie, they'll have to pick someone else.

MILLIE NODS HER APPROVAL.

MILLIE

Pick! Pick!

LAURA

(NOW COMPOSED) Mr. Patrick . . . I think you'd better call someone else . . . I'm afraid she's a little nervous.

PATRICK

All right. Thank you very much. Say, how about you?

LAURA

(NOW NERVOUS) Me?

PATRICK

Yes. Don't be nervous.

LAURA

Well . . . I . . . well . . .

MILLIE

(NOW THAT SPOTLIGHT IS OFF HER) Go ahead, Laura.

LAURA

What do you mean, go ahead?

MILLIE

11 I mean go ahead. If you win something we'll split it . . . don't be a baby.

OTHER WOMEN REACT TO THEIR CONVERSATION.

LAURA

When did you get so brave?

MILLIE

Laura. . . we can't lose . . . you're smart . . . you're sexy . . .

LAURA

Millie!

PATRICK

(LOOKING AT WATCH) I'm afraid we'll have to choose . . .

MILLIE

She'll do it. (THEN PLEADING TO LAURA) Laura . . . do it.

LAURA

12 (ANGRY GLANCE AT MILLIE) Well . . . okay . . . I'll do it.

PATRICK

How about a little encouragement for the lady?

WOMEN APPLAUD. MILLIE STARTS OUT OF STUDIO. LAURA IS ON HER WAY UP TO STAGE.

PATRICK

(CONT'D) Wonderful . . . wonderful . . .

LAURA

(TO MILLIE) Where are you going?

MILLIE

13 To call Jerry to tell him to watch me.

LAURA

You're not on.

MILLIE

14 It's the same thing . . . (MEANINGFULLY) Partner!

LAURA REACTS.

FADE OUT:

END OF TEASER

ACT I

FADE IN:

INT. ALAN BRADY'S OFFICE—DAY

BUDDY AND SALLY ARE ON SOFA. MEL IS STANDING NEAR ALAN'S DESK. ALAN IS
15 SEATED BEHIND DESK. ROB IS PACING AND TALKING . . . REFERRING TO PAPER
IN HAND.

ROB

And . . . uh . . . we think that in the new format we should do the second
dance number before the big sketch.

SALLY

I'm not sure.

ALAN

I like it.

SALLY

16 Now I like it.

BUDDY

I like it.

MEL

I like it.

ALAN

What do you know—look at that tie you're wearing.

17 ROB LOOKS AT MEL'S TIE, THEN AT HIS OWN. THEIR TIES ARE IDENTICAL. ROB
TRIES TO COVER HIS UP.

ALAN

(CONT'D) Let's not waste time—what else have you got there?

ROB

(HANDING HIM PAPER) A list of the guest stars we'd like to get on the
show.

SALLY

You'll notice they're mostly men . . .

ALAN

You made up the list, huh?

SALLY

Who else?

ALAN

18 Okay. Now listen. Remember, these advertising guys gotta be romanced, so I'll do all the talking.

SALLY

I'll do the romancing.

ALAN

If I need any help, I'll ask for it.

MEL

19 Right, if Alan needs any help, he'll—

ALAN

(TO MEL) Shut up, Mel.

MEL

20 Yessir.

ALAN

(LOOKING AT WATCH) Okay . . . we'll grab a quick bite and then get over there.

THE PHONE RINGS . . . MEL ANSWERS IT.

BUDDY

I'm not too hungry.

ALAN

I'm treating.

BUDDY

I'm starving.

MEL

(TO PHONE) Hello?

ALAN

Shut up, Mel . . .

MEL

(WHISPERS) Rob, it's for you.

ALAN

Speak up, Mel.

MEL

21 It's for . . . (LOUDER) The phone is for Rob.

ALAN

So shut up and give it to him. Come on, dress me. (HANDS HIS JACKET TO MEL)

MEL

Yessir.

ROB CROSSES TO PHONE.

ALAN

Make it snappy, Rob.

ROB

(CROSSING) Thanks, Mel. Hello . . . Ritch? Is anything wrong?

OTHERS DIRECT ATTENTION TO ROB.

ROB

22 (CONT'D) Huh? Ritch . . . (TO GROUP) My son. (BACK INTO PHONE)
Yes . . . I'm working . . . I'm in an important meeting. Ritch, what . . .
(SIGHS) Uncle Alan, Uncle Mel, and Uncle Buddy.

SALLY GETS HIS ATTENTION.

ROB

(CONT'D) And Uncle Sally. Ritch . . . what do you want?

BUDDY

23 He calls once a day with a new riddle he heard in school.

SALLY

Then we use them on the show.

ROB

(SURPRISED) Uncle Jerry said Millie said Mommy's on what?

SALLY

This one's tougher than usual.

ROB

24 What television show? Oh . . . those dumb tickets I got her. (LOOKS AT
WATCH) Yeah . . . okay, Ritch . . . okay . . . (TRIES TO HANG UP) Okay,
boy . . . yeah . . . yeah. (THINKS) Uh . . . I give up . . . an unlisted banana.
(SMILES) Right . . . okay . . . See you tonight, pal. (HANGS UP)

BUDDY

What's an unlisted banana?

ALAN

Rob . . . what was that?

ROB

25 Laura is a contestant on the Johnny Patrick show.

SALLY

When?

BUDDY

Who cares . . . what's an unlisted banana?

ROB

Today . . . now!

BUDDY

What's an unlisted banana?

ROB

I got the tickets for her and Millie . . .

BUDDY

Rob . . .

ROB

26 (TO BUDDY) What's long and yellow and seldom rings?

BUDDY

(LIKE HE GOT IT) An unlisted banana!

ROB

(LOOKS AT WATCH) Listen . . . why don't you all go on ahead to lunch. I'd like to stay here and watch her. Okay, Alan?

ALAN

27 Okay, Rob. We'll be at the Purple Peacock.

SALLY

Hey, I'd rather watch the Johnny Patrick show. It's not as fattening as lunch.

ALAN

28 Johnny Patrick . . . he's the one who's so rough on the contestants.

BUDDY

Yeah. One day I saw him get an airline pilot so confused he admitted he was afraid to fly.

SALLY

And he made a mother admit she hated her own kid.

ALAN

My kind of guy. Let's stay and see what he gets Laura to admit. Mel, tune
29 the set . . . make it clearer. We'll all stay.

MEL

Yes, sir . . .

ROB

Oh, you don't have to stay.

BUDDY

Yeah, I'm starved.

ALAN

We'll all stay!!

BUDDY

30 That's what I said. (SITS) Why don't we all stay.

SALLY SITS ON HIS LAP.

BUDDY

(CONT'D) This is no time for romance. Get a chair.

SALLY

What about gallantry?

BUDDY

No time for that, either. Get a chair.

SALLY

Thanks, Sir Galahad. I hope Laura wins something I can borrow.

BUDDY

31 I hope she's on first. I'm so hungry I could eat an unlisted banana . . .

THEY ALL LAUGH AS WE
TIME DISSOLVE TO:
INT. TELEVISION STUDIO
JOHNNY PATRICK IS TALKING TO ANOTHER CONTESTANT.

PATRICK

So . . . Mrs. Warner, in your "pay as you go" journey from New York
to Quebec you ran out of gas in Quincy, Mass. . . . but thanks for playing
the game.

MUSIC PLAYOFF AND APPLAUSE.

PATRICK

32 (CONT'D) And now our next traveler is a lovely little lady from New
Rochelle, New York. Mrs. Laura Petrie . . .

MUSIC PLAY ON: APPLAUSE.
NOTE: INTERCUT SHOT OF MILLIE APPLAUDING WILDLY.
WHEN INDICATED CUT BETWEEN STUDIO AND OFFICE.

BUDDY

33 It's about time.

LAURA CROSSES TO PATRICK . . . OBVIOUSLY A BIT NERVOUS.

PATRICK

So . . . it's Laura Petrie.

LAURA

Yes, it is.

MILLIE

(TO WOMAN) That's my friend—shh!

WHEN INDICATED CUT BETWEEN STUDIO AND OFFICE.
CUT TO OFFICE:

ALAN

Hey, Rob . . . she looks good.

ROB

Yeah . . .

CUT TO STUDIO:

PATRICK

(THINKING) Petrie . . . Petrie . . . is your husband in television?

LAURA

34 (SMILES) Yes, he is.

PATRICK

I thought the name was familiar.

CUT TO OFFICE:

SALLY

Here's some free publicity, Rob.

ROB

(DREADING) I hope not.

CUT TO STUDIO:

PATRICK

Ladies and gentlemen . . . this little lady happens to be married to one of the most talented men in our business.

SHOT OF ROB CRINGING.

LAURA

Thank you. I think he is.

PATRICK

Ladies and gentlemen, she's married to the producer of that wonderful
35 show, "The World In Trouble," Dave Petrie . . .

BIG APPLAUSE . . .
REACTION SHOT OF ROB LOOKING SHEEPISH AND OTHERS LAUGHING AT HIM.

LAURA

No . . .

PATRICK

He's not producing it anymore.

LAURA

No . . . he's not my husband.

PATRICK

Well . . . we let the cat out of the bag there.

LAURA

No. He never was.

PATRICK

Ho . . . ho . . .

LAURA

No, you see . . . (SMILES PROUDLY) . . . my husband is *Rob* Petrie. (WAITS
36 FOR A BIG REACTION. NOTHING)

PATRICK

Who?

LAURA

Robert Petrie.

PATRICK

37 I'm afraid I never heard of him.

LAURA

He's the head writer of the Alan Brady show.

PATRICK

38 (TEASING) Is that still on?

REACTION SHOTS FROM OFFICE.

LAURA

Of course it is.

PATRICK

Tell me, Mrs. Petrie . . . is the show any better than it used to be?

LAURA

39 Oh, yes. (CAUGHT) I mean, no.

AUDIENCE LAUGHS.

ROB

Boy, I'm hungry.

PATRICK

Well, what do you mean?

LAURA

I mean . . . it was always good.

PATRICK

Of course. You're a little nervous.

AUDIENCE LAUGHS.
(IN OFFICE) ROB REACTS SHEEPISHLY.

PATRICK

(CONT'D) (WINKS) . . . (ASIDE) Tell me, Laura . . . between us . . . what's Alan Brady really like?

ALAN

40 Nobody make a sound.

ROB STIFFENS.

LAURA

(CONFIDENTIALLY) He's a very fine, talented man.

ALAN

Let's hear it. A sigh of relief all around.

ROB

41 She's cute.

BACK TO STUDIO:

PATRICK

I agree. Alan Brady is an extremely talented man.

SHOT OF ALAN REACTING.

ALAN

42 You know, this guy's very good.

LAURA

My husband always says how exhilarating it is to work for a man as gifted
as Alan.

SHOT OF ROB REACTING RELIEVED.
BACK TO STUDIO:

PATRICK

43 She had to say that, folks.

ROB

No, she didn't.

PATRICK

(SETTING HER UP) Tell me . . . is he any easier to get along with now?

LAURA

(TAKING THE BAIT) Oh, yes . . . unh, no! (TRYING TO GET OUT OF IT) Uh,
he's the same.

PATRICK

Come on, now, the truth. Is he still a screamer?

LAURA

No . . . uh . . . he's not that way anymore.

PATRICK

Oh?

LAURA

(HELPLESSLY) Well . . . uh . . . as far as I know he was never that way.

PATRICK

44 Mrs. Petrie . . . you're a wonderful sport.

SHE BEAMS.
IN OFFICE . . . ROB HEAVES SIGH OF RELIEF . . . AS OTHERS REACT ACCORDINGLY.
BACK TO STUDIO:

PATRICK

45 Now, we'll see if you can win some prizes right after this word from
Jabboes.

CUT TO OFFICE AND STAY FOR FOLLOWING.

SALLY

Buddy, I think you'd better get your cello.

ALAN

(TURNING DOWN VOLUME) How do you like that creep . . . trying to get
Laura to say I was all those rotten things.

                              ROB

(JUMPING IN) I hope you noticed she didn't.

                              ALAN

46 Yeah . . . she's okay, Rob.

                              BUDDY

Yeah, she almost put her foot in your mouth.

ROB SMILES.

                              MEL

(LOOKING AT WATCH) Say . . . if we're going to eat and get to that meeting
we'd better go.

                              ALAN

47 Shut up, Mel . . . and what are you doing in my chair?

                              MEL

I don't know. (GETS UP)

                              ALAN

Okay, let's go.

                              ROB

Yeah, it's late and Laura won't mind if we don't watch the rest.

                              SALLY

Hey . . . don't you want to see if she wins anything?

                              ALAN

It's not really important what she wins. The important thing is . . . she
didn't lose.

                              ROB

Hunh?

                              ALAN

48 Your job.

                              ROB

(NODDING) Yeah. Right.

                              ALAN

Let's eat.

                              BUDDY

Good idea.

                              ROB

49 (TO TV SET) Good luck.

AS THEY EXIT WE
DISSOLVE TO:
INT. TV STUDIO—DAY
FIFTEEN MINUTES LATER.
LAURA IS AT THE END OF HER QUESTIONING . . .
MUSICAL FANFARE. LAURA BLINKS HEADLIGHTS.

PATRICK

(REFERRING TO LARGE MAP) All right. Let's see what Laura Petrie . . .
the writer's wife . . . won on her "pay as you go" trip from New York to
California . . . a hair dryer . . . (POINTS TO PHILADELPHIA)

REACTION SHOTS OF MILLIE.

PATRICK

50 (CONT'D) (PITTSBURGH) A vacuum cleaner . . . (TO CLEVELAND) a
rotisserie . . . (POINTS TO LOS ANGELES) . . . an eight-millimeter movie
projector.

APPLAUSE.

PATRICK

(CONT'D) It was wonderful having you with us, Laura. Come back again,
won't you?

LAURA

(SWEETLY) Well . . . I'll try.

STARTS TO GO OFF.

PATRICK

Oh . . . I meant to ask you.

LAURA

Yes?

PATRICK

Have you ever been to Alan Brady's house?

LAURA

Oh, yes . . . many times.

PATRICK

Does he wear his toupee at home?

LAURA

51 Oh, yes. He wears it all the time. (HER EYES WIDEN IN HORRIBLE REALIZA-
TION)

PATRICK

You mean Alan Brady is bald!

LAURA

Well, no.

PATRICK

Then why does he wear a toupee? (LAUGHS)

LAURA

Well, well . . .

PATRICK

(LAUGHS—TO AUDIENCE) Well, gals, the secret is out. She said it and she
knows. Alan Brady is bald and you learned it here! How about that, folks?
52 Aren't we devils?!

LAURA

No, no . . .

PATRICK

(TURNS TO HER) Oh, don't worry, Laura. I'm sure Alan will understand.

LAURA

Oh, no, he won't . . . you don't know him. He'll go . . . oh . . .

PATRICK

What? What? He'll what?

LAURA

(FAST) Nothing . . . nothing . . . he'll do nothing. He's a wonderful man. Thanks for the prizes.

STARTS OFF.

PATRICK

(SHOUTING AFTER HER) And thank you for the scoop. Well, ladies, are we having fun?

53 AUDIENCE YELLS "YEAH" AND APPLAUDS.

FADE OUT:

END OF ACT I

ACT II

54 INT. PETRIE KITCHEN—NIGHT.
LAURA IS PREPARING VEGETABLES FOR SALAD: CARROTS, CELERY, TOMATOES, RADISHES, LETTUCE, ETC.
MILLIE IS PACING.

LAURA

How could I have been so stupid!

MILLIE

You weren't stupid. You won four prizes. Look, I'll take the dryer and the . . .

LAURA

Forget the prizes, Millie. I told America that Alan Brady is bald!

MILLIE

So, a lot of men are bald.

LAURA

Yeah, but they're not big TV stars, my husband's boss, and the vainest man in the world.

MILLIE

Is Alan that vain?

LAURA

When Alan had his tonsils out, Rob and I went to visit him in the hospital
and he was wearing a hat.

MILLIE

In the hospital? That's crazy.

LAURA

55 Now you know why I'm worried.

MILLIE

What kind of a hat?

LAURA

Millie!

MILLIE

Well, if Rob hasn't called by now . . .

LAURA

What?

MILLIE

If Rob hasn't called by now . . . (THINKS) Uh . . .

LAURA

(IMPATIENTLY) Well, what?

MILLIE

Well, I was hoping you could finish it with something like maybe nobody
saw the program.

LAURA

56 (SIGHS) Even if they didn't see it, they're bound to find out about it.

MILLIE

Laura, people say things on that program every day and you don't hear
about it.

LAURA

But nobody ever said Alan Brady was bald. That's big news!

MILLIE

You know, I never knew it. How bald is he?

LAURA

57 Oh, Millie, please!

SOUND: ROB'S CAR DRIVING INTO GARAGE. LAURA STIFFENS.

LAURA

(CONT'D) Millie, Rob's home. Will you stay with me?

MILLIE

Gee, I wish you hadn't asked that.

LAURA

Why?

MILLIE

Cause you're not gonna like the answer. Good-bye and good luck.

AS MILLIE EXITS, ROB ENTERS FROM GARAGE.

MILLIE

(CONT'D) Hi—I see you're home.

ROB

Hi.

LAURA

(WEAKLY) Hi . . .

ROB

(LIGHTLY) Boy, did you louse up a day for us. Alan is furious.

LAURA

(NODDING, LIKE SHE EXPECTED IT) Furious . . . are you?

ROB

58 No, it wasn't really your fault.

LAURA

Right! Rob, you're wonderful. I've been thinking you'd kill me. I've been worried all day.

ROB

Worried? How did you know about it?

LAURA

Rob, what are you talking about?

ROB

Alan. We had a meeting to go to but we stayed in the office to watch you.

LAURA

(CONFUSED) Then you did watch me.

ROB

Yeah, and it got late so we had to run for a cab and Alan slipped and sprained his ankle and he blames you. Did you win anything?

LAURA

You said you watched.

ROB

Not the whole thing. Just your interview. We were all proud of the way you handled yourself with that Patrick rat. Alan said you saved my job. What did you win?

LAURA

59 A dryer . . . a rotiss . . . (STARTING TO CRY) . . . a rotisserie . . . a vac . . . a vac . . . (MAKES SUCKING SOUND) Oh, I'm so unhappy!

ROB

Why?

LAURA

Because you didn't see the end of the show.

ROB

Well, honey, I had to work.

LAURA

Rob . . . at the very end of the show I didn't handle myself too well with that Patrick rat.

ROB

(SMILES) Ahh . . . What did he do? Get you to say something embarrassing?

LAURA

Yes.

ROB

(BABYING HER) What was it?

LAURA

60 That Alan Brady is bald!

ROB TAKES IT FOR A SECOND. THEN GINGERLY RELEASES LAURA AND KIND OF HOLDS HER OFF AT ARM'S LENGTH.

ROB

You . . . (POINTS TO TOP OF HEAD)

SHE NODS.

ROB

(CONT'D) That Alan has no hair?

SHE NODS.

ROB

(CONT'D) . . . on the air?

SHE NODS.

ROB

(CONT'D) (PATHETICALLY) Sweetheart, beloved . . . you did know that was a secret, didn't you?

LAURA

Yes!

ROB

(RAVES AND SCREAMS) Sure! What's the fun of telling it if it isn't a secret!

LAURA

He tricked me.

ROB

(DRIVING) Okay . . . okay . . . he tricked you . . . he's tricky . . . but telling
61 the world about Alan's wig. Oh, boy, are we in trouble.

LAURA

You saw the way he asked questions. (HELPLESSLY) You don't know what to answer.

ROB

I'm surprised you didn't tell him about Alan's nose job!

LAURA

62 I didn't know Alan had a nose job.

THIS STOPS ROB SHORT IN HIS TRACKS. HE REALIZES HE TOO HAS OPENED UP A BIG MOUTH.

ROB

(DOWN) Oh. Yeah. It used to be a secret.

LAURA

(A LITTLE ON THE ATTACK) I thought we had no secrets.

ROB

(INDIGNANT) Hold it! You're mad at me for not telling you a secret in the middle of an argument where I'm mad at you for telling a secret?!?!

LAURA

I'm not sure, but you see how you can blurt something out when you're excited. And I wasn't trying to trick you.

ROB

63 I just hope through some fabulous miracle Alan won't hear about it.

LAURA

Millie suggested that.

ROB

What a day. Now I'm thinking like Millie.

LAURA

(PLAINTIVELY) Rob . . . I don't know what to do.

THE PHONE RINGS.

ROB

(POINTS TO PHONE) Answer it. Alan'll tell you. (SHE SHAKES HEAD "NO." HE BREATHES DEEPLY AND PICKS UP PHONE) Hello. (RELIEVED) Buddy. (SHE BREATHES A SIGH OF RELIEF. ROB'S FACE DARKENS) How did you find out? (LAURA REACTS) Sally. Then how did . . . uh hunh . . . (TURNS TO LAURA) She read it in the paper.

LAURA

(FEARFULLY, TO ROB) Alan?

ROB

(LISTENING, WAVES HER OFF) Yeah . . . right . . . uh hunh . . . oh boy . . .
64 okay, Buddy . . . thanks, pal. I'll see you tomorrow . . . maybe. (HE HANGS UP)

LAURA
(AWAITING HER DOOM) Well?

ROB
(THINKING) The item in the paper read . . . the question whether Alan Brady is bald was answered today on television by the wife of the future ex-writer of the Alan Brady show. And they gave my name.

LAURA
Oh, my . . . will it make you feel better if I tell you how really sorry I am?

ROB
65 No . . . but if it makes you feel better, go ahead and tell me.

HE KISSES HER LIGHTLY.

LAURA
What do you think Alan'll do?

ROB
(WINCES) Not what. How? How will he do it?

DISSOLVE TO:
INT. ROB'S OFFICE—DAY
ROB, THE DOOMED MAN, IS ON TELEPHONE.

ROB
(ON PHONE) Yeah, Val . . . well, has he said anything to you about it? (WINCES) Did you tell him I've been trying to call? What did he say to that? He shouldn't talk like that. Does his leg hurt?

BUDDY ENTERS.

ROB
(CONT'D) Well, look . . . just tell him I'm ready for him whenever he's ready for me. Right . . . bye! (HANGS UP) (TO BUDDY) Hi.

BUDDY
(CROSSING TO DESK WITH HIS COFFEE) Hmmmph. You're still here!

ROB
He won't fire me. It'll look bad in the papers.

BUDDY
Yeah . . . it looks bad to fire a guy the same day you kill him.

ROB
He's not gonna kill me.

BUDDY
Well, he ain't gonna give you a raise.

ROB
Whatever he's going to do . . . I wish he'd do it fast. Has anyone ever lost his job because of his wife?

BUDDY

Who was Marie Antoinette's husband . . . the guy without the head?

ROB

Oh, I could get fired.

BUDDY

What else did you do to Laura?

ROB

What do you mean . . . "what else"?

BUDDY

66 After you kicked her and punched her and yelled at her, and broke her purse mirror.

ROB

After I yelled I didn't do anything to her . . . except apologize for yelling.

BUDDY

You apologized?

ROB

Yeah. How come after they do something wrong we end up apologizing?

BUDDY

Don't ask me. Pickles don't do anything wrong.

ROB

Oh, come on.

BUDDY

67 She don't do anything.

DOOR OPENS AND SALLY ENTERS. SHE APPROACHES ROB . . . CAUTIOUSLY.

SALLY

Hi, Bud . . .

ROB TURNS AND SMILES TO HER AND WAVES.

BUDDY

Morning, Sal . . .

SALLY

(LOOKS AROUND ROOM. LEANING IN TO ROB) Where's Laura?

BUDDY

She's posing for a statue of her mouth for the Smithsonian Institution.

SALLY

Where's Laura?

ROB

She's at home.

SALLY

No . . . she's here.

ROB

Where?

SALLY

I don't know where but I saw her get in the elevator.

ROB

The elevator?

SALLY

Yeah, that little room in the lobby that goes up and down.

ROB

68 In this building?

SALLY

Yes, I saw her just as the doors closed. I figured she came here.

ROB

I don't understand. Where did she go?

BUDDY

To the roof. She's gonna jump.

ROB

No . . . Alan's office.

SALLY

She's got a better chance jumping.

ROB STARTS OUT.

BUDDY

Where are you going?

ROB

To protect my wife from protecting me.

HE BOLTS OUT.

BUDDY

(CALLING AFTER HIM) Don't do it, Rob. Save yourself. After a reason-
69 able period you can find another girl and remarry.

CUT TO:

INT. ALAN BRADY'S OFFICE—DAY

IT IS THE SAME TIME. ALAN IS SEATED BEHIND DESK. A HUGE WRAPPED FOOT
IS PROPPED UP ON THE DESK. A CANE IS ON THE DESK. HE IS WEARING A HAT
ON THE DESK ARE A SERIES OF TOUPEES ON FORMS. MEL IS STARING AT THEM

ALAN

70 (STEAMING—WAVING AT TOUPEES) There they are, Mel . . . a thousand
dollars worth of useless hair. What am I supposed to do with them?

MEL

(THINKING ABOUT HIS OWN HEAD) Alan . . . could I . . .

ALAN

71 No . . . I'd rather make a coat for my wife. (HITS ONE FORM WITH CANE) Pick it up, pick it up!

MEL

(PICKING IT UP) Alan, I can't tell you how sorry I am about this whole mess.

ALAN

72 (ROUNDS ON HIM) You can't tell me anything. Get your hands off my hair.

BUZZER RINGS. ALAN PICKS UP PHONE.

ALAN

Yes, what is it? (EYES WIDEN) Mrs. Petrie???

MEL

Rob's wife?

ALAN

73 No, his brother. (TO PHONE) I know his wife. Send her in. (HANGS UP) Laura Petrie's crazy. I knew it. She's crazy.

MEL

I've always felt . . .

ALAN

You never felt anything, Mel.

KNOCK ON DOOR.

ALAN

(CONT'D) Come in! The door, Mel, get the door.

MEL

(CROSSING TO IT) Yessir, yessir.

MEL OPENS THE DOOR AND LAURA MEEKLY WALKS IN AS MEL EXITS. AFTER A MOMENT, SHE OPENS HER MOUTH TO SPEAK.

ALAN

74 Wait! Don't say a word! Let me look at you. (TO TOUPEES) Fellas, there she is—take a good look at her. She's the one who put you out of business. (TO LAURA) So your husband is letting you take the rap all by yourself.

LAURA

Oh, no. If Rob knew I was here he'd kill me.

ALAN

Good. I'll call him.

LAURA

Alan . . . uh . . . please . . . Rob . . . as you know . . . uh . . .

ALAN

(YELLING) What, what, what???

LAURA

75 How's your foot?

ALAN

(HOLDING LEG UP) How does it look?

LAURA

Ooh!

ALAN

(KNOCKS FOOT) Ow!

LAURA

Ahh!

ALAN

Eeh!

LAURA

Oh! Does it hurt?

ALAN

Laura, what the heck are you doing here?

LAURA

Well, I . . .

ALAN

If you like to look at ruins why don't you go to Greece?

LAURA

Alan . . . you're not ruined . . . really.

ALAN

My leg . . . my head . . . What are you after now . . . my liver?

LAURA

I just wanted to see you personally to apologize . . . and . . . uh . . . try to explain.

ALAN

76 What's to explain, you have a big mouth.

LAURA

I do, I know, but . . .

ALAN

If you wanted a free dryer and a rotisserie I woulda gotten them for you. I'd have bought you a house . . . a showplace!

LAURA

(LAUGHS WEAKLY) Alan . . . please . . . you don't have to do that. May I say something?

ALAN

You have more to say?

LAURA

Well, I've been thinking about it . . . and, well, for instance, I think you
77 look very nice . . . uh . . . without . . . your . . . uh . . .

ALAN

It's hair! (TAKES HAT OFF, PUTS IT ON AGAIN)

LAURA

Well, yes . . . I've . . . I've . . . now, believe me, I'm not saying this
because I'm in trouble . . . although goodness knows, I am.

ALAN

Oh, no.

LAURA

But, sincerely . . . really sincerely, and you can ask anybody . . . I've
always liked you better without your . . .

ALAN

78 It's hair . . . hair . . . ! (THROWS HAT ON DESK) You didn't have any
trouble saying it yesterday! (THEN) When did you ever see me without
my hair?

LAURA

Well . . . uh . . . a couple of times. Remember that time on your boat
when you fell overboard . . .

ALAN

(ACCUSINGLY) The time you bumped into me.

LAURA

No . . . no . . . you tripped over Rob.

ALAN

79 (TO TOUPEES) Did you hear that, fellas? The whole family hates me. I
should have fired him then.

LAURA

And the time you had your tonsils out at the hospital.

ALAN

(REMEMBERING) Yeah . . . so?

LAURA

I remember telling Rob, and I told him to tell you . . . did he ever tell
you? I told Rob to tell you how nice and natural and warm you looked
. . . (SLOWLY) that way.

ALAN

(DISGUSTED) Sort of a father figure . . . right?

LAURA

Oh, no . . . just the opposite . . .

ALAN

80 A bald mother figure?

LAURA

(SMILES) No, Alan . . . a very interesting mature real person.

ALAN

(STEADILY) A little more snow in here and we can ski.

LAURA

(WEAKLY) No . . . (HE STARES AT HER) I really like your hair . . . not on . . . uh . . . you without it.

ALAN

If this is so, then why didn't you tell me in private?

LAURA

I didn't feel it was my place.

ALAN

No, your place is on network television.

LAURA

But it was an accident.

ALAN

So was Custer's last stand. (POINTS TO TOUPEES ON DESK) Would you like a scalp to hang on your belt?

LAURA SHUDDERS.

ALAN

81 (CONT'D) (PICKS UP TOUPEE AND FLOPS IT ON HEAD) See this clever one —this one made people say, "Hey, isn't Alan losing his hair?" (SHE DOESN'T KNOW WHAT TO DO. HE PUTS ANOTHER ONE ON TOP OF THAT) This is my summer rug . . . crew cut. (LAURA DOESN'T KNOW WHAT HE'S GETTING AT. PUTS ANOTHER ONE ON) This one is my "Alan, you need a haircut" one. Any suggestions what I might do with these, Laura?

LAURA

82 Well, there must be some needy people . . .

ALAN

Needy bald people! Mrs. Petrie . . .

ROB ENTERS EXPECTING TO SEE LAURA BEING MURDERED.

ROB

83 (SEES ALAN WITH ALL THE TOUPEES ON HIS HEAD) Hold it! (THEN BACK TO LAURA) Why did you come here?

LAURA

Because it was my fault and I didn't want you to take the blame and possibly get fired.

84 THEY NOW ARGUE, COMPLETELY FORGETTING ALAN WHO REMAINS WITH THE THREE TOUPEES ON HIS HEAD.

ROB

But it's a man's place to take the blame and possibly get fired. I'm responsible for you. Why didn't you say something to me?

LAURA

If I did you wouldn't have let me come.

ROB

Right . . . I would not have let you. You shouldn't be here.

ALAN

85 Hi, Rob. Remember me?

ROB

(TURNING) Oh, Alan. (REACTS TO ALAN IN THREE WIGS) Whatever you were going to say to Laura . . . I wish you'd say it to me.

ALAN

Okay . . . if that's the way you want it. Rob . . . you're a beautiful girl.

ROB

(LAUGHS) Alan, I . . .

ALAN

No, let me finish, sweetheart. You're a beautiful girl.

ROB

Thanks.

ALAN

If I had seen you an hour after she opened her mouth on TV, I would have killed you. But I've been thinking, and it's interesting you like me without my rug because my secretary likes me that way, too . . . and my wife. That's three in favor.

ROB

86 I always told you I like you bald.

ALAN

Good, that's four. My butcher is five. It's a regular trend. (RISES) Now, the fact that five dumbbells like me bald is not the only reason I've decided to be adorable about this mess.

ROB

You're going to be adorable?

ALAN

(LIMPS OVER TO ROB) The fact is . . . this incident took a big strain off my brain. It's tough keeping a secret like this. But now that it's out I feel better.

LAURA

You . . . you . . . mean you're happy that I told?

ALAN

(DISDAINFULLY) Happy? (TO ROB) They're perfect. You not only have to forgive them for their destruction, but you have to be happy. (TO LAURA—SMILES) All right. I'm happy.

LAURA

I am, too.

ALAN

87 (TO ROB) You happy, too?

ROB

I'm happy.

ALAN

We're all happy. Happy days are here again.

HE SITS IN CHAIR AND LAURA PUSHES THE COFFEE TABLE OVER SO THAT HE
CAN PUT HIS ANKLE UP.

ALAN

(CONT'D) Don't try to make up, Laura. Sure, I'm an established genius
. . . my publicity man says that, if anything, my hair was holding me
back.

ROB

Well, I wouldn't say that.

ALAN

Be smart—don't say anything. I'm letting you off the hook.

LAURA

88 Why?

ROB

Honey . . .

ALAN

(TO ROB) She'll kill it for you yet. This thing had to happen sooner or
later and the way it turned out I'm getting a lot of sympathy and publicity.

ROB

Yeah, that was great stuff in that column.

ALAN

They're taking before and after pictures tomorrow. I may get the front
and back cover of Newstime . . .

ROB

Boy, how about that, honey. I bet you never thought this would work out
so well.

LAURA

89 (BLITHELY TRYING TO MAINTAIN THE GOOD MOOD) Never! Maybe I ought
to go on television and tell about your nose.

ROB STIFFENS.

ALAN

(GETTING STEAMED—TO ROB) You told her about my . . .

LAURA

(QUICKLY) I don't know anything. Ask Rob. I always said I liked you
without your nose.

ROB

She loves it, she loves it!

ALAN

(MENACINGLY TO ROB) Did you tell her about my capped teeth, too?

ROB

90 (LOOKING) Do you have capped teeth?

ALAN

No!

ROB

See how easy it is to blurt something out when you get excited?

ALAN

(STARTS CHASING ROB AND LAURA OUT) Get out of here, both of you!
Out! Why don't you come to my house? Then you can tell all about my
wife's . . .

AND THEY'RE ALL OUT THE DOOR.

FADE OUT:

END OF ACT II

TAG

FADE IN:

INT. KITCHEN—NIGHT.

ROB IS AT THE TABLE TRYING TO READ NEWSPAPER. MILLIE AND LAURA ARE
DISCUSSING DISTRIBUTION OF PRIZES.

MILLIE

Laura . . . it's only fair . . . you got into trouble so you should have
first choice.

LAURA

(RESIGNED) Okay, Millie . . . I guess I'll take the vacuum cleaner . . .

MILLIE

(SOFTLY) Ooooh.

ROB REACTS WITH A CONCEALED SMILE. LAURA BREATHES DEEPLY.

LAURA

Millie, you said I could have first choice.

MILLIE

Yeah . . . but I didn't think you'd pick that.

LAURA

You pick.

MILLIE

No, you pick. You won.

ROB RISES QUICKLY AND CONFRONTS THEM.

                              ROB
May I settle this?

                              LAURA
Please.

                              ROB
We have four prizes, Millie. Pick a number from one to ten.

                              MILLIE
(CONFUSED) Ooooooh . . . oooh . . . uh, nine.

                              ROB
Nine. Laura?

                              LAURA
Uh . . . three.

                              ROB
Good. (TO MILLIE) A color.

                              MILLIE
Red.

                              LAURA
Yellow.

                              ROB
Great. (TO MILLIE) Your favorite tree.

                              MILLIE
Weeping willow.

                              LAURA
The mighty oak.

                              ROB
(TAKES SLIGHTLY BUT RACES ON—TO LAURA) Your favorite planet.

                              LAURA
Earth.

                              MILLIE
She picked my planet.

                              LAURA
Millie.

                              MILLIE
All right, give me Pluto.

                              ROB
Okay. Laura is three yellow oak earth . . . Millie is nine red willow
Pluto. So . . . Millie gets the dryer and the vacuum, Laura gets the
rotisserie and the projector. That's it.

                              MILLIE
Wonderful . . .

LAURA

Rob . . . how did you arrive at that?

ROB

What's the difference, we got there.

HE STARTS OUT. LAURA FROWNS.

MILLIE

Laura . . . I'll trade the vacuum . . .

ROB POPS HEAD BACK IN.

ROB

Millie . . . who's your favorite singer?

MILLIE

Frank Sinatra.

ROB

Then you've gotta keep the vacuum cleaner.

HE EXITS.

LAURA

He's right.

AS MILLIE LOOKS CONFUSED, WE

FADE OUT:

THE END

SCENE-BY-SCENE ANALYSIS OF THE SCRIPT

1. The "teaser" introduces the home audience to a typical daytime giveaway quiz, a kind that has become a familiar abomination. What we see is *authentic* and *fast*. The purpose of this teaser is to put Laura into a situation that is going to imperil Rob. All teasers should manage two other things besides getting the main story in motion: to set mood and be fun to watch.

   Note in the opening directions the overload of adjectives given to Johnny Patrick. We know the writers hate him, even in their imaginations. We know we'll hate him, too. We're told to. Everything is immediately comprehensible. This is to be an idiotic formula show, with a geographic hook as its main idea. We're witnessing the selection of contestants and the byplay that goes with the dreary jokes and phony cordiality of such shows.

2. "Hack it!" and "Love ya!" say a great deal in a few seconds. The emcee is a raucous jerk and a hypocrite. But he has real contact with the female jungle he is about to exploit. We *know* such emcees. We also know such contests. A map and the sign "Pay as you go" are enough.

3. Response to the irresistible Patrick creature quickly shows us a difference between Millie and Laura. We know most of the emcee's jokes are "set" jokes, that he uses them in every warm-up. He winks (sly devil), kids the audience, and gets a contestant off the stage. Why? So we can move quickly

forward with the Millie-Laura scene. Slight though it is, it yields much in the way of character differentiation. Plus a lot of fun.

4. Reference to sex here is not in itself funny, but the writers know their cast. Millie (Ann Morgan Guilbert) has no more sex appeal than a pile of unsorted laundry.

5. There is a slight flare-up. Laura "calls" Millie and challenges her. This gets the moment in motion.

6. Here we have a fine characterizing line. It turns Millie in for being bitchy, ungrateful, and greedy. She's just come for the loot. Her snide remark about Rob instantly draws Laura's loyal response. Millie is a bleak and doughy bundle, the complete opposite of chic and therefore a *fine foil* for Laura. How could anyone stand a woman like Millie—gossipy, suspicious, insensitive, envious? Easy. These women are best friends! This is comedy. Without the sharpness of these contrasting types, the writers would have nothing to work against. (Always go for such contrast in your own work.)

7. "I already thanked you for that" is another way of saying, "For heaven's sakes, stow it!" Millie is a real magpie. From the brief time we've been on the air, consider how much we know of the three—Patrick, Millie, and Laura. Patrick is beautifully enthroned as a chill-hearted, gas-headed ape, Millie a monolith of me-first. Of importance to writers is to note how swiftly yet how accurately a portrait can be drawn, not by description but by *insinuation*—the short but revealing sentence, the side-glance, the inflection, the quick but telling sample.

8. The writers of this script have a perfected instinct for pace. Between Millie's "blind intuition" and the calling out of her name there's no delay. It comes at once. In the same sequence, note the opposite values given to Laura's "Oooh!" (pleased surprise) and Millie's (pure dread). Millie is going to hedge.

9. Millie's backing off necessarily gets Laura displayed, something she has not sought.

10. She gets pushed into the act. Of course it is the mechanical device by which the writers effect the shift (from Millie to Laura), but the mechanics of it are well hidden. How? So much is revealed of the characters of these two that our entire attention is focused on what each will now do, not on how. Getting Laura before the cameras, remember, has been the primary purpose of the teaser. Now we're nearly there.

11. Millie's character now promptly turns into a disaster area. She's just proved herself a total coward. But what does she say to Laura? "Don't be a baby."

12. Then she practically pushes Laura to the stage.

13. Next Millie has the gall to phone her husband. But does she phone him to watch Laura? No, ". . . to watch *me*."
    Note how consistent the writers have been in posing and arranging the posture Millie has now assumed.

14. She is now shameless—and acquisitive.
    We've got a hot situation, well started. It contains more than enough comic tension to hold the audience through the first commercial. With Millie scooting

off to alert her husband, her mouth set in a grin of booty, our interest is zeroed in on one thing now:

How will Laura do?

How Laura will do is a handy thing to have hanging about. It is a useful moving part of the larger mechanism of the story, a moving part that Persky and Denoff, the writers of this teleplay, can lower into the right slot at the moment it will deliver its worst (actually its best) impact.

15. But a situation is not a story, only the beginning of one. Where it's going is quickly indicated with the opening scene of Act I. We are in the office of the greatest package of self-love in television—Alan Brady. Important to us? Of course. He is Rob's boss. With the scene change, we get alterations in atmosphere, mood, and purpose. Shoptalk is brief, but it's enough to get the sense of professionalism of what these people do.

In much less than a full minute, we find Alan Brady to be a bully of extraordinary vanity—powerful, successful, detestable. He holds the live-or-die privilege over all these people. Ruthless? Altogether. No one survives but sycophants. Tremendous comedy values have been brought up from this reservoir, notably in the satanic way Brady treats his own brother-in-law, Mel. (There has seldom been a more perfect piece of casting than the assigning of the role of Mel to Richard Deacon. Any time he's on, it's impossible to look away.)

Mel lives in a perpetual whirl of humiliation. Yet we love to see him pulverized. Why? Because he himself is a horrid, sneaky toad who harasses the writing staff whenever he can get away with it. Here again, with Mel and Alan, we have such a rich contrast of types, the groveler and the scourge, that any time they are seen together we know we're going to hear the lash whistle and crack.

16. Comic obsequiousness opens this scene.

17. The fearsome presence of Alan makes itself felt at once (the necktie bit) and gives Rob a fine moment of distressed pantomime. No one in television can handle these quick flushes of apprehension better than Dick Van Dyke. He can suggest apoplexy by a finger wiggle. The dialogue is fast, uncomplicated— not so much advancing the story as setting the characters and their relationship to the big boss. And setting Alan Brady's self-regard.

18. ". . . so I'll do all the talking." Mention was made earlier of the use of insinuation or intimation to set out a character where he becomes instantly recognizable. But the vanity of Alan Brady is proclamatory. He does it for us.

19. This scene is a typical squelch—Brady the bully, Mel the cringer.

20. As a piece of play-making, why do we get so much of this right here? The writers are doing it deliberately and for this practical reason: when poor Laura has to face this ogre, he must be truly formidable. So we early find him so.

21. "Shut up, Mel." "Speak up, Mel." Squashing Mel is an Alan Brady reflex. Do we enjoy it? You bet. Mel is a worm.

22. A happy domestic intrusion by Ritch. Is it really an intrusion? No. The story hasn't yet started to move. Note three things: how much fun the writers can

wring from the simplest, most natural exchanges—the schoolboy riddle, in this case. Also, how each member of the company gets his share of the dialogue. Finally, how each one uses his (or her) share *characteristically*.

23. The riddle-a-day is a quick filler, so fast it doesn't slow the pace. It also suggests more fun on the way. And it brings a nice family feel to this moment.

24. Start of the running gag ("unlisted banana"). Plus the television show Laura is on. "Those dumb tickets." This downgrades the Johnny Patrick show, and does it in three words.

25. But now the Johnny Patrick show is hooked into *our* show. Now it is a moving part of the plot. Now it is important. They can belittle it, as Buddy does ("Who cares?"), but that doesn't belittle it to us. *We* care. So does Rob. Note also in this stretch of dialogue the emphasis on the unlisted banana. Why so? The writers are preparing to snap it.

26. As they do here, and with a neat reverse.

27. Rob is eager to watch his wife as a contestant—but he doesn't want the others to watch. This is part loyalty, part apprehension. To his relief, they start for lunch.

28. Here our attention sharpens. Brady knows who Patrick is now: ". . . rough on the contestants."

29. Reversal on the lunch plans. Now they'll stay. This tightens it even more.

30. Another nudge of comic sycophancy.

31. Here is one more bounce of the bananas gag. From the point of view of pacing, we now expect to witness the wreckage, and fear Alan Brady will, too.

32. This scene wastes no time on the geography game. We know enough.

33. The main thing here is to get Laura *on*. There is good use of intercutting throughout this sequence. Consider the apprehension that hovers over Rob's head. Consider, also, the large number of contrasting reactions the cameras can quickly pick up. Intercutting accelerates pace and excitement. Use it.

34. Here we have a cheerful buildup that is extremely pleasing to Laura—getting her husband a big plug—only to have the emcee smear it up, insinuate an illicit flavor to Laura's connection to the Petrie he knows.

35. This is the Patrick technique at work, prying and pressing. He's almost saying, "We really caught you then."

36. Laura's delicious moment just stands there, not happening.

37. Patrick never *heard* of Rob. This is adding insult to injury.

38. Good friction here plus professional rivalry.

39. Now we get the first evidence of the diabolical side of the Patrick technique—how he trips and traps his contestants, gets them to stumble, manipulates them. Patrick is exciting to watch, even though we hate him, because he *is* crafty. Here he unabashedly uses the classic ploy: Have you left off beating your wife? He asks Laura if the Alan Brady show is any better than it used to be. Any answer will injure Alan Brady (and torture Rob).

40. There is good staging in these lines: "What's Alan Brady really like?" and "Nobody make a sound." Real suspense.

41. Instant relief.

42. Having been flattered publicly, Alan Brady now reverses his estimate of

Patrick. Notice this: *all the lines* are in character with respect to the person delivering them.

43. Intercutting here makes good comic contradiction possible. Though both scenes (Brady's office and the studio) are essentially stationary—one of them stand-up, the other sit-down—intercutting keeps the entire sequence moving with great speed and lively expectation. A lot is riding on the answers, a lot more than the rotisserie.

44. Laura's struggle with a heartless prosecutor, her unending loyalty to Rob, her gallant reaching out for escapes—all this would win the jury over to her side no matter what the charges. For this one instant she's on top, though we know she won't stay there long. Why not? If she bested the villainous creep who's persecuting her, the show would be over before it got rolling.

45. We cut the scene, which has made its first point, with the interruption for a commercial sell.

46. We know Laura didn't "put her foot in your mouth." But we do know something else, that she presently will.

47. Brady scourges Mel again. This action gets the group in motion.

48. The job threat, the heart of the Brady-Petrie relationship.

49. Rob addresses the TV set. This has great charm. It is really an offering of love.

50. Reaction shots of greedy Millie, already coveting the loot, already arranging the split to suit herself. An authentic note about quiz giveaways: the tawdry merchandise we see on all these shows. It provides an illusion of reality.

51. Patrick's ambush of Laura is a complete success. She commits her worst blunder. There is nothing she could say that would be more damaging to the Brady ego. He's bald.

52. Patrick's true stripe is now in garish display. He gloats. "Aren't we devils?" is in the same category as "Love ya!" He crucifies guests for the savage gratification of a savage audience. Again note how *consistent* the speech is for every character. After tripping Laura, he tries to squeeze his advantage for one more revelation. Laura has no weapons with which to oppose him. She's done her best, yet it's come out for the worst. She knows Rob will now be fired. She is worse than defeated. She is routed.

53. Comic sadism here: "Are we having fun?" It puts in one more nail. Vile Patrick has ravished the innocent.

54. The Petrie kitchen (one of the neatest, most hospitable in all television) provides sharp contrast with what we've just experienced. Millie is already confiscating her share. Laura is right to the point. She knows what she did—"I told America that Alan Brady is bald!"

55. The strong structuring of the Brady vanity has precise purpose: Laura is to collide with it later. This same strip of talk has a marvelously comic detour by the mentally vagrant Millie: "What kind of a hat?"

56. Here Millie redeems herself an inch or two.

57. We get another peek into her little mind.

58. Millie runs as Rob enters. The exchange here provides fine comic suspense. Notice how many character values are displayed. Laura, aside from her basic naïveté, has a cagey quality, quick on the pickup. "Is-it-just-possible-I-didn't-

get-caught" is implicit in all she says and thinks. "Alan said you saved my job." But she knows now that she's lost it for him. And so there's hell to pay.

59. Her breakup in this scene is a delicious and moving moment. Mary Tyler Moore does these better than anyone in television.

60. Great comic pantomime and fine interplay here when Laura snaps it right out, almost defiantly, "That Alan Brady is bald!" Rob's bitter reaction, salted with sarcasm—"What's the fun of telling it if it isn't a secret!"—has important plot connections. (He's soon to make the identical blunder, under somewhat equivalent circumstances.)

61. "Oh, boy, are we in trouble." And oh, boy, does the audience know it.

62. Here the writers ignite another fuse, the secret about Brady's nose job. This is not only a superlative use of comic sense, but it is structurally neat. This *new* secret about the Brady vanity will be part of the finish.

63. Husband-and-wife fury is close enough to reality to be recognized by the viewers. And Laura—in any woman's opinion—has a good defense. It's a fair parallel, what she blurted out on the show and what Rob has just blurted out in the kitchen.

64. Here the directions for line reading and line value are all blunt, unmistakably clear. (Yours should be also.)

65. Because we know there is real love in this marriage, an ideal marriage in all ways, all of its honest disturbances affect our feelings, but all its distractions and social dismantlings are fun. The two elements are kept in balance.

66. Buddy's crack about Rob's savagery is a great touch. How so? The audience knows that Buddy knows Rob to be the gentlest man in the world.

67. Pickles, a total cipher, is "present" in most shows, though never seen. A brief effort was made to cast her but was dropped. So many references had been made to her that when she did physically materialize, she did not resemble the audience's collective (or individual) image of her.

68. Notice *consistency* here again. Each character has his own way with a wisecrack. This is a mark of the professional.

69. Buddy cheerfully throws salt in the wound.

70. This scene provides more lacerations of Mel by Brady, and under conditions in which our enjoyment of their warfare can be total. This Carl Reiner scene, his pantomimes and takes with the gallery of bewigged forms, is to my mind one of the funniest sequences ever delivered by this show. Or any other. At the start, Mel wants one of the toupees. Brady is insulting. Mel is as bald as a bowl.

71. Brady sends a form crashing to the floor. "Pick it up, pick it up!" *Grovel, grovel.* Both in character.

72. "Get your hands off my hair" is explosively funny.

73. Here Mel is the irredeemable flunkey.

74. Now the animation and personification of the mounted toupees. Brady addresses them as if expecting them to respond.

75. Laura has tried to compose herself for this burning-at-the-stake.

76. Nobly she takes the fire. There is no quivering, no begging, no attempt at extenuation.

77. But she can't say the word "hair."

78. It's good for another bounce.
79. The toupees—a ring of blank marionettes—are consulted.
80. "A bald mother figure?" It would be difficult to top this line. Note how normally it seems to follow his previous line; note, also, that the writers didn't have to reach for it.
81. There are unusually rich pantomime opportunities in this scene, with Carl Reiner trying on the toupees one by one. He's suffering. But we love it—he's got it coming to him.
82. There is sad bravery in Laura's hope, "There must be some needy people."
83. Rob, as Galahad, has come in to face up to everything, as he invariably does. Here the extravagant absurdity of Alan, festooned with toupees, makes no impression on Rob at all. He sees it, but doesn't react to it.
84. Rob's not reacting makes possible a rich and riotous tableau.
85. Still sarcastic, Alan Brady wants to be recognized.
86. Here we have good, sarcastic kidding about his baldness.
87. We're over the worst. The action is beginning to go down now.
88. Dick Van Dyke's use and control of inflections is so versatile, his single word "honey" is made to mean, "For goodness sake, don't you know enough to stop while you're ahead!"
89. Now the nose job comes out. Things could get no worse.
90. Rob now tries to use, in his own defense, the same defense Laura put up in the kitchen scene. It is a nice reversal.

This script, not only as a script but as a teleplay that delivered a continuous barrage of believable fun, has been pulled apart with considerable vigor. With all the show's components, major and minor, laid out on the table one by one, as we have done here, it is possible to appreciate each single part for its own contribution, for its intrinsic fun. Furthermore, when the script is disassembled this way, we can discern how each element has been coupled into the larger structural mechanism of the whole. What keeps it running, how emotion takes the place of speed when we have to slow down—all these factors are now visible. It would be difficult to make any deep cuts in this script without losing values we need. It would be hard to make small cuts without jeopardizing coherence and quick comprehension.

Note the *physical* appearance of these pages of dialogue. I call them "open pages." I've emphasized the importance of open pages for the fast pacing of dialogue to all my students at Temple University. I made the emphasis some years before to other students at NYU.

There is another way to analyze story values and scripting. Begin at the end; don't begin at the beginning. Most writers know their finish before they start to fashion their introduction. Most magicians have already finished their trick long before they let *you* see its surprise explode. They've just been padding the act with patter and digital flutter.

In the case of "Coast to Coast Big Mouth," could not the reasoning have gone something like this?

"Let's have a show that is built around Alan Brady's sensitivity to his baldness."

"Right. We'll get Rob in bad someway and threaten his job."

"Let Laura get him in bad, not knowing she's putting him in danger."

"Not knowing, until it's too late."

"Maybe let Laura and Millie stumble into something. Maybe a PTA meeting. Maybe Ritchie and his friends are in false faces. Mr. Clean false faces, and Rob brings one to the office. Puts it on."

"No. No good. Alan Brady is never without his rugs."

"Maybe the open secret of Brady's baldness could be *publicly* revealed. Come out on some Joe Pyne type show."

"Or come out innocently on some game show."

"With a killer-type emcee. A giveaway show that the dames go for."

"Laura wouldn't go to one."

"No, but Millie would. Millie might make Laura come along."

"And the emcee could set up Laura. Get spontaneous admissions out of her. Before she knew she was being had."

That would be enough to start.

Such conversations between the great team that wrote so many of the Dick Van Dyke shows (and innovated so many others) have taken place every time they sat down to put a new one together.

But how did they learn? Where did they start? What setbacks did they have to survive? How did they reach their present position? And especially how did they accomplish it while still so young? Here are some clues:

> We started our joint career while working at Radio Station WNEW in New York. We met there in 1955 while working in the Continuity Department. We started writing jokes, jingles, and special material. After writing for many nightclub performers, we got our first television job out here in California in 1961, working for Steve Allen. That show was short-lived, which propelled us into a period of unemployment. We worked on the Andy Williams show in 1962.
>
> After that season we decided to write half-hour shows, primarily because we wanted to fortify our craft as writers. We wrote a few episodes for the *Joey Bishop Show,* the *Bill Dana Show, McHale's Navy,* and then wrote one for Carl Reiner. He liked our work and said we could do as many as we wanted for the *Dick Van Dyke Show.*
>
> This being the best show on the air, we jumped at the chance and stayed with it for three years. During that period we did some specials, including the *Julie Andrews Special.* We then created a series for Marlo Thomas called *That Girl* and are the Executive Producers of this series. We also created and produced the CBS show *Good Morning, World,* which, as you know, is no more.
>
> Last year we wrote the *Sid Caesar Special,* and this past season we wrote and produced the *Bill Cosby Special.*
>
> We are now out of work.
>
> /Signed/ Bill Persky and Sam Denoff

7

GOMER PYLE

McHale's Navy, Hogan's Heroes, F Troop, Sgt. Bilko, and thirty others of
greater or lesser inspiration would suggest to any mind—whether approving or
disapproving of this kind of entertainment—that service comedies of one branch or
another will always have a slot in television schedules. They should, too.

About thirty-three million living Americans have been in uniform. This figure
keeps advancing as the seasons do.

Happy-go-lucky extravaganzas like *Gomer* are easy to ridicule—but they aren't
easy to write.

"Pyle succeeds with a big audience," wrote one of my students, "and easy to see
why: a happy revelation to viewers that they've finally found someone dumber than
they are. (Don't be too sure, citizens.) "

And another: "*Gomer Pyle* is successful because it's idiotic. Idiocy is one of the
seven virtues of television comedy. The other six are innocuousness, blandness,
fraudulence, simplicity, plasticity, and Doc."

And of Gomer's sergeant: "Carter is a typical sergeant with an extra two inches
added to the mouth."

This always makes for a lot of classroom fun. But I always kept a stick to flog
them with and the students knew this. I might at any time assign them to *write* one
of these things. And often did.

In another part of this book I've recorded the class response to the problems that
beset a show now long gone—*The Legend of Custer.* The class, after deriding most
of the goings-on, suddenly reversed itself upon being told to shift its point of view
from persecutor to repairman.

No writer can make any progress in television unless he can bring an honest
defense to the shows he works on. If he can't do this, if the temptation to derision
is too strong, he should sign off and try another. Unless you are a professional critic,
the panning should begin and end in conversation. It should never find its way to
the typewriter. The work of putting shows together is too tough, that of condemning
too easy.

Another basic for writers-who'd-like-to-get-there: you can't walk into a producer's office and tell him his show stinks. If the show is in trouble, he already knows it. If it's not, your comment has no meaning.

Before making anyone do any work on his own interpretation of *Gomer Pyle,* I read to the class a thoughtful piece of criticism of a show that, to me, had seemed doomed from the very start—you may remember it—*Dundee and the Culhane.* My own reasons for thinking this show would fail are not important. The following student comment I felt to be very apt:

"No western can make room for a Fred Astaire type—never in a continuing role. The light presence, the fine speech, the splendid acting of John Mills make everyone look like an unwashed bum. But this show's *principal* problem is with its language.

"Language is on three separate levels. In a single scene you hear the precise, clipped English of John Mills. On top of this, the more precise *legal* speech in the trials. The 'western' talk that everywhere forces itself in sounds out of its own groove. The different language levels don't add interest. They confuse; they dilute and distract. This doesn't quicken the viewer's interest. It does the reverse—it alienates him."

That is a penetrating observation. And the class to whom I read this (that week studying *Gomer Pyle*) recognized its thoughtfulness.

"If you can't take the show *Gomer Pyle* seriously—and I'm not insisting you should—you must take the show's elements seriously. For example, what is the basic difference between *Gomer Pyle* and *Bilko?*"

Ridicule vanished.

"In *Bilko,*" wrote one student, "it's the rascal and his machinations. In *Pyle,* it's the buffoon and his blunders."

Another response: "*Bilko* is management. *Pyle* is labor."

A third: "The basic difference between *Gomer Pyle* and *Sgt. Bilko* is this: in *Pyle* everyone works for the best and bungles it. In *Bilko* everyone works for the worst and makes it."

I asked this: "Who is Gomer?" and received this: "Gomer is the country boy adrift in civilization, a stereotype that dates back to Rousseau and the Natural Man concept. Tarzan is another variation."

I asked if the *Gomer Pyle* show were a true original or derivative.

"Derived. The sergeant's role, as victim of Gomer's bungling, lets us identify with Gomer, an aspect of their interplay that is reminiscent of Laurel and Hardy."

"More heisted than derived," said another. "They just took Dagwood and Dithers out of the office and put them in uniform."

Anyone familiar with the *Blondie* strip and series will appreciate the appositeness of this. Both are fair comments, if unfinished.

In every student, the whole mechanism of his mind, the whole challenge to his talent, takes a sudden affirmative turnaround when he leaves the plush seat of the audience and faces the bleakness of the typewriter. And when a student, about to make his first try at a Gomer story, compresses the Gomer character into this— "scared but incorruptible, gullible but game"—you know that you, as teacher, have made a little progress.

Time had a most revealing column on Jim Nabors, very appealing and human. And it appeared the same week we were screening film and studying scripts of the show. The behind-the-scenes peek at this unusual natural, the revelation of the size of the money, the big-business talk by his agent, all helped to persuade reluctant minds and educated types—those with the typical university built-in resistance to Gomer—that if they were indeed good enough to write for him, they'd be in the big time. Here is *Time*'s story:

SUCCESS IS A WARM PUPPY
(From *Time*, November 10, 1967, copyright Time, Inc. 1967)

Nabors is both a representative and a caricature of the noble American rustic. As Gomer, a leatherneck Pfc., he wears a gee-whiz expression, spouts homilies out of a lopsided mouth and lopes around uncertainly like a plowboy stepping through a field of cow dung.

He is a walking disaster area.

When his drill sergeant chastises him for "taking the taxpayer's money without putting in a day's work," the hapless recruit returns part of his paycheck—and fouls up the bookkeeping system of the entire Marine Corps. Yet in the end, Gomer's goodness always wins out. He is, in short, an innocent out of step with the swinging 60's, which must explain why the Nielsens love him so.

Nabors, who offstage is only slightly less gentle than Gomer, went to Los Angeles in 1958 not to feed his ambition but to foil his asthma. He worked as an apprentice film cutter, sang on amateur nights at a club called The Horn. TV's Andy Griffith dropped by one night, liked his country-bumpkin patter between songs and offered him a walk-on role in his series. Nabors says he was as nervous as a cat in a room full of rocking chairs, but Griffith assured him that "all I had to do was act like one of those fellows down home who sit around the gas pump reading comic books." Shucks, that was easy, and Nabors soon became a regular on the show. *Gomer*, naturally, was a spin-off.

Though he will make $500,000 this year, Nabors is hardly the type to go Hollywood. His fans like to think of him as "jes folks," and he knows on which side his cornbread is buttered. He lives alone in a six-room house in unchic Studio City with a swimming pool that, by Hollywood standards, is little more than a glorified bathtub. No dual-exhaust Belchfire sports car for him; his speed is a Rambler station wagon. He leaves the wheeling and dealing to his manager, Dick Linke, a Hollywood slicker who limits Nabors to a weekly allowance of $75, pours the rest of his money into California real estate.

"Jim is a warm puppy," says Linke, who fully expects him to soon out-earn his other top client, Andy Griffith. "I figure another year of Jim doing Gomer, then on to Broadway. Then back to Hollywood for the movies. I've got another Al Jolson on my hands. You see how in his act I got him dropping down on one knee like Jolie? He hasn't got that voice throb yet, but it's coming, it's coming."

This is one of the shows that university people feel they are above watching. But the men who wrote *Gomer Pyle* don't draw on their Ivy League backgrounds. Most don't have them.

Here is some down-to-earth talk from a tough professional, Jack Elinson, a *Gomer Pyle* writer—"telling it like it is":

"My brother Iz started in the business just writing jokes as a hobby. He used to send topical gags to Winchell and eventually became one of Winchell's biggest contributors. Then Walter O'Keefe, who was a pretty prominent radio comedian at that time, started noticing Izzy's stuff in the papers and asked him if he'd like to work on his radio show. Naturally, Iz jumped at the chance and that was the beginning of his career.

"Iz had no formal education in writing. He just had a funny bone—something they can't teach you in school. Colleges can teach you how to write. But they can't teach you how to write funny. It has to be inbred.

"When I got the bug to make up jokes, Izzy suggested I start the same way—by sending gags to Winchell, which I did. That was my basic training and it later led to work in radio, then to television. My particular 'break' was having Iz already in the business. He was able to open those first few doors for me. After that, the words I myself put on paper had to carry me through.

"I think that's how most writers break into the business today—they're helped by other writers. New writers, with anything at all on the ball, seem to be zooming to the top a lot faster than we did in our day. We'd have to have a whole season, and a successful one, before they'd give us a nominal raise. Nowadays if a writer shows he's got the stuff, he's immediately given the top fee. Good comedy writers are so scarce, producers want to lock them up when they're discovered. So they're willing to pay the money.

"As far as the networks are concerned, I don't believe they're making any honest effort to develop new writers. Right now, they're not even making any honest effort to develop anything new for television. They are taking the easy way out with movies and letting it go at that.

"Right now there's a pall of gloom over this town, about the state of TV. They all feel we're about to enter a giant recession. Writers, actors, and everybody else connected with the business are genuinely worried about where the work will be coming from if the movies continue to gobble up the prime time. This isn't a very encouraging thing to tell budding writers, I know, but it's the truth.

"Of course, I think writers are in a better position than any of the others. Even if they're not being paid for it right there and then, they can go ahead writing and their work can pay off later. Maybe this recession will be a good thing. It will force a lot of us into writing plays and scenarios, which we've all talked about doing but never got around to. We've been too busy grinding out the TV series. Often in the past, writers who couldn't get work in TV ended up writing that smash play or picture, simply because there wasn't anything else to do. So, ironically, they became much more successful than the average TV writer.

"Agents—good agents, that is—are always important to the new writer, but as I said before, it's usually the established writer who can really help the guy coming up. I know of so many writers in this business today who are here simply because they were recommended by other writers. Then, after they're established, they can begin to maneuver and do themselves some good.

"Summing it up, despite the above negatives, I would say that the opportunities are better than ever for the new writer. All I know is that I go to Writers' Guild meetings and see all these young faces. In fact, they're so young, I feel like kicking their tails. *Who sent for them?*

"But whether we like it or not, they're coming—they're *here!*—and we veterans have to just hope they're not too much better than we are. After all, we'd like to keep working, too. An awful lot of Cadillacs and swimming pools depend on us."

Jack Elinson's credits include:
Coproducer and writer: *Danny Thomas Show*
Producer: *The Bill Dana Show*
Producer-Writer: *Run, Buddy, Run*
Writer: *Danny Thomas Show, Andy Griffith Show, The Real McCoys, Jimmy Durante, Garry Moore, Ed Wynn, Johnny Carson.*
The point Elinson makes here (of older writers helping younger writers to come along) was also made to me by Sam Bobrick, who gave this further emphasis: "Young writers are sympathetic to the even younger writers."
One of the most practical pluses in this whole vexed area of writing is represented by Sheldon Leonard, a man of ferocious demeanor (gangster roles as an actor—he could outstare Bogart) but of an unusually perceptive response to writers, what they are, what they need, how to get their best, how to turn them into producers or producer-writer teams. Leonard has an unexpected sensitivity to writing, a quick understanding of writers and their craft, what they really mean to the industry and how they can be best protected, best used.
Sheldon Leonard is truly innovative, as seen in his early uses of the sixteen-millimeter camera (in *I Spy*), his iconoclastic philosophies of production, his throwing away everything that is worn-out or useless. But it is in his quiet development of new writers, new teams, his quick recognition of exact values, and his more exceptional recognition that good writers very often are poor talkers (less and less so in "verbalized" Hollywood)—it is in this area that Leonard's contributions are of immense though seldom recognized value. It is possible that teams such as Kleinschmidt and McCraven, Peggy Elliott and Ed Scharlock, Jerry Belson and Gary Marshall would not be operating as such without Leonard's influence.
All writers who have ever worked for him say the same thing, that he's the finest man in the business, with the quickest, most intuitive response to writers. Through Sheldon Leonard the stature of the writer has improved. He's given them dignity, respect, and self-respect, given them more to say, more room to work in, more opportunity to expand their own capacities, more confidence, more money, more breaks.

In a mood quite different from any other in this book come the following words of Leonard Stern, creator of *The Good Guys, He and She, The Hero, Run, Buddy, Run, I'm Dickens, He's Fenster,* and regular writer over many seasons on *The Honeymooners, Sgt. Bilko,* and the *Steve Allen Show.*
Leonard Stern has won every award there is, including the Emmy and the Peabody. Among the nationally acclaimed comedians he has introduced to television are Bill Dana, John Astin, Louis Nye, Tom Poston, Don Knotts, and Don Adams.
Stern began in radio, more than twenty-five years ago, after majoring in journalism at Columbia. He did special material for Milton Berle and worked on such

radio shows as *Take It or Leave It,* the *Dinah Shore Show,* and *Abbott and Costello.* He also wrote a number of the *Ma and Pa Kettle* scenarios.

I have extracted what I feel are his most illuminating comments from an informal lecture delivered at CBS a year ago and titled "The Comedy Writer in Television." And I have also included some fragments from the question-and-answer period that followed his talk. Writers will find some of Stern's comments to be a bit salty, some wry, some bittersweet, many of them close to cynical, but no reader can walk away from what Stern had to say about his own work without the feeling that he had made a true effort to level with his audience, not only in the briskness of his responses but in his frequent acknowledgment of hurt and bafflement.

Here is part of the seminar:

> I have been writing comedy for television since 1953. When I first started, I was innocent about the lunacy that prevails in all echelons of the business. I now accept all this. Perhaps my personal experiences over the past fifteen out of twenty years will give you an idea of the evolution, the mercurial changes of comedy material on television.
>
> Prior to entering television, I was writing motion pictures. At that time there was enormous fear that the giant of television would eliminate movies. This fear was so deep-rooted that most motion picture companies reduced their production by eighty percent. Work being at a minimum, I was most receptive to an offer to work in New York on the *Jackie Gleason Show.*
>
> I was most interested in *The Honeymooners.* Up until this time it had only been a ten-minute segment on his show. I felt *The Honeymooners* could easily expand to an hour. I was looking forward to exchanging ideas with Jackie and selling him on my premise. I had known Jackie as a friend. There was a time when we had shared a room in Las Vegas, where he was appearing, very unsuccessfully, in a nightclub. But he was big now.
>
> The power in the early days of comedy television was in the hands of the comedian: Milton Berle, Gleason, Lucille Ball, Sid Caesar. You didn't submit a concept to them. It came from the performer. For example, *The Honeymooners* was a Gleason idea. So was the highly imaginative thought of having Art Carney portray a sewer worker.
>
> This power of which I speak was so absolute in those days that no one offended a star. Networks, agencies, other performers, producers, directors, writers—all subjugated their wishes to those of the star.
>
> In the early days of television comedy—comedy was funny. There is logical thought behind this paradoxical statement. Most of the comedians knew what was funny, what was right for them. The shows were done in front of an audience (Gleason, Caesar, Lucille Ball, Danny Thomas, *Bilko*). If the material didn't work, the comedian died. The next week's show had to be funny or grand-scale replacements were made—usually among the writers.
>
> Comedy content in shows started to decline when comedians were all used up, or because they grew tired of the medium and abdicated. Once the comedians were replaced by actors and the studios dictated the form of the show, the comedy content lessened severely. Sometimes it was totally absent.
>
> As the "new" comedy became the thing, there was less of a demand for laughter in comedy. The more talented comedy writers deserted. Consequently, in the middle years you had very few truly funny shows, a lot of bad ones,

and a few which emphasized whimsy and gentle humor, such as *Father Knows Best.*

This depreciation of comedy was of great concern to me. When I became a producer on my own, I wanted to go back to the big laugh show. *Dickens and Fenster* was my first show. I wanted to play it in front of an audience. I knew that in front of an audience we would have to earn our laughs. I wanted to legitimately challenge the audience, to prove what we'd brought. I always hated putting a laugh track into a show. It's a cheat. You're out of gas and you're getting a tow. You're stealing it. Danny Thomas, Dick Van Dyke, and Lucy were all live audience shows. Each of them was unquestionably funny, and I can't help but believe that part of the reason was that they tested their material against an audience.

I hope you don't infer that I feel all shows should be done in front of an audience. There are many excellent shows that are designed not to be, such as the *Andy Griffith Show.* I am involved in one, *Get Smart.* We are fortunate in having Don Adams, a truly funny man, as the star. And he is a welcome return to the past. He demands that the scripts be funny. Initially the gimmick idea of the show caught on, but today I think it owes its popularity to Don Adams. He has transcended the show.

A few years back in *He and She* we tried to reestablish big laughter in situation comedy, while at the same time keeping it current by making our characters reflect today's thinking. It failed by narrow marginal statistics, and yet in its failure became a peculiar type of success. Everybody started to revere it, perhaps disproportionately so. Because it was no longer around, it acquired stature—"the dearly departed." Incidentally, the same thing is true of *The Honeymooners.* There are only thirty-nine of them on film, and they've been rerun some twenty-odd times each—a phenomenal record. But because they're the only record on two monumental artists, they're revered and given disproportionate kudos.

The actual producing of a comedy show is no different from the producing of any show. The producer is always dependent upon the writers if the concept is about people, and dependent upon the public if the show revolves around a gimmick. I think when *Bewitched* came out everybody tried to climb aboard with their own version of the "believable supernatural" show. Then the networks declared the gimmick show out. Yet when *I Dream of Jeannie* succeeded, it was back in again. After feeble attempts to emulate *Jeannie* failed, the ghost was given up until *The Ghost and Mrs. Muir* worked. So any season now someone is going to get another one of those invisible people on the air—possibly us.

To me, speaking as writer, the most difficult type of comedy to write is that based upon character differences, contrasts, and confrontations. Because of the paucity of writers skilled in this area, you are more apt to see gimmick shows and soft comedy on the air.

The depreciation of the appreciation of writers' skills has hurt us as far as content is concerned. This lack of respect for the importance of writing is reflected in shows' budgets. Let me cite you some examples:

The Gleason show was budgeted (it was an hour then, mind you) at around fifty thousand dollars. The writing budget was, in those days, somewhere around twelve thousand dollars. Today a one-half-hour show costs close to ninety thousand dollars and the budget for writers is thirty-five hundred dollars. Nearly twenty-five percent of the budget was once allotted to writing. Now it is closer to four percent. This, as much as anything else, explains why so many gifted writers have moved out. Neil Simon might still be in television had they thought to recognize and pay for his skills.

Nat Hiken created *Sgt. Bilko*. I worked on that show. I cannot say I wrote *Bilko* because only Nat was able to truly write this imaginative show. Television let him go by, and when you think about it, it is very sad that most of today's good dramatic writers and directors, who were spawned in television, are now no longer connected with the medium.

Television is simply not respectful of its creative artists.

I have always considered a pilot a deceit. You spend four hundred thousand dollars for one show and then, should you sell it, you attempt to duplicate it for eighty-five or ninety thousand dollars. This is totally impossible. Or take the situation where you have, say, a Reginald Rose write your pilot. You cannot afford to meet his price for subsequent episodes. Nor are there comparable skills available at a lesser price. What do you do? You don't sacrifice the series. You continue it, painfully aware that more often than not there is a severe loss of quality. What is the solution? How do you hold gifted writers?

On the shows that we've attempted, we've tried to reestablish the staff concept. That means we guarantee the people who are working on the show employment for forty weeks. This insures that they are with us physically, emotionally, and creatively when we need them.

Though it works for us, the staff concept has not generally prevailed. Today most writers and directors are forced to free-lance. Because of this they are unavailable on anything amounting to a regular basis. It is not uncommon for a man to direct a show and then not make it to the first cut. He can't be there to help edit because he's on another job. Consequently you often have to edit without knowing what he had in mind!

Prices have escalated so much that I don't know the solution. Maybe some realistic support by the networks is the answer.

All of us are interested in the machinations involved in selling a show. It is difficult to present an idea of any originality because of the preconceived notions and taboos indelibly set in the buyers' minds. Yet what is most appealing is the unconventional, the new, the pattern breaker. Here are two shows from early television which I feel would be most difficult to sell today. Let me show you the difficulties I, as a salesman, might encounter in today's marketplace if these were the two packages I had to sell. I will play both parts. The conversation would go somewhat like this:

Writer: How do you do, sir.
Buyer: Hello.
Writer: I have a new show.
Buyer: New show. Good. Always interested in a new show. What's its name?
Writer: *The Honeymooners*.
Buyer: Interesting. Young couple, starting out in life?
Writer: No, sir. They're not young, they're about thirty-five, thirty-eight.
Buyer: Why do you call them the honeymooners?
Writer: Well, that doesn't matter. We can change the title, it just seemed amusing.

Buyer: Yes, amusing. What is it about?

Writer: Well, sir, you see, there's this man who's a bus driver and he—

Buyer: No, no. Who's interested in a bus driver? That's too mundane, most people don't care—

Writer: Well, sir, we can skip the bus driver. It's actually his relationship with his wife and his best friend who's a sewer worker that matters. The two men—

Buyer: Hold it! What does the other fellow do?

Writer: He's a sewer worker.

Buyer: When do you expect this show to go on?

Writer: Well, prime time. Eight, eight thirty.

Buyer: While people are eating you're going to have a sewer worker on? You know, young man, they don't have sewers in Kansas. What's your other idea?

Writer: It's a show called *I Love Lucy*.

Buyer: Good title. Young couple, starting out in life?

Writer: Well, they're not so young, they're about thirty-five—

Buyer: How many children?

Writer: No children.

Buyer: That's not good. Thirty-five, without . . .

Writer: Well, sir, we won't . . . the fun is that she's a nut, eccentric, and they have friends upstairs with whom they relate and she makes a great deal about the fact that they—

Buyer: They should be young.

Writer: Well, they're not old in the old sense. You see, the wife, she tries to help her husband with his orchestra and his nightclub . . .

Buyer: Orchestra and nightclub . . . you're going to do a show-business show?? —There hasn't been a successful show-business show on the air ever!!!

Writer: Well, we won't trade on that, sir. She'll make much more fun of the way he speaks—

Buyer: What do you mean the way he speaks?

Writer: He has an accent. He's a bandleader.

Buyer: What kind of an accent?

Writer: Cuban.

Buyer: A Cuban bandleader! ! ! ! ?

My own evolution on *Get Smart* is funny. I started out as the producer and then we had to make room for a writer so I became the executive producer. Then we hired two permanent writers and I was no longer the executive producer. Now my credit comes at the end of the show and says something about my being in charge of production, whatever that is. I think I'm just one staff writer away from being off the program entirely.

Because of the enormous costs of a show produced today, the demand is for immediate success, more than ever before. This, as much as anything, explains the disproportionate reliance on gimmick shows. Gimmicks, if they work, happen immediately. *Get Smart* is a case in point. Initially it could have been called a gimmick show, and had it not succeeded I doubt whether we would have lasted beyond thirteen weeks. We are now in our fifth season and, as I mentioned before, a marvelous evolution has taken place. Don Adams has *become* the show. People relate to him, not to the spy background.

When I was on the Steve Allen show, we featured for the first two years Don Knotts, Louis Nye, and Tom Poston. Those three men gave the show impact. Many of our expressions, such as "nooop," "hi ho, Steverino," and "why not?" were the "sock it to me" of their day. The impact of the show started to diminish almost in direct ratio to the characters we added in the subsequent years. The men were gifted comedians, enormously talented— Bill Dana, Tim Conway, Dayton Allen, Pat Harrington, Jim Nabors, Gabe Dell. But it is impossible to write a one-hour show that involves that many people and give equal time to all the performers. Equal time becomes important if there is no one *star* on a show. Watch your favorite variety shows. If they start to disintegrate, you will know that it is the internecine warfare that is doing it more than anything else. Invariably one performer wants to know, "Why is my part so small?" Soon enmity and rivalry prevail. It is unfortunate. It's called living, I think.

People ask me what we do at Talent Associates to promote new writing talent. What we've done is the only thing I know to do, buy outside scripts and hire new writers. As a matter of fact, if you will look at the *Laugh-In* staff, four of those men started with us, contributing to *Get Smart*. Whenever we see something on paper that is legitimately funny, we'll make room for the talent in some way. I wish there was a way of teaching comedy writing. You can teach the theory. You can indicate desired content. But you can't make a funny bone. You can only develop one that exists.

The movies are such severe competition for writing talent that it is very difficult to hold onto those that you do find and develop. A case in point: Jerry Belson and Gary Marshall. Six or seven years ago Gary and Jerry were writing the Joey Bishop show. They went from that to the *Dick Van Dyke Show*, then to producing *Hey, Landlord*, which they created. Now a few short years later they have their own motion picture company. Their first movie, with Debbie Reynolds, did very well. They obviously don't need or desire the grueling weekly schedule of television. We in our office now hire only masochists.

You rise or fall on the strength of your personalities. *The Fugitive* made David Janssen. But it is equally true that David Janssen made *The Fugitive*. Envision a physically less attractive actor running from the police and it is not inconceivable that you would want him caught. Comedy is no better off.

Sophisticated comedy today is suffering from a lack of training grounds for both performers and writers. S. N. Behrman and Phillip Barry comedies are simply nonexistent. There isn't any place where future Robert Montgomerys, Henry Fondas, or Melvyn Douglases can cut their wit and wisdom teeth. This is an enormous loss. When you gave Spencer Tracy a scene, he made it unique because of his inherent charm. Today the emphasis is in totally another direction. Actors feature their *neuroses!*

Television was a medium of dialogue in its early days. Right now *form* is taking precedence over content. Interesting to me is how the movies are employ-ing television commercial concepts in the making of their pictures. There are smash cuts, overlapping dissolves, and all forms of graphic arts. Today, if you try to put a story together, you learn it isn't there. Words are used as a last resort. But it won't be ever thus. I think we will come back to story ideas and words. Save your dictionaries.

Questions from the floor:

Q: Is there a prescribed formula which assures a comedy show of getting on the air?

A: I would say so.

Q: Will you tell us what it is?

A: Provided you don't take notes. Actually there are certain shows more apt to receive consideration than others because of one frightening thing—they are more familiar. A gang comedy, a group of individuals fighting the system or authority, is usually safe fare to serve the potential buyer. *Bilko, McHale's Navy, F Troop, Gomer Pyle* are of this genre.

Q: How many writers of comedy are there? How many men write comedy?

A: Those *are* two questions. There are about fifty gifted comedy writers. There are about two hundred who write comedy. When I say two hundred men write comedy, I don't necessarily limit it to television. That includes those who write books and plays as well. I find that most of the successful comedy writers stopped writing as soon as they became affluent. Or were easily recognized at a party. Forget being affluent. Being recognized at a party is enough.

Q: We have not established whether or not the transition is going to take place. For the first fifty years the film industry really didn't say very much, and then it stepped out in the last ten years and said a great deal, and it's been pretty well accepted. The question is: do you think something like this could happen to television?

A: It will regress or progress depending on what is required for survival. The absence of a movie audience, one weened away by television, forced the movies to explore areas, attitudes, and perversions never before brought to the screen . . . subjects which right now would not be permitted on television. Unless you live in Palm Springs. I don't remember who said it, I think it was me, that impending disaster is consistently the prime reason for innovation and change in thought and ideas. Try to remember that. I think it's going to be the best sentence tonight.

May I ask myself a question which just occurred to me? How many of today's provocative movies will they be able to show in prime time? Answer: This will be determined by the need for an audience. Of course, sometimes you do get a change in programming as a result of one man's tenacious pursuit of an ideal or an idea. . . . You never get it by a committee decision.

Q: Aren't you, by treating the contemporary subjects in a comedic vein, actually tending toward satire? Could you take a show like *The Good Guys* and all of a sudden start making jokes about the current scene without actually changing the whole concept of the show?

A: Yes and no. That is not as ambivalent as it seems. If we would be exclusively satirical, we would be bending the format and misrepresenting what we had sold, but by sprinkling the show with contemporary references, we enhance its value, I think, by making it a show of today. What we have to avoid is being topical. Topical jokes are ephemeral. Let me put that another way. If we were to discuss a subject such as a specific strike, say the teachers' strike or the sanitation men's strike in New York, this would be disadvantageous. A few years from now the specifics of the strike would be forgotten. And if they *were* remembered, that very fact would make the show seem dated. But there is nothing wrong with doing a story about a strike. Say Claudia were to be a member of the cashiers' union and she was called out on strike. There seems to be something inherently funny about a wife being forced to strike against her husband. Eventually a fight ensues and they are not speaking. Now when they go to bed, she won't cross the picket line. . . . Give me a moment. I want to write that down.

Q: Now, I've been watching the so-called youthful revolution for many years and I'm just curious to know whether anyone has done any research to find out if some of the lack of respect for authority the young people have may not have been from the overuse of television.

A: In my own household our children are discriminating in their choice of shows. As some of you may know, I produce *Get Smart,* and yet my nine-year-old daughter last year steadfastly watched *My Three Sons* in preference to *Get Smart.* This year we haven't had to face that problem —we don't allow her to live with us.

8

THE PRICE OF TOMATOES

One of the destructive clashes that will always be present in network television—at least in the structure we have now—is the clash between business people and program people. Program people do not make program decisions. Business people make program decisions. These business people often have the title of program executives, but they are not program people. They are business people.

This same collision course exists also in most advertising agencies. Most copywriters are at the mercy of nonwriters, at the mercy of men and women who themselves could not write an entertaining memo. They are "account" people, business people.

Commercial artists in advertising agencies are similarily subjected to the most awful critical nonsense of which English is capable. To be sure, art directors very often can help out by translating (and translate is the right word) what the artist is doing, and by explaining why he's doing it that way. Art directors can make clear to clients, account executives, and other members of that vast congregation of the hard-of-hearing what is happening in the picture, and why it is good advertising.

Because their world is special, perhaps arcane, artists suffer fewer invasions and humiliations than writers do. Writers are unprotected. No executive is afraid to pick up a piece of copy and "rework" it. But he is afraid to pick up a paintbrush, for he knows he'd then really parade his foolishness. He's not afraid to pick up a pencil if the page is already filled. But give the same executive a blank page, tell him to fill it, and he'll faint.

This explains much of the forced or the eunuchoid or the bleached, leached quality of so many of America's ads. Committee work. Nonwriters hacked them to death. Nonwriters took out the buzz. Nonwriters dismembered them, wrung them, boiled them.

The artwork is usually better than the copy. It's less thumbed and fingered.

In the network area, the absence of program people in top programming jobs is, to my mind, the source of its worst blunders. And its most expensive. The scarcity of skillful program builders, the scarcity of programming judgment in network program departments, can be explained—to some extent defended—by the fact that networks don't do much building anymore. They do a good deal of financing but they create less and less as the seasons pass.

I observed many years ago that the typical American business success is a man who is scared to death of emotion, afraid to show it, that he equates it with softness or weakness or with something less than the hard professionalism that got him where he is; that he must be ruthless. Show me a ruthless man and I'll show you a man who never created anything.

In the advertising business this refusal to recognize, assess, and use the raw material of emotion—whether it appears in the lyric of a coffee jingle or in one of the graphic arts or in a block of copy or in the unfolding of a dramatic show—this refusal is costly. Yet advertising is crowded with executives who feel their tough-guy, man-on-the-move image is threatened if they acknowledge either the existence or the value of human feeling, or if they permit themselves to respond to its allures and beckonings. They're afraid to show feeling, afraid to be caught at it. They'd sooner be caught in a motel with the wrong girl.

They resemble a bunch of battlewise generals who remain stony-eyed at mass burials.

It's-smart-to-be-ruthless is a proper posture, no doubt, for the men involved in most of the world's big industries. But the advertising executive who has fenced himself out of the world of *feeling* is either dense or myopic or hypocritical. Or all three. I've worked in five large advertising agencies. In twenty-five years I have never heard a top advertising executive make a speech that was fit to listen to. Not one. Anywhere. Ever. What was said was poorly said. And what was thought was no more stimulating than a side dish of unsalted parsnips. They all keep making the same speech year after year. They're afraid to say anything with feeling. Or to say anything new. Of course, they never know how dull they've been. They're the president of the agency. Who's going to tell them?

It is appalling what a hundred-thousand-dollar salary can immunize a man against, how stock options can inflate self-regard and block off a bright man from further teaching.

There are a few exceptions. There are even a few executives who can write. And a few copy chiefs who have published. But it is criminally and professionally wasteful of the American advertising executive to bypass the value of human feeling. And it is stupid. It is stupid because his business *lives* on it. Emotion is the core of effective advertising. The value just referred to is a real and palpable one; it is a money value.

In television the situation is not so well hidden as it is in advertising. Each year a new fleet of hopefuls is hauled from the hangars, revved up, and let go. A few of these fly. But why are there so many disasters? Why are there so many when there are at the same time so many sharp businessmen who abhor losses more than they abhor fines and taxes?

I believe it comes back to the matter of emotion. I believe it is that basic. I believe the greatest weakness in television today is the scarcity of the program executive who can make a true judgment on a written property, who knows how to do this by instinct and by the hard practice of the years, who knows because he has himself put his hand to the building of some of these happy constructs. It seems to me a wasteful oversight on the part of top management—from the very beginning of network television right up to its form as we know it today—that only two men with the ultimate responsibility of network television programming have ever published anything.

One of these men is David Levy, the other is Hubbell Robinson. I don't believe I've missed anybody.

Wouldn't you think in the course of more than two decades of television storytelling that *some* executive—one, at least—might have thought it a good idea to hire a man from a book publishing firm, for instance, or a magazine, a man who had spent his professional life buying material that would entertain, amuse, hold, or fascinate the public? Hire a man who had a success record in the purchase of popular fiction? In the handling of writers? In the reading of popular tastes?

Television has never looked in this area for help. Yet what is written is still the most important single fact and factor of this whole business. And expertise in evaluating what the man wrote remains television's weakest, most unpeopled area.

Right next to the cemetery of junked pilots is the orphanage of banished scripts. It is painful to report that the great script we will next explore was flatly rejected by a high-level network program executive. I shall make no further comment about it. There's no need to. It makes its own.

"Why doesn't *McCall's* print more good stories?" Some years ago this question was put to its then editor—Herb Mayes—and he gave it instant reply: "Because we don't get them. We only get six or seven fine stories a year."

The same answer will explain the long slow death of the anthology efforts in television drama. If any dramatic series could be sure of a story as moving as "The Price of Tomatoes" and at a frequency rate of one in three, this type of television entertainment would be with us through the remainder of the century.

I wish any reader who is going through this book for the purpose of improving his own skills as a television storyteller would stop right here and read "The Price of Tomatoes." Read it uncritically. Read it for the sole purpose of receiving its emotional impact.

Marks of professional skill, true signs of the true craftsman, are visible on every page. We shall look at every page and point these out.

THE PRICE OF TOMATOES
by
Richard Alan Simmons

Copyright © 1962 by Four Star Television

ACT I

FADE IN:

1 EXT. WHOLESALE PRODUCE MARKET—CRANE SHOT—ESTABLISHING—DAY. OUR DOWN ANGLE ESTABLISHES THE VITALITY OF A WHOLESALE PRODUCE MARKET: TRUCK-AND-TRAILER RIGS, PILES OF CRATES, BOOTHS, OFFICES, DEALS BEING MADE IN THE STREET. THE LOCALE IS EL PASO. MANY OF THE WORKERS ARE MEXICAN AND SOME OF THE BOSSES WEAR BROAD-RIMMED HATS.

WE DESCEND NOW PAST A SIGN THAT READS, "EL PASO PRODUCE CENTER." THE
FOCUS OF OUR ATTENTION BECOMES A RELATIVELY NEW TRUCK BEARING THE
LEGEND "FRESCO AND SON, EMPIRE PRODUCE SERVICE, CINCINNATI." SWINGING
TO ITS REAR, WE SEE A HANDFUL OF WORKERS LOADING CRATES OF TOMATOES
UNDER THE EYE OF A FOREMAN WITH A CLIPBOARD. THE TRUCK BED IS ALMOST
FILLED.

FOREMAN

(CHECKING CLIPBOARD) Fifteen hundred lugs. Thirty to go.

HE TAPS A STACK OF CRATES.

2 EXT. AT SINK—MED. SHOT—DIMITRI FRESCO. A FEW YARDS FROM THE TRUCK,
A MAN STANDS SHAVING AT AN OUTDOOR SINK, A TOWEL OVER HIS SHOULDER.
THIS IS DIMITRI FRESCO, AGE IN THE MID-THIRTIES, NATIONALITY AMERICAN,
EXTRACTION GREEK, TEMPERAMENT MERCURIAL, A MAN OF WILD AND REST-
LESS ENERGIES.

FRESCO

(SHOUT TO FOREMAN) Thirty-two, Mr. Wiseguy!

3 ANGLE ON FOREMAN—FRESCO IN B.G.

FOREMAN

Two just loaded!

FRESCO, THE SOAP STILL ON HIS FACE, COMES TOWARD US.

FRESCO

(SUSPICIOUSLY) Let's see what they're loaded with.

HE STOPS A CRATE AS IT IS ABOUT TO BE SWUNG ABOARD.

FRESCO

Rip this one.

FOREMAN

(TO A WORKER) Show him.

THE WORKER RIPS THE TOP OFF THE CASE. IT IS MARKED "PRODUCT OF
MEXICO."

4 TWO SHOT—FRESCO AND FOREMAN. ANGLE INCLUDES OPEN CASE OF TOMATOES
PACKED 5 X 6. IT TAKES ABOUT TWO SECONDS FOR FRESCO TO EXAMINE THEM
TO HIS DISSATISFACTION.

FRESCO

Aw, come, on, can't you read tomatoes? I said pink to greens!

FOREMAN

So this lug's a little green.

FRESCO

So let 'em be a little pink!

FOREMAN

(TO WORKER; BEDEVILED) Give him what he wants.

5 EXT. OFFICE—UP ANGLE SHOT—MICHAELS. MR. MICHAELS, A HEFTY PRODUCE
   DEALER, STANDS ON THE PORCH OF A SECOND-STORY OFFICE APPROACHED BY
   AN EXTERIOR FLIGHT OF STAIRS.

MICHAELS

Hey, Fresco!

6 EXT. OFFICE PORCH—MED. SHOT—MICHAELS.

MICHAELS

(THUMB JERK TO INTERIOR) Your call to Cincinnati.

HE EXITS TO INTERIOR.

7 DOWN ANGLE SHOT—TO FRESCO AS HE COMES UP TO US ON THE DOUBLE
   (HIS CHARACTERISTIC FORM OF LOCOMOTION) AND EXITS INTO OFFICE.

8 INT. MICHAEL'S OFFICE—TWO SHOT—FRESCO AND MICHAELS—DAY. AS FRESCO
   ENTERS, MICHAELS IS SEATED AT HIS DESK, COUNTING A MASSIVE WAD OF
   BANKNOTES. HE INDICATES THE PHONE.

FRESCO

(TO PHONE) Hello? . . . Yeah, this is Fresco, put her on. (HAND OVER
PHONE TO MICHAELS) How's the count?

MICHAELS

Forty-eight hundred. You always pay cash?

FRESCO

When you start your own business, you pay cash. (TO PHONE) Hello,
Ma? . . . No, nothing's wrong.

9 CLOSER ANGLE ON FRESCO. AS HE SPEAKS, HE WIPES THE SHAVING SOAP FROM
   HIS FACE WITH A TOWEL.

FRESCO

(STILL TO PHONE) Let me speak to Pop . . . (EXPLOSIVELY) Well, where
is he? . . . Look, you tell him this: tell him the rain washed out every vine
between Cincinnati and the border. . . .

SOUND OF O.S. TRUCK PULLING UP.

FRESCO

(CONTINUES) Yeah, I just picked up a load of Mexicans . . . No, Ma,
tomatoes!

10 TWO SHOT—MICHAELS AND FRESCO. MICHAELS IS LOOKING CURIOUSLY FROM
   WINDOW.

MICHAELS

Looks like your competition.

FRESCO CARRIES PHONE TO WINDOW.

11 POV DOWN ANGLE SHOT—SINDELL TRUCK. ANOTHER TRUCK IS SLOWING TO
   STOP. THERE ARE TWO MEN IN THE CAB.

12 EXT. PRODUCE MARKET—CLOSER ANGLE—SINDELL TRUCK. IT STOPS SO THAT

WE CAN READ THE LEGEND PAINTED ON ITS SIDE: "SINDELL BROTHERS, CIN-
CINNATI."

13 INT. OFFICE—AT WINDOW—MED. CLOSE SHOT—FRESCO. HE STARES DOWN
FROM THE WINDOW WITH AN EXPRESSION OF LOATHING.

FRESCO
(TO PHONE) The Rumanians just got in. Tell him I'll call him back—
tonight, sometime . . . Yeah, fine, Ma. I'm eating like a horse.

HE SLAMS PHONE ONTO CRADLE, TOSSES TOWEL ASIDE, AND CROSSES TO DOOR.

FRESCO
(CONTINUES) Thanks, Mr. Michaels. See you next time.

MICHAELS
Have a good run.

FRESCO
It better be good. I bet the whole bankroll.

14 EXT. OFFICE PORCH—MED. SHOT—FRESCO AS HE EMERGES FROM OFFICE AND
PAUSES, LOOKING DOWN TO:

15 FRESCO'S POV—DOWN ANGLE SHOT—SINDELL BROTHERS. THE SINDELL
BROTHERS, JERRY AND AL, HAVE EMERGED FROM THEIR CAB. THEY CROSS TO
FRESCO'S RIG AND LOOK IT OVER. JERRY SAYS SOMETHING AND POINTS UP TO
THE OFFICE. AL CROSSES TO THE STAIRS.

16 EXT. ANGLE AT BASE OF STAIRS—FRESCO AND AL SINDELL AS FRESCO DESCENDS
AND PASSES AL ON HIS WAY UP.

AL
(THROWAWAY) What do you say?

FRESCO
Hiya.

CAMERA PANS FRESCO TO PICK UP HIS JACKET BY THE SINK AND TO CROSS TO
JERRY SINDELL AS HE PUTS IT ON. JERRY STANDS BY THE DRIVER'S DOOR TO
FRESCO'S CAB.

17 EXT. AT FRESCO'S CAB—TWO SHOT—JERRY AND FRESCO AS FRESCO CROSSES
INTO SCENE AND YANKS CAB DOOR OPEN.

JERRY
Your own rig, huh?

FRESCO
(A COOL REMOTENESS) Yeah, mine, Jerry. Me and my old man.

JERRY
How you like it on your own?

FRESCO
We like it anywhere we don't have to work for you.

HE GETS INTO THE TRUCK. JERRY GRINS, NO HARD FEELINGS.

JERRY

How's the tomato market?

FRESCO

What tomatoes?

JERRY

Come on, Fresco, what's the good of fighting? We get the first loads into Cincinnati, we can buddy-up and make our own price.

FRESCO

Yeah, well, I'll tell you, buddy-up. I got a load, but *you,* you ain't got no load. You got to make a deal and stack fifteen-hundred lugs. That makes *me* first into Cincinnati, right?

THAT'S WHAT JERRY GETS FOR BEING NICE.

JERRY

Okay, pal. You better be ready to fly that thing.

FRESCO

(A GLARE) Contact!

HE HITS THE STARTER. JERRY SLAMS THE DOOR SHUT.

18 INT. TRUCK—MED. CLOSE SHOT—FRESCO—DAY. HIS MOUTH COMPACTED INTO A GRIM LINE, HE SHIFTS GEAR.

19 EXT. FULL SHOT—THE TRUCK AND JERRY AS THE TRUCK STARTS FORWARD. JERRY SPRINTS TOWARD THE STAIRS TO MICHAELS' OFFICE.

DISSOLVE TO:

20 EXT. HIGHWAY—FULL SHOT—FRESCO'S TRUCK—NIGHT. THE TRUCK RUNS THROUGH A DRIVING RAIN.

21 EXT. WINDSHIELD SHOT—NIGHT (PROCESS) AS THE SWINGING WINDSHIELD WIPER REVEALS FRESCO HUNCHED OVER THE WHEEL AND MUNCHING ON A TOMATO.

LAP DISSOLVE TO:

22 EXT. HIGHWAY (ANOTHER LOCATION)—ANGLE ON FRESCO'S TRUCK—NIGHT. THE RAIN HAS STOPPED. OUR ANGLE EMPHASIZES THE WET HIGHWAY AS THE TRUCK APPROACHES US.

23 EXT. HIGHWAY—LOW POSITION SHOT—FRESCO'S TRUCK—NIGHT—AS THE TRUCK SLAMS THROUGH A DITCH AND THROWS UP A PLUME OF RAINWATER.

LAP DISSOLVE TO:

24 EXT. GAS-LUNCH STOP—ESTABLISHING SHOT—NIGHT. FRESCO'S TRUCK PULLS UP TO A GAS-STATION-LUNCHROOM AND FRESCO VAULTS FROM THE CAB. HE ADDRESSES A YOUNG MEXICAN ATTENDANT NAMED PEREZ, THRUSTS A CREDIT CARD AT HIM. THE TERRAIN IS WET AND PUDDLED AND WE HAVE THE SCENE OF A RAW AND INCLEMENT NIGHT.

FRESCO

Top it off, huh?

PEREZ

You bet.

HE MOVES TO THE TANK CAP AS FRESCO RACES FOR AN EXTERIOR PHONE BOOTH NEAR THE CLOSED LUNCHROOM. NOW PEREZ GLANCES TOWARD THE STATION OFFICE, LOOKS BACK AT FRESCO, CROSSES TO ENTER THE OFFICE. THERE IS A WOMAN THERE, SEATED PASSIVELY. WE SEE PEREZ SPEAK TO HER AND INDICATE THE TRUCK. THE WOMAN GLANCES AT IT, LOOKS QUESTIONINGLY BACK TO THE ATTENDANT.

25   INT. PHONE BOOTH—FRESCO—NIGHT.

FRESCO

(TO PHONE; YELLING) Fresco—F-R-E-S-C-O—Fresco, reverse charges.

HE FISHES FOR A CIGARETTE AND MATCH UNTIL:

FRESCO

Pop? I'm heading home. Yeah, she told you right. Fifteen-hundred lugs, fresh out of Mexico . . . three-fifty a lug . . . Will you quit worrying? It's like money in the bank. Five-by-sixes, pinks to greens—beautiful!

NOW HE SCOWLS AS HE LOOKS OUT TOWARD HIS TRUCK AND SEES:

26   POV WINDOW SHOT—TRUCK, PEREZ AND WOMAN—NIGHT. THE WOMAN IS CLIMBING INTO THE PASSENGER SEAT OF FRESCO'S TRUCK AS THE ATTENDANT FEEDS GAS TO THE TANKS.

27   MED. CLOSE SHOT—FRESCO (EXT. ACTION IN B.G.)

FRESCO

(QUICKLY) Listen, Pop, talk to Charlie Schwartz from Holiday Markets. Tell him we'll take care of him. Five-and-a-half a lug or we go elsewhere. . . . (GRIM GLANCE TO WINDOW) I gotta go now . . . Forget the Sindell Brothers! I got a three-hour lead. Listen, call Joanie. Tell her I'll be in Tuesday morning and I love her. And quit worrying! It's my savings, too!

HE HANGS UP AND RAMS OUT OF THE BOOTH.

28   EXT. SERVICE STATION—AT TRUCK—PEREZ, THE WOMAN, FRESCO—NIGHT. PEREZ IS MAKING OUT THE CHARGE SLIP AS FRESCO CROSSES INTO SCENE AND WRENCHES THE CAB DOOR OPEN.

FRESCO

(TO WOMAN) You—out!

THE WOMAN LOOKS TO PEREZ. HE SHRUGS. SHE GETS OUT. PEREZ GIVES FRESCO THE CHARGE SLIP AND PENCIL AS:

PEREZ

(NO ACCENT) I told her maybe you'd give her a lift.

FRESCO

(SCRIBBLING NAME) You're a real sport.

HE HANDS THE SLIP TO PEREZ; BUT AS HE ACCEPTS THE RECEIPT, HIS GAZE (NOT WITHOUT A SUDDEN ELEMENT OF RELUCTANT COMPASSION) IS ON THE WOMAN.

29 POV SHOT—THE WOMAN. HER NAME IS ANNA BEZA. SHE IS IN HER THIRTIES AND,
AS WE SHALL SEE, IN THE FINAL STAGES OF PREGNANCY. UNDER THE HARSH,
ACTINIC STAB OF THE FLUORESCENTS, HER FACE IS PALE AND FRIGHTENED.
SHE WEARS A THIN COAT HELD TIGHTLY ABOUT HER THROAT WITH ONE HAND.
NO HAT. HER MANNER, FOR THE MOMENT, IS CHARACTERIZED BY A KIND OF
INSULAR PASSIVITY.

CAMERA TILTS DOWN: HER PREGNANCY—HER BARE LEGS—HER SHABBY SHOES
PATHETIC ON THE WET ASPHALT.

30 THREE SHOT.

FRESCO

No riders. Company rules.

HE CLIMBS INTO CAB.

PEREZ

She just wants to go down the road.

ANNA

(A SOFT, MIDDLE-EUROPEAN ACCENT) To my sister's house.

FRESCO

Where?

ANNA

I show you. Please.

PITY GROWS IN FRESCO LIKE A BOIL ON THE NECK. HE SHOVES THE DOOR WIDER.

FRESCO

(IMPATIENTLY) Come on, come on, let's go!

THE WOMAN AWKWARDLY CLIMBS IN NEXT TO HIM AS HE SLIDES BEHIND THE
WHEEL AND HITS THE STARTER. PEREZ CLOSES THE DOOR AND WAVES TO HER
AS THE TRUCK BEGINS TO ROLL.

LAP DISSOLVE TO:

31 INT. FRESCO'S TRUCK—CLOSE SHOT—PHOTO-AMULET—NIGHT. AN AMULET
CONSISTING OF A FAMILY SNAPSHOT AND A GREEK ORTHODOX CROSS DANGLES
FROM A CHAIN ON THE DASHBOARD.

FRESCO'S VOICE

Ninety-thousand winter tomatoes.

32 INT. TRUCK—TWO SHOT—FRESCO AND ANNA—NIGHT. ANNA SITS WEARILY,
HER HEAD BACK.

FRESCO

(CONTINUES) You know how many tomatoes that is?

ANNA

(A WAN SMILE) No.

FRESCO

Well, I'm telling you, that's one big bunch of tomatoes, lady. First ones
into Cincinnati, I'm really in business.

ANNA'S EYES ARE CLOSED NOW. SHE IS NOT REALLY LISTENING TO HIM. HE GLANCES AT HER FACE.

FRESCO

(CONTINUES) You shouldn't travel around in your condition.

ANNA

(EYES OPEN; CONTENTEDLY) I will have my baby—in my sister's house.

FRESCO

What about your husband?

ANNA

(SIMPLY) He is dead now.

FRESCO

(A COMPASSIONATE GLANCE) Oh. That's tough.

ANNA

(NOT UNDERSTANDING) Tough?

FRESCO

Hard.

ANNA

Life is hard. (A FAINT SMILE AS SHE REMEMBERS) I will have my baby.

FRESCO MAKES A POINT OF TALKING NOW, AS IF CHIPPING THE EDGE FROM THIS PAINFUL CONDITION OF HAVING A BABY WITHOUT A HUSBAND.

FRESCO

I got four kids myself. (GRINS; GLANCES AT HER) That's really married, huh? The last two, they were born while I was on the road, (GRIMLY) working for the Sindell brothers. The Rumanian thieves. What an outfit.

ANNA

I am Rumanian.

FRESCO, REALIZING THAT HE HAS MADE A GAFFE, HASTENS TO UNDO IT.

FRESCO

Yeah, well there's all kinds. (THUMB IN CHEST) Me, I'm Greek.

HE REACHES BACK TO AN OPEN LUG AND HANDS ANNA A TOMATO.

FRESCO

(CONTINUES) Here, keep up your strength. Compliments of Fresco and Son.

ANNA REFUSES THE GIFT.

ANNA

Tomatoes—(HEADSHAKE)—I don't like them.

FRESCO THROWS IT BACK INTO THE BOX.

FRESCO

(INCENSED) You don't like 'em. In Cincinnati those things'd run you fifty, sixty cents a pound!

ANNA

I am not going to Cincinnati.

FRESCO

(EYES ON ROAD) Where's this sister of yours live?

ANNA

San Francisco.

FRESCO THROWS HER A HORRIFIED GLARE AND HITS THE BRAKES.

33 EXT. HIGHWAY—FULL SHOT—FRESCO'S TRUCK—NIGHT—AS IT SCREECHES TO
A HALT AT THE EDGE OF THE HIGHWAY—JUST PAST A SIDE ROAD.

34 INT. TRUCK—TWO SHOT.

FRESCO

Are you nuts?!

ANNA

I go to San Francisco.

FRESCO

(RAGING) Well, this is Texas, lady! Don't you know that?

ANNA

Yes.

FRESCO

Then what'd you tell me "down the road"?

ANNA

To make a beginning.

OUTRAGED, FRESCO HURLS HIMSELF FROM THE CAB.

35 EXT. TRUCK—ANGLE ON FRESCO AND ANNA. ANNA'S FRIGHTENED EYES FOLLOW
FRESCO AS HE DASHES AROUND TO THE DRIVER'S DOOR AND WRENCHES IT OPEN.

FRESCO

(BELLOWING) You want to go to Frisco you take a bus, you don't make
trouble for people!

ANNA COMES DOWN FROM THE CAB.

ANNA

I am sorry.

SHE STARTS TO WALK DOWN THE ROAD IN THE HEADLIGHTS OF FRESCO'S TRUCK.
AT THE SAME TIME, ANOTHER TRUCK, COMING FROM THE OPPOSITE DIRECTION,
SLOWS BESIDE FRESCO. THE DRIVER'S NAME IS CASEY. HE LEANS TO THE
PASSENGER WINDOW.

CASEY

Any trouble?

FRESCO CROSSES TO HIM.

36 AT CASEY'S TRUCK—TWO SHOT—CASEY AND FRESCO.

> FRESCO

Naw. It's okay.

> CASEY

(LOOKS CURIOUSLY AFTER ANNA) Who's she?

37   POV SHOT—ANNA AS, VIOLENTLY ALONE, SHE CONTINUES DOWN ROAD.

38   BACK TO CASEY AND FRESCO.

> FRESCO

Some kind of nut.

> CASEY

Better watch yourself, pal. (GESTURE DOWN ROAD) Roadblock. Immigration cops picked up a bunch of wetbacks. They're still looking for some dame.

HE WAVES AND ROLLS THE TRUCK AS FRESCO STEPS BACK. NOW LATTER CROSSES THOUGHTFULLY TOWARD HIS OWN CAB, LOOKS DOWN THE ROAD TO:

39   POV SHOT—ANNA STILL MOVING AWAY FROM US IN THE HEADLIGHT BEAMS. SIMULTANEOUSLY, WE HEAR THE HOWL OF AN APPROACHING SIREN.

40   MED. CLOSE SHOT—FRESCO. SOUND OF APPROACHING SIREN OVER SHOT. FRESCO CHEWS FURIOUSLY AT HIS LIP, SUDDENLY BURSTS INTO A RUN TOWARD ANNA AS CAMERA ANGLE WIDENS.

41   ANGLE ON ANNA AND FRESCO. SIREN CLOSER NOW. ANNA TURNS IN RESPONSE TO SOUND OF FRESCO'S APPROACH. HE GRIPS HER ARM AND THRUSTS HER OFF THE ROAD.

> FRESCO

Down!

HE PULLS HER DOWN BEHIND SOME BUSHES.

42   EXT. BUSHES—ANGLE TO HIGHWAY. AN IMMIGRATION PATROL CAR SPEEDS BY AND SIREN BEGINS TO FADE. CAMERA ANGLES BACK FOR TIGHT TWO SHOT, ANNA AND FRESCO.

> FRESCO

Listen, where'd you come from tonight? (NO ANSWER) Come on, I ain't going to bite!

> ANNA

Mexico.

> FRESCO

(APPALLED) Mexico. (RUNS A DISTRAUGHT HAND OVER HIS FACE) Great. That's great. (GLARING AT HER) Any papers?

> ANNA

(A BEAT) No. Please—it was a necessary thing . . .

> FRESCO

(A BOMB GOING OFF) Lady, you got some nerve!! You know what happens if I get picked up with you?

ANNA'S EYES BEGIN TO BRIGHTEN WITH TEARS.

ANNA

(A PLEADING HEADSHAKE) Please . . .

FRESCO

Yeah, "please!" The license, the truck—everything goes!

ANNA IS CRYING SOFTLY NOW, HER HANDS PRESSED TO HER FACE. IT IS AS IF FRESCO'S FURY WERE HER FINAL, UNBEARABLE BURDEN. BUT NOW PITY IS CLAWING ONCE AGAIN AT FRESCO'S SOUL. HE TRIES, WITH ONLY LIMITED SUCCESS, TO MODULATE THE ANGER IN HIS VOICE.

FRESCO

(CONTINUES) Well, what's so important you had to jump the border?

ANNA

I have my baby here.

FRESCO

Where?

ANNA

(DIRECTLY, ALMOST CHALLENGINGLY) United States.

43 MED. CLOSE SHOT—FRESCO AS HE SHAKES HIS HEAD IN AMAZEMENT, HALF TURNS AWAY.

FRESCO

Boy, that's one for the books.

HE UTTERS A BRITTLE LAUGH. SUDDENLY ANNA'S HAND WALLOPS HIM ACROSS THE CHEEK.

FRESCO

(CONTINUES) Hey!

CAMERA ANGLES FOR TWO SHOT. NOW THERE IS A RAGE IN ANNA TO MATCH HIS OWN.

ANNA

You don't laugh.

FRESCO

Who laughed?

ANNA

(FIERCELY) Not at me! Not at my child! I wait too long for this!

FRESCO

Well, I did a little waiting for that truck of mine!

HE GESTURES DOWN THE ROAD.

ANNA

Then go! Drive your fine truck!

SHE MOVES FROM BUSHES TO HIGHWAY. FRESCO LEAPS AFTER HER AND SEIZES HER ARM.

44 EXT. OF HIGHWAY—TWO SHOT—FRESCO AND ANNA.

FRESCO

You know what they got down there? They got a roadblock to catch
people like you. Now come on!

HE TURNS FROM HER, WALKING SWIFTLY TOWARD HIS TRUCK. ANNA, CONFUSED,
REMAINS MOTIONLESS.

45 WIDER ANGLE—FRESCO AND ANNA AS FRESCO TURNS TO HER.

FRESCO

(IMPATIENTLY) I said come on!

ANNA MOVES UNCERTAINLY AFTER HIM.

46 AT TRUCK—FRESCO AND ANNA. FRESCO IS ALREADY THERE AS ANNA MOVES
INTO SCENE. STILL UNCERTAIN, SHE LOOKS THROUGH OPEN DOOR TO PASSENGER
SEAT, LOOKS AT FRESCO.

ANNA

I get in?

FRESCO

Boy, you're thick. Sure, get in!

A SMILE OF SUDDEN HOPE. SHE GETS IN. FRESCO CLOSES DOOR AND RUNS TO
THE OTHER SIDE OF THE CAB.

47 INT. TRUCK—TWO SHOT AS FRESCO GETS IN.

FRESCO

(BLUNTLY) I'm gonna get you off this road.

ANNA'S FACE STILL BEARS HER TEARS. HE PULLS A FRESH HANDKERCHIEF
FROM GLOVE COMPARTMENT AND THRUSTS IT AT HER. SHE TAKES IT GRATE-
FULLY.

FRESCO

(CONTINUED) There's a place over that way called Claro. (HE WAVES
TOWARD SIDE ROAD) They got a bus stop. (HE STARTS THE ENGINE) I
dump you there, you go to San Francisco, I go to Cincinnati and good
luck to you.

ANNA

Thank you.

FRESCO

(A NOD) Believe me.

NOW THEY BECOME AWARE OF A SIREN APPROACHING FROM OPPOSITE DIREC-
TION TO THE FIRST PATROL CAR. FRESCO LOOKS BACK ONTO THE ROAD.

48 EXT. ANGLE ON TRUCK AS THE TRUCK HEADLIGHTS ARE EXTINGUISHED. SOUND
OF SIREN DRAWS CLOSER AS FRESCO RAMS THE TRUCK INTO REVERSE, SHIFTS
GEARS, AND SWINGS DOWN THE SIDE ROAD. NOW ANOTHER IMMIGRATION
PATROL CAR COMES TEARING DOWN THE HIGHWAY. IT SLOWS AS IT REACHES
THE SIDE ROAD, AS IF THE DRIVER WERE CONSIDERING AN INVESTIGATION.

BUT THEN IT PICKS UP SPEED AND THE SIREN HOWLS LOUDER AS THE CAR
CONTINUES DOWN THE MAIN HIGHWAY AND WE

FADE OUT.

ACT II

FADE IN:

49 EXT. SIDE ROAD—LOW POSITION SHOT—FRESCO'S TRUCK—NIGHT. THE TRUCK
APPROACHES AND STREAKS PAST US.

50 INT. TRUCK—FRESCO AND ANNA—NIGHT. A MOMENT OF SILENCE. IN FRESCO,
COMPASSION AND IRE HAVE STRUCK A BALANCE. ANNA IS EATING A TOMATO.
SHE GRANTS HIM A SMILE AS IF TO SAY, "NOT SO BAD." HE PULLS OPEN THE
GLOVE COMPARTMENT AND HANDS HER A SMALL CONTAINER.

FRESCO
Salt.

SHE APPLIES THE SALT, TAKES ANOTHER BITE, LOOKS AT FRESCO.

ANNA
You are tired.

FRESCO
Why should I be tired? I slept two days ago.

A PAUSE.

ANNA
(TIMIDLY) The bus . . .

FRESCO
Yeah, the bus.

ANNA
I have no money.

FRESCO
(A GLANCE) So I'll lend you the money! I'm getting off cheap, you know
what I mean?

51 POV WINDSHIELD SHOT—THE ROAD AS THE HEADLIGHTS SLICE INTO THE
DARKNESS.

52 INT. TRUCK—TWO SHOT.

FRESCO
You could've waited in Mexico—had your kid. They would've let you in.

ANNA FINISHES THE TOMATO AND CAREFULLY WIPES HER HANDS ON HIS
HANDKERCHIEF. SHE LEANS HER HEAD BACK.

ANNA
Sometime. I have waited too long for the papers. Now my child will have
American life.

FRESCO RUNS A WEARY HAND OVER HIS FACE.

FRESCO

Some life. (GLANCES AT HER) You can't even get a Social Security card. How you gonna work?

ANNA

(SIMPLY) I will go back to Mexico.

FRESCO

So what's the point?

ANNA

My sister will keep my child. (A DREAMY, CONTENTED QUALITY) A year —three years. My time will come.

FRESCO

(WASHING HIS HANDS OF IT) Okay, you want to be crazy, be crazy.

DISSOLVE TO:

53 EXT. CLARO BUS STOP—TRUCK AND ESTABLISHING SHOT—NIGHT. THE HAMLET OF CLARO IS THE QUINTESSENCE OF ARIDITY. THE ONLY SIGN OF LIFE OR LIGHT IS THE BUS STATION WHICH IS A COMBINATION TICKET OFFICE AND SOFT DRINK STAND. A DESICCATED WOMAN TENDS THE STAND. LOUNGING THERE ARE A COUPLE OF YOUNG, BUCOLIC MORONS DECKED OUT LIKE TELE-VISION COWBOYS. A JUKE BOX IS SHRIEKING THE MOST JAGGED KIND OF ROCK-AND-ROLL. THE TRUCK DRIVES UP AND STOPS. FRESCO GETS OUT AND COMES AROUND TO OPEN ANNA'S DOOR.

FRESCO

End of the line.

HE HELPS HER OUT. NOW, AS ANNA'S FEET TOUCH THE GROUND, SHE GIVES A LITTLE MOAN OF PAIN AND GRIPS HER STOMACH. FRESCO, ABOUT TO TURN TOWARD THE STAND, WHIRLS BACK TO HER.

54 TWO SHOT—THE YOUTHS. ONE OF THEM SMIRKS AND NUDGES THE OTHER.

55 ANGLE ON CLARO WOMAN. BEHIND THE COUNTER, SHE LOOKS UP FROM A DOG-EARED RECORD BOOK. SHE HAS CAUGHT THE SCENT OF MISERY AND HER THIN LIPS PART IN A GRIMACE.

56 TWO SHOT—FRESCO AND ANNA. ANNA'S FIGURE IS BENT BY THIS FIRST LABOR PAIN. HORROR SETTLES INTO FRESCO'S BONES.

FRESCO

What's the matter?

ANNA BITES HER LIP, SHAKES HER HEAD.

ANNA

A pain . . .

FRESCO LAYS HIS HAND ON HER STOMACH.

57 ANGLE ON TWO YOUTHS. ONE OF THEM UTTERS A HOOT OF LAUGHTER.

58 FRESCO AND ANNA. FRESCO SHOOTS THE O.S. YOUTHS A SULPHURIC GLARE, THEN:

> FRESCO

(TO ANNA) You got a pain all right! You deserve all the trouble you're gonna get.

> ANNA

I did not know—so soon . . .

> FRESCO

(BELLOWING) Everybody knows! Can't you count up to nine?

HIS ARM SUPPORTS HER NOW. THE PAIN IS EASING. ANNA TRIES TO EXPLAIN.

> ANNA

The time, it was—so confused . . .

> FRESCO

Yeah, well, you save it all for the bus driver!

HE STRIDES TOWARD THE STAND.

59 AT STAND—GROUP SHOT—FRESCO, THE WOMAN, THE YOUTHS AS FRESCO COMES TO THE COUNTER. WE SEE A RACK OF WRAPPED SANDWICHES.

> FRESCO

Coffee!

THE WOMAN TURNS TO DRAW IT. FRESCO EYES THE TWO YOUTHS. THEY RETURN HIS STARE SULLENLY.

> FRESCO

(TO THE WOMAN) When's the next bus?

> WOMAN

Where to?

> FRESCO

West. San Francisco.

60 EXT. AT TRUCK—ANGLE ON ANNA. THE PAIN HAS LEFT HER NOW. SHE RUNS A HAND THROUGH HER HAIR, WIPES HER MOIST FOREHEAD WITH FRESCO'S HANDKERCHIEF. SHE LOOKS FORWARD.

61 POV SHOT—THE STAND, FRESCO, ET AL. FRESCO REMOVES HIS WALLET FROM HIP POCKET AND DRAWS OUT SOME MONEY.

62 EXT. AT TRUCK—ANGLE ON ANNA. SHE LOOKS AT THE HANDKERCHIEF, REMEMBERS THAT IT IS FRESCO'S. SHE FOLDS IT VERY CAREFULLY AND PLACES IT ON THE SEAT. NOW SHE SHIVERS, DRAWS THE COAT CLOSER ABOUT HER THROAT. FRESCO COMES INTO SCENE. HE CARRIES A COVERED CONTAINER OF COFFEE AND A COUPLE OF WRAPPED SANDWICHES.

> FRESCO

Get in.

> ANNA

The bus . . . ?

> FRESCO

No bus till morning. Get in.

SHE DOES SO. HE SLAMS THE DOOR AND MOVES AROUND TO DRIVER'S SIDE.

63 INT. TRUCK—ANNA AND FRESCO. FRESCO GETS IN, THRUSTS COFFEE AND SANDWICHES AT HER. ANNA RECEIVES THEM BLANKLY.

> FRESCO
> (EXPLOSIVELY) Well, I can't leave you here!

HE STARTS THE ENGINE.

64 EXT. ANGLE ON TRUCK AS THE TRUCK PULLS OUT OF THE BUS STOP.

LAP DISSOLVE TO:

65 INT. TRUCK—TWO SHOT—FRESCO AND ANNA. ANNA HOLDS THE COFFEE AND SANDWICHES NUMBLY.

> FRESCO
> The woman says there's a doctor about a mile down this way. A white house. Watch for a white house.

> ANNA
> (FAINTLY) Thank you.

> FRESCO
> (VIOLENTLY) Don't thank me!

> ANNA
> (YELLING) Why do you yell?

> FRESCO
> The Sindell brothers beat me into Cincinnati, I'll spend the rest of my life eating those lousy tomatoes!

HE GESTURES TOWARD THE BACK, CONTINUES TO CHEW QUIETLY ON HIS WRATH.

> FRESCO
> (CONTINUES) I pick 'em. Boy, how I pick 'em.

ANNA IS CALMLY LIFTING THE LID FROM THE COFFEE CONTAINER. SHE PASSES IT TO HIM.

> FRESCO
> Eat!!

HE DRINKS, LOOKS AHEAD, REACTS, AND SPINS THE WHEELS AS THE TRUCK BUCKS.

66 POV WINDSHIELD SHOT. DIRECTLY AHEAD, THE SIDE ROAD DETERIORATES INTO A BRIEF STRETCH OF RUTTED MUD.

67 INT. TRUCK—TWO SHOT—ANNA AND FRESCO. ANNA'S WIDE GLANCE FLICKS TOWARD FRESCO.

> ANNA
> The road . . . ?

> FRESCO
> What road? There ain't no road!

HE FIGHTS THE WHEEL.

68 EXT. DETERIORATED ROAD—LOW ANGLE—NIGHT—AS THE TRUCK SPRAYS THROUGH A DITCH.

69 EXT. FULL SHOT—THE TRUCK—NIGHT—AS IT SKIDS, SWERVES, AND COMES TO A CIRCUS STOP.

70 INT. TRUCK—FRESCO AND ANNA—NIGHT. THE ABRUPT STOP HURLS ANNA HEAVILY AGAINST DASH AND WINDSHIELD. FRESCO'S HANDS FLASH AT THE EMERGENCY BRAKE AND IGNITION KEY. THEN HIS WHOLE CONCERN IS FOR ANNA AS HE GRIPS HER SHOULDERS. PANIC STILL SHOWS IN HER FACE.

FRESCO
(SEARCHINGLY) You all right?

ANNA
(WAN NOD) I think.

FRESCO
Don't think! I gotta know!

ANNA
All right.

FRESCO
All right.

HE RELEASES HER AND TURNS TO RE-START THE ENGINE. ANNA WATCHES NERVOUSLY AS FRESCO FEROCIOUSLY SHIFTS GEARS AND POURS POWER TO THE WHEELS.

71 EXT. LOW ANGLE CLOSE SHOT—POWER WHEELS. THE TRUCK'S POWER WHEELS SPIN FUTILELY AGAINST MUD.

72 INT. TRUCK—TWO SHOT. AGAIN FRESCO SHIFTS GEARS, SMITES HIS FOREHEAD, TURNS OFF THE ENGINE.

ANNA
We are stuck?

FRESCO
Stuck, yeah, that's the word, lady, that's it. Stuck.

HE RAMS HIS DOOR OPEN AS ANNA IS SEIZED BY ANOTHER LABOR PAIN. HE TURNS BACK TO HER AND UNFASTENS HIS WRIST WATCH AS:

FRESCO
This your first baby?

ANNA
Yes . . .

FRESCO
(THRUSTS WATCH AT HER) Okay, you keep track of those pains. Time 'em. (HE DOESN'T SEEM TO BE GETTING THROUGH) You know? Count!

ANNA
Yes . . .

FRESCO ROLLS HIS EYES UPWARD AS IF IN PRAYER FOR STRENGTH.

FRESCO

"Yes."

73 INT. TRUCK—ANNA. THE PAIN IS RELEASING HER NOW. SHE NOTICES A PHOTO-GRAPH IN A SMALL CIRCULAR FRAME: AN AMULET DANGLING ON A CHAIN THAT ALSO BEARS AN ORTHODOX CROSS. SHE LOOKS CLOSER.

74 INSERT—PHOTOGRAPH. A FAMILY SNAPSHOT, TIGHTLY GROUPED: FRESCO, HIS WIFE AND FOUR CHILDREN. SOUND OF CAB DOOR OPEN.

75 INT. TRUCK—ANNA AND FRESCO. ANNA LOOKS UP AS FRESCO OPENS DOOR AND YANKS HIS KEYS FROM THE DASH.

ANNA

(THE PHOTOGRAPH) You have a fine family.

FRESCO

Don't worry, they're gonna starve.

76 EXT. TRUCK—FRESCO AS HE TURNS FROM CAB TO APPLY A KEY TO THE PAD-LOCKED TOOL BOX JUST BEHIND THE TRACTOR. THE LOCK IS RECALCITRANT. HE WRENCHES AT IT . . .

FRESCO

Come on, come on!

FINALLY THE LOCK IS FREE AND FRESCO IS PAWING AT FIENDISHLY SNARLED TIRE CHAINS AND AN AXE AND A SHOVEL AND SOME SHORT TWO-BY-FOURS.

77 INT. TRUCK—ANNA. SHE PICKS UP ONE OF THE SANDWICHES, UNWRAPS IT. BUT SHE DOES NOT EAT. INSTEAD SHE LEANS HER HEAD BACK AGAINST THE SEAT, DREAMING OF THE CHILD WITHIN HER BODY. SHE REMEMBERS TO LOOK AT THE WATCH.

DISSOLVE TO:

78 EXT. TRUCK LOW POSITION SHOT AT DRIVE WHEELS—FRESCO—NIGHT. FRESCO WORKS IN THE DITCH, PACKING THE TWO-BY-FOURS AND TIRE CHAINS INTO THE DUG-OUT AREA IN FRONT OF THE WHEELS. HE IS WELL GRIMED WITH MUD AND GREASE.

NOW HE BECOMES AWARE OF THE SOUND OF AN APPROACHING MOTORCYCLE. A PARALYZING THOUGHT. HIS EYES SLIDE ROADWARD. SOUND OF MOTORCYCLE SLOWING AS IT COMES ON. AND THE HEADLIGHT BEAM. HIS EYES SQUEEZE SHUT AGAINST THIS NEW MENACE. HE OPENS THEM. MOTORCYCLE WHEELS AND A BOOTED LEG, HIGHLY OFFICIAL IN APPEARANCE. HE RISES AS ANGLE WIDENS.

FRESCO FACES A UNIFORMED MOTORCYCLE OFFICER.

OFFICER

Hi. What's the trouble?

FRESCO

Me? No trouble. (EYES BACK ON WHEEL) Great little roads you build around here.

79 INT. TRUCK—ANNA. SHE VENTURES A GLANCE OUT THE WINDOW, PULLS BACK AND PRESSES HER CHEEK AGAINST THE SEAT. THE TRUCK HEADLIGHTS ARE ON.

OFFICER'S VOICE

This piece got kinda washed out.

80 EXT. TRUCK—FRESCO AND MOTORCYCLE OFFICER. THE OFFICER GETS OFF HIS CYCLE AND COMES CLOSER TO FRESCO.

OFFICER

Truck like yours, you shouldn't even *be* on it.

FRESCO

Yeah, well, I'm heading back to the main highway.

OFFICER

What brought you out here?

FRESCO

(WORKING AT CHAIN) Just visiting a friend of my old man's. You know —the doctor. The white house down there.

HE GESTURES DOWN THE ROAD. THE OFFICER CONSIDERS THIS.

OFFICER

From now on, you better stay clear of these side roads. You want any help?

FRESCO

Naw. You go ahead.

THE OFFICER MOVES BACK TO HIS MOTORCYCLE, IS ABOUT TO MOUNT IT WHEN HE LOOKS CURIOUSLY TOWARD THE CAB. NOW HE CROSSES TO OPEN THE DOOR.

81 MED. CLOSE SHOT—FRESCO WATCHING. HE COULD DIE.

82 INT. TRUCK—ANGLE ON OFFICER. WE SEE ONLY THE OFFICER. ANNA IS NO LONGER THERE. HE REACHES IN TO PRESS A SWITCH ON THE DASHBOARD.

83 EXT. TRUCK HEADLIGHTS AS THE HEADLIGHTS ARE EXTINGUISHED.

84 EXT. TRUCK—ANGLE ON OFFICER AND FRESCO AS THE OFFICER MOVES BACK TO HIS MOTORCYCLE.

OFFICER

You wouldn't want to get stuck with a dead battery.

HE STARTS THE MACHINE, WAVES AND DRIVES OFF.

85 ANGLE ON FRESCO. HE BREATHES AGAIN AND MOVES QUICKLY WITH CAMERA TO SNATCH OPEN THE DOOR OF THE CAB. NO SIGN OF ANNA.

FRESCO'S WORRIED GLANCE SWINGS AROUND. THEN HE DARTS PAST THE FRONT OF THE TRUCK TOWARD THE OPPOSITE SIDE.

86 EXT. OTHER SIDE OF TRUCK—FRESCO. HE COMES AROUND AND SUDDENLY FINDS HIMSELF STARING AT ANNA. HAUNTED AND SOULFUL, SHE IS STANDING WITH HER BACK AGAINST THE SIDE OF THE TRUCK.

FRESCO IS TORN BETWEEN FLAYING AND HUGGING HER. HE RAISES A QUIVERING FINGER.

FRESCO

You . . .

WORDS FAIL HIM. HE SHAKES HIS HEAD AND ADJUSTS HIS CHEMISTRY BY MOVING TO TAKE UP THE AXE AND CHOP WILDLY AT TWIGS AND BRANCHES FOR FILL. HE GATHERS UP AN ARMLOAD AND RUSHES TO THE DRIVE WHEELS.

87   LOW POSITION SHOT—AT DRIVE WHEELS—FRESCO. HE KNEELS AND SHOVES THE FILL INTO THE DITCH, ALONG WITH CHAINS AND TWO-BY-FOURS. SUDDENLY ANNA IS THERE WITH ANOTHER ARMLOAD, THRUSTING IT UNDER THE WHEELS.

FRESCO

What are *you* trying to do?

ANNA

To help.

FRESCO

(WORKING) You helped enough already!

ANNA

Why do you speak like that?

FRESCO

Because we're stuck in the mud, lady! That's Rumanian mud and we're never gonna get out of it!

ANNA SHAKES HER HEAD AT THE PHENOMENON OF THIS MAN.

ANNA

You are like a child.

FRESCO

Yeah, a child.

ANNA

With you always there is no hope. Always the end of the world!

FRESCO

(RESENTFULLY) What are *you*, some big expert or something?

ANNA

For hope, yes! Every day of my life I make a miracle. To be here now— even this place: a miracle!

FRESCO

Well, you can pass another miracle and get us outa this place!

WITH THIS, HE RISES AND STARTS TOWARD CAB. AS ANNA TURNS TO GO WITH HIM, ANOTHER PAIN. SHE GRIPS HER STOMACH AND FRESCO'S ARMS LEND HER A COMFORTING PRESSURE.

FRESCO

How long's it been?

SHE LOOKS AT THE WATCH ON HER WRIST.

ANNA

Twelve minutes.

THEY STARE AT EACH OTHER; TWO FRIGHTENED PEOPLE.

FRESCO

Scared?

SHE NODS, BIG-EYED.

FRESCO

I'm an authority. My wife told me all about it. Four times.

HE HAS RAISED HIS HANDS IN A GESTURE. NOW HE STARES DOWN AT THEM: THEY ARE FILTHY. HIS GLANCE COMES SLOWLY UP TO HERS.

FRESCO

You get in the truck, huh? Just sit down.

HE HELPS HER INTO THE TRUCK, SLINGS HIS TOOLS BACK INTO THE BOX, AND THEN MOVES TO SLIDE INTO DRIVER'S SEAT.

88 INT. TRUCK—FRESCO AND ANNA. ANNA WATCHES ANXIOUSLY AS HE STARTS THE ENGINE, SHIFTS, AND CAREFULLY FEEDS POWER TO THE WHEELS.

89 INT. TRUCK—CLOSE SHOT—FRESCO'S FOOT ON ACCELERATOR.

90 EXT. LOW POSITION SHOT—DRIVE WHEELS. THE WHEELS CHEW FUTILELY AGAINST THE FILL.

91 INT. TRUCK—FRESCO AND ANNA. AN EXCHANGE OF GLANCES.

FRESCO

(GRIMLY) Miracles. Some miracles.

HE TRIES THE ACCELERATOR AGAIN.

92 EXT. CLOSE SHOT—DRIVE WHEELS. THE WHEELS ARE GRIPPING NOW, SLOWLY BEGINNING TO MOVE THE TRUCK.

93 EXT. FULL SHOT—THE TRUCK AS IT LURCHES FREE OF THE DITCH AND ROLLS ACROSS THE REMAINING SECTION OF WASH ONTO THE ROAD, DRIVING AWAY FROM US.

94 INT. TRUCK—FRESCO AND ANNA (PROCESS). FRESCO TURNS A GRIM AND THREATENING GLANCE ON ANNA, AS IF CHALLENGING HER TO SAY, "I TOLD YOU SO." HER BROWS ARCH AND SHE MAKES A DISMISSING LITTLE HAND GESTURE. THEN SHE SETTLES HERSELF CONTENTEDLY BACK IN THE SEAT. FRESCO TAKES A DEEP BREATH AND ROLLS HIS EYES UPWARD.

ANNA DARES A GLANCE AT HIS FACE AND GRINS AT HIS DISGUST. ANOTHER GLARE FROM HIM AND SHE LOOKS AWAY. THEN SHE IS WATCHING FRESCO AGAIN. THE SIDE OF HIS FACE IS STILL STREAKED WITH MUD. ANNA UTTERS AN INCONGRUOUSLY GIRLISH GIGGLE. FRESCO HURLS HIS GLANCE AT HER.

FRESCO

What's so funny?

ANNA

Oh, you are a terrible sight.

STARING AHEAD AGAIN, HE NODS SOURLY.

FRESCO

Yeah, some face I got.

ANNA

Not the face, the mud.

SHE DABS AT HIS CHEEK WITH HER HANDKERCHIEF. THIS SIMPLE OFFERING OF CONCERN STARTLES FRESCO. HE SHOOTS ANOTHER GLANCE AT HER.

ANNA

Watch the road, please.

HE DOES SO. ANNA LEANS BACK IN HER SEAT.

FRESCO

Thanks.

ANNA

(IMITATING HIM GRUFFLY) "Don't thank me!"

AND AGAIN FRESCO LOOKS AT HER. HE GRINS.

FRESCO

Tough, huh?

ANNA

Oh, yes. Very tough.

NOW FRESCO LOOKS AHEAD AND REACTS TO:

95 POV WINDSHIELD SHOT—WHITE HOUSE—NIGHT. THE WHITE HOUSE IS COMING UP. IT STANDS ALONE AND IS RATHER IN NEED OF PAINT. SOME LIGHTS ARE ON.

96 INT. TRUCK—TWO SHOT.

FRESCO

(NOD AHEAD) There's your doctor.

97 MED. CLOSE SHOT—ANNA. HER EYES SCAN THE HOUSE AHEAD.

98 EXT. WHITE HOUSE—FULL SHOT—THE TRUCK—NIGHT—AS IT DRIVES UP AND STOPS. FRESCO MOVES AROUND TO ANNA'S DOOR AND OPENS IT.

99 EXT. TRUCK—ANNA AND FRESCO. HE HELPS HER DOWN. CAMERA PULLS BACK AS THEY START TOWARD THE FRONT STEPS OF THE HOUSE. SUDDENLY FRESCO'S EXPRESSION TIGHTENS AND HE STOPS. ANNA GLANCES AT HIS FACE.

ANNA

What is it?

GRIMLY HE POINTS TO:

100 EXT. HOUSE—SIGN. A LARGE SIGN IS SET UP IN FRONT OF THE HOUSE. IT READS: "CLEMENT C. CONNELL, PHYSICIAN—DOCTOR OF ASTROLOGICAL THERAPY." CAMERA EMPHASIZES THIS SECOND LINE.

101 TIGHT TWO SHOT—FRESCO AND ANNA STARING AT THE SIGN AS WE

FADE OUT.

ACT III

FADE IN:

102 EXT. WHITE HOUSE PORCH—TWO SHOT—FRESCO AND ANNA—NIGHT. A LITTLE
SIGN ABOVE A BELL HANDLE SAYS: "RING FOR DOCTOR." FRESCO TURNS THE
HANDLE. A BELL RINGS IN THE HOUSE. FRESCO AND ANNA EXCHANGE GLANCES.
NOW HE HAMMERS ON THE DOOR.

FRESCO

Hey!

NO ANSWER. HE TRIES THE KNOB. THE DOOR OPENS. HE MOTIONS ANNA TO
FOLLOW AND STEPS INSIDE.

103 INT. PARLOR-RECEPTION ROOM—ANNA AND FRESCO—NIGHT. FRESCO CLOSES
THE DOOR BEHIND THEM. THEY LOOK AROUND. WE ARE IN A SORT OF DINGY
PARLOR-RECEPTION ROOM. THERE IS A FLIGHT OF STEPS AND A HALL LEADING
TO BACK OF HOUSE. MORE IMMEDIATELY, THERE IS A DOOR BEARING THE SIGN:
"DOCTOR'S OFFICE."

FRESCO

(A SHOUT) Doctor!—Dr. Connell—Anybody here?

SILENCE. HE GLANCES AT ANNA AS SHE MOVES TO DOOR TO DOCTOR'S OFFICE
AND PRESSES IT OPEN. SHE GLANCES AT FRESCO. HE SHRUGS. THEY GO INTO
THE OFFICE.

104 INT. CONNELL'S OFFICE—FRESCO AND ANNA—NIGHT—AS THEY ENTER. STILL
NO SIGN OF THE DOCTOR. THERE IS A COUCH, A DESK, A BOOK CASE SERVING AS
AN INSTRUMENT CABINET. THE OFFICE IS NOTEWORTHY NEITHER FOR CLEANLI-
NESS NOR NEATNESS. A SECOND DOOR LEADS TO THE REAR PART OF THE HOUSE.
SOME UNWASHED DINNER DISHES LIE ON THE DESK. MINOR INSTRUMENTS ARE
STREWN HAPHAZARDLY ABOUT. FOR ATMOSPHERE, WE INCLUDE SOME SORT OF
WEIRD MECHANISM SURMOUNTED BY A BANK OF LIGHT BULBS. ON THE WALL
NEAR THE DESK IS A LARGE AND COMPLEX ZODIACAL CHART. OTHER CHARTS
ARE ON THE DESK AS WELL AS A ZODIACAL GLOBE.

AS FRESCO AND ANNA TAKE ALL THIS IN, THEIR UNEASINESS INCREASES.

FRESCO

(SHOUT) Hey!

HE LOOKS AT THE LIGHT-BULB MACHINE, CURIOUSLY PRESSES A BUTTON. THE
LIGHT BULBS BEGIN TO FLICKER. HE GLANCES AT ANNA, WHO IS LOOKING AT
ONE OF THE INSTRUMENTS. SHE SETS IT DOWN AND GIVES FRESCO A WAN SMILE.

FRESCO

(WITHOUT CONVICTION) Any port in a storm, like they say.

ANNA

He is not a real doctor?

FRESCO

Yeah, well—guess he's a doctor, all right. He's just got different ways, you know? (SHOUTS AGAIN) Hey, Doc!

ANNA SITS WEAKLY ON THE COUCH. FRESCO CROSSES TOWARD DOOR TO REAR OF HOUSE.

105 AT SECOND OFFICE DOOR—ANGLE ON FRESCO. HE OPENS THE DOOR AND FINDS HIMSELF FACING DR. CLEMENT CONNELL IN THE FLESH. HE IS A PLUMPISH, MIDDLE-AGED MAN, SLEEPILY FASTENING AN UNCLEAN SMOCK; ONE WONDERS IF PERHAPS HE IS NOT SLEEPY BUT A LITTLE DRUNK.

CONNELL

(CURTLY) Yelling won't help.

FRESCO

I got a lady here.

HE MOVES BACK INTO THE ROOM AS CONNELL ENTERS.

106 INT. CONNELL'S OFFICE—FRESCO, ANNA, CONNELL.

FRESCO

She's got to be delivered, you know what I mean?

CONNELL SITS AT HIS DESK AND ADOPTS A PROFESSIONAL MANNER.

CONNELL

Terminal gravidity.

ANNA

Please?

CONNELL

The technical term for your condition.

HE BEGINS RUMMAGING AROUND HIS DESK, LOOKING FOR A PAPER WHICH HE WILL LAY OUT.

FRESCO

Listen, I got to get moving. What kind of a deal you want to look after her?

CONNELL SHOOTS HIM A PALE, EVALUATING GLANCE, THEN CONTINUES SEARCHING AS:

CONNELL

You folks passing through?

FRESCO

Yeah.

CONNELL

(EYES ON DESK) Does she want the baby?

FRESCO

Come again?

CONNELL

I asked does she want the baby?

ANNA

(AN ANGRY EDGE) What kind of a question is this?

FRESCO

Sure she wants it!

CONNELL

(A SEARCHING GLANCE AT THEIR FACES) Of course.

CONNELL FINDS THE PAPER HE IS LOOKING FOR AND SETS IT ASIDE.

CONNELL

(TO ANNA) I'm pleased to see you're not putting yourself in the hands of one of those medical doctors. Are you both believers?

ANNA

(TO FRESCO; IN CONFUSION) What does he ask?

FRESCO

(TO CONNELL) What do you mean "believers"? Believe in what?!

CONNELL

(HE TOUCHES THE GLOBE) The ways of wisdom.

A LITTLE MOAN FROM ANNA AS THE PAIN ATTACKS AGAIN. CONNELL REMAINS SEATED. FRESCO MOVES TO HELP HER SINK ONTO THE COUCH.

FRESCO

(TO ANNA) Take it easy . . . (TO CONNELL) I believe in tomatoes and she believes in American babies! That's it.

CONNELL'S EYEBROWS ARCH. HE STUDIES ANNA.

CONNELL

How often are those pains coming?

ANNA

Ten minutes . . .

CONNELL

The important factor is the propitious moment of birth.

ANNA AND FRESCO WATCH CONNELL AS HE MOVES TO PICK UP A HYPODERMIC SYRINGE AND FILL IT FROM A VIAL TAKEN FROM THE BOOKCASE.

ANNA

(FRIGHTENED) What do you do?

107 UP ANGLE MED. CLOSE SHOT—CONNELL FILLING THE SYRINGE.

CONNELL

This'll give us time to work out a proper analysis. (A GLANCE TOWARD FRESCO) The cost for delivery and four days' care is three hundred dollars.

108 TWO SHOT—FRESCO AND ANNA. THE FIGURE HITS FRESCO WITH SHATTERING IMPACT.

FRESCO

Three hundred . . . (TO ANNA) Look, we better get your sister on the phone. You know her number?

ANNA

I have it—here.

SHE FUMBLES FOR A SCRAP OF PAPER IN HER POCKET AND GIVES IT TO FRESCO. HE CROSSES TO SNATCH UP PHONE AS CAMERA ANGLE WIDENS TO INCLUDE CONNELL.

FRESCO

(TAPS PHONE CRADLE) Operator, I want to make a call to San Francisco.

CONNELL'S GLANCE SNAPS UP FROM THE SYRINGE. FRESCO MEETS IT AS:

FRESCO

(TO PHONE AND CONNELL) Yukon 6-0710. Reverse charges! . . . Yeah, I'll wait.

CONNELL INDICATES THE PAPER ON THE DESK.

CONNELL

(TO ANNA) You'll have to sign this.

FRESCO'S TROUBLED GAZE SWITCHES TO ANNA AS SHE COMES TO THE DESK.

ANNA

You explain, please?

CONNELL

Standard professional procedure. Even those medical doctors do this—in case of accident.

HE LAYS A PEN ON THE FORM. SLOWLY, UNCERTAINLY, ANNA PICKS IT UP.

109   MED. CLOSE SHOT—CONNELL WATCHING BEADILY.

110   MED. CLOSE SHOT—ANNA. HER GAZE GOES TO:

111   MED. CLOSE SHOT—FRESCO. HE STILL HOLDS THE PHONE. HIS EYES ARE ON ANNA.

112   THREE SHOT—ANNA, FRESCO, CONNELL. ANNA LOOKS DOWN AT THE FORM, IS ABOUT TO SIGN AS:

FRESCO

(EXPLOSIVELY) You ain't signing anything!

CONNELL

I'm afraid she . . .

FRESCO

(SLICING IN; TO PHONE) Never mind! The call's canceled. Where's the nearest hospital around here? . . . Yeah, I mean a regular hospital!

CONNELL

(RESENTFULLY) You're making a mistake, mister!

FRESCO IGNORES HIM, SCRIBBLES AN ADDRESS ON ANNA'S SLIP OF PAPER.

FRESCO

Thanks. (HANGS UP; MOVES TO ANNA) Let's go.

ANNA

(CONFUSED AND FRIGHTENED) Perhaps it is easier if I stay . . .

FRESCO

No dice. If this guy's a doctor, I'm a college professor.

HE STEERS HER TOWARD DOORWAY AS:

CONNELL

(WITH GLINT OF VENAL ANGER) Just a minute, professor! (FRESCO TURNS
TO HIM) There'll be a ten-dollar consultation fee.

FRESCO STARES AT HIM WITH CONTEMPT, TAKES OUT HIS WALLET AND SLAPS
A BILL ON THE DESK.

FRESCO

A real bargain.

HE EXITS WITH ANNA.

CONNELL

(A WASPISH SHOUT AFTER THEM) Take her to a medical doctor and see
what happens!

SOUND OF DOOR OPEN AND SLAM. CONNELL SLUMPS INTO DESK CHAIR, STARES
SOURLY AT THE TEN-DOLLAR BILL, THEN OPENS DRAWER AND TAKES OUT A
BOTTLE OF LIQUOR. HE HOLDS IT UP TO THE LIGHT. IT IS ALMOST EMPTY. HE
RIPS OUT THE CORK AS WE

DISSOLVE TO:

13 (OMITTED)

14 EXT. ROAD—ANGLE ON FRESCO'S TRUCK—NIGHT—AS IT APPROACHES AND
ROARS PAST.

15 INT. TRUCK—CLOSE SHOT—ANNA—NIGHT. HER HEAD RESTS AGAINST THE
SEAT. HER FACE IS GLAZED WITH PERSPIRATION. THE BOUNCING OF THE TRUCK
BRINGS AN ANGUISH OF DISCOMFORT. CAMERA ANGLE WIDENS TO INCLUDE
FRESCO HUNCHED OVER THE WHEEL. HE GLANCES AT HER.

FRESCO

How do you feel?

ANNA

There is not much time.

FRESCO

(BITTERLY) If I ever get outa this one . . .

HE GRABS THE PHOTOGRAPH-AND-CROSS AMULET AND KISSES IT. ANNA HAS
ROLLED HER HEAD TO LOOK AT HIM.

ANNA

The hospital is far?

FRESCO

Back on the main highway.

ANNA

(LOOKING AHEAD) How long?

FRESCO

Twenty minutes maybe.

HE WIPES HIS MOIST PALMS ON HIS JACKET AND BEGINS TO STEAM AGAIN, BLASTING AT THE FIENDISH DISPARITY BETWEEN HIMSELF AND THE REST OF THE UNIVERSE.

FRESCO

Boy, that must be some sister you got!

ANNA

She is a good person.

FRESCO

Yeah, well, *she* oughta be driving this truck, not me!

THIS PRIES A LITTLE LAUGH FROM ANNA.

ANNA

Rosa? I can't imagine this.

FRESCO

The least she could've done is met you at the border.

ANNA

(REFUSING THIS) Always you make the worst of things!

FRESCO

Too bad.

ANNA

Yes, it *is* too bad!

FRESCO

What are you getting sore about?

ANNA

My sister—you speak this way, you don't even know her!

FRESCO

What's so special to know?

ANNA

When I wrote her I will cross the border, she answers that this is a wrong thing. She says she will send money and I must wait; until I have the papers.

FRESCO

Well, you should've listened to good sense!

ANNA

No.

FRESCO

No. Not you.

116 CLOSE SHOT—ANNA. HER HEAD IS RESTING BACK AGAINST THE JOUNCING SEAT AGAIN. SHE SPEAKS SIMPLY, IN SMALL, STRENGTH-CONSERVING SENTENCES. THE FRAGMENTS ARE LACED TOGETHER WITH LITTLE BITES OF EMOTION, LANCES OF PAIN, SLIVERS OF MEMORY.

ANNA

My sister is first to come to America—many years ago. A good place. Good for children. I was a child then. My father says we will go to her—to Rosa. We make plans. Then comes the time of the Iron Guard, the Fascists. To leave—is more difficult now. So he works—he saves—he plans. And then the war. The Nazis come. We plan for after the war. And then—is the turn of the Russians. My father dies. My mother. I am married now.—I have a husband. We plan again. He becomes ill. But still we escape—to Turkey. From Turkey to Mexico. Again we wait. A child grows in my body. My husband dies. Now I am done with fine plans. With waiting. I know what I will have for my child. This land. This life.

117 TWO SHOT. HER HEAD TURNS TOWARD FRESCO. HIS LIPS ARE PRESSED INTO A GRIM, EMPATHIC LINE. HE DOES NOT LOOK AT HER.

ANNA

You understand?

FRESCO

If I understood anything, I'd be rich.

ANNA

(THIS IS IMPORTANT TO HER) Please. You understand?

FRESCO

Yeah, sure I do. My old man came from Greece, didn't he? (A MUMBLED AFTERTHOUGHT) So he can go bankrupt in his old age.

MORE PAIN. ANNA'S HAND GRIPS FRESCO'S ARM.

ANNA

How long?

FRESCO

Pretty soon, pretty soon!

HE DRIVES THIS WAY FOR A FEW BEATS AND THEN REACTS TO:

118 WINDSHIELD SHOT—A BRIDGE. THE HEADLIGHTS PICK OUT A BRIDGE COMING UP. IT IS UNDER REPAIR AND LANTERNS ARE SET OUT. PILES OF PLANKS AND BUILDING MATERIALS LIE NEARBY.

119 EXT. AT BRIDGE—ANGLE ON TRUCK—NIGHT—AS TRUCK STOPS AT APPROACH TO BRIDGE.

120 EXT. CLOSE SHOT—SIGN. A SIGN READS: "BRIDGE UNDER REPAIR—MAXIMUM LOAD 25,000 LBS."

121 INT. TRUCK—TWO SHOT. FOR FRESCO, THIS IS THE FINAL MINISTRATION OF AN ANGRY DIVINITY.

FRESCO

Great! That's all I needed!

HE POUNDS THE WHEEL AND LOWERS HIS HEAD ONTO FOLDED ARMS.

ANNA

What does it mean?

FRESCO

(HEAD UP; DEFEATED) The bridge'll take about twenty-five thousand pounds. We've got thirty thousand in the load and another ten thousand in the truck. So you figure it out.

ANNA

Then we go another way.

FRESCO

Another way'll take two hours.

THEY SIT FOR A MOMENT IN HELPLESS SILENCE.

ANNA

Perhaps you would like to yell a little.

FRESCO

Why?

ANNA

For the soul.

FRESCO LOOKS AT HER. HE GRINS. THE GRIN FADES.

FRESCO

(WORKING UP STEAM) All right!

FRESCO

(BELLOWING) All right, so what's another law! I might as well bust this one, too!

HE BANGS THE DOOR OPEN.

122 EXT. AT BRIDGE—ANGLE ON FRESCO—NIGHT. FOR A MOMENT HE INSPECTS THE SPAN. THE HEADLIGHT BEAM REVEALS SOME LOOSE CONSTRUCTION PLANKS SCATTERED OVER THE ROADBED. ANNA EMERGES FROM THE TRUCK AS FRESCO RUNS TO PICK UP A BOARD AND HEAVE IT OUT OF THE WAY. HE IS LIFTING ANOTHER AS HE SEES ANNA BENDING TO ONE OF THE PLANKS.

FRESCO

You pick that up, I'll hit you with this one! (SHE STRAIGHTENS) Now walk! The other side!

CAMERA PANS AFTER ANNA AS SHE STARTS ACROSS THE BRIDGE.

123 ANGLE ON FRESCO. FRESCO WIPES THE PALMS OF HIS HANDS AGAINST HIS TROUSERS AND CROSSES TO ONE OF THE BUTTRESSES AT THE SIDE OF THE

BRIDGE. HE SLAMS IT WITH THE HEELS OF HIS HAND, AS IF GAUGING ITS STRENGTH, AND THEN LOOKS DOWN TO THE TERRAIN BELOW.

124 EXT. FAR SIDE OF BRIDGE—ANGLE ON ANNA—NIGHT. ILLUMINATED IN THE HEADLIGHT BEAM, ANNA STANDS TENSELY, WATCHING. NOW SHE STRUGGLES AGAINST THE GRIP OF ANOTHER PAIN.

125 TRUCK SHOT—FRESCO LOOKS AT ANNA, THEN WALKS TO THE CENTER-LINE OF THE SPAN. CAMERA DOLLIES WITH HIM AS METHODICALLY, ALERTLY HE WALKS THE LENGTH OF THE BRIDGE. HIS EYES SWING FROM SIDE TO SIDE OVER THE ROADBED BEFORE HIM. ONCE HE DROPS TO ONE KNEE, INSPECTING MORE CLOSELY. THEN HE CONTINUES TO THE FAR SIDE OF THE BRIDGE AND TWO SHOT WITH ANNA. FOR A MOMENT THEY STARE AT EACH OTHER. THEN:

FRESCO

(DRY-THROATED) Okay, we try it.

ANNA

(RAPT WITH CONCERN) If it breaks . . .

FRESCO

If it breaks, it breaks.

ANNA

(HEADSHAKE) No! Not this! Not for me!

FRESCO

It's got nothing to do with you! I gotta move those tomatoes.

ANNA

(ANOTHER HEADSHAKE) You smash your fine truck . . .

FRESCO

Look, you didn't believe in the signs at the border, what do you believe in that one for?!

HE STABS A FINGER AT WEIGHT SIGN. ANNA'S EYES ARE BRIGHT WITH TEARS. SHE KISSES HIS HAND. FRESCO STARES AT HER. HIS MOUTH TIGHTENS. HE TURNS AND RUNS ACROSS THE BRIDGE.

126 EXT. TRUCK—ANGLE ON FRESCO AS HE COMES INTO SCENE AND GETS INTO TRUCK, SLAMMING DOOR.

127 INT. TRUCK—FRESCO GRIMLY STARTS THE ENGINE, FLICKS THE HEADLIGHTS OFF AND ON AGAIN.

128 EXT. FAR SIDE OF BRIDGE—MED. SHOT—ANNA. SHE SQUINTS AGAINST THE HARSH LIGHT OF THE HEADLAMPS.

129 EXT. TRUCK—WINDSHIELD SHOT—FRESCO—SHOOTING THROUGH WINDSHIELD, WE SEE HIM DELIVER A HASTY KISS TO THE AMULET AND RELEASE THE BRAKE.

130 EXT. TRUCK SIDE OF BRIDGE—ANGLE ON TRUCK. IT STARTS TO ROLL TOWARD US, DIRECTLY INTO CAMERA, FILLING THE SCREEN AS WE

FADE OUT.

ACT IV

FADE IN:

131 EXT. BRIDGE—HEAD-ON TRUCK ANGLE—NIGHT—AS THE TRUCK CREEPS SLOWLY TOWARD US AND ONTO THE BRIDGE.

132 EXT. FAR SIDE OF BRIDGE—ANGLE ON ANNA WATCHING IN AN AGONY OF ANXIETY.

133 INT. TRUCK—ANGLE ON FRESCO. HIS FACE STIPPLED WITH PERSPIRATION.

134 EXT. BRIDGE—FULL SHOT—THE TRUCK MOVING DEAD SLOW.

135 EXT. BRIDGE—LOW POSITION SHOT—TRUCK WHEELS TURNING SLOWLY. NOW A GRINDING, CREAKING SOUND AS THE BRIDGE REBELS AGAINST THE STRAIN.

136 EXT. FAR SIDE OF BRIDGE—ANNA. HER HAND GOES TO HER MOUTH. SOUND OF CREAKING.

137 INT. TRUCK—FRESCO. SOUND OF CREAKING.

138 EXT. BRIDGE SUB-STRUCTURE—CLOSE SHOT—BEAMS—NIGHT. SOUND OF STRAIN. THE BEAMS ARE SHAKING. DUST SIFTS DOWN.

139 EXT. BRIDGE—LOW POSITION SHOT—TRUCK—WHEELS MOVING OVER THE BRIDGE.

140 INT. TRUCK—CLOSE SHOT—FRESCO'S AMULET PHOTOGRAPH AND CROSS ARE CLANKING ON THEIR CHAIN.

141 EXT. BRIDGE—ANGLE ON TRUCK EMPHASIZING DRIVE WHEELS. (NOTE: WE MAKE THE PRODUCTION ASSUMPTION THAT THE BRIDGE HAS A FALSE ROADBED.) NOW THE WHEELS BREAK THROUGH AND THE TRUCK DROPS SEVERAL INCHES.

142 EXT. FAR SIDE OF BRIDGE—ANNA. SHE SCREAMS.

143 INT. TRUCK—FRESCO. FRANTICALLY HE BRAKES THE TRUCK AND SITS MOTION-LESS FOR A MOMENT, AFRAID TO BREATHE, AFRAID TO MOVE. THE SILENCE IS FRACTURED BY SOUND OF CREAKING. GINGERLY FRESCO OPENS THE DOOR AND GETS OUT.

144 EXT. FRONT OF TRUCK—ANGLE ON FRESCO AS HE MOVES TO INSPECT THE DRIVE WHEELS AND THE BROKEN PLANKING.

145 EXT. FAR SIDE OF BRIDGE—ANNA. SHE STARTS TOWARD FRESCO BUT IS SUD-DENLY SEIZED BY A SPASM THAT LEAVES HER GASPING AND HOLDING TO THE BRIDGE FOR SUPPORT.

146 EXT. BRIDGE—ANNA AND FRESCO. FRESCO LOOKS TOWARD ANNA.

FRESCO

How's your schedule?

ANNA

(HAND HOLDING TO A SUPPORT) The last one—three minutes.

FRESCO DARTS TOWARD THE BRIDGE RAILING AND CLIMBS OVER IT TO INSPECT THE TERRAIN BELOW.

147 ANGLE ON ANNA AS SHE MOVES TOWARD RAILING. SHOOTING DOWN AND PAST HER, WE SEE FRESCO SCRAMBLING DOWN THE SLOPE TOWARD THE SUB-STRUCTURE OF THE BRIDGE.

148 MED. CLOSE SHOT—ANNA AS HER FRIGHTENED EYES TRACK FRESCO.

149 EXT. SUB-STRUCTURE OF BRIDGE—ANGLE ON FRESCO AS HE MOVES IN, COMING DIRECTLY ON CAMERA AND LOOKING UP TOWARD BRIDGE UNDER-PINNING. HE WIPES PERSPIRATION FROM HIS EYES. SOUND OF CREAKING AS THE BRIDGE RESPONDS TO STRAIN.

150 POV UP ANGLE—BRIDGE STRUCTURE. WE SEE A SEGMENT OF THE TRUCK TIRE PROTRUDING THROUGH THE FRAGMENTED BRIDGE BED. DIRT TRICKLES DOWN. AN ADJACENT BEAM OR PLANK CRACKS AND SPRINGS FREE, AS IF TO INDICATE THE RAPID WEAKENING OF THE ENTIRE STRUCTURE.

151 MED. CLOSE SHOT—FRESCO. HIS UPWARD GLANCE HOLDS FOR A DREAD MOMENT. THEN HE TURNS AND RUNS TOWARD SLOPE AND ROADWAY.

152 EXT. BRIDGE—FRESCO AND ANNA. ANNA MOVES TOWARD FRESCO AS HE COMES OVER THE BRIDGE RAILING. THEY LOOK AT EACH OTHER. THEN:

FRESCO

I said wait over there! (HE INDICATES FAR SIDE OF BRIDGE) And don't go stomping too hard!

A BEAT AND SHE TURNS FROM HIM, CROSSING AGAIN TOWARD THE FAR SIDE OF THE BRIDGE. FRESCO WHIPS TOWARD HIS TRUCK, LOOKS AGAIN TOWARD ANNA BEFORE HE OPENS THE DOOR, THEN GETS IN.

153 EXT. TRUCK—ANGLE ON FRESCO THROUGH WINDSHIELD AS HE ALLOWS POWER TO TRICKLE INTO THE WHEELS.

154 EXT. BRIDGE—LOW POSITION SHOT—DRIVE WHEELS. THE WHEELS TEAR AGAINST THE PLANKING WITHOUT EXTRICATING THEMSELVES FROM THE GASHED BED.

155 EXT. FAR SIDE OF BRIDGE—MED. CLOSE SHOT—ANNA WATCHING—WATCHING.

156 INT. TRUCK—ANGLE ON FRESCO. HE MOISTENS HIS LIPS AND BEGINS TO SHIFT DELICATELY BETWEEN LOW AND REVERSE GEARS SO AS TO THROW THE TRUCK INTO A GENTLE ROCKING MOTION.

157 EXT. BRIDGE—ANGLE ON TRUCK ROCKING AGAINST THE PRESSURE OF THE EMBEDDED WHEELS.

158 EXT. BRIDGE—CLOSE SHOT—DRIVE WHEELS TEARING INTO THE PLANKING AS THE BRIDGE ROCKS.

159 EXT. BRIDGE SUB-STRUCTURE AS THE STRAIN IS TRANSLATED THROUGH ANOTHER BUCKLING BEAM.

160 EXT. BRIDGE SUB-STRUCTURE—UP ANGLE SHOT—PROTRUDING WHEEL CHEW-ING AGAINST THE SHATTERING BED.

161 EXT. FAR SIDE OF BRIDGE—VERY CLOSE SHOT—ANNA, HER HAND RAISED TO HER MOUTH.

162 INT. TRUCK—ANGLE ON FRESCO. HE SLIDES THE TRANSMISSION INTO NEUTRAL, WIPES THE PERSPIRATION FROM HIS FACE, HESITATES AND THEN VIOLENTLY SLAMS THE TRUCK INTO LOW GEAR AND APPLIES POWER AGAIN.

163 EXT. BRIDGE—LOW POSITION SHOT—DRIVE WHEELS. THE WHEELS SPIN AGAINST THE TORN BED AND FINALLY TEAR FREE.

164 EXT. ANGLE ON TRUCK. THE TRUCK IS MOVING ACROSS THE BRIDGE AS WE HEAR A MAJOR CRACKING SOUND. SIMULTANEOUSLY, WE HAVE A SUDDENLY CANTED CAMERA ANGLE TO COUNTERFEIT A TRANSVERSE LURCH OF THE BRIDGE. FRESCO POURS POWER TO THE TRUCK AND ROLLS SAFELY ONTO THE FAR SIDE.

165 EXT. FAR SIDE OF BRIDGE—THE TRUCK, ANNA, FRESCO. ANNA MOVES QUICKLY TO PASSENGER SIDE AS DOOR OPENS AND FRESCO EMERGES. IGNORING HER, HE GATHERS UP AN ARMLOAD OF FLARES AND "DANGER" SIGNS FROM BEHIND THE SEAT AND RACES BACK ACROSS THE BRIDGE. ANNA LOOKS AFTER HIM, TURNS TO START PAINFULLY INTO THE TRUCK, SLIPS AND ALMOST FALLS.

166 EXT. ORIGINAL SIDE OF BRIDGE—FRESCO. FEVERISHLY HE SETS OUT FLARES AND SIGNS, SWINGS A COUPLE OF WOODEN HORSES TO BLOCK THE APPROACH TO THE BRIDGE, AND RUNS BACK TO THE TRUCK.

167 EXT. FAR SIDE OF BRIDGE—THE TRUCK, ANNA. ANNA STANDS LEANING AGAINST THE TRUCK. HER SHOULDERS ARE SHAKING. SHE IS SOBBING. FRESCO RUNS INTO SCENE, STOPS, GENTLY TURNS HER TOWARD HIM.

FRESCO
(NORMAL VOICE) Don't cry. You hear me? (YELLING AGAIN) You don't have to cry! You're going to be okay!

ANNA
(HEADSHAKE) You almost die. You do this and you could die . . .

AND AS FRESCO STARES AT HER, HE REALIZES THAT ANNA'S TEARS ARE FOR HIM.

FRESCO
Listen, you want to worry about something, worry about the tomatoes!

HE HELPS HER INTO THE CAB AND MOVES AROUND TO DRIVER'S SIDE.

168 INT. TRUCK—ANNA AND FRESCO. FRESCO GETS IN. HE BANKS OFF THE EMER GENCY BRAKE AS:

FRESCO
(A TORTURED NON SEQUITUR) Those Sindell brothers, huh? Those Rumanians are killing me!

HE IS DRIVING AGAIN.

169 EXT. ANGLE ON TRUCK AS IT HURTLES DOWN THE ROAD, GROWLING FROM ONE GEAR TO THE NEXT.

LAP DISSOLVE TO

170 EXT. HIGHWAY—RUN THROUGH SHOT—THE TRUCK—NIGHT.

171 INT. TRUCK—ANNA AND FRESCO. ANNA'S FACE CONTORTS. A HALF STIFLED SCREAM. SHE BITES AGAINST HER HAND. FRESCO SHOOTS A GLANCE AT HER. HE IS DRIVING BRUTALLY NOW, SHOVING THE RIG WITH HIS OWN STRENGTH, HIS VOICE RISING IN A CLIMACTIC HYMN TO HIS OPPRESSIVE GODS.

FRESCO

You're going to have your baby in America! In a hospital! That's my promise—me, Fresco!

FRESCO

(CONTINUED) (ANOTHER GLANCE AT HER) You ever know me to break a promise? (EYES ON ROAD) Just cooperate! You have that kid now, I'll make an issue!

ANNA SHAKES HER HEAD AND TRIES TO SMILE.

ANNA

Not yet.

FRESCO

"Not yet." (A SNARL) What do *you* know about it?!

HE HUNCHES OVER THE WHEEL.

DISSOLVE TO:

172 EXT. HOSPITAL—ESTABLISHING SHOT—DAWN. A SMALL, SINGLE-STORY HOSPITAL STANDS JUST OFF THE HIGHWAY. CAMERA PANS TO FRESCO'S TRUCK APPROACHING AND SLOWING FOR TURN INTO DRIVEWAY.

173 EXT. HOSPITAL DRIVEWAY—A SIGN. A SIGN READS "HOSPITAL PARKING." THE TRUCK DRIVES OUT FROM CAMERA AND STOPS. FRESCO EMERGES AND RACES TO ANNA'S DOOR.

174 EXT. HOSPITAL—AT ANNA'S SIDE OF TRUCK—FRESCO—AND ANNA AS FRESCO HELPS HER OUT, SUPPORTING HER HUDDLED FIGURE.

FRESCO

Let's go to work.

CAMERA PULLS BACK AS THEY CROSS TOWARD HOSPITAL ENTRANCE. ANGLE NOW INCLUDES AN IMMIGRATION PATROL CAR. FRESCO STOPS.

175 CLOSE SHOT—DOOR PANEL ON PATROL CAR. A SEAL AND LEGEND READING: "U.S. IMMIGRATION SERVICE."

176 TWO SHOT—FRESCO AND ANNA—DAWN. ANNA LOOKS AT FRESCO. HIS MOUTH TIGHTENS. THEY START FORWARD AGAIN TO HOSPITAL ENTRANCE. AS THEY REACH IT, A UNIFORMED IMMIGRATION OFFICER COMES OUT. HE STOPS, CURIOUSLY EYEING THIS MAN AND WOMAN. FRESCO STANDS ROOTED AT ANNA'S SIDE, BOTH ARMS SUPPORTING HER. THEN:

FRESCO

(A SNARL) Come on, you got a busted arm or something? Open the door!

IMMIGRATION OFFICER

(HE GRINS) I'm with you, Daddy-o.

HE HOLDS THE DOOR OPEN. FRESCO AND ANNA GO IN. THE OFFICER GRINS AND MOVES TO HIS CAR.

177 INT. HOSPITAL RECEPTION ROOM—FRESCO, ANNA, ADMITTING NURSE—DAWN. WE HAVE THE ADMITTING DESK, COUCHES, A COUPLE OF WHEEL CHAIRS, A TELEPHONE BOOTH, SWINGING DOORS TO A HOSPITAL CORRIDOR. ALSO, SOME FLOWERS ON THE DESK, PICTURES ON THE WALL; IN SHORT, A DIFFERENT WORLD.

THE ADMITTING NURSE IS WORKING OVER SOME PAPERS AS FRESCO AND ANNA ENTER. SHE LOOKS UP AND BLINKS. THEY MAKE A WEIRD APPEARANCE: FRESCO GRIMED BY HIS NIGHT'S LABORS, ANNA SHABBY AND THREADBARE AND OBVIOUSLY ON THE IMMINENT EDGE OF HER PRIVATE MIRACLE.

NURSE

Wow. (TO A VOICE BOX) Dr. Rubell—right away, please.

SHE MOVES TO ANNA AND GUIDES HER FIRMLY INTO A WHEEL CHAIR.

NURSE

(CONTINUES) You sit here and don't move.

ANNA

(WANLY) Thank you.

FRESCO

(TO ANNA) Okay, huh? (PATS HER SHOULDER) Okay.

THE NURSE TAKES A PAD AND PENCIL FROM THE DESK.

NURSE

(TO FRESCO) What's the lady's name, hon?

FRESCO LOOKS AT ANNA.

FRESCO

She wants your name.

ANNA

Anna. Anna Beza. B-E-Z-A.

THE NURSE WRITES THIS DOWN AS DR. RUBELL ENTERS THROUGH SWINGING DOORS. HE WEARS HOSPITAL WHITES AND A STETHOSCOPE. HE IS VERY YOUNG

NURSE

(INDICATING ANNA) One delivery.

178 TWO SHOT—ANNA AND RUBELL AS THE DOCTOR COMES TO ANNA. HE GRINS AND HIS TOUCH IS SOLID REASSURANCE.

RUBELL

Easy, mama. The doctor's here.

HE PLUGS IN STETHOSCOPE EARPIECES.

179 TWO SHOT—FRESCO AND NURSE.

NURSE

(EYES ON PAPER) Are you the husband?

FRESCO

What do you mean "husband"? I ain't even a friend!

THE NURSE LOOKS UP IN SURPRISE.

180 TWO SHOT—ANNA AND RUBELL AS THE DOCTOR REMOVES STETHOSCOPE.

RUBELL

Cut it kind of fine, didn't you?

ANNA ANSWERS WITH A WAN AND FRIGHTENED SMILE. RUBELL GUIDES THE
WHEEL CHAIR TOWARD CORRIDOR DOORS. CAMERA ANGLES TO INCLUDE FRESCO.

RUBELL

(TO FRESCO) You going to stick around?

FRESCO

Yeah, well, I'd like to, but I got a job to do . . .

HIS ARM IS EXTENDED TOWARD EXTERIOR BUT HIS EYES GO TO ANNA'S FACE.

181 CLOSE SHOT—ANNA. FRESCO IS HER ONLY FRIEND. HER EYES ARE LARGE AND
PLEADING. SHE SAYS NOTHING.

182 THREE SHOT—ANNA, RUBELL, FRESCO.

FRESCO

(TO RUBELL) How long?

RUBELL

Brother, we ain't got time to talk about it.

HE SHOVES THE DOOR OPEN AND IS WHEELING ANNA AWAY AS:

FRESCO

(A SHOUT) Okay, I'll wait!

THE DOORS SWING SHUT. FRESCO TURNS DISTRAUGHTLY INTO SHOT WITH THE
NURSE. HE FEELS CALLED UPON TO SHOUT AN EXPLANATION.

FRESCO

People shouldn't be alone when they have babies!

HE CROSSES O.S. TO THE PHONE BOOTH.

83 MED. CLOSE SHOT—NURSE. SHE LOOKS UP AND SMILES.

84 AT PHONE BOOTH—MED. CLOSE SHOT—FRESCO AS HE THRUSTS A DIME INTO
SLOT AND DIALS INFORMATION.

FRESCO

I want to call San Francisco . . . (FINDS ADDRESS SLIP IN POCKET) Mrs.
Rosa Stern—S-T-E-R-N. Yeah, the number is Yukon 6-0710. (VIO-
LENTLY) Who do you think? Me! I'll pay!

HE IS PUMPING COINS INTO THE SLOTS AS WE

DISSOLVE TO:

85 EXT. HOSPITAL—FULL SHOT—FRESCO—DAY. FRESCO IS KNEELING BY THE
DRIVE WHEELS, REMOVING THE LAST OF THE TIRE CHAINS. HE HAS HAD THE
OPPORTUNITY TO WASH AWAY THE GRIME OF HIS NIGHT'S ADVENTURES. RISING,

HE OPENS TRUCK DOOR AND TOSSES CHAIN INTO STORAGE COMPARTMENT. DR. RUBELL EMERGES FROM HOSPITAL AND LIGHTS CIGARETTE. FRESCO GOES TO HIM.

186 TWO SHOT—FRESCO AND DR. RUBELL.

> FRESCO
>
> Anything?

> RUBELL
>
> Something.

> FRESCO
>
> What?

> RUBELL
>
> A boy.

> FRESCO
>
> No kidding.

HE GRINS.

> RUBELL
>
> She says she'd like to see you.

FRESCO'S GRIN FADES.

> FRESCO
>
> No.

HE TURNS AND FURIOUSLY SLAMS THE TRUCK DOOR SHUT.

> FRESCO
>
> No!

LAP DISSOLVE TO:

187 INT. HOSPITAL ROOM—ANGLE ON ENTRANCE—DAY. THE DOOR OPENS SLIGHTLY AND FRESCO ENTERS WITH THE HUSHED MANNER PECULIAR TO HOSPITAL VISITORS. HE CROSSES TO THE BED AND INTO SHOT WITH ANNA. A WINDOW, ITS SHADE UNDRAWN, FACES ONTO THE HIGHWAY.

ANNA'S HAIR IS BOUND BACK WITH A WHITE TOWEL. SHE IS AT ONCE EXHAUSTED AND RADIANT. SHE IS CONTENT. FOR HER, THE MEMORY OF THE WOMAN IN THE TRUCK IS ALREADY GROWING DIM.

> ANNA
>
> Hello.

> FRESCO
>
> (SOFTLY) How do you feel?

> ANNA
>
> So good.

> FRESCO
>
> Now you're the mother of an American. For that you get a medal.

> ANNA
>
> (SHE SMILES) An easy thing—you know?

FRESCO

You think so, huh?

FROM THE HIGHWAY OUTSIDE, WE HEAR THE APPROACH OF A HIGHBALLING TRUCK. FRESCO MOVES QUICKLY TO THE WINDOW.

188 INT. HOSPITAL ROOM—AT WINDOW—FRESCO AS HE APPROACHES, LOOKS OUT PAST CAMERA AND REACTS TO:

189 POV WINDOW SHOT—SINDELL BROS. TRUCK—DAY. THE SINDELL BROS. TRUCK IS ROARING PAST THE HOSPITAL.

190 EXT. HIGHWAY—CLOSE SHOT—SINDELL BROS. TRUCK—DAY. EMPHASIZING THE LEGEND "SINDELL BROS., CINCINNATI," AS THE TRUCK DRIVES PAST.

191 INT. HOSPITAL ROOM—FRESCO AND ANNA—DAY. FRESCO TURNS FROM THE WINDOW AND BACKS ANXIOUSLY TOWARD THE DOOR.

FRESCO

Look, I gotta go, Anna. I got some heavy driving.

ANNA

(AN EAGERNESS) I ask them to bring my son. You wish to see him?

FRESCO'S HEART SINKS. ONE WOULD EXPECT HIM TO PICK UP A CHAIR AND BELT HER WITH IT. BUT HE IS QUITE A MAN, THIS FRESCO. HE JUDGES THE PRIDE IN ANNA'S FACE AND NODS.

FRESCO

Yeah. Yeah, I guess I'd like that. (RETURNS TO WINDOW; A RESIGNED GESTURE) Those Sindell Brothers—it'll take another one of your miracles.

ANNA

Then I will pray.

FRESCO

(A BEAT) You better pray for those immigration people. You tell them how things were, Anna. I bet they ain't so tough. (A GRIN) They might even thank you for your contribution.

SOUND OF DOOR OPEN. THEY LOOK TO:

192 ANGLE ON NURSE. SHE ENTERS WITH THE INFANT. FRESCO GOES TO THEM.

FRESCO

Sure. He's beautiful.

193 INSERT—CLOSE SHOT—THE INFANT (STOCK)—DAY.

194 ANGLE ON FRESCO, ANNA, NURSE. ANNA REACHES FOR THE CHILD AND THE NURSE PLACES HIM IN HER ARMS.

NURSE

Five minutes now.

SHE EXITS.

FRESCO

(TO ANNA) You be proud. (BACKS TOWARD DOOR) Oh, I called your sister. She's flying out here to take care of you. From now on, you go through life without me, okay?

ANNA

Okay. (THEN) How are you called?

FRESCO

What?

ANNA

Your name.

FRESCO

Oh. Dimitri. It's kinda foreign. Dimitri Fresco.

ANNA LOOKS AT HER BABY, TOUCHES HIS FACE.

ANNA

Good.

FRESCO GIVES HER A LITTLE WAVE AND IS GONE.

LAP DISSOLVE TO:

195 EXT. HOSPITAL—ANGLE ON FRESCO—DAY. HE IS IN HIS TRUCK, TURNING THE ENGINE OVER. CAMERA PANS TO HOSPITAL ENTRANCE AS DR. RUBELL EMERGES. HE WEARS AN OPEN RAIN COAT OVER HIS WHITES.

196 EXT. TRUCK—ANGLE ON FRESCO. HE SEES THE DOCTOR, REACHES BEHIND THE SEAT TO AN OPEN LUG, AND MAKES A BENEDICTION.

FRESCO

Hey, Doctor! Have a tomato.

HE THROWS A TOMATO.

197 MED. SHOT—RUBELL. SURPRISED, HE CATCHES THE TOMATO AND WAVES.

RUBELL

Thanks.

198 EXT. TRUCK—ANGLE ON FRESCO.

FRESCO

Don't thank me! They came cheap.

HE GUNS THE TRUCK FORWARD, SWINGING AROUND THE HOSPITAL DRIVE AND ONTO THE HIGHWAY.

199 EXT. HIGHWAY—MED. LONG SHOT—THE TRUCK—DAY—ACCELERATING DOWN THE HIGHWAY TOWARD A BEND.

200 EXT. HIGHWAY AROUND BEND—FULL SHOT—FRESCO'S TRUCK. FRESCO'S TRUCK SWEEPS AROUND THE BEND AND CAMERA PANS TO DISCOVER THE SINDELL BROTHERS' TRUCK IN A DITCH. JERRY AND AL ARE ON THEIR KNEES AT A WHEEL. THEY APPEAR TO BE ARGUING VIOLENTLY.

201 INT. FRESCO'S TRUCK—ANGLE ON FRESCO AS HE SPOTS THE SINDELL BROTHERS' TRUCK AND LETS OUT A WHOOP OF JOY. HE GLANCES AT THE LEFT-HAND SIDE MIRROR, BOUNCES JUBILANTLY AND LAUGHS A WILD, TRIUMPHANT LAUGH.

NOW HE SNATCHES UP HIS AMULET AND KISSES IT, SETTLES DOWN IN HIS SEAT AND HEADS FOR HOME, FEELING AS STRONG AS MOUNTAINS.

202 EXT. HIGHWAY—REAR OF FRESCO'S TRUCK. FOR AN INSTANT OUR SHOT EMPHASIZES THE PAINTED WORD "CINCINNATI" ON THE REAR OF THE TRUCK. THEN IT IS ROLLING AWAY FROM US AS WE

FADE OUT.

THE END

Note one thing at the very start: the *authority* with which the opening scene is set. The writer has asked for a crane shot. This elevation, not extreme, gives us a swift panoramic sweep of the field. Which in turn gives the viewer the opportunity to inhabit the mood of the story, to witness the kind and quality of characters who will likely people it. And hints of the action—"deals being made in the street," the word "vitality."

The mark of *authority* here can be stated in two words: dispatch and economy. Nothing flossy, nothing fancy, no "writing"—just blunt, serviceable description.

Look at paragraph one of Shot 1. The writer, Richard Alan Simmons, always knows what camera angle he wants and asks for it. You will see that this is consistently observed through the whole of the script. Again, it is never fancy, just clear, direct, and simple. But the principal ingredient of this same paragraph is the definitiveness with which the outdoor set is described. It has movement, color, reality. It tells propmen and set decorators all they need to know. It stamps an immediate impression on our eyes and feelings.

Paragraph two of this same shot introduces other values. Quick eyes will pick up the fact that "Fresco and Son" is a new firm, and that it's a long way from home headquarters.

Look now at the effective *isolation* given to Fresco, the physical isolation. Do this in your own work. Set off your principals. Let your viewers see them alone, long enough for physical appearance and character overtone to register.

The outdoor sink is a fine touch. Better still is the use made of it. This outdoor shaving, because no notice is taken of it by the others, further stamps the activity in this wholesale market as being authentic. Obviously it's there for the convenience of truck drivers. You know you're looking at the real thing, that "this is the way it is."

Instinctively we're buying what we're looking at.

We are given a few fine adjectives about our leading man. They add up to an interesting person. But good or bad? We aren't told. The playing will reveal this, how the man responds to the thrusts and crises into which he's about to be thrown.

"Thirty-two, Mr. Wiseguy!" Fresco contradicts the foreman.

What qualities in Fresco does that remark denote? Quite a few: suspicion, caution, hawk-eyed attention to detail, sassiness, aggressiveness. The action at once confirms all this: "Fresco, the soap still on his face, comes toward us."

Any doubts now about Fresco's being on the ball? See how *early* the author is setting the primary forces of his hero. Already he is beginning to fascinate us, though we don't know why. It may be his brutish brevity, or the near swagger that goes with his movements, or the presence of his quality of challenge. We know he wants his way and we know he'll make a tough adversary. We don't know whether we like him. But it isn't important. Yet.

Shots 3 and 4 show us a great deal more, and we sponge it up as each item begins to deliver its meaning and thus take hold of our feelings. Note the *consistency* of all of Fresco's words and actions. "Let's see what they're loaded with." "Rip this one." "Can't you read tomatoes?"

The speech and action through this moment suggest that the writer was there, that he saw, that he listened, that he picked up some of the idiom of the trade: "Lug" for crate, for example. Or "Can't you read tomatoes?" (i.e., "Don't you know a green one from a ripe one?"). All of it petulant, hurried, and pushy.

How much more needs to be said to the actor playing the foreman than that one word "bedeviled" for that one spot? It says everything. And it also makes its own comment as to the *effect* Fresco has on others. Fresco not only talks tough, he is tough. Almost everything he says is accompanied or followed by *action*.

This is an important key to his whole character. Its impacts are being felt and delivered already, and we've seen this hustling ball of energy for less than a minute. He gets what he wants.

Notice the neat, unassertive, but unmistakable way our geographical orientation is made clear: a stencil on a crate top. We've previously seen the sign "El Paso Produce Center" and some Mexican faces and Mexican hats. If you missed these on the way by, you've now been told flat out where you are.

We've been looking down, or looking across at and parallel to, the scene and the characters in this action so far. Now in Shot 5 we look *up*. Do this in your own work. Mix up your shots. Give relief and contrast and variety to the eye. Keep inviting it to inspect new corners, new elevations, new surprises. Keep the eye busy. Get in the habit of this.

Shots 6 and 7 emphasize "Cincinnati," insinuate a good relationship between Fresco and the produce dealer, give us a good visual contrast, and further build the character, through adding another characteristic, of Fresco. On an earlier page I mentioned consistency. Notice throughout this script how consistently this new attribute is respected: Fresco being "on the double." He vaults to loading platforms, he leaps into his truck's cab, leaps down from it. He seems able at any moment to belt somebody, to take charge of anything with his hands. He's never still. Even when stationary, he's coiled.

Did it help Richard Alan Simmons, in the writing of this script, to know that his leading man was to be Peter Falk? You bet. You won't have this luxury in your first triumphs. It has to be earned. But it will sharpen your own disciplines, in building your characters line by line and scene by scene, if in your imagination you *are* writing for a specific actor, one you admire, one whose tricks you respect, whose capacities you wish to exploit. So always *think* you know who your principals are going to be. And write for them. You'll write with greater assurance if you do. It's the best way I know to avoid the blur of generality, the quickest way to bring out sharpness in character outline. Depth of character comes later, but believable contours of character can be achieved even by beginners.

Can the student writer pick out the scene, or perhaps the line, where the viewer is beginning to cheer for Fresco? Or beginning to want to? Yes, he should be able to by the time we've experienced the little exchange in Shot 8. He's bold and tough and practical, but he's also just starting out on his own.

Stop for a moment right here. What adjectives has Fresco already earned in our brief acquaintance? You may make your own list, but mine would give this much to Fresco already: that he is slangy, impulsive, confident, resourceful, scrappy, strong, responsible, competitive, hard pressed, self-driven. I'd say also that he's a gambler but that he's nonetheless absolutely straight about money and about any obligation he's decided to assume.

Have any plot items been planted as yet? There is the suggestion of one, neatly buried (as such should be) in Shot 9. "The rain washed out every vine between Cincinnati and the border." Good use, as you know, is very soon to be made of the weather factor, good story use as well as good picture use. It is, in fact, one hell of a ride this man is about to take on, and take us on. The casual mention of heavy rain is a conversational throwaway to Fresco's mother, but it has more meaning than that to us. We're going into it.

There is good action and good television in Shot 10. Look at it again. It says and shows a lot. And all in a matter of five or six seconds. Remember the two words, dispatch and economy, mentioned many times in this book. Here's a fine example of both at once. We get a tingle out of this little scene. And our first knowledge that a competitive factor is to be involved. It is a good, photographable piece of business to have Fresco, while still on his long-distance call, lug the phone to the window and peer down. Shot 11 limns in the kind of competition it is, Shot 12 names it, and 13 says all we need know about Fresco's reaction: "loathing."

We have met the enemy.

The direct "tosses towel aside" is neither casual nor careless. It just means man-in-a-hurry. Directions aren't decorations and never should be. Television does not have the time for James M. Barrie cuteness. Here the small bit with the shaving towel, and his disposal of same, adds a dimension to the expanding character of Fresco.

Note, in Shot 13, Fresco says "Mister" Michaels. His surliness at the loading platform is a true part of his character, but his (for him) courtesy and appreciation toward Michaels establishes a good relationship between the two. Their relationship is not important to the main story, but see how nimbly and naturally the little scene with Michaels in the office tells us so very much about Fresco.

Shot 14 is a good exit line. This is a big gamble, "the whole bankroll." Note contrast of camera angles in Shots 15 and 16. This keeps the eye busy, and also sets up the importance of the Sindells.

In Shot 16, the one slang word "hiya," though it is not possible to tell from the script, always gets a huge and sudden laugh from viewers. Peter Falk's response to Jerry's salutation was so monstrously casual, it was cutting. Which he meant it to be. When Falk said that line, it really came out, "Out of my way, scum."

This is another advantage to the writer in knowing who is to play what role. From their year of experience together in *Trials of O'Brien,* Simmons knows Peter Falk's techniques, that he makes much more use of his hands and of quick, expressive articulations of his head than he does of voice or face or speech cadence.

In Shot 17: "We like it anywhere we don't have to work for you." This is the clincher. Battle is joined. We now take sides. And we even enjoy Fresco's impudence when he mimics Jerry and reverses the whole idea of a partnership: "Yeah, well, I'll tell you, buddy-up." This is really quite withering. And we at once see that a shot of adrenalin gets pumped into Jerry's bloodstream. After such a put-down, Jerry *has* to lick him. We know there is bad blood in this contest. We know the Sindell brothers have accepted the challenge because Jerry "sprints toward the stairs."

We know for sure that we're going to witness a race. It's hard to believe, isn't it, that we could be persuaded to care so much about a load of tomatoes?

What else do we know? That Fresco, though the underdog, is a rough competitor, that he has a grudge, that the odds are against him, that failure will ruin him and his father, that he has the boldest possible stripe of true venture instinct.

And that he's nice to his mother. (This is always good.)

Shot 23. Angle of camera again. Use these tricks and contrasts. Here, if you saw and remember this great show, you can no doubt recall the effectiveness of having the camera close to the road surface. It was so close, you could smell the rainwater pools.

Especially useful to new writers—and a habit that is not hard to develop—is the use of a certain *type* of word—action words here—which, more quickly and more fully, lets us know our leading man, his intents, energies, and skills. Does he "press" the starter? Never. He "hits" it. He "vaults," "rams," "slams." Does he offer his credit card at the filling station? No, he "thrusts" it. He's all gristle. We sense submerged rage in him all the time, but not at the truck, always at circumstance or at people in his way.

All gristle? Yes. Anything else? Yes. He is all heart.

Another useful word, another valuable habit for any television writer, is isolation. In Shot 24, Simmons, the scriptwriter, wants to concentrate, briefly, on the woman. Wants her to register. Her story, as we know, has parallel urgency to Fresco's. See how naturally, how expeditiously, the writer manages this.

We're talking here about isolation, about seeing the main thing without distraction. Is the lunchroom busy? No. It's closed. Its only occupant is the seated (pregnant) Anna. And how alone she is! How unlikely that anyone in her condition would be there and *be* alone. How wretched! We see all, at once. Does Fresco? Not yet. The business at the outdoor phone booth occupies him. The action is continuous. We don't *stop* in order to inspect Anna. She is a moment among other moments. He sees her cross the drive-in area, then climb into the cab of his truck. He scowls but continues talking to Pop.

We like him more and more. This gruff young fellow is enormously responsible. In being able to hide his own concern and yet maintain the morale of others—his mother first, now Pop—he shows a fine courage of his own. And leadership.

Where are the actual lines that prove his courage? Easy. Look at Shot 25. Is Fresco worried about his trip? Sure, why not? Weather is against him. So are the Sindells. All he has in his favor is time. And nerve. But what does he say to Pop? "Will you quit worrying?"

Now look at the last two lines of Shot 13. Read them aloud. Look at the impact that is now delivered right here in the line, "It's like money in the bank."

He's projecting his most optimistic self into the phone, an optimism he doesn't really feel, when he looks out the window of the phone booth at more trouble. This is the second time he's inherited one problem while on the phone trying to deal with another.

Do you appreciate the invisible mechanics that are here working? Working to build and stimulate story interest and character involvement both at once? One more thing—and it makes Fresco our hero for sure: "Tell her I'll be in Tuesday morning and I love her" (his wife).

We've been on the air only six minutes, but there isn't very much more we *need* to know about Fresco, is there? Certainly not for the dramatic load he must carry in this story. And all the qualities he's been given will be put to use and repeatedly tested.

Did the writer ever describe Fresco? In the way, for example, that Thomas Hardy described Eustacia Vye or James Barrie described Maggie Wylie? No, he didn't. He gave us clues as to background ("extraction Greek"), and this much more, "temperament mercurial, a man of wild and restless energies." That's all. Then the writer put Fresco *in action,* and let us see for ourselves the exact sort of person there is here. Let us see it by what Fresco *does.*

Do the same, in all your television work.

You know, from the scowl, that Fresco is going to be rough on the girl. He doesn't open the cab door. He "wrenches" it open. "You—out!" In his own mind he's all through with her, permanently and right now. He's that sort. She's in the way. Get rid of her. Primitive. Efficient. Deal with anything the instant it comes up.

Could Fresco have shouted from the phone booth, "You—out!" before Anna gets into his truck? Yes. But think how much more poignant and affecting to let her get seated, and then be ejected.

There are more structural reasons than that. It gives each one a chance to inspect the other, and it gives us a chance to inspect both. Mostly it reveals another compartment in the emotional reservoir of Fresco: "reluctant compassion," Simmons has called it. He doesn't like to have to do anything nice. Or to be seen doing such. The sort who claws off his hat in a cathedral and is relieved when mass is over.

In Shot 29 we envision Anna almost completely with the quick lines, "thin coat held tightly . . . with one hand. No hat." Her legs are "bare," shoes "shabby"—and "pathetic on the wet asphalt."

Fresco takes in the full situation. Does it affect him? It nearly knocks him apart. He *identifies* with her distress, inhabits it, knows the feeling. And very soon we know why: four kids of his own. He's been through these dynamics. He knows what they are.

Does Fresco have humor? Yes. A lot of it. "You know how many tomatoes that is?"

"No."

"Well, I'm telling you, that's one big bunch of tomatoes, lady."

Shot 32 is a fine example of television writing. See how spare it is. Writing lean is always harder than writing fat. And almost always it is very much more effective. Look at 32 again, and then close the book. Besides the information that is given us, what more do we know about the *feelings* of these two?

Notice, too, the difference in speech types, speech patterns, word choices, phrases. Each of the two characters has his (her) own. Neither is well educated; both are intelligent and perceptive. There is much hidden emotion, by its being unspoken, in the reactions these two have to each other's disclosures. Fresco has just impugned the Rumanian people; his response to Anna's immediate revelation that she also is Rumanian calls for some charming backpedaling.

What could you say of Anna before we leave this little scene? That she is honest, practical, realistic, patient, seeing, that she, like himself, is a person of no-nonsense. Negative? No. Just blunt, direct, and in a jam. Truthful? Yes. But she's just lied, hasn't she? Yes, she has. Can you be both a truth teller and a liar? Sure. We all are.

"Then what'd you tell me 'down the road'?" he rages.

"To make a beginning," she answers.

Is his outrage justified? Indeed, yes. He's been bad. How at fault is Anna? Entirely. How heavily do we blame her? Not very. She'll take her lumps. She's already taken more than most women could survive. She's told a white lie, maybe a gray one, but she's a good woman in a bad fix. Is Fresco justified in bellowing? Of course. In throwing her out? Yes, even that. She *is* trouble. And at a most awkward, unwanted time.

That is why this is a story.

There is some good television in Shot 35. Male readers will appreciate it better than the women. There is a brotherhood among all transcontinental truck drivers. They share the same hazards, and in this sharing they respect and help each other, as Casey does now in this brief scene.

Two other important pieces of playmaking: one, how quickly, economically, and believably we're warned about the roadblock and a wetback "dame." Good, fast plotting, invisible as such in its naturalness.

The other item: the isolation of Anna, mournfully retreating as if being scourged by the headlights, "violently alone." Could you turn your back on this? Could Fresco? This taut little moment is a fine example of dispatch.

The police siren punctuates what Casey has just reported. And it forces a decision from Fresco. He's not going to abandon the woman till he knows more.

The short strip of talk (Shot 42) says much about both, and in very few words. Almost all their talk is sparse. Fresco wants her to level with him. This is not too hard for her; she's a woman who has spent all her brief years leveling with life, and on its terms, never hers.

The practical side of his nature operates him now: "Any papers?" etc. His involvement with Anna, even out of the best of motives, can ruin him, ruin his business, wreck his family. What really gets him? That she's taking these risks and gambles so her baby can be born in the United States. With no flag-waving, no sentimental sludge about the melting pot, he knows all he needs to know about Anna. And he buys it. In an oddly contorted way, he even celebrates it: "That's one for the books." And he gets whacked across the face for it. Anna thinks he's deriding something quite sacred to her. Now *she's* outraged—a fine dramatic reversal, most effective.

Does it offend him? Not much. He's too tough, too honest within his own feelings. (There is nothing dishonest in any part of this television play.) We are in the presence of real people, in a real situation. Is it believable? Entirely. Is it melodramatic? It verges on it, but there is no cheapening descent into it. The protagonists aren't manipulating anything. They are being closed in on by trouble not of their making. They are enormously vulnerable.

Fresco's last line, "Believe me," says many things, including "You're welcome," "Good riddance," "Good luck," "You take it from here," and "I've had it." His laconism has many keys.

The action in Shot 48 is just right. It would be hard to improve on this for a first-act curtain.

At the beginning of Act II, there is a touch of symbolism: Anna is eating a tomato, and liking it. She'd spurned the offer of one earlier. But Fresco is about to inherit another problem. Anna has no bus fare. Added up quickly, Anna is nothing but problems to Fresco. She's dead broke. She's "wanted." She's on the verge of giving birth. And she's going the other way. Is Fresco being had? Indeed so. And being hard? That, too, though it is tempered throughout by his unspoken tenderness: "So I'll lend you the money! I'm getting off cheap, you know what I mean?" He's being hard in order to hide his feelings.

There is effective juxtaposition (in Shot 52). "Now my child will have American life." And Fresco's bitter, "Some life."

This man is about exhausted. But he has fifteen hundred miles yet to drive, all without relief.

Anna's line, "A year—three years. My time will come," carries great heroism and determination. This exchange has true characterizing power. Anna doesn't want to be a burden to anybody. She'll go back to Mexico to earn her own living, separate herself from her baby just to be sure the baby has every chance at a good start.

Any woman in the viewing audience will instantly respond to what this means. Anna's willingness to make such a sacrifice will grab any woman who has ever borne a child, shake her, and tear her up. But see how *lean* the dialogue is, no speeches, no big black blocks of talk, no heroic philosophizings, just honest short jabs at the truth, the eloquence of brevity, the clean line of simple talk, of people saying what they mean and feel.

Read aloud the description of Claro (Shot 53). Think what great help these few lines are to the producer, and to the set decorator. Note the isolation opportunities the little depot offers—no clutter, no extra people. The writer never floods his pages with camera directions, just gives what he wants. The same with his people, the clanking "television cowboys."

Now both Anna and Fresco are in real trouble: the baby is on the way and no help yet.

In the production itself a line was added that is not here. And, like all of Simmons's lines, it was short but full of meaning. It had to do with Fresco's response to the tawdry cowboys. In the script he "shoots the o.s. youths a sulphuric glare." In the actual show he hurled a sarcastic line at them, referring to their ogling of the pregnant woman: "What's-a-matter—you never see a truck before?"

It had this effect: it stopped them cold. Though it was a two-to-one situation, both these caparisoned phonies knew that Fresco could bang their heads together.

Do we expect a facing off? No. In a western, yes, but not in a fine piece of work like this. No dramatic need for it. The cowboys are beneath Fresco's notice, and his swift contempt, with no response from these fake heavies, says it all: they *know* they are papier-mâché tough guys.

In Shot 62 there is an exquisite touch. Anna is taking leave of Fresco and returns his handkerchief. She's so stunned by the bad news about bus service that she's not aware he's offering her something to eat. Look at the power of those two simple adverbs, "blankly," "numbly."

"No bus till morning" is one frustration too many. He's had quite a few already, enough to excuse his exasperation and his only cruelty—"You deserve all the trouble you're gonna get" (Shot 58). But he is only getting started on his own list.

Without looking at the script, pause at this point and set down your own list of the frustrations he's already met. Then add those you remember from your earlier reading of the story. Your list might look a bit like this:

Not getting the right kind of tomatoes, as the loading ends
Having trouble explaining his situation to his mother
Interrupted while shaving
Bothered by the competition he hates, who now want to make a deal
Inheriting a lady passenger he doesn't want
Finding she's a "wetback"
That she's pregnant
Wanted by the police
Penniless
Trying to find a doctor when labor sets in
Finding a doctor who is a quack
His truck stuck in the mud
His truck halted at a bridge unsafe for such a load as his
His plan to drop Anna at bus depot aborts when he finds there will be no bus
Frustrations of time (the Sindells creeping up on him)
Delay when he's interrogated by the motorcycle cop
Anna's obstinacy
The wait at the hospital
The efforts to phone San Francisco
The sighting of the Sindell brothers' truck sailing by the hospital

Any reader of this drama could add to the list, according to his or her definition of frustration or response to it. To some, for example, the very fact of Anna's genuine warmth could be interpreted as a frustration. If Anna were a crude or thankless person, she'd be easy to deal with despite the desperateness of her predicament. At least, she'd be a lot easier to set down and abandon. But she's endearing. And mature. And in many ways she's Fresco's superior, something he seems often to recognize. At least he surely recognizes her basic nobility. This keeps churning through him, forces him to try harder, disallows him the right to cut her adrift. So it could be argued that her very goodness does represent a continuing frustration to him. If she were evil she could be dismissed.

That's a pretty good lineup of headaches. While still on this particular point, it is important to see how the dramatist managed to load the story with such a number of reverses and to do so without letting these slow down his tale or bore or depress the viewer. He used seven different devices. Use them yourself, or use their mechanical counterparts, in your own storytelling. Here they are:

1. Most important, we are solidly interested in what is to happen to the principals.
2. This interest is due far more to the quality, to the recognizability, of the people created than it is to the respective predicaments into which each one has been flung.
3. Constant new revelations of their expanding characters keep adding to our interest.
4. Short, playable dialogue.
5. Quick glints of humor at tough and unexpected moments.
6. Continuous scenic and atmospheric contrast.
7. The impact delivered by the races against time, hers for the baby, his for the delivery of his cargo.

In any serious television drama, built for intelligent viewers, remember this:
Character is better than plot.
Emotion is better than action.

Let us go through the rest of Richard Simmons's script. Shot 65 has a sadly understandable flare-up on the part of Fresco. Circumstances have now just about badgered him to death. His nerves are so frayed that he'd be a dangerous man in a fight. And it would take little to start one. "Don't thank me!" he hollers. Anna rises to it. She yells right back, "Why do you yell?" (Jump ahead now to Shot 94 and see what happy use Simmons made of this outburst.)

In the line, "Boy, how I pick 'em," is there any self-pity? None. Never with either of these two. Here his sarcasm is boiling rage at frustration.

Shot 68—truck "sprays" through ditch. This is a sight word, and it paid off well in the playing, a fine shot. Consider how *visually* this writer's mind holds tight to the television aspects of his storytelling. He misses no trick, no delight, no plus or emphasis. He lets the camera take the story where he wants it to go, and he constantly urges the camera to do its own underlining.

In his building and perfecting of the characters he wants us to know, his two principals, though they can talk, are essentially nonverbal. Both are good. Both are basic, rather than primitive. Both have ideals, codes even, great industry, great belief, and a special kind of fierce honor. All this with a minimum of talk.

Note in Shot 72 "We are stuck?" See how this little turn of phrase maintains the consistency of what we first met in Anna. She's foreign—a Rumanian fresh out of Mexico.

In the same sequence, we have a fine example of the hard practicality of Fresco. He's in charge now and there is no turning back, no transferring the problem to some other. He's stuck with it. Defeated? No. Just on it, pragmatic. He hands her his watch, makes her time her pains ("I gotta know!").

In Shot 76 the repetition, "Come on, come on!" projects his great irritation, as had his chilling sarcasm just before.

Consider how much more sharply Fresco's battle has been conveyed by having this man, accustomed to purple profanity, refraining from using any at all. This leads at once to a great secret of good writing:

Never overlook the effectiveness of restraint.

Shot 77: "Instead she leans her head back against the seat, dreaming of the child within her body." If male viewers did not pick up what was in Anna's mind at this moment, there was no woman who missed it.

Shot 78 here gives Peter Falk his best single moment to turn on the special magic of his pantomime skill. Read the simple sentences that describe what is now descending upon him, and the effects of these as he anticipates their possible consequences. What could be worse? "His eyes squeeze shut." He winces with dread. But he has to play it out anyhow. And he knows it. He's caught, and he knows that. There will be no explaining Anna. Who wouldn't wince, in the paralyzing second to which he must now steel himself?

Shot 79: "This piece got kinda washed out." Do you recall where we were first told of this? And how? Look back to Shot 9. See how well used the item is—so casually mentioned the first time. Yet we've dealt with rain ever since we took off. A practice to remember: if you don't plan to use it, don't put it in. *Use it or lose it.* This will save you time, will help keep your script clean and support your story's consistency. I've mentioned it before.

In Shot 80 Fresco does some quick but plausible imagining. We all know what's going to happen if the highway policeman goes around to the cab, if he begins to interrogate Anna, her obvious condition notwithstanding. And around he goes! It's a great moment of suspense and it delivers two surprises: The police officer merely turns off the headlights to save juice; and Anna has vanished. Shot 86 provides Peter Falk with another great instant of confused but eloquent responses.

See what a professional page Shot 87 represents. How moving, how sad, how comical, how revealing. And emotionally how very much more mature the girl is than this well-weathered, well-married roughneck. "You are like a child." And he is. But her trust and her thanks and her idealism all show through this little moment, all shining despite the mud and the desolation and the overhang of dread. "With you," she chides, "always the end of the world." With her? "Even this place: a miracle."

Her faith is absolute. It is unshakable.

Near the end of this scene, there is an instant of exquisite tenderness. Fresco: "Scared?" and the direction, "She nods, big-eyed." We need no more. He'll go all the way now. See it through.

In Shot 94, filled with delicious opportunities for them both to pantomime, expert use is made of the trick of the sudden juxtaposition of feelings, the sudden reversal of them, too. Anna giggles. Fresco is a sight. How *human* all this is! And there is also fine use made of a process shot. (Description and use of the process shot appear in the chapter on *Tarzan*.)

Anna's concern about the mud on Fresco's face and her effort to clean him up with her handkerchief really reach him. She hasn't been with this fellow very long, yet she knows him completely. When it's needed, she is a schoolteacher being patient with a foot-stamping third-grade brat. Now she has a lovely chance to pay him back, and she mimics him: "Don't thank me!" (We've heard this line before, as noted. See how beautifully it explodes here.)

There is great kidding all through the little scene in the truck cab. All the male viewers have the same feeling about Anna: She's a great kidder and she'd be wonderful fun to be with. A great sport, a girl with humor, resilience, and companionability. She's such a fine creation that it's too bad she's fiction. Writers can't expect a better reaction than that. And no actress could have brought more to the role than Inger Stevens.

This cheerful moment is suddenly over. And something foreboding, perhaps sickening, is put right in front of us. Is this doctor for real?

Another fine curtain.

No one answers the bell. Fresco, not one to wait long for anything, begins to shout. Both poke around. Our findings become sinister. Instruments are strewn about. Unwashed dishes are visible. So is a zodiacal chart. Is this the man to deliver Anna's baby? Anna, who has lived in direct confrontation with reality her whole life, instantly knows fraud. She can smell it. "He is not a real doctor?" Fresco stalls and hopes. But we sense that he also knows.

See Shot 105. Here the dramatist has told the actor playing Dr. Connell *exactly* what to project: "One wonders if perhaps he is not sleepy but a little drunk."

The doctor throws his college-degree vocabulary around a bit to emphasize his professionalism, knowing they wouldn't know that gravid means pregnant. Then suddenly he ruptures the atmosphere with his familiar and cynical, "Does she want the baby?" Think of the agonies this woman has already borne to have this child! And now this! For her, the room swims. But at once it gets even worse: "I'm pleased to see you're not putting yourself in the hands of one of those medical doctors."

Consistent with his character and equally as outraged as is the cautious but witnessing Anna, Fresco bursts out with his line about "I believe in tomatoes and she believes in American babies!" Which is his way of saying, "Cut out this crap and get busy!"

We have some fine action through here: the shock about the money—three hundred dollars is big money to Fresco, bigger still to the penniless Anna. For the third time we have an alarming occurrence while Fresco is on the telephone, this time with Connell trying to sign up Anna and so be clear "in case of accident."

From the phone Fresco sees trouble (as he saw the Sindells, as he saw Anna when she mounted his cab). This time there is an element of horror, a smell of death. Or butchery. He screams from the phone, "You ain't signing anything!" Immediately, while still in contact with the operator, note the words Simmons has used: "slicing in." "Ram." "Slam." "Thrust." "Wrench." These are Fresco words. (The thing to note here is consistency.)

A measure of Anna's increasing desperation is caught in her pitiful line, "Perhaps it is easier if I stay . . ." This is close to heartbreak.

These two just escape the charnel attentions of a boozy quack. In their quick departure, with Fresco slamming down the money, the action as performed in the show itself did not include the final business that ends Shot 112 in this reprint. It ended this way: "Sound of door open and slam. Connell slumps into desk chair, stares sourly at the ten-dollar bill, then opens drawer." We did not see his hand come out with the whiskey bottle, did not see him hold it up to the light, did not see him rip out the cork. No need to. *We know all about Connell.*

Anna has a hurry-up line in Shot 115: "There is not much time." The imminence of her delivery gives to the pacing of the script the same sort of urgency that the word *stretto* ("faster and faster") gives to an orchestral piece. It quickens the beat.

Simmons is so adept at character carpentry that we feel, just from the fragments that come to Anna's mind about her sister Rosa, that we know her.

The only real biographical fill-in we get appears in Shot 116. Do you think Anna would have taken Rosa's advice if she hadn't been carrying a child? In any case, we understand Anna completely, understand her haste, her hard determination, her bypassing the law. She has *tried* to do everything according to the book. All her life. But bureaucracy has finally overturned her. "I am done with fine plans. With waiting." Who blames her? Never Fresco, surely. (Nor the audience.)

Suddenly we are thundering right into the worst frustration and the biggest hazard we have met, a bridge that warns against the load we're pushing. What is Anna's concern now? Herself? It is for him. Think what nobility this lends her! Her tears are also for him—he's had to put up with too much. She kisses his hand. It is a charming, moving gesture, a blessing, a recognition of what he's done, a prayer for what he must now take on.

This bewildering emergency carries us into Act IV. And in its mechanical structuring it is not dissimilar to some of the inventions that moved the *Tarzan* script from one act to another.

Don't laugh at *Tarzan* just because it's not your kind of show. For the serious television writer, or sincere candidate thereto, *any* show is your kind of show, if it has made its way.

The suspense that is maintained unbroken from the truck's approach to the bridge to the creaking but successful crossing represents some of the best action television I have ever seen or read. Almost all of it is self-explanatory. The quick cuts to Anna's face merely emphasize what we're already feeling. The concern for each other, without the other being aware, is unusually moving and real. This is indeed a breathless moment. And it is a real tour de force that it could be made to come off after the vicissitudes, alarms, and heavy risks we have already survived.

There is a deeply affecting moment in Shot 167: "Fresco . . . realizes that Anna's tears are for him." And another one in Shot 171, as if he might have said, "This is my proclamation to the world." It's the happy business of his promise to Anna that she'll have her baby in a hospital. And in America.

We know we're home when the camera picks up the sign "Hospital Parking."

The script here reprinted includes the short scene of possible trouble at the very last moment with the Immigration Service. But it was found to be unnecesary in final rehearsals. It took away more than it added. The show was "running for a curtain," as the expression goes, and the audience had been plagued to the limit of its tolerance. So the scene was scrubbed. Not seen, it was not missed.

The hospital sequence, the irritation of Fresco in having to wait, his real concern and benevolence in phoning Rosa, the suppression of his eagerness to be in motion again, the jolt he gets when the Sindells roar by, the impatience he feels while waiting to be shown the new baby, his taking leave of Anna, the tomato tossed to the doctor—all this, beautifully and cleanly set out, should now bring back to the reader the two words that were stressed at the opening of our thorough look at this script: the words *dispatch* and *economy*. From Shot 177 to the very end these two qualities of professional work are in fine display.

And who but the poorest sport could deny Fresco his primitive joy at the unexpected sight of the "Rumanian bandits" piled up in a ditch?

As a caution to new writers, remember this was the script that won an Emmy, after having been rejected by a network program executive. I mention this so that you will better know the reality of the risks. These are always present to threaten the sweetness of rewards.

Richard Alan Simmons, a former journalist from Toronto, Canada, has been active in Hollywood since 1948, first in radio, then in pictures and television. He wrote over thirty films, many of which you certainly have seen—*Beachhead, Shield for Murder, The Private War of Major Benson, Woman on the Beach, Fuzzy Pink Nightgown.*

In television his work was prominently seen in the field of anthologies, including the Alcoa-Goodyear and the Dick Powell shows. His versatility soon brought him the ideal title of writer-producer, the function he enjoyed in the work just examined —"The Price of Tomatoes." He exercised the same controls over many other award-winning shows: "The Last of the Big Spenders," "The Glorious 4th," "Three Soldiers," "The Prison," and "The Doomsday Boys."

Do you remember *The Trials of O'Brien* that also starred Peter Falk? It was the work of Richard Alan Simmons and was recognized as a high-water mark in meaningful contemporary television. Universal has made his *Art of Love* and his comedy *Skin Game,* and Simmons is currently with that company, writing and producing theatrical films and preparing several new series. He has already brought forth *Fear No Evil* and *Lock-Stock and Barrel.* He has also recently finished a screenplay, *Fandango.*

He has his own views about who the writer's enemy is:

"It is my belief that the creator's primary struggle is not within the network nor the advertising agency but with himself and the audience, the idea being to attack with sufficient strength to overcome surfeit and distraction, and so *nail* the viewer that, in spite of himself and the confined medium, he has a valid emotional experience. I am also convinced that the writer has a significant edge if he happens to be his own producer."

9

JUDD FOR THE DEFENSE

Paul Monash, one of the real heavyweights of the television writing industry, did most of the scripting of the successful courtroom drama I'd like briefly to discuss in these pages. He did not do all of the scripting, however. And this is not unusual. In the present case large contributions were made by Harold Gast, whose credits are almost as vast and varied as are those of Monash.

Actually, and very often, a one-hour script in a series as expensive and prestigious as *Judd*, or any series that has large star value, may have received attention from as many as five or six writers. But only one or two will receive credit on the crawl at the end of the show.

Let us first acquaint ourselves with the contents of the story, a story that in the hands of an amateur writer would collapse. Why? For one thing, the principal character is in an impossible jam from which Clinton Judd makes an effort to extricate him.

So what's new about that, you ask. This is new: the character is a black. He is a habitual criminal. He is and he remains completely unsympathetic. In real life it would take a man of heroic idealism to spend time unraveling such a man's problem when all he gets in return is cynicism, sass, and ingratitude. The man—Jesse Aarons (who was superbly played by Brock Peters)—is not only bitter, he is vengeful, primitive, and dangerous in the extreme. Yet Paul Monash has contrived to make us very much want to see this social outcast get a fair hearing.

How does he manage it? Here is a good trick: he manages it by getting the viewer fascinated in the *case*, not in the man. It is a peach of a device. (It is also in the public domain. Reach in and help yourself.)

We the audience, and Clinton Judd the hero, put up with the rages and outrages of the defendant. Monash sees to it that Judd takes all this without letting it jiggle his aim. What does this accomplish? Much. It builds and enhances the character of our leading man, and does so through a fine exercise of concentration and restraint. (Restraint is always more effective than blowoff.)

Here is another value in this story: though black versus white is an ingredient, it is not the main theme. Human justice is the main theme. Much of the appeal is to

298

ethics, to our mind, to reason, to sense, to fairness. And though our feelings are many times grabbed and shaken, our judgments are never blurred by emotion. True, the overtone and the menace and the coloration and the sense of potential explosiveness that the black ingredient brings to this is a large part of its tension. The blacks hate the whites, and the whites—most of them—bear a chilling indifference to the plight of Jesse Aarons. The governor controlling these pressures is Judd. Without Judd the black would still be doing life.

Here is the first page of the play's three-page prologue:

"Commitment"
PROLOGUE

FADE IN:

1 EXT. JUDD'S HOUSTON OFFICE BUILDING—NIGHT. ESTABLISHING. (MOST OF THE LIGHTS SHOULD BE OUT; THIS IS QUITE LATE—AND THAT IS QUITE IMPORTANT.)

2 INT. GARAGE—ELEVATOR DOOR—NIGHT. IT OPENS—AND CLINTON JUDD, ESQ., STEPS OUT.

CAMERA TRACKS PARALLEL TO JUDD (AT ABOUT A DISTANCE OF FIFTEEN FEET) AS HE WALKS THROUGH THE UNDERGROUND GARAGE. IT IS, AS NOTED, LATE AT NIGHT—POOLS OF SHADOW, FEW CARS PARKED. MOVING WITH JUDD, CAMERA UNCOVERS A MAN (JESSE AARONS) STANDING BEHIND A POST, CONCEALED. (OH, IF JUDD WERE LOOKING FOR SOMEONE, HE WOULD SEE JESSE; BUT HE IS MOVING DIRECTLY AND PURPOSEFULLY TO HIS CAR.) CAMERA HOLDS JESSE IN THE F.G., AS JUDD APPROACHES HIS CAR. THEN CAMERA MOVES FORWARD, FROM BEHIND JESSEE, TOWARD JUDD. (WE GET A SENSE OF BULK IN JESSE; HE SHOULD BE A POWERFULLY BUILT NEGRO.) JESSE (AND CAMERA) STOPS, WITH:

JESSE

Mr. Judd!

JUDD TURNS. AND CAMERA MOVES FORWARD WITH JESSE.

JESSE

I gotta talk to you.

HE STOPS, AND JUDD LOOKS AT HIM, CAREFULLY.

3 JESSE—JUDD'S POV. DRESSED IN DENIMS, WITH AN ILL-FITTING JACKET. JESSE HAS A TOUGH, SCARRED FACE; A LOT OF PEOPLE WOULD BE FRIGHTENED BY HIM. (JUDD DOES FEEL UNEASY.) HIS AGE IS DIFFICULT TO DETERMINE; PUT IT IN THE THIRTIES.

JESSE

And don't tell me to come to your office.

4 SCENE. AS JUDD STUDIES HIM, CAUTIOUSLY. (THE GARAGE IS EMPTY—AND JESSE IS BIG.)

JUDD

(FLAT) All right, I won't.

See how much the first thirty seconds of this prologue fling into the imagination of the viewer. What are the moods or the physical impacts that so quickly take hold of us?

Three things, right off the bat. The sinister lighting in Shot 1. Next, the sight of a man concealed, obviously waiting to get Judd. Third, especially note the clever use of the camera here. Look again at the direction given: "Jesse (and camera) stops." And quite fearfully so do we.

This is a great big spread of freeze-motion on which to rivet that opening line. What else?

In Shot 3, as Judd takes in the unexpected, see the clues the writer has scattered here, not only what is here to look at physically, but clues suggesting how Carl Betz might play this reaction: "Judd does feel uneasy."

The physical power of the black man, the minatory suggestiveness of his motions, his thorough distrust of the world, his own terrible emergency—all this is economically displayed or insinuated.

And all of it in less than one minute.

Let us look at a few more secrets. There is a most appealing and illuminating line, early in the play: "Jesse looks at him with a bitterness which goes beyond the moment all the way into race memory." To any sensitive performer, those words say much. They reemphasize the mood in which Jesse's character is to be sustained; they underline the kind of poison he spits out at all those about him—people, institutions, motives. They're all one to him. All situations are traps. All people are liars.

What I am saying is simple. The characterization of Jesse Aarons would catch the eye of a sociologist, for Jesse is a fascinating, well-constructed antisocial. What I am urging you to do, when creating these things, these people, yourself, is to put backgrounds behind them. Suggest where they've been. Suggest what they've done. Do it economically. A quick revelation will suffice. Always, in television, you're in a race against time. You are not writing a novel. You have only these few minutes, so be brief.

I'm not going to go through the Monash script, excellent though it is. No need. Compare Judd's situation to that of the heroes in three other unrelated shows in this book: *Tarzan, Run for Your Life*, and "The Price of Tomatoes." Each leading man in each of these completely different stories is nonetheless beset by risk and problems that would cause any other man to quit. The quality of their heroism is often equal to the size and obstinacy of the struggle, the spirit brought to it, and the persistence with which they're willing to stay in the fight.

In this script everything is against Judd (as, of course, it always is): his client, the police, the DA, the evidence, even Ben, his own assistant. Did Tarzan have it any easier? Or Ben Gazzara? Or Peter Falk? No. If things had been easy for them, they wouldn't have been heroes. Television is in the heroics business, and that isn't bad. Monotonous, maybe, but not bad.

Monash (and Harold Gast) in the present story add a good ground-base of suspense. You must have suspense in any courtroom story. The reason is simple. You're in the melodrama business as well as in the heroics business. One of the deep rumbles of this ground-base: when the dangerous black Jesse Aarons was escaping, he hit a man, one Morley. Morley remains unconscious through most of the show. We dip into his condition frequently, quick question-and-answer mostly. Is Morley still alive?

Another suspense constituent: Aarons's court-appointed defender in the previous trial didn't do a good job. He botched the case. Where is he now? A night clerk "in one of those downtown hotels," we're told. You know what that means. Everybody knows what that means. He's in a down spiral and probably still on the sauce. (If you already sense that this same shabby, no-good, irretrievably booze-crazed lawyer-bum finally comes through, you would be quite correct.) But Monash keeps the man's ineptitude in focus, which in this case means Monash always keeps him just a little fuzzy. Nice piece of mystery writing here: instead of "who killed Mrs. Pankhurst?" it is "guess who redeems himself at the last minute." He is never oversold as a drunk. When you wish, or need, to surprise your reader, viewer, listener, try giving *equal value* to your parade of suspects. Don't make the real culprit too interesting.

Frustrations borne by the hero: he can't find this drinking lawyer. All he knows is that the man no longer practices law. Jesse, the defendant, claims an alibi. It can't be established. There are three or four other frustrations. Their defeatism is only briefly scattered by one little quiver of good news. Jesse, who hates everybody including Judd who is trying to get the black an honest trial, suddenly realizes how hard Judd is working for him, how thoroughly he has gone over the material, and he says, "You *really* been looking into this!" But he erases it all a moment later: "But he tricked me, Mr. Judd—just like you did." A good mix, puzzling yet appealing. You learn, by practice, to make up believable, plausible frustrations.

In constructing the character of Jesse Aarons, Paul Monash has created a person at once so pitiable and so hateful that any fine character actor would want to play the role. Try for this, even with your lesser characters. There was an actor of large accomplishment (Nicholas Joy), whose work I often saw and always admired, who said a valuable thing about playwriting, and it goes for television writing, too: "Any play is a fine play if every character in it—even the least important—is so well drawn and so honestly set into the story that any fine actor in the world would want the part."

Here is a short scene from the second act. Just read the scene. Don't read the comment that follows. Why is it so effective?

The setting is simple. Judd and Reed (Reed is the typical tough DA) are standing before the judge. Judd is trying to get a new trial for the black. The DA opposes. But the camera is on the people at the defense table, on Jesse and the lawyer (the drinking lawyer—his name is Creighton) who bungled Jesse's case some years earlier. We *hear* this dialogue:

JUDD

And our motion, Your Honor, is simply to grant him that fair trial now.

REED

The State opposes this motion, Your Honor. Jesse Aarons very recently broke out of State Prison . . . (CREIGHTON WILTING UNDER THE HEAT OF JESSE'S STARE)

> REED
>
> (o.s.) And assaulted a police officer who now lies between life and death. If this officer should die . . .
>
> JUDD
>
> (o.s.) That is precisely the point, Your Honor! Jesse Aarons might be charged with Murder in the First Degree . . .
>
> THE BENCH—JUDD, REED, JUDGE.
>
> REED
>
> He most certainly would be charged!
>
> JUDD
>
> In which case, it would be very difficult to guarantee him an impartial trial on the *other* charge.
>
> REED
>
> Is my learned colleague saying that a man who commits two murders is entitled to more consideration than a man who commits only one? (THERE IS SOME LAUGHTER FROM THE BAILIFFS AND CLERKS)

You know by now that the initials "o.s." stand for offscreen. We hear an off-screen clash between Reed and Judd, but we *look* at the effect of this clash as it works over the face of Creighton. It is beginning to break him. The jam that Creighton has put Jesse Aarons in is now possibly about to be compounded. How to prevent such? Creighton's conscience begins to work. It revives his manhood. Long lost, it now threatens to come alive.

After the laughter at Reed's incinerating challenge (the best line in the play, by the way), the dramatist uses the moment to see Jesse's reaction: raw sarcasm.

I want you to see Creighton's scene. It is quite short. As a piece of acting (by William Windom) it was one of the best-delivered I ever saw in television. Note the words, not of Creighton's speech, but the words Paul Monash has set among the sentences to indicate the changing intensities that are called for here. "There are tears in his voice." (There were tears running down the actor's face.) It seemed a moment of self-crucifixion. And of resurrection, too, perhaps?

Here it is:

Revised—"Commitment"

41 THE BENCH—THE JUDGE.

> JUDGE
>
> I'm inclined to agree with you there, Mr. Judd. Proceed with your argument.
>
> JUDD
>
> May it please the Court . . . And without intending any criticism of his court-appointed lawyer . . . I submit that it is important to ask why Jesse Aarons—a man who had stoutly maintained that he was innocent—suddenly change his plea to guilty.
>
> A CRY FROM OFF:

CREIGHTON'S VOICE

(O.S.) I'll tell you why!

42 THE DEFENSE TABLE—CREIGHTON. UNABLE TO BEAR JESSE'S GAZE ANY MORE, HE IS RISING TO HIS FEET . . . AND BEN'S RESTRAINING HAND ON HIS ARM DOES NOT STOP HIM.

CREIGHTON

Because his lawyer needed a drink!

43 THE BENCH—JUDD TURNING IN SHOCK . . . A STUNNED SILENCE PREVAILS . . . JUDD GLANCES AT THE JUDGE, WHO NODS PERMISSION. CAMERA GOES WITH JUDD AS HE STRIDES TO CREIGHTON FOR A WHISPERED CONSULTATION.

JUDD

Creighton, I never wanted you to go as far as this . . .

CREIGHTON

I want to.

JUDD

(TURNING) Your Honor, this is Ira Creighton, of counsel, who was the attorney of record. He would like to approach the bench.

44 THE JUDGE LOOKING GRIM.

JUDGE

You may do so, Mr. Creighton.

A44 ANGLE ON DEFENSE TABLE. JESSE TURNS TO JUDD, WITH FURY.

JESSE

You not doin' it to me again, you hear? You not goin' turn me over to him so he can sell me out, this time, too! You not doing this for me— you're doing it for him!

JUDD TURNS TO HIM SILENTLY. BEN GRABS JESSE'S ARM AND PULLS HIM INTO THE CHAIR.

BEN

Jesse, sit down!

CREIGHTON WALKS TOWARD THE JUDGE.

B44 ANGLE ON THE JUDGE AS CREIGHTON COMES UP, LOOKING UP AT THE BENCH. THERE IS A STILLNESS IN THE COURTROOM, AS THOUGH A TERRIBLE SENTENCE WERE TO BE HANDED DOWN.

CREIGHTON

It was three o'clock in the afternoon, Your Honor. A time when anyone feels beat. But if you start out beat in the morning, by three o'clock, you're desperate. (BEAT) I had told my client that the prosecution was offering a deal for murder two. And he had told me no—he was innocent. At this point, my mind was not on his problem—it was on that bar across the street. So, I stepped over to Mr. Reed—he may remember the conversation.

45 SHOT AT REED. HE NODS.

46 ANGLE ON CREIGHTON.

CREIGHTON

I said to him, "Let me give you my answer first thing tomorrow. Will you agree to a continuance?" He said no. I wouldn't get the same deal tomorrow—take it or leave it right now. Your Honor, I don't blame Mr. Reed for playing his hand as hard as he could. He couldn't see how my hand . . . was shaking. (BEAT, AND NOW HIS VOICE RISES IN SELF-TORMENT) I then returned to my client, and I said, "We have no defense . . . Jesse, if you don't take the deal, you'll go to the chair . . ." He said to me—(THERE ARE TEARS IN HIS VOICE) "Mr. Creighton! I've got no one to trust but you!" I said to him, "Jesse! I am telling you the truth, so help me God!" (ANGUISH) But I was telling him only *half* the truth! The other half was in that bar across the street! (LOWERING HIS HEAD) So we made the deal. And I had my drink. And that's . . . why Jesse Aarons changed his plea.

47 FULL SHOT—THE SCENE. THE SILENCE HOLDS FOR A MOMENT . . . AND THEN THE JUDGE CLEARS HIS THROAT.

JUDGE

Mr. Judd . . . Mr. Reed . . .

BOTH LAWYERS APPROACH THE BENCH, FLANKING CREIGHTON, WHO TURNS AS THOUGH TO CRAWL BACK INTO THE WOODWORK . . . BUT JUDD TAKES HIM BY THE ARM, WARMLY, APPRECIATIVELY, HOLDING HIM THERE WITH HIS COL-LEAGUES.

JUDGE

In view of this remarkable . . . (WHAT TO CALL IT?) statement . . . And in view of the points presented in the brief by Mr. Judd and Mr. Caldwell . . . I will order a new trial in the case of Jesse Aarons . . .

48 SHOT AT DEFENSE TABLE. BEN LOOKING AT JESSE . . . BUT ALL THAT JESSE DOES IS SIT BACK, RAISE HIS HEAD, AND HEAVE HIS BIG CHEST IN A DEEP, DEEP BREATH . . .

Even after a display so honest, so painfully self-purgative, Jesse Aarons is unmoved. But this isn't a story about a nice guy who got a bum rap. It is about justice, nothing more. Jesse Aarons is a criminal who hates, who robs, who carries weapons, who is despised by his own people, who will never go straight, who doesn't want to, doesn't believe in it, and doesn't want to learn how.

And remember this, structurally it isn't important that Jesse is a black. It is important atmospherically and that is all. Jesse does not even have to be a sub-merged member of a minority group. He just has to be one thing: he has to be irredeemable.

We saw almost no violence in this show, yet it tingled from the opening scene. And it is *full of movement*. But how do you get movement into a story (or a scene) as stationary as a courtroom?

There are some concrete things to know, to remember, to use.

For example, in one of the acts of this play, seventeen different directions were given to the camera. This kept the eye refreshed. So long as the eye is refreshed, the mind is busy.

Another item: amateur writers waste a lot of time swearing in witnesses. Professionals don't do this. At least, they do very little. But how can you avoid swearing in a witness if you're going to put him on the stand? Easy. Bring your scene on with the witness *already* giving testimony. So, avoid swearings in. They are too familiar. Like countdowns at Cape Kennedy. And they are all stage waits. Unless you need the close-up of a face, leave them out.

You can also skip from one witness to another, the presumption being that the witness was sworn before.

Another device: changing of witnesses. Changing from one *type* of witness to another. Changing to a quick moment of humor, or to a quick moment of the totally unexpected. Changing the questioners—from direct to cross. Changing cameras to pick up a string of quick reaction shots.

The epilogue of this play had some fine mordant ironies. It never tried to suggest a converted Jesse. But Jesse knows he has been in the presence of integrity. He also knows there is enough humanity even in the world of the white man for one of its members painfully to recondition himself in order to do the right thing by a black he has injured.

Television will always have a series built on courtroom drama. The reason is not hard to get at: there is drama in courtrooms.

The reader may have noticed the word "Revised" at the top of the quoted play-script. This is common. It is inevitable. Everything in television gets rewritten several times. In radio, we were always rewriting right up to air time. Now that most television is taped or filmed, the rewrites, while as common (and expensive), have achieved a certain amount of order—appropriated from the movie industry—by putting new rewrites on different-colored pages. Some producers insist on their own sequence of colors: white first, then pink, blue, yellow, orange, amber, green. Quite a challenge on the resources of the stock department!

Before me now is an old *Custer* script.

The title page is sky blue. It reads "Custer." Under that, "Glory Rider" (the name of the episode for that week). Then "Written by Jack Turley." At bottom left, "2548." (Each page must carry the production number.) Bottom right, "Final, June 7, 1967."

Final? Yes, but what a struggle! On page 2, we are no longer sky blue. We are pink. It is the first revise of the Cast List. There were three revises of this *one* page. See next page. Can you figure it out? Try. The first revise of the Cast List bore the date June 8. The second, a day later, June 9. It is apple green. What's the difference between the two? The third Cast List is on blue again (blue for final).

All that can be seen from these changes is that while Trooper Lawson survived (in the cast), Trooper "Rio" got lost. Poor chap.

We have a revised page 7 (green) for June 9.

We have two pages (1-X and 2-XX) called "Additional Scenes." Yellow. Things return to blue for a spell, and then we get a pink revise for page 11. Another pink for 15. A revised 21 (green) of June 9. A pink revise for page 23. Six more pages of "Additional Scenes" (on yellow) between pages 28 and 29. One more of blue, followed by a single page (yellow) of "Additional Scenes." Next, two pages on orange paper, dated August 2! (That is a long time to wait for a rewrite. Some writer no doubt had a White Sulphur Springs breakdown.)

The main thing: new material must be dated and must carry the same production number as all the others (on every page). Cast and crew must throw out all the old stuff and keep refreshing their own "master" as it comes to them. The reason for changing color is to simplify directions and to keep day-by-day track of the script's development. Any change, however minute, requires throwing the entire page away and processing a new one. From the writer's point of view, it all does add to the arduousness of the work, and adds also, quite often, to the seeming futility of it.

REVISED—"GLORY RIDER"—JUNE 8, 1967
CAST LIST

CUSTER
BUSTARD
CALIFORNIA JOE
CRAZY HORSE
TERRY

KERMIT TELLER
SIOUX BRAVE
CAPTAIN KESTER (AT FORT WALLACE)
TROOPER LAWSON
TROOPER "RIO"

TROOPERS OF 7TH U.S. CAVALRY
DROVERS: COWHANDS AND VAQUEROS
PIEGAN INDIANS
SIOUX FIGHTING WARRIORS

REVISED—"GLORY RIDER"—JUNE 9, 1967
CAST LIST

CUSTER
BUSTARD
CALIFORNIA JOE
CRAZY HORSE
TERRY
TROOPER "RIO"

KERMIT TELLER
SIOUX BRAVE

CAPTAIN KESTER (AT FORT WALLACE)
TROOPER LAWSON

TROOPERS OF 7TH U.S. CAVALRY
DROVERS: COWHANDS AND VAQUEROS
PIEGAN INDIANS
SIOUX FIGHTING WARRIORS

CAST LIST—FINAL

CUSTER
BUSTARD
CALIFORNIA JOE
CRAZY HORSE
TERRY

KERMIT TELLER
SIOUX BRAVE
CAPTAIN KESTER (AT FORT WALLACE)
TROOPER LAWSON

TROOPERS OF 7TH U.S. CAVALRY
DROVERS: COWHANDS AND VAQUEROS
PIEGAN INDIANS
SIOUX FIGHTING WARRIORS

Typical Background of a Successful Television Dramatist

In Paul Monash we have another writer with much of the same kind of drive and storytelling power that belong to Rod Serling. I remember much of his early work in radio many years ago when we were both at Young & Rubicam. Paul was anchor writer for a popular half hour called the *Mollé Mystery*. This would be somewhere in the mid-forties, before television. But the story inventiveness of the man, then quite a young fellow, was established. It kept displaying itself week after week.

Monash is a New York product, received a B.A. degree from the University of Wisconsin, an M.A. from Columbia. He worked as a seaman in the merchant marine. He's been a newspaper reporter and a high school teacher. He also served with the U.S. Army Signal Corps during World War II, and then lived for three years in Europe, working for the United States government.

He's been writing for television or motion pictures since 1952. He is one of the real "five-hundred-thousand-dollar-a-year-men." What did he have to do to get there? His list of credits—as writer or producer or creator, or all three—is truly immense.

He wrote the two-parter that launched *The Untouchables*. And it was this show, this show alone, that shoved ABC into direct rivalry with its big brothers, thus really putting American Broadcasting in the big time.

Peyton Place, as a soap opera at night, in prime time, twice a week—a completely unheard-of (and unlikely) gamble—was his own daring concept. It was, and is, a television landmark. One may hack at it but no one can dispute its success.

Paul Monash created *Cain's Hundred* and served as its executive producer.

He has written for *Philco Playhouse, Studio One, Theatre Guild of the Air, Desilu Playhouse*. His "Helen Morgan Story" was seen on *Playhouse 90*, and his splendid biography of the electrical genius, Steinmetz ("The Lonely Wizard"), won the Emmy Award in 1958. He's written two novels, *How Brave We Live* and *The Ambassadors,* both published by Scribner's.

Paul Monash joined 20th Century-Fox Television as an executive producer in 1962, and is with them now. Probably you saw *Butch Cassidy and the Sundance Kid*.

When he created *Judd,* Monash insisted on Carl Betz as the star. *TV Guide* had an interesting backstage look into this part of the evolution of that show. Here is part of it:

" 'Carl was the master stroke,' Monash recalled, 'The network had other ideas—Chuck Connors, Martin Landau. But I wouldn't do it without Carl. . . .' Monash prides himself on his casting sense," said *TV Guide*. "Years before, Betz had moonlighted from the serenity of his *Donna Reed* chores with some heavyweight drama in a local little theatre—plays like *Night of the Iguana* and *Krapp's Last Tape*. Monash had seen his work, liked it and remembered it.

" 'Adding to Betz's attractiveness,' says Monash, 'was the fact that we didn't have to give away any points. Chuck Connors would have demanded part ownership in the show. . . . Betz made no such demands. . . . Financially he was well fixed. And critically he was a smash.' "

10

RUN FOR YOUR LIFE

Appreciable time is being spent in this book in revealing to the new writer, or to any writer making his first stab at television, how successful shows originate, who had to do what to make the thing come off. Though the true genesis of one successful series may be quite different from that of another, there is always this one thing in common—a fortunate convergence of the right people.

Run for Your Life made a lot of money for everyone involved with it. But did it begin as a series? No. It had its origin as a spin-off in the *Kraft Theatre of Suspense*.

The spin-off was an underwater thriller that starred Ben Gazzara. Was it a creation of pure originality at that time? Again, no. *Run for Your Life* was derived from an unproduced property owned by Universal. Roy Huggins, perhaps the most versatile of imaginations that contemporary television has produced, gave to this property the *form* it has now. Jo Swerling, the series producer, compressed the property referred to above to a *single page of story*.

This page was then given to Luther Davis to build into a pilot script for a show that was to last for a full hour. Was this one page enough? Yes. It had the guts of the idea that carried the show though several successful seasons.

When I say this one page was enough, I mean it was enough for a veteran who knew what to do with it. Whenever you look into the background of any established performer—whatever his medium—you find an overwhelming amount of hard work you never heard of. And much failure. The list of George Abbott's Broadway flops would leave you gasping, as no doubt it did his backers at the time.

Most of the public—and this should include all its writers-to-be who haven't published anything or sold anything as yet—have a fixed belief that the big names in the entertainment world were somehow always out there in front. The truth is that very few have had it big from the start. Most had a lot of slugging to do to get where they are now. But most of them *did* the slugging—and this is the tough partition that separates the men from the boys.

What preparations, for example, had Luther Davis been through that made possible his conversion of a one-page story from Jo Swerling to the commencement of a series that delighted millions for many years?

He had been through quite a lot. It began to show early. And he began to work hard at it early. He wanted to write drama. And he went to a pretty good place to find out how the thing is done, the Baker '47 Workshop at Yale. In New Haven Luther Davis applied himself at once, became one of the editors of the Yale *Lit*, finished the drama courses, graduated, then decided to see the world. You can't blame him. His hometown was Brooklyn.

He worked his passage on a freight ship that took him to Indonesia. He lived for many months in what many have reported as the most romantic spot on our whole planet—the island of Bali. He was there when it fell to the Japanese. He went to Singapore. He was there when this British stronghold also fell. He wrote these stories and sent them to the United States, where they were immediately bought and published by the old *Liberty* magazine.

Returning to the United States, he went to work for *Collier's*. In a single year he sold the magazine twenty-four pieces. Ten of these were written in collaboration with John Cleveland, later killed in the war. At the time Luther Davis met him, Cleveland was doing a series of interviews with Hollywood celebrities. (This was a time when there were such.)

Davis joined the air force, serving in the Orient, though in the somewhat less romantic areas of New Delhi. Frederic Wakeman, whose meteoric rise as a popular novelist had been given an impressive lift with *The Hucksters*, preceded the advertising story with a war story he called *Shore Leave*, a story that Luther Davis, with his trained dramatist's eye, at once saw as a play.

He wrote the play and called it *Kiss Them for Me*. He wrote the play while he was in service, another sign of hard discipline. (Could you do it?) The play succeeded.

Interesting notes in passing should include the fact that the show introduced Judy Holliday and Richard Widmark to Broadway. Jayne Meadows was also in the show, though she was already well known. The production won the Derwent Award for "Best Play" of 1945 and it got Luther Davis a job with MGM. He's worked on the West Coast since.

The signs of the professional-to-be are quickly visible to any teacher of the craft of writing. Less noticeable to the public, however, is the *constancy* with which the path to success is pursued. Most quit. Writers go on writing. In the case of Luther Davis, he had the special credentials (magazine background plus a fat Broadway success) that give a most useful commercial sheen to the large colony of writers who are (and were) making it in California.

What does this mean? It means he has enjoyed the luxury to be sought after. But he did the work to get there. That is the main thing.

Look at these credits:

Pictures: *The Hucksters* (Clark Gable, Deborah Kerr, Ava Gardner)
          B.F.'s Daughter (Barbara Stanwyck, Van Heflin)
          Black Hand (Gene Kelly)
          A Lion Is in the Streets (James Cagney)
          Lady in a Cage (Olivia de Havilland)

His television credits include original plays for *Bus Stop, Ford Star Time, Chrysler Theatre, Kraft Theatre of Suspense, Ironside, Stage 67*. He created and produced the ABC series *The Double Life of Henry Phyfe*. For his teleplay "End of the

World, Baby" he won the Edgar Allan Poe Award, given by the Mystery Writers of America. "Fame Is the Name of the Game" is his work. So is the television adaptation of "Arsenic and Old Lace."

Ever since the subsidence of what came to be known on television as the anthology series, networks and producers have been digging about, hunting for the form or the formula that will deliver dramatic series durable enough to survive many seasons, the same star and same unit having a new, though vigorous, experience each week.

There are sharp economic reasons for wanting such. Many of these forms, original, imitative, or lifted (*Garrison's Gorillas*), have paid off. Each has, or seeks to have, its own thing. Half-hour comedy had been cleaning up for years and years in both radio and television—a bonanza that conceivably may have had its origin in a soap opera of nearly forty years ago, *Lorenzo Jones*. This was supposed to amuse middle- and lower-class American housewives and it did. All the writers had to do was fashion a stupid man and keep him stupid. They succeeded in doing this. Lorenzo was so stupid he could get lost in his own cellar. And did. This gave confidence to women who had little.

Though general improvements have occurred, they haven't been too fast. Some of the gimmicks, however, have shown remarkable hardihood. And most of them have tested their producers severely.

When you tease out and pin back the skin of certain shows—take, for example, the trio of *Maya, Guns of Will Sonnett,* and *The Fugitive*—and when you coldly inspect their insides, the biotic mechanisms aren't too different. To be sure, the skins, the skeletons, and muscle power of these three shows are quite different. And their habitats are altogether different. But in each of the three, the *viable element is the same*. It is the element of *search*.

Someone-important-to-someone-else is missing. "We must find him." In two cases—*Maya* and *Will Sonnett*—the missing person was Dad.

When so simplified, the big question as to the survivability of the series, on a commercial basis, is also simple. How important can this search be made to *us?* Can we be persuaded to care? If so, how much?

In this area, actors and writers carry most of the load. When shows do fail, however, no one in the whole rickety history of show business has ever been known to acknowledge error, though *Maya,* for me, hung up a new record for no-talent acting. And not very much was planned, either for Dad or the audience, on the great faraway day when he might, conceivably, turn up. In *Maya* it all ended in a massive histrionic sprawl that took an odd quality of spiritual discipline merely to witness. The tiger turned in a no-show. Toward the end, it was so bad even the elephant looked away.

Probably this show failed because it was horrible everywhere. Most aren't this bad. Most make a bold try. Most have a good underpinning of intelligence to support them. But its main ingredient—where's Dad?—gave to *Maya* its excuse for being, exactly as the same question supplied a rationale to the long treks we've taken with Will Sonnett's father and son.

There was nothing wrong in either show with that central idea. In one, the workmanship was poor. In the other, excellent.

What about *The Fugitive?* The element here had a double edge to it. The man

doing the searching was himself in flight. He held our sympathy on both sides
of his torment, as pursuer and as pursued. It was all in sharp focus. And it was
convincingly, often stunningly, sustained by the superior acting of David Janssen,
a fine skill long hidden in the factory-built mediocrity of *Richard Diamond*.

What has any of this to do with *Run for Your Life?* Quite a lot. It has a success
formula.

With a man like Roy Huggins at the controls, *Run for Your Life* had every
chance to come in strong and remain so. I've mentioned *The Fugitive*. Roy Huggins
created that. He also created *Cheyenne, Maverick,* and *77 Sunset Strip*. He doesn't
resemble the popularly accepted idea of a TV producer. He is scholarly, sober,
solitary, has secured a master's degree and is a candidate for his Ph.D. (in political
science) at UCLA.

Though I hate the word, once the indispensable "gimmick" has been built
into the hull, not much notice need be taken after the launching. We know it's
going along with us. Occasional reference is enough to keep everything floating
for the full extent of the voyage.

As writers, most of you will be anxious to prise out the secrets of commercial
properties that have enjoyed large success. This is proper. Most of this book is
concerned primarily with that very problem. Consider the momentum that was
built up in *Run for Your Life* through the careful week-to-week exploitation of
the single inertial force that propelled it. What was that force? It was this—
an attractive, well-educated, well-built man of wide interests and unlimited courage has a year to live, maybe two years. He happens to be a lawyer. What does
he plan to do with this "stay of execution"?

What would *you* do with it? If you were given that much and no more? It's an
intriguing thought for anyone, irrespective of his circumstance or training. What
could you build it up to?

It becomes more intriguing if we add the extra fillip about money: he has the
means to do what he wishes. Anything else? One more: though widely known and
well connected, he's not spoken for, owes no man a thing. And no woman. Think
what such dramatic availability can do to the imagination of the average woman!
Or even to the unaverage woman, if there is such. More piquantly, think what
such a complete package can do when it appears under the name of Ben Gazzara.

Paul Bryan (Ben Gazzara) opted to fill his last days with as much adventure,
as much travel, girls, and excitement, as he could possibly pack in. Will Sonnett's
son and his father pushed their search into one dangerous shoot-out after another.
David Janssen, though running all the time, was also in relentless pursuit of the
real killer, and through that the securing of his own vindication. Once the killer
was found, he could level off and be normal. Which would, of course, mean the
end of the series (as it did).

Paul Bryan's human predicament, though held together by tough and dependable
cordage, was a bit different. He seemed to be taking great pleasure in cheating
death, postponing or outwitting it, doing so by deliberate face-to-face confrontations with life in all its forms and tangles.

And he doesn't always prevail. Many endings, as in the script to be seen next
are sad. If you watch repeats of this, you'll see. For himself he has utterly no
concern. Death will catch him anyway. So his willingness to take risks has no limit

The uses made of this freedom would tempt most writers and producers into the groove of the television stereotype. It has been avoided here by the *quality* of storytelling. Paul Bryan will move in on any situation that interests him. He'll help anyone in trouble if the values involved suggest he should act. He's not afraid to get hurt since he's on the way to his own funeral anyhow.

In his teleplay, "The Committee for the 25th," Luther Davis, with some good help from Tom Allen, has taken on one of America's toughest adversaries, the controls of Las Vegas gambling. Or he has permitted Ben Gazzara to take them on. And Ben has quite a go at it. The play's title has special significance. It refers to the 25th Amendment to the Constitution. At the time the play was written, we didn't have a 25th amendment. (We do now. It deals with presidential disability and succession.) The amendment proposed in the script Luther Davis has written would outlaw gambling in all fifty states. (Open gambling is already prohibited in forty-nine.)

There is no preaching. The situation here dramatized is its own preachment. It fights the special kind of corruption that goes with the glitter of Nevada, glitter plus a backstage focus on attitudes and practices that may serve to explain the condition of epidemic cynicism that is devouring the American idea like cancer.

The script supplies a great range of contrasts: of purposes in conflict, methods of operation, criminal attitude, love-hate, good-bad, objective assessment, and passionate intervention.

Scenic contrasts, from the Byzantine garishness of the gambling house to the tranquillity of the Grand Canyon, make their own comment and erect an authentic reredos before which the action takes place.

A skillful cast, each member bringing his particular value to this shocking story, made each moment, each scene, something never to be forgotten. The girl (Sarah Sinclair) entrapped by heroin was played by Brooke Bundy. Wendell Corey appeared as her father. The heavy, Carl Cappi, was played by Edward Asner. Peter Broco had the role of the gentle-appearing but irretrievably villainous Cana.

Writing is a lonely job. When I asked Luther Davis what he'd advise new writers trying to make the weight in television, his answer was quick: "I'd tell them to avoid it." But somehow I don't think he really meant it.

(The profession of acting is lonely, too. Who could wish for a more solid skill than Oskar Werner's? He could: "I would never become an actor again.")

RUN FOR YOUR LIFE

"The Committee for the 25th"

Teleplay by Luther Davis

Story by Tom Allen

Copyright © 1966 by Roncom Films-Huggins Productions

FADE IN:

1 EXT. SPECTACULAR SIGN SAYING "LAS VEGAS"—NIGHT—LONG SHOT (STOCK)
—BLINKING ON AND OFF.

2 INT. LINE OF SLOT MACHINES IN LOUNGE OF HOTEL—NIGHT—SHOT STARTS CLOSE ON A MACHINE. CAMERA PANS PAST SEVERAL MACHINES BEING WORKED AND COMES UPON PAUL BRYAN JUST PUTTING A COIN INTO SLOT OF ONE MACHINE . . . HE HAS JUST ARRIVED, AND CARRIES SUN GLASSES, A HAT, SOME MAPS; BEHIND HIM STANDS A CONCAVE, DISPIRITED YOUNG BELLBOY HOLDING PAUL'S SUITCASE. PAUL PULLS THE LEVER, WATCHES THE WHEELS TURNING—IS READY TO MOVE ON, BUT PAUSES AND REACTS TO A SINGULAR DISPOSITION OF THE WHEELS . . . THERE IS A CASCADE OF COINS. PAUL LAUGHS, DELIGHTED, AND STARTS TO SCOOP UP COINS:

PAUL

(TO BELLBOY) Jackpot! I'm in Vegas two minutes and I hit a jackpot!

BELLBOY

(SPIRITLESSLY) Hooray.

PAUL GLARES AND GATHERS UP HIS WINNINGS.

PAUL

Thanks. I nearly felt good there for a minute.

BELLBOY

That's just to hook you; you'll put it all back and a lot more besides.

PAUL

I see. Are you hooked?

BELLBOY

Man, everybody in Vegas is hooked, one way or another. (STARTS AWAY WITH THE SUITCASE) Everybody in the world is hooked, one way or another.

PAUL GRIMACES HIS DISAGREEMENT AND FOLLOWS.

PAUL

How old are you to be so cynical?

BELLBOY

How old do you have to be?

WE PAN OR TRUCK THEM ALONG MORE SLOT MACHINES . . . AS THEY CROSS WE BECOME CONSCIOUS OF VERY AGGRESSIVE DANCE MUSIC, FRUG-ISH IN BEAT.

HERE CUSTOMERS AT THE SLOT MACHINES, MEN AND WOMEN, ARE LOOKING UPWARD AND OFF, MERELY GLANCING AT THEIR MACHINES. PAUL SEES A MAN FOCUSING OFF AND UP WITH MUCH LEER; PAUL LOOKS IN THAT DIRECTION:

3 INT. GLASS CAGE IN LOUNGE—NIGHT—FROM PAUL'S POINT OF VIEW. HANGING OVER THE SMALL DANCE ORCHESTRA IS A GLASS CAGE; IN IT SARAH SINCLAIR DANCES IN A VERY BRIEF FRINGE DRESS. SHE IS TWENTY-ONE, MARVELOUSLY LITHE AND ATTRACTIVE; HER MOVEMENTS ARE ALMOST IDLY PROVOCATIVE; HER WRISTS ARE IN FRONT OF HER EYES AS IF SHE WERE

IMMERSED IN SOME PRIVATE REVERIE, BARELY CONSCIOUS OF THE FACT
THAT SHE IS ON PUBLIC EXHIBITION.

4 FAVORING PAUL. HE GIVES A LITTLE SMILE OF MAN-TO-MAN APPRECIATION
TOWARD THE BELLBOY WHO MAKES A LONG SUFFERING SHRUG AND STARTS
OFF AGAIN.

PAUL

(FOLLOWING) Isn't there anything you like?

BELLBOY

Not girls in glass cages.

PAUL GLANCES UP ONCE MORE—HIS EXPRESSION ALTERS AS HE THINKS HE
RECOGNIZES HER:

5 HIS POINT OF VIEW OF SARAH IN HER GLASS CAGE. SHE HAS REMOVED HER
HANDS FROM IN FRONT OF HER FACE . . . IS DANCING WITH HER EYES
CLOSED . . .

6 PAUL AND BELLBOY.

PAUL

I know her!

BELLBOY

Bully for you.

PAUL

Is her first name Sarah?

BELLBOY IS STARTLED BY THE UNEXPECTED ACCURACY OF THIS; THEN HIS
MANNER BECOMES MORE SUSPICIOUS:

BELLBOY

Sarah what?

PAUL

Isn't she Sarah Sinclair?

BELLBOY

I'm paid to carry your bag, show you how the air-conditioner works,
maybe bring you some ice. Conversation you are going to have to get
from somebody else.

WHAT HAD BEEN BADINAGE HAS NOW BECOME SOMETHING HARDER; PAUL'S
EXPRESSION SOBERS; HE HANDS HIS MAPS, ETC., TO BELLBOY.

PAUL

Put all this in my room and bring me the key. I'll be over there.

BELLBOY

Yes, sir.

HE GOES OFF ACROSS LOUNGE. WE STAY WITH PAUL WHO CROSSES TO A
COCKTAIL TABLE AT FRINGE OF THE LOUNGE.

7 FAVORING BELLBOY, WHO PASSES ANOTHER TABLE, A BANQUETTE, AND GOES TOWARD THE MAN WHO SITS THERE . . . THIS IS CARL CAPPI, A WELL-BARBERED, CONSERVATIVELY DRESSED DINER OF ABOUT FORTY; HE OWNS THE HOTEL, OR AT LEAST FRONTS FOR IT, AND SITS TALKING QUIETLY INTO A TELEPHONE ON TABLE.

BELLBOY

(SOFTLY) Mr. Cappi? Excuse me . . .

CAPPI FINISHES A RATHER LONG SENTENCE, AND THEN TURNS TO LOOK AT BELLBOY:

CAPPI

(GENTLY) Yes, son, what is it?

BELLBOY

The feller sitting at sixteen, he knows Sarah. Called her Sarah Sinclair.

CAPPI

Thank you, son.

BELLBOY

Yes, sir.

BELLBOY GOES OFF; CAPPI CAREFULLY DOES NOT LOOK IN THE DIRECTION BELLBOY INDICATED AS TABLE SIXTEEN. HE HANGS UP THE TELEPHONE AND THEN, AND ONLY THEN, ALLOWS HIMSELF TO LOOK TOWARD TABLE SIXTEEN.

8 PAUL AT TABLE SIXTEEN FROM CAPPI'S POINT OF VIEW—LONG SHOT. PAUL IS BEING SERVED A DRINK BY A PRETTY WAITRESS IN TIGHTS; PAUL'S ATTENTION IS ON THE CAGE O.S.:

9 CLOSER ON PAUL. HIS EXPRESSION SHOWING INTEREST, APPRECIATION—AND PUZZLEMENT; WHAT IS THIS PARTICULAR GIRL DOING THERE, OF ALL PLACES?

10 SARAH FROM PAUL'S POINT OF VIEW. THE SAME INTROVERTED SEXUALITY; HER DANCE REACHES ITS CONCLUSION AND MUSIC STOPS.

11 WIDER ANGLE INCLUDING PAUL AND SARAH AS SHE COMES OUT OF HER DISPLAY CASE AND STARTS ACROSS IN THE GENERAL DIRECTION OF CAPPI'S TABLE . . . AS SHE PASSES PAUL'S TABLE, HE RISES:

PAUL

(SOFTLY) Hello, Sarah. Does your father know where you are?

SHE STARES AT HIM—RECOGNIZES HIM AND SMILES BROADLY:

SARAH

Mr. Bryan!—I mean Paul. I must remember I'm a big girl now. (HER EXPRESSION CHANGES; SHE LOWERS HER HAND WHICH SHE HAD STARTED TO OFFER) What brings you to the City of Schools and Churches?

PAUL

I'm just—here for the waters, as they say. I saw you and—*does* your father know you're here?

SARAH

Does yours know you're here? Grown-ups don't keep in hourly touch with their parents.

PAUL

Okay, Sarah, you're a grown-up. How about having a drink with me?

HE HOLDS CHAIR—SHE HESITATES—LOOKS TOWARD CAPPI'S TABLE—LOWERS HER VOICE:

SARAH

When the shows are all over, around four in the morning, some of us go to a soda fountain down the road—"Brownies." What's to keep you from wandering in there? I mean, you could want a milkshake or a box of cookies, or something.

PAUL

I feel that I'm going to want a milkshake or a box of cookies.

SHE SAYS NO MORE BUT STRIDES OFF ACROSS THE ROOM. WE STAY ON PAUL WHO SITS AGAIN AND SIGNALS FOR A WAITRESS.

12 SARAH FROM HIS POINT OF VIEW AS SHE SITS AT CAPPI'S BANQUETTE; CAPPI IS TALKING ON TELEPHONE—DOESN'T SEEM TO NOTICE HER; A WAITER APPEARS AND IS TAKING HER ORDER.

13
thru OMITTED
22

23 INT. SODA FOUNTAIN—NIGHT—SHOT STARTS ON TWO MILK SHAKES. WE PULL BACK AND SEE SARAH AND PAUL AT COUNTER—WE CAN PRESUME IN A CORNER OF THE SODA FOUNTAIN; IN FRONT OF PAUL IS AN EASILY IDENTIFIABLE BOX OF COOKIES HE HAS PURCHASED TO TAKE TO HIS ROOM. HE AND SARAH TAKE LONG PULLS ON THEIR STRAWS AND SMILE AT EACH OTHER WITH APPRECIATION.

SARAH

One thing you have to say about Vegas, they can sure shake milk.

PAUL

What else can you say about it?

SARAH

Everything. It's where we're going. The whole world.

PAUL

(SURPRISED) Vegas?

SARAH

Sure, right here, this is the world of tomorrow, not all that space stuff.

SHE NODS OFF.

24 SHOOTING ACROSS SODA FOUNTAIN—POINT OF VIEW. WE SEE A MIDGET

AND A CHORUS GIRL WORKING A SLOT MACHINE; HER SLACKS ARE VERY TIGHT; THEY GAMBLE VAGUELY, NOT MUCH INTERESTED.

25 PAUL AND SARAH.

PAUL

A midget and a chorus girl gambling at five in the morning is the world of tomorrow?

SARAH

(IMPATIENTLY) No, man, no. They're looking inside themselves, don't you see? What you *do,* that's just to move muscles, like you've got to stand or sit or something. But inside the head, *there's* somewhere to go.

PAUL

Is that where you've been?

SARAH

I celebrated my nineteenth birthday two years ago by marrying exactly the guy my father said I shouldn't.

PAUL

And?

SARAH

He was a mess.

PAUL

Daddy was right, eh?

SARAH

As I remember it, you used to be a nice guy.

PAUL

Daddy was right, eh?

SARAH

Do I look as if I'm hurting anywhere?

PAUL

You look and sound as if you died some time ago. About a hundred and ten pounds of some of the most beautiful girl anybody's ever seen, an I.Q. up in the hundred and sixties if I remember something I once heard about you . . . enough money to go anywhere . . .

SHE SUDDENLY SHAKES HER HEAD WITH GREAT VIOLENCE.

SARAH

Where's to go? (INSULTINGLY) "Enough money to go anywhere?!"

SHE GETS OFF STOOL; CLEARLY IS LEAVING.

PAUL

Good-bye. Thanks for the milkshake.

SARAH

Good-bye. (STARTS OFF; PAUSES) Look—is there anything I can do for you while you're here?

PAUL

I don't know. Want to come see the Grand Canyon with me tomorrow?

SARAH

The Grand Ca—(SHE LAUGHS) That's your idea of where's to go?

PAUL

I never saw it. Seems to me everybody ought to see the Grand Canyon before he dies.

SARAH

(WAGGING HER HEAD) Good night. If you see Dad around, give him my love.

PAUL

I won't be seeing him—but okay. Good night.

SHE STARTS OUT—PAUSES AS SHE PASSES THE SLOT MACHINE WHERE THE MIDGET AND CHORUS GIRL WERE GAMBLING—THEY'VE GONE NOW. SHE PAUSES, AND, WITH THE STRANGE BLANK COMPULSIVENESS OF VEGAS, PUTS A COIN INTO THE MACHINE—CLEARLY HAS FORGOTTEN PAUL . . . MACHINE CLICKS THRICE—NO WIN . . . SHE STRIDES OUT WITHOUT A BACKWARD GLANCE.

26 INT. HOTEL CORRIDOR—DAY—LONG SHOT TOWARD ENTRANCE FROM OUTSIDE. A MODERN CORRIDOR, GROUND FLOOR; WE CAN SEE GLASS DOORS AND RIGHT OUTSIDE SOME POTTED CACTUS; PAUL ENTERS, DRESSED AS WE LAST SAW HIM, KEY AND THE BOX OF COOKIES IN HIS HAND, AND COMES TOWARD ROOM DOOR NEAR CAMERA. JUST AS HE NEARS IT, AND AS HIS KEY IS ABOUT TO ENTER THE LOCK, A MAN'S HAND ENTERS SHOT FROM BEHIND CAMERA AND GRABS PAUL BY THE WRIST.

27 WIDER ANGLE. A TOUGH-LOOKING MAN WE'LL KNOW AS CHARLIE IS THERE IN SLACKS AND A SPORT SHIRT. BEHIND HIM, SIMILARLY ATTIRED, IS STEVE, THE CAPTAIN OF WAITERS WE MET IN THE LOUNGE—AND WHOM WE SHOULD RECOGNIZE; A THIRD MAN IS BEHIND THEM; HE IS A RATHER ATHLETIC INDI-VIDUAL WEARING TRUNKS AND CARRYING A TOWEL OVER HIS ARM.

CHARLIE

You Mister Albert Smith from Yonkers, New York?

PAUL LOOKS DOWN AT THE HAND ON HIS WRIST—AND WE GATHER THAT THE GRASP HURTS.

PAUL

No, I'm not.

HE TRIES TO WITHDRAW HIS HAND.

CHARLIE

This is Smith's room.

PAUL LOOKS AT HIS KEY, AND OPENS THE DOOR WITH IT . . . LOOKS IN.

PAUL

No, this is my room. (LOOKS DOWN AT THE HAND ON HIS WRIST AGAIN)

My name's Bryan, Paul Bryan, from San Francisco. Would you mind letting go of my wrist?

STEVE

I think it's the same guy that won at poker two nights ago. I'd almost swear this is Smith.

PAUL

I was at the road races in Riverside, California, two days ago.

CHARLIE

The man we want is a race driver, too.

PAUL

I'm not. I'm a lawyer. If you'll take your hand off my wrist, I'll prove it.

CHARLIE DOES SO AND PAUL HANDS HIM HIS WALLET. ALL THREE LOOK AT SOME OF THE IDENTIFICATION.

STEVE

Seems to be named Bryan, all right. Going to be in Vegas long, Mr. Bryan?

PAUL

Few hours.

STEVE

Then back to San Francisco?

PAUL

Why do I get the feeling you never thought I was an Albert Smith from Yonkers, New York?

CHARLIE

You're going to leave Vegas in a few hours and then where will you be going?

PAUL HESITATES AND THEN DECIDES TO TELL THEM.

PAUL

I'm going to look at the Grand Canyon.

CHARLIE

Alone?

PAUL LOOKS AT HIM VERY CLOSELY NOW.

PAUL

Why?

STEVE

We recommend you go alone. We recommend you go in a few hours just as you said, and that you don't take anybody with you.

PAUL

Like who?

THE ATHLETIC INDIVIDUAL MAKES A SUDDEN MOVE AND WITH A LIGHTNING (UNDERCRANK?) GESTURE SHOVES PAUL'S FINGERS FROM THE FRAME OF

THE DOOR, AGAINST WHICH HE WAS LEANING, INTO THE DOORWAY ITSELF; AT THE SAME TIME CHARLIE MAKES AN EQUALLY QUICK MOVE AND BRINGS THE DOOR CLOSED; PAUL CRIES OUT IN PAIN; CHARLIE GRABS PAUL'S RIGHT WRIST AND HOLDS HIS FINGERS THERE.

CHARLIE

(TRANSPARENTLY) Hey, fellers, be careful, you want to mash Mr. Bryan's fingers?

28 FAVORING PAUL SWEATING IN PAIN.

29 GROUP SHOT.

STEVE

Lot of people think that you can't get hurt in Vegas, they think it's just a fun town.

CHARLIE

That's very dumb. You can get hurt in Vegas.

PAUL

I feel the truth of what you're saying.

SUDDENLY, THE DOOR IS OPENED; THEY LET GO OF HIS WRIST, AND ONE OF THEM GIVES HIM A GENTLE SHOVE INTO HIS ROOM.

30 INT. PAUL'S ROOM—DAY—AS HE STAGGERS IN, HOLDING HIS FINGERS WHICH HURT. BEHIND HIM CHARLIE STICKS HIS HEAD IN FOR A MOMENT; TOSSES IN THE BOX OF COOKIES WHICH PAUL DROPPED.

CHARLIE

Don't forget your cookies.

HE CLOSES THE DOOR SOFTLY. ALONE, PAUL WIGGLES HIS FINGERS, SHAKES HIS HAND IN THE AIR TO COUNTER THE PAIN HE FEELS, AND THEN SEES TELEPHONE ON OTHER SIDE OF THE ROOM. HE STRIDES TOWARD IT DECISIVELY, PICKS IT UP IN A SWEEPING GESTURE:

PAUL

(INTO TELEPHONE) Operator, I want the local—(HE BREAKS OFF, REALIZING HOW SHADOWY HIS REPORT WOULD BE—FROWNS)

OPERATOR'S VOICE

(ON FILTER) Yes, sir? Hello . . .

PAUL

Never mind. Wake me up in about three hours, will you. I'm going to get a little sleep.

OPERATOR'S VOICE

(ON FILTER) Yes, sir . . .

PAUL HANGS UP, GLARES AT HIS FINGERS AND BEGINS TO WRAP A HANDKERCHIEF AROUND THEM.

31 INSERT.

ROUGH BUT TALENTED LINE DRAWING (PENCIL ON OUTSIDE OF FOLDED

WHITE SCRATCH PAPER) OF A GIRL RESEMBLING SARAH HOLDING HER FINGER TO HER LIPS IN A GESTURE FOR SILENCE . . . PAUL'S LIGHTLY BANDAGED RIGHT HAND COMES INTO SHOT AND PICKS THE PAPER UP . . .

32 EXT. PAUL'S CAR IN HOTEL PARKING LOT—DAY. PAUL HAS JUST OPENED DOOR OF CAR AND PICKED UP THE SCRAP OF PAPER; HE GLANCES OVER HIS SHOULDER—WE SEE A BELLBOY APPROACHING WITH PAUL'S SUITCASE. PAUL SURREPTITIOUSLY OPENS THE NOTE AND READS IT, WHILE GESTURING FOR BELLBOY TO PUT SUITCASE IN REAR SEAT.

33 INSERT NOTE. "OKAY, I WOULD LIKE TO SEE THE GRAND CANYON. I'LL BE WAITING AT 22A LA MIRADA STREET . . . SHHH! I'M SNEAKING OUT!"

34 BACK TO SHOT. PAUL, PUZZLED, SOMEWHAT AMUSED, POCKETS THE NOTE WITH ONE HAND AS HE TIPS THE BELLBOY AND PREPARES TO GET INTO DRIVER'S SEAT OF HIS RENTED CONVERTIBLE.

35 CLOSE SHOT—SUN GLASSES—ELABORATELY STYLED, MODERN SUN GLASSES FOR A WOMAN—THEY'RE BEING PUT ON . . .

36 EXT. FRONT SEAT OF PAUL'S OPEN CONVERTIBLE—DAY—TWO SHOT PAUL AND SARAH (PROCESS). THEY'RE SPEEDING ALONG A FLAT NO-OTHER-TRAFFIC HIGHWAY IN THE DESERT—MUCH FEELING OF SUN . . . HE HAS HIS SUN GLASSES ON, AND SARAH, SITTING BESIDE HIM, HAS JUST MODELED A PAIR OF HER OWN FOR HIM; SHE WEARS SMART LOOKING SLACKS; HER HANDSOME OVERNIGHT CASE IS ON REAR SEAT BESIDE HIS SUITCASE.

SARAH

These—? (TAKES ANOTHER EXTREME PAIR OF SUN GLASSES FROM HER PURSE) Or these . . . (STILL ANOTHER—YELLOW BEN FRANKLINS) Or these . . . ?

PAUL

Depends on whether you want to look like Ben Franklin or a moth.

SHE LAUGHS AND THEN LOOKS AT HIM VERY DIRECTLY:

SARAH

Today everything about me is up to you.

PAUL

A moth.

SHE PUTS ON THE LARGEST PAIR, AND SINKS DOWN LOW IN THE SEAT WITH A SIGH.

SARAH

The hours I keep, I've only been seeing the sun at dawn—I thought it had become a large bloodshot eyeball, like everything else.

PAUL

"The sun is a bloodshot eyeball"—Las Vegas show girl's view of the world.

SHE CHUCKLES, PLEASED.

SARAH

I like that, I like to think of myself as a Las Vegas show girl.

PAUL

Why did you come today?

SARAH

Oh—you know. (GIGGLES HAPPILY DEEP IN HER THROAT AND GESTURES VAGUELY)

PAUL

No, I don't know.

SARAH

(IMPATIENTLY) Just to *see*. You know.

PAUL

(PATIENTLY) To see what, Sarah?

SARAH

Oh—if people still really do—everything, drive cars back and forth, talk to each other, "How do you do, Mrs. Fleriot, how are your *beau*tiful petunias, yatayatada; may I ask you to dinner sometime?—ten gallons, please, and check the oil; great heavens, so that's the Grand Canyon? Now I have to see the Louvre; will the entire Second Form please stand up, yatayatayata, *never* wear high heels with slacks, don't forget your white gloves in town, say please, dear, servants are people; I never stay in London during the Season, it's all become so vulgar; God bless Swiss banks, my numbered account saved my life; a Cardinal is called Your Grace; don't ski into sunset; two hamburgers medium, hold the onions. . . ."

SHE SUDDENLY SLIDES EVEN FURTHER DOWN INTO THE SEAT, PRESSING HER KNEES AGAINST THE DASH; HOWLS WITH LARGELY PRIVATE, VERY GOOD-HUMORED, GIRLISH LAUGHTER, THE BACKS OF HER WRISTS AGAINST HER FACE SOMEWHAT AS IN HER DANCING PERFORMANCE . . . AS SHE LAUGHS SHE MOVES HER BODY A TRIFLE AS IF DANCING IN HER OWN MIND.

37 FAVORING PAUL—PUZZLED—HALF SMILING, NOT SURE WHAT HIS REACTION SHOULD BE.

SARAH

(THROUGH HER LAUGHTER) Hey—

38 FAVORING SARAH. SHE IS STARING AT HIS BANDAGED HAND RESTING ON HIS KNEE —HE IS STEERING WITH HIS LEFT HAND.

SARAH

(SOMEWHAT SOBERED) What happened to your hand?

HE GLANCES AT HER BRIEFLY.

PAUL

It got stuck in a door.

SHE SUDDENLY, SURPRISINGLY, TAKES HIS HAND IN HERS AND KISSES IT. PAUL LOOKS EMBARRASSED—REMOVES HIS HAND.

SARAH

What's the matter?

PAUL

(GRINS) I don't know—just not used to having my hand kissed; seems sort of un-American.

SHE SMILES A TRIFLE MYSTERIOUSLY, TAKES HIS HAND AND KISSES IT AGAIN.

SARAH

(ALMOST AS IF BY ROTE) Oh, Paul, I'm doing just great here, I have a good feeling about my life at last, and a real direction. I'm taking singing lessons, and acting lessons, and I've found my town, Vegas is my town!

PAUL

(CONCEALING HIS PRIVATE SARCASM) A real fun town, eh?

SHE GLANCES AT HIM COVERTLY AND THEN NODS.

SARAH

Fun in the sun.

SHE KISSES HIS HAND AGAIN.

PAUL

I don't intend to see your father, but if I should run into him, and if he should ask me, I'd say that you're well and happy and have found your town. Is that maybe why you came today? So I'd give a good report?

SARAH

I don't know. I don't think so. Maybe.

PAUL

If it is, that's done. Now, what kind of trouble are you in and how can I help?

SHE PUTS HIS HAND BACK ON HIS KNEE AND MOVES AWAY FROM HIM.

SARAH

I'm not in any trouble of any kind.

PAUL

Then why did three monkeys threaten me and suggest that I leave town alone?

SHE DOESN'T ANSWER FOR A MOMENT. THEN SHE SLOWLY SLIDES UPRIGHT AGAIN.

SARAH

Well—did you—try anything funny in the casino? Try to cheat or anything?

PAUL

This is me, Sarah, Paul Bryan. I wouldn't cheat at gambling, least of all in a casino which I hear is controlled by the mob.

SARAH

Everything's controlled by something. (SHRUGS)

HE TRIES TO CONCEAL HIS IRRITATION; GLANCES TOWARD SIDE OF ROAD:

39 INSERT POINT OF VIEW—ROAD SIGN SAYING THAT THEY HAVE PASSED FROM NEVADA INTO ARIZONA.

40 BACK TO SHOT.

PAUL

(AN IDLE COMMENT) We're in Arizona.

SARAH

Yatayatayata. . . .

SHE IS AFFLICTED WITH MORE GIRLISH LAUGHTER; SLIDES DOWN IN THE SEAT AGAIN . . . HE GLARES AT HER.

41 EXT. SCENIC VIEW OF THE GRAND CANYON—DAY—FROM A HIGH ANGLE (STOCK)—AS BEAUTIFUL A TOURIST SHOT AS CAN BE FOUND.

42 EXT. A BENCH BACKED BY PINE TREES—DAY—TWO SHOT PAUL AND SARAH LOOKING DOWN AND OFF AT THE VIEW. PAUL SEEMS QUIETLY IMPRESSED. SHE IS FUMBLING IN HER PURSE—PUTS ON HER BEN FRANKLIN SUN GLASSES AND PEERS AT THE VIEW AGAIN. HE GLANCES AT HER TO SHARE THE EXPERIENCE; SHE PANTOMIMES A LADYLIKE YAWN.

PAUL

I must take you on more trips.

SARAH

The whole world is on a trip, and it may not be back.

PAUL

How about a donkey ride down to the bottom?

SARAH

You have got to be kidding! (LAUGHS GOOD-HUMOREDLY) All right! All right, Paul! Where do we get a donkey?

PAUL

(PLEASED, LEADING HER OFF) This way, Madame!

43 EXT. SCENIC VIEW OF GRAND CANYON—DAY—LONG SHOT (STOCK)—A VIEW OF A TRAIN OF BURROS WITH TOURISTS ATOP.

44 OMITTED.

45 INSERT. SIGN "CANYON VIEW MOTEL"—A TOURIST ON A BURRO IS ITS LOGO.

46 INT. MOTEL ROOM—DAY—FULL SHOT. GNARLED LITTLE PROPRIETOR WEARING COWBOY BOOTS AND BLUE JEANS IS SHOWING THEM SARAH'S ROOM. PAUL CARRIES HER OVERNIGHT CASE—PROPRIETOR CARRIES PAUL'S CASE.

PAUL

All right, Sarah?

PROPRIETOR

It's the best room we got.

SARAH

(RESTLESSLY) It's fine . . . (TAKING HER CASE) I'll just get right in the shower. . . .

PROPRIETOR

I'll bring up some ice and like that.

SARAH

A shower for me. I'm sure you want one too, Paul.

PAUL

(GRINNING) We're going.

SHE FLASHES AN AUTOMATIC SMILE BUT HER IMPATIENCE IS CLEAR.

PROPRIETOR

(OBLIVIOUS) How'd you like the canyon?

SARAH

Oh, it was peachy keen, peachy keen. . . .

PAUL

Great.

ANOTHER QUICK NERVOUS SMILE—SHE HOLDS THE DOOR. . . .

PROPRIETOR

(CROSSING TOWARD WINDOW) You can see Sunset Point from here. . . .

SARAH

Not now!

PAUL

Come on, show me my room.

PROPRIETOR

(A TRIFLE SULKY) Okay . . . (STARTS OUT) Seems a shame, separate rooms, such a pretty couple.

SARAH LAUGHS, BUT TIGHTLY.

PAUL

That's life, one can't have everything. Now, would you please show me my room!

HE AND SARAH GRIN AT EACH OTHER—SHE TAUTLY—AS PROPRIETOR RELUCTANTLY LEADS PAUL OUT. WE STAY WITH SARAH WHO STANDS FIRM, HER OVERNIGHT CASE IN HER HANDS, UNTIL THEY HAVE GONE OUT AND CLOSED THE DOOR BEHIND THEM. THEN SHE TAKES A DEEP BREATH AND HER POSTURE AND POSE OF COMPETENCE DISSOLVES—SHE SLUMPS, REVEALING A KIND OF INNER EXHAUSTION. SHE RAISES HER HEAD, GOES TO BED, OPENS THE SUITCASE, AND, WITH SLOW, CLUMSY, DRAINED GESTURES, PAWS THROUGH IT FOR SOMETHING. SHE FINDS A PLASTIC CASE, OPENS IT, TAKES OUT A VERY BUSINESSLIKE LOOKING HYPODERMIC NEEDLE, NEATLY ARRANGED WITH A TIP OF COTTON ON ITS POINT . . . SHE HAS THIS IN HER HAND WHEN THERE IS A CLICK FROM DOOR AND SHE LOOKS IN THAT DIRECTION. PAUL STANDS THERE, HER COMPACT IN HIS HAND. THEY LOOK BLEAKLY AT EACH OTHER.

PAUL

(AFTER A MOMENT) What is it, heroin?

SARAH

No. I don't know. They make it up specially for me. Some cocaine, I know, maybe some heroin too . . . and a couple of other goodies—put them all together they spell Mother.

PAUL

How long have you been hooked?

SARAH

I don't like the word.

PAUL

Are you hooked?

SARAH

Look, you need oxygen, you have to breathe to live, but you don't say you're "hooked" on air. You're not strung out on air, Sarah, this is your life. (SHE KISSES THE PACKET) I love you.

PAUL

How old are you? Twenty-one?

SARAH

". . . an I.Q. up in the hundred and sixties," yatayata, let me alone now, Paul, it's grown-up time.

PAUL

You're a grown-up?

SARAH

I will be in a minute if you'll let me take my fix!

PAUL

How much does it cost you a day?

SARAH

Nothing, not one little penny.

PAUL

They give it to you because they love you?

SARAH

He. He gives it to me because he loves me.

PAUL

Who's "he?"

SARAH

(A VICIOUS IMPATIENCE NOW) Paul, get out of here! I'm not very good at giving these to myself and—

PAUL STRIDES ACROSS THE ROOM AND GRABS THE SYRINGE FROM HER.

SARAH

Listen, Paul, it's after six o'clock, I'm due, I'm due right *now*!

SHE GIVES A CRY OF RAGE AND IMPATIENCE AND RUSHES TOWARD HIM JUST AS DOOR FROM HALL IS OPENED AND CAPPI APPEARS THERE.

> CAPPI
>
> (TO PAUL) Get out of here, Bryan.

SHE RUNS TO HIM.

> SARAH
>
> (HAPPILY) Oh, Cappi!

CAPPI PUTS ONE ARM PROTECTIVELY AROUND HER WAIST.

> SARAH
>
> Please, Cappi, give me my cocktail, it's cocktail time. Oh, I'm glad to see you!

> PAUL
>
> (TO CAPPI, WITH LOATHING) So you hooked her.

> CAPPI
>
> Nobody hooks anybody, people hook themselves.

> SARAH
>
> (TO PAUL) Give me that syringe.

PAUL LOOKS AT HER, DOESN'T MOVE. CAPPI OPENS THE HALL DOOR AND GESTURES; STEVE AND ANOTHER OF THE MEN WHO THREATENED PAUL BEFORE APPEAR; CAPPI NODS TOWARD PAUL. THEY START TOWARD HIM.

47 FAVORING SARAH. SHE WHIMPERS AND HIDES HER FACE IN CAPPI'S CHEST.

48 FAVORING PAUL. BACKING AWAY, STILL HOLDING SYRINGE. . . . KNOCK ON DOOR —ALL FREEZE; CAPPI MAKES A VICIOUS GESTURE TOWARD THE BATHROOM AND THE TWO MEN SLAP HANDS OVER PAUL'S FACE, SILENCING HIM, AND DRAG HIM INTO THE BATHROOM. CAPPI GOES TO THE DOOR TO CORRIDOR WHERE THERE'S ANOTHER KNOCK.

> PROPRIETOR'S VOICE
>
> It's some ice, you want it in here, or in the other?

CAPPI OPENS THE DOOR.

49 INT. CORRIDOR—PROPRIETOR HOLDING A TRAY WITH A PLASTIC BAG OF ICE AND SOME GLASSES ON IT.

> CAPPI
>
> That's just great, thanks. (TAKES IT)

> PROPRIETOR
>
> It's a quarter for the ice.

CAPPI HANDS HIM A BILL AND SLAMS THE DOOR; IMMEDIATELY THEREAFTER THERE IS A CRASH SOUND—WE CAN PRESUME THAT PAUL TRIED TO ESCAPE FROM THE MEN'S GRIP IN THE BATHROOM O.S. PROPRIETOR STOPS, PUZZLED AND WORRIED—ANOTHER LOUD SOUND.

PROPRIETOR STARTS BACK TOWARD THE DOOR WHICH IS SUDDENLY OPENED FROM WITHIN—STEVE STANDS THERE. HE SMILES TOOTHILY, AND MENACINGLY.

STEVE

When you get down to the office, call up and tell me what time it is.

PROPRIETOR

(STARTS TO CONSULT WRISTWATCH) I can tell you what—

STEVE

I want office time, on the telephone.

PROPRIETOR

Yes, sir.

HE GOES OFF UP THE HALL; STEVE WAITS UNTIL HE'S SURE HE'S GONE AND THEN RE-ENTERS THE ROOM.

50 INT. MOTEL ROOM. THE OTHER THUG BENDS OVER PAUL, WHO IS RECUMBENT AND MOTIONLESS OVER THE FOOT OF THE BED . . . CAMERA PANS TO DEEP CHAIR IN WHICH SARAH SITS, BACKS OF HER HANDS OVER HER FACE AS IN HER DANCE, HER BODY MOVING A LITTLE AS IF IN THE DANCE; CAPPI SITS ON A STRAIGHT CHAIR BESIDE HER, ADMINISTERING DRUG INTO HER VEIN.

CAPPI

(GENTLY) Feel better, baby?

SHE TAKES HIS HAND AND KISSES IT. CAMERA ZOOMARS IN TOWARD HER AND THERE IS A LOUD DISCORDANT NOTE OF MUSIC.

DISSOLVE TO:

51 INT. CLOSE SHOT—NIGHT—SARAH WITH HER HANDS IN FRONT OF HER EYES. THEN WE REVERSE ZOOMAR AND SEE THAT SHE IS DANCING IN HER GLASS CAGE IN THE LOUNGE OF THE HOTEL, HER BODY MOVING SINUOUSLY. . . .

52 INT. BANQUETTE—NIGHT—CAPPI. HE IS WATCHING HER IDLY WHILE TALKING BUSINESS QUIETLY INTO TELEPHONE—WE CAN'T HEAR HIS WORDS; HIS PRIVATE BODYGUARD, STEVE, HOVERS IN B.G. NEITHER NOTICES PAUL ENTER SHOT BEHIND THEM. HE LOOKS LONG AND HARD AT CAPPI; HE DOESN'T HAVE ANY BANDAGES OR MARKS ON HIS FACE. HE MOVES FORWARD AND SITS AT CAPPI'S TABLE. STEVE STEPS FORWARD QUICKLY, PROTECTIVELY, HAND GOING TO GUN IN SHOULDER HOLSTER, AND CAPPI MAKES A SIMILAR MOVE. PAUL HOLDS UP BOTH HIS HANDS ABOVE TABLE EDGE—BOTH ARE BANDAGED. CAPPI AND STEVE RELAX.

CAPPI

You're a real stupid man, Bryan, coming back to Vegas.

PAUL

I have a question, Mr. Cappi; you may want to consult your attorney before answering.

CAPPI

I doubt it. What's the question?

PAUL

You've been charged with the commission of felonies in Arizona, based on charges brought by me, such as assault with a deadly weapon, assault with intent to commit bodily harm, and conspiracy. A request has been made that you be extradited to face trial in Arizona. Are you willing to waive extradition and appear voluntarily for trial?

CAPPI COVERS A SMILE OF REAL AMUSEMENT, AS DOES STEVE.

CAPPI

I don't have to consult with my attorney, I don't waive nothing, nobody is going to extradite me, you are out of your mind. I have at least a dozen taxpaying Nevada witnesses from right in this hotel who will swear I never left Las Vegas that night.

STEVE

Two dozen . . .

PAUL

I haven't mentioned any particular night.

CAPPI

You mention it, I'll cover it.

SOUND OF APPLAUSE O.S.—THEY TURN TO LOOK:

53 LOUNGE OF HOTEL—FULLER SHOT—NIGHT. LOUNGE IS NOT FULLY OCCUPIED, BUT PEOPLE ARE APPLAUDING SARAH WITH ENTHUSIASM . . . SHE HAS FINISHED HER STINT AND IS COMING TOWARD CAPPI'S BANQUETTE.

54 BANQUETTE.

PAUL

I have a call in to Sarah's father, he's up around the Rogue River somewhere salmon fishing.

CAPPI

I never seen anybody work so hard to get his mouth stopped. You, Steve?

STEVE

(LAUGHING GOOD-HUMOREDLY) Sure beats me. (TO PAUL) Nobody pushes Mr. Cappi here around, don't you know that? You as stupid as you sound?

PAUL

Do I sound stupid? Is this some pre-Statehood Nevada mining town? Or is this an American city in 1966?

55 FAVORING SARAH—AS, NEARING THE TABLE, SHE SEES PAUL—HER EXPRESSION SHOWS INSTANT SYMPATHY AND CONCERN:

SARAH

Paul! Oh, Paul, forgive me for—

CAPPI

(CUTTING ACROSS HER WORDS) He's called your old man.

HER EXPRESSION CHANGES.

SARAH

Any time I want to call my father *I'll* call him.

PAUL

Sarah, I'm bringing charges against your friend Cappi. I'm going to ask you to testify about what happened the other night.

SARAH IS SILENT, DISTURBED. SHE SHAKES HER HEAD.

CAPPI

Didn't Sarah tell you, friend? She and I aren't just an item. It's the real thing. (SMOOTHLY) Why don't you wise up and just forget the whole megillah, huh?

PAUL

Sorry. Can't do that.

SARAH

Paul, Paul, leave me alone!

PAUL

Can't do that either. I don't like your friend, don't like the way he made that "real thing" between you.

HE RISES AND EXITS THE SHOT. CAMERA COMES DOWN TO CAPPI.

56 EXT. CITY OF LAS VEGAS OFFICE BUILDING—DAY—LONG ESTABLISHING SHOT (STOCK)—AN IMPRESSIVE MODERN BUILDING.

57 INT. OFFICE WITHIN—DAY—SHOT STARTS ON ASSISTANT DISTRICT ATTORNEY. A WELL-EDUCATED YOUNGISH WESTERNER IN STANDARD CITY CLOTHING EXCEPT FOR A COWBOYISH SLIPKNOT NECKTIE:

ASSISTANT D.A.

. . . Mr. Bryan, I'm an Assistant District Attorney, not a miracle worker!

CAMERA PULLS BACK TO SHOW PAUL SITTING IN VISITOR'S CHAIR IN THE ASSISTANT D.A.'S OFFICE; PAUL CARRIES A FILE OF DOCUMENTS.

PAUL

I'm not asking for miracles, just my rights under the law—(TAKES OUT PAPERS) Here's a sworn deposition from the proprietor of the motel, giving a perfect description of Cappi and his chief assistant and describing certain—sounds—he heard while I was being beaten up. (RATTLES ANOTHER PAPER) Another perfect description of Cappi by the man who picked them up at the little airport there and took them to the motel.

ASSISTANT D.A.

There's nothing I can do unless the Governor of Arizona requests extradition. You know that. And it'll probably never happen, because when the chips are down, your witness won't appear, or they'll suddenly lose their memories. Mr. Bryan, I live in Vegas, and I know what I can get done and what I can't. With Cappi you're licked—he's one of the boys.

PAUL

The boys?

ASSISTANT D.A.

The mob, Mafia, Cosa Nostra, whatever you call it this week. Here in

Vegas, it's headed up by a quiet little fellow named Joey Cana, who's very close to your friend Cappi.

PAUL

Preliminary hearing is scheduled for tomorrow, three P.M. Under Arizona law, you could be present as an observer for the state of Nevada. I'd like to have you there.

ASSISTANT D.A.

I'll be there. (RISES) You know you could die of what you're doing, don't you, Mr. Bryan?

PAUL

(A SMALL SMILE) It happens to all of us. Hadn't you heard?

58 INT. LOUNGE OF HOTEL—NIGHT—SARAH IN HER GLASS CAGE. SHE'S DOING A REAL NUMBER THIS TIME—SINGING INTO A MIKE WHILE DOING HER DANCE—EVEN WHILE SINGING SHE KEEPS HER EYES CLOSED AND/OR COVERED AND MAINTAINS THE SAME REMOTE MANNER, WHICH SEEMS TO BE THE HALLMARK OF A CERTAIN KIND OF MODERN SEPARATENESS IN DISCOTHEQUES.

59 AT A TABLE BELOW—PAUL IS SITTING WATCHING—A MAN WHO COULD ONLY BE MR. SINCLAIR SITS BESIDE HIM—AS HE WATCHES HIS DAUGHTER, HIS EXPRESSION IS DEEPLY HURT, INQUIRING, AND A LITTLE SHOCKED. HE IS IN HIS MIDDLE FIFTIES, A QUICK MAN WITH AN EXPRESSIVE, VULNERABLE FACE.

60 TWO SHOT—PAUL AND SINCLAIR. PAUL PUTS HIS HAND SYMPATHETICALLY ON SINCLAIR'S ARM. SINCLAIR LOOKS AROUND AT THE PEOPLE NEAREST THEM:

61 INT. TWO SHOT—TWO DRESSED-UP COWBOYS—FROM SINCLAIR'S POINT OF VIEW—GAPING UP AT SARAH WITH LOOSE LIBIDINOUS LEERS.

62 INT. LOUNGE—ANOTHER TABLE—NIGHT—A CUSTOMER. THIS GENTLEMAN IS SOMEWHAT ELEGANT, PERHAPS EUROPEAN, LOOKING UP AT SARAH WITH A VERY KNOWING, CYNICAL SNEER: "I KNOW WHAT YOU WANT, BABY, AND I MAY JUST BE PERSUADED TO ACCOMMODATE YOU . . ."

63 FAVORING SINCLAIR. TURNING FROM THIS SURVEY OF THE LOOKERS-AT-HIS-DAUGHTER, NEARLY DOWNED BY EMBARRASSMENT, INJURED PRIDE, PARENTAL CONFUSION—AND SIMPLE UNHAPPINESS.

HE GLANCES AT PAUL.

64 TWO SHOT.

SINCLAIR

You never had any children, did you, Paul?

PAUL SHAKES HIS HEAD.

SINCLAIR

I think I could understand it if she'd been an unhappy child—or a rebellious one—or if my late wife and I had misbehaved or—Paul, Sarah was—a no-problem child, a beloved child . . . (HE BREAKS OFF, HIS EXPRESSION HARDENS) Where is her gangster friend, her "pusher" I believe the word is. . . .

PAUL

He runs the casino here and fronts for the hotel—(HE NODS TOWARD
CAPPI)

65 INT. HOTEL LOUNGE—NIGHT—POINT OF VIEW OF CAPRI—TALKING CHARM-
INGLY AND SOFTLY TO A SQUARE COUPLE WHO ARE GUESTS AT HIS TABLE FOR A
MOMENT—STEVE HOVERS BEHIND THE TABLE.

66 PAUL AND SINCLAIR.

PAUL

I've talked to the Assistant District Attorney here, and gathered some
hearsay. Apparently Cappi has a wife and three children stashed away in
Cleveland—most of these boys do—in places like that—or Phoenix or
Detroit. He found Sarah when she was at low ebb right after her marriage
broke up. He introduced her to the stuff she takes. I can't even find out
what it is he mixes for her—some kind of exotic, expensive combination.
It keeps her tied to Cappi. I think he gets a large kick out of having a rich,
socialite girl friend.

SINCLAIR'S EYES HAVE ROVED TOWARD CAPPI'S TABLE.

SINCLAIR

I wonder how old *his* children are?

PAUL

Three daughters, the eldest seventeen.

SINCLAIR

What would *he* do to someone who took his daughter and—

PAUL

(SHRUGS) He'd do something you won't let yourself do.

SINCLAIR

(SOFTLY) And that's his strength, isn't it? . . .

THEIR EYES GO TOWARD SARAH WHOSE NUMBER IS ENDING.

67 WIDER ANGLE AS SARAH, STILL BLINDED BY LIGHTS AND NARCISSISM, COMES
OUT OF HER CAGE TO GOOD APPLAUSE. AS SHE PASSES A TABLE OF DRUNKEN
MEN ONE MAKES A GRAB FOR HER WHICH SHE SIDESTEPS WITH BORED AND
PRACTICED EASE.

68 CLOSER ON SARAH HEADING TOWARD CAPPI'S TABLE, OBLIVIOUS TO ANYTHING
ELSE—THEN HER EYES WANDER TOWARD PAUL'S TABLE—WIDEN—SHE STOPS
SHORT.

69 SINCLAIR AND PAUL FROM HER POINT OF VIEW. SINCLAIR SLOWLY RISES IN HIS
PLACE, WATCHING HER GRAVELY. PAUL RISES TOO.

70 WIDER ANGLE. SARAH HESITATES, LOOKS TOWARD CAPPI'S TABLE, AND THEN
SLOWLY APPROACHES HER FATHER.

71 AT PAUL'S TABLE—AS SHE REACHES IT.

SARAH

Hello, Daddy.

SINCLAIR

Hello, Sarah. I—enjoyed your—performance. . . .

PAUL

Sit down.

HE HOLDS CHAIR FOR HER; SHE SITS A TRIFLE UNWILLINGLY.

SARAH

(TO HER FATHER) Thank you.

SINCLAIR

(A SOMEWHAT GRIM SMILE)—It's not exactly what we had in mind when
we gave you all those ballet lessons.

SARAH

I don't think an entrechat would be very safe in that cage.

SINCLAIR

You—look fine.

SARAH

(TO PAUL) You've told him everything. All the seamy details.

PAUL

Everything.

SARAH

(DRILY) Thanks. (TO HER FATHER) Sure I look fine. One thing about
being an addict, I never catch cold any more. Remember how many colds
I used to have?

SINCLAIR

(EXPLODING) My God, Sarah, how can you sit there and talk about being
an addict!—

PAUL PUTS A RESTRAINING HAND ON SINCLAIR'S ARM—

SARAH

Would you prefer to talk about the weather?

SINCLAIR

You're coming home with me right now . . . You can even come in that
thing you're wearing if you want!

SARAH

Can I? That's very kind of you.

PAUL

Sarah, he wants to help you.

SARAH

I'm over twenty-one, I've found a marvelous life—who wants help? I think
you need help, both of you. (SHE RISES) Why don't you both try a pop.
I'll see if I can hustle a fix for both of you. (LAUGHS) You'd be kind of
cute turned on, Paul. You, too, Dad!

SINCLAIR

(ANGRY) You make "Dad" sound like a dirty word!

SARAH

Yes, I do.

SINCLAIR IS HURT, DISMAYED, AWARE THAT HE SHOULD NOT HAVE REACTED.

SINCLAIR

Sarah—I'm sorry I raised my voice to you. I apologize. You're my daughter and you're ill. Please let me help you.

SARAH

You still don't get it. I'm not ill. I'm fine. Fine.

SINCLAIR

No one's "fine" who needs—

SARAH

That's the way it is, and I'm too strung out to change. Daddy, I'm way in. You're way out. (SHE STARTS OFF TOWARD CAPPI'S TABLE; PAUSES) Would you like to meet Cappi?

SINCLAIR

I think I'll spare myself that, if you don't mind.

SARAH

Beneath you?

SINCLAIR

If you ever change your mind—and want me—just pick up a telephone.

SARAH

Thanks. Enjoy your stay in Vegas. It's a real fun town.

SHE STRIDES OFF TOWARD CAPPI'S BANQUETTE. WE STAY ON PAUL AND SINCLAIR AS THEY RESUME THEIR SEATS. THEIR EYES MEET.

SINCLAIR

I did everything wrong, didn't I?

PAUL

I doubt if there's much about this situation in Dr. Spock's book.

SINCLAIR SHOOTS HIM A GRATEFUL GLANCE.

SINCLAIR

Thanks.

72 OMITTED.

73 INT. HEARING ROOM—DAY—FULL SHOT. THE HEARING OFFICER IS BEHIND DESK IN STREET CLOTHES; PRESENT ARE PAUL, SINCLAIR, THE ASSISTANT D.A. WE MET IN LAS VEGAS, AND ANOTHER OFFICIAL OR TWO, ON CHAIRS AND COUCH. ALL ARE LOOKING TOWARD THE MOTEL PROPRIETOR WE SAW BEFORE. HE SITS ON STIFF CHAIR IN FRONT OF DESK. PAUL IS STRIDING ACROSS ROOM TOWARD THE MAN, HIS MIEN ANGRY.

74 FAVORING PAUL.

PAUL

But, you described him entirely differently in your affidavit!

75 TWO SHOT—PAUL AND PROPRIETOR. PROPRIETOR LOOKS DOWN AT HIS HANDS
AND SAYS SHEEPISHLY:

PROPRIETOR

Well, that's the way I remember him now.

PAUL

Tall and blond?

PROPRIETOR

Yes, sir, a tall blond man, or maybe reddish hair. I didn't *study* the man.

PAUL

And you didn't hear any sounds of a beating?

PROPRIETOR

I heard some sounds. But I didn't see anything and I can't swear *what* I
heard.

PAUL

Why did you say you did, in the affidavit you swore to?

PROPRIETOR

Well—you was sort of pushing me into it.

PAUL

(TURNING AWAY) I see.

76 WIDER ANGLE. PAUL GESTURES DEFEAT TO THE HEARING OFFICER, WHO SIGHS
AND RUFFLES SOME DOCUMENTS.

HEARING OFFICER

All right, ask the taxi driver to come in, please. . . .

JUMP CUT TO

77 BIG HEAD CLOSEUP—TAXI DRIVER—A COLORED MAN, HIS EXPRESSION UNHAPPY
AS HE SAYS:

TAXI DRIVER

All I can say is I just didn't get a good enough look. I couldn't identify
nobody. I know that much for sure.

CAMERA ZOOMARS IN THROUGH HIS FACE TO:

78 CLOSEUP—ASSISTANT DISTRICT ATTORNEY—HIS EXPRESSION SORROWFUL:

ASSISTANT D.A.

(GENTLY) It's the same old story, Mr. Bryan—we're used to it. Money
and power correctly applied—to produce fear, or greed, or both—I'm
afraid they can make the law look pretty sick.

79 CLOSEUP—PAUL. DEFEATED AND ANGRY; WIPES HIS JAW WITH HIS HAND
WHICH STILL HAS A BANDAGE ON IT (A STILL SMALLER BANDAGE—THIS IS THE
LAST BANDAGE OF A DIMINISHING SERIES).

PAUL

I'm sorry I wasted everybody's time. Very very sorry.

HE RISES INTO CAMERA.

80 INT. HOTEL LOUNGE—NIGHT—MED. SHOT OF SARAH IN HER GLASS CAGE. A QUICK CUT FROM A LOW, TILTED ANGLE—AS SHE DANCES. . . .

81 CLOSEUP—SINCLAIR. PRESUMABLY AT THE BAR IN THE LOUNGE, BUT SHOT SO CLOSE AS TO BE PLACELESS EXCEPT FOR THE MUSIC WHICH TIES IT INTO ABOVE SHOT; HE IS LOOKING UPWARD AND OFF AT HIS DAUGHTER, HIS EXPRESSION SAD AND LOST AND DEFEATED.

82 EXT. SPECIAL EFFECT SHOT OF A JET POD OF A JET AIRLINER—NIGHT—CLOSE SHOT—STOCK. ENGINE BEING STARTED WITH A ROAR OF SOUND.

83 EXT. PASSENGER WALKWAY AT LAS VEGAS AIRPORT—NIGHT—TRUCKING WITH SINCLAIR. WE SEE SINCLAIR AND SOME OTHER PASSENGERS MOVING TOWARD PLANE GATE . . . SIGNS IN B.G. ABOUT "TO PLANES—PASSENGERS ONLY" AND WE HEAR P.A. ANNOUNCING A DEPARTURE TO RENO AND SAN FRANCISCO. SINCLAIR CARRIES AN ATTACHE CASE AND A HAT; HIS WALK IS HEAVY AND DEFEATED . . . HE PASSES A SLOT MACHINE WITH A SIGN SAYING: "LEAVING LAS VEGAS—FUN IN THE SUN—COME BACK, PARDNER." SINCLAIR GRIMACES HIS DISTASTE; HE PAUSES—BECOMES CONSCIOUS OF THE P.A. SYSTEM:

P.A.

(FILTER) Mr. Dwight W. Sinclair is wanted at the information counter— Mr. Dwight W. Sinclair, San Francisco passenger, please go to information counter.

SINCLAIR HAS REACHED AIRLINE OFFICIAL TAKING TICKETS—HESITATES— STARTS TO RETREAT:

AIRLINE OFFICIAL

The plane will be taking off right away, sir. . . .

SINCLAIR

When's the next flight?

AIRPORT OFFICIAL

Not until tomorrow morning.

P.A.

Mr. Dwight W. Sinclair—information counter, please. . . .

HE IS IN SOME DOUBT WHAT TO DO—PAUL RUNS INTO SHOT: HE IS A BIT DISHEVELED, VERY KEYED UP WITH ENTHUSIASM:

PAUL

Dwight!—

SINCLAIR

Was that you paging me, Paul?

84 TWO SHOT.

PAUL

Yes. Remember what that Assistant D.A. said, "money and power correctly applied . . ." He said they could make the law look pretty sick?

SINCLAIR

Unfortunately, it's true.

PAUL

You have money and power, and there's no reason we can't find a way to "correctly apply" it.

AIRPORT OFFICIAL

Boarding, sir.

SINCLAIR

I'll be right there. (TO PAUL) She's a grown-up, she made that clear, she seems to have the life she wants.

PAUL

Dwight, you know that isn't true. You know that was the drug talking.

SINCLAIR

(RESEARCH, CHECK) There are something like a million and a half people in jail in the world right now, for real crimes. All those people have parents, many of whom aren't guilty of anything; I don't think I'm guilty of anything. I will not punish myself for her crimes.

AIRLINE OFFICIAL

This is the last call, sir, it really is.

SINCLAIR

I'm coming. Thanks, Paul—thanks very much, but good-bye.

85 FAVORING PAUL STANDING FIRM, ANGRY, UNWILLING TO ACCEPT DEFEAT.

86 WIDER ANGLE AS SINCLAIR STARTS FOR THE GATE; SINCLAIR PAUSES TO ADD:

SINCLAIR

If she ever wants help I'll help her, but I'm not going to go on my knees to her!

PAUL

(QUIETLY) Suppose your wife were still alive. Mothers don't mind kneeling so much.

SINCLAIR WINCES—PAUSES—TURNS. HE COMES BACK TOWARD PAUL AND THEY START BACK AWAY FROM THE BOARDING AREA.

87 INT. ANOTHER GAMBLING CASINO—NIGHT—WIDE PANNING SHOT (STOCK). STYLE OF DECOR IS NOTICEABLY DIFFERENT THAN IN CAPPI'S HOTEL; MUCH PLAY GOING ON—MONEY AND HIGH LIFE . . . AN ORCHESTRA, EITHER SEEN OR UNSEEN, PLAYS AN IDENTIFIABLE TUNE WHICH REMAINS UNDER NEXT SHOT.

88 INT. A PLUSH CORRIDOR JUST OFF THE CASINO—NIGHT—PAUL AND SINCLAIR.

THEY ARE WALKING SIDE BY SIDE, HAVE CHANGED TO MORE DRESSY CLOTHES
THAN WHEN WE LAST SAW THEM AT THE AIRPORT; THEY APPROACH AN IMPRES-
SIVE PAIR OF DOUBLE DOORS—TRY THE DOORS—THEY ARE LOCKED . . . THEY
LOOK AT EACH OTHER IN SOME PUZZLEMENT—THEN PAUL SEES SOMETHING
JUST ABOVE—NUDGES SINCLAIR—THEY LOOK UP AND WATCH THE LENS OF A
REMOTELY CONTROLLED CLOSED CIRCUIT TV CAMERA SEARCHING THE COR-
RIDOR BEHIND THEM. . . .

89 FAVORING PAUL AND SINCLAIR.

PAUL

(WHISPERING) We seem to be on closed circuit television.

90 WIDER ANGLE—THE CAMERA LOOKS DOWN AT THEM AGAIN—THERE'S A CLICK
AND THE DOOR OPENS. THEY ENTER.

91 INT. CANA SUITE—NIGHT. IT'S A VERY EXPENSIVELY FURNISHED OUTER OFFICE;
THERE ARE DESKS WITH ELECTRIC TYPEWRITERS, ADDING MACHINES, ETC.—
ALL UNTENDED AT THE MOMENT. DOOR FROM INNER OFFICE OPENS AND MR.
CANA ENTERS. HE IS THIN, HUMORLESS, ABOUT SIXTY-FIVE, NEATLY DRESSED
AS FOR A DAYTIME BOARD MEETING IN CHICAGO, ILLINOIS; HE HAS A SLIGHT
ITALIAN ACCENT MIXED WITH A MIDDLEWESTERN AMERICAN ONE; WEARS
SLIGHTLY TINTED STEEL-FRAMED GLASSES LIKE VITO GENOVESE'S.

PAUL

Mr. Cana?

CANA

That's right. You're the man that telephoned.

PAUL

Paul Bryan, yes. This is Mr. Sinclair.

CANA

You was a senator or something, wasn't you, Mr. Sinclair?

SINCLAIR

Mayor. San Francisco.

CANA

Good steaks in San Francisco.

SINCLAIR

We also pride ourselves on our Italian restaurants.

CANA

I'm a steak man. (HIS GAZE WANDERING TOWARD PAUL) You the one that
said you had something important, Mr. Bryant?

PAUL

Bryan. (HE HOLDS UP HIS HANDS WHICH HAVE SCARS ACROSS THE FINGERS)
Bryan. (SHARPLY) Something very important. We want your help. To
put Carl Cappi behind bars for eight or ten years.

CANA

What's the matter, you lose at the tables, bad loser or something? He runs honest tables.

PAUL

We hear you're sort of his boss.

CANA MAKES A DISGUSTED SOUND WITH HIS LIPS AND CALLS OFF INTO HIS INNER OFFICE.

CANA

Bring me a black coffee. (TO PAUL AND SINCLAIR) I got a lot of work to do tonight, leaving town for a while in the morning. He runs one casino, I run another casino, who's boss, what's this boss talk?

A VERY PRETTY AND VERY YOUNG GIRL IN A THEATRICAL, TIGHT EVENING GOWN COMES OUT OF THE INNER OFFICE CARRYING A STEAMING MUG OF COFFEE.

CANA

All I keep here is coffee, you have anything you want out at the bar. (TO THE GIRL) Call the bar, say anything these gentlemen want. (STARTS TOWARD ANOTHER PAIR OF DOORS, PRESUMABLY LEADING INTO ANOTHER SUITE) Good-bye.

PAUL

I think you'd better listen to us. We may be about to start something that'll put you and your friends out of business.

CANA

(AT DOOR) You so big you're going to change state law? Do you know what percentage of state taxes we pay, the gambling industry? Eighty per cent! (MUTTERS AND EXITS) Put us out of business!

92   FAVORING PAUL. HE GOES TO THE DOUBLE DOORS AND TRIES THEM; THEY'RE LOCKED; HE CALLS THROUGH THEM:

PAUL

We have bigger ideas than trying to change state law. We have much bigger ideas. Did you ever ask yourself how the other forty-nine states feel about open gambling? We're going to ask those states—we're going to form a committee to support an amendment to the federal constitution.

HE LOOKS TOWARD SINCLAIR, WHO SIGNALS THAT PAUL HAS SAID IT VERY WELL PAUL LOOKS AT THE GIRL, WHO SMILES EMPTILY.

GIRL

(INDICATES DOOR TO CORRIDOR) Ask for Florence, she's a cute blonde, or Harriet, she's a brunette but she's got a gassy figure.

PAUL LOOKS AT THE DOUBLE DOORS AGAIN.

PAUL

Mr. Cana? Did you hear me, did you understand me?

SINCLAIR

We'll send him a telegram.

PAUL STARTS TO TURN AWAY, RELUCTANTLY, WHEN THE DOUBLE DOORS SUDDENLY OPEN. CANA IS THERE.

CANA

(BY ROTE) "Thirty-five thousand people in this state earn their living out of gambling or related."

SINCLAIR

We have a feeling that about two hundred million other Americans are suspicious of open gambling; some of us—Mr. J. Edgar Hoover, to name one—think that it makes a window through which a lot of very unsavory people get illegal money into legal circulation; a sort of hole in the wood-work through which a lot of unpleasant, rather slimy things creep.

PAUL

Forty-nine states have outlawed your kind of gambling, Mr. Cana. They don't like it. Do those sound like good odds to you? Forty-nine to one? In fact, it only takes you thirty-eight states to pass an amendment.

CANA

You guys are crazy—outa your skulls!

PAUL

Mr. Sinclair has decided to make all his personal resources—which come to over a hundred million dollars—available to set up a committee for an amendment to the Constitution of the United States. The last amend-ment, the twenty-fourth, was ratified by thirty-eight states in less than a year and a half. The twenty-fifth just might get passed in even less time. Forty-nine to one. Those aren't your kind of odds, Mr. Cana.

SINCLAIR

And I can assure you that many of my friends will come in, too. Several are quite—solvent and even *more* influential.

CANA

(TO GIRL, MILDLY, ABOUT COFFEE) I thought I told you I don't like it this hot.

HE HANDS MUG BACK TO HER AND THROUGH FOLLOWING SHE SITS SOLEMNLY BLOWING ON HIS COFFEE FOR HIM.

CANA

The American people *like* to gamble. They come up here, they gamble, they see a few topless showgirls, they swim and sit in the sun, why do you want to make trouble?

GIRL

(SUDDENLY) Gambling built this town.

SINCLAIR

I don't think the hotels or golf courses or the sunshine would disappear—(TURNS TO CANA AGAIN) Your man Cappi supplies my daughter with narcotics. I want that stopped. I want him stopped.

PAUL

Another small point—he had me beaten up. I want him sent to jail the way any other citizen who did that to me would be sent to jail.

CANA

You think I'm a jury or something?

PAUL

I think if you say the word, witnesses will recover their memories and a jury will send Cappi to prison.

CANA SHOOTS A SHARP LOOK AT PAUL, TRIES THE COFFEE, FINDS IT STILL TOO HOT, HANDS IT BACK TO HER, AND SHE BLOWS HARDER.

CANA

You fellas been reading do-gooder propaganda. There ain't nothing I can do for you. In fact, there ain't nothing I'd do for you even if I could. (NODS) That's the way you come in. Use it.

PAUL AND SINCLAIR TURN AND START OUT.

PAUL

You could use just a little more imagination, Mr. Cana. Nothing lasts forever.

SINCLAIR RAISES HIS HAND IN A KIND OF GOOD-BYE, BUT DOESN'T LOOK BACK. THEY CLOSE THE DOOR BEHIND THEM. CANA TAKES THE COFFEE MUG FROM THE GIRL AND SIPS IT.

CANA

(MILDLY) Now that's just right.

93 & 94 OMITTED

95 INT. CORRIDOR—PAUL AND SINCLAIR AS THEY WALK AWAY FROM MR. CANA'S SUITE, THEIR MANNER DISPIRITED.

PAUL

He didn't even nibble at the bait. I'm sorry.

SINCLAIR

It was worth a try; I'm glad we tried. Let's get the early plane in the morning.

PAUL

I have one chore I have to take care of.

SINCLAIR

What?

PAUL

I found where my friend Steve—Cappi's strong-arm boy—parks his car. I want to say good-bye to him.

SINCLAIR

Paul, that's not your style.

PAUL

No. It's *their* style—and they showed me how it goes, twice. (PAUSES
AND HOLDS OUT HIS HAND) Dwight—sorry about tonight. I'll see you on
the plane in the morning.

SINCLAIR

Would you mind very much if I went along with you?

THEY EXIT TOGETHER.

96 EXT. PARKING LOT—NIGHT—STEVE'S CAR. THE SAME PARKING LOT WE SAW
PAUL IN EARLIER; MOONLIGHT IS REFLECTING FROM THE ROOF OF ONE
RATHER HANDSOME CAR PARKED ALONE ON THE LOT HERE. . . .

97 EXT. BESIDE HEDGE NEARBY—NIGHT—PAUL AND SINCLAIR SITTING ON A ROCK
BESIDE HEDGE. SINCLAIR IS SUCKING ON A PIECE OF LONG GRASS.

SINCLAIR

I haven't tasted fresh long grass since I was a kid.

PAUL

Be careful—up here it's probably loco weed or something.

SINCLAIR LAUGHS AND HANDS PAUL A PIECE.

SINCLAIR

As they say in Vegas, everybody's hooked on something—join me.

PAUL

Dwight—you can really walk away from Sarah like this? Leave her alone
in this—place?

SINCLAIR WINCES, WAGS HIS HEAD.

SINCLAIR

She married a nothing—I warned her he was nothing—she knew I was
right—now she can't admit failure. Maybe she's as stubborn as I am.
Paul, she was an only daughter. Maybe I brought her up too much as a
son. Sometimes I think she wanted to be me—I'm—an irritation to her
—a goad—in some way I'm the worst thing for her. I'm all she has—
and I'm the worst thing for her. If cutting off an arm would help her—but
it wouldn't. I'm all she has and I'm the worst thing for her. That's why
I have to leave.

PAUL

(GENTLY) It's easy to be an expert when you don't have children.

SINCLAIR

Have some, Paul—more than one.

PAUL

Not this trip.

HE BREAKS OFF—SIGNALING FOR SILENCE. WE HEAR ONE PAIR OF FOOTSTEPS
. . . PAUL PEERS OFF AROUND EDGE OF BUSH.

98 EXT. AT STEVE'S CAR—NIGHT—STEVE—AS STEVE STRIDES UP TO IT, YAWNING,
    UNFASTENING HIS BOW TIE AS HE WALKS. PAUL COMES UP BEHIND HIM.
    STEVE HEARS AND SPINS AROUND. PAUL HITS HIM A HARD RIGHT TO THE JAW
    . . . ONE TO THE STOMACH—ANOTHER TO THE JAW. STEVE GRUNTS, STARTS
    TO CRUMPLE, PRODUCES HIS GUN . . . PAUL KNOCKS THE GUN OUT OF HIS
    HAND AND HITS STEVE AGAIN; STEVE SINKS DOWN AGAINST HIS EXPENSIVE CAR.

                              PAUL
    (LOOKS AT HIM, PRETENDS TO GASP) Oh, I'm sorry, I thought you were
    Albert Smith from Yonkers, New York.

    HE TURNS ON HIS HEEL AND STRIDES AWAY, RUBBING HIS FIST, BUT HAPPY, AS
    HE WALKS OFF.

                              PAUL
    And so we say farewell to the City of Churches and Schools.

99 INT. SINCLAIR'S HOTEL ROOM IN LAS VEGAS—DAY—SHOT STARTS ON SUITCASE
    SUITCASE IS MONOGRAMMED "D.W.S."—SINCLAIR'S HANDS ARE CLOSING IT
    . . . PULL BACK. WE SEE THAT HE IS JUST FINISHING PACKING. PAUL, FULLY
    DRESSED TO TRAVEL—HIS SUITCASE BESIDE THE DOOR TO CORRIDOR, WHICH
    IS OPEN—IS SPEAKING INTO TELEPHONE:

                              PAUL
    . . . that's right. To take us to the airport, tell him. (HANGS UP, SAYS
    CONVERSATIONALLY) Taxi's on its way.

    ASSISTANT DISTRICT ATTORNEY APPEARS IN DOORWAY. WITH HIM IS A DEPUTY
    WHO WEARS WESTERN HAT.

                          ASSISTANT D.A.
    You won't need a taxi, the Assistant District Attorney will transport you
    personally. It's a service we only give to honored guests—and you two
    are kings. Emperors—
                            SINCLAIR
    What?

    ASSISTANT D.A. GRINS AT DEPUTY.

                          ASSISTANT D.A.
    (FULL OF WONDERMENT) The impossible has happened—Paul's wit-
    nesses in Arizona have gotten their memories back, both of them! And
    those people here who swore Cappi was with them that day—they've
    decided he wasn't. How did you do it?

                              PAUL
    Simple. Joey Cana has one higher loyalty than his friendship with Cappi
    . . . affection for his pocketbook—or the *mob's* pocketbook. That's the
    one we appealed to.

    PAUL AND SINCLAIR SHARE LOOKS OF TRIUMPH. SINCLAIR HOLDS OUT HIS HAND
    TO PAUL.

SINCLAIR

(SHAKES PAUL'S HAND) I wish you'd been my campaign manager, I'd have won a third term.

DEPUTY

What's more, Mr. Bryan, one of the monkeys who beat you up has volunteered to turn state's evidence.

ASSISTANT D.A.

Volunteered! Do you understand the novelty of that word in these circumstances?

DEPUTY

I hear Carl Cappi is tearing mad.

THE YOUNG BELLBOY WE MET IN OPENING—NOW WEARING A CIVILIAN SPORT SHIRT ABOVE UNIFORM SHOES AND TROUSERS—APPEARS IN CORRIDOR AND RAPS ON DOORJAMB.

BELLBOY

Mr. Sinclair, could I see you a minute, sir?

SINCLAIR

Yes? What is it?

BELLBOY

(NERVOUSLY, IN A LOWERED VOICE) It's about your daughter, sir. . . .

SINCLAIR MOVES SWIFTLY TOWARD THE DOOR.

SINCLAIR

(TO ASSISTANT D.A. AND DEPUTY) Sit down. I'll be right back.

00 INT. CORRIDOR—DAY—AS SINCLAIR STEPS OUT WITH BELLBOY, WHO LEADS HIM DOWN THE HALL TO SARAH, WHO WEARS SOMETHING PRETTY DOMESTIC AND A PAIR OF LARGE SUN GLASSES.

SARAH

Hello, Daddy.

SINCLAIR

Are you all right?

SARAH

No, I'm not. I'll need a fix in an hour and I don't know where it's going to come from. I'm not all right at all, if I don't have a fix pretty soon, I'm going to crash.

BELLBOY

She's climbing the walls already. Mr. Cappi won't talk to her or anything. He's awful mad. (INCREDULOUSLY) Is it true he might be put in jail?

SINCLAIR

Yes, it's true.

BELLBOY MAKES A GESTURE OF HIS INCREDULITY.

SARAH

You said to come to you if I needed help. Well—I need help.

SINCLAIR

(TO BELLBOY, REACHING INTO HIS POCKET) Thanks very much. . . .

BELLBOY

No, no. (AWKWARDLY TO SARAH) I'll be around.

SARAH

Thanks, Sammy.

HE WAVES AND EXITS; SARAH TURNS TO HER FATHER AND SAYS QUIETLY—THE ONE THOUGHT IN HER MIND:

SARAH

My teeth are beginning to chatter already, I know it hasn't started yet, I mean I know I'm being previous and silly, but it's coming and it'll be a beaut, please get started. I haven't any money and I'm going to be pretty shook up before very long. I'll give you the names of everybody I know who might have connections of their own.

SINCLAIR

(CALLING) Paul! (TO SARAH) Sarah, I'm going to help you—but not that way.

SARAH

What? What did you say?

SINCLAIR

You're going into a hospital.

SARAH SEES PAUL COMING, TURNS, AND STRIDES AWAY FROM THEM, ANGRY AND NERVOUS; SHE MAKES A GRIN OF PAIN AS SHE WALKS. . . .

PAUL'S VOICE

(SHARPLY) Sarah!

SHE PAUSES—PAUL AND SINCLAIR ARE COMING HASTILY TOWARD HER.

100-A WIDER ANGLE—THREE SHOT.

PAUL

Sarah—take what your father's offering.

SARAH

A bed in a hospital?

PAUL

You don't have any choice! After what's happened to Cappi, do you think anyone here will help you? They won't go near you! Your father's way, at least you'll get some medication to help you through withdrawal.

SARAH

Then what? After—withdrawal?

SINCLAIR

Then we'll see, we'll try to—reach each other, Sarah—try to. . .

SARAH STARES AT HIM IN CONFUSED DEFIANCE.

SINCLAIR

(TAKING HER ELBOW) All right. Come along, now.

SARAH

"Come along now" . . . you think you've got me back to being twelve years old again!

SINCLAIR

Somebody has. I don't think it was I.

THE BELLBOY ENTERS WITH SINCLAIR'S LUGGAGE.

SINCLAIR

Sarah . . . ?

A BEAT . . . THEN THEY START DOWN THE CORRIDOR.

101 EXT. IN FRONT OF HOTEL—DAY—FAVORING TAXI DRIVER AS HE WAITS NEXT TO HIS CAB, ONE OF SEVERAL PARKED IN FRONT . . . CAMERA PANS FROM HIM AND HIS CAB TO A CAR PARKED ACROSS THE STREET—HOLDS FOR A MOMENT AND THEN ZOOMARS IN TOWARD THE CAR AS MUSIC HITS.

102 OMITTED

103 INT. PARKED CAR—DAY—CAPPI. CAPPI SITS BEHIND THE WHEEL—HE HOLDS A BROWN PAPER BAG ON THE SEAT BESIDE HIM, HAS HAND ON IT AS WE HAVE SEEN IT REST ON TELEPHONE AT HIS BANQUETTE . . . HE IS STARING OFF TOWARD THE HOTEL, HIS EXPRESSION SHOWING HATRED, PERTURBATION . . . HOW DID JACK RUBY LOOK AS HE ENTERED THE DALLAS POLICE STATION? HE GUNS THE ENGINE EXPERIMENTALLY TO MAKE SURE IT HASN'T STALLED. . . .

104 INT. ENTRANCE HALL TO HOTEL—DAY—PAUL, SINCLAIR, SARAH, ASSISTANT D.A., DEPUTY, AND BELLBOY. AS THE PARTY HEADS TOWARD THE ENTRANCE DOORS—SARAH AND SINCLAIR ARE IN THE LEAD; SINCLAIR IS KEEPING A PROTECTIVE ARM AROUND HER WAIST; A BELLBOY OF THIS HOTEL CARRIES PAUL'S AND SINCLAIR'S SUITCASES. THEY REACH GLASS AREA NEAR MAIN DOOR.

105 INT. CAPPI'S CAR. CAPPI TAKES REVOLVER FROM THE PAPER BAG AND BEGINS TO AIM IT, USING THE INSIDE OF HIS ELBOW AS A REST.

106 EXT. LONG SHOT FROM BEHIND CAPPI TOWARD ENTRANCE DOOR—DAY. WE SEE THE GROUP JUST INSIDE THE MODERN GLASS FRONT—SARAH AND SINCLAIR ARE AT REVOLVING DOOR AND ABOUT TO STEP INTO IT. . . .

107 INT. HOTEL ENTRANCE HALL—DAY—FAVORING SINCLAIR AND SARAH. JUST AS SHE STARTS INTO THE REVOLVING DOOR, SHE STUMBLES; SINCLAIR SUPPORTS HER WITH ONE HAND. THERE IS MUCH PATERNAL TENDERNESS AS HE DOES SO—PAUL COMES UP BESIDE THEM; HE AND SINCLAIR LOOK AT EACH OTHER OVER SARAH'S HEAD . . . A SHARED LOOK OF UNDERSTANDING AND SYMPATHY. . . .

SARAH

(PULLING HERSELF TOGETHER WITH SOME DIFFICULTY) Thanks. Sorry. Okay.

SARAH IN THE LEAD, SINCLAIR FOLLOWING—THEN PAUL, THEN ASSISTANT
D.A., THEN DEPUTY—THEY ALL GO THROUGH THE DOOR. . . .

108 EXT. IN FRONT OF HOTEL—DAY—MED. SHOT THE GROUP—AS THEY COME
DOWN TOWARD DRIVEWAY, STARTING TO SEPARATE INTO TWO GROUPS . . . A
SHOT RINGS OUT—

109 FAVORING PAUL, WHO STOPS SHORT, LOOKING AROUND . . . THE OTHERS
DON'T SEEM TO RECOGNIZE THE SOUND AND CONTINUE ON THEIR WAY . . .
HE LOOKS TOWARD THE DEPUTY, WHO IS JUST COMING OUT, THE LAST TO
COME THROUGH THE REVOLVING DOOR.

110 FAVORING DEPUTY. LIKE PAUL, HE KNOWS THERE HAS BEEN A SHOT BUT HASN'T
YET APPLIED THE KNOWLEDGE TO HIS OWN GROUP—THEN THERE IS ANOTHER
SHOT HEARD—THIS TIME HE DOES UNDERSTAND THAT THE SHOOTING IS VERY
CLOSE . . . HE PRODUCES HIS OWN GUN AS HE HURRIES OUT. . . .

111 EXT. IN FRONT OF HOTEL—DAY—PAUL. ANOTHER SHOT RINGS OUT: WE HEAR
RICOCHET SOUND VERY CLOSE. . . .

PAUL

Get *down*—

HE STARTS TO RUN FORWARD, CROUCHING. . . .

112 WIDER ANGLE. THE OTHERS HAVE PAUSED; ASSISTANT D.A. IS RUNNING TOWARD
SARAH AND SINCLAIR, WHO ARE STARTING TO GET DOWN NEAR SOME SHRUBS
BESIDE WALK . . . THE DEPUTY IS RUNNING FORWARD, GUN RAISED . . .
ANOTHER SHOT IS HEARD. . . .

DEPUTY

Hit the ground!

113 INT. CAPPI'S CAR—DAY—CAPPI. CAPPI IS TAKING CAREFUL AIM. . . .

114 EXT. IN FRONT OF HOTEL—DAY—THE GROUP—LONG SHOT. ALL HAVE HIT
THE DECK EXCEPTING ONLY DEPUTY, WHO IS AIMING CAREFULLY TOWARD
THE CAR IN THE APPROVED FBI MANNER . . . SHOT RINGS OUT . . . DEPUTY
SPINS AND FALLS. . . .

115 FAVORING PAUL—DEPUTY IN B.G.—AS DEPUTY FALLS, OUT OF COMBAT . . .
PAUL RUNS CROUCHINGLY TOWARD THE GUN . . . ANOTHER SHOT IS HEARD
. . . PAUL LEAPS ONTO THE GUN AND ROLLS INTO THE BUSHES BESIDE THE
WALKWAY THERE. . . .

116 PAUL AMONG THE BUSHES. ONE MORE SHOT IS HEARD, AND PAUL LIFTS HEAD,
QUICKLY AIMS, FIRES. CAPPI RETURNS THE FIRE AND PAUL FIRES AGAIN.

117 LONG SHOT TOWARD CAR. CAPPI HAS BEEN HIT. PAUL AND ASSISTANT D.A.
RUN FORWARD.

118 AT CAR. THEY LOOK INTO CAR.

119 INT. CAPPI'S CAR—DAY—CAPPI. HE IS DEAD.

120 PAUL AND DEPUTY AND ASSISTANT D.A.

SINCLAIR'S VOICE

Paul! Paul!

THEY TURN.

121 FAVORING SINCLAIR. HE IS STANDING OVER SARAH—

SINCLAIR

(TURNING TO CALL INSIDE) Somebody get a doctor! Call an ambulance . . . !

122 PAUL ET AL. RUNNING TOWARD SINCLAIR. THE DEPUTY GETS TO HIS FEET, APPARENTLY NOT BADLY WOUNDED.

123 SINCLAIR.

SINCLAIR

She's been hit. I thought he was aiming at me, but—it was Sarah.

THE OTHERS START TOWARD SINCLAIR AND SARAH.

124 FAVORING SARAH. HER SUN GLASSES, BROKEN, LIE BESIDE HER; SHE IS MOVING A LITTLE IN PAIN. SINCLAIR KNEELS BESIDE HER. . . .

SINCLAIR

A doctor's coming, honey, it'll only be a minute, we're only a minute away from that big new hospital . . .

PAUL ENTERS SHOT; KNEELS TOO . . .

SARAH HAS CLOSED HER EYES. SINCLAIR TRIES TO FIND HER PULSE. HE PUTS HIS HEAD NEXT TO HER BREAST, LISTENING FOR HEART BEAT . . . THE ASSISTANT D.A. KNEELS BESIDE HER, TOO. SINCLAIR LIFTS HIS HEAD, A STRICKEN EXPRESSION ON HIS FACE.

ASSISTANT D.A.

(FEELING NO HEARTBEAT) She's dead. I'm sorry, Mr. Sinclair. She was a fine—(HE BREAKS OFF; FINISHES LAMELY)—a fine girl.

SINCLAIR RISES AND CAMERA RISES WITH HIM. PAUL RISES INTO SHOT, TOO. IN THE DISTANCE, A SIREN SOUNDS.

SINCLAIR

(LOOKS TOWARD SOUND) You didn't get your felony conviction—and I didn't save my daughter's life. We both failed. And that old—Mafia—goat—Mr. Cana—he's still running his private show.

PAUL

Maybe.

SINCLAIR

Maybe?

PAUL

Maybe that committee is a better idea than we thought it was. Maybe it's as reasonable a proposition as we made it sound. Joey Cana thought so.

SINCLAIR

Maybe it is . . . (HE LOOKS DOWN AT HIS DAUGHTER'S BODY OUT OF FRAME BELOW . . . HIS EXPRESSION SOFTENS; HE BEGINS TO SQUAT DOWN) Maybe it is. . . .

HE DISAPPEARS BELOW FRAME LINE; PAUL AND ASSISTANT D.A., THEIR EXPRESSIONS GRAVE, LOOK DOWN AT HIM AS MUSIC HITS AND WE:

WHIP PAN TO

125 CLOSE SHOT—RANK OF SLOT MACHINES. THE WHEELS ARE SPINNING. OVER THIS, SUPER:

126 MED. SHOT—LOOKING DOWN AT SARAH. THIS SUPERIMPOSED SHOT FLASHES ON AND OFF IN A STACCATO RHYTHM LIKE THE NEON SIGN IN OPENING SHOT OF SHOW.

FADE OUT

THE END

11

TWILIGHT ZONE

Rod Serling very early in the *Twilight Zone* series perfected an original and shivery opening. It was (and is) a fine signature that establishes the show at once. It is filled with foreboding and loneliness, strongly setting the mood for the stories he tells, which involve suggestive fragments of mystification, invisible evil hidden in visible beauty, unusual odysseys by unusual men arriving at unexpected non-destinations. Metempsychosis, *déjà vu* run clear to a finish, precognition left in midair.

His stories mix the juices of the science fiction theater with those of the preter-natural and the supernatural. He is at home in the chemistry of all three.

His characters have outline only but need no more than this. They are used pretty much as message carriers for his ideas, as pushcarts to carry the furniture of his stories. The quality of their individual character almost never has anything decisive to do with the manipulation of the story. The stories overwhelm the characters.

At the same time he gives his characters an edge or a basic quality, something immediately seen and immediately familiar. He not only doesn't want his characters to influence his story. He doesn't even want them to get in the way of it. So they are all one-dimensional. And that is what they should be. This is something almost universally observed in television's long parade of westerns. Right away you know who you're supposed to like. And hate. In *Twilight Zone* Rod Serling is quite right to keep his people this bold, this stark. Everyone has a punch card sticking out of his shirt front. Dickens did the same.

Serling's language or talk is undifferentiated between one character and another. Lines could be swapped and interchanged. The point is simple: the thing has got to be *said,* and for the progress of the story it often matters little who does the saying of it. His language is everywhere lean. No nifty words. Just plain Anglo-Saxon two-syllable stuff that gets things said quickly and clearly.

Serling is going for instant and universal comprehension. And he gets it. You never come away from his theater wondering what you saw.

351

He repeats words occasionally, as you'll notice. In this play "aimless" and "nondescript" stand out. But it's deliberate. It's a form of underlining. Theodore Dreiser used the same technique. Rod Serling wants to be sure you get the picture *exactly* before he starts to move anything around. He wants to get you in the mood, and this is his atomizer to spray you into acceptance.

He has other bench marks. His contrasts are abrupt and startling. What does he really want to accomplish in *Twilight Zone?* Pure entertainment. He wants to startle, to awaken, to stun, to excite, to shake, to frighten, to impale. To edify? Almost never. Mostly he wants to stretch your mind by forcing it to go with the shape of his imagination. He wants to see your mouth hang open in a transfixion of wonder, surprise, or terror. He wants you to receive a shock of some sort, one that he has hurled from the darkness of his technique into the quick of your feelings. You never saw it coming. It is just suddenly there. Right in front of you. He wants to see you hold back a scream. Time after time you will find it is Rod Serling's adroit employment of contrast that has managed this.

To see this device at work, look at Shot 7. From his loneliness and his near surrender to despair, we see Corry asleep. Then, wham! You, the viewer, are quite as excited as Corry is. Motion and sound have broken in on the stillness, both bound tightly in the hold of surprise. It is *sudden.* That is the thing.

And that is the way with most of Rod Serling's contrasts, with his scene endings, his time and temperature changes. If he were conducting an orchestra, you would be able to hear his stick whistle when it came down for a quick cutoff.

Is the dialogue artificial? Much of it. Much of it is awkward besides. One actor will turn unnaturally to another and say something quite unlikely (actually, of course, he is saying it to *us*). Something that is mechanically out of place, out of place logically and very often emotionally too. For example, see Carstairs's lines in Shot 9. But we need the information and we need it now. So we get it now.

In the same shot, note the direction, "Corry wets his lips and tries to keep the supplication out of his voice." Think how valuable that line is to the actor playing Corry, how much it tells him of how to do and what to feel. And how much it tells the director, too. We know, just from the reading, the precise voice timbre Serling wants to get out of Corry. We know the taut look he wants Corry's face to assume.

Our visitors have only fifteen minutes. And they have bad news. But are we oriented yet? Where does the viewer, by this time, think he is? In terms of geography where does he think he is? Who are the characters Adams and Carstairs? Spacemen or prison guards? They are both, and they work grandly, almost ostentatiously, at their impersonalism. But do we know where we are? Does the script reader know more than the viewer at this point? Or is it the other way round? No. We don't know how our visitors got here beyond a "sound of engines." Have we been clued in on anything? No. The camera has never looked at the spaceship. The beat-up vintage car seems to have fulfilled its purpose as a pure sign we must be earthbound. Has to be.

Presently we get another Serling surprise (and he has really staged the line). After its careful buildup with phrases like "this kind of punishment," "unnecessarily cruel," the payoff line hits hard: "They may . . . imprison you on earth like the old days."

So we aren't on earth at all.

Corry's reaction to Adams's barbs is fairly standard. It probably surprised few viewers, though it surely surprised Adams. We felt like slugging him ourselves and felt good when somebody else did it for us (an item in the "violence" controversy that should be given equal time!). Adams is given a good reason to remain sour during the rest of the scene. This is routine. But look at the preparation we have for the next surprise, the box. It's contraband of some kind. It was smuggled aboard the spaceship. It's illegal. Allenby's own colleagues, though they have hefted it, don't know what's in it. What is so special about it that the contents can't be revealed till the ship is out of sight? It can't even be discussed. Obviously something unique has entered the picture, or is about to enter. We've *got* to know what's in that box.

And presently we do. But not at all in the way you or I would write it. In the way only Serling would.

We never do see this packaged IBM-RCA-Bell Lab doll in her box. The girl is already making herself at home in Corry's shack. And no one, not one person in the whole United States, tuned out at the end of Act I. Think how rapidly this pushed forward the story.

Serling has resisted another temptation in the interest of expediting his story. He has bypassed most of the getting-to-know-you routine. Most writers would bring it in for sure. And many would luxuriate in it. But there is no need, even though he is telling a love story. Serling skips it. We pick up with Alicia at a time when we can face fundamentals right away. *Is* she a woman? Corry's terrible need of companionship has underscored the entire play. Surely such a treasure (and a girl besides!) can't be allowed to turn out a counterfeit. Corry just couldn't take that. So he won't. He just won't. He tells her she's flesh and blood. She says she's plastic. He says she has tissue. She says she's a machine.

Well, if she is a machine, she's been damn well programmed, wouldn't you say? And by a most feeling computer-feeder. She can gather firewood and she can cook. Other skills, of course, come to mind.

Corry's falling in love is real and touching. It never gets mucky. (No need, and with four commercials no time either.) The diary device is not "device-y." It was established earlier and well used.

The machine-made human companionship of Alicia has made up for the appalling skimpiness of his life on this bare asteroid. It has done much more than that. Corry has found love. The desert blooms. For four years he's had nothing but a bent jalopy. Now he has Alicia. He wants nothing more.

What a fine irony we are wrung with now! He can't take her back to earth.

(In passing, note the near mislaying of Carstairs. I believe he has only one line in Act II. But this is not a serious mistake.)

The shattering of Alicia's face by Allenby's bullet was as convincing an illusion as I ever saw in television. Her face cracked like a smashed clock. Coils of wire sprang from her eye socket. From the open mouth—serene and half-smiling—

came forth a gout of circuitry. The chest opened. Tubes, wires, relay terminals. Strange musical sounds came from inside her as she disintegrated, with one system after another coming apart.

This story is Rod Serling at his *Twilight* best. What a neat idea! Prisoners sentenced to life are transported to satellites. A very special kind of solitary.

Turning to a matter of production now, think how the cost of this production was kept down by never showing the spaceship. There was no mock-up of it on the ground. We saw a section only. And it was carpentry, not hardware. I have mentioned these habits of economy in other chapters: in *Tarzan, The Flying Nun,* and *Get Smart.* Get in this habit yourself. Anyone can ask for opulent sets, but the real pro cuts all the production costs he can think of.

This show had little but the desert, the flivver, and the shack. It was filmed in the Mojave in two and a half days.

THE TWILIGHT ZONE
"The Lonely"
by Rod Serling

ACT I

FADE IN:

1 EXT. SKY NIGHT. SHOT OF THE SKY . . . THE VARIOUS NEBULAE AND PLANET BODIES STAND OUT IN SHARP, SPARKLING RELIEF. AS THE CAMERA BEGINS A SLOW PAN ACROSS THE HEAVENS—

NARRATOR'S VOICE

There is a sixth dimension beyond that which is known to man. It is a dimension as vast as space, and as timeless as infinity. It is the middle ground between light and shadow—and it lies between the pit of man's fears and the sunlight of his knowledge. This is the dimension of imagination. It is an area that might be called the Twilight Zone.

THE CAMERA HAS BEGUN TO PAN DOWN UNTIL IT PASSES THE HORIZON AND IS FLUSH ON THE OPENING SHOT (EACH WEEK THE OPENING SHOT OF THE PLAY).

WE ARE NOW LOOKING AT AN EMPTY PATCH OF DESERT, AN ARID, DULL, NONDESCRIPT PIECE OF LAND, ITS MONOTONY BROKEN ONLY BY OCCASIONAL SCRUBBY, DYING CACTUS, A FEW SAND DUNES THAT SHIFT NERVOUSLY AND SPORADICALLY IN A WIND THAT PROVIDES THE ONLY MOTION AND THE ONLY SOUND TO AN OTHERWISE STAGNANT SCENE. THE CAMERA PANS LEFT VERY SLOWLY UNTIL IT IS ON A—

2 LONG SHOT—A COTTAGE THAT SITS ALONE IN THE DESERT. THIS IS A RAMSHACKLE, TWO-ROOM AFFAIR MADE OF CORRUGATED STEEL, DRIFTWOOD, AND OTHER NONDESCRIPT MATERIAL. ALONGSIDE IS A BEAT-UP, VINTAGE 1930s SEDAN. BEYOND AND BEHIND THIS IS A TINY TOOL SHED THAT HOUSES A SMALL GENERATOR. A LIMP WIRE EXTENDS FROM THE SHED TO THE SHACK.

NARRATOR'S VOICE

(OVER THE PAN) The residence of Mr. James W. Corry; a shack, a shed, and an old sedan. With a front yard made up of sand and scrub that stretches to infinity.

AT THIS POINT WE SEE CORRY COME OUT OF THE HOUSE. HE'S DRESSED IN JEANS AND A THREADBARE SHIRT. HE LOOKS UP TOWARD THE PALE SKY AND THE STRANGE SICK, WHITE GLEAM OF THE SUN, SHADES HIS EYES, WALKS OVER TOWARD THE CAR AND STOPS, LOOKS AT IT, TOUCHES IT WITH HIS HAND, THEN LEANS AGAINST IT AND STARES ONCE AGAIN TOWARD THE HORIZON.

3 MED. CLOSE SHOT ACROSS THE CAR LOOKING AT CORRY. HE'S A MAN IN HIS EARLY FORTIES OF MEDIUM HEIGHT, PERHAPS A LITTLE MORE MUSCULAR THAN MOST MEN. HIS FACE WAS ONCE A STRONG FACE; IT IS NO LONGER. THERE IS NO WILL LEFT AND NO RESOLVE. WHAT WE SEE ON IT NOW IS RESIGNATION; A SENSE OF DULL, PERVADING HOPELESSNESS. HE RATHER AIMLESSLY OPENS THE CAR DOOR AND, LEAVING IT OPEN, SLIDES IN TO SIT IN THE DRIVER'S SEAT AND LOOK OUT THE FRONT WINDSHIELD. THE CAMERA MOVES AROUND SO THAT IT'S SHOOTING THROUGH THE FRONT WINDSHIELD TOWARD HIM.

NARRATOR'S VOICE

There is a ritual even to loneliness. For twice a day Corry will leave his shack, go over to look at the car . . . touch it . . . sit in its front seat, stare out of its windshield, and perhaps succumb to a wishful daydream that he was at the wheel and the car was on a highway and there was someplace to go. (A PAUSE NOW) This would have to be just a wish because where this man is, there are no highways, and there are no places to go, no people to see, no spots to visit. Mr. Corry is all alone . . .

4 CLOSE SHOT—CORRY AS HE GETS OUT OF THE CAR AND STARES ACROSS TOWARD THE HORIZON.

NARRATOR'S VOICE

For the record, let it be known that James W. Corry is a convicted criminal placed in solitary confinement. And it matters little that confinement in this case stretches as far as the eye can see. This is a prison without people; without their talk and their laughter; without sound save the wind. It is an exile far worse than a dungeon at the far end of the earth.

THE CAMERA PANS SLOWLY UP TOWARD THE SKY TO WHERE WE SEE A SHOT OF THE EARTH.

NARRATOR'S VOICE

Because Mr. Corry has been banished to a place beyond the earth!

5 MED. SHOT—CORRY. CORRY, SHOULDERS SLUMPED, IS WALKING IN A KIND OF DRAGGY, AIMLESS SHUFFLE, GOES BACK TOWARD THE SHACK AND WALKS INSIDE.

CUT TO:

6 INT. SHACK—FULL SHOT—THE ROOM. THE INSIDE, LIKE THE EXTERIOR, IS MAKESHIFT AND LOOKS TEMPORARY. THE FURNITURE IS MADE OUT OF PACKING CASES. THERE'S AN AGED WIND-UP VICTROLA, AN ICEBOX. THE BED IS DISHEVELED AND DIRTY. HE WALKS OVER TO A SMALL, RICKETY TABLE, TAKES OUT A DOG-EARED LEDGER, OPENS IT, AND RIFLES THROUGH THE PAGES SLOWLY AND RATHER AIMLESSLY. THEN HE TAKES A PENCIL, SITS DOWN, AND STARTS TO WRITE. THE CAMERA MOVES IN VERY SLOWLY AS HE VOICES ALOUD THAT WHICH HE IS WRITING.

CORRY'S VOICE

Entry . . . approximately fifteenth day, sixth month . . . the year, four. (HE SMILES NOW GRIMLY) I'm finding lately that everything is pretty much an approximation. I've been here about four years—that's close enough. When a man is reduced to just sleeping and waking . . . eating and drinking . . . when all that's left is just survival . . . you don't have to have a second hand to document the beginning and the middle and the end of days that are all alike. It's better to be vague about it. It's a service to the mind not to be reminded that your life is made up of a vast silence and each moment is a breaking point that somehow you live through . . . but never really want to.

HE PUTS THE PENCIL IN HIS MOUTH AND STARES STRAIGHT AT THE WALL FOR A LONG MOMENT, THEN HE TURNS IN HIS SEAT TO LOOK OUT THE WINDOW, RISES, CROSSES OVER TO STARE OUT THE WINDOW, THEN RETRACES HIS STEPS BACK TO THE TABLE, LOOKS DOWN AT THE OPEN LEDGER, AND, WHILE STANDING, CONTINUES TO WRITE.

CORRY'S VOICE

That's not the way. Not what I just wrote. You can live with despair without giving in to it and I can't give in to it. I must think of other things. So the mind can remain alive—I have to think of other things. (A PAUSE. NOW HE SITS AS HE WRITES) There'll be a supply ship coming in soon, I think. They're either due or overdue and I hope it's Allenby's ship because he's a decent man and he'll sneak things in for me to read. (HE STOPS WRITING FOR A MOMENT, LOOKS DOWN AT THE LEDGER, THEN CONTINUES TO WRITE) Like he brought in the parts to that antique automobile. I was a year putting that thing together—such as it is. A whole year putting an old car together. (A PAUSE) But thank God for that car and for the hours it used up and the days and the weeks. It's odd but time isn't the only approximation. Everything else is, too. Who I am, what I am, what I believe in. It's all hazy now. It's only the sand that's real and the horizon and the pale sun that doesn't look like a sun at all. That's all that's real anymore. And the loneliness. Oh, God . . . the loneliness.

HE SLOWLY LETS THE PENCIL DROP OUT OF HIS FINGERS, LOOKS DOWN AT THE BOOK. HIS EYES CLOSE, THEN HE SLUMPS FORWARD, BURYING HIS FACE IN HIS ARMS, LEANING AGAINST THE TABLE.

DISSOLVE TO:

7 EXT. SHACK—DAY. THROUGH THE WINDOW WE CAN SEE CORRY SLEEPING, STILL BY THE TABLE. THERE'S THE DISTANT ROARING SOUND OF ENGINES, A FLASH OF LIGHT THAT SHINES AGAINST THE SIDE OF THE SHACK AND ENTERS THE WINDOW. WE SEE CORRY START, AND RISE, AND RACE TO THE DOOR, FLINGING IT OPEN, PEERING OUT OVER THE LANDSCAPE.

CUT TO:

8 EXT. DESERT—LONG SHOT—A GROUP OF THREE MEN DRESSED IN SIMPLE UNIFORMS NOT UNLIKE PILOTS OF TODAY. THE CAMERA STAYS DIRECTLY ON THEM AS THEY APPROACH.

INTO THE FRAME FROM BEHIND THE CAMERA COMES CORRY, WHO IS RACING OUT TO MEET THEM. HIS FINGERS CLENCH AND UNCLENCH AT HIS SIDE. HE TAKES A FEW FAST, STUMBLING STEPS TOWARD THEM, THEN, THINKING BETTER OF IT, STOPS AND THEN, GIVING IN AGAIN, RUNS TOWARD THEM AGAIN.

9 CLOSE SHOT AS THEY SUDDENLY MEET A FEW FEET FROM ONE ANOTHER. THE HEAD OF THE SPACE GROUP STOPS. THIS IS ALLENBY, A MAN IN HIS FIFTIES. HE NODS A LITTLE CURTLY.

ALLENBY

How are you, Corry?

CORRY

All right.

THERE'S A SILENCE NOW. ADAMS, ONE OF THE OTHER TWO SPACEMEN, LOOKS AROUND.

ADAMS

So this is your private world, huh, Corry? You'll forgive an observation . . . but it's a hellhole!

CARSTAIRS

But it makes for simple living, Adams. This is Corry's kingdom and you can make a complete inventory of it by picking up a handful of sand. Because that's it. That's all of it. It's six thousand eight hundred and thirty-three miles north to south, five thousand miles east to west. It has two salt lakes and a scrubby little mountain range a hundred miles due east. It has Corry's shack here and that's it. That's all of it!

THE CAMERA IS ON CORRY'S FACE NOW. HE WETS HIS LIPS. HE WANTS TO SAY SOMETHING WITH DESPERATE URGENCY. ALLENBY SEES THE LOOK, LOOKS AWAY A LITTLE UNCOMFORTABLY FOR A MOMENT.

ALLENBY

We've only got a fifteen-minute layover, Corry.

CORRY WETS HIS LIPS AND TRIES TO KEEP THE SUPPLICATION OUT OF HIS VOICE.

CORRY

Nobody's checking your schedule out here. Why don't we have a game of cards or something?

ALLENBY

(SHAKES HIS HEAD) I'm sorry, Corry, we're on our way home now.

CORRY

So what's a couple of hours? Come on. I've got three bottles of beer I've saved. We can play some cards, tell me what's going on back there—

ALLENBY

(WITH AN EMBARRASSED LOOK AT THE OTHERS) I wish we could, Corry, but like I said—we've only got fifteen minutes—

CORRY

(HIS VOICE RISING AND GETTING SHAKY AS IF LOSING CONTROL) Well . . . well, what's a lousy couple of hours to you? A card game. (HE NODS TOWARD THE OTHERS) How about you guys? You think I'll murder you or something over a bad hand?

ALLENBY

(QUIETLY AND FIRMLY) I'm sorry, Corry. (HE STARTS TO TAKE CORRY'S ARM) Let's go to the shack—

CORRY FLINGS OFF HIS ARM, NOT IN ANGER, BUT IN DESPERATION.

CORRY

All right. Two minutes are gone now. You've got thirteen minutes left. I wouldn't want to foul up your schedule, Allenby. Not for a . . . (HE LOOKS AWAY) Not for a lousy game of cards. Not for a few bottles of crummy beer.

THEN HE LOOKS UP SLOWLY, TURNS TO LOCK EYES WITH ALLENBY. HE SEEMS TO CATCH HIS BREATH FOR A MOMENT.

CORRY

(CONT'D) Allenby . . . what about the pardon?

ADAMS

(SQUINTING UP TOWARD THE SKY, HIS VOICE VERY MATTER-OF-FACT) You're out of luck, Corry. Sentence reads fifty years and they're not even reviewing cases of homicide. You've been here four now. That makes forty-six to go, so get comfortable, dad, huh?

HE LAUGHS UNTIL HIS EYES REACH ALLENBY'S. ALLENBY STARES AT HIM, THEN WETS HIS LIPS AND LOOKS AWAY. ADAMS'S LAUGH DIES OUT.

10 TRACK SHOT AS THE THREE MEN HEAD TOWARD THE SHACK. CORRY'S EYES ARE DOWN, STARING AT THE SAND WHERE HIS FEET MAKE CRUNCHY SOUNDS AS THEY SINK DOWN OVER THE CRUST OF THE TOP LAYER. ALLENBY, ALONGSIDE OF HIM AS THEY WALK, LOOKS AT HIM INTERMITTENTLY.

11 DIFFERENT ANGLE AS THEY REACH A SMALL KNOLL. OVER THEIR SHOULDER WE SEE THE SHACK AND CAR SITTING THERE IN MUTE, UGLY LONELINESS. CORRY STOPS INSTINCTIVELY TO STARE AT THEM.

12 CLOSE TWO SHOT—CORRY AND ALLENBY.

CORRY

It just crossed my mind, Captain. (HE RAISES A FINGER UP SLOWLY TO POINT TOWARD THE SHACK) This is ninety percent of the view I'm gonna have for the next forty-six years. Just what I'm looking at right now. That shack, that miserable car, and all that desert and this is my company for the next forty-six years.

ALLENBY TOUCHES HIS ARM COMPASSIONATELY WITH AN INSTINCTIVE GENTLENESS.

ALLENBY

(QUIETLY) I'm sorry, Corry. Unfortunately we don't make the rules. All we do is deliver your supplies and pass on information. I told you last time there's been a lot of pressure back home about this kind of punishment. There are a whole lot of people who think it is unnecessarily cruel. Well, who knows what the next couple of years will bring? They may change their minds, alter the law, imprison you on earth like the old days.

CORRY

(TURNS TO STARE INTENTLY INTO THE OLDER MAN'S FACE) Allenby, I have to tell you something. Every morning . . . every morning when I get up I tell myself that this is my last day of sanity. I won't be able to live another day of loneliness. Not *another* day, and by noon when I can't keep my fingers still and the inside of my mouth feels like gunpowder and burnt copper and deep inside my gut I've got an ache that won't go away and seems to be crawling all over the inside of my body, prickling at me, tearing little chunks out of me—and then I think I've got to hold out for another day, just another day. (THEN HE TURNS TO STARE AT THE SHACK) But I can't keep doing that day after day for the next forty-six years. I'll lose my mind, Allenby.

ADAMS

You should have thought of that before you killed a man.

CORRY WHIRLS AROUND TO STARE AT HIM. HIS FEATURES CONTORT. THERE'S AN ANIMAL-LIKE GROWL THAT SHOUTS OUT DEEP FROM HIS THROAT AND SUDDENLY, LOSING ALL CONTROL, HE LUNGES AT ADAMS, HITTING HIM TWICE, CRUNCHING, DESPERATE BLOWS THAT SMASH AGAINST ADAMS'S FACE AND PROPEL HIM BACKWARD TO SPRAWL FACE FIRST IN THE SAND. ALLENBY AND THE OTHER OFFICER GRAB CORRY'S ARMS.

ALLENBY

(SHOUTING) Easy, Corry, easy!

GRADUALLY CORRY LETS HIS BODY RELAX, GOING THE ROUTE FROM A TREMBLING, SHAKING AGUE TO A HEAVY, TIRED MOTIONLESSNESS.

13 MED. CLOSE SHOT—ADAMS—AS HE RISES FROM THE SAND, GINGERLY TOUCHES THE BRUISE ON HIS FACE.

ADAMS

I wouldn't worry about going off my rocker, Corry. It's already happened. Stir crazy they used to call it. Well, that's what you are now. Stir crazy.

ALLENBY

(TAKING A STEP TOWARD HIM TO KEEP HIM BACK) Back off, Adams. You and Carstairs go back and get the supplies. Bring them over to the shack.

ADAMS

(BRIDLING) What's the matter—the con doesn't have any hands and feet?

HE POINTS TO CORRY.

ALLENBY

Go ahead, do as I tell you. And the big crate with the red tag—handle that one gently.

CARSTAIRS

How about the use of his buggy there? Some of the stuff's heavy.

CORRY

(AS IF SHAKEN OUT OF A DREAM, SOFTLY) It isn't running today.

ADAMS

(LAUGHS) It isn't running today! What's the matter, Corry—use it too much, do you? (TO CARSTAIRS) You know, there's so many places a guy can go out here. There's the country club over the mound there and the seashore over that way and the drive-in theater, that's someplace around here, isn't it, Corry?

ALLENBY

Knock it off, Adams, and go get the stuff.

ADAMS AND CARSTAIRS TURN WITH ANOTHER LOOK TOWARD CORRY AND START BACK ACROSS THE DESERT. ALLENBY TAKES CORRY'S ARM AND THE TWO MEN WALK TOWARD THE SHACK.

14 LONG SHOT—CORRY AND ALLENBY AS THEY WALK PAST THE CAR AND THE SHED AND INTO THE SHACK.

15 INT. SHACK—FULL SHOT—THE ROOM. CORRY GOES OVER TO SIT ON THE BED TO STARE NUMBLY ACROSS THE ROOM AT NOTHING. ALLENBY CROSSES OVER TO THE ICEBOX, TAKES OUT A JUG OF WATER, LOOKS AROUND THE ROOM AND THEN OVER TO CORRY.

ALLENBY

Glasses?

CORRY

(MOTIONS) Paper cups. On the shelf there.

ALLENBY UNSCREWS THE JAR AND SNIFFS, MAKES A FACE, THEN POURS SOME WATER INTO A CUP, TAKES IT IN A QUICK GULP.

ALLENBY

We've got some fresh on board. They'll be bringing it over.

CORRY NODS NUMBLY. ALLENBY PULLS UP A CHAIR SO THAT HE'S SITTING DIRECTLY OPPOSITE CORRY.

ALLENBY

(CONT'D) Brought you some magazines, too. Strictly on my own.

CORRY

(NODS) Thanks.

ALLENBY

And some microfilm. Old vintage movies. Science-fiction stuff. You'll get a kick out of it.

CORRY

(NODS, LOOKS UP UNSMILING) I'm sure I will.

ALLENBY BITES HIS LIP AND LOOKS AT CORRY FOR A LONG, SILENT MOMENT, THEN HE RISES AND CROSSES TO THE WINDOW.

ALLENBY

I brought you something else, Corry. It would mean my job if they suspected. (THEN HE TURNS TOWARD CORRY) It would be my neck if they found out for sure.

CORRY

What would that be—a forged pardon? Not that it matters, Allenby, but I'm rotting here for performing a public service. You know the man I killed?

ALLENBY

(NODS) I knew him and I knew the case. I knew it very well. Do me a favor, Corry? Please don't press me. I've heard it before.

CORRY

You know he was a monster, don't you? You know he was responsible for the death of my wife. A drunken joyride—

ALLENBY

(CUTTING HIM OFF) I know, Corry. I know all about it. (HE RETRACES HIS STEPS BACK OVER TO THE CHAIR AND SITS DOWN) This is off the record, now. This is just one guy to another. Do you know what it's like stopping here four times a year? It's miserable, Corry. It's miserable having to look and see what's happening to you . . . having to look into your face. (THEN HE TURNS AWAY AND HIS VOICE IS TIGHT) It's miserable to have to see any man in agony.

CORRY

You touch me, Allenby. (HE POUNDS HIS CHEST) Right here. That's where you're getting me.

ALLENBY

You want to hear me out?

CORRY

(NODS) Go ahead.

ALLENBY

I don't care what you did. To put a man on an asteroid with no company except the sky—and the wind and the desert . . . I don't care what you did, Corry, I don't think this is human.

CORRY IS ON HIS FEET. HE LAUGHS A TORTURED, AGONIZED LAUGH.

CORRY

Will you do me a favor, Allenby? Will you hold back on the sympathy? That's something I can't digest now. It sticks in my craw. It makes me sicker than I am. It stinks, Allenby, so please shut your mouth, will you? Will you shut your mouth?

THERE'S A LONG, LONG SILENCE. ALLENBY RISES AGAIN.

ALLENBY

I can't bring you freedom, Corry. I can't even bring you a hope so I brought you the next best thing.

HE LOOKS ACROSS THE ROOM AND OUT THE WINDOW.

16 LONG SHOT—THROUGH THE WINDOW. ADAMS AND CARSTAIRS ARE BOTH LUGGING A SMALL METAL CART LOADED DOWN WITH CRATES AND SUPPLIES. THEY ENTER THE AREA OF THE SHACK TO BRING THE CART UP CLOSE TO THE FRONT DOOR. THE TWO OF THEM TAKE A HEAVY CRATE OFF THE TOP OF THE PILE, A RED TAG FLUTTERING FROM ONE END. THEY LAY IT DOWN IN THE SAND.

CARSTAIRS

(CALLS) You want this big crate opened up, Captain?

17 MED. CLOSE SHOT—ALLENBY.

ALLENBY

(CALLS OUT) Not yet. Stay out there. I'll be right out.

18 TWO SHOT—CORRY AND ALLENBY.

CORRY

I'll bite, Captain. What's the present? (HE LOOKS BRIEFLY THROUGH THE WINDOW) What is it?

HE RISES, GOES OVER TO THE WINDOW TO STARE OUT AT THE LONG, REC-TANGULAR BOX.

19 MED. LONG SHOT—THROUGH THE WINDOW—AT THE BOX AS IT LIES IN THE SAND.

20 MED. CLOSE SHOT—CORRY AS HE TURNS BACK TOWARD THE ROOM.

CORRY

If it's a twenty-year supply of puzzles—lots of luck—I'll have to decline with thanks. I don't need any puzzles, Allenby. If I want to try to probe any mysteries—I can look in the mirror and try to figure out my own.

ALLENBY

(CROSSES OVER TO THE DOOR, OPENS IT, TURNS BACK TO CORRY) We've got to go now. We'll be back in three months. (A PAUSE) Are you listening to me, Corry? This is important.

CORRY STARES AT HIM.

ALLENBY

(CONT'D) When you open up the crate there's nothing you need to do. The . . . item has been vacuum packed. It needs no activator of any kind. The air will do that. There'll be a booklet inside, too, that can answer any of your questions.

CORRY

You're mysterious as hell.

ALLENBY

I don't mean to be. It's just like I told you, though—I'm risking a lot to have brought this here. (HE POINTS TO THE DOOR) They don't know what it is I brought. I'd appreciate your waiting until we get out of sight.

CORRY

(UNEMOTIONALLY) All right. Have a good trip back . . . Give my regards to . . . (HE WETS HIS LIPS) . . . to Broadway. And everyplace else while you're at it.

ALLENBY

Sure, Corry. I'll see you.

HE GOES OUT THE DOOR, MOTIONS TO THE OTHER TWO MEN. THEY START TO FOLLOW HIM.

CUT TO:

21 MED. CLOSE SHOT—CORRY STANDING AT THE DOOR.

CORRY

Allenby!

CUT TO:

22 REVERSE ANGLE—ALLENBY AND THE OTHER TWO—CORRY'S POV. THE THREE MEN PAUSE TO LOOK TOWARD THE SHACK. IN THE FOREGROUND IN FRONT OF THEM WE SEE THE LONG CRATE LYING ALL BY ITSELF IN THE SAND.

CUT TO:

23 MED. CLOSE SHOT—CORRY. HE WALKS DOWN THE STEP AND STANDS NEAR THE BOX, POINTS TO IT.

CORRY

I don't much care *what* it is. For the thought, Allenby. For the . . . for the decency of it . . . I thank you.

24 MED. SHOT—ALLENBY.

ALLENBY

You're quite welcome, Corry.

HE TURNS AND THE OTHER TWO FOLLOW HIM.

25 LONG ANGLE SHOT LOOKING DOWN AT THEM AS THEY SLOWLY TRAMP ACROSS THE SAND AND DISAPPEAR OVER THE LINE OF DUNES.

26 MED. CLOSE SHOT—CORRY. HE WATCHES THEM GO, SHADING HIS EYES AGAIN AT THE SUN, THEN VERY SLOWLY HE LOOKS DOWN AT THE BOX. HE STARES AT IT FOR A LONG MOMENT, THEN HE KNEELS DOWN TO FEEL OF ITS SIDES AND FINALLY FINDS THE TWO RELEASE CATCHES. HIS BOTH HANDS GO OUT TO TOUCH THEM SIMULTANEOUSLY. HE PUSHES THEM AND VERY SLOWLY THE TOP OF THE BOX OPENS.

27 TIGHT CLOSE ANGLE SHOT—LOOKING UP AS FROM INSIDE THE BOX TOWARD CORRY'S FACE AS HE STARES INTO IT. HIS EYES SUDDENLY WIDEN WITH ASTONISHMENT.

CUT ABRUPTLY TO:

28 MED. CLOSE SHOT—INSERT SECTION OF SPACECRAFT. WHAT WE ARE SEEING IS JUST PART OF A HATCH AND A METAL LADDER. CARSTAIRS IS JUST CLAMBERING UP THEM TO DISAPPEAR INSIDE THE SHIP. ADAMS STARTS TO FOLLOW HIM. HE PAUSES HALFWAY UP TO LOOK TOWARD ALLENBY WHO IN TURN IS STARING OFF INTO THE DISTANCE.

ADAMS

Captain—just man to man, huh?

ALLENBY

What?

ADAMS

What did you bring him? What was in the box?

29 MED. CLOSE SHOT—ALLENBY AS HE SLOWLY SCRATCHES THE BEARD STUBBLE OF HIS SQUARE JAW.

ALLENBY

(VERY SOFTLY AS IF TO NO ONE IN PARTICULAR) I'm not sure really. Maybe it's just an illusion—or maybe it's salvation!

THEN HE TURNS, MOTIONS ADAMS UP THE LADDER, AND THEN FOLLOWS HIM UP.

DISSOLVE TO:

30 EXT. THE SHACK. THE TOP OF THE BOX HAS BEEN OPENED AND AS THE CAMERA PANS OVER IT TOWARD THE SHACK WE SEE THAT IT IS EMPTY. THE CAMERA CONTINUES TO PAN OVER TO THE SHACK.

DISSOLVE THROUGH TO:

31 INT. SHACK. CORRY STANDS AT THE FAR END OF THE ROOM STARING OFF BEYOND THE CAMERA. HE HAS A BOOK IN HIS HAND WHICH HE SUDDENLY SEEMS TO REMEMBER. HE LOOKS DOWN AT IT, STARES AT THE COVER FOR A LONG MOMENT, THEN OPENS IT WITH BOTH HIS HANDS. HE STUDIES IT PERPLEXED FOR A LONG MOMENT; THEN HE LOOKS UP AGAIN. THEN HE LOOKS DOWN AT THE BOOK AGAIN AND SLOWLY HE READS ALOUD.

CORRY

You are now the proud possessor of a robot built in the form of woman. To all intent and purpose this creature is a woman. Physiologically and psychologically she is a human being with a set of emotions, a memory track. The ability to reason, to think, and to speak. She is beyond illness and under normal circumstances should have a life span similar to that of a comparable human being. Her name is Alicia.

VERY SLOWLY CORRY'S HEAD RISES. SLOW PAN SHOT ACROSS THE ROOM TO A SHOT OF ALICIA WHO SITS IN A CHAIR LOOKING BACK AT HIM. THE CREATURE IS

NOT BEAUTIFUL. THERE'S SOMETHING TOO IMMOBILE—TOO EMOTIONLESS ABOUT HER FEATURES. THE EYES THAT LOOK BACK AT HIM SHOW NEITHER RESIGNATION NOR INTEREST, ONLY AWARENESS. SHE'S DRESSED IN A SIMPLE, LOOSE GARMENT THAT NEITHER ADDS TO NOR DETRACTS FROM HER FEMININ- ITY. CORRY TAKES A FEW HESITANT STEPS OVER TOWARD HER.

CORRY

Can you . . . *can* you speak?

32 CLOSE SHOT—THE GIRL.

ALICIA

(LOOKS UP AT HIM) Of course. What is your name?

A SLOW FADE TO BLACK:

END ACT I

ACT II

FADE ON:

33 EXT. THE SHACK—LONG ANGLE SHOT LOOKING DOWN AT CORRY. HE'S PERCHED ON A LADDER AND IS JUST PUTTING ON THE FINISHING TOUCHES TO A STONE CHIMNEY. HE LOOKS OFF TOWARD THE HORIZON, SMILES, AND WAVES.

34 LONG SHOT—LOOKING ACROSS THE SAND AT ALICIA. SHE'S CARRYING TWIGS AND KINDLING. SHE WAVES BACK AND STARTS TO WALK TOWARD THE SHACK.

35 MED. CLOSE SHOT—THE YARD—AS CORRY COMES DOWN THE LADDER. HE SMILES AT THE GIRL, TOUCHES HER ARM, POINTS TO THE TWIGS THAT SHE'S PUT DOWN ON A PILE.

CORRY

That's fine, Alicia. Did you have to go very far out?

ALICIA

Quite far this time. Will this burn, Corry?

CORRY

(KICKS AT THE TWIGS WITH A FOOT) Should burn very well.

HE TAKES OUT A PIPE AND LIGHTS IT, SQUINTS UP AGAINST THE SUN TO LOOK AT THE CHIMNEY.

CORRY

I'm just afraid that chimney will burn with it. (HE POINTS) It isn't really rock. It's clay of some sort. I don't know whether the clay here is like the clay back home.

ALICIA

(SIMPLY) I don't either.

CORRY TURNS TO STARE AT HER. ALICIA MEETS HIS LOOK WITH A HALF SMILE.

ALICIA

More questions, Corry?

CORRY

(SMILES) That's the pattern, isn't it? Suddenly you say something that reminds me that—

HE STOPS ABRUPTLY.

ALICIA

(GENTLY) Go ahead, Corry, say whatever you want and ask whatever you want to. (SHE SHAKES HER HEAD) You can't hurt me.

HE STARES AT HER FOR A LONG MOMENT.

CORRY

You're so . . . you're so . . .

ALICIA

Real? I *am* real, Corry. And I have a mind and I have a memory. (AND THEN VERY GIRL-LIKE, COCKING HER HEAD AND LAUGHING) And I am real, that's all.

HER HAND TOUCHES HIS AND HE SUDDENLY TAKES IT AND HOLDS IT. HE LOOKS DOWN AT IT, FEELING OF THE FINGERS FOR A LONG MOMENT. THEN HE LOOKS UP TO SEE HER WATCHING HIM. HE LETS LOOSE OF THE HAND.

ALICIA

(SOFTLY) Not like flesh, Corry?

CORRY

It *is* flesh. And underneath are veins and muscles. Tissue.

ALICIA

It's plastic, you know, Corry.

CORRY

(HIS VOICE RISING) No! (AND THEN QUIETER) No, Alicia. It's flesh and blood. Do you remember what I told you about things in relationship to other things? Well, this is a part of it. What *you* are. You exist in relationship to me and therefore you are what I need you to be. (HE LOOKS DEEP INTO HER FACE) Do you understand me?

ALICIA

I try, Corry.

CORRY

Well, well, think of the shack here. A million miles away on earth . . . it's a shack. It's corrugated steel and imitation glass and scrap metal. But here it's a house. Do you understand, Alicia? In our context—it's a house. (HE TAKES HER SHOULDERS AND AS IF SPEAKING TO A CHILD) Now also back on earth perhaps you'd be something else. I don't know—maybe a . . .

ALICIA

A machine.

CORRY

(HURRIEDLY PUSHING THIS ASIDE) Whatever! Here you're flesh and blood,

Alicia. You're a fellow human. You're a companion . . . (THEN HE SMILES, TOUCHES HER FACE) Come, we'll have an early dinner tonight.

ALICIA

(WALKING WITH HIM TOWARD THE HOUSE) Drive in the car tonight? Look at the stars?

CORRY

(LAUGHS) That's right. Tonight we'll drive in the car and look at the stars.

ALICIA

Point them out to me again tonight, Corry? Orion. Rigel. Centauri.

THEY'RE AT THE DOOR AND CORRY OPENS IT, MOTIONS HER IN.

CORRY

We'll see, Alicia.

THEN HE FOLLOWS HER INSIDE.

36 INT. SHACK. THE GIRL BUSIES HERSELF TAKING DISHES OUT. CORRY TAKES OUT THE LEDGER, LOOKS ACROSS AT HER. THEY CATCH EACH OTHER'S LOOK AND THE GIRL SMILES.

ALICIA

Or the poetry. You could read me the poems again.

CORRY

You like those, huh?

ALICIA

Very much.

CORRY RELIGHTS HIS PIPE, LEANS BACK IN THE CHAIR SURVEYING HER.

CORRY

Our tastes are alike, Alicia. Everything that I like to do—you like too.

ALICIA

That's our nature, Corry. We adapt to you. We become a . . .

CORRY

A part of me.

ALICIA

That's right. I've become a part of you. (THEN SHE TURNS AWAY) And now I'll get dinner ready.

CORRY RISES AND PICKS UP THE LEDGER, CHECKS THE PENCIL, EXAMINES ITS POINT, THEN WALKS OUT.

37 EXT. SHACK—PORCH—DAY—MED. CLOSE SHOT—AS HE SITS IN THE HOMEMADE ROCKER. HE LOOKS OFF TOWARD THE HORIZON AND THEN SLOWLY BEGINS TO WRITE AS WE HEAR HIS VOICE.

CORRY'S VOICE

Alicia has been with me now for eleven months. Twice when Allenby has brought the ship in with supplies I've hidden her so that the others wouldn't see her and I've seen the question in Allenby's eyes each time. It's a question I have myself. It's difficult to write down what has been the sum total of this very strange and bizarre relationship. It is man and woman, man and machine, and there are times even when I know that Alicia is simply an extension of me. I hear my words coming from her. My emotions. The things that she has learned to love are those things that I've loved.

HE STOPS ABRUPTLY AS HE LISTENS TO ALICIA SINGING FROM INSIDE THE SHACK. HE SMILES AND THEN CONTINUES TO WRITE AGAIN.

CORRY'S VOICE

(CONT'D) But I think I've reached the point now where I shall not analyze Alicia any longer. I shall accept her here simply as a part of my life— an integral part.

HE CONTINUES TO WRITE SILENTLY NOW, TURNING THE PAGE TO CONTINUE ON THE OTHER SIDE, AND THEN HE STOPS, PUTS THE BOOK AND PENCIL DOWN, RISES, GOES TO THE DOOR, AND STANDS THERE LOOKING AT ALICIA. SHE TURNS TO SMILE AT HIM AND HE ENTERS THE ROOM. THE CAMERA MOVES BACK SO THAT IT IS SHOOTING AT THEM THROUGH THE OPEN DOOR AND ACROSS THE LEDGER BOOK WHICH LIES FACE UP. WE HEAR CORRY'S VOICE.

CORRY'S VOICE

(CONT'D) Whatever Alicia is, wherever she came from, whether her father and mother are chemistry and electricity and she came out of a mold—I don't care anymore. I'm not lonely any longer. Each day can now be lived with. (A PAUSE) I love Alicia. Nothing else matters.

DISSOLVE TO:

38 EXT. DESERT—NIGHT—LONG SHOT—LOOKING UP TOWARD A MOUND OF SAND —AS HAND IN HAND ALICIA AND CORRY RACE DOWN TOWARD THE CAMERA. HE STOPS HER ABRUPTLY AND POINTS TO THE SKY.

CORRY

And, Alicia, look. That's the star Betelgeuse. It's in the constellation of Orion. And there's the "Great Bear" with its pointer stars in line with the Northern Star. And there's the constellation Hercules. You see, Alicia?

HE TRACES A PATH ACROSS THE SKY WITH HIS UPRAISED HAND AND HER EYES FOLLOW IT. THEN HE TURNS TO LOOK DOWN AT HER FACE UPTURNED IN THE HALF LIGHT.

ALICIA

(SOFTLY) God's beauty.

CORRY

(NODS) That's right, Alicia. God's beauty.

SUDDENLY THE GIRL'S EYES STOP AS THEY TRAVERSE ACROSS THE SKY. SHE POINTS.

ALICIA

That star, Corry? What's that star?

39 CLOSE SHOT—CORRY AS HE STARES AT SOMETHING IN THE SKY.

CORRY

That's not a star. That's a ship, Alicia.

ALICIA

A ship?

VERY SLOWLY THERE'S A RAY OF LIGHT THAT PLAYS ON BOTH THEIR FACES ANE GETS BRIGHTER AND LARGER. ALICIA MOVES CLOSER TO HIM.

ALICIA

There's no ship due here now, Corry. You said not for another three months. You said after the last time it wouldn't be for another—

CORRY

(GENTLY) Go back to the house, Alicia. Stay out of sight. Go ahead.

SHE TAKES A FEW STEPS AWAY FROM HIM, STILL SEARCHING THE SKY, LOOKING TOWARD THE LIGHT.

ALICIA

Corry—

CORRY

(HIS VOICE LOUDER) Go back to the house, Alicia.

THE GIRL CONTINUES TO WALK ACROSS THE DESERT, DISAPPEARING INTO THE NIGHT BEYOND THE LIGHT OF THE APPROACHING SHIP. CORRY STANDS THERE MOTIONLESSLY STARING UP.

DISSOLVE TO:

40 EXT. DESERT—NIGHT—LONG ANGLE SHOT LOOKING UP AT THE TOP OF THE DUNE AS THREE SPACE-SUITED FIGURES APPEAR. ALLENBY IS IN THE FORE-GROUND. HE TAKES OFF HIS HELMET, WIPES HIS FACE, PEERS DOWN AT SOME-THING BELOW.

ALLENBY

Corry? Is that you? The shack was dark. We were worried.

CORRY

I'm all right. You have trouble?

ALLENBY

No, we had no trouble.

HE MOTIONS THE OTHERS TO FOLLOW HIM AND THEY WALK DOWN THE DUNE TO STAND CLOSE TO CORRY.

ALLENBY

This is a scheduled stop.

ADAMS

We've got good news for you, Corry.

CORRY

(LOOKS FROM FACE TO FACE) I'm not interested.

THE OTHERS EXCHANGE LOOKS OF SURPRISE.

ALLENBY

You better hear what it is.

CORRY

You heard me, Allenby. I'm not interested.

ALLENBY

You will be. This I guarantee!

CORRY TAKES A FEW BACKWARD STEPS LOOKING PARANOIACALLY FROM ONE TO THE OTHER.

CORRY

Allenby, give me a break, will you? I don't want trouble.

ALLENBY

We don't either.

ADAMS

(TO ONE OF THE OTHERS) He gets worse! If we'd come a month later he'd have been eating sand or something.

CORRY NOW TURNS AND STARTS TO WALK AWAY FROM THEM, OCCASIONALLY LOOKING OVER HIS SHOULDER.

ALLENBY

(CALLS OUT TO HIM) Corry!

41 TRACK SHOT—CORRY, AS HE WALKS FASTER AND FASTER AND IS ABOUT TO BREAK INTO A DEAD RUN.

CUT TO:

42 LONG SHOT—OVER CORRY'S SHOULDER LOOKING AT ALLENBY WHO NOW SHOUTS.

ALLENBY

Corry!

HE RUNS, CRUNCHING ON THE HARD SAND, TO COME UP CLOSE TO CORRY. HE GRABS HIM, WHIRLS HIM AROUND.

ALLENBY

It's this way, Corry. Your sentence has been reviewed. They've given you a pardon. We're to take you back home on the ship. But we've got to take off from here in exactly twenty minutes. We can't wait any longer. We've been dodging meteor storms all the way out. We're almost out of fuel. Any later than twenty minutes, we'll have increased our distance and I'm not sure we'd make it.

CORRY STARES AT HIM AND THEN AT THE OTHER MEN WHO HAVE COME DOWN THE DUNE BEHIND HIM.

43 TIGHT CLOSE SHOT—CORRY. HIS EYES DART ABOUT, GOING WIDE AS THE SENSE OF WHAT'S BEEN SAID TO HIM SEEPS IN. HE TRIES TO SPEAK, BUT FOR A MOMENT NOTHING COMES OUT.

CORRY

Wait a minute, Allenby. Wait just a minute. (HE CLOSES HIS EYES (TIGHTLY, THEN OPENS THEM) What did you say? What did you just say about a—

ALLENBY

(FILLING IT IN) A pardon.

ADAMS

(COMING UP ALONGSIDE) But it won't do any of us any good unless you get your stuff together and get ready to move, Corry. We've only got room for about fifteen pounds of stuff, so you'd better pick up what you need in a hurry and leave the rest of it behind. (THEN WITH A GRIN, LOOKING OFF IN THE DIRECTION OF THE SHACK) Such as it is.

CORRY

(STRUGGLING TO KEEP HIS VOICE FIRM BUT ALREADY IT BEGINS TO SHAKE WITH JOY AND EXCITEMENT) Stuff? My stuff? I don't even have fifteen pounds of stuff!

HE LAUGHS UPROARIOUSLY, TURNS, AND AGAIN STARTS TO WALK TOWARD THE SHACK.

44 TRACK SHOT—ALL OF THEM AS THEY WALK. CORRY'S VOICE GOES UP AND DOWN IN UNCOMFORTABLE LAUGHTER, A COMBINATION OF NERVES, RELIEF, AND ALMOST UNBEARABLE EXCITEMENT. THE WORDS SPEW OUT AS HE WALKS.

CORRY

I've got a shirt, a pencil, and a ledger book. A pair of shoes. (THEN HE THROWS BACK HIS HEAD AND LAUGHS AGAIN) The car you can keep here. That'll be for the next poor devil.

ALLENBY

(EVENLY) There won't be any next poor devil. There won't *be* any more exiles, Corry. This was the last time.

CORRY

Good! Wonderful! Thank God for that!

THEY CONTINUE TO WALK AGAIN.

CORRY

(CONT'D) We'll let it rest here, then. The farthest auto graveyard in the universe! And Alicia and I will wave to it as we leave. We'll just look out of a porthole and throw it a kiss good-bye. The car, the shack, the salt lakes, the range. The whole works! Alicia and I will just—

HE STOPS ABRUPTLY, SUDDENLY CONSCIOUS OF THE SILENCE AND THE LOOKS.

45 PAN SHOT—ACROSS THE FACES OF THE OTHER MEN AS THEY STARE AT HIM.

ADAMS

(HIS EYES NARROW) Who? Who, Corry?

46 TIGHT CLOSE SHOT—ALLENBY. HIS EYES CLOSE FOR A MOMENT.

ALLENBY

(SOTTO) Oh, my dear God, I forgot her!

47 GROUP SHOT—CORRY'S EYES MOVE AROUND FROM FACE TO FACE.

CORRY

Allenby—(AND THEN ACCUSATIVE) Allenby, it's Alicia—

CARSTAIRS

(WHISPERS UNDER HIS BREATH TO ADAMS) He's out of his mind, isn't he?

ADAMS

Who's Alicia, Corry?

CORRY

(LAUGHS UPROARIOUSLY) Who's Alicia? Adams, you idiot! Who's Alicia! You brought her! You brought her here in a box! She's a woman—(AND THEN HE STOPS, LOOKS AWAY FOR A MOMENT, SOFTLY, THEN LOOKS TOWARD ALLENBY) A robot. (AND THEN ONCE AGAIN LOOKS AT ALLENBY) But closer to a woman. She's kept me alive, Allenby. I swear to you—if it weren't for her—

HE LOOKS AROUND AT THE CIRCLE OF SILENT FACES THAT STARE AT HIM.

48 CLOSE SHOT—CORRY.

CORRY

What's the matter? You worried about Alicia? (HE SHAKES HIS HEAD) You needn't be. Alicia's harmless. I tell you she's like a woman. And she's gentle and kind and without her, Allenby, I tell you without her I'd have been finished. I'd have given up. (A LONG PAUSE AND THEN VERY QUIETLY) You would have only had to come back to bury me!

49 GROUP SHOT.

ADAMS

(TO ALLENBY) That's what you wouldn't let us look at, huh? The crate with the red tag—

CORRY

(TO ALLENBY) Sorry, Captain, but I had to let it out—

ALLENBY

That's all right, Corry. That's all over with, but unfortunately that's not the problem—

CORRY

(AGAIN WITH A HIGH UNCONTROLLED LAUGH) Problem? There aren't any problems! There are no more problems left on heaven or earth! We'll pack up fifteen pounds of stuff and we'll climb in that ship of yours and when we get back to that beautiful green earth—

50 TIGHT CLOSE SHOT—CORRY. HE SUDDENLY STOPS, BUT HIS LIPS FORM THE
WORDS "FIFTEEN POUNDS."

CORRY

(HE WHISPERS IT) Fifteen pounds. (AND THEN HE SHOUTS IT) Fifteen
pounds? (HE LOOKS FROM FACE TO FACE AGAIN) You've got to have
room for more than that. Throw out stuff. Throw out equipment. Alicia
weighs more than fifteen pounds.

51 GROUP SHOT.

ALLENBY

(QUIETLY) That's the point, Corry. We're stripped now. We've got room
for you and nothing else except that ledger of yours and the pencil. (HE
SHAKES HIS HEAD) You'll have to leave the robot here.

CORRY

(SHOUTING) She's not just a robot! Stop talking about her as if she were
a machine or something. This is a woman, Allenby. This is like flesh
and blood.

ALLENBY

(SHAKES HIS HEAD, HIS VOICE QUIET) This is a machine, Corry. This is
wires, magnetos, and electrodes with a plastic covering.

CORRY

(WITH SHEER DESPERATION) But you don't know her, Allenby. You
don't know Alicia. She's like a human being. You leave her here—it'd
be murder. Worse than murder. Oh, my God, Allenby, you can't leave
her behind—(HE BACKS AWAY FROM THEM FRIGHTENED AND STARTS TO
RUN) No! No, Allenby, you can't leave her behind! I won't let you. I'll
stay here myself, then, but you can't leave Alicia here. No, you can't.
(AND THEN SCREAMING) Alicia! Run, Alicia! Run!

52 LONG ANGLE SHOT—LOOKING DOWN—AS CORRY RACES TOWARD THE SHACK
FOLLOWED BY THE OTHERS.

CUT ABRUPTLY TO:

53 INT. SHACK—AS CORRY SMASHES OPEN THE DOOR AND RACES INSIDE ONLY TO
FIND THE ROOM EMPTY. HE STANDS IN THE MIDDLE OF THE ROOM LOOKING
AROUND AND THEN OVER TOWARD THE DOOR AS ALLENBY ENTERS FOLLOWED
BY THE OTHER MEN.

ALLENBY

Where is she, Corry?

CORRY

I don't know. But you're not going to get her.

ADAMS

We don't want her, Corry. We just want you to get your gear packed and
let's get out of here. (HE LOOKS AT HIS WATCH, NERVOUSLY TO ALLENBY)
We've only got about ten minutes. How about it, Captain?

ALLENBY

(GENTLY) Come on, Corry.

CORRY

(BACKS FURTHER INTO THE ROOM) No! I'm not leaving, Allenby. I told you that. I can't leave.

ALLENBY

You don't understand. This is our last trip here. This is anybody's last trip. This is off the route now. That means no supplies, no nothing. That means if you stay here you die here. And that way, there'd be a day, Corry, when you'd pray for that death to come quicker than it's bargained for—

CORRY

(ILLOGICALLY, HALF WILDLY) I can't help it, Allenby. I can't leave her behind. And you won't take her. So that means I stay. (AND THEN, LOOKING OVER HIS SHOULDER WILDLY, HE SCREAMS) Alicia! Alicia, stay away! Don't let them see you! Don't let them get you! Stay away, darling—

54 CLOSE SHOT—ALLENBY AS HE HEARS THIS TERM.

ALLENBY

Corry, listen to me. She's not a woman. She's a machine. I saw her get crated, shoved in a box—

CORRY

(SHAKES HIS HEAD) I don't care.

ALLENBY

She's a machine, Corry. She's a motor with wires and tubes and batteries.

CORRY

(SCREAMING) *She's a woman!*

ALLENBY WETS HIS LIPS, BITES HIS LIP FOR A MOMENT, STANDING THERE UN-SURE, NOT KNOWING WHAT TO DO. THROUGH THE WINDOW, OUTSIDE IN THE YARD WE SEE ANOTHER MEMBER OF THE CREW WALK TOWARD THE YARD, PAUSE NEAR THE SHACK.

CREWMAN

Captain, Captain Allenby?

ALLENBY

What?

CREWMAN

Captain, we've got just four minutes left. Begging your pardon, sir—but we've got to take off! If we wait longer than that, sir, we'll have moved to a point too far out. I don't think we'll make it, sir!

ADAMS

(HIS VOICE FRIGHTENED) How about it, Captain Allenby, leave him here!

ALLENBY

We can't leave him here. Sick, mad, or half-alive, we've got to bring him back. Those are the orders.

HE TAKES ANOTHER STEP TOWARD CORRY, WHO BACKS AGAINST THE WALL.

ALLENBY

Corry, now it isn't just you. Now it's all of us. So that means we can't talk any more and we can't argue with you. We simply just have to take you!

HE MAKES A QUICK MOTION WITH ONE HAND. ADAMS AND CARSTAIRS TAKE A STEP INTO THE ROOM TO FLANK ALLENBY AND TO MOVE IN TO CONVERGE ON CORRY. CORRY, WITH A KIND OF ANIMAL SHOUT, BULLS HIS WAY PAST THEM, PUSHING ADAMS OUT OF THE WAY, AND BOLTS OUT OF THE DOOR.

CUT TO:

55 LONG ANGLE SHOT—LOOKING DOWN ON THE DESERT—AT THE FIGURE OF CORRY AS HE RACES, STUMBLING, FALLING, PICKING HIMSELF UP AGAIN. HIS VOICE CAN BE HEARD SHOUTING OVER AND OVER AGAIN.

CORRY

(SHOUTING) Alicia! Alicia!

56 DIFFERENT ANGLES OF HIM RUNNING. THE OTHERS IN PURSUIT.

57 LONG ANGLE SHOT—LOOKING UP TOWARD A DUNE—AS HE SUDDENLY APPEARS AT THE TOP AND STARES DOWN. CAMERA SWEEPS TO THE LEFT AND DOWN FOR A SHOT OF ALICIA STANDING ALONE DOWN IN THE DEPRESSION OF THE SAND.

58 FULL SHOT—THE PLACE.

CORRY

Alicia!

BEHIND HIM ALLENBY AND THE OTHERS APPEAR. CORRY STARTS TOWARD THE GIRL. CARSTAIRS TACKLES HIM, AND THEN ADAMS POUNCES ON HIM. THEY HOLD HIM TIGHT AS HE SHOUTS.

CORRY

Alicia, run. Run, Alicia.

ALLENBY TAKES A FEW STEPS DOWN THE DUNE AND STOPS HALFWAY DOWN. HE LOOKS BACK AT CORRY.

ALLENBY

I'm sorry, Corry. I don't have any choice. (A PAUSE. HIS VOICE IS QUIET) I have no choice at all.

59 CLOSE SHOT—HIS HAND AS IT UNBUCKLES THE GUN HOLSTER ON HIS BELT.

60 TIGHT CLOSE SHOT—CORRY. HIS EYES GO WIDE.

CORRY

(SCREAMS) No, Allenby! No! She's a human being!

61 FLASH SHOT—BEHIND ALICIA—LOOKING STRAIGHT UP AT THE DUNE AT AL-LENBY WHO TAKES THE GUN OUT AND FIRES THE GUN DIRECTLY INTO HER FACE.

62 FLASH SHOT—CORRY. HE PULLS AWAY FROM THE OTHERS, SCREAMS, AND COVERS HIS FACE.

63 ANGLE SHOT—LOOKING UP TOWARD THE BACK OF ALICIA—AS VERY SLOWLY SHE CRUMPLES TO THE SAND, BLOTTING OUT THE CAMERA MOMENTARILY.

64 CLOSE SHOT—CORRY. HIS FINGERS CONVULSIVELY MOVE AWAY FROM HIS FACE AND FALL TO HIS SIDE. HE TAKES THREE SLOW STEPS DOWN THE DUNE TOWARD THE CRUMPLED FIGURE. THEN HE LOOKS DOWN. PAN SHOT WITH HIS EYES TO A CLOSE SHOT OF ALICIA'S HAND CLENCHED TIGHTLY. A FURTHER PAN SHOT ACROSS HER ARM AND SHOULDER TO THE BACK OF HER HEAD. THEN A VERY SLOW PAN SHOT TWO OR THREE FEET ACROSS THE GROUND TO A SHOT OF THE REMNANTS OF A BROKEN MACHINE, TWISTED AND BENT WIRES, A CRACKED EYE, A COUPLE OF FRAGMENTS OF PLASTIC, ALL THE REMAINS OF A FACE.

65 GROUP SHOT—THE MEN WITH CORRY IN THE FOREGROUND. A FEW FEET BEHIND HIM ALLENBY, AND THEN ON THE DUNE ARE THE OTHERS. CREWMAN COMES INTO THE FRAME IN THE BACKGROUND.

CREWMAN

It's got to be now, Captain Allenby!

ALLENBY

(NODS, SOFTLY) It *will* be now! (THEN HE TURNS TO CORRY) Come on, Corry. It's time to go home.

NOW NUMBLY, WITHOUT DIRECTION, CORRY ALLOWS HIMSELF TO BE LED UP THE DUNE AND ACROSS THE DESERT.

66 LONG ANGLE SHOT—LOOKING DOWN ON THEM AS THEY WALK. THE LIGHT FROM THE SHIP GETS BRIGHTER AND BRIGHTER AS THEY APPROACH IT.

67 CLOSE GROUP SHOT—AS THEY PAUSE FOR A MOMENT. CORRY LOOKS BACK AT THE CRUMPLED FIGURE IN THE DISTANCE, THEN AGAIN TURNS AND BEGINS TO WALK.

68 TRACK SHOT—WITH THEM AS THEIR FEET CRUNCH ON THE SAND, PAST THE SHED, THE CAR, AND ALL THE REST OF IT.

ALLENBY

(ALONGSIDE CORRY) It's all behind you now, Corry. All behind you. Like a bad dream. A nightmare . . . and when you wake up you'll be on earth. You'll be home.

CORRY

Home?

ALLENBY

That's right. (A LONG PAUSE, PUTTING HIS HAND ON CORRY'S ARM) All you're leaving behind, Corry, is loneliness.

69 TIGHT CLOSE SHOT—CORRY'S FACE AS TEARS ROLL DOWN HIS CHEEKS. HIS EYES MOVE DOWN TO THE SAND BY HIS FEET AND FOR A MOMENT HIS FACE IS IMPASSIVE AND IMMOBILE. HE NODS SLOWLY.

CORRY

I must remember to . . . I must remember to keep that in mind!

THEN HE TURNS TO WALK AHEAD OF THE OTHERS.

70 LONG ANGLE SHOT—LOOKING DOWN AT THE LITTLE GROUP OF MEN AS THEY PASS THE SHACK AND THEN MOVE AWAY INTO THE NIGHT TOWARD THE DISTANT LIGHT THAT FLICKERS ON THEM, BECKONS THEM AWAY. THE CAMERA PANS THEM AND UP INTO THE STARRY NIGHT SKY.

NARRATOR'S VOICE

Down below on a microscopic piece of sand that floats through space is a fragment of a man's life. Left to rust is the place he lived in and the machines he used. Without use they will disintegrate from the wind and the sand and the years that act upon them. All of Mr. Corry's machines . . . including the one made in his image, kept alive by love but now . . . obsolete . . . in the Twilight Zone!

A SLOW FADE TO BLACK

THE END

New Paths and New Inventions

If you will here recall the backgrounds of some of the writers whose work or whose theories are in this book, think how many of them had to do other things before they could make a breakthrough as writers. I mentioned this in chapter one. Most writers have had to go through a solitary trek of some kind, some for many years, before establishing their right to be heard or coming to the notice of the public. Jack Kerouac zealously peddled the manuscript of *On the Road* for five years before he found a publisher. If you wish a tougher example than that, how many copies of *Moby Dick* did Herman Melville sell in the first edition? A thousand? No. How about seventeen? That was it. That's the figure.

It seems sensible to me that if you can't get aboard a television show as one of its writers, it is nonetheless extremely important to be *physically* connected to the industry, to be physically bound up in it in some way, to be a participant, to be where it's happening, to be close enough to hear everything, to meet people, and to have people meet you.

With this in mind, consider a practical example. How much do you know about CATV? Cable television? Community antenna TV? It has many names. There are three or four aspects of CATV that could be of importance to you. It is spreading. It is good. It is going to be everywhere. It is changing television already. It is expanding and improving programs. It is on the threshold of originating programs. It wins friends everywhere it's installed. It's simple. It is going to change the character of networks. We are at the end of an era and we are moving into a new one.

One of the most dynamic figures in communications today is Irving B. Kahn, head of the TelePrompTer Corporation. Every time he talks about the future of television, he makes your mind jump about a foot. He has made the minds of movie theater owners jump a lot more than a foot. In New York they've jumped clear down to City Hall, claiming that the cable invader is presently going to charge viewers for what they are now getting for free. "Unfair competition."

The rapid evolution of CATV has been fascinating to watch. It began so simply and so innocently, bringing excellent television reception into rural or remote areas where regular service was poor or impossible. It cleared up the fuzzy pictures. It brought in clear ones. New ones. An antenna on top of a hill and a wire going into your own personal set did the job. The antenna merely intercepted what was already going by and redirected it locally.

The coaxial cable (about as thick as a pencil) has now made it possible to feed thirty-six different programs into the average receiver. That is a lot of programs. But where would so many programs come from? The transmitting sources can't feed that many. Not enough channels. Local program originations therefore seem inevitable. This means work for writers, and probably work very close to where they are presently living. If cable TV comes in big, you won't have to move to the Coast.

An important breakthrough takes a practical turn in September, 1971. To stimulate competition and to open up new producing sources, a new FCC policy prohibits individual television stations from accepting more than three hours, at night, of network programming. Show material will have to be found to fill seven half-hour periods a week on about 650 stations. Syndicated shows will of course move into many of these "holes," but many more will be open to local programming ingenuity. It definitely means that hundreds of new opportunities for creative impulses all over America will very soon be available. This FCC plan has been talked about for years. It is now here and it will affect nighttime programming, especially in those cities which are not among the top forty in size, like no impact thus far felt by the industry.

Jack Gould, radio and television editor of the *New York Times,* has been studying the dramatic advance of cable television since it started. You will be interested in a few of his comments:

> One of the more interesting capabilities of a cable system is that it can be broken up into neighborhood entities, something already the subject of experimental tests. A cable system is potentially one way of decentralizing the mass media, allowing viewers to see a program of direct pertinency to their own area.
>
> In this connection, respected electronic concerns are working on methods whereby questions might be asked on one empty channel and viewers could give a variety of responses merely by touching one of an array of buttons, such as electronic voting either yes or no, in a public opinion survey. Computerized tabulations could record the outcome in a matter of seconds, and presumably consign human pollsters to limbo.
>
> If electronics could be the means of restoring a sense of local involvement through neighborhood television, participatory democracy might be retrieved in an interesting way. At the least, the idea is worth a thought and goes beyond the movie theatre owner's fear of a box office in the home.

Although Irving Kahn, more than any single individual, is driving the forces of cable television where they are dramatically paying off, of comparable excitement, and also in the field of new marvels, is inventor Peter Goldmark of CBS. His name perhaps is not well known to most, but it is hugely respected throughout the communications world.

Years ago, while I was still at CBS, I was one of several who had the pleasure to watch Peter Goldmark's first private demonstration of color television. What he had then was better than what we have now. In a long wrangle with RCA, CBS lost the color fight only because the Goldmark invention could not be adapted to the then universal black-and-white receiving set. Goldmark is not a man who can be discouraged. After three years of quiet tinkering in the CBS lab, he revolutionized the recording business with his development of long-playing discs. After six years he produced EVR (electronic video recording). In a very few years, set owners all over the world will be using EVR. It enables you to put the visual material you want into your own set, to see what you want when you want it.

Of his own invention Goldmark has said: "EVR is not just another tool in the audiovisual kit. It's a new medium, a new dimension. For the first time in video history it can free the individual set owner from complete dependence on the programmer and broadcaster."

You may keep and play your favorite shows at any time. They are transferred to a tiny cartridge of such astonishing effectiveness—a new and stunning triumph of miniaturization—that the entire content of a twenty-four-volume encyclopedia can be filmed and stored in a single cartridge. Its retrieval system is so sure, it can pick out any page or paragraph. The public is now beginning to build libraries of shows, concerts, specials, great comedy routines, educational material, historic speeches—all the best of the endless procession that is now, for the most part, so indiscriminately tuned in.

The energies and imaginations of men like Irving Kahn and Peter Goldmark are remaking the public's attitude toward its favorite plaything, vastly multiplying its uses, perfecting its pictures, and forever taking the impersonal, intrusive element out of your home set. More and more it will be doing what you want it to do. And for the television writer it will begin to remove the transitoriness of his labors and give him the dignity of permanence.

PART V / SOAP OPERA

12

LOVE OF LIFE

Roy Winsor, one of the most adroit manipulators of this most ridiculed sub-division of television programming, has no illusions about what he does, why it works, and how to give it a shot when it threatens to drag.

In three previous books I have defended the right of American women to watch and listen to this kind of entertainment, and shall bypass the temptation to do so again here. Perhaps it is sufficient, in its own defense, to note that *Love of Life* has been on the air for twenty and a half years. That is about eighteen and a half longer than the average television show. So there must be something to explain its special durability.

John Hess and Roy Winsor created *Love of Life* in 1950. It went on the air in September, 1951. It was an original. It was first seen as a fifteen-minute, five-a-week strip, not a half-hour. Unlike many early shows, *Love of Life* supplied its cast with no prompting devices. "I believed then, and do now," says Winsor, "that actors would become the characters they were playing. If they got stuck, they could ad-lib their way out of their difficulties. They'd have to. They knew it. And it worked."

I will now set down a list of questions that I put to Winsor, and give you his straight answers—I should say his instantaneous answers—to each one. Roy Winsor is never in doubt about anything, as you will soon see.

Q: What is the value of pretaping?
A: We do pretape, but we produce the show as if it were live. We can't afford to redo parts where mistakes are made. The main advantage of tape is to accommodate a performer from time to time who has a schedule conflict. By tap-ing ahead you can resolve these conflicts.
Q: On cast contracts do you guarantee so many appearances a week? A month? A quarter?
A: We draw them for a year, guaranteeing anywhere from thirteen to twenty-six performances in a thirteen-week cycle.
Q: Any satisfactions to you as producer, or to the audience, that the show is presented in color?

A: I don't think the addition of color has meant a damn thing.

Q: Your anchor writer, Bob Shaw, lives in Beverly Hills. Do you have interminable phone conversations? Or long memo exchanges?

A: Neither. We require Bob Shaw, at his expense, to visit us here in New York every four to six weeks. He can afford the fare.

Q: Today's show dissolved out of a commercial into a kitchen scene with Van's mother *seeming* to continue with the same commercial. Close-ups on food being prepared. Strong talk about economy—the commercial merging right into the show. Was this deliberate?

A: No. Pure accident. A long time ago, during dress, we learned that an actor on the show was appearing in one of the commercials. On the commercial he was clean-shaven. On our show he had a moustache. We had to shave him.

Q: Last week, Van's mother was reminiscing about making home brew and there was a fine explosion in the cellar. This coincided exactly with the explosion of the Lipton's [tea and soup] magician materializing on the screen, pawing his way out of the smoke to sell chicken broth, etc. Was this enough separation, in your view as producer, between show and sell?

A: No. Commercial integration or control is a thing of the past. I have nothing to do with commercials. They are sold and then plunked into the program, always without thought or taste.

Q: How long has *Love of Life* been shortchanged by the five-minute news spot at twelve twenty-five?

A: *Love of Life* has always been a twenty-five-minute show.

Q: How does this affect the writer? And the flow of the show?

A: The writing is affected in the sense that the commercials arrive faster than they would on a full thirty-minute program.

Q: Does this affect your Nielsen?

A: Yes. It depresses the Nielsen figures critically.

Q: *Love of Life* gives frequent plugs to *Against the Storm,* and vice versa. What has your being producer of both these shows to do with the cross-plugging schedule?

A: Both programs are owned by American Home Products.* It makes obvious sense to promote their own stuff all they can.

Q: How does Tess become pregnant if John is sterile?

A: Aha! Tune in during the weeks ahead! Millions wonder the same thing! But here is the answer: Tess was pregnant when she married John. (Millions will wonder, pregnant by whom? And we'll let that one haunt them for many weeks.)

Q: It is my view that the *storytelling* for radio soaps and TV soaps is exactly the same. My question: isn't the *burden* of story invention identical for both media? Ditto the continuity of episodic revelation? The *pace* of disclosure? The Friday hook?

A: Agree. The difference we *try* to bring to programs now is to make the story grow out of character. Or out of characters who have more than a proto-

* No longer true. CBS now owns them.

typical interior. And I think our subtext or subplotting tries for a bit more in content, in real problems really looked at, than some of the early radio soaps. And I think this is helping us move from cartoon to drama.

Q: Ninety percent of the action in television soap operas is in one of two places, living room or kitchen. Maybe an occasional corner-fold for baby's bath. Why-be-active-if-you-can-save-money-being-inert sort of thing. Is that right?

A: Perfectly. The reason is economy. When I created *Search for Tomorrow* years ago for the Biow Company, I insisted on a bare-stage technique. And not only because of economy but because close-ups on a small tube are what serials are all about.

Q: Your mention of close-ups puts this one back in my mind. Isn't the soap opera close-up, in television, the same thing that the five-second "beat" was in radio soaps?

A: Exactly the same.

Q: Doesn't this mean, then, that writers of television soap operas don't think in terms of television because they don't *need* to think in those terms?

A: Agree.

Q: Then why should aspiring TV writers seek work there?

A: Because they have a better chance to get it.

Q: Where is *Love of Life* in the Nielsens?

A: It's in the first ten. Often in the top five.

Q: Has *Love of Life* ever been repositioned?

A: No. We've always been where we are right now.

Q: What about the competitive factors you have to fight?

A: They change. NBC is giving us trouble right now. The American housewife likes serials or she likes game shows but seldom likes both.

Q: Your Nielsen has been hurt by your show being bobbed that five minutes for the CBS news break. How about your cost-per-thousand?

A: Because of our budgets, our cost-per-thousand [CPM] is lower than that of any other program in the universe!

Q: In terms of pure economics, what is your view of the contribution of television soap operas to a network's wealth?

A: Without any doubt, we are the bread and butter of the entire edifice.

Q: You occasionally headline a star. But does your show ever create a new star?

A: I think we do. At least we give promising talent a fine chance to discover itself. We're the gym they train in before they go into the arena.

Q: Examples?

A: Quite a few. Did you ever hear of Warren Beatty before he hit it with *Bonnie and Clyde?* Probably not. But he was on *Love of Life* for three years. Learned a lot about acting. James Franciscus, while still at Yale, played for a long time on *The Secret Storm.* Lee Lawson played Barbara on *Love of Life.* The Hamlet in *Rosencrantz and Guildenstern*—a big smash—was on *Secret Storm.* Joanna Roos is playing an important role in *Love of Life.* Claudette Nevins, with a big role right now in *Plaza Suite,* has been an important character for us in *Love of Life* for many months now.

Q: What about sex in the soaps today?

A: Much better. Very much. Program Practices is more relaxed than in years past. However, this gives us no license to turn either *Love* or *Storm* into orgies of mass reproduction because we still feel we must reflect, in the serials, such sub-conscious (or conscious) American archetypes as "Mother is okay," "adultery gets you in trouble," "hard drinking is a poor substitute for fearless self-examination." But we have wider margins in which to play more honest shows, truer stories. We aren't so immediate, so contemporary, as the published fiction of today's short stories or novels. We never will be. And never should be. But we are more honest than we were in radio days. At the same time, characters on serials, during the past five years, have been boozing it up and smoking like a fare-thee-well.

Q: But you've not lost contact with heaven, home, and mother?

A: Oh, no. I really believe that no matter how garish or nutty so many of today's social aberrations seem to be, the home, the hearth, popcorn at a ball game, a good five-cent nickel, and Christmas Eve around the tree with the teenies—that these constitute what America is all about.

What size audiences do these shows really pull? Agnes Eckhardt Nixon, soap opera's first "Cinderella girl" (in the money from her first start, at age twenty-two), wrote an interesting piece for the Sunday *New York Times* (July 7, 1968) and gave some as-of-then figures:

"Of the 33 programs presented during daytime viewing hours, 12 are serials, seven of which are in the top ten in daytime ratings. Each one of these 12 serials is watched by an average of 6,830,000 viewers—men, women, and children. This is more people, in one day, than saw *Life With Father* during its nine years on Broadway. And when one multiplies that number by 12 shows, five days a week, 52 weeks a year—that is either a lot of arrested development or a lot of enter-tainment."

Who do you have to be to play in this league?

Look at these credits for Robert J. Shaw, head writer for *Love of Life:*

Pilot script and forty originals for *Hawaiian Eye* (Warner Bros.)

Twenty originals for *The Lieutenant* (MGM-TV and Norman Felton)

Checkmate—twenty-three originals for Revue Productions

More than a dozen for each of the following: *The David Niven Show, 77 Sunset Strip, Robert Taylor Detectives, Matinee Theatre, Schlitz Playhouse*

In radio Shaw was the sole writer of *Mr. District Attorney* for eleven years! He was sole writer for *Valiant Lady* for two. He created and was head writer of *Front Page Farrell* for four years.

His work has been heard on the *Somerset Maugham Theatre, U.S. Steel, Ponds Theatre, Climax, Danger, Studio One, Kraft Theatre,* and *Suspense.*

In March, 1964, Shaw was the first writer contracted by 20th Century-Fox to participate in preproduction preparation, development of story line, and writing of scripts for *Peyton Place.* He's done over fifty of these episodes.

Do you wonder he can pay his fare to New York?

The credits of Roy Winsor, the show's producer, go back as far as Shaw's do. He was agency producer-editor of some of radio's most indestructible daytimes: *Ma Perkins, Houseboat Hanna, Lone Journey, Woman in White, Vic and Sade, The Goldbergs, Hymns of All Churches, The Light of the World, Kitty Keane, The Man I Married, Sky King,* and *True Confessions.*

Winsor was an actor for five years (four of which were college years) in the Wharf Theatre, Provincetown, Massachusetts. He is a Harvard graduate, with an A.B. and a magna cum laude, which is not so good as a hot Nielsen but not often seen in television.

Besides the television shows he now produces (*Love of Life* and *Secret Storm*), Winsor has created and produced *Search for Tomorrow, Hotel Cosmopolitan, The Public Life of Cliff Norton, Nothing But the Best,* and *Ben Jarrod.*

I mention these credits for a reason beyond their mere cataloging. In the case of writers and of writers-to-be, one thing should have got through to the reader by now: a writer becomes a writer by one route only—by never stopping.

Too many young writers feel they'd have it made if only they had an agent. This is the popular notion. But think of the writing problem from the point of view of the agent. In all truth, asks the agent, why *should* he take you? He never heard of you. No one ever heard of you. Most agents have another frightening question: what *else* have you written?

What's your answer?

The question I am putting here is as blunt as the above. Do you *deserve* the attentions of an agent? Have you earned this right? Money is the name of the game. Can you make money for *him?*

Isn't this closer to the real truth? You've written a TV script that you now want someone to peddle for you.

I'll say this, if you are a writer who is really writing, it is easier to write a first novel and get a contract for it than it is to write a first television play and get a check for it.

If you are an unknown, you have to go where the action is. You have to go to the West Coast. I said this in chapter one. The matter seems to need continuing emphasis. Unrecognized writers don't want to have to believe this, but it is the truth.

Another thing about agents. They like clients who can perform in more than one arena. Why? They're easier to sell. Books, magazine articles, stories, radio and television appearances—things that get your name before people—all this helps an agent help you.

Agents hate clients who have no credits. Agents are in business to make a living. They are in no other business. Certainly they are not in the business of training writers. They are in the business of representing them. That is all.

Though the networks have grown rich out of writers, they have done little to train new talents, and since agents won't teach you—who will? Perhaps you shouldn't break your heart to find out. At the same time, besides taking courses, there is a way you can get a hard professional appraisal of what you have written, a hardheaded evaluation of the true worth of your writing skills as these skills exist right now. And it doesn't matter what you've written, whether poem, essay, play, story, or libretto. You can write to the Westport, Connecticut, Famous Writers School.

Here is some advice to new writers:

1. Don't write something and then wait for something to happen to it. Do a piece and forget it.
2. Never look back.
3. Always have something in the typewriter.
4. Keep a notebook. Jot down your thoughts. If you don't do this, they get away from you.
5. Know your subject but don't swamp your pages with research.
6. "Never write about anything you don't know anything about."
7. Develop a fixed habit of work and of *daily* output.
8. If you are writing on a familiar subject, bring a new interpretation to it.
9. Ignore reviews.
10. Don't ignore criticism.
11. Do what your editors tell you.
12. Always work from a plan. Why so? At the very least, what you have done will have structural coherence; it will have form.

Writers write. Nonwriters talk about it. From the point of the mechanical as well as the emotional, I would say that a writer is nothing more than this: a man who can take unlimited loneliness, weariness, and disappointment and go right on working as if nothing had happened.

Here is episode #4,620 of *Love of Life*. It is the customary Friday cliff-hanger, bringing the action and the emotional crescendo a little farther ahead, repeating a few items conversationally so viewers who missed an episode or two can still stay with the story.

What has been discussed in another chapter in regard to splitting the hour show or the ninety-minute show into three or four acts represents a mechanical problem that has been cruelly compounded in the daytime serial, and almost ludicrously compounded in this particular daytime—only twenty-five minutes. Yet it must have its regular number of interruptions to accommodate the commercials the sponsor pays for.

You can understand Roy Winsor's bluntness about this aspect of daytime television. Some readers will remember that it was on this very rack that Garry Moore finally gave up daytime—too many commercials. It was degrading and bastardizing his shows, and he quietly sent up his challenge to headquarters: stop choking my show to death or I quit. They didn't stop and he quit.

Winsor, a healthy cynic, stayed with the agony and drives around Westchester County in a Rolls-Royce. Garry Moore had other shows beckoning.

In any case, bring your best effort to whatever you write. But in television, until you are a writer-producer, leave your idealism at home.

Perhaps as much as any other script in the book, this example of playable dialogue represents something I keep emphasizing: open pages. Open means playable.

LOVE OF LIFE
by Robert J. Shaw

CAST: SETS:

    ED   JOHN'S OFFICE

    JOHN   ROSEHILL INN

    BRUCE   STERLING PATIO

    VAN

    TESS

PATRONS & PERSONNEL   TIME:

AT THE ROSEHILL INN   DAY

ACT I

FADE IN: INT. JOHN'S OFFICE—DAY (10:00 AM). ED STANDS WAITING WHILE JOHN CONCLUDES A PHONE CONVERSATION.

JOHN

(TO PHONE) I agree, Father. Payment ought to be in Swiss francs. Exactly. I'll bring it up at the board meeting next week. Fine. (BEAT) How's the weather in Madrid? All right? (BEAT) Well, I'm glad to hear it. (BEAT) Yes, I will, Father. I'll tell her tonight. (BEAT) Good to talk to you. (BEAT) Yes, soon. (BEAT) Good-bye.

HE HANGS UP, AND MOTIONS ED TO A CHAIR.

JOHN

Sorry to keep you waiting, Bridgeman. My father was calling from Madrid. Sit down.

ED

Thank you. I'm afraid the May reports aren't quite ready, Mr. Randolph. I hope to finish them this afternoon.

JOHN

No problem. If you do finish them, just leave them here on my desk.

ED

I'll make sure of it.

JOHN

Actually, I didn't call you in about the reports. I have good news for you.

ED

Oh?

JOHN

You're doing a good job, Bridgeman. In fact, you're doing more than a good job. You've taken on additional responsibilities and you're handling them very well indeed. I'm not unaware of that.

ED

That's nice of you to say, Mr. Randolph.

JOHN

I've done more than just say it. You'll find a twenty percent increase in your next salary check.

ED

Why, that's . . . that's handsome of you, sir. I am deeply grateful.

JOHN

I'm grateful for your good work. And if I may be personal for just a moment, I was delighted to hear that things are going well for you at home.

ED

Clare and I are trying, Mr. Randolph. At the moment, I'm content with just that. We *are* trying.

JOHN

(PUZZLED) I'm sorry. I'm not sure I understand. I was talking about Sally.

ED

Oh, I'm sorry. I thought you meant something else. You see, sir, Clare and I are trying to . . . how shall I say it? Put our house in order. Straighten out our lives, as it were, while we still can.

JOHN

I'm glad to hear it. It's rather difficult to express, but I believe you have great potential. Not only here, but in other areas as well. As a family man, for example, and as a father. How is Sally? Getting along all right? (HE SEES ED FROWN) I'm sorry. Is something wrong?

ED

To tell you the truth, Mr. Randolph, it's too soon to tell. Sally's experience with drugs has had an effect. A very . . . disturbing effect. Whether it's permanent or not, we just don't know.

JOHN

What kind of effect?

ED

Apparently there's been some brain damage.

JOHN

Oh, no!

ED

Outwardly, she seems quite normal, except that she can't write. It's a matter of correlation, apparently, between the brain and her hands.

JOHN

Ed, I'm shocked. And deeply sorry. Can something be done?

ED

Something has to be done. We're seeing about therapy for her now. I haven't told Clare, incidentally. I thought that could wait.

JOHN

Of course. Well, again, I'm extremely sorry. And if there's anything I can do, anything at all, I want you to tell me.

ED

You've done a great deal already. You can see now why I'm grateful for the raise.

JOHN

Keep me advised, Ed. I mean that. For Sally's sake, and for yours, too.

FADE OUT

ACT II

FADE IN: INT. STERLING PATIO—DAY (5:00 PM).
WITH WHAT COULD BE BLOODY MARYS OR TOMATO JUICE.

JOHN

Bridgeman wasn't explicit, but apparently it's some form of brain damage.

BRUCE

That's tragic. I hadn't heard.

JOHN

Ed's keeping it quiet. In fact, he hasn't even told Clare.

BRUCE

It's not uncommon, you know. Sally took an overdose of speed—a concentration of amphetamine.

JOHN

Yes, I know.

BRUCE

Damage to the central nervous system is often the result. What are they doing about it?

JOHN

Ed mentioned therapy.

BRUCE

That can be a long process. And not always successful.

JOHN

You used the right word, I think. Tragic. The damage youngsters do to themselves. The sometimes irreparable damage.

BRUCE

The worst part is, kids themselves won't believe it can happen.

JOHN

I know. (BEAT) Incidentally, I hope you won't mention Sally's difficulty to Bill Prentiss. I'm not sure Ed wants it known.

BRUCE

Oh, I wouldn't. Actually, Van and I see very little of Bill these days.

JOHN

Isn't he living with you?

BRUCE

Technically, yes. But he's out early in the morning and by the time he gets back from working for Tammy at the theater he's off to The End.

JOHN

I'd heard he was working at the theater again this summer. This may sound strange, coming from me, but there's a lot to admire in Bill. His job at The End, his recording activity, working at the theater—one could hardly call him lazy.

BRUCE

Far from it.

JOHN

As long as we're talking about him, Bruce, tell me. Has he accepted the divorce pretty well?

BRUCE

The young are resilient, John. They bounce back.

JOHN

They can bounce, period. I'm an authority on the subject.

BRUCE

Oh?

JOHN

I imagine you've heard. Tess is moving back to Carrie's at the Potting Shed.

BRUCE

Really?

JOHN

Then you hadn't heard?

BRUCE

No. I don't think Van has either.

JOHN

She will, I'm sure. As I recall, the Potting Shed belongs to Van's mother.

BRUCE

Yes, it does. Oh, Carrie has an interest in it, but the original money came from Sarah.

JOHN

Well, the way things look, Sarah's going to have a tenant. Two tenants, really. Tess and the baby.

BRUCE

Look, I . . . I don't want to get into something that's none of my business . . .

JOHN

Nonsense. I brought it up.

BRUCE

It's just that I thought . . . that is, I assumed . . . (HE STOPS) Look.
Maybe we'd better change the subject.

JOHN

You assumed Tess and I would be married again.

BRUCE

Frankly, yes.

JOHN

So did I.

BRUCE

Are you saying you won't?

JOHN

Oh, no. Nothing like that. At least, I hope it's nothing like that. And in
a way, I can understand Tess's point of view.

BRUCE

That isn't always easy.

JOHN

What it comes down to, I think, is that Tess feels she's being manipulated.
By my mother, and to a certain extent, by me. This decision to move back
to Carrie's is really a blow for freedom, a desire to make up her own
mind. As I say, I can understand it.

BRUCE

You don't seem too upset about it.

JOHN

Just a bit disappointed, I'd say. Forgive me, Bruce. I had no intention
of pouring out my troubles. We must sound like two old biddies gossiping
over a shrimp salad.

BRUCE

I don't mind.

JOHN

Actually, I'm grateful. I like to think I've made good friends here in
Rosehill, but there are very few to whom I can talk this way. I'm afraid
you're stuck, Bruce. You're one of them.

BRUCE

I consider you a good friend, John. I'm not sure I'm much help, but I
certainly don't mind listening.

JOHN

I'm well aware that mother and I have managed Tess. I think we meant
well. Still do, but nevertheless, a certain amount of resentment is only
natural.

BRUCE

You really think Tess resents you?

JOHN

I hope not. In fact, really to lay it on the line, there's only one thing I want Tess to understand. I'm in love with her, I want very much to marry her, and in time—in due time—I shall.

FADE OUT

ACT III

FADE IN: INT. STERLING PATIO—DAY (5:00 PM).

VAN

(AMAZED) She's moving back with Carrie!

BRUCE

So John said at lunch, honey.

VAN

Well, I'll be . . . I really will be darned! Mother hasn't said a word.

BRUCE

She will. Give her time.

VAN

Darling, for heaven's sakes, don't stop there. And put down that paper.

BRUCE

What?

VAN

Tell me the rest. What did John say?

BRUCE

I just told you. He thinks Tess may move out of the Rosehill Inn and back to the Potting Shed.

VAN

But why? Didn't John say why?

BRUCE

(SHRUGS) I guess Tess likes to be independent. Something like that.

VAN

Have Tess and John had a fight?

BRUCE

No! For Pete's sake!

VAN

Something's happened, though. That much is obvious.

BRUCE

Van . . .

VAN

What?

BRUCE

Will you stop making a big thing out of it?

VAN

But, darling, it is a big thing. Oh, wait till I tell Diana.

BRUCE

Why don't you tell Charles, too? He can work it into his next TV show. Sort of a news bulletin.

VAN

Very funny. (BEAT) So, she won't do it. What do you know?

BRUCE

She won't do what?

VAN

Tess. She won't marry John.

BRUCE

Honey, I never said that. I'm serious, now. I never said anything like that. And neither did John. In fact, it was just the opposite.

VAN

What was?

BRUCE

What John said this noon.

VAN

You see? There is more. Bruce, you can be so infuriating. Tell me!

BRUCE

Honey, for your information, when two grown men have lunch, they do not sit there and discuss things like that.

VAN

Like what?

BRUCE

Like who's going to marry who.

VAN

Whom.

BRUCE

Thanks a heap.

VAN

Go on. What did John say?

BRUCE

Just that he wants to marry Tess.

VAN

That's hardly news.

BRUCE

That's what I'm trying to tell you.

VAN

Everybody knows he wants to marry her. But does Tess want to marry him? Now, that's something else again. It really is. Darling, start from the beginning. I want to hear exactly what John had to say.

FADE OUT

ACT IV

FADE IN: INT. ROSEHILL INN—DAY (6:00 PM). TESS AND JOHN ARE SEATED, WITH DRINKS.

JOHN

Father said the weather in Madrid has been perfect. June is pleasant there, as I recall.

TESS

It always sounds so marvelous. Just to say, oh, by the way, I was talking to Spain this morning.

JOHN

Father and I talk at least once a week.

TESS

I know. (BEAT) Can I ask you something about him?

JOHN

About Father? Why, of course.

TESS

You seem to like him, John. The way you just said, you talk to him a lot.

JOHN

Certainly I like him, Tess. Whatever made you think I didn't?

TESS

I've never been sure what to think. It just seems so funny. Amanda lives here with you, and your father lives way off in Madrid.

JOHN

We have large holdings in Spain, Tess. Throughout Europe, in fact.

TESS

Is that why he doesn't live with Amanda? Because of business?

JOHN

You know, you have rather a remarkable way of pointing up a question. No, it's not a matter of business. Sometimes I wish that were the answer.

TESS

I guess it's none of my business.

JOHN

Of course it is. Anything about me is your business. And to answer your question, Mother and Father have remained good friends.

TESS

Good friends? They're married.

JOHN

Yes, and to stay that way—to remain friends *and* man and wife—they find it best to live apart. Does that make any sense to you?

TESS

I guess so.

JOHN

They're both very strong personalities, Tess.

TESS

Your mother sure is. Sometimes I'm scared to death of her.

JOHN

Oh, now, come on, the Duchess adores you. You know that.

TESS

She's been wonderful to me. You both have. That's one reason it's so hard to . . . well, to do what I think is right.

JOHN

And that's what?

TESS

Move back to Carrie's.

JOHN

I see. You're going through with that, are you?

TESS

I have to.

JOHN

No one "has" to do something if she doesn't want to, Tess. May I speak quite frankly?

TESS

Sure.

JOHN

Are you concerned about expenses? The suite upstairs, Miss Blodgett's salary, all that?

TESS

I can't let your mother go on paying for all that, John.

JOHN

Would you let me?

TESS

No. That would be the same thing.

JOHN

I think you'll have to explain that. The same thing?

TESS

I can't let Amanda pay for me, or you, either, because then you'd never be sure. I'd never be sure myself.

JOHN

I'm still a bit confused. Sure of what?

TESS

We'd never be sure why I married you again.

JOHN

I see.

TESS

It's kind of hard to explain, but don't you see? If you or your mother are paying for me, then it might be that I'd marry you because I had to. Because I owed you so much. If I'm back living at Carrie's, and *then* we got married, it would be for just one reason.

JOHN

What reason?

TESS

Because I wanted to. I didn't have to. I wanted to. (BEAT) Does that make any sense?

JOHN

You know, dear, in your own way—your own, curious, often unfathomable way—you never cease to amaze me.

TESS

Is that good or bad?

JOHN

It's delightful. What you've just said, the way you've just explained yourself—is surely one of the nicest things you've ever said to me.

TESS

It's just the way I feel.

JOHN

Then move back to Carrie's by all means. Provided, of course, you understand one thing.

TESS

What?

JOHN

You'll be pursued, you know. Boxes of candy, flowers, my fraternity pin, you name it. If you like, I'll arrive nightly and howl under your window.

TESS

I'd love it.

JOHN

And I love you. (HE TAKES HER HAND) Remember that, Tess. Just that, and we'll be fine. I love you.

FADE OUT

ACT V

FADE IN: INT. JOHN'S OFFICE—DAY (6:15 PM). THE OFFICE IS EMPTY, AND THE DOOR IS OPEN. WE HEAR ED'S VOICE IN THE OUTER OFFICE.

ED'S VOICE

I told Mr. Randolph I'd put these reports on his desk, Mrs. Willy. You lock up, if you want to. I'll turn out the lights.

AFTER A MOMENT, ED ENTERS. HE CROSSES AROUND THE DESK, AND PLACES A REPORT ON THE BLOTTER.

FOR A MOMENT, HE SEEMS INCLINED TO LEAVE. THEN HE LOOKS AROUND, ADMIRING THE SANCTUM, AND QUITE OBVIOUSLY HIS IMAGINATION BEGINS TO WORK.

FINALLY HE SITS IN JOHN'S CHAIR, AND BEGINS TO ASSUME THE POSTURE OF AN EXECUTIVE, ENJOYING IT.

JOHN'S VOICE

(FILTER) You're doing a good job, Bridgeman. In fact, you're doing more than a good job. You've taken on additional responsibilities and you're handling them very well indeed.

ED

(EXPANSIVE) Think nothing of it, John, old man.

JOHN'S VOICE

(FILTER) I believe you have great potential. Not only here, but in other areas as well.

ED

(NODS) Other areas. Yes, that's quite true, sir.

JOHN'S VOICE

(FILTER) As a family man, for example, and as a father.

ED FROWNS, FOR THIS IS NOT A COMPLETELY PLEASANT AREA. HE ALLOWS HIMSELF TO SINK INTO DEEP, AND TROUBLED, THOUGHT.

ED'S VOICE

A family man. A father. Can that be true? After all these years, can that really come to be? Ed Bridgeman, a man of potential? A family man? A father? Not the Ed Bridgeman *I* know. Oh, never. Why, he's a . . . he's a . . . (BEAT) Well, go on, say it. What is he? A bum? A wanderer? A man born without one iota of responsibility? Isn't that the real Ed Bridgeman? Of course it is. He walked out on his wife and child, didn't he? You bet he did, and more than once. Just disappeared into thin air. Gone for years at a time without a care in the world. That's a man of potential? Oh, now, come on! Ed Bridgeman? Never. (PAUSE) Now wait a minute. That was before. That's all in the past. We're talking about the *new* Ed Bridgeman. Right? Right! The family man. The father. (BEAT) The father. (BEAT) Oh, Sally, Sally, how can I help you? If ever I wanted to make it up to you, if ever you needed me, it's now. Right now. But how? What do I do? How can I help you? Only God can do that now. Only God. Do I pray for you, my dearest? Is that now the only answer? (BEAT) Would God help me, do you suppose? Me, of all people? Would the dear Lord help *me* to help *you*? Would *He* help *me*?

HE PAUSES, AND THEN COMES OUT OF HIS REVERIE. HE STANDS UP, PLACES THE CHAIR JUST AS HE FOUND IT, AND TURNS OUT THE DESK LIGHT.

HE CROSSES TO THE DOOR, AND THE LIGHT FROM THE OUTER OFFICE ILLUMI-NATES HIM. HE PAUSES, AND THINKS.

> ED
> "Let each man think himself an act of God,
> His mind a thought, his life a breath of God;
> And let each try, by great thoughts and good deeds,
> To show the most of Heaven he hath in him."

HE PAUSES, AND THEN SEEMS TO FILL WITH DETERMINATION.

> ED
> And let each try.

HE TURNS OFF THE LIGHTS, TURNS, AND EXITS.

CUT TO:

INT. STERLING PATIO—DAY (7:00 PM).

> JOHN
> This is unforgivable, Van. I should have phoned.

> VAN
> Nonsense, John, we're glad you dropped in. Can you stay for dinner?

> JOHN
> Thanks, no. Mother and I are due at the Carlsons'. In fact, I'm late now.

> BRUCE
> How about a drink, John?

> JOHN
> I really haven't time, Bruce. I only stopped in because . . . well, to be honest, I'm so darned pleased about something, I wanted to tell you.

> VAN
> You look pleased.

> JOHN
> I am. I had a drink with Tess a few minutes ago, and she's decided to move back to Carrie's.

VAN

And that pleases you?

JOHN

Wait till you hear her reason.

BRUCE

Oh?

JOHN

I can't use her exact words, I'm afraid. Tess has rather an oblique way of expressing herself.

VAN

We know.

JOHN

But her thinking is beautiful. Really beautiful.

VAN

It must be. You're actually bubbling.

BRUCE

What'd she say?

JOHN

Tess has decided that as long as she stays at the Inn, as long as mother is paying for her, she could never be sure why she married me again.

VAN

I'm sorry. I think I've lost you.

JOHN

It's simple, Van. And quite wonderful. Tess won't marry me because she's obligated. Therefore she's going to move back to Carrie's where she *isn't* obligated.

BRUCE

And then what?

JOHN

And marry me, of course. But not out of obligation, Bruce. But purely and simply because that's what she wants to do.

VAN

Tess explained all that?

JOHN

That, and more. Do you wonder I'm pleased?

VAN

No, I don't. And I'm pleased for you, John. Once in a while, I think, we underestimate Tess.

JOHN

I don't.

BRUCE

You're prejudiced.

JOHN

Of course I'm prejudiced. She's going to be my wife.

FADE OUT

Story Projection for "Love of Life"

What kind of story plan do the writers of soap opera serials work from? Who determines where the story is to go? And how fast it ought to get there? Where its climaxes are to be spotted? Does the same writer who does the dialogue also do the story planning?

The boss of any production is the producer himself. In the case of *Love of Life,* Roy Winsor, the producer, is a bit more than Mr. Big. As co-creator of the show more than twenty years ago, he has exercised tremendous power over every aspect of the show, more than in the case of most daytime serials. In every sense *Love of Life* is this man's baby, or was until CBS bought it from him a year ago. The care and culture of this hardy perennial is so firmly set and so easily grasped that the show represents a fine model to work from.

Why do I say this? Because it has everything. And all of it bare as a winter tree, even to the attitudes of those doing the work. In advertising there is one basic rule and it goes like this: don't mess with a campaign that's working. In soap operas the same order obtains. Usually. Clients have pretty much learned to keep their hands off the daytime schedule, at least as backseat drivers. The temptation to interfere is less because there is nothing glamorous about the shows. And the work itself seems so arcane that most clients don't try to decipher it. Agencies pay some attention, but mostly to the ratings, the share, and the cost-per-thousand—or CPM, as it's known (M standing for thousand). This is so low for most daytimes that it alone guarantees the continuation of this kind of entertainment forever.

Story projections are of three kinds: the week-by-week projection, the three-month projection, and the long. The long projection is the most important, of course, and in reality it constitutes an outline for a novel. It is pure invention. The shorter ones are refinements. The long projection lays out the excitements and frustrations through which our characters are to be hauled for the next six months, even the next full year. Clients (who pay the tab) like to know the story will maintain a steady flow of emotional struggles and disintegrations. Advertising agencies like the positive assurance that these collisions will never cease. They like to be able to report this regularly to their clients. The story projection is the producer's promise to them both.

It will be useful for the student, or the aspiring writer, to arrange his schedule so that he can regularly watch *Love of Life* over a period of time. I suggest a minimum of twenty shows, or four weeks. You will presently realize the show has its own rhythms; that it would be possible to draw a graph or profile of highs and lows, to spot those exact places where new plot material is being introduced, to anticipate coming frictions and see what great use of these is made when they finally hit—Friday's friction, of course, is to bring you back Monday.

The principal advantage to a regular screening of the show is this: it will bring rich and rewarding meaning to the long story projection you are to see now. Roy Winsor will take story ideas from anybody. In fact, he very much seeks them from his writers, editors, and assistant producers. He studies all that comes in, redoes it, and then integrates the new material into the flow of what is going by now —passing the baton to a new runner, as it were.

You won't understand the *emotional* potential of what you are about to read unless you know the characters who are carrying the story now, and unless you know what they all mean to each other. Read the projection anyhow. Then make the disciplined effort to watch the show for several weeks. And then come back to this same outline and study it once more. It will have quadrupled its meaning and its worth, its worth to you. I earlier reminded you that one of the first reasons you should pay some attention to this part of the television spectrum is that it is easier for a writer to get started on a soap than on any other series or type on the schedule.

Here now is the basic material that took *Love of Life* through most of its delicious torments for more than a year. It has a title (they all do). Roy Winsor has called this projection "Extended Visit."

EXTENDED VISIT

Sarah Dale, Will Dale's widow of fifteen years and the mother of Meg Andrews and Vanessa Sterling, has lived all her life in Barrowsville, a small farm town of five thousand persons, northeast of Albany.

When Meg Andrews left New York after the murder of her husband, she went to live with her mother. In Barrowsville, Meg gave birth to Abby, now ten or eleven years old. Once Meg was back on her feet, she went to work for John Cerdone, an innkeeper, a minor hoodlum, a married man, and the father of three. Meg became his mistress and, in time, part owner of his inn, the Three Lanterns.

When in time Meg's reputation as a Jezebel became known to Mrs. Dale, there were many violent quarrels, which ended when Mrs. Dale ordered Meg out of her house. That was five years ago. Meg and her then six-year-old daughter moved to River Junction, about thirty miles away but in the direction of the Three Lanterns. Meg and her mother have not spoken to each other since Meg was forced to leave.

At the time our story begins (the week of December 11), Mrs. Dale telephones Van in Rosehill to say that she has had a stroke. When Van reaches Barrowsville, she finds that her mother, sixty-four or sixty-five, is frightened and now very conscious of being alone because, even though she is ambulatory, she will no longer be able to work as a clerk in Mr. Winton's General Store. Mrs. Dale then faces self-confinement.

What we now set about playing as our story is the all-too-familiar problem of what to do with an aged, dependent parent. Since it is the Christmas season, Van and Bruce insist that Mrs. Dale spend the holidays in Rosehill. She readily accepts.

After Van and Bruce return to Rosehill on December 15 (with Van promising to return next week to bring her mother to Rosehill), we see Mrs. Dale happily preparing to move out of her home, not to pay a visit to Van but to move out of her own home for good. She talks to a friend, a real estate man, and sells her house for twenty thousand dollars. Except for a few favorite pieces of furniture (a rocking chair, a lamp, some pictures, etc.), she also sells the rest of her household goods. The sale of everything amounts to twenty-seven thousand dollars. This, added to her savings of seventy-five hundred dollars, means that Mrs. Dale is worth about thirty-five thousand dollars. And, of course, she draws Social Security because her husband, Will, was covered when he worked as foreman of a small Barrowsville mill.

A word here about Mrs. Dale. We envision her as a pleasant, pathetic, God-fearing, church-going woman whose point of view toward life, morals, etc., was firmly fixed by the vestiges of Victorianism that were still very present in the twenties. She is self-righteously negative toward the attitudes, morals, and license of today. She never angrily or violently expresses her protest, but quietly sits in judgment of a world into which she will never quite fit. In Barrowsville, she had her church and her friends who thought as she did; when she is established in Rosehill, she will be alone, a fish out of water.

Bruce and Van have no idea when Mrs. Dale comes down for Christmas that she has assumed she will stay there forever. (Incidentally, we should see Mrs. Dale clucking to a Barrowsville friend or two—or even to her minister—about how wonderful it is to have a daughter like Van who knows a daughter's obligation to a parent. We should see enough of Sarah's world to realize that she will be a stranger, a foreigner, in her new "home.")

Bruce and Van make Sarah happy during the holidays. Then Sarah springs her surprise. She gives Van and Bruce a check for twenty-five thousand dollars, most of the money realized from the sale of the house. The Sterlings are stunned. "Ma! What's *this* for?" Sarah, her eyes twinkling through two small but real tears, says, "It's the least an old woman can do who's homeless and has found a home. The money is for you. In gratitude—and to use. I'm not expensive—and I have my savings and Social Security. This check is yours—for your kindness and for putting up with me."

From the foregoing, which is merely a series of incidents, we begin our story. Its theme is the problem a married couple face when their household is changed and possibly even destroyed by their sense of obligation to a homeless parent. This is a common problem today. We believe that it will find great empathy with the viewer.

Van and Bruce don't know what to do. Both of them know that the situation can become intolerable. Over a period of time, Sarah's presence aggravates the Sterlings' sense of helplessness. She slowly imposes her rigid way of life on both Van and Bruce. "Who was that on the phone, Van?" "Don't you think Mrs. Carlson is a little stuck-up?" "Now, that Diana is pretty, all right—but you say she isn't *married* to Mr. Lamont?" "You *do* insist on candles at dinner, don't you? Lands, when I was a girl, we were glad to get rid of them!" "Don't you drink a little too much, Bruce?" Etc.

None of what Sarah says is vicious. It's merely another viewpoint from another world and another time. It finally drives Bruce up the wall. Charles is his confidant, Diana is Van's.

Two events now occur to advance the story from the first stage. One snowy night on his way home from the high school, Bruce's car skids as he tries to avoid hitting a woman who, blinded by the snow, is hurrying to cross the street. Bruce stops his car and takes her to the hospital. (We play the concurrent excitement.) Bruce is very badly shaken up. (Don't forget that Bruce's first wife, Gay, was killed in an accident.)

The woman is Lucy Beale, thirty-five, and a widow. She is beautiful and articulate. She was married to a very successful New York lawyer, fifteen years her senior, who was exposed for a stock transfer swindle and committed suicide. Lucy left New York and returned to Rosehill, her hometown. She lived with her parents for a while and now lives in a beautiful apartment overlooking the river. She is a writer of monographs on historical sights to be found up and down the Hudson Valley and throughout the upper regions of New York State, gives slide lectures, etc. Bruce has heard of her, of course.

Bruce, being Bruce, has a deep sense of guilt about the senseless accident. He visits Mrs. Beale in the hospital. When she's released—in a few days because her injuries were minor, a broken arm and superficial lacerations—Bruce takes her to her home.

Because of Sarah's presence in the Sterling household, Bruce visits Lucy more and more frequently. She's stimulating and she's a very good listener. Obviously Bruce reluctantly—he's sure he loves Van—is falling in love with Lucy.

At about this time, who shows up in Rosehill but Meg! Van welcomes her heartily because Van is worried about Bruce, but, to her surprise, Van learns that Meg has only one reason for the visit: money. Meg has finally learned what her mother did—sold the family house and moved to Rosehill. Where's the money? Van says, "In the bank. It's yours. All of it—if you'll give mother a home. She's destroying mine!"

Meg is glad to oblige, but Sarah won't even see her. When the meeting is forced upon Sarah, she denounces Meg as a cheap prostitute. Meg is furious. She's entitled to half the estate. "She's not dead!" Van screams. "Get out, get out!" Meg's visit forces Van to act. She must get her mother out of the house. She must.

During the time that Bruce is more and more absent from the house because of Mrs. Beale, Sarah constantly disparages him to Van. Sarah and Bruce have very little to say to each other, so Sarah, unable to change Bruce into her image of a son-in-law, justifies Bruce's rejection of her by shaking her head over him as a lost soul.

We come now to the climax of the story. The easy solution, of course, would be to have Mrs. Dale die. Then Van might be able to reestablish her home. This is wrong. It's too pat, too easy.

Van investigates an old folks' home. Sarah flatly rejects the idea. When Van says, "But I'm losing my husband because of this situation!" Sarah says, "Good-bye to bad rubbish!" Van is desperate. She pleads with Bruce. He won't admit he loves Mrs. Beale. He simply cannot live in his own home with Sarah there as the ghost at every meal and meeting.

It's possible that old Aunt Carrie, who, as far as we know, is still working for Mickey, might come to the rescue. She and Sarah are much alike. By this time they will know each other. Aunt Carrie and Sarah could live together happily and forever after—and, a key point, Sarah would return to a milieu in which she is happy—church, warm milk, prejudice, suspicion, and self-righteousness.

Say that Carrie is our savior. What, then, about Bruce and Van? We suspect that Bruce would not quickly forget Mrs. Beale. In fact, we think that Bruce's relationship with her reaches a point where scandal raises its thorny head. Bruce is forced to leave his job as principal of West High, and he's out of work. Because he cannot quite bring himself to divorce Van, Mrs. Beale grows tired of Bruce and refuses to see him. In a way he's relieved.

When Van realizes that Bruce is headed for trouble, she goes to work. She easily manages to find a job selling real estate (she did this before) and then, whether or not she will take back a penitent Bruce, she will be a working woman and we will have her out of that kitchen for as long as we choose. As a woman with a job, we can place Van where her involvement in future stories will be easier to achieve than in her present role as a nosy intruder.

It seems to us that between the Tess-John-Bill story, which ends in Tess-Bill married, and "Extended Visit" (the Sarah Dale story), we have story material for at least a year. Furthermore, at the end of each story we have characters so affected and changed by the events of the year that the distant future opens up many fresh story possibilities.

I would like to end this chapter with an "inside" note, permission to reprint it having come from Roy Winsor. On another page I mentioned attitude. Here we have a fine example of it and in a double-edged way: attitude toward each other of the team that maintains *Love of Life* and the attitude (or intimations of it) of the group, and more particularly of Winsor, toward the work itself. It is a bit like running a garage or car wash. It is barren of illusion. It professes no idealism. It is not cynical but it is ultrarealistic, no-nonsense. It is bold, direct, challenging, extremely candid. Its purpose is blunt. It is trying to find out what's the matter with some of the other shows, coming from the same office, that aren't doing as well as *Love of Life*.

Here it is, unedited. Winsor has titled this memo "The Importance of Character."

FROM: Roy Winsor
TO: Staff
SUBJECT: THE IMPORTANCE OF CHARACTER

Last Sunday night I viewed *Bonanza*. The plot was so puerile that a puer would have rejected it as boyish. The plot was Swiss cheese. Two things, however, struck me as I watched my cuticle-picking confreres: no one challenged the plot; and each person was filled with empathy for the characters. Why? Here is a very successful program. As story and as plot, it was claptrap. Compared to it *Tarzan* and *Dr. No* are *War and Peace*. What is *Bonanza*'s appeal? If we know, we might learn something to apply to our shows, present and future.

What I think is this: *Bonanza* is filled with prototypes, 18th century "Humour" characters. The father is God. One son, "Hoss," is a simple peasant; another is a frustrated intellectual, "Adam"; and the youngest is "Nature Boy."

What is unique is that the producer and writer never allow variations on their prototype characters. Mr. Cartwright remains Godlike at all times, even, I suspect, when naked. "Hoss" can never be anything but ingenuous. And so on.

Now let us apply this to our programs. *Love of Life* is successful because we have adhered to the principle of prototype. If we create a Glen to be a villain, he is a villain. This is a major function of the job of producer-editor.

An even more important function of the producer is to force his imagination to envisage a character or a situation, either of which then can be worked into a story and then into a plot.

We have two programs which are not nearly so good as *Love of Life*. One is *The Secret Storm* and the other is *The Widening Circle*. More about *Circle* later.

On *The Secret Storm,* we have, for too long a time, presented actors to whom we have given names but—and I am speaking very broadly, of course—not character. The so-called characters are not quickly enough known to the viewer as good, bad, clever, furtive, wise, equivocal, etc. I think that I can prove this with an example: why did Peter marry Myra or Myra, Peter? We have never really known the answer to this question. If Peter Ames is similar to Mr. Cartwright in *Bonanza;* if he is a self-righteous man; if he is almost always absolutely sure of himself; if all these things are true, he would be attracted to a person who needs his kind of strength. This might be Myra. The point, however, is this: our producer and our writer(s) should calculatedly have known in advance that every time we saw Myra we should have seen her as the kind of person who, eventually, would marry Peter. And what kind of a Myra would that have been? A Myra who was mercurial, impulsive, charming, somewhat confused, struggling for a direction in life? Peter would have been there to supply that need. Then, in marriage, Myra would have become restless. This would have led to defiance and that, in turn, might have led her to Nick Cromwell—BECAUSE HE SHOULD HAVE BEEN VERY MUCH LIKE HER.

You see, once we decide who our characters are, and once we determine to keep them consistent, we can present characters with whom the viewer feels instant empathy. Most important of all, such characters could not stand around and talk. To any except the most trivial subject the characters would bring an *attitude*. When attitudes clash, there is conflict, and that's what this business of drama is all about.

I urge each of us—and I'm the biggest sinner of all, I do believe—to DEFINE CHARACTER IN THE VERY SIMPLEST TERMS, AND THOSE TERMS ARE IN PROTOTYPES. Richard the Third is unquestionably evil. Micawber always equivocates. Uncle Vanya and his ilk will always suffer, and Cleopatra will always make the pyramids blush. If we start with prototypes, and if we can keep characters based on those prototypes consistent, then a writer, within the orderly confines of the prototype, can work to make those prototypes credible, rich, real, and effective.

I mentioned *The Widening Circle*. Everyone likes this idea. Why? I think that I know why: the buyer likes it because it's about a girl who has suffered a mental breakdown and is trying to rejoin society. The character is a PROTOTYPE. *That* is what caught the attention of the buyers. Forget our idealistic prattle about studying life as it really is. We can get so lost in our own personal frustrations that we are in danger of overlooking the fact that we are in business to entertain people. We can tackle any subject, but only through characters whose natures are rooted in recognizable and easily identifiable prototypes.

I am going to rewrite the entire presentation of *The Widening Circle* because I want us to be certain that when we are told to put the program on the air, we know exactly the nature of each of our characters so that they will instantly be known and understood by the viewer. This, I believe, is the only way to create characters with whom the viewer can identify. Once that identification occurs—and *Bonanza* proves the importance of quick recognition of types—we have viewer participation in whatever story we want to tell. Also, our stories will move faster, harder, and more excitingly because we will not be able to attenuate for the simple reason that our protypical characters, kept consistent, could never just stand around and review or indulge in small talk.

If you disagree with this essay, say so. If you find it to be right, please apply it. Now!

13

PATROL

Here is an unusually interesting original by a student writer. He'll make the weight some day.

In the chapter dealing with soap operas, the point is made that television—as a sort of added dimension to radio—brings little to most of these living room dramas, that their interminable stories can be followed without looking at the screen. This is true of many television shows, even of some of the big nighttime shows.

Steve Shapiro, a graduate student who was in two of my sessions at Temple University, created the script you are to see next, in part as a protest against "radio with pictures," but more as an experiment in pure television. Can a convincing and coherent story be told in television without any dialogue at all? That is what this writer was going for.

No word is spoken. Not one. The entire story is projected by sound, pictures, acting, and background music. But I believe you will agree the story has great force.

This is a bold effort. Given a good cast and a sensitive director, the play would not only come off; it could be quite overwhelming. Shapiro's major purpose: to make *television* do all the work without benefit of a verbal interpreter. His own comments are most illuminating:

"The following paragraphs are a summary of the particular reasons I chose to do the story as I did. My reasons were two, one dealing with form, the other content.

"Television has often been criticised as being little more than radio with pictures. If a viewer were to not look at but only listen to most of today's programming, he would miss very little story. I wanted to create a drama that was entirely visual; stimulating thought, feeling, and emotion by what is seen rather than heard.

"If the production is a good one, I believe the viewer will, consciously or otherwise, supply any dialogue the characters *might* have spoken, i.e., the viewer would have spoken if he were there.

"I hope the story itself will suggest an antiwar theme to the viewer. The episode involving the tank illustrates the cool professionalism that men can bring to almost

everything, especially killing. The simultaneously youthful and grotesque appear
ance of the dead German tank commander gives the lie to the belief that war i
romantic or noble.

"This theme is further explored by the situation of the Old Woman and Child
political innocents, who are representative of those who generally do the sufferin
but are carefully omitted when war is glamorized. Their rejection of the American
(the perennial good guys) is a rejection of the idea of 'right' or 'wrong' of war
To their empty bellies, dead relatives, or ruined homelands, morality runs a poo
second.

"These events only serve to create an atmosphere for the primary confrontatio
between the German and American soldiers. Both are essentially the same: cold
weary, and resigned. The difference between them is an artificial one. It exists i
the color of their uniforms and shape of their helmets. For a short time they tak
leave of their roles as soldiers playing at war and become simply men who shar
a common agony, the intense cold."

PATROL

by Steve Shapiro

EXTERIOR. EXTREMELY COLD WINTER NIGHT. ARMY FRONT LINE.

CAMERA PANS a succession of foxholes showing soldiers sleeping. There i
snow on the ground and the men look dirty, worn, and tired. They range i
age from youth to middle age. CAMERA HOLDS on the last foxhole. CLOSE T
the face of SGT, also sleeping. After a brief moment, his eyelids flutter an
open. CAMERA HOLDS on his face as he visibly forces himself to waken. Hi
expression is a mixture of weariness, boredom, and resignation. He looks a
his watch.

CUT TO

SGT'S WRIST WATCH. It shows 12:00.

CUT TO

ECU SGT'S FACE as he makes up his mind to get up.

SUPER CREDITS

CAMERA MOVES BACK to show his companion sleeping. The SGT reaches ove
and silently nudges the sleeping CPL. CPL makes an unintelligible grunt a
he, too, wakens silently and looks at his watch. He nods and gets up, movin
about mechanically.

DISSOLVE TO

LINE OF FOXHOLES as the two men go along silently waking up four othe
men. The frozen breath of the men can be seen.

DISSOLVE TO

OVERHEAD ANGLE of MEN climbing out of their foxholes and lining up for
final check. The MEN are heavily bundled and again their frozen breath
evident as each man goes through his own ritual of trying to warm up a littl
while he is waiting.

ANOTHER ANGLE, CLOSER. The SGT goes around to each man and checks h
gear. CAMERA TRACKS parallel to SGT as he moves back to the front of the lin

raises his hand above his head and brings it forward in a "move out" gesture.

CAMERA HOLDS as the men move away into the still darkness.

CREDITS END

FADE OUT

ACT I

FADE IN on FIELD at NIGHT. LONG SHOT on men approaching, slowly and mechanically. CAMERA HOLDS as the men draw near and pass by, showing MCU's of their faces. The faces are lined, weary, and resigned.

DISSOLVE TO:

GROUND LEVEL ANGLE of a dirt road with little pools of frozen water and snow. CAMERA IS FACING IN FRONT of men. CAMERA HOLDS as the backs of legs come into view first as the men walk on screen. More of the men can be seen as they walk past the camera and along the road.

CUT TO:

FRONT ANGLE of PATROL. A rumbling sound is heard in the background.

CUT TO:

MEDIUM SHOT of the SGT as he raises his hand for the PATROL to stop as he listens for the sound. With a sudden realization, he recognizes it as a tank and motions for the platoon to scatter.

CUT TO:

POV of tank driver, catching a glimpse of a figure darting to the side of the road.

CUT TO:

SCENE

The tank goes slightly off the road in pursuit of the shadowy figure.

CUT TO:

YOUNG PVT behind a tree as the tank in the background fires its machine gun into the woods. He is trying to hold his breath and not run any farther as fear registers on his face.

CUT TO:

POV FROM REAR OF TANK. It is slightly off the road facing into the woods looking for the figure. Another figure approaches along the ground, kneels by the rear of the tank, and pulls the pins of two grenades before throwing them into the tread area of the tank. After throwing the grenades the figure gets up, runs, and dives to the other side of road.

CUT TO:

CPL diving into a ditch on the other side of the road. There is an explosion.

CUT TO:

TANK with smoke billowing from its side. The 50 mm gun of the tank fires a few short bursts and then is quiet. CAMERA HOLDS as the sound of the tank's motor is heard uselessly trying to move the tank.

CUT TO:

SGT in ditch waving his hand.

CUT TO:

SCENE

TWO MEN get out of a ditch and run across the road.

CUT TO:

REAR OF TANK. The men approach just as the top hatch begins to open. One of the MEN climbs up onto the tank as a GERMAN turns to face him. The PVT on the ground shoots the GERMAN, who slumps over, half in and half out of the hatch. PVT on the ground looks up at PVT on tank who drops another grenade into the open hatch and dives off.

QUICK CUT FROM:

PVT hitting the ground BACK TO TANK and HOLD as it explodes.

CUT TO:

PATROL approaching the tank slowly, cautiously, from different directions. CAMERA TRACKS parallel to SGT as he climbs aboard to peer into the tank hatch. He turns back to the dead GERMAN and rolls him over.

CUT TO:

ECU of dead GERMAN. It is the face of a very young man. The eyes are open and the mouth agape in a grotesque stare. CAMERA PULLS BACK to include SGT. The SGT closes the eyelids and climbs down slowly.

CAMERA HOLDS alongside the tank as the PATROL moves off down the road into the distance.

CUT TO:

PATROL walking along a small ravine.

DISSOLVE TO:

ECU of a PVT's foot as it steps on a frozen puddle, breaking through.

DISSOLVE TO:

LONG SHOT THROUGH A FARMHOUSE WINDOW of a quiet winter night scene. One at a time, shadowy figures dart from tree to tree and bush as the patrol moves on the farmhouse.

CUT TO:

EXTERIOR OF FARMHOUSE

The men are moving carefully up to the farmhouse. The first to reach the building is the SGT. He inches along the wall and toward the door and waits for his men to join him.

CUT TO:

MEDIUM ANGLE of MEN approaching the SGT at the wall.

CUT TO:

CU of SGT's FACE as he looks back to see that all of his men are with him.

PAN ALONG WALL showing the rest of the PLATOON.

CUT TO:

ANOTHER ANGLE, SGT's FACE as he signals one minute by holding up one finger and pointing to his watch. CAMERA MOVES BACK to show MEN circling the farmhouse and each stopping at a window or door.

CUT TO:

CU OF SGT's WATCH WITH SECOND HAND ON 11. FREEZE FRAME ON EACH SECOND AND JUMP OUT THROUGH TO ECU OF WATCH AS SECOND HAND SWEEPS TO 12.

CUT TO:

MEDIUM ANGLE SGT kicking in the door as the OTHERS go in through the windows and rear door.

CUT TO:

The doors bang open and the SGT is silhouetted against the door with his rifle at the ready. CAMERA CLOSES SLOWLY as the expression on his face softens.

CUT TO:

SGT'S POV. CAMERA PANS the interior of a single, disordered room. There is some broken furniture, an overturned stove, etc. In a darkened corner an OLD WOMAN is huddling with a small CHILD. Both are silent, shivering, and scared, cowering in the darkness.

CUT TO:

FACES OF SOME OF MEN looking guilty for their intrusion. The YOUNG PVT steps forward. He takes his overblouse off, then a sweater. He puts the jacket back on.

CUT TO:

POV of OLD WOMAN and CHILD as the YOUNG PVT approaches them and kneels down.

CUT TO:

ANOTHER ANGLE as the OLD WOMAN and CHILD stare at his gun. The YOUNG PVT reaches back and gives the gun to one of the other men.

CUT TO:

OLD WOMAN and CHILD staring in fear at the PVT. CAMERA MOVES BACK to include all three. The YOUNG PVT takes his sweater and offers it to the OLD WOMAN. She hesitates and then refuses, shaking her head.

CUT TO:

YOUNG PVT looking perplexed. He looks back to the others for reassurance.

CUT TO:

FACES OF OLDER MEN looking sympathetically skeptical.

CUT TO:

ANOTHER ANGLE. YOUNG PVT as an idea comes to him. He reaches into his coat and pulls out a candy bar. He holds it up so that the OLD WOMAN and CHILD can see what it is. The CHILD is hesitant.

CUT TO:

CU OF PVT. He smiles and nods his head yes while pushing the chocolate toward the CHILD.

CUT TO:

CU of OLD WOMAN and CHILD. The CHILD is about to accept, but the OLD WOMAN holds the CHILD close to her.

CUT TO:

ECU of OLD WOMAN'S FACE. There is hate and fear in her eyes as she spits at the YOUNG PVT.

CUT TO:

ECU of YOUNG PVT as his face registers shock and surprise. He is about to offer again, but a hand is placed on his shoulder. CAMERA MOVES BACK to show SGT reaching down for the candy bar. He takes it and the sweater. The CAMERA TRACKS with the SGT as he goes over and places the candy bar and sweater on the table, along with another candy bar from his own pocket. He walks slowly out the door. The others follow, placing candy and another sweater on the table as they exit.

CUT TO:

CU of table as candy and the sweater drop onto it. CLOSE TO ECU of candy and sweater on the table and

DISSOLVE TO:

CU of OLD WOMAN AND CHILD as the door is heard to close.

CAMERA MOVES IN FOR ECU as we

FADE OUT.

ACT II

GROUND LEVEL ANGLE of MEN silhouetted against the sky as they are again on patrol.

DISSOLVE TO:

OVERHEAD ANGLE THROUGH TREE BRANCHES showing the PATROL passing by underneath.

DISSOLVE TO:

FRONT ANGLE OF SGT approaching, stopping, and putting his hand up above his head to stop the PATROL. He points to his left and the MEN disappear into the woods in the direction he has pointed.

CUT TO:

FACE OF A PVT TO A CU OF HANDS GRIPPING A GUN TO CU OF A DIFFERENT FACE TO FEET WALKING ACROSS THE FROZEN GROUND TO REAR POV OF MEN MOVING THROUGH WOODS TO FACE OF CPL TO OVERHEAD ANGLE TO FOUR GERMAN SOLDIERS, apparently also on patrol. They are gathered around a fire, trying to warm themselves. Their guns are away from them, standing with the butts on the ground and the muzzles together, pointing skyward, forming a pyramid. SOL I is briskly rubbing his hands together over the fire. SOL II has his back to the fire with rear flap of his coat raised, trying to warm his rear. SOL III is trying to thaw out the German equivalent of C rations. SOL IV is just huddled close to the fire. Their faces are as weary and bored and tired as the Americans'. As the CAMERA PANS the scene, breaking twigs and other evidence of the approach of the PATROL can be slightly heard in the background. CAMERA CLOSES TO SOL III. He stiffens, eyes searching for movement, but does not go after his gun.

CUT TO:

SOL I. He, too, has heard the movement. His eyes also search for some sign. He looks at SOL III.

CUT TO:

SOL III looking back at SOL I.

CUT TO:

CU of SOL II. Like the others, he has heard movement. He tries to nonchalantly look around for its source.

CUT TO:

SOL IV by the fire. He remains still.

DISSOLVE TO:

SGT'S POV. He sees the four GERMAN SOLDIERS sitting by the fire.

CUT TO:

SGT'S FACE. HOLD BRIEFLY BEFORE CAMERA PULLS BACK SLOWLY as he motions to the others to encircle the fire.

CUT TO:

CU of SGT'S GUN as he releases the safety catch. QUICK CUT THROUGH PATROL releasing the safety catches of their guns.

CUT ONE-AT-A-TIME TO:

FACES OF GERMAN SOLDIERS as they each hear the distinct clicks of safety catches being released. Their faces show concern and realization, but they do not move any farther away from their positions.

CUT THROUGH:

REAR POV'S of AMERICAN SOLDIERS approaching the GERMANS around the fire.

DISSOLVE TO:

LONG SHOT of GERMANS at their places and the PATROL standing on the edge of the clearing in a circle around them with their guns ready. The GERMANS still have not physically noticed the PATROL'S presence. CAMERA HOLDS on scene as we

FADE OUT.

ACT III

FADE IN on the PATROL standing around the edge of the clearing as the GERMANS remain immobile in their earlier positions. CAMERA CLOSES IN SLOWLY on SGT as he remains motionless, trying to decide what to do.

QUICK CUT TO:

FACES OF THE PATROL showing similar expressions.

CUT TO:

ANOTHER ANGLE ON SGT as he takes a few cautious steps toward the fire. CAMERA PULLS BACK to show the rest of the PATROL doing the same thing. The GERMANS remain as they were.

QUICK CUT FROM:

FACE OF SOL I TO FACE OF YOUTHFUL PVT. TO the FIRE to a CU of PVT'S FOOT walking on the frozen ground. TO an OVERHEAD ANGLE of the PATROL stopped very near the GERMAN SOLDIERS.

DISSOLVE TO:

GROUND LEVEL SLOW PAN OF GERMANS still immobile, apparently waiting. The extreme cold should now become visually most obvious, from the SOLDIERS' frozen breath to the snow-covered ground to shivering on the part of the GERMANS who have yet to move. CAMERA PANS SCENE TO SGT'S FACE AND HOLDS for a moment as he again is confronted with a decision. His expression slowly softens and he looks down at his gun.

CUT TO:

MENACING CU OF FRONT OF MUZZLE AND SGT'S MITTENED HAND holding the rifle.

CUT TO:

SOL IV'S FACE, expressionless in his shivering.

CUT TO:

SGT looking questioningly at his men for help in making up his mind.

CUT THROUGH:

PATROL'S FACES AND BACK TO SGT'S, holding on him briefly.

CAMERA MOVES BACK:

ANGLE INCLUDES SOL IV and the SGT kneels by the fire, pauses, looks around again, and places his gun on the ground beside him. He then nonchalantly tries to warm his hands by the fire. CAMERA PULLS FARTHER BACK as the rest of the PATROL follow the example of the SGT.

DISSOLVE TO:

OVERHEAD ANGLE of all of the men huddled by the fire. The GERMANS still have not moved and the PATROL is kneeling close to the fire with their guns at their sides. HOLD BRIEFLY.

DISSOLVE TO:

CU OF FIRE. CAMERA MOVES BACK to show SGT and SOL IV by the fire. SGT takes out a pack of cigarettes and lights one. SOL IV's eyes follow his actions and look longingly at the cigarette. This is the first movement of any kind by any of the GERMANS. The SGT looks from the cigarette package to SOL IV's haggard face.

CUT TO:

ECU OF SOL IV'S FACE

CUT TO:

ANOTHER ANGLE, CU SGT'S FACE. He silently takes the cigarette from his mouth and leans over to offer it to SOL IV. CAMERA PULLS BACK TO SHOW SOL IV accepting it with a slight nod. SOL III leans across the fire and offers the SGT some of the food he has been warming. The SGT also accepts with a nod.

CUT TO:

WEARY FACES OF PATROL AND GERMANS

CUT TO:

ECU FIRE

DISSOLVE TO:

ANOTHER ANGLE. SOL IV finishing the cigarette, throwing it away, and offering an almost silent sigh. CAMERA MOVES BACK to show SGT finishing the food and handing back the plate to SOL III. SOL III takes it without looking at the SGT. SOL IV and SGT again confront each other with their eyes.

CUT FROM:

ECU OF SGT'S EYES TO EYES OF SOL IV TO SGT

DISSOLVE TO:

ANOTHER ANGLE. LONG SHOT. HOLD BRIEFLY.

DISSOLVE TO:

GROUND ANGLE IN FRONT OF SGT reaching for his gun.

CUT TO:

ANOTHER ANGLE. LONG SHOT as the PATROL again follow the SGT's example.

CUT TO:

SGT rising slowly. CAMERA MOVES IN FOR CU OF SGT AND HOLDS as he slowly backtracks into the woods.

DISSOLVE TO:

LONG SHOT of the PATROL following SGT'S actions. The GERMANS again sit as if they haven't noticed the PATROL'S PRESENCE.

DISSOLVE TO:

ANOTHER ANGLE. REAR POV as the PATROL slowly backs into the woods toward the CAMERA.

DISSOLVE TO:

OVERHEAD ANGLE GERMANS sitting by the fire and ZOOM OUT SLOWLY as we

FADE OUT.

CU of a SOLDIER'S foot as he is backing up. CAMERA MOVES BACK to show the SOLDIER trip over a branch and fall. As he lands, his gun goes off.

CUT TO:

ECU OF A MUZZLE OF A RIFLE in another SOLDIER'S hands as it fires.

QUICK CUT THROUGH:

DIFFERENT ANGLES ECU'S OF OTHER GUNS as they fire as if by reflex action.

CUT TO:

LONG SHOT of PATROL standing still to assess the situation.

ZOOM IN SLOWLY ON SGT AS CAMERA MOVES TO DIFFERENT ANGLE FOR ECU OF SGT'S FACE, fixed and emotionless. HOLD BRIEFLY. CAMERA MOVES BACK as SGT moves in to look at the dead GERMANS. Methodically he performs the ritual of turning one over to make sure of death.

CUT TO:

MEDIUM SHOT. ANOTHER ANGLE. The rest of the PATROL follows his example.

CUT THROUGH:

CU'S of FACES of AMERICANS. All of their expressions are also wooden, immobile, and emotionless. They are soldiers, unconsciously performing what they have been trained to do.

CUT TO:

ECU OF AN UNKNOWN FACE, alert and appearing to have just heard a foreign sound. CAMERA MOVES BACK to show a GERMAN SGT at the head of a patrol similar to the AMERICAN PATROL. He puts his hand up above his head to stop his men. He points to his left and the GERMAN PATROL disappears into woods in the direction he has pointed.

CUT FROM:

FACE OF A GERMAN PVT TO A CU OF HANDS GRIPPING A GUN TO A CU OF A DIFFERENT FACE TO FEET WALKING ACROSS THE FROZEN GROUND TO REAR POV OF GERMAN PATROL MOVING THROUGH WOODS TO FACE OF GERMAN CPL TO OVERHEAD ANGLE TO AMERICAN PATROL around the fire in the same positions as the FIRST GERMAN PATROL. As the CAMERA PANS the scene, breaking twigs and other evidence of the approach of the SECOND GERMAN PATROL can be slightly heard in the background.

DISSOLVE TO:

LONG SHOT THROUGH WOODS OF AMERICAN PATROL AROUND FIRE as the GERMAN PATROL can be seen approaching the FIRE. ZOOM OUT SLOWLY as we

FADE OUT.

As an interesting contrast in some of the basic techniques of radio and television respectively, especially in terms of technical directions, compare a sample page of any TV script with the simplicity of Milton Geiger's story, "In the Fog." It is a radio classic in its own right. The experience of one reading will show you why, and it will remain with you for a long time.

Radio had something that television doesn't have: a tremendous power to insinuate, to suggest, to lure—yes, even to haunt. Radio extracted the best from the imagination of each individual listener. It made you look over your shoulder, as a good story does. It didn't tell you all. It was sightless, so it couldn't. Thus it compelled *you* to furnish, from your own emotional chemistry, what did not go down on the page, what did not come out, as words or sounds, from the speaker. Radio was a much more personal thing than television. For anything that really caught our own moods and imaginations, we invested the show with our own private interpretations and reactions. We brought our own daydreams into it and let the program enrich these, as listeners do, for example, in their responses to music.

Here is "In the Fog"—a play without sight, just as "Patrol" is a play without the sound of words, a pure contrast of radio and television elements.

IN THE FOG

MUSIC—DOWN BEHIND NARRATION.

NARRATOR

It is a dense, foggy night somewhere in Pennsylvania. An automobile feels its way slowly over the misty hills. Suddenly, a blur of swaying light swims before the driver's straining eyes. Dimly, the figures of two men materialize out of the darkness. Each carries a rifle under his arm. One wears a canteen slung over his shoulder. The other wears a tattered jacket that looks as if it once belonged to some kind of uniform. The men set themselves squarely in the path of the oncoming automobile; one lifts his lantern, while the other levels his rifle menacingly at the man behind the wheel.

MUSIC—OUT.

SOUND—DRONE OF AUTOMOBILE AT LOW SPEED.

EBEN

(OFF . . . STRANGELY) Stop! In the name of mercy, stop!

ZEKE

Stop, or we'll shoot!

SOUND—GRIND OF BRAKES . . . ENGINE IDLES.

DOCTOR

(MORE ANGRY THAN AFRAID) What—what do you men want?

ZEKE

(COMING ON) You don't have to be afraid, mister.

EBEN

We don't aim to hurt you.

DOCTOR

(INDIGNANTLY) That's very reassuring! I'd like to know what you mean by stopping me this way!

ZEKE

What's yer trade, mister?

DOCTOR

I—I'm a doctor. Why?

ZEKE

A doctor, hey?

EBEN

Then you're the man we want.

ZEKE

He'll do proper, I'm thinkin'.

EBEN

So you'd better come out o' that thing, mister.

DOCTOR

You understand, don't you, that I'm not afraid of your guns. You may take anything of mine you like, but don't imagine for one moment that I'll be quiet about this to the authorities.

ZEKE

All right. But we're needin' a doctor right now.

DOCTOR

Oh, has anyone been hurt?

EBEN

It's for you to say if he's been hurt right to the finish.

ZEKE

So we're askin' ye to come along, doctor.

DOCTOR

Very well. If you'll let me get out of here.

SOUND—DOOR OPENS . . . SLAMS METALLICALLY.

DOCTOR

(INTERROGATIVELY) Well. Take me to your man. Where is he?

EBEN

Yonder.

ZEKE

Under the tree, where he fell. He's bad wounded, we're a-fearin'.

DOCTOR

I don't know you men, you know. Do you suppose I could have a better look at you?

ZEKE

Why not? (PAUSE) Raise yer lantern, Eben.

EBEN

Aye. (PAUSE)

DOCTOR

(APPALLED . . . GASPS) Good Lord!

ZEKE

(IMPASSIVELY) That's Eben. I'm Zeke.

DOCTOR

But great heavens, man, what's happened!? Has—has there been an accident or—or—or what? Your faces, streaked with dried blood. It's in your hair, in your beards! What's happened?

ZEKE

Mischief's happened, stranger.

EBEN

Mischief enough.

DOCTOR

But . . .

ZEKE

So if ye'll be comin' along, we'd be ever so much obliged, that we would.

DOCTOR

(STILL SHOCKED . . . LOW) Yes, yes, of course.

EBEN

(OFF A LITTLE) This way, doctor. Follow the lantern.

ZEKE

(RUMINATINGLY) Mischief's happened, that's what. Enough to last these parts a good long while and a day.

DOCTOR

I don't like this. I don't like it at all!

ZEKE

Can't say we like it better'n you do. What must be must. There's no changin' or goin' back, and all's left is the wishin' things were different.

DOCTOR

There's been gunplay!

ZEKE

(MILDLY BITTER) Ye'r tellin' us they's been gunplay.

DOCTOR

And I'm telling you that I'm not at all frightened. It's my duty to report this. And report it I will!

ZEKE

(CASUALLY SARDONIC) Aye, mister. You do that.

DOCTOR

You're arrogant about it now, yes! You don't think you'll be caught and dealt with. But people are losing patience with you men, you—you—moonshiners! Running wild, shooting up the countryside!

ZEKE

(UP) Hear what he says, Eben, moonshiners!

EBEN

(OFF) Here we are. (PAUSE . . . ON) And there's yer man, doctor.

ZEKE

(ANXIOUSLY) He ain't stirred since we left 'im.

DOCTOR

All right, let's have that light, will you? (PAUSE) Closer. So.

EBEN

Like this?

DOCTOR

Yes. That's good. Now help me with his shirt. No, no, don't take it off; just tear it. Yes . . .

SOUND—RIPPING OF CLOTH, CLOSE ON-MIKE.

DOCTOR

That's good. Now bring that lantern still closer and . . . (DEEP BREATH . . . LOW) Dreadful, dreadful!

ZEKE

Reckon it's bad in the chest like that, heh?

DOCTOR

His pulse is positively racing! How long has he been like this?

ZEKE

A long time, mister. A long time.

DOCTOR

Well—(WITH DECISION) You! Hand me that bag! Hurry!

ZEKE

(TENSELY) Aye, captain.

SOUND—RATTLE OF BAG.

DOCTOR

Open it!

SOUND—RATTLE OF INSTRUMENTS AS BAG IS OPENED AND RUMMAGED THROUGH.

DOCTOR

All right, now lend me a hand with these retractors. Draw back on them when I tell you to. Hold it!

SOUND—DEEP BREATHING, TENSELY . . . ON-MIKE.

EBEN

How is he, mister?

DOCTOR

More retraction; pull back a bit more. Hold it!

EBEN

Bad, ain't he?

DOCTOR

Bad enough. But the bullet didn't touch any lung tissue so far as I can see right now. All I can do is plug the wound. I've never seen anything like it!

EBEN

Ye'r young. Lots o' things you never seen.

DOCTOR

(PAUSE . . . DEEP BREATH) There. So much for that. Now, then, give me a hand here.

ZEKE

(SUSPICIOUSLY) What fer?

DOCTOR

We've got to move this man! We've got to get him to a hospital for treatment, a thorough cleansing of that wound, irrigation. I've done all I can for him here.

ZEKE

I reckon he'll be all right, 'thout no hospital.

DOCTOR

Do you realize how badly this man is hurt?

EBEN

He won't bleed to death, will he?

DOCTOR

I don't think so. Not with that plug in there. But . . .

ZEKE

All right then. (A DISMISSAL) We're much obliged to ye.

DOCTOR

But I tell you that man is dangerously wounded!

ZEKE

Reckon he'll pull through, now, thanks be to you.

DOCTOR

(ANGRILY) Well, I'm glad you feel that way about it! But I'm going to report this to the Pennsylvania state police at the first telephone station I come to!

ZEKE

We ain't stoppin' you, mister.

EBEN

The fog is liftin', Zeke. Better be done with this, say I.

ZEKE

(SLOWLY . . . SADLY) You can go now, mister, and thanks. We never meant a mite o' harm, I can tell ye. If we killed, it was no wish of ours. What's done is done, though.

EBEN

(AS SADLY) Aye. What's done is done.

ZEKE

Ye can go now, stranger. On your way. We don't want no more trouble. There's been trouble enough and grievin' enough an' we've had our share. Aye. Our share and more. We've killed, and we've been hurt fer it. We're not alone, either. We ain't the only ones. (PAUSE . . . SIGHS) Ye can go, now, doctor.

EBEN

Aye. An' our thanks to ye. You can go now, an' thanks. Thanks, mister, in the name o' mercy. (FADING . . . HOLLOW) In the name o' mercy we thank you, we thank you, we thank you . . .

MUSIC—BRIDGE BRIEFLY.

SOUND—FADE-IN DRONE OF AUTOMOBILE ENGINE . . . FAST . . . CAR GRINDS TO STOP . . . DOOR OPENS AND SHUTS METALLICALLY.

ATTENDANT

(COMING ON) Good evening, sir. Fill 'er up?

DOCTOR

(IMPATIENTLY) No, please. Where's your telephone? I've just been held up!

ATTENDANT

No!

DOCTOR

Do you have a telephone?

ATTENDANT

Find one inside, pay station.

DOCTOR

Thank you!

ATTENDANT

(STOPPING HIM) Er . . .

DOCTOR

Well? You were going to say something?

ATTENDANT

Sort of looking fellers were they?

DOCTOR

Oh. Two big ruffians, with rifles. They won't be hard to identify. Bearded, both of them. Faces and heads bandaged and covered with dirt and blood. Friend of theirs with a gaping chest wound. I'm a doctor, so they forced me to attend him.

ATTENDANT

Oh. (ODDLY KNOWING) Those fellers.

DOCTOR

Did you know about them?

ATTENDANT

Yeah, I guess so.

DOCTOR

They're desperate, I tell you, and they're armed!

ATTENDANT

That was about two miles back, would you say?

DOCTOR

Yes, just about that. Now, if you'll show me where your phone is and tell me the name of that town I just went through—(PAUSES ON QUESTIONING NOTE . . . NO ANSWER) I say . . . (ANNOYED) What town was that back there?

ATTENDANT

(ODDLY . . . QUIETLY) That was Gettysburg, mister . . .

DOCTOR

(STRUCK) Gettysburg!

MUSIC—IN VERY SOFTLY, POIGNANTLY, BACKGROUND, "JOHN BROWN'S BODY."

ATTENDANT

(QUIET AND SOLEMN) Gettysburg, and Gettysburg battlefield. (PAUSE . . . FOR EFFECT) When it's light and the fog is gone, you can see the gravestones. Meade's men and Pickett's men and Robert E. Lee's.

DOCTOR

Then, those—those men . . .

ATTENDANT

On nights like this, well, you're not the first they've stopped in the fog, nor the last.

DOCTOR

(SOFTLY . . . DISTANTLY) Gettysburg, and the dead that never die!

ATTENDANT

That's right, I guess. (PAUSE . . . DEEP BREATH) Fill 'er up, mister?

DOCTOR

(DISTANTLY) Yes, fill 'er up . . . fill 'er up.

MUSIC—"JOHN BROWN'S BODY" UP STRONG . . . CASCADE OF DISTANT TRUM-
PETS FADING AWAY INTO "TAPS" AND ORCHESTRA IN THEN . . . FULL AND OUT.

14

PLOTS, PLOTTING, AND SYNOPSES

The entire purpose of this chapter is to remove the terror and the mystery from this area of writing popular fiction. Among the most fearsome of all writing problems, plotting is always mentioned first. That is to say, it is always mentioned first by nonwriters.

However, it is actually the least of the professional's problems.

For those writers who haven't written for television and for those student beginners who want to get there because they hear it pays well (there is no better reason to write), it should be comforting to realize they are *continuously* in the presence of the very answers they seek.

How so?

Stop looking at television to enjoy it. *Start* looking at it to dissect it.

Put a pad on your lap. Write down every one of the story's essentials as it reveals itself—or as it promises to reveal itself but then suddenly fools you by doing something else. Don't wait for the end of the story to write its plot. You'll likely miss the very trick you're trying to uncover. Write it as the story is unfolding. Allow yourself to be trapped or intrigued or waylaid or deceived. Do this for your own benefit. There is no better way to unlock the author's secret than to permit yourself to be guided according to his story plan—his plot—as if you were just another enraptured beholder, which in every way except one you are.

The one way in which you are different is this: you are the only person watching that television show who is mercilessly going to go back over it, scene by scene, challenging everything that happened, every motivation that caused it to happen, and every character's response to the stimuli with which the writer has pricked him. You are going to find out why it worked.

You are going after the real basic—validity. Without that, nothing is believable. Suppose you enjoyed the story while it was in progress, enjoyed it perhaps for its fine acting or its speed of storytelling or the magic of its atmosphere. Then suppose you find, upon reviewing your notes and your memory together, that the conclusion should not have, *could* not have derived from the buildup of story material preceding it.

What must you determine from this? You must accept the judgment that the story was a cheat and that you've been had.

Only you *haven't* been had. You've made a diagnosis, learned something. You've been a secret witness to an interesting, instructive postmortem. You don't have to worry about the departed corpse. You didn't write it. It was some other body snatcher who lugged in that one. You may learn how to reoxygenate the very corpse another writer's clumsiness has permitted to expire.

This skill has only one requirement: the disciplined intention to watch television for a purpose other than pleasure. That purpose is profit.

Your first efforts in this new area, with its acknowledged intent to spy, will be awkward. You won't be able to read back all your notes. I suggest you make them as legible as possible and that you do so during commercials. You'll need to know exactly what your notes mean if the words are to separate the raw materials of story from the fascination of a fine production. A fine production can hide many flaws. A fine production can hide a fraud.

You'll write too much. You will also leave out clues of importance. How so? You'll leave them out simply because you didn't recognize them as clues while they were going by. The writer fooled you. He conned you. (That's part of his craft.) But after forty or fifty such sessions, you'll be harder to deceive. And you will also have taken this great forward step:

You will be *thinking* in terms of plot and motivation.

After honest practice and the beginnings of self-reliance, you can start the more professional refinements of economy, of not saying so much, of saying only what needs to be said in order to display the story's power, its arrangement, its tricks.

Plot synopses should do a bit more than tell the story. They should report the story's special individuality. They should reveal the story's special twist, its special use of suspense, reveal its special surprise if it has one.

A good plot synopsis should make a complete statement to the uninformed, to the person who did *not* see the show. And this statement, without decoration, should be sufficiently meaningful to make clear the real dimensions of the story.

Think of the synopsis this way: that you, and not someone else, have written the story and that you now want an editor to buy it, but that the editor is giving you only *one minute to interest him.*

A skeleton, then? Yes. But a skeleton with articulating joints. This skeleton must get up and jump. Accordingly, more than anything else, you must be *specific.* The nonspecific is deadening, wasting. The specific moves, shows, activates, convinces. It doesn't just promise. It lays down the cash.

Your plot synopsis must have two virtues. It must be complete. Yet it must be concise. At first, in trying for completeness you will overwrite. In trying for conciseness, you'll miss things.

Start your practice of story dissection with these rules:

1. Don't let your personal preferences intrude.
2. Don't be flippant.
3. Don't editorialize.
4. Don't try to make a script evaluation.

5. Don't try to "write." Just try to be clear.
6. Use the present tense at all times.
7. Don't use the word "foil" or any other shorthand word that doesn't do the job.
8. Don't condescend.
9. Reread your work. Cut every irrelevance.

Here's a good question to keep in mind while putting any synopsis together: "Could a professional writer reconstruct the television show I've just seen on the basis of what I've just written?"

If he could, then you've done your job. Of course, you don't know for sure, since your work won't be put to that test. Nevertheless, this is the *obligation* that is incumbent upon you. And if you keep looking at this obligation, you're more certain to meet it.

Let's now study a few synopses. First, we'll give our attention to several that clearly reveal how *not* to do it.

"Lucy and Carol become airline stewardesses. They pull all sorts of blunders on their first trip. Lucy has eyes for one passenger and offers him all sorts of comforts which are obviously unwanted."
Don't say "all sorts of." Much better to give us just one.

"This was the regular *Hazel* show."
This says nothing, even if you are a regular viewer.

"Soon he is deeply entrenched in a myriad of petty difficulties."
This says nothing. Neither does this: "Everything soon reaches an impasse." Such a statement is gloriously empty of picture, information, and usable reference.

Here's one that starts out well enough, then suddenly aborts its mission: "Bank robbery. Fourteen-year-old boy sees where the loot is stashed. Boy's grandfather also stumbles upon the cache. Police suddenly find the two with the money. The boy had found it in a shack, and so admits. Hours later the police find a body in the same shack. It's up to Perry Mason to prove the boy and his grandfather had nothing to do with the robbery or the murder."
What's missing here is so central, its omission is almost comical. Begin with: Did Perry Mason find them innocent? If so, how?

"*Green Acres* is a typical improbable situation comedy in the true tradition of *Beverly Hillbillies*. Dissimilar to a good situation comedy, the situation is unlikely and not comic. It is inundated with canned laughter inserted at nonhumorous times."
Do we know anything yet?

"The situation was one in which the husband and wife—two sophisticates from New York who moved to a farm—were trying to convince the ignorant townspeople to go on a trip to Paris. The purpose of this maneuver was to create a bond between farmers of both areas. The wife explained that at least 112 dresses and four coats, three of them fur, were needed. The townswomen confessed to owning only three dresses and one coat."

Well, we have a start, anyhow. Here's the closing paragraph:
"This is possibly the humor that could be seen by the middle-class viewer. As in any comedy, when people are taken from their natural habitat and placed in a new situation, there forms a humorous note. However, in this particular program, the situation was 'cute,' but the acting and humor were strained, as was probably the writer."

This violates most of the rules—the first three, especially. It is just poor reporting. The viewer hasn't told us much of what he saw. He's told us how he felt about it. We're not interested in that. We'd like to know, since it sounds like the very center of the story, whether anyone got to Paris and, if so, how and what happened. (This is the only television show I don't have the physical courage to watch. Perhaps this also happened to the student somewhere along the way.)

"*Dragnet*—this punchy, fast-talking, quick-cutting, old-time detective favorite could very aptly be tagged the series with the plot that never changes. In last week's episode, Sergeant Friday and his straight-faced aide, Officer Gannon, broke up a tricky con game operated by a gypsy spiritual reader, Mother Marie.
"As in other *Dragnet* episodes, the plot centers around Friday and Gannon and the way they employ their powers of detection to foil the fiendish plans of all criminals operating in the Los Angeles area. The boundaries of the *Dragnet* plot dictate that these hardened, almost cynical officers must always get their man. In this respect, the plot has become somewhat hackneyed. As a matter of fact, it would be a delight to see the good guys stumped at least once. In general, though, the plot succeeds because it places two no-nonsense police officers in suitably lifelike situations."

This attempt grounds itself by violating rules three and four. There is only one sentence that relates to the analysis we seek: "Sergeant Friday . . . broke up a tricky con game operated by a gypsy spiritual reader."

"Patty fails a 'typical teenager' contest and enrolls in a modeling school to regain her confidence."
Does this say anything? Yes. A lot. Now read the next sentences:
"She decides models make a lot of money and possess a great deal of glamour." This adds little. Already implicit in first sentence. "This changes her attitude and she then actively tries to become a model." How? "She succeeds" (how?) "but appears to create an unresolvable situation" (which is what?) "when her plans didn't work out as expected." Why not? "The final solution" (which is what?) "is happily attained in the closing moments and we are prepared for the next episode."
If the essential story is not reconstructible from your plot synopsis, you've failed. The above synopsis of a Patty Duke *show, therefore, is a failure. We don't know the how of anything.*

See how much better done this is:
"The guest star, Carol, recently moved to Patty Duke's hometown, where Carol becomes a classmate of hers at Brooklyn Heights High School. Carol is a shy girl and, because she is new there and has no friends, she is extremely introverted.

Patty, who is very popular, decides to help Carol overcome this shyness. Patty and her boyfriend Richard teach Carol to dance, cheerlead, etc. Patty tells Richard to take Carol out on a date.

"Soon Patty becomes upset because Richard and Carol are dating on a regular basis. Carol becomes captain of the cheerleaders and runs for class president, the office Patty presently holds. So Carol and Patty are opponents again. Patty's father rationalizes the situation and tells Patty that if she wins the election her original battle will be lost, that being to help Carol. Patty campaigns for Carol. Carol wins the class presidency, and Patty and Richard get back together."

This is fine. The writer has condensed all the values of the show, missed nothing, wasted no words.

"The exiled ruler of Vaisca has been captured by the Vaiscan secret police chief, together with microfilm containing the names of Vaiscans involved in a plot to overthrow the new government. The Mission Impossible team is assigned to rescue Nikolai Curzon, who is being returned to Vaisca for interrogation, and to recover and destroy the microfilm. A Vaiscan plane carrying the Deputy Chancellor home from the United States will stop to pick up Stahl, the secret police chief, and Curzon —the rescue will be made from the plane.

"Cinnamon poses as a famous French astrologer and tells the Vaiscan Vice-Chancellor, who is waiting at the airport, that the Chancellor is in grave danger. Rollin, impersonating the Chancellor on a phone tap, convinces the Vice-Chancellor that an attempt was made on his life and asks that the astrologer accompany the Vice-Chancellor back to Vaisca.

"Barney and Rollin are concealed in Cinnamon's luggage, together with an automaton copy of Curzon. They gain access to the compartment where Curzon, under heavy sedation, is being kept by cutting a hole through to him from the baggage compartment. They first substitute a microfilm implicating the Vice-Chancellor for the real one in the plane's safe. The secret police chief, on an astrological tip from Cinnamon, looks at the microfilm and arrests the Vice-Chancellor and his deputy. Then he contacts the Chancellor by radio.

"Barney has wired the radio so that Rollin, in the baggage compartment, can once again impersonate the Chancellor. Rollin tells Stahl to land the plane at an airport near the chief executive's country estate, to drop off the astrologer, and then to proceed to the capital, where Stahl will be in charge. Then Rollin and Barney place the automaton by an emergency door and rig it to open the door on an electronic signal. When Stahl comes to investigate the emergency door alarm, he sees 'Curzon' open the door and get sucked to his death.

"When the plane lands at the airport near the country estate, Phelps and Willy, posing as the Chancellor's servants, pick up Cinnamon and her luggage, containing Barney, Rollin, and Curzon. As the plane prepares to continue to the capital, Phelps releases the three from the luggage and burns the original microfilm."

This is a fine compression of a Mission Impossible *plot. In such shows (include* Star Trek, I Spy, Run for Your Life, Voyage to the Bottom of the Sea) *the plots are often necessarily complicated. Deliberate mystification is part of their fun. Thus they can't be squeezed as tight as the plots for comedy and straight drama—straight drama, that is, as opposed to melodrama. Nor squeezed as tight as the involved kind of storytelling we often find in the science fiction category.*

"Jethro gets a crush on a movie starlet but becomes dejected when she calls him a 'creep,' runs over his foot with her car, and sics her dog on him. The starlet, Kitty, changes her tune, however, when she discovers that Jethro's Uncle Jed owns the studio where she works. Jethro, armed with a love charm from Granny, again meets Kitty, who now willingly goes home with him to meet his family. When they arrive, however, she suddenly shifts her affections from Jethro to his Uncle Jed."

This is a fair statement of a representative Beverly Hillbillies *show. Remember, these things aren't supposed to be imperishable.*

"A six-foot, arm-wrestling girl in a mining camp town sets out to 'court' the new constable. He is quite put off by her mannish ways. When she realizes this, she goes to the doctor's wife, the only other woman in town, and asks if she will teach her to be a lady. When she completes her lessons in demureness, domesticity, and baking, she sets out after the constable again, and gets him."

Much the same comment applies to this sample of Death Valley Days *as to* Beverly Hillbillies *above. It's warm and funny, and reasonably believable and human, and quite awful. But think how long the show ran. Respect the factors that gave it durability.*

"Tarzan interrupts a witch doctor's attempts to 'cure' a little boy, takes the boy to the local M.D. The jealous witch doctor then kills the M.D. The M.D.'s son, come to pick up his father's personal notes, instead takes his place when he hears the story.

"His mother plots with a disreputable district officer to have him returned to the States. The witch doctor forces the officer to empower him to carry out the deportation order, an order Tarzan has refused to allow. Tarzan is jailed for his interference, but the chief of the tribe supports the M.D. The ambitious witch doctor sees this as a chance to become chief and he declares war.

"Tarzan breaks out of jail, with help from Jai and an elephant, and arrives at the village in time to help the chief's forces defeat the witch doctor's men. In a last desperate foray, the wounded witch doctor holds a knife at the throat of the M.D., but Tarzan reminds him that the M.D. is the only one who can save him. He capitulates and everyone is happy, including the mother, who decides to stay and help her son as she had refused to help his father."

There is much villainy here, but most of it is pretty well motivated. This story, creditably summarized above, was strong enough and literate enough to win the attention of Helen Hayes—who played the city-bred but provincial mother—and her son, James MacArthur, who played the young M.D. Many of America's best actors and actresses appeared as guests in this series. Though it's off the air, it will return. Have no fear. A new Tarzan is pounding his chest this minute, somewhere.

"Trouble arises when Morticia's former beau visits the Addams household. Jealous Gomez hires a maid to seduce him. Both husband and wife become convinced that their marriage has become triangular—Morticia believing Gomez has become smitten with the maid, and Gomez being certain that she will leave him for her ex-suitor. Happily, the two visitors leave in marital togetherness when the boyfriend discovers the maid is rich in stocks."

In my view, the basic component in the fine Addams Family *series has almost nothing to do with its deliberate grotesqueries, although many of these were egregious. It has to do with the vast love these spooky people have for each other. This aspect runs right through the series. The above synopsis, brief but sufficient, notes the implicitness of love as being the pivot on which this neat but tiny plot revolves.*

"Bill Davis returns from a party and casually mentions that Carole Haven was there. The thought of Carole Haven, a beautiful movie star, talking to their uncle excites Bill's three adopted children, and especially sixteen-year-old Cissy. The phone rings. It's Carole herself and she'd like to go out to dinner with Bill.

"At dinner, fans recognize Carole and keep interrupting their conversation.

"The next night, they have dinner at Bill's house and Carole meets the children. They love her. The following days she takes them shopping and tells them she might be leaving for Spain to do some filming. The children are sad.

"Carole goes to her agent and tells him she's going to abandon her career and get married. When Bill arrives, she tells him what she has done. Bill tells her she wouldn't like being married because it's not glamorous. He advises her to go to Spain and do the film. 'We'll be here when you get back.'

"After some time elapses, she sends a package from Spain. It contains gifts for the children and a publicity release announcing that Carole expects to make another six pictures within the next three years."

This synopsis of a standard Family Affair *show rings most of the chimes that have kept this show in the top five for many seasons. The emotional tugging, the looking-back-over-the-shoulder at love that was, love that even yet might be, the enriched poignance of a civilized man and three sweet kids who need "mothering"— all make for a strong formula. In this episode, it's all here but Sebastian Cabot.*

The hard work we did in the disciplines of plotting and synopses at Temple University brought forth a new respect for the mechanics of storytelling. Without the technical preparation this gave my students, I doubt that their appreciation of "The Final War of Olly Winter" (one of the best pieces of work ever presented by the *CBS Playhouse*, or any other playhouse anywhere, anytime) would have been so acute, so quick, so responsive. They were enormously involved in the experience.

There are so many aspects of writing that are paralleled in the other arts, one is always tempted to cite them. Here, for instance, at the time my advanced class sat down to watch the brief moment in the lives of two lost people, their participation in the story was enriched by their having had to struggle with some of the materials themselves. They were playing in the orchestra, as it were, not just sitting in the presence of a recital. They were part of it. Their eye and ear were informed.

Phrasing meant more; pauses, gradations, inflections, camera uses, lighting, sound, close-ups. We had been through a good deal of hard professional television—the shows themselves and the scripts that became the shows. The students had become a knowing audience, enormously critical, yes, but sympathetically so, for now they were beginning to know how truly hard writing is.

Story dissection had played a large part in their creative growth. They were maturing. They were growing into an acceptance of the lonely labor of writing, growing into a sharp recognition of when they were in the presence of excellence, and of the signs and criteria that separated it from successful commercial trivia.

It came to me, during those semesters, that the great turning point in any writer's serious attempt to professionalize his work occurs when he starts to *think of himself* as a professional. When does that happen?

In my classes at Temple I had some fine sensitivities. All were overwhelmed by the experience of the production of "Olly Winter." This beautiful, haunted story of an inexorable journey to bitter death, to the meaningless rubbing out of a lost but gallant man only a few hours after the promise of some sort of purpose in life had crossed his path—the dramatic experience of this brought forth many of the encomiums the story and the performances deserved.

No doubt you saw this show. It represented one of the great moments in television's generally flaccid parade of self-imitating flatness. I will never forget this show. Nor will any who saw it. (It brought overnight recognition to the wide range of talents with which Ivan Dixon is endowed.)

I asked the students at Temple University what the most memorable line was in the Ronald Ribman script. Every student had a line, or a moment. All had one—a sure sign of progress. Ivan Dixon (Olly Winter, a black GI) has begun to fall in love with the slender Vietnamese woman he has found and protected. Neither understands a word the other says, of course. So what they do and say very often has a double poignance. Here is one entry: "Oh, lady, if there were just a little world for you and me!"

Upon his return to "civilization" (Brooklyn), after seeing too much of the Asian jungle, all Olly wanted was a cement "lawn." (Of course, he never got back.) Now, after his relationship with the little Vietnamese girl has begun to mature, he wants something else—a greenhouse. Why? "Keep the sun in my house all day."

"Who is Olly?" I asked. "What does he represent?"

"Olly is the figure of a lot of GIs in a lot of wars," wrote one student, "wandering around in a strange country, not knowing why he's there or who the enemy is. Olly shows the true dichotomy of the Oriental and the Occidental mind when he tells the little Vietnamese girl that her country is ignorant, that 'They ought to get with it,' 'Get rid of this jungle. Put on shoes, so you won't get little bugs in your feet. Get factories.' (He shows an odd pride in the 'accomplishments' of the American system, not realizing how absurd it would all sound to the girl were she to know what he is saying.) The script then points up one of the deep problems of this war, of any war, hot or cold, after the casual burial of two nameless and faceless peasants: (Olly) 'People got to be more than holes in the dirt.' "

They were catching essences, though many were never stated in the script.

I asked the class to explain the play's title and got this:

"The previous 'wars' implied in the title are not limited to military conflicts, as the expert use of flashbacks throughout the show soon reveals. Olly has always been involved in violent struggles, either in terms of family distress, personal survival, or in fighting for his own dignity as a man. The current 'war' in the title is both the obvious one in Vietnam and the more subtle war for basic understanding and communication between humans. Surely the jungle is also the U.S., the girl an American, and the Vietcong guerrillas a white vigilante group of citizens. Olly is the modern tragic figure, painfully forced to live the present in terms with the past, to live his own life in terms of his inevitable death. His reward is in the final victory of personal honor and understanding, over the imbecile demands of a society which condones the murder of persons guilty only of compassion for their fellow men."

Here is a thoughtful reaction: "Ribman's moving from the slangy to the poetic, while the soldier pours out his heart to a girl who can't understand a word of it, is most effective. Such lines as the following are very touching: 'The world is moving. I sit here quiet and I feel it. Round and round. The old houses come down' (we saw them coming down in one of the Brooklyn flashbacks); 'Sisters die' (another flashback showed us this); 'Little babies sit in the clearing and don't know what happened to them. You eat crazy fruits' (the Vietnamese girl has just given him some), 'fruits you never seen before. You sleep in jungles. You open your eyes and it's twenty years later and nobody knows your name.' (Another flashback from Olly's boyhood days.) This is affecting to watch and listen to. But," concludes this student, with rare insight, "I think more was said in scenes of *silence* than in scenes with speech."

A recognition of the high quality of the acting in this production, as well as the writing, was caught by this student: "Ivan Dixon was so completely credible, one felt a Congressional Medal of Honor should have been presented his widow—though there was and is no widow. This is a high compliment to Dixon."

Another student noted this parellel: "Olly is all alone in the world, and we know he was early orphaned. So also with the girl; worse, she's a young widow. I notice too they both fall forward, into the sun, when killed. The dog, running in circles after the two principles are killed, seems in itself to be an expression of the uselessness of war: men going around in circles, killing each other, achieving nothing at all."

In addition to the pluses in this production, I asked the class to catch such technical errors as came to their notice, and I got quite a few, many of which had escaped me altogether. (Nothing so quick as young eyes.)

"Tiny blocks of wood that floated the water lilies were visible. It destroyed some of the romance of the scene."

So many students today have had military training, it's impossible to fake in this area. Even tiny mistakes are caught:

"Olly's fatigue clothes had dress stripes. Noncombat. And white name plates. In the jungle, combat fatigues would have *muted* rank insignia. Anyhow, Olly needed no artificial identification; his dark skin was a vivid enough marker."

"The cartridge belt feeding the machine gun didn't move, although the gun was firing."

"I got the feeling Olly was always walking around the same pile of dirt."

"When Olly tore the girl's clothes off, he really ripped them. A few minutes later they were intact. Did she stash another in her purse?"

"In one spot, Olly chopped so hard in the jungle, the whole set shook."

"The same 'jungle' was used after the cast had moved to a new spot."

"The drowned man raised his head to breathe."

"The sound effects had the brittle tone of studio production. Too often you knew you weren't outside."

These aren't negative or picky. They are positive and sharp.

Most of the students got all the symbolism, everything Ronald Ribman wanted to hit us with:

"The approach differs vastly from the stereotyped war picture in which the Negro, if a hero, is a minor one. In this play, Olly is America."

"The play is an excellent portrayal of man fighting in a primitive country where communication between self and those around him is almost nonexistent, and, at the same time, a portrayal of actual primitive attitudes and conditions that prevail in America, in regard to one human and his treatment by others. Our 'culture' is supposed to be highly developed, even sophisticated. Actually, and in its own special way, it is just as primitive as Vietnam's, the people as savage, their torments as unprotected."

"The fine use of flashbacks in this play set up an ironic comparison between the hot violence of the war in Southeast Asia and the cold, dispossessed, but no less savage condition of the poor—especially the Negro poor—in American cities, cities Olly refers to as 'civilization.' Olly's father, mother, and sister are all trapped and then ground to their own deaths by the American 'system,' or lack of any system at all (just as destructive), exactly as the Vietnamese villagers are."

"The play is not so much anti-war as pro-people."

I asked them what use of dissolves they could remember, and at once got many effective ones, including these two:

"The weeds of his father's grave site blend into the jungle weeds of the battle-field."

"The hand stroking the pet cat becomes a hand putting a gun together."

And finally a question on the impact delivered to the viewer after an accumulation of flashbacks: "The development of the flashback technique as here used kept steering the viewer's mind to one thought and underscoring it: a sense of time. The sum total is not the seventy-two hours of the action in the war. It is both an instant and a lifetime."

Where Do You Send What You Write?

Over and over again students have come to me with stories, or story plans, or with a carefully prepared synopsis of something they wish to write "for television," and when I ask them what show it is intended for, they always have the same answer:

"For any producer who'll buy it."

Let us kill this notion right here. There *is* no such producer. No such network. There is no "open market" in television. The most exciting plot in the world would almost certainly be returned unread.

Why is this the case?

You have to *aim* at something. You have to aim at a show that is on the air *now*. Or at the very least you have to aim at a category or type of show that is on the air now.

Your story should fit, and fit exactly, the tight corners as well as the open spaces in which that series is working. Study the episodes week by week till you know the flavor and the character range, the type of fun or excitement that represents the guidelines for the series.

That is the reason I assign my own students the mental exercise of creating new plots for *existing* shows. I never give any class the assignment to write a plot for a story that "some producer" or "some magazine" might buy. Too vague. Too chancy.

If you do have a good story idea that you feel might interest a magazine editor, know the magazine. If you don't know it, get acquainted with it. Even that won't help much. Your chances are not very good because so little fiction is being published in popular magazines these days. And so many magazines are dying! But in television, even though thousands of scripts are bought each year, nothing could be more wasteful of your time than to make a blind submission. It can only end up on the desk of a blind reader who won't read it. Why should he read it? To whom can *he* send it? For what show? He can't send it anywhere except to the producer he's working for.

Let us assume, however, that you have been following a series with real attention, with cold objective evaluation. You know the kind of story the series carries, who the star is, what he handles best, who the costar is, what their relationship is, what kind of emergencies they have to meet, and how they meet them. You know the kinds of places in which the action is likely to take place, the nature and amount of the action.

In the matter of dramatizing issues of the day—the large, in contrast to the merely topical—you know how far you can go, or what you have to skirt or bypass and how to do that. You are sensitive enough to discern what the show's taboos are. All shows have them.

Another thing, don't create enemies inside your show. There are plenty of them outside. Make friends. And when studying shows, take note of the shows' sponsors: who they are, the products they sell, the way the products are displayed and merchandised, what they avoid saying about themselves, what they avoid showing, the nature of their "settings," both natural and psychological. Most of the products sold by television are entirely respectable and enjoy wide public acceptance.

What about building a new show? The atmosphere of a show has a tremendous lot to do with its effectiveness as an advertising message carrier. If you are thinking in the bolder regions of "something new," think first of *wide popular acceptability*. It must be clear to all, for example, that the thinking behind the success of *Bronson* was exactly this simple: it is the mechanizing of Clint Walker, the lifting him off his horse and setting him on a motorcycle. It is the *Cheyenne* formula given a gas engine and a new rider, *Cheyenne* on better roads. Nothing new, nothing at all, has been added. Bronson pokes about aimlessly, pure, merciful, ready, perceptive, brave, unattached, doing good, preventing or correcting trouble, leaving hearts athrob once a week, just as Clint Walker did—a sexy Boy Scout patrol leader, noble as Tarzan, YMCA as Dick Clark.

Who can fight anything so sanitary?

Some of the same quality of preliminary inquiry went into my considerations of the suitability of the story that became *The Flying Nun*. Could anyone knock it? Perhaps. But probably only at the start. There was just too much tidal power of conformity. Nuns take vows of chastity, poverty, and obedience. They don't smoke or drink. Most nuns are humorous (certainly, for television, they'd have to be). Most nuns are fun to be with.

Enemies? Sure. There are Protestants who will always hate anything Catholic. But there was a change to note. The non-Catholic world, even the anti-Catholic world, had within the past few years—principally through the visible humanitarianism of the late Pope John XXIII and his "opening of the windows" message—been obliged to reassess its views of this venerable system, just as the church had been obliged to reassess its own views of itself, a process of self-inspection that will surely last out the century.

This, of course, has been the experience of many other institutions—we are living in an age of direct challenge—which have found themselves obligated to adjust their own concepts to accommodate and to absorb the relentless dramatic changes breaking over the heads of all of us. It has become imperative to try to relate to these evolutions, to survive among them, and, if possible, to recover lost vigor and find new meaning in the process of alterations.

In thinking about a nun, for television, and in thinking about the Catholic Church, I realized that yesterday the Catholic Church meant something to Catholics only, but today the Catholic Church means something to everybody. I felt that today it had more friends and fewer enemies than at any time since St. Peter. Thus, when thinking in the broad terms of an entire new series, it is necessary to turn over all the stones that one can see. (Note some of the reasons, stated in another chapter, for the flat failure of many of television's new shows.)

When thinking in the more confined terms of selling a story to a show that is already running, just observe the fence laws. They're well posted. Just study the series.

The above is a suggestion to save you time and labor and it might be expressed as simply as this: before putting your imagination to work, use your mind. Pick out a show you like, analyze its basic nature, feel its fabric, then think toward that model all the time.

Playwrights don't have to do this. But for television dramatists, it is imperative. And again, for a very simple reason. The anthology market is dead. What you write must meet the specifications of a series. The basic elements for doing so are all delineated in this book. Nor is it important that some of the shows reprinted herein are no longer in network production. Comparable formulas are here, comparable entertainments now being televised, with comparable standards, requirements, and frameworks. And most good series live on as repeats.

Of some practical help will be your own scrutiny of the newspaper television pages describing local entertainment in the community in which you now live. Get acquainted with the local station productions. Though their budgets are small, their needs are often large and their opportunities open. It doesn't too much matter *how* you start. Just consider the histories of the television writers whose records are here in this book. They all had their share of turndowns, early bewilderments. Some, as you've seen, still carry a large load of doubt, though all, please note, did a huge amount of work. Shows of the type of *Lamp Unto My Feet* are good risks for new writers. And such shows give them a chance to have work bought and produced.

Similarly, shows like *Look Up and Live* readily take the offerings of unknowns and will pay six or seven hundred dollars for a script. Don't belittle the productions of any of the educational stations in your neighborhood, or within reach of your set. They need scripts. They haven't much money to pay you, but this field is getting better every month and one day soon will truly bloom.

A great many stations all over the United States have annual "festivals of the arts" excitements. Try for them. Winners get extremely useful notice, useful to themselves in their struggle to get their careers in motion.

The thing you need to do is to get your nose under the wire. It doesn't matter at the beginning what kind of pasturage is on the other side of the fence. It's where you want to be. It's where you have to be.

Another thing: think in terms of the university nearest you. Very often television plays are usable for their dramatic schedules. If you can't see your production on a tube, you can at least see it "standing up." Every time your work is put through a new process, no matter what and no matter how amateurish, you learn something of value. And you make new contacts.

The Shubert Foundation offers fellowships so that student writers can go on working. This is for playwriting. But it is so closely related to your own basic problem of dramatic expression that this opportunity should be explored by every student. If you succeed in getting one of these fellowships, you know for sure that you will see your work produced as a play by the drama department of a university.

Many stations scattered all over the country do something similar to the popular annual activity of WGBH-FM in Boston. This station has been running a radio drama contest for at least two years now. Some stations are doing the same for television. The well-known editor and short-story anthologist, Whit Burnett, runs a contest for college students each year. It's quite a generous bag: screen plays, TV scripts, radio. Good prizes and good publicity.

None of this is big and none of the above is national. But, nonetheless, these are good places to get first experiences. Real prestige attaches to some of the awards.

On a national basis both CBS and NBC have put time and money aside to encourage the newcomer. NBC's Sunday afternoon TV experiment has brought forth a number of new names. The CBS *Repertoire Workshop* is open to showcase presentations by new playwrights. In both cases the budgets are small. And they require a format that is the reverse of the splashy. This means minimum sets and small casts. Several important things can happen if you land a script on either of these outlets. You do get paid, not heavily, but fairly. You have a chance to work closely with your own materials as your story goes through the production process. You are continuously in the presence of professionals. You can see your work under most advantageous conditions. Perhaps most important of all, *others* will see your work, and your name, under those same conditions.

Remember, no one starts big.

Never despair. Remember there are such producers as Leonard Stern. He may live to regret his generosity in stating his office's willingness to read everything that comes in!

APPENDIX I

THE McLUHAN MYTH

Charles S. Steinberg has been CBS Television vice-president for public information since 1959. He had filled two big spots for CBS prior to that. He joined CBS Radio in 1957 as director of press information. The following year he was promoted to director of information services for CBS Television.

Before CBS brought Steinberg into its family, Warner Bros. had made good use of his skills. He served this motion picture colossus for fourteen years in two capacities, educational director and eastern director of public relations.

The *Television Academy Quarterly* carried this introductory paragraph about Steinberg's article "The McLuhan Myth":

> In this issue a television network executive and trained Social Scientist, Charles S. Steinberg, makes a frontal assault on the Toronto prophet and upon that cult which has built up around his work. The medium cannot truly dominate the message it transmits, argues Steinberg, and computers will never substitute for man's conscious and continuing need to define his moral position in relation to the condition of his life. Scoring McLuhan for generalization and for deprecating the contributions of serious communications research, Steinberg insists that most of McLuhan's observations about television are useless, inaccurate, or both.

THE McLUHAN MYTH
By Charles S. Steinberg

As with most phenomena, it is difficult to tell how the McLuhan cult began. To his admirers, Marshall McLuhan burst upon the narrow world of communications like a colossus, flaying unmercifully the conventional wisdom of the old fogeys who teach mass media in the universities and offering the new religion of electronic technology. To his detractors—and they are increasingly vocal in and out of the academic community—McLuhan is all shadow and no substance, giving off irritating puffs of smoke rather than a hard, gem-like flame.

Harold Rosenberg's discovery of McLuhan's *Understanding Media* in *The New Yorker* is probably as responsible as anything else for the emergence of McLuhanism as the "in" thing in the current dialogue over television and other mass media. Rosenberg's name for it, "philosophy in a pop key," may well have been the genesis of the McLuhan cult. Certainly, McLuhan's converts have been few in the field of serious scholarship in mass communications, for most scholars in the mass media are disinclined to take him seriously.

His style and approach are neither scholarly nor logical. He has either discarded or reversed every conventional approach to the study of mass media. And it is not at all surprising that those to whom McLuhan would appeal are the devotees of pop art, high camp, rock and roll, and the ritualism of the contemporary tribal dances. In a sense, McLuhan's is the popular philosophy of the age of the discotheque. Philosophy in a pop key is, after all, modern voodooism in which electronic technology will ultimately extend our consciousness outward into the world around us. McLuhan has caught on, precisely because he is an amalgam of camp and voodoo, medicine man and lay divine. He is the high priest of pop.

McLuhan's thesis has the impact of a brilliantly contrived piece of advertising copy: "the medium is the message." It is alliterative, it sounds profound, it titillates the imagination. And it is categorical. Either one accepts this thesis or one rejects it out of hand. There is no room for ambivalence. To buy it is to become convert to McLuhan's pop philosophy, with McLuhan playing the piper and his disciples singing the tune. The medium is the message: this is the quintessence of McLuhan's creed as expressed in depth in *Understanding Media.*

Rosenberg has called *Understanding Media* a book about humanity, "as it has been shaped by the means used in this and earlier ages to develop information." But that is precisely what it is not. It is a book which, like all pop art, is curiously detached from humanity with the computer representing the modern golden calf. Media are amputations of our physical self and, therefore, nonhuman.

McLuhan's philosophy, indeed, is an alienation of humanism. It is regressive in that it stumps for a return to a tribal era. What the electric light has wrought is not progress but atavism, a turning back to a pre-literary period. The printing press was not a sign of progress, but an obstacle in the way of progress. It brought man out of the cohesiveness of his tribal period into a modern social fragmentation that has proved disastrous. What may yet save us all is the new electric technology. This will bring us forward into a new, creative global consciousness which will ultimately envelop all of society in a pantheistic union.

Despite the fact that McLuhan's books are not conventional treatises on mass communications, one has the obligation nevertheless to approach them by using some of the conventional criteria. Of any serious work, the reader has the right to ask certain basic questions. What has the author set out to do? How convincingly does he do it? How valid are his arguments? How tenable are his conclusions? What are his recommendations?

In terms of these yardsticks, at least, McLuhan's hypothesis defies definition, not because it is brilliant and beyond criticism, but because it is repetitive to a point of dullness. It is an uneasy blend of neo-Freudian psychology, sociology and historiography. It is incredibly confusing in its citation of innumerable secondary sources, because McLuhan airily disdains to cite chapter and verse and the reader has no idea whether the idea and the authority are accurate or paraphrase.

Marshall McLuhan's "cool" world has been compared to the "other-directed" society of Reisman's *The Lonely Crowd,* but the analogy is false. Reisman's inner, outer and other directed societies have not only logical, but historical precedent. McLuhan's "hot" and "cool" media are mere labels for such media as radio or television. It is never satisfactorily explained why radio is "hot" and television "cool." They are what they are, McLuhan says, high participation or low participation media, but how they got that way is your guess as well as mine.

Nevertheless, McLuhan is a social and academic success and *Understanding Media* is a national best-seller. The success of both only serves to underscore the paucity of original thinking on the effects of mass media. Because there is no genuine scholarship, a spurious facsimile has found a receptive audience. This is particularly evident because the message is provocatively off-beat.

No paraphrase reveals the tenuousness of the McLuhan creed better than McLuhan himself. Fiction, for example, subverts fact while McLuhan tosses off some of the most politically naive convictions of our time. "It is no accident," he writes, "that Senator McCarthy lasted such a very short time when he switched to television." McLuhan would have us believe that "neither the press nor McCarthy knew what happened." This, of course, is political and journalistic nonsense. The press and the public knew very well what happened. What happened was Joseph Welch, who peeled the hide off McCarthy in full view of millions of Americans. McLuhan either did not watch the hearings or he is abysmally ignorant of one of the most striking effects of television as a medium of mass communication.

Similarly, the statement is made that Nixon was superior to Kennedy on radio, but inferior on television, because he offered a "high definition" image on the "cool medium," while Kennedy emerged triumphant because his image had a "blurry, shaggy texture." Many political observers feel, on the contrary, that Kennedy's image was singularly clear and well defined. What is more revealing, however, is McLuhan's total rejection of what either Kennedy or Nixon had to say about the issues involved. The message is overwhelmed by the medium, and appearance obliterates reality.

Philosophically, McLuhan is a self-styled operationalist. "In operational or practical fact," he says, "the medium is the message." This is the cardinal point in the McLuhan scheme. Since the medium is the message, substance or content are not only irrelevant, but even to consider their importance is absurd. The electric light is "pure information" and best exemplifies the current automated technology which is "integral." The period of print and of machine technology, on the other hand, was fragmented. What we are witnessing is nothing less than catastrophic change—a radical metamorphosis—from a print-oriented to an electronic-oriented society. The phonetic alphabet and the printing press, which moved man out of his tribal Eden, were disastrous inventions, but there is hope that the new electric technology will return man to the sophisticated innocence of tribalism.

McLuhan's media go far beyond the conventional mass communicators, such as radio and television. Media are not only extensions of our own nervous systems, but extend literally into all phases of our society. Money is a medium, as are the wheel, clothing, the motor car, weaponry and the bicycle. These are no less media than the book. And as we move into the cool presence of the future, the world will tend to become anti-literary or even non-literary—a world in which pop art and the comic strip may well displace the conventional literary tools of book and play.

In a characteristically puzzling statement, McLuhan concludes that the paper-back book suddenly became acceptable in 1953, although "no publisher really knows why." But the fact is that every publisher knows why. The paper-back book became a best-selling commodity because it was cheap, and readers who heretofore could not afford the rapidly increasing price of cloth-bound books were now able to buy both classic and contemporary books at a fraction of their previous cost. The why of paper-back books was discussed in depth by Kurt Enoch, who pioneered in this field, and by Irita Van Doren and a panel of critics and publishers in a forum on "The Future of Books in America," published by *The American Scholar*.

Few will dispute the fact that electric technology is having an enormous impact on modern society. What *is* disputable is McLuhan's conviction that the good or evil wrought by electronic media has no relevance to their content. They do not even function as conduits or circuits outside ourselves. They *are* ourselves. As such, the effects of technology "do not occur at the level of opinions or concepts." They simply affect patterns of perception. Print, for example, was responsible for individualism and nationalism, but this effect could never be determined by an analysis of print content. What, one then asks, *did* determine the effect of print? McLuhan unfortunately does not provide the answer, but it is clear that the print media—Thomas Paine's *Common Sense* for example—had no part in shaping society. By print media, McLuhan does not mean the great books of the Western world, but rather the medium of print itself. What the printing press issued pales by comparison to the effect of the press itself—which is another way of saying that the message is inherent in the medium and to hell with content.

The difficulty one has with this hypothesis is that it is beyond definition and beyond rational proof. One accepts or rejects it as one accepts or rejects any dogma. It is as easy to assert that the medium is the message as it is to proclaim that God is dead. Neither is supportable by scientific evidence and there is no method capable of reducing either to proof. McLuhan is in very close proximity to the religious mystic.

Similarly, the contempt for the content of mass media renders absurd all previous studies in both content and effects of mass communication. In such a sweeping generalization the contributions of Bernard Berelson, Wilbur Schramm, Paul Lazarsfeld and a host of other serious scholars are dismissed as the babbling of innocent children.

Although the publishers classify it as sociology, *Understanding Media* genuinely defies classification, except as a kind of off-beat philosophy of history. The basic themes—the medium is the message, all media are extensions of our nervous systems—are endlessly repeated to evolve into a neo-Hegelian thesis and antithesis, out of which we arrive at a synthesis of all the senses. Or, as McLuhan coins it, a "synesthesia." Thesis: Tribal society was integrated, functional and individualistic. Antithesis: The emergence of print de-tribalized man and fragmented society. Synthesis: The new electric technology returns man to a golden, tribal era again. Human society can look forward to a brave new world in which our nervous systems become extended into the electro-magnetic technology and "it's but a further stage to transfer our consciousness to the computer as well."

Now, a statement like this must either be taken rhetorically or it must be taken literally. If it is rhetorical, then McLuhan is enjoying his own private joke, while his disciples take him seriously. If he is literal in what he says, then the transference of consciousness to the computer can only mean a total abandonment of ethics and an abdication of value judgments. What we confront is a new theology in which the computer resolves—or explains away—all of the moral dilemmas of modern man. If the implications were not absurd, they would be frightening to contemplate. By this "technological extension of consciousness," man becomes serf to the computer, which is precisely what critics like Lewis Mumford see as a real and present danger. In his return to tribalism, man would serve electric technology with the fidelity that society once worshipped the totem pole. McLuhan's deity is the electric light and it is not electric technology which serves us, but toward which we develop "servo-mechanisms." All of our conscious awareness, and our knowledge as well, are trapped in the entrails of the computer. The problem of free will versus determinism is, once and for all, resolved. But the price is costly. We are confronted with the spectre of what Rene Dubos has called "undisciplined technology."

Is there an escape hatch from this dilemma? McLuhan is obviously uncomfortable with it, for he seeks a way out through art. The artist can save us, he says, but characteristically he does not say how. For art, too, does not exist either for its own sake or for society. Art is but another bulwark against the inevitable blows to our psyche. From Hans Selye, the medical expert on stress, McLuhan derives the notion that any extension of ourselves brings about a state of physiological numbness. But, as in the case of other authorities upon whom McLuhan draws, the analogy is both awkward and untenable. There are medical experts who would quarrel with his statement that "the function of the body . . . is to act as a buffer against sudden varieties of stimulus in the physical and social environment." To say that art serves to lessen the numbing effect of technology is to take art out of the media category. It becomes a non-medium, a psychological barrier against the onslaught of the extension of consciousness. McLuhan's view of art is that it is, in short, not aesthetic but anaesthetic.

The reader is confronted with similar dilemmas in the case of literature, as well as the "orthodox" mass media of press, radio and television. In McLuhan's world of tomorrow, electric technology can do without literature—or literacy. This nonprint oriented world "does not need words any more than the digital computer needs numbers," for literature and language will be bypassed in favor of a "general cosmic consciousness." Now, if the meaning of this kind of verbalizing is to be taken literally, it is obviously absurd. If it is meant to shock, as so much of McLuhan appears to be, then the shock is not one of recognition, but of bewilderment. What is happening is a complete consignment of all the values of Western man to a kind of nonverbal limbo, dominated by a computerized, push-button tribal society in which the medium, as message, simply exists as electric technology with no meaning beyond its own existence.

Since the medium is its own message, the literate man acts with complete detachment from emotional involvement. The non-literate individual, however, reacts with an explosive emotional charge. But how reconcile this with the great protest literature that has influenced the course of civilization by the very impact of its message to mankind? And, if radio and television threaten to make literature extinct, how account either for the proliferation of books in this television age or, for that matter, for the impact of at least some of the literature of motion pictures and television?

In the McLuhan philosophy, the answer is that print is moribund while television functions purely as electric technology and not as a conduit for program content. From a strict and literal interpretation of medium as message—and McLuhan gives no hint of poetic license or rhetoric—it does not matter whether television covers the news in depth, whether it tackles the great issues of our time or whether it presents a *Death of a Salesman* or not.

At the same time, and with characteristic paradox, McLuhan expresses the belief that television demands a "creative participant response." But response to what? The logic can only point to response to the medium itself and not the message, in which case the response could be neither creative nor participant. Is the conventional wisdom absurd in asking that mass media extract creativity not only from the viewer, but from the purveyor of content as well? Do those who produce television programs or publish books err in their effort to juxtapose form with content? On the other hand, if content is to be ignored in favor of pure form, the consequences are appalling for our conventional way of conducting the whole business of mass communication. We need concern ourselves no longer either with the creative or moral effects of mass media. Electric technology—the message—is, like beauty, its own excuse for being.

McLuhan's presentation for this hypothesis is repeated so relentlessly that one cannot quite determine whether he is being deadly serious or perpetrating a gigantic joke. In his tilting with the conventional wisdom, he is a swinger, a cool man, an anti-establishmentarian, an advocate of flux and change. The status quo and the conventional wisdom irritate him.

But in the long run his separation of form from content and his deification of electric technology are spurious and self-defeating. Form and substance, whether in art or in life, defy dissolution. They are integral and inseparable. To split them arbitrarily is to deny either aesthetic or moral credence to either. Value judgments are "out" and electric technology is "in."

What is troublesome—and dangerous—about this philosophy is that it does not touch anywhere on the social, political or moral implications of the electric technology. Clearly, McLuhan has small regard for the ethical implications of mass media. The effect of communication for good or evil is irrelevant if the medium, rather than the content, is the message. Yet, McLuhan cites "concern with *effect,* rather than meaning" as a basic change wrought by electric technology. But effect with respect to what? We can speak of the effects of mass media in terms of the substance conveyed by print, radio or television. But what effect, other than numbness, can one expect of pure electric technology?

Even when McLuhan draws upon sex to drive home a point, he cannot escape from the consequences of the medium as message philosophy. "The open mesh silk stocking is far more sensuous than the smooth nylon," he says, "just because the eye must act as hand in filling in and keeping the image, exactly as in the mosaic of the television image." Those males who have an eye for mesh silk stockings would quarrel with this erotic analysis, insisting that it is not the fibre of the stocking but what's in it that counts. And, as in mass media, McLuhan tends to neglect what's in it. The mesh stocking, like the electric conduit, becomes important, while the limb is relegated to limbo.

Throughout the book one comes upon opinions, offered with the no-nonsense firmness of a categorical imperative, but clearly rejected by facts. Northcote Parkinson, for example, is used as the statistical source to show that bureaucratic structures function and proliferate in inverse ratio of the work to be done. This is analyzed by McLuhan in terms of the movement of information, with total disregard of the simple fact that *Parkinson's Law* was a serio-comic commentary on the organization of 20th-century bureaucracy, and that Parkinson scarcely intended his book to be accepted as serious sociological dogma.

Although the expressed purpose of McLuhan's books is "to understand mass media," the effect is to obscure and confuse. There is no way to refute the claim that electric technology is "pure information without any content" except to dismiss this kind of thinking as semantic nonsense. The electric light is not information. Its function is to provide illumination and to convey information. It has made the communication of information easier and quicker, and perhaps more efficient. But it is not "pure information" because there is no such modality as pure information unless, in the final analysis, McLuhan is writing elaborate rhetoric rather than fact.

This constant subversion of semantics is what is both irritating and amusing about the McLuhan hypothesis. What he has structured is not a philosophic system, but a series of feints or probes. Some of these are extraordinarily provocative, but they tend to fall apart upon close examination and they bear neither the stamp of scientific truth nor moral evaluation. Who can disagree with McLuhan when he says that the electronic age has created "problems for which there is no precedent." But here again he confuses rightness of statement with rightness of reason. He has come forth with another brilliant half-truth, and it is this confusion between rhetoric and reality which is at the root of the confusion and the spuriousness of his thinking. It is not media which create problems without precedent, but the way in which media are used. It is not the medium, but the message, which causes concern.

In the McLuhan world, it's not the broadcast but the beep that matters. It is, truly, a world of all shadow and no substance. And, while it may provide a provocative bull session for campus cut-ups, it makes little sense to the responsible communicators who are concerned with the impact and effect of mass communication in a democratic society. Indeed, the final irony is that McLuhan must resort to several hundred pages of print medium to present his case against the effects of the phonetic alphabet. Marshall McLuhan envisions a brand new electric world, but his own approach to it is tribal and fragmented.

APPENDIX II

OF MIKES AND MEN —
THE HIDDEN STORY

BY JOAN WALKER

My reason for including this interesting article is fully explained by the first sentence of the second paragraph.

Richard Nixon, in the course of his recent television rounds, has indicated that he now believes what has been bruited about by others for years—namely, that he lost the 1960 election because he had such a bad makeup job during the first televised debate with John Kennedy. According to such reasoning, which is pretty prevalent, results of the 1968 election may not hinge on the course of the war in Vietnam or on the amount of crime in the streets or on the identity of the Republican nominee. They may hinge on the lavaliere microphone that Lyndon Johnson had hidden under his jacket during his press conference last November. That was the press conference where, for the first time, Mr. Johnson left the lectern with the Presidential seal and stationary microphone on it. The long microphone cable that ran from his lavaliere mike to a microphone input in the wall gave him mobility, and he used it. He walked up and down the platform, clenched his fists, raised his arms, drew curves in the air, and generally gestured away in a performance that brought to the TV screen the debut of what has been described variously as "the real Johnson," "the old Johnson," the new Johnson," or "the new old Johnson." Whichever it was, it was effective use of television, and that is what wins ball games.

It's about time the microphone got some attention. There's always talk about the visual side of television—the makeup jobs, the hair pieces, the blue shirts, the well-lighted set, the too-loose choreography, the good profile versus the bad profile, the *image*—but relatively little about the sound side of things.

The mikes are all over the place. On situation comedy shows they are nearly always out of sight overhead on a boom. On panel shows they're in the panels, on the panel members, and sometimes sticking up at the panel members from modernistic swivel chairs. On drama shows they are mainly overhead on a boom. They are also sometimes being handheld by a soundman who has them on the end of a "fishpole," and stashed away around the set. Sometimes a soundman, his fishpole pointed at the actors, is just out of camera range crouched in the kneehole of a kneehole desk, or strapped to a speeding automobile, or swimming next to a small boat, or flat on his back under a deathbed. Microphones are behind pieces of furniture in living-room sets. In barroom scenes, you can bet there's a mike in the neck of at least one of those whisky bottles. If actors are talking around a desk in an office, there is a mike somewhere on that desk, say in the pencil jar. For a cafeteria scene in one "Naked City," the soundman instructed the two actors to "Just talk into that basket of rolls." For the ubiquitous courtroom scenes, there's definitely a mike in the witness box, and you can be pretty sure the judge has one either behind his artfully arranged law books or behind the water carafe he doesn't pick up and pour from.

On their regular shows, Huntley and Brinkley and Walter Cronkite all use lavaliere microphones, just like the one the President used. They all hide their mikes under their buttoned jackets. When Peter Jennings had his news show, it was easy to hide his because, as the most clothes-conscious of the evening newscasters, he has very high lapels on his suits. Hugh Downs almost flaunts his, just tossing it around his neck and leaving it outside his jacket in full view of the "Today" audience. Barbara Walters, like most ladies, tries to hide hers under her dress. A lavaliere mike can absolutely ruin the lines of a Donald Brooks.

Some sound quality is lost with body mikes, which is why they are no good for, say, a Leontyne Price. For most television performers, they are good enough. After all, what can you lose from a staff announcer's voice? (Also, our receivers are not as delicate as they might be.) Body mikes are not good enough for Frank Sinatra. On Frank Sinatra specials, there are mikes, visible mikes, *everywhere*. He always sings with a mike right in front of his face, not hidden inside his shirt. That is why the sound is better on a Frank Sinatra special.

Then there are the wireless microphones. They consist of a small microphone that is, depending on the sex of the wearer, clipped onto a bra or attached to a tie, shirt, or breast pocket. A cord then goes, inside the clothing, to a transmitter which is about the size of a cigarette pack and which is usually, no matter what the sex, somewhere around the hip hidden in a pouch. From the transmitter—say between the dress and the slip or down the trouser leg—dangles about 18 inches of tiny wire. It is the antenna. The wearer, thus rigged, is a walking radio station operating on an FCC-approved frequency. He is subject to interference but, under the right conditions, he has a great deal of mobility. Wireless mikes are used extensively in nightclubs and in the theater, especially in musicals. Her wireless mike is the reason Pearl Bailey can murmur "back where I belong" and IT COMES OUT LIKE THIS. The wireless mike is essential for some documentaries, especially those involving non-pros—policemen, firemen, welfare recipients, hospital patients, drug addicts. With a mike staring at him or with cables snaking all over the floor, the subject of a documentary is acutely conscious of the equipment, and becomes self-conscious. With a wireless mike, he soon forgets that every word he says is being broadcast. Thus comes verisimilitude, even television vérité.

Without a wireless mike, NBC could never have done that famous "Comedian Backstage" in which Shelly Berman blew his top. Without a wireless mike, "The Violent World of Sam Huff," the good old "Twentieth Century" that CBS reran

New Year's Eve, would not have been as effective. With it attached to the Giants' linebacker during a game, the audience got to hear the huddles and the grunts and all the pounding thumping football noises. Without a wireless mike, Daniel Moynihan and Frank McGee would not have been anywhere near as moving as they were when they walked through the rubble of the aftermath of the Detroit riots in a documentary last September. Cables trailing after them would have ruined the effect.

Where the wireless mike really came into its own, of course, was on "Person to Person" (1953–1961). Without it, there would have been no "Person to Person"; and Lee Bailey's "Good Company" would not have had even its short life this season. After all, viewers can't pretend they've been invited into a celebrity's private home for a personal tour if the celebrity, while modestly reminiscing about his trophies, is drooling cables wherever he goes. But, while the wireless mike made the show possible, it gave the "Person to Person" crew more trouble than all the celebrities put together. Men and show folk, used to the camaraderie of the locker and the dressing room, presented few problems when it came to rigging them. (Two categories of men used to be difficult: Englishmen and anyone who affected bow ties. It seems that English tailors don't provide pockets for transmitters, and that was before the day the transmitter pouch was invented. As for the bow-tie wearers, they just had to switch to four-in-hands until microphones got smaller. RCA has a microphone today that is great for a bow tie: It is one inch long and the width of a man's little finger.) The ladies presented the problems. For instance, Kathleen Winsor, although she had written "Forever Amber" and married Artie Shaw, was so shy that she refused to be wired by a strange technician. A technician had to explain the procedure to her maid, and the maid did the rigging. It worked except that the technician forgot to mention that the sensitive side of the mike should be *away* from the skin, with the result that Miss Winsor's heartbeat was audible to all throughout her stint.

In those days it took bouffant skirts to hide the transmitters, but some slim women, like Constance Bennett and Lillian Gish, were not about to hide their figures in bouffant skirts. (Miss Gish had a slim-lined Valentina, and that dress was going to be on that show.) Their transmitters had to be taped to their inside lower thighs with the same elastic bandage football players use on bum knees. That is where the transmitters still go when the dresses are tight.

As one soundman put it, "With show folk, it's OK to hook a mike to their brassieres, but if it's a personage, like Mrs. Roosevelt or Jackie Kennedy, well, you do something else." Mrs. Kennedy is not only a personage; she also has a voice that is so small that a boom has trouble picking it up. "Person to Person" solved her problems by rigging the then-Senator Kennedy and having *him* do the walking around while she sat still and talked into a hidden, stationary, close-up mike. On other occasions, when she needed to be rigged, she agreed with alacrity, and her secretary did the rigging.

APPENDIX III

HOW TO PROTECT AN IDEA

BY THEODORE R. KUPFERMAN

Mr. Kupferman is general attorney and vice-president of Cinerama Productions Corporation; formerly a member of legal departments of National Broadcasting Company and Warner Brothers Pictures; arranger and editor of "1953 Copyright Problems Analyzed"; former chairman of Copyright Committee, Federal Bar Association of New York, New Jersey and Connecticut; and former New York judge. This article is reprinted from The Hollywood Reporter, *November 12, 1954.*

Over the years in my work in the legal departments of motion picture and broadcasting companies, certain questions of a practical yet legal nature have been repeatedly presented to me, either by employes of the companies or by those with whom they deal.

I have, therefore, on the theory that there are universal questions, culled from my notes the one item which most often evoked queries:

"How Do I Protect an Idea?"

You start out with an idea, but you cannot protect an idea as such. It is only the embodiment of the idea or its concrete expression that can be protected under the law. This means that your idea must be expressed in the form of a story or a drama or simply set forth in plain English on a piece of paper before it can be considered for protection.

Once that idea is expressed on paper, which we will hereinafter call your "work," it is the possible subject for some form of legal protection either by common law copyright, statutory copyright, unfair competition or contract.

Common law copyright exists for your written work as long as it is not "published." Published in this sense means made available to the general public. E.g., if you print a book for private distribution and give out copies to close friends only, the work is not considered published, but if you put one copy of any work in the public library for general distribution, even if the work never has been printed and the library copy is typewritten, it is considered published.

The concept of publication is tricky. You would think that a hit play which has been seen by thousands of people would be considered under this definition as published, but the early copyright law as it developed in England considered these performances as restricted publication. One reason for this may be that nothing in writing is made available to the public and so there is really nothing upon which to put a copyright notice or to send for registration. On this basis, a television play would not have to be copyrighted in the sense that it should have a copyright notice and be registered, although the law on this point has not yet been decided. A court recently held in a much criticized decision (Shapiro Bernstein & Co. vs. Miracle Record Co., Judge Igoe) that distributing records of a song before copyrighting the song was publication. The decision was criticized on the ground that inasmuch as a record is not acceptable for copyright registration, an act not susceptible of obtaining statutory copyright should not have the effect of divesting it.

If a work is published, unless it bears a proper copyright notice, it falls into the public domain, which means it is free for all to use.

fuller discussion at some other time, but for unpublished works which already have

Statutory copyright for published works is a field in and of itself and a subject for common law copyright it may still be desirable to obtain statutory copyright by registration.

If you have a copyright registration, you get the benefit of the federal provisions on damages, your work is on file and thus shows that you must have written it at least before the filing date, and if you sue for infringement, the defendant cannot claim that you have altered your work in order to make it more like the one you claim is an infringement. On the other hand, common law copyright continues forever, but, once registered, your copyright term is 28 years from registration plus additional 28 years if you file for renewal. This is the same term as for a published work except that there the term begins on publication.

There is a difference in the copyright law with respect to registering unpublished and published works. A published work gets statutory copyright by having the proper copyright notice and registration is just a formality. An unpublished work gets statutory copyright by registration under a special provision of the law.

Assuming that you would prefer to register your unpublished work, you will find that only a limited class of unpublished works can be accepted by the Register of Copyrights for registration under the law. This limited class of works includes only dramas, musicals, songs, and lectures or sermons. It does not include books nor does it include ideas or stories done in narrative rather than dramatic form.

Therefore, if before publication you want to register it, your work should be set forth in dramatic form with dialogue, somewhat in the nature of a play or set up in the nature of a lecture for oral delivery. When you've done that you write to the Register of Copyrights in Washington for application Form D if it is a dramatic composition, or Form C if it is a lecture. You return the completed form, which is prepared in duplicate, with a fee of $4 and one copy of your work, and the Copyright Office returns to you as your Certificate of Copyright one of the duplicate forms.

If your work is sent for registration as a lecture and does not seem to be a lecture, the Copyright Office will question you as to whether it has actually been prepared for a lecture or speech. Therefore, if there is no possibility that your work can be considered a lecture, it is best to set it up in dramatic form for registration in Class D.

If it is not possible for you to prepare your work in dramatic or lecture form or you prefer not to register, what other protection can you have?

The objectives we have in mind are those already set forth such as establishing a date of creation of the work and proving its content. This can be done by enclosing a copy in an envelope and sending it to yourself by registered mail. When received put this registered letter away in a safe place without breaking the Post Office seals on the envelope. The date on the envelope will prove that the content was conceived and expressed at least by that date and the seals will prove that the content was then as you now claim.

Some people have the mistaken idea that statutory registration or the registered mail method is the ultimate in protection.

It must always be kept in mind that these are merely methods of establishing your claim and that, unlike patents, in this field of copyright and literary property, the question is not who thought of it first, but rather did the defendant create his work independently, even if he did it after you, and therefore, the means of your protection can only lend themselves to preventing theft or proving the theft once it has occurred.

Once you have established the creation and content of your work and the submission of it to a third party, you have at least laid the necessary groundwork for pressing your claim.

Naturally, the above discussion is in only very general terms, and if you have any specific problem, it would be wise to consult your own lawyer.

INDEX

451